UNCLE SAM AND US

Globalization, Neoconservatism, and the Canadian State

Can Canada survive?

In response to widespread fear about the impact of globalization on Canada, Stephen Clarkson has written an erudite but highly readable book about Canadian government in a new era.

Taking as his yardstick the relatively generous and active state constructed under John Diefenbaker, Lester Pearson, and Pierre Trudeau, he proceeds to identify the changes – for better or for worse – that occurred under Brian Mulroney and Jean Chrétien, who signed transformative treaties and adopted right-wing policies.

Uncle Sam and Us shows how the prime institutions of the international economic order established in the 1990s – the North American Free Trade Agreement and the World Trade Organization – have reconstituted national governance in Canada. Taken together, NAFTA and the WTO impose on the federal government, the provinces, and their cities a 'supraconstitution' that has constrained authority that was once the exclusive preserve of democratically elected legislatures.

Clarkson looks at how the Canadian state's principal economic functions have been altered. He tackles the issues that have the most powerful effect on Canadian society – those related to social, labour, environmental, and cultural policies. He also appraises the foreign-policy limits set by Canada's vulnerability to 'Uncle Sam,' which was dramatized on September 11, 2001, when Washington temporarily blockaded all cross-border trade.

This comprehensive study concludes that the Canadian state has been weakened more by ideologues than by global forces. So the hope for restoring the quality of their society remains in the hands of Canadian voters, should they elect politicians who reaffirm values of social justice, ecological sustainability, and civic democracy. The clock can't be turned back, but globalization can be humanized if citizens push their governments to rebalance the international rules that have unleashed transnational corporations while hobbling democracy.

STEPHEN CLARKSON is Professor of Political Economy at the University of Toronto. He is the author of *Canada and the Reagan Challenge* (1982), which won the John Porter prize, and co-author, with Christina McCall, of *Trudeau and Our Times, Vol. 1: The Magnificent Obsession* (1990), which won a Governor General's Award, and *Trudeau and Our Times, Vol. 2: The Heroic Delusion* (1994), which won the John Dafoe prize.

The Woodrow Wilson International Center for Scholars

Lee H. Hamilton, Director

About the Center
The Center is the living memorial of the United States of America to the nation's twenty-
eighth president, Woodrow Wilson. Congress established the Woodrow Wilson Center in
1968 as an international institute for advanced study, "symbolizing and strengthening
the fruitful relationship between the world of learning and the world of public affairs."
The Center opened in 1970 under its own board of trustees.

   In all its activities the Woodrow Wilson Center is a nonprofit, nonpartisan organization, supported financially by annual appropriations from the Congress, and by the contributions of foundations, corporations, and individuals. Conclusions or opinions
expressed in Center publications and programs are those of the authors and speakers
and do not necessarily reflect the views of the Center staff, fellows, trustees, advisory
groups, or any individuals or organizations that provide financial support to the Center.

Uncle Sam and Us

Globalization, Neoconservatism, and the Canadian State

Stephen Clarkson

UNIVERSITY OF TORONTO PRESS
Toronto Buffalo London

and

WOODROW WILSON CENTER PRESS
Washington, D.C.

University of Toronto Press Incorporated
Toronto Buffalo London
Woodrow Wilson Center Press
Washington, DC
www.wilsoncenter.org
Printed in Canada

ISBN 0-8020-3758-5 (cloth)
ISBN 0-8020-8539-3 (paper)

Printed on acid-free paper

National Library of Canada Cataloguing in Publication

Clarkson, Stephen, 1937–
    Uncle Sam and us : globalization, neoconservatism, and the
Canadian state / Stephen Clarkson.

    Includes bibliographical references and index.
    ISBN 0-8020-3758-5 (bound).   ISBN 0-8020-8539-3 (pbk.)

    1. Canada – Economic conditions – 1991– 2. Canada – Social
conditions – 1991– 3. Canada – Politics and government – 1993–
4. Conservatism – Canada. 5. Canada – Foreign relations – United
States. 6. United States – Foreign relations – Canada. 7. Globalization.
8. International economic integration. I. Title.

    FC635 C59 2002   971.064'8   C2002-902596-6
    F1034.2.C59 2002

University of Toronto Press acknowledges the financial assistance to its
publishing program of the Canada Council for the Arts and the Ontario
Arts Council.

University of Toronto Press acknowledges the financial support for its
publishing activities of the Government of Canada through the Book
Publishing Industry Development Program (BPIDP).

This book on the state of the Canadian state
is dedicated to
Clare Margaret McCall Monahan
and to
Talia Chloë Clarkson Lewis
in the hope that it will be there for their generation
as it has been for their grandparents'

Contents

1 Not Whether, but Which Canada Will Survive 3
2 The Peripheral State: Globalization and Continentalism 14

I The Polity: Reconstituting the Canadian State

CHANGE FROM WITHOUT

3 Continental and Global Governance 37
4 NAFTA and the WTO as Supraconstitution 49

CHANGE FROM WITHIN

5 The Federal State: Internal Trade and the Charter 75
6 The Municipal State: Megacity and the Greater Toronto Area 99

II The Economy: Reframing the State's Functions

THE MACRO ECONOMY AND THE MANAGERIAL STATE

7 The Taxing State: From Lord Keynes to Paul Martin 127
8 The Banking State and Global Financial Governance 138

THE OLIGOPOLISTIC ECONOMY AND THE REGULATORY STATE

9 Financial Services: National Champions at Risk 151
10 Telecoms: From Regional Monopolies to Global Oligopolies 169

THE EXTERNAL ECONOMY AND THE INTERNATIONALIZING STATE

11 The Trading State 187
12 The Investing State 203

THE MICROECONOMY AND THE INTERVENTIONIST STATE

13 The Residual State: Accommodation at the Federal Level 233
14 The Industrial State Goes Provincial 259

III The Society: The Contradictions of Neoconservatism

15 The Civil State: Social Policies under Strain 281
16 The Working State: Labour Relations under Stress 305
17 The (Un)sustainable State: Deregulating the Environment 329
18 The Cultured State: Broadcasting and Magazines 354
19 The Diplomatic State: Lockstep under Hegemonic Dominance 381

20 The Post-Globalist State and the Democratic Deficit 407

   Notes 429

   Acronyms 491

   Acknowledgments 497

   Author Index 503

   Subject Index 513

UNCLE SAM AND US

Globalization, Neoconservatism, and the Canadian State

1 Not Whether, but Which Canada Will Survive

'Stephen, will Canada survive?' a physicist friend of mine asked out of the blue as we drove back to Toronto after a summer concert at the Sharon Temple, that Quaker oasis of colonial beauty where music and nature can still be experienced in serene harmony. Although the bluntness of his question took me by surprise, such apocalyptic fears have been widespread ever since neoconservatism and trade liberalization sparked anxiety in the 1980s about globalization's perverse impact on Canada's political, economic, and social systems.

A Simple Question ...

Canadians like my friend are not alone in harbouring concerns about their state system's sustainability. Everywhere in the world people are experiencing high levels of anxiety about the social cohesion, economic performance, and political viability of their state structures in the wake of the dual strengthening of local neoconservatism and global trade governance. Even in the United States, which emerged from the Cold War as the world's undisputed 'hyper-power,' anger is rife about the country's loss of sovereignty to transnational corporations (even though most of them are American) and to global institutions' behaviour (although the United States has been instrumental in defining their structures and hosts many of them).

Throughout newly industrializing Asia, the devastating combination in 1997 of an exchange rate crisis and government austerity measures imposed by the International Monetary Fund (IMF) shook these countries' capacity to promote their own interests. In Latin America, market contagion provoked a run on Brazil's currency, which in turn pushed neighbouring Argentina into a severe economic crisis that led to the government's calamitous default of 2002. In their far more stable context, the European Union's fifteen member states focused on a related debate about their governments' ability to sustain their domestic social policies, having entrusted to the European Central Bank much of their economic management.

Situated somewhere between these extremes of externally determined dysfunctionality and self-imposed truncation, Canadians at the beginning of the new millennium doubt that their political system can perform its expected functions in the wake of three radical changes associated with globalization: the landmark continental treaties the government of Canada implemented with the United States – the Canada-United States Free Trade Agreement (CUFTA) in 1989 and the North American Free Trade Agreement (NAFTA) in 1994 – and its subsequent entry the next year into the World Trade Organization (WTO) to which, by 2002, 143 other states belonged.

Several factors make it difficult for both citizens and experts to ascertain how much the new global governance constrains the Canadian state. A shift in the managerial paradigm of both elected politicians and their bureaucrats away from government activism makes it hard for scholars to determine whether a reduction in policy activity results from their fear of falling afoul of the new global rules or their belief that less government is better government. Such 'non-decision-making' is also notoriously resistant to empirical observation: outsiders can rarely tell to what extent NAFTA has inhibited state actions that might have been taken in its absence. Finally, Canadian governments may be renouncing such popular practices as supporting national enterprises not because of externally dictated constraints but because of a self-imposed determination to eliminate their budget deficits.

Canadians are aware that their federal and provincial governments and municipal administrations have made numerous efforts to rein in their activities. These include:

- *withdrawal* by Ottawa from social assistance, forestry management, manpower training, and other fields formally under provincial jurisdiction in which it had been active
- *downloading* of federal authority both to the provinces in fields of joint jurisdiction such as immigration and in overlapping areas such as environmental regulation and to Native band councils on land management

- *privatization* of federal and provincial crown corporations, which shrinks the public sector and diminishes governments' capacity to shape economic development
- *deregulating* economic sectors such as transportation and diminishing the rigour of such existing regulatory regimes as food inspection
- *cutting* government expenditures by reducing the coverage of programs such as unemployment insurance, education, and health care
- *downsizing* the federal, provincial, and municipal civil services, which then have trouble enforcing the regulations and administering the programs that remain nominally in force
- *offloading* the taxation burden from corporations to citizens in the form of consumption taxes and user fees

The starkest social effects of these political changes are obvious to the most casual observer who stumbles across a homeless person lying on a city sidewalk or has to pay a new airport tax when boarding a flight. Vital public institutions, such as the Canadian Broadcasting Corporation and the 'National Film Board, are now shadows of their former, robust selves. Telephone, electricity, and natural gas are no longer price-controlled services provided through a state-regulated monopoly. Crown corporations that helped constitute the state and its identity, such as Air Canada and Canadian National Railways, have been sold off and are run as private monopolies, nominally answerable to shareholders who are as likely as not American.

The country on which my friend, as a civic activist, environmentalist, and university professor, had projected his hopes and ideals indeed seemed finished. The Canada he loved was toast. So in asking whether the country would survive, he was implicitly begging a couple of other questions. Did these indicators of social and institutional degeneration result from *external* forces or from decisions made by *domestic* political actors? And were they reversible in the sense that the Canada of his dreams could re-emerge in reality?

Valid though these questions were, answers could not easily be found through reading the huge and contentious literature that has sprung up about the current state of the nation-state. To start with, there is confusion about the nature of the external forces to which states are now subjected. Since no one agrees even on the meaning of crucial terms, I would like to clarify how the three concepts of globalization, global governance, and globalism will be used in this book.

Globalization is, of course, the dominant buzzword of our times and bears a heavily determinist load. Voters are told that governments must cut budgets because the irresistible force of globalization requires fiscal austerity. But if we consider the basic claims – political, ideological, economic, social, environmental, cultural, and technological – made for the phenomenon, we can see that the novelty of globalization is quite relative.

- *Politically,* globalization is thought to be destabilizing existing centres of authority and security, with new power centres emerging at every level, from the local to the international.[1] This is not a new phenomenon. Since long before the term was coined, imperial powers have destabilized their colonies' political systems. But much of what is today called globalization is the product of decisions made by nation states, particularly the most powerful.[2] In the wake of the catastrophe of September 11, 2001, the United States has proven that the state system, if it wants to, can regain control by clamping down on terrorist organizations' use of global capital markets for money laundering.
- *Economically,* markets trade round the clock. Transnational corporations (TNCs) locate components of their production process wherever they can minimize their costs. Distribution systems are now organized on a global basis in order to recuperate the huge investments made to develop new high-tech products. It is nevertheless true that some TNCs have operated globally for decades, some for centuries.
- In *social relations*, globalization is restructuring the way in which people live and how they relate to each other. But societal transformation across vast distances has been proceeding since long before Europeans sailed to the New World in the fifteenth century.
- *Environmentally,* the fragile envelope that sustains plant and animal life on earth is under increasing strain, but threats to human survival from industrialization antedate the recent discovery of globalization and would continue even with lower levels of technological, cultural, and economic interconnectedness.
- In *cultural expression*, the production and diffusion of information and entertainment have become worldwide through the use of satellite transmission. Again, this reality is undeniable but needs to be put in the perspective of world religions, which were crossing the seven seas hundreds of years ago.

- *Technologically,* the computer and the internet have obviously accelerated information exchanges, but such fundamental breakthroughs as the telegraph and telephone had already created a universal society by the early twentieth century.

Any debate over globalization's novelty is bound to be sterile. Because it has become so, well, globally accepted, I want to use the word to stand for the current, post–Cold War phase of these political, economic, social, environmental, cultural, and technological trends.

Global governance. Long before the millennium, most European states had already experienced *transnational* governance through supranational continental institutions, which evolved fitfully in the years after 1945 into today's European Union. Canada had resisted formalized transnational governance until it implemented CUFTA in 1989. Continental governance including Mexico came a few years later with NAFTA, although this agreement's institutions were of doubtful effectiveness.

Globalization did bring one innovation in the 1990s whose importance no one should dismiss. The WTO is an institution of *global governance* that is both new and powerful. While it had deep roots in the half-century-old General Agreement on Tariffs and Trade (GATT), the World Trade Organization constituted a major development in *global governance* as an institution providing a mode of regulation for the current phase of globalized capital accumulation. The Canadian state's almost-simultaneous entry into both continental and global liberalizing regimes in 1994 and 1995 allows me to posit global governance after globalization as a second exogenous – or external – variable in my inquiry

Globalism. I use globalism to label the ideological corollary of globalization and global governance. Inspired and theorized by neoclassical economists, this paradigm maintains that a state's ability to protect its markets *ought to be* constrained. As the world economy then becomes more integrated, corporations can achieve the greatest economies of scale by operating on a worldwide basis, producing their goods and services at the lowest prices for the greatest benefit of consumers.[3]

As with the discourse on globalization, sceptics about globalism can validly object that this is not the first time that a doctrine has been universalized. A century ago, conservative laissez-faire was orthodoxy in the industrial world's governing circles. Half a century later, a more progressive Keynesianism was the global ideology endorsed by elites throughout the capitalist world. For this reason, I term *neoconservative* globalism the policy paradigm that currently justifies and promotes globalization as necessary, beneficial, and desirable.

To identify neoconservative globalism as a universal ideology raises the danger of obscuring the role of *domestic* political actors. Neoconservative ideas are not imposed mechanically by the American Enterprise Institute, Harvard University's Department of Economics, or the *Wall Street Journal*, although U.S. think tanks and research faculties have articulated the attack on liberal Keynesianism, and corporate-controlled mass media have popularized these ideas to the general public. However, when Premiers Ralph Klein, Mike Harris, or Gordon Campbell took up this paradigm in Alberta, Ontario, and British Columbia, they were agents both of globalization and of domestic pressures. Depending on its political base, neoconservatism can be considered either an external or a domestic expression.

The adjective 'neoconservative' will also serve to distinguish the ideological system favouring globalization and its corresponding global governance from the ideas expressed by those individuals and groups who have awakened to realize that their jobs, their health, the quality of their environment, and certain other values they hold dear are affected, even threatened. Anti-globalization ideologies have mobilized citizens in waves to protest the policies, processes, and practices of globalization's institutional embodiments. In anti-globalist organizations, 'Seattle,' 'Washington,' 'Windsor,' 'Calgary,' 'Prague,' 'Quebec,' and 'Genoa' have become code names for voluble, visible, and globally televised demonstrations organized by various transnationally connected opposition networks against (respectively) the WTO, the World Bank, the Organization of American States, the World Petroleum Association, the IMF, the Free Trade Area of the Americas, and the Economic Summit. As with neoconservative globalism, populist globalism generates transnational solidarities while remaining rooted in domestic politics.

So far, this preliminary discussion has treated globalization, global governance, and neoconservative globalism as if they were independent variables and exogenous factors in the analysis. This is because this book's prime question is the extent to which these recent manifestations of ever-greater transnational integration have affected the

Canadian state. Readers can rightly object to this being too simple-minded an intellectual agenda. When we come to such questions as the nature of global governance or the role of Canadian direct investment abroad, we will see that Canada has not been entirely passive in the face of external forces. The following chapters analyse globalization as a double-edged phenomenon, something that happened to us as well as something that we have caused to happen.

Other problems citizens encounter in the globalization literature are inherent in social science itself, which cannot take for granted the *meaning* of the facts that bombard us. For instance, we may read that in 2000 Canada exported $360 billion worth of goods to the United States and imported $268 billion of U.S. goods. Presented as raw data, the mind-boggling magnitude of these figures escapes most of us. We may get a better feel for the importance of trade to the country's economic health when the exports are translated as 40 per cent of Canadian gross domestic product and the imports as 30 per cent. Only when we compare these proportions with those of other countries do we learn that the Canadian economy has become extraordinarily 'open.' When these Canada-U.S. trade numbers are presented as 85 per cent of Canada's total exports and 74 per cent of its imports for that year, we can see how overwhelmingly dependent Canada is on trade with one single economy. And when these figures are then compared to the levels that obtained just before CUFTA came into effect in 1988 – 74 per cent for exports and 66 per cent for imports – we see how far Canada's integration in the American economy has advanced under free trade.

Grasping the significance of a fact also involves making a judgment, and making a judgement invokes one's core values. Those who celebrate the *fact* of Canada's growing openness to foreign trade as a welcome increase in its international integration generally embrace a value system giving top priority to economic growth. They see Canada's continental integration as a passport to its global economic success. Those who bewail their country's growing economic dependence on the American market espouse values such as political autonomy, social equality, labour rights, and environmental sustainability. They tend to see Canadian integration in the American system as entrenching an unwelcome reliance on factors beyond national control.

Confusion over facts is linked to confusion over values. This appears in the globalization debate as an emotive element that is rife in many analysts' work. In June 2000, at a Harvard University conference on the crisis of the multilateral trade system, even world-famous economists demonized 'them' – protesters at the WTO's meeting in Seattle the previous autumn – condemning them as either ignorant of elementary economics or outright demagogues, if not fascists.

An equally Manichean view of a world caught in a titanic struggle between the forces of evil (transnational capital and neoconservatives) and the forces of good (environmentalists, labour activists, and other representatives from civil society) permeates the non-governmental organizations (NGOs) leading the attack on globalization. Their publications rarely refer to the works of mainstream economists, just as neoclassical economists consistently ignore the publications of their critics.

This dialogue of the deaf extends to government's role in the economy. Neoconservatives start from the position that any interference in the economy by politicians is a mistake. Who governs least governs best. NGOs representing environmentalists, labour unions, or human rights activists also tend to distrust the state, because they see it as captured by neoconservatives, but they believe that better government policies should be part of the solution. They can point to some of the great success stories of the last half-century as those of interventionist states, both in Europe and in Asia, that created competitive advantage for their firms. Bombardier, BC Hydro, and Nortel in its former glory would not have become triumphs of Canadian capitalism without active state support.

My analysis takes the Keynesian welfare state that was developed under the prime ministerships of John Diefenbaker, Lester Pearson, and Pierre Trudeau from 1957 to 1984 as the standard against which to assess the neoconservative state that has been reconstituted by Prime Ministers Brian Mulroney and Jean Chrétien. In doing so I want to foreswear both a nostalgia for what cannot be restored and a teleology that ascribes to the state certain roles that it *should* play.

If concerned men and women are understandably confused about the fate of their state, it is equally appropriate if they are sceptical about the policy solutions to which they are exposed, whether in thirty-second sound bites from TV commentators or thirty-page articles in learned journals. Citizens have been plied with a stream of these neoconservative panaceas. In the mid-1980s, free trade was the solution for Canada's productivity problem. The country took the plunge, but a decade later Canadians learned their economy's productivity was still in crisis. The new magic bullet became cutting corporate taxation levels in order to attract capital. Or reducing personal income taxes to stem the brain drain. Or adopting the American dollar to stabilize the currency.

No one can deny the heavy element of subjectivity that pervades this discussion. What may be a half-full glass for one analyst who sees an impressively efficient healthcare system may be half empty for another who emphasizes the cracks that are appearing in the structure as the expensive and inefficient U.S. model looms large. Because of the highly emotional and even arbitrary bases on which many arguments about globalization are developed, I hope this book will offer readers thorough, solid information and a clear, if necessarily complex, analysis of the central issues in Canada's survival dossier.

... Deserves a Complex Answer

There is one simple answer that I chose not to put forward in response to my friend's simple query. I could have replied that of course Canada will survive if only because the United States would not want to annex it. Adding nine provinces to the American union, not to mention Quebec and the territories, would upset the delicate balance of power the Democrats and Republicans have achieved in the U.S. Congress. Canadians lean heavily towards the Democrats even in Alberta, the country's most conservative and American province. Accommodating 24 million people – Quebecers presumably would opt for independence rather than annexation – accustomed to state-supplied medical care would present the American polity with an immediate crisis.

But my friend's question was not about whether the geographical *space* now known as 'Canada' would survive. Obviously, it would remain on the map, stretching over a vast terrain from the American border all the way to the North Pole. The issue was in what form and with what content the political, juridical, economic, societal, and cultural entity we call Canada would continue to exist. This question in turn breaks down into two problems – one external, the other internal. The conundrum about outside forces has been on everyone's lips: was globalization causing Canada to lose control of its destiny? Also widespread as a public concern was whether the neoconservative governing paradigm has eviscerated the social achievements that have been integral to Canadians' sense of their national identity.

I am by no means the first social scientist to address the Canadian survival question. Some scholars have explicitly raised the spectre of Canada's dismantling.[4] Others have poured scorn on this concern, insisting that Canada will persist even though its distinctiveness is far less notable than nationalists claim.[5] On the whole, the debate has pitted those on the left, who put a high value on Canada's unique identity and believe government helps sustain its difference, against anti-nationalists on the right, who dismiss most state policies as responses to special interests trying to feather their own nests.

I agree that Canada is not about to disappear. But I also argue that the changes wrought to the political legacy of the Diefenbaker-Pearson-Trudeau period by neoconservative politicians in the two decades of the Mulroney-Chrétien era have been significant, in some cases seriously endangering the country's social fabric, economic vitality, and environmental sustainability.

I address these problems in the following chapters by distinguishing the *structural* changes to the Canadian state from its *functional* workings. Looking in part I at innovations in Canada's institutional structure will take us from the reconstitutionalizing effects on the federal and provincial governments of the new trade regime to the way that neoconservatism has reframed our cities.

Having established the effects of globalization on the *political* framework of government, the rest of the book looks functionally at the major policy areas of principal interest to Canadians. Part II contains eight chapters on *economic* policy, while part III deals with the more *societal* state functions of social, labour, environmental, cultural, and foreign policy.

After we have looked at the structural and functional changes wrought by globalization and neoconservatism on the Canadian political system, two general propositions will become clear. In the first place, the new forms of global governance – in whose construction Canada participated if only in a supporting role – have indeed significantly restructured the Canadian political system. In this reconstituted political space, neoconservativism has inspired Canadian politicians and their bureaucrats to adopt policies that have had a substantial, parallel, and direct impact on the country's fibre.

If I am right in this second step of the argument, there is a double answer to my friend's question. To start with, the issue is not *whether*, but *which* Canada will survive. Then, even if Canada's *form* has been partially determined by outside forces, its *content* has been determined mainly by agencies and agents that the public ultimately controls. So if citizens want a different Canada that embraces the kind of values that my friend holds dear, they will have to elect politicians who have the same sense of social justice. And they will have to be willing to pay the price for more egalitarian, sustainable, and progressive government.

Before we engage in this two-part analysis, we need to think more about how globalization challenges our notion of the state and what is special about the Canadian condition in North America, the subject of chapter 2.

2 The Peripheral State:
Globalization and Continentalism

For several months after the federal election of November 21, 1988, had confirmed that Canada would ratify the Canada-United States Free Trade Agreement (CUFTA) over which Brian Mulroney had successfully fought his campaign, I mentally wore a black armband. I was in mourning for the exuberant, liveable, creative, hopeful Canada that my generation had tried to build and that 'free' trade seemed to have condemned to a lingering death. I had shared, and helped articulate in my research, the concerns of the millions who opposed Mulroney's deal. Deeper integration in the American system, we believed, would doom the efforts of many generations to build a better society on the northern third of the continent. CUFTA signalled the end of Canada as we knew it. It would strike at the heart of the government structures and programs in which we had lodged so much of our shared identity.

As I look back with greater serenity and detachment at the aftermath of this political battle, CUFTA has proven to be what both camps in the debate expected: a historical turning point from which there could be no return. It also turned out to be just the first round in a series of Canadian engagements with those broader economic and political forces that we now call globalization and that affect all countries. To situate Canada in its wider political-economy context, the next few pages will unpack both the concept of the state and that of globalization.

The Emergence of the Territorial State

Our starting point in attempting to understand the *Canadian* state under globalization should be to understand the changing quality of all states over time. This enterprise requires us to come to grips with a general truth about human beings and the societies they construct:

they experience constant change. As civilizations have risen and fallen, the political forms they have taken – their state structures – have also changed. Think of the small, but fiercely independent city states of ancient Greece. Think of the vast imperial states created by the Romans or the Byzantines. Think of the tiny feudal domains characteristic of the Middle Ages in Europe and of the victorious monarchies that later coalesced from their ranks through armed force and diplomatic guile. In 1648, when the Peace of Westphalia was signed after thirty years of devastating religious wars, the emergent kingdoms recognized each others' sovereign right to order their internal (particularly religious) affairs without outside interference. That watershed treaty marked the dawn of our own era: the state had become identified not just with religion, but with territory, with nationality, with military might, with sovereign power, and increasingly with language and even ethnicity.

What many refer to as the Westphalian or nation-state I call the 'sovereign' or 'territorial' state, because 'nation' is a highly contested concept in Canada among Quebecers and Aboriginals. This type of state is a relatively recent phenomenon, at the most 400 years old, and, for those that emerged from European colonial rule, under 50 years of age. If we join Max Weber in defining states as the institutions that divide the surface of the globe into discrete territorial units within each of which the government enjoys sovereignty – that is, a monopoly over the legitimate means of violence within its borders and a mutual recognition with other states of their right not to be interfered with from without – we must acknowledge that we are embellishing a notion of statehood from the very specific, nineteenth-century, Euro-American intellectual context of modernity. In this framework the idea of the modern state became endowed with many politically significant features that are now seen to constitute the essence of 'stateness':

- The modern state has a *constitution*, which creates governing institutions and determines how they are to operate in the political process.
- The modern state operates a government on *representative* and electoral principles, which allow it to call itself democratic.
- The modern state creates a public *bureaucracy*, which transmutes power into impersonal modes of authority.
- The modern state creates *rights* for its members, who enjoy special liberties, entitlements, and obligations as a consequence of their status as its citizens.
- The modern state also controls the market activities carried on within its borders, which are understood as *its economy*.

- Giving expression to its monopoly over the legitimate use of *coercion*, the modern state has armed forces to deal with threats to its sovereignty from without and police forces that repress threats to public order from within.
- The modern state fosters a *culture* that constructs its citizens' distinctive national identity and promotes a multitude of symbols such as a national flag and anthem, a national airline or broadcasting system.
- The modern state nourishes a *public domain*, which can be thought of as unalienated lands and natural resources and public spaces such as parks, streets, and buildings to which everyone enjoys free access.

Having sketched in the outlines of the ideal Weberian state, we need immediately to recognize that such a pure construction can never exist under contemporary conditions. No territorial state is ethnically homogeneous. No territory can be perfectly guaranteed against invasion or sabotage, as Americans learned on September 11, 2001. No economy can operate autarchically. No identity can be reduced solely to citizenship. No culture could be entirely contained within national boundaries. However inadequate Weber's notion of the state might be as a description of every political society's complexity, it helps direct our understanding empirically of what states actually *are* and our attitude normatively about what states *should be*.

The Canadian State

In the light of the sovereign modern state's evolution, it is immediately obvious that the Canadian version has been sovereign and modern only in theory. Canadian governments never fully controlled their economy, which has had high levels of trade dependence linked to imperial control. They have never been able to protect their borders without the help of the armed forces provided by their current protector – France, Britain, or the United States. Canada's culture has never come close to being fully self-generated. In these respects Canada was 'postmodern' long before modernism. Only in the political sense did it enjoy sovereignty, with complete control over its democratic processes, its bureaucracy, its courts, its police forces, and, eventually, its constitution.

Staple-Exporting Colony

Once the Americas were discovered by Europeans, who called them their 'new world' and wrested them from the hands of their native populations, they were ipso facto internationalized. What we now think of as 'Canada' is the present result of an evolving set of power struggles. First the military wars for dominance among the European monarchies decided the location of frontiers between their colonies far across the Atlantic Ocean. These conflicts continued within North America between settlers and Aboriginals, then between the colonies and their imperial centres, and later still among the three emerging Mexican, American, and Canadian states.

As a periphery first to Paris and later to London, the Canadian economy was from its inception part of a global commercial network, vulnerable to the political whims of the hegemon and subject to the world market's fluctuating demand and prices for its products. The long and painful transition on the northern half of North America from an Aboriginal to an industrialized economy was driven by an early form of globalization: the overseas demand from metropolitan France, then England for the 'staples' their explorers had found in this wild land mass – fish to start with from Newfoundland's Grand Banks, fur brought by native trappers to exchange for guns or liquor, later timber hacked from the virgin forests, and then wheat grown where the land was cleared of its remaining stumps.

Whether the colonial economy enjoyed boom or suffered bust depended on the play of *external* factors that had led to its creation in the first place. Transportation technology dictated how quickly cargoes could cross the Atlantic and make intercontinental commerce possible. Consumer demand in the motherland was the sine qua non of a peripheral economy. When fur hats were the rage in Paris, the beaver trade boomed in Nouvelle France. When they fell out of fashion, it plummeted. The availability of metropolitan capital was equally basic to establishing a colonial enterprise. When the Gentlemen Adventurers of England Trading into Hudson Bay pooled their financial resources in 1672 in the hope of making fortunes for themselves, a new era began in Canada.

Emerging Dominion (1867–1911)

Ever since Westminister created the Dominion of Canada through the British North America (BNA) Act some two centuries later, the postcolonial Canadian state has reconstituted itself in several strikingly different incarnations. From its inception, the Dominion's constitution was established under that of Britain, which exercised a supraconstitutional control of the Dominion's foreign and commercial policy, signing treaties with Washington and declaring war on Canada's behalf.

The central government in Ottawa controlled the territories and managed internal, country-wide affairs with its military, judicial, and economic powers defined in the BNA Act. Meanwhile the provinces shared sovereignty with the central government, having competence in resource management, schools, roads, welfare, and establishing municipalities.

Under John A. Macdonald and Wilfrid Laurier, who governed in most of the years from 1867 to 1911, the young Dominion had a minimal state structure as these leaders strove to use a centralized, party-driven, patronage-fuelled parliamentary politics to build what they called a 'nation.' This first phase of national policy connected a grouping of disparate colonies and territories to the British imperial centre through their eastward-oriented, staple-exporting economy using the first industrial revolution's technology of steam and telegraphy.

If we understand markets as overlapping systems of power that states try to manage to their greatest benefit, we can see Macdonald's National Policy of 1879 as his attempt to use the four simple policy tools at his disposal to create a more state-directed market out of the disparate colonial economies he had helped cobble together at Confederation. Ottawa appropriated millions of acres occupied by Aboriginals and used them as bait for enticing immigrants to risk roughing it in the wilds and clearing the bush for cultivation. The young federation's creditworthiness, which was greater than that of its constituent colonies, allowed it to float bonds in London and run deficits in order to finance the railway construction needed to open up the prairies to settlement and farming. The federal government's commerce power enabled Ottawa to institute a tariff that would generate revenue and induce would-be entrepreneurs from Britain or the United States to install their factories alongside those of local businessmen, protected from the competition of foreign imports. Lastly, Ottawa's Patent Act created a use-it-or-lose-it incentive to induce inventors to apply their new techniques commercially in Canada or to forfeit the right to exploit them in Canada.

These efforts of the fledgling Canadian state at fostering economic development by import substitution mimicked the pattern of other countries emulating British industrialization, but with two major differences. Vast though its territory may have been, Canada's population was too tiny to consume the primary products it harvested, and its manufacturing capacity was too embryonic to produce the range of finished goods it needed. Having refused to join the American colonies in cutting its economic umbilical cord, British North America retained the imperial market for fish, for timber from its watersheds, and for agriculture in the midwest. Even the new manufactured goods produced in central Canada found an external market that, at the end of the century, was secured by imperial preference rates, which gave Canadian exports privileged access to British consumers.

Canada's second distinguishing characteristic of capitalist development via tariff protection was its active encouragement of foreign investors. Chancellor Bismarck used the tariff to protect infant industries while they matured within the German customs union and empire, but he was careful to exclude foreign capitalists from taking over the commanding heights of the economy. Canada's disregard for the nationality of its immigrant entrepreneurs paid off handsomely for several decades. By the turn of the twentieth century, the young Dominion had the seventh-largest manufacturing economy in the world, on a par with Japan and somewhat ahead of Sweden. Its farm-implement industry was – to use the jargon popular a hundred years later – globally competitive, as was apparent when Massey Harris exhibited its mechanical reaper at the Paris World Fair of 1889. The product of a partnership between two Americans who had settled in Upper Canada, it became the prototype of a revolutionary new entrepreneurial form by establishing fully owned and controlled operations in many other countries to manufacture and market its burgeoning range of farm machinery and tractors.[1]

Federal Consolidation (1911–1935)

The Canadian state developed from the Conservative prime ministership of Robert Borden to that of R.B. Bennett (1911–1935) on the basis of a brokerage politics whose conflicts were mediated by a culture of inter-regional compromise and a newly meritocratic bureaucracy. The political class's defiant reliance on an individualistic, laissez-faire liberalism proved incapable of preventing capitalism's ultimate collapse in the early 1930s, when Canada was granted de facto autonomy from Westminster.

Canada may have helped invent the transnational corporation (TNC), but it ultimately became its victim, as this new technique of corporate management allowed entrepreneurs abroad to retain ownership and control of their production processes. The technology of the second industrial revolution (based on electricity, the telephone, radio, and the internal combustion engine) spread into Canada mainly by branch plants exploiting their intellectual property under foreign licence. At the same time, Canada shifted from shipping staples across the Atlantic for the British market to mining minerals or making newsprint, along with many other staples, to be sent south to satisfy a voracious U.S. demand. The most advanced Canadian industries in the twentieth century – automobile manufacturing, chemicals, petroleum, electrical equipment, pulp and paper – evolved in large part as American-owned branch-plant operations. Their technologically dependent relationship with their headquarters across the border and the resulting restricted scope for their Canadian managers' entrepreneurial initiative provoked a long, sometimes-bitter – and still-unresolved – debate about the liberating or constricting consequences of foreign direct investment.

Nationality of ownership became irrelevant when boom turned to bust. The moral crisis of capitalism precipitated by the Crash of 1929 and by increased protectionism, which turned serious recession into the Great Depression, produced intense pressure on politicians to remedy the social distress and dislocation that spread across the country. Liberals, who had been taught to believe that the state's role was to leave the economy to its own devices, were emboldened by new thinking in the 1930s from John Maynard Keynes in England about how the state could save capitalism by regulating and humanizing it. Galvanized by the need to marshal the country's resources for total war against fascism, Liberal politicians and their British-trained civil servants in Ottawa under Prime Minister William Lyon Mackenzie King revolutionized the state's role in directing the economy during the early 1940s. They fixed prices to contain inflation. They rationed distribution to husband supplies. They created crown corporations to produce necessary goods, such as synthetic petroleum, or to provide services not offered by the private sector, such as trans-Canada air transport.

State Keynesianism (1935–1984)

Following this heady experience with state-mobilized capitalism, Canada's rulers relaxed their near-total control of the economy's functions but retained the general role of manager. They could justify their continuing involvement in managing the market by invoking Keynes's two-track formula for state activism: on one level, counter-cyclical macro-economic adjustment, and, on the other, direct transfers to individuals through public spending on social programs such as unemployment insurance and baby bonuses, publicly provided medical care, and old age security.

The governments of King and Louis St Laurent (1935–1957) pioneered their Keynesian mode of regulation under the aegis of a central government supported by a consociational consensus of the country's political, corporate, and media elites. Complementing this Keynesianism was a 'Fordist' consensus that was worked out on the factory floor. State-regulated collective bargaining granted organized labour a share in the returns produced by mass-production manufacturing under conditions of growing productivity rates and an increasingly acquisitive society, whose consumerism was activated by the insistent taste-making of the mass media.

The Keynesian formula produced a remarkable economic success. From the end of the Second World War in 1945, it presided over a 'mixed' economy, in which the federal and provincial public sectors, with considerable governmental bureaucracies, some strategic crown corporations, and many regulatory bodies, coexisted with a tariff-protected private sector. Its technologically advanced industries were in most cases dominated by American companies, which supplied consumer goods from their local branch plants and operated alongside a few Canadian-owned sectors – most notably, the steel industry, the pulp and paper sector, the banking oligopoly, and the regional telephone monopolies. Thanks to the Fordist compromise between management and the trade unions, wages went up in conjunction with productivity, so that annual real income rose dramatically, from $12,000 per capita in 1961 to $17,000 in 1971 and $22,000 in 1981.[2]

The reference point for my assessment of the Canadian state under globalization is the next period, initiated during John Diefenbaker's turbulent incumbency (1957–63), after which Lester Pearson (1963–8) and Pierre Trudeau (1968–84) attempted to consolidate a social security state. Although Canada has always been a fundamentally liberal country, deeply sceptical of coercive and concentrated state action, Keynesianism was based on a more activist liberalism, which wove market functions into the social fabric, subordinating moderately liberalized trade and international capital movements under the pax Americana to the interests of domestic macro-economic management.

The achievement of formal political sovereignty occurred in 1982 when Westminster passed the final act that ceded to Canada the sovereign power to amend its constitution, now the Constitution Act, 1982. Britain's vestigial and de jure supraconstitutional authority over Canada had long been replaced by the United States's informal but de facto supraconstitutional suzerainty.

The Canadian-American Relationship as a Constitutional Order

Keynes did not deserve all the credit for Canada's postwar economic success. Even if Ottawa had followed his prescriptions religiously – and Liberal politicians violated them whenever they proved uncomfortable – Canada's capital market was too integrated in the U.S. financial system for Ottawa and the provinces ever to follow the Cambridge economist's advice to the letter. Only myopia kept Canadians from recognizing how much their economic success was due to growth in the U.S. economy, to which theirs was as firmly attached as a caboose to a freight train by links that were societal, cultural, and political as well as economic.

Along with intense investment and trade, the cross-border flow of people, ideas, fashion, culture, sports, and societal organizations had developed a constitution-like stability. U.S. relations with Canada had unobtrusively developed a number of behavioural conventions that expressed the two states' interests in mutual co-operation without setting up formal institutions to govern their relationship.

The United States had long applied a strategy of maintaining Canada as a complementary economy while preventing it from becoming a competitive one, freely admitting its raw materials but slapping high tariffs on its manufactured exports aimed at the U.S. market.[3] Washington never officially formulated a comprehensive set of demands concerning how the federal and provincial governments to the north should – or, more important, how they should not – behave. For its part, Canada resisted institutionalizing its crucial bilateral relationship, preferring to deal with its overwhelming neighbour either on an ad hoc basis, issue by issue, or in multilateral forums, where it could form alliances with other countries on specific problems it had with Washington.[4]

Despite Canada's integration in North America not being formalized by any overarching document or institution, there were clear portents by the mid-1960s that this continental dyad was developing an unwritten, convention-based order, demonstrating the eight features considered characteristic of a constitution.[5]

- *The will* to manage North America as a common community had been palpable since intense military and economic co-operation began in the common effort to mobilize the continent's resources during the Second World War.
- *Basic norms*, understood as regularized constraints on behaviour, were worked out by the civil servants and politicians responsible for managing the relationship. Both sides tacitly agreed that Canada should not overtly criticize American foreign policy. As quid pro quo, the United States was not to bully Canada. These principles were actually elaborated into a doctrine dubbed 'quiet diplomacy' to indicate that Canadian-American conflicts were to be mediated as much as possible by bureaucrats behind closed doors in order to keep political tensions at bay.[6] One such rule, derived from the need *quietly* to manage a relationship between two highly unequal states was the norm of not 'linking' issues. This meant, for instance, that a conflict over a cultural matter, such as Ottawa's legislating out of business the Canadian edition of the American *Time* magazine, was not to be complicated by U.S. threats of retaliation affecting bilateral trade in, say, steel.
- Formal *policy-making institutions* did not exist beyond the military entity created by the North American Air Defence Command (1957), but continental policy making took place within such sub-systemic, private-sector institutions as TNCs, American trade unions with Canadian branches, sports conglomerates such as the National Hockey League, professional associations such as the Canadian Medical Association, and the production and distribution networks of the mass entertainment industry.[7] Within each of these economic or cultural sectors, the overwhelming weight of the American system compelled the Canadian component to play by the Americans' rules. Many aspects of Canadian policy operated in lockstep with their American counterparts to the extent that, for instance, the formally autonomous Bank of Canada's me-too interest rate behaviour earned it the sobriquet of 'the thirteenth district' of the Federal Reserve Board. Similarly, the power of New York's stock exchanges induced Canadian exchanges to adapt their own rules to those of the larger system. All Western countries were integrated within the economic imperium created by a dominant U.S. dollar and experienced some degree of dependence. But in Canada's case, the handful of formal and the multitude of informal institutions generated a unique stability of expectations, predictability of behaviour, and regularized

co-operation between the hegemon and its nominally sovereign but deeply dependent neighbour, which continually legitimized the relationship by calling it 'special.'

- Washington accepted tacit *limits* to the exercise over Canada of its enormous structural power, provided that Ottawa supported U.S. anti-communist foreign policy abroad.
- American corporate citizens enjoyed *rights* of access to Canadian resources and markets. Canadian firms, even if mainly branch plants of U.S. TNCs, had certain rights as well: access to bidding for Pentagon defence contracts, for instance. Citizens of both countries generally enjoyed greater mobility in being able to emigrate to each other's country than did people from other states.
- Because the Canadian-American system was not formally institutionalized, it lacked any *judicial process* for resolving disputes. Conflicts were dealt with through diplomatic negotiations or subsystemically within, for example, the U.S.-dominated labour movement.
- *Enforcement* of the rules of this intuitively understood bilateral game was made possible by the high level of trust that developed among the relevant decision-makers in each political system. On the American side, knowledge that there were so many U.S. interests involved in the relationship militated against letting any particular dispute get out of hand. On the Canadian side, the understanding that the United States could at any moment unleash damaging retaliatory measures required extremely careful responses to American pressure. Otherwise, once Canada became the object of political agitation in Congress, civil diplomacy gave way to threatening U.S. demands that Ottawa change its errant ways or be punished.[8]
- Significant *amendments* to this largely unwritten entente were made only after extensive consultations or negotiations generated specific agreements such as the Auto Pact of 1965.
- *Ratification* of this special relationship took the form of the two nations' leaders making ritualized references, as they waxed eloquent during bridge-opening ceremonies and after banquets, about the marvels of the world's longest undefended border.

Neither capital contemplated aborting the deeply routinized bilateral relationship, which seemed to be progressing sector by sector towards the two economies' full integration – until 1971. On August 15 of that year, under the balance-of-payments strain caused by his massive imperial overstretch in Vietnam, President Richard Nixon detached the U.S. dollar from the price of gold and imposed a surcharge on all imports. 'Nixonomics' was unleashed on the world to deal with the United States's global economic problems, but closer to home it broke bilateral conventions developed over previous decades, threatening to throttle Canadian exports and close down American direct investment. Although the U.S. president forebore at the last minute from precipitately torpedoing the Auto Pact, he went out of his way to end the special relationship unilaterally. He travelled to Ottawa the following spring to declare pointedly before a joint session of Parliament that Canada should think of itself as an independent state.

Exploring the Third Option (Increased National Autonomy) (1972–1984)

The Nixon bombshell ushered in a decade and a half of instability in Canada's relationship with its hegemonic neighbour, in which a phase of apparent autonomy prepared the way for a formal reconstitutionalization of its subordinate position. Trudeau commissioned a review of the American relationship that laid out three possible options, of which the first was maintaining the status quo and the second was pursuing deeper continental integration. Taking Nixon's advice to heart, the Trudeau government chose the third option of diversification to reduce dependence. Over the ensuing decade the Liberal government introduced many measures aimed at re-establishing federal control over the economy. After decades of treating U.S. firms as good Canadian citizens (an approach that was later known as national treatment), federal policies started discriminating in favour of Canadian capital. Most salient in the mid-1970s were agencies established to screen foreign direct investment (the Foreign Investment Review Agency) and to promote domestic ownership of the economy (the Canada Development Corporation). Then in 1980 came the Liberals' ambitious and notorious National Energy Program (NEP), which was designed to channel economic rents from resources into industrial development. This assertion of authority by the Canadian state over its economic space marked the apogee of its attempt to construct a dominant territorial state and to slow integration – at least at the political level.

Nixonomics and Ottawa's 'Third Option' response interrupted for a decade and a half the steady maturation of an informal Canada-U.S. regime. The U.S. State Department felt it could do nothing about

Ottawa's moderately nationalist response to its own government's chauvinism. Trudeau was a difficult politician to influence, since he was so largely indifferent to American values. Nettled when a continental energy deal was aborted, Washington held its breath and waited for Trudeau to leave the stage.[9]

Since Canadian business was no longer operating as though the national market was its bailiwick, the Trudeauites' efforts to shore up a mode for regulating a national economy came too late. The NEP's politically catastrophic dénouement two years later signalled the disjuncture between activism in a weak state and its economy's inability to resist the hegemon's gravitational pull. The failure of the Trudeauites' unusually progressive budget of 1981 marked a watershed in the Canadian state's trajectory of continual growth.[10] From that moment it began a gradual, tortuous, and bumpy slide towards a neoconservative reconfiguration along overtly continental lines.

By the 1970s Canadian firms were already encountering difficulty competing in their own market because of declining tariff protection. In their quest for survival they searched for space in the American market where they could invest and participate in a regime of corporate accumulation that was becoming increasingly continental in its orientation. How they fared there depended on forces largely beyond Ottawa's control, since its trade policy could do little except watch out for Canadian interests as the United States negotiated with its partners in the GATT the gradual reductions of the tariff rates that countries imposed on their imports. Trade negotiators were little-known officials with an obscure expertise that was respected more at GATT's headquarters in Geneva than it was in Ottawa. Trade commissioners were second-string civil servants and sometime diplomats in the federal Department of Industry, Trade and Commerce (IT&C) whose primary, and generally losing, struggle was to have their liberalizing goals in the trade and commerce sections prevail over the protectionist proclivities of their counterparts in the industry side of the department.

When nationalists in the federal Liberal caucus lost their battle in the early 1980s to enhance the interventionist thrust of federal industrial policy, the Trudeau government took the first, tentative steps towards considering commercial policy as an alternative route to boosting the economy's performance.[11] It moved the trade commissioners' service from IT&C and integrated it in the foreign service in what turned out to be the bureaucratic equivalent of a reverse takeover. Having been marginal in their old structure, the small band of liberalizing trade commissioners became the driving force in their new home.

The first indication of trade policy's dominance in Canadian foreign policy thinking came in an interdepartmental trade policy review. Although the report favoured total free trade as the solution, the timid recommendation that emerged in late 1983 was merely to propose several sectors to the United States for consideration as candidates for managed free trade arrangements similar to the Auto Pact. Even sectoral free trade seemed too bold for the politics of the period, if not for the times themselves. When discussions with Washington concerning a number of possible sectors, such as computers and transportation equipment, failed to produce a potential deal that would equitably balance gains and losses on the two sides, the idea was dropped – to the great relief of a government whose caucus was dominated by economic nationalists from Ontario.

Choosing the Second Option (Increased Continental Integration) (1984–)

The victory of Brian Mulroney's Tories in the 1984 federal election does not itself flag the turning point for Canada's radical shift in the neoconservative direction. The bilingual anglophone labour lawyer and manager of a staples-extracting branch operation who hailed from the Quebec resource hinterland was unabashedly pro-capitalist and pro-American – an admirer of Ronald Reagan and his British booster, Margaret Thatcher. But his intellectual capacities were modest, his ideological convictions negotiable, and his policy positions opportunistic. During his campaign for the Progressive Conservative Party's leadership in 1983, Mulroney had poured scorn on the very idea of free trade as a way to shore up his position in Ontario and to attack his challenger, John Crosbie. As leader of the opposition he had taken positions in favour of universal medicare and official bilingualism that seemed to guarantee greater continuity for the interventionist welfare state than did the state-shrinking ideas about cutting government spending and reducing the federal deficit that John Turner expressed while campaigning a year later to succeed Trudeau as Liberal leader.

Nor can the shift to neoconservatism in Canada be credibly presented as the extension of an irresistible tidal wave that was driving Keynesianism onto the rocks on every national shore. To be sure, there was a changed ideological context in the early 1980s. Margaret

Thatcher had swept to power in Britain in 1979 with her militant program to decimate the welfare state. The Iron Lady's unflinching, 'there-is-no-alternative' conviction certainly bolstered support for Ronald Reagan's campaign in 1980 to get government off the backs of business and powered her second majority victory in 1983. In the Antipodes, New Zealand had become the neoconservative exemplar – a once-generous welfare state that had cut its services to the bone. But continental Europe was steadfastly resisting the new siren song. And, in the Far East, two dazzling new dragons, Taiwan and South Korea, were about to bring in welfare state measures in the wake of dramatic moves to democratize their previously authoritarian (and parsimonious) states.

While the corporate base for an increasingly vocal Canadian neoconservatism in the mid-1980s was the foreign- and domestically owned TNCs grouped under the powerful lobby known as the BCNI (Business Council on National Issues), its institutional base had been the federal Department of Finance ever since the Conservative Michael Wilson, a product of the Toronto business community, had become its minister. Wilson's first economic statement, issued in the autumn of 1984, had already challenged the nostrums of the previous forty years.

According to the finance department's revised wisdom, the state's proper role was no longer to pursue internal equilibrium by attempting to manipulate aggregate demand. Past efforts to do so by running budgetary deficits had not reduced unemployment levels while succeeding only in accumulating a monumental national debt. Efforts to develop microeconomic and interventionist industrial strategies had failed. Instead of pursuing state activism, government ought to liberate the market from excessive regulation so that the economy could play the central role in job creation and growth that was deemed to be its proper function. This neoconservative analysis knitted macroeconomic, industrial, and trade policy together into a coherent pattern that buried Keynes.

Although this argument was coherent, its persuasive power within Mulroney's cabinet was limited. By the late summer of 1985, however, the prime minister faced a serious dilemma. Despite his huge majority in the House of Commons, he was leading a scandal-wracked government. Worse, it was wallowing in indecision because he had not managed to give it a clear direction. One day after a not-so-euphoric celebration on September 4 of his first anniversary in office, Mulroney received an unlikely gift from the gods – or, rather, an unintended gift from his predecessor.

Three years earlier, when Trudeau's efforts at post-Keynesian, micro-economic interventions were being widely denounced as failures, he had agreed to launch an arm's-length review of the Canadian government's policy options. He appointed his former finance minister, Donald S. Macdonald, to chair a royal commission on the Economic Union and Development Prospects for Canada and to recommend an agenda for what it was assumed – with typical Grit hubris – would be the Liberal Party's next period in government, as it led the country towards the new millennium. As events unfolded, Macdonald did indeed provide an agenda for the governments that took Canada into the twenty-first century. But the action program he designed was to reverse – not perpetuate – the trail blazed by the Trudeauites. And it was executed not by state-friendly liberal governors who were wary of the market, but by market-friendly conservative officials who were wary of the state.

Macdonald's recommendation of free trade coupled with a rejection of Canada's historical commitment to an active state offered an immediate solution to Mulroney's agenda problem.[12] The 'optics' were excellent. Its three thick volumes were the product of $21 million spent on academic research and public consultations. Given his impeccable Liberal credentials, Macdonald's prescription could not be accused of partisan, pro-Tory bias. Nevertheless it would steal the thunder from John Turner, now leader of the Liberal opposition. Better still, the report's anti-statist positions fitted nicely with those being put forward in Finance by Wilson.

In Macdonald's vision, trade policy would play a new, central role in Canada's economy. It was his belief that, in a geographically fragmented market largely open to foreign imports after three decades of steady tariff reduction, manipulating domestic demand could no longer provide the impetus for industrial development. Rather than encourage economic development with the industrial-policy stimuli of various hands-on, state-provided carrots, trade liberalization offered a large, threatening stick: it would force firms to become competitive with their international rivals or face extinction. Keynesian-era incentives were to give way to globalization's Damoclean sword. If they rose to the challenge, made a leap of faith, and survived the cold shower of competition – all clichés popular among trade liberalizers – entrepreneurs would find pots of gleaming gold. Access to global markets would create the virtuous circle caused by economies of scale: falling costs would accrue from rising sales and engender greater profits, allowing more investment in new technologies and so further expansion. The way to liberate the market was to abandon protectionism and statism and to opt for global free trade.

But there was an impediment in the trade liberalizers' program. GATT was so weak as a forum for arbitrating trade conflicts that it was dubbed sarcastically the 'general agreement to talk and talk.' In the mid-1980s, when a proposed round of negotiations on difficult new issues such as services and investment seemed irredeemably blocked by extensive differences between the European Union (EU) and the United States, leading economic bureaucrats in Ottawa became convinced that the only way to pre-empt a new wave of congressional protectionism threatening Canada's vulnerable export dependence on the U.S. market was to negotiate a bilateral deal directly with Washington.

Once Mulroney accepted the prescription (notwithstanding clear indications that he did not really understand it),[13] he allowed no shilly-shallying. In October 1985, when he wrote to Reagan formally requesting negotiations between the two countries, he started a process that would start to reconstitute the Canadian state. Replacing Trudeau's Third Option with the previously unthinkable second option of increased continental integration, he reversed thirteen years of his predecessor's efforts to increase Canada's parlous autonomy vis-à-vis the United States. At the same time he renounced the protectionism that had been his party's core belief since John A. Macdonald had announced the National Policy in 1879. Rejecting Canadian governments' longstanding instinct to resist formalizing their relationship with the United States, Mulroney embraced trade liberalization with a determination bordering on zealotry. Free trade had become in his mind a panacea for Canada's ills, and nothing could stop him achieving it.

He put in place believers who would implement the program without deviating from his objective: making a deal with Washington at virtually any price. The chief trade negotiator, Simon Reisman, was a business lobbyist and former deputy minister of finance who turned his appointment into a heaven-sent opportunity to make his mark on history. Having been impressed by the toughness and commitment demonstrated by Derek Burney from the Department of External Affairs in organizing Canada's so-called Shamrock summit with Reagan in March 1985, Mulroney appointed the diplomat to the partisan position of principal secretary to maintain discipline in the Prime Minister's Office (PMO) during the negotiations. Those people with doubts or minds of their own were marginalized, whether it was Pat Carney, the trade minister who was nominally in charge and whom Reisman systematically ignored, or Sylvia Ostry, the Ottawa mandarin who was the most seasoned Canadian bureaucrat in international economic negotiations but was relegated to the multilateral GATT negotiations that were apparently going nowhere.

For its part, the United States in the mid-1980s was apprehensive. Its economic hegemony was being challenged by the resurgence of rival states in Europe as well as in Asia, which had used their governments to create competitive advantages for their national champions. Washington had been strengthening its already-powerful unilateral measures to strong-arm individual countries to change policies it felt too restrictive of American exporters or investors and too generous to their competitors. But using the blunderbuss of retaliatory threats on a country-by-country basis was not a satisfactory process because it generated disproportionate displays of ill will. And, in the case of the EU, which had become as powerful as the United States, and Japan, on whose capital exports the U.S. was increasingly depending, crude retaliatory threats were decreasingly effective and sometimes even counterproductive. More important, Americans knew that their economic success in the twenty-first century lay in exploiting their global lead in the information-based sectors, just as their success in the twentieth century had been based on exploiting their regional lead in manufacturing.

To ensure that its high-tech and knowledge-driven corporations could profit from their superiority and prevent other countries from pirating their knowhow, Washington wanted to expand the reach of the global trade rules administered by GATT to include investment conditions, the sale of services, and intellectual property rights. However, the prospects for such a transformation of the international economic order were bleak. The Uruguay Round – GATT's eighth – of multilateral trade negotiations, which had been dragging on since 1986, was in gridlock. As a second-best expedient, Washington decided to use bilateral negotiations with compliant partners in its own immediate sphere of influence as a strategic tool. 'If a multilateral treaty is not negotiated to our satisfaction,' the Americans were hinting heavy-handedly to their commercial rivals, 'then we will continue to negotiate one on one, proceeding beyond Israel, Canada, and Mexico to our next most compliant trade partners until the most obdurate amongst you are completely isolated.' By this tactic, Washington intended to establish important precedents for the ongoing multilateral talks and exert pressure on the Uruguay Round palavers.

When negotiations began in 1986, it seemed unlikely that an agreement would be reached because Ottawa's positive aim (exemption from U.S. trade-remedy legislation) and the defensive goals that Macdonald had advised (not to negotiate the politically sensitive issues of culture, energy, agriculture, and the Auto Pact) were unacceptable to the U.S. negotiators, who aggressively targeted what they viewed as objectionable Canadian policies while adamantly refusing to put their own protectionist policies on the table. An inherently unequal match made more asymmetrical by the urgency with which the PMO defined the need for an agreement and the inflated claims that the government made about the gains expected from 'free' trade meant that it was negotiating on its knees with the world's most powerful nation. Ottawa made the major concessions on the big questions – some of them even before negotiations started. Washington made a token concession in accepting the creation of a novel dispute settlement process. The two negotiating sides may have represented neoconservative governments, but only the Canadians seemed to believe their own rhetoric. While Ottawa boasted it was divesting itself of significant powers to monitor foreign direct investment or to set energy prices, the American state refused outright to limit its own sovereignty.

Having come close to electoral defeat in 1988 over this politically risky strategy, the Mulroney government found itself in 1991 reluctantly obliged to negotiate still more invasive concessions the moment Mexico City and Washington became serious about developing their own economic agreement. Apprised of this unanticipated negotiation, Ottawa feared that the advantages it claimed to have won in CUFTA might be lost if Mexico worked out its own deal with the United States. Volunteering warships from the Canadian Navy to support the American 'Desert Storm' war against Iraq, Mulroney prevailed on President George Bush to turn the Washington-Mexico City dialogue into a trilateral effort to establish an agreement on continental market integration. Canada was duly admitted to the talks, where CUFTA was used as the template for negotiations.[14]

Apart from its many provisions explicitly concerning Mexico, the North American Free Trade Agreement (NAFTA) deepened CUFTA by expanding its institutional structure, changing the dispute settlement mechanism, altering the Auto Pact, broadening the investment provisions' coverage, and, alongside many smaller changes, adding what was to prove a politically explosive capacity for foreign corporations to sue host governments. NAFTA increased the revised trade rules' limits on Canadian and Mexican policies (particularly in introducing tough intellectual property rights benefiting U.S. pharmaceutical industries) and reduced their effect on U.S. sovereignty (weakening the dispute settlement process).

When NAFTA showed the EU how far the United States was able to go in incrementally pushing forward its international trade agenda on investment, agriculture, services, and intellectual property rights, and when President Clinton's enthusiasm about Asia Pacific Economic Co-operation suggested that he might be developing a U.S.-led Pacific-rim trade area, Brussels realized it was time to give up its GATT stonewall-ing. The American strategy for breaking the Uruguay Round's logjam had proved successful. But the astonishingly impressive results institu-tionalized in the World Trade Organization (WTO) in 1994 had a 'con-stitutional' significance for its signatories that surprised trade analysts everywhere.

Reconstituting GATT as the World Trade Organization

Since the early 1980s, the Canadian trade policy community has held firmly to a clear and simple credo. As a mid-sized state, Canada is bet-ter off in a *rules-based* system with a dispute settlement mechanism strong enough to enforce the rules than it is in a *power-based* system in which might defines right. The corollary of this axiom argues that Can-ada is better off in a *multilateral* rules-based system, in which it can form alliances with countries of various sizes but similar national interests, than in a *bilateral* one with the world's only hyperpower. Both positions beg important questions: Who gets to make the rules? In whose interests are they written? How are they interpreted when they are applied: in what kind of tribunal, and with what kind of judges and legal processes?

In practice, GATT's rule-making process itself was based on the world's existing power system. Unlike the United States's control over NAFTA's contents, agreements with the EU and Japan had to be worked out in the tough Uruguay Round. As a result, the WTO's glo-bal rules incorporated norms favouring these three regional powers' general interests, as well as the specific objectives articulated by their globally competitive corporations.

For this reason, multilateralism does not necessarily present Canada with a real escape from a U.S.-defined supraconstitution. Indeed, much of the constraint that the WTO imposed on the Canadian state in the first few years of its existence has been an application of Uncle Sam–driven demands that Canada comply with Uncle Sam–inspired rules on behalf of Uncle Sam–based pharmaceutical and entertainment giants – as we shall see in the next two chapters.

PART I

The Polity:
Reconstituting the Canadian State

CHANGE FROM WITHOUT

We need to examine in what way the evolution of continental and global levels of governance affects the freedom formerly enjoyed by the sovereign state to run its own affairs. We do this in chapter 4. But the relationship between national and external constitutional orders is not a zero-sum game in which the creation of higher governance levels causes only losses at lower ones. A decline in a state's internal sovereignty may be partially offset by its capacity to exercise external sovereignty through participating in the deliberative processes at the continental and global levels that establish the norms, regulations, and disciplines it subsequently imposes on itself. In Canada's case global governance in economic matters starts on the continent with the North American Free Trade Agreement before moving to global institutions like the World Trade Organization (chapter 3).

3 Continental and Global Governance

When I was asked by CTV News to comment on the tens of thousands of demonstrators who had converged on Seattle to protest during the World Trade Organization's second ministerial meeting, my interviewer wanted me to answer two questions. Why were trade unions and environmental organizations hurling invective, if not stones, at an institution that dealt with commerce rather than labour or the environment? And why was so much upset being expressed then, in November 1999, rather than in 1995, when the WTO was first established?

I said the answers lay in the WTO's dual reality. It had been created out of the General Agreement on Tariffs and Trade as an international economic institution but with such extraordinary power that its rules on trade, investment, and services turned out to trump international labour conventions and multilateral environmental treaties. The trade unions and environmental movements had been asleep at the switch during the long years from 1986 to 1994 when the GATT's Uruguay Round of negotiations had followed their halting course behind closed doors. Only when they realized how serious was the damage done to their interests by the WTO did they belatedly react and target it as a serious problem. They had awakened finally to the importance in their lives of global governance.

We will see in the next chapter that NAFTA's rules arguably have a more constraining supraconstitutional impact on Canadian governments than do those of the WTO. But before looking at the way that NAFTA and the WTO have reconstituted the Canadian state, we need to understand what kinds of continental and global governance they have established.

NAFTA as Continental Governance

The very desire to negotiate the broad sets of economic rules contained in NAFTA established the first prerequisite for a formalization of the United States's relationship with its two neighbours, because it indicated the *will* of all three countries' economic and media elites to have North America's regime of accumulation guided by a common neo-conservative vision. However, the desire for a continental rule book did not include the wish to have a strong supranational governance that might resemble in any way the elaborate structures of the European Union. In fact, an integrated North American market is being forged by corporations operating continentally thanks to NAFTA's new investment and trade rules[1] but without a corresponding mode of governance for the continent.

What was striking about CUFTA's institutional structure was its almost complete absence. No policy-making institutions were established beyond the Canada-United States Trade Commission, which was set up on paper but not in practice. With neither a supranational secretariat nor a permanent address, it consisted merely of periodic meetings of the two countries' trade ministers who had powers to decide a limited number of issues such as how to implement recommendations to resolve arbitrated disputes.[2]

NAFTA told a slightly different story, that of minimal institutional deepening in the interests of maintaining maximal member-state sovereignty. It created as its executive body a North American Free Trade Commission, which consisted of once-yearly powwows by the three countries' trade ministers, who retained final authority to supervise NAFTA's institutional mechanisms, resolve disputes over interpreting its text, and take whatever steps might be necessary for its future development. NAFTA's decision-making was to be by consensus, which meant that each 'party' retained a veto over common business. In effect, the executive side of North American governance consisted of little more than the two bilateral Canada-U.S. and Mexico-U.S. relationships supplemented with a newly animated relationship between the two peripheral parties, all under the umbrella of the agreement.

However flimsy as a structure, the Free Trade Commission has substantial potential powers beyond supervising the work of NAFTA's various working groups and commissions. Chief of these is the authority to make interpretations of NAFTA's clauses and annexes that would be binding on arbitration tribunals set up under Chapter 11.

This power, which is in the hands of the three parties' trade ministers and could transform the impact of the agreement and create further norms, is a potentially supraconstitutional feature of the new continental governance. Through it, if the heads of government and the trade ministers from the three NAFTA states wish to interpret an existing norm, they can do this without any reference to their executives, their legislatures, their courts, or their publics.[3]

CUFTA's non-existent secretariat morphed into NAFTA's never created International Coordinating Secretariat, an agency that was to register complaints, organize the dispute panels, and co-ordinate the agreement's many working groups. Instead, each country established within its trade bureaucracy a NAFTA office to monitor ongoing disputes.

Even more invisible to the public, NAFTA has several dozen working groups, working subgroups, committees, and subcommittees that are mandated to examine particular common issues, typically those requiring a harmonization of some standard important for continental economic integration, such as the rules applying to the transportation of hazardous waste.[4] Other ad hoc groups are set up by the three governments to report on common problems such as the expansion of the continental energy market. Staffed by government officials and by employees of corporations with interests in the particular field, these groups act as a channel of communications among the various policy communities that take the place of continental governance in North America. Whether they operate with greater or lesser intensity, they remain well shielded from scrutiny by voters or even legislators in the three states whose functions they in part pre-empt.[5]

Some institutional deepening can be seen in NAFTA's two more narrowly mandated organizations, which were established following supplementary negotiations insisted on in the early 1990s by a newly elected Clinton administration anxious to appease its labour and environmental supporters.

First, the North American Agreement on Labour Co-operation (NAALC) created a trinational Commission for Labour Co-operation (CLC) whose executive was made up of the three national governments' labour ministers.[6] After some delay, a secretariat headquartered in Dallas (but subsequently moved to Washington) was set up to report on each country's labour laws and to encourage compliance with them. The object of this exercise in symbolic politics was to assuage U.S. trade union concerns about the export of jobs caused by the social-dumping effect of Mexico's lax enforcement of its legislation on workers' rights. Since labour law comes largely under provincial jurisdiction and since few provinces signed on to the NAALC, the CLC has minimal import for Canada beyond encouraging some labour unions to exchange information with their Mexican counterparts, as we shall see in chapter 16.

Second, the North American Agreement of Environmental Co-operation, NAFTA's other side deal, created in Montreal the Commission for Environmental Co-operation. This tripartite organization, whose professional secretariat was given supranational standing (even if its budget came directly from the three governments), constituted the most promising aspect of continental governance, because it incorporated citizens directly in its processes, although its actual effectiveness has been found wanting, as we shall see in chapter 17.

Apart from the labour and environmental organizations, whose substance remains very much in doubt, NAFTA has not created a proactive entity with the executive or legislative power to regulate the newly liberalized continental market it established. Nor does it have the dynamic capacity to make new rules when they appear needed or the authority to interfere with any of its member-states' sovereignty – apart, that is, from the considerable limitations on their autonomy dictated by the trade agreements' many stipulations.

CUFTA and NAFTA are significant legal documents that have been toughly negotiated, ceremoniously signed, solemnly ratified, and formally implemented in the legislation of the three negotiating parties. Although the language of trade agreements expresses a studied symmetry, in which each 'party' has rights and obligations, they betray in practice a noticeable disparity in their respective ratification processes. Canada and Mexico have adopted these undertakings as if they were treaties and have passed the necessary legislation to implement them and make the required changes in their existing laws. The United States participated in the same formal process of passing implementation legislation. However, NAFTA specifies that any subsequent act of Congress can amend this legislation. Washington's future protectionist measures will apply to Canada with the slight proviso that they must explicitly mention Canada. This means that the peripheral states do not have in NAFTA a guarantee against the hegemon's changing the rules of the continental game without their consent.

Nor is there anything in continental governance that might give the two neighbouring states some say in or influence over the hegemon's policy-making. Apart from the three parties' agreeing informally to alter practices established by NAFTA, the agreement would require new negotiations and legislative implementation to be amended. If Mexico and the United States do not want to accede to Canada's desire to reword the expropriation clause in Chapter 11, this amendment will not happen. Consensus, which gives a veto to each member-state, constitutes a high hurdle for achieving normative change and gives the document more constitutional substance. However, this rigidity could condemn NAFTA to irrelevance in the longer run if other trade regimes such as the WTO are more capable of generating new rules in response to changed circumstances.

De facto asymmetry characterizes NAFTA's formally symmetrical clause defining how any 'party' can abrogate the agreement: it needs only to give its partners six months' notice of its intention. The threat of abrogation has a very different weight in the hands of Washington than in those of Ottawa or Mexico City. American interests would be affected – but not radically so – if Canada or Mexico defected from NAFTA. Disaster would be the assumed impact on either of the peripheral states should the United States abrogate. Following their virtually complete integration in the continental economy, they would be forced to their knees if Washington threatened to terminate its participation in the agreement, a technique it used when it forced Hawaii to join the United States late in the nineteenth century.

NAFTA was carefully designed to prevent any form of continental governance from developing. In the name of their own sovereignty, the three governments have already taken steps to hobble the supranational autonomy of the Commission for Environmental Co-operation. In the interests of perpetuating their separate systems, they are firmly resisting the creation of a North American monetary union that might clone the EU's Monetary Union.[7] Far from encouraging greater political integration, its two English-speaking member-states are carefully monitoring their borders to obstruct unwanted immigration from Mexico. President Vicente Fox pushed Washington to regularize the illegal status of millions of Mexicans in the United States, but it responded to its new concern with terrorism by building up, not cutting down, its border controls.

CUFTA and NAFTA do indeed represent a sea change for the two peripheral members of North America. Far from producing a system of continental governance in which Mexico and Canada would have had some influence, their texts have reconstituted American hegemony in the form of an economic rule book that establishes an unevenly liberalized market and a set of supraconstitutional constraints on the policy-making options of both Canada and Mexico. That NAFTA does not limit the United States's traditional use of its power became clear following the catastrophe of September 11, 2001, when Washington specified in great detail what security measures it expected Canada to take. The failure of the three governments to call a special meeting of its Trade Commission further indicated that NAFTA was tertiary in its importance as a form of governance for dealing with issues that the United States considered urgent.

Autonomy does not mean equality. Indeed NAFTA appears to have increased the power asymmetry between the hegemon, whose legislative and administrative orders are little affected, and its neighbours, which have had to make significant changes (in Canada's case) and counter-revolutionary transformations (in Mexico's case). The agreement's critics considered its provisions as both too intrusive in pre-empting decisions that should more properly be made in its two peripheral member states and too ineffectual in disciplining the continental hegemon. The first defect was soon intensified and the second defect partly remedied when, in 1995, some 130 states signed the landmark treaty creating the World Trade Organization, to whose judgments even the United States would in principle have to submit.

The WTO as a Prime Regime of Global Governance

A patchwork quilt of institutions purporting to establish a system of international management has been growing ever since the Atlantic powers started planning a new global order during the Second World War. On broad political, social and cultural matters, the system took the form of the United Nations itself and its many ancillary organizations, such as UNESCO (for promoting culture), the World Health Organization (for controlling disease), and the International Labour Organization (for enhancing labour standards).

For managing the world economy, the Bretton Woods agreement of 1944 established a pair of far more powerful international financial institutions (IFIs). The International Monetary Fund (IMF) was to supervise how countries managed their exchange rates and to help them when their currency ran into difficulties because of poor trade figures or speculative pressures. The International Bank for Reconstruction and Development (World Bank) was to provide development capital to help countries rebuild their economies. When the U.S. Congress failed to ratify American adhesion to the International Trade Organization (ITO), which had been designed in 1947 to be the third pillar of the international financial structure, the ITO's complementary General Agreement on Tariffs and Trade (GATT) became by default the gradually consolidating site for resolving international trade problems.

Later on, other organizations firmed up as important building blocks in the architecture of global economic management. The Bank for International Settlements developed as a forum for central bankers to monitor each others' regulation of their national banking systems.[8] The Organization for Economic Co-operation and Development (OECD) emerged as the locus for researching global economic problems and negotiating a policy agenda for the industrialized economies' commercial needs. More technically specialized agencies grew up for the regulation of specific problems – for example, the World Intellectual Property Organization (WIPO). At the same time, mixed bodies developed in response to both private- and public-sector needs for common standards – the Codex Alimentarius, for instance, linked government representatives with scientists, farm organizations, and global agribusiness to work out criteria for acceptable levels of toxins and pesticides in food. And in the private sector, the growth of transnational law firms and international commercial arbitration started displacing state regulation of international commercial matters, particularly dispute settlement.

Approximately 300 of the 3,900 international organizations relate to economic matters.[9] Sovereign states have created these bodies by signing treaties or making agreements that commit them to observe the principles contained in their charters, to provide them financial support, and to supply personnel or delegates to their meetings. States sign and join, presumably having calculated that it is in their best interest to do so. They continue to belong for the same reason, accepting a contract that gives up a morsel of their freedom to manoeuvre in exchange for the benefit they expect to accrue from membership in the particular entity.

Small, economically desperate countries have suffered the most palpable loss of sovereignty through being obliged to reconstitute their regimes as a precondition for aid from the IMF or the World Bank, each of which requires recipients of their support to restructure their political economies on neoconservative lines. Large, but not major, countries such as Canada consider the derogation of power acceptable because they gain external influence – getting a voice in the policies of the mul-

tilateral organization in question – even if they lose internal sovereignty
to the extent that they are bound by that organization's conventions. In
the typical specialized institution, which is little more than a secretariat
set up to manage the international community's response to a universal
problem such as global warming or ozone-layer depletion, member
states carefully prevent the emergence of any supranationality that
might impinge on their powers.[10] In most areas, Canada considers its
loss of sovereignty minimal, because the values enshrined in these
organizations express the norms of liberal industrial societies.

Each international organization has its own constitution – that is, a
set of generally written principles governing its operation. The WTO's
establishes a strikingly uneven institutional structure with a legislature
given to paralysis, a wiry administration, a powerful judiciary, and no
coercive capacity of its own.

The WTO has no executive worthy of the name. Rather, it inherited
from the GATT an informal 'green room' process in which a self-
appointed group of dominant countries sets the agenda.[11] Its director is
mandated to run not a policy-making body but a lean secretariat while
supplying the organization with some leadership.

The WTO's legislative body – the ministerial conference – is a mam-
moth gathering of trade ministers from all member states, who con-
vene biennially. Operating on the basis of consensus, it gives all the
ministers the opportunity to address, and in principle resolve, their
common problems. As the débâcle in the ministerial meeting in Seattle
proved in 1999, it is for all intents and purposes an inoperable body
unless a global consensus has been forged. Two years of fence-mend-
ing with Third World members generated enough consensus among
the membership that the 2001 conclave at Doha in the Arab emirate of
Qatar did yield an agreement on the agenda for the next round of rule-
making negotiations. Between the biennial 'ministerials,' members
participate in the WTO's ongoing decision-making business through
its general council, its many policy committees (some of which facilitate the development of a negotiating agenda), and the intergovernmental activities of their diplomatic delegations, in which the
Canadian trade embassy staff is constantly involved.

The WTO inherited from the GATT both a headquarters in Geneva
and an effective secretariat of 500 officials, including a staff of legal
experts who constitute the institution's historical memory and administrative energy. The secretariat administers over a dozen complex
trade agreements and provides bureaucratic support for the dispute

panels. A review body monitors member-states' conformity to their new obligations and provides a forum for developing the policy agenda. While this institutional structure has been criticized for being too elaborate for its small budget to support – a Mercedes Benz without gas, as the Canadian trade expert Sylvia Ostry famously described it[12] – it has potential for refinement as it matures. Although its executive is virtual, its legislative is ineffectual, and its administrative organs are stretched, the WTO's judicial mechanism is extraordinarily powerful, as we shall see shortly.[13]

Canada and WTO Governance

As the archetypal hegemonic state, the United States is the dominant global rule maker. Weak states that inhabit the periphery of the world power circle are rule takers, having to accommodate the rules imposed on them. That Canada exists in a zone between hegemon and periphery can be seen from its being partly rule maker and partly rule taker. However formless NAFTA may be, Canada participates in this fourth level of governance by its presence in its dispute settlement actions and in its sectoral working groups. As for its fifth level of state architecture, the WTO allows Ottawa to promote its interests by helping make the rules. Alongside the IMF, the World Bank, the United Nations, the OECD, UNESCO, the G7/8 Economic Summits, and a host of other functional institutions and in the light of NAFTA's institutional near-vacuum, the WTO offers another, but more significant global site where Canadian trade representatives can operate proactively.

Canada's voice in multilateral trade policy is greater than its actual size might lead one to expect. In 1990, for instance, half-way through the long Uruguay Round, Canada was the country that proposed creating a more authoritative institutional structure to strengthen the somewhat ineffectual GATT. This proposal, consistent with Canada's multilateralism, helped transform GATT into the much-more-substantial WTO, with its binding dispute settlement process.[14] In the current negotiations on services, Canadian officials retain their active role.

Even many of those who believe the WTO marks considerable progress over the GATT are highly critical of its distinct tendency to favour corporate interests at the expense of environmental and social concerns. To the extent, then, that the WTO can be considered part of Canada's fifth level of governance, Canada's continued participation is contested more vigorously than it is in any other international institution. And the more the WTO's raison d'être is questioned, the more likely its legitimacy is to atrophy. In the meantime, its members' continuing determination to support it will depend on its institutional qualities and the effects of its decisions.

In the jockeying for advantage that characterized states' behaviour in the post-Cold War era, the recognition of a commonality of interests on any issue was a significant accomplishment. The transformation in 1995 of the weak, consensus-driven GATT into a muscular membership organization with international legal personality and impressive power indicated that a shared *will* did exist – at least among those officials representing their governments[15] – to reorder the global economic system. How strongly that collective international desire persists will determine the WTO's effectiveness in the years ahead. The massing of protesting NGOs at the WTO's intended launch for its next, 'Millennial' Round of negotiations at its tempestuous biennial ministerial in 1999 in Seattle indicated how shallow and contested was that commitment outside the narrow confines of the transnational community of trade advocates. Support for the WTO varied from state to state, with Third World countries considerably more antagonistic to it than their industrialized partners who controlled its rule-making processes.

Canadians' will to participate in the WTO is divided between the unapologetic fervour of the trade community and the equally fervent opposition of many citizens active in environmental NGOs and trade unions. Prime Minister Chrétien's acceptance of trade liberalization was even more wholehearted than his slightly qualified endorsement of continental free trade. His own anti-protectionist beliefs were the natural product of his roots in the Quebec resource-producing hinterland, his mentorship in the 1960s under the Liberal finance minister, Mitchell Sharp, and the close connections he made during his years in major economic cabinet portfolios first with Montreal's, then with Calgary's, and finally with Toronto's business communities. When he became prime minister his policy environment was largely neoconservative. His trade officials in the Department of Foreign Affairs and International Trade were true believers in trade liberalization, with little sympathy for the social-democratic concerns about state sovereignty, environmental sustainability, or social program survival voiced by diplomats elsewhere in the department as well as by citizens' groups such as the Council of Canadians and its media-savvy gadfly, Maude Barlow. His ministers for international trade, first Roy

MacLaren, then Sergio Marchi, and ultimately Pierre Pettigrew, were staunch spokesmen for their department's orthodoxy that the more trade agreements signed by Ottawa, the better it would be for Canada. Even when Canada lost ruling after ruling before WTO dispute panels, Pettigrew insisted that Canada was benefiting because the rules were being clarified.

This belief that striking down government regulations was an essentially positive phenomenon was not widely shared outside the country's political, media, and business elites. Within labour unions, among environmentalists, throughout the cultural community, and in the many other sectors of civil society which looked to the state for support and had developed an unprecedented coalition in opposition to free trade in the mid-1980s, economic liberalization at the global level became just as objectionable as CUFTA and NAFTA. In 1997 and 1998, the anti–free trade coalition, which had almost prevailed in the 1988 federal election but then had failed to mobilize effectively against NAFTA during the next federal campaign in 1993, rallied its troops. Joining forces with counterparts in countries as disparate as France, Australia, and India, the Council of Canadians helped generate such vehement opposition to the Multilateral Agreement on Investment (MAI) being negotiated under the OECD's auspices, that this attempt to universalize the powerful rights contained in NAFTA's Chapter 11 for TNCs' global investments was aborted when the French government officially walked out of the talks.[16]

Encouraged by their successful campaign against the MAI, the anti-trade liberalizers next targeted the WTO itself. While Canadians did not play the lead role in organizing the protests that helped stop the WTO's Seattle ministerial gathering in 1999 from launching the Millennial Round of global trade negotiations, their supportive presence suggests that the Canadian will to sustain the WTO is far from firm. Active participation by Canadian NGOs in subsequent protests at the regular meetings of the IMF and World Bank (Washington, April 2000, and Prague, September 2000), the Organization of American States (Windsor, Ontario, June 2000), and the Summit of the Americas (Quebec, April 2001) indicates that the government's commitment to neoconservative globalization remains hotly contested.

The WTO's 2001 ministerial meeting in Doha firmly kept international NGOs at a distance from the deliberations. But the attention they paid to the proceedings was an indicator of the WTO's importance as a new forum for global governance.

Ottawa's effectiveness does not necessarily reassure representatives of Canada's civil society who are excluded from both negotiations of new rules and the adjudication processes that interpret them. NGOs can simply lobby from the outside, although since Seattle, they have had increasing success in being heard. In sum, whether through citizens' groups, corporate lobbyists, or the governments' official representatives, this international economic institution has given the Canadian state a new means to project itself on the global level of governance.

Canadian participation in continental and global governance is an activity dominated by the central government, which gives a privileged role to corporate representatives. Provincial governments, NGOs, and individual citizens are politely but firmly kept from the table. The variable geometry of Canada's representation in these transnational governance forums reverses when we look at the impact of these economic regimes on the Canadian political system. NAFTA and the WTO's supraconstitutional presence in the Canadian legal order affects all citizens, interest groups, and governments, however they are represented abroad.

4 NAFTA and the WTO as Supraconstitution

At 10 o'clock one Sunday evening in the autumn of 1986 my phone rang. It was the president of the Canadian Club of Toronto, who wanted to talk about a serious problem she had with her lunch meeting scheduled for the next day. The American senator booked to speak about the ongoing negotiations over a Canada-U.S. trade agreement had just cancelled. Would I fill his shoes?

Having followed the contentious debate very closely, I agreed to take up the challenge. Fifteen hours later I stood up in front of several hundred business people in the Confederation Room of the Royal York Hotel and made what I thought was a persuasive case why the two countries would not reach an agreement. My logic was straightforward: Canada wanted something that the United States would not give. Ottawa's prime negotiating objective was to obtain 'secure access' for Canadian exports to the U.S. market. This required the United States to exempt Canada from its protectionist trade legislation. But everything I knew about Congress told me that U.S. politicians would never agree to abandon their precious powers to add special countervailing or anti-dumping duties to imports that threatened the interests of American business and the jobs of American workers.

In part of my prediction I was proven right: the United States refused to waive the right to use its trade remedy legislation against Canada. Where I turned out to be wrong by a country mile was in underestimating the urgency of Brian Mulroney's desire for a deal with Washington, even if it meant sacrificing his stated goal.

Had I been invited back in 1992 to address the chances of a successful Mexican-U.S.-Canadian trade negotiation, I would have been less confident in my scepticism. But I would have erred again in misreading the Mulroney government's willingness to sign an agreement whose implications for Canada's constitutional order neither he nor his officials understood. They thought that the

North American Free Trade Agreement was just an inclusion of Mexico in CUFTA. It turned out to be a greater straitjacket on Canada (and Mexico) than its Canadian (or Mexican) negotiators realized at the time they signed it. What they had done was to add an external tier to the country's constitution, one that was shortly to be joined by hundreds of the WTO's even more intrusive rules.

When a country signs a treaty it partly *internationalizes* the state's legal order to the extent that domestic laws are harmonized with the norms embodied in the accord. Before the advent of the new global trade order, even hundreds of international organizations (IOs) did not constitute a significant constitutional challenge to the conventional nation state, whose legal sovereignty was not compromised. If a state strongly disagreed with an IO's mandate, it could abrogate its commitment – as the United States and Britain did by withdrawing from UNESCO because they considered that its policies responded too much to Third World concerns. Nor was a government bound to comply with a ruling by an international body that it considered adverse to its interests or incompatible with its culture. Canada has occasionally been willing to flout international law that challenges a constitutional norm,[1] but generally it has self-consciously played a model role: when it has been shown to be in violation of a multilateral convention that it has signed, it has mended its ways.

In sharp contrast with most international organizations, the WTO creates a new mode of economic regulation with such broad scope and such unusual judicial authority that it has transformed not just the nature of global governance, as we saw in the previous chapter, but the political order of each of the 144 states that had become members by 2002. For Canada, the WTO's economic rules are complemented by NAFTA's parallel set of provisions. Since Parts II and III look at the specific impact of these regimes' individual rules, I offer in the following pages the minimum amount of detail necessary to explain the constitutional significance for Canada of the five major elements of NAFTA and the WTO – their norms, limits on government, rights, adjudication procedures, and enforcement mechanisms.

Norms

Constitutions typically entrench certain inviolate principles or norms that are above the reach of any politician to alter, and both NAFTA and the WTO have done this.

NAFTA

NAFTA established several government-inhibiting principles to be applied to all policies, regulations, and actions of member states. In agreeing that CUFTA should enshrine the principle of 'national treatment,' Canada was not simply reiterating a commitment that it had made in 1948. In GATT, national treatment stipulated that member states treat *goods* that had entered their economy from abroad in the same way as they treated domestically-produced items. In other words, they agreed not to discriminate against foreign-made products once they had cleared border barriers such as tariffs.

CUFTA was a pioneering document in this regard, since for the first time a trade agreement brought the vast, but uncharted territory of business *services* under norms that had so far applied only to goods. Under economic liberalization, 'national treatment' would henceforth apply not just to physical objects but to services such as banking operations and insurance contracts, legal and architectural work, education and health care.

A further innovation was to apply trade rules to *investments* as well as to goods. This means that signatories commit themselves to treating foreign investors the same way as they treat domestic entrepreneurs – a concession that Canada had long resisted because of its economy's high proportion of foreign direct investment. The federal government had not wanted to abandon economic development policies that tried to promote domestically owned firms as national champions and discriminated against foreign capital. National treatment for foreign investors required amputation of that limb of government dedicated to supporting domestic enterprise.

In the event, the government's acceptance of national treatment constituted the loss of a power that for ideological reasons it did not want to keep. By committing itself to offering American and Mexican companies the same incentives that it might give domestic firms to boost their prospects, it engaged itself, the provincial governments, and their successors in perpetuity to desist from the kinds of industrial strategies that had formed the core of much of federal and provincial policy activity for twenty years. It touted national treatment as the way to prevent any repetition of Pierre Trudeau's use of post-Keynesian, interventionist approaches to generate economic growth of the type that had culminated with the (in)famous National Energy Program of 1980. If CUFTA or NAFTA tied the government's hands, this was a plus for the Conservative prime minister, not a minus – a clear illustration of

how international agreements can be used to constitutionalize a
domestic ideological position. The aim was to let market forces do
their economic job free of political control and prevent future politicians of a different persuasion from messing things up ever again.

The right of establishment was a second supraconstitutional principle that was pregnant with potential effects because it guaranteed foreign corporations' ability to do business in the economy and so qualify
for national treatment.

These norms are supraconstitutional because they control government behaviour even though they are not part of the Canadian constitution. They may not necessarily have been implemented in specific
legislative changes, but they remain as prescriptions to which NAFTA
partners may appeal if they feel that Canada is not fulfilling its obligations.

WTO

GATT's normative apparatus was often thought to have no more significance for its member states' political orders than any of the other
high-sounding declarations that constitute the conventions of international treaty law. GATT's trade principles were reformulations of conventions that had gradually emerged in the course of several centuries
of international commerce. States actually paid considerable heed to
these principles, because they had learned that, in the long run, they
profited from practising them and being seen to do so. Otherwise their
competitors could have good reason to cheat.

Along with national treatment, the 'most-favoured nation' (MFN)
norm in GATT's Article 1 rules out discriminating among trading partners even for reasons of social or environmental policy. Now that they
are part of the WTO's normative structure, this and other basic trade
principles are supraconstitutional because they are mandatory for its
members, unlike international commitments that Canada has made by
signing, for instance, the many conventions on labour rights sponsored
by the International Labour Organization. As well, the interpretation
of the WTO's norms is far more expansive than that of identical norms
under the GATT. Even when government measures are formally neutral vis-à-vis nationality, the WTO may strike them down if in practice
they bias the competitive conditions in favour of domestic service providers (national treatment) or of particular foreign providers (most
favoured nation).[2]

We can see the intrusiveness of the WTO's rules most easily by look-ing at how rulings on disputes over services have been brought within the scope of global economic governance. In the case that Japan and the EU brought against the Auto Pact, the panel ruled that allowing domestically produced services to count in meeting Canada's mini-mum value-added standard for a car to qualify for duty remission con-stituted de facto discrimination against foreign service providers and so a violation of national treatment for 'like' services.[3] Canadian trade negotiators had included the wholesale market for motor vehicles in the commitments that they had made in signing the General Agree-ment on Trade in Services (GATS) and had erroneously thought that NAFTA's exemption from GATT rules as a free trade area protected the Auto Pact from the application of GATS.[4] A citizen can hardly be expected to comprehend such complexities when the Canadian gov-ernment's own legal experts had misunderstood their implications.

The existence of these supraconstitutional norms in NAFTA and the WTO is only one pressure that the external trade regimes exert over states' regulatory behaviour. There is also a process of external over-sight that applies transnational scrutiny to the Canadian state's behav-iour. The United States Trade Representative's Office keeps federal and provincial policies under regular review, reporting annually to Con-gress about Canadian compliance with its obligations in NAFTA. The WTO's Trade Policy Review Mechanism reviews Canada's compliance with these norms every two years. At these reviews trading partners cannot force changes, but they ask about governmental measures that interfere with their investments or trade and so put Canada's govern-ing elite on the defensive if it is found dilatory in restraining its protec-tionism.

With its broader membership, its more symmetrical balance of power among the major regions, its more inclusive provisions, and its more legitimate institutions, the WTO has compounded the impact of CUFTA and NAFTA on Canada's political order by producing a more generalized set of norms that will apply more authoritatively to its members, including the United States.

Limits to Government Policy

Beyond the general norms that it establishes, a constitution also sets limits to what governments can do in specific policy domains. By sign-ing CUFTA, NAFTA, and the WTO, Canada undertook to make immediate changes in a wide range of legislation and regulations. CUFTA's investment chapter raised the size of a corporation whose foreign take-over would be subject to review from $5 to $150 million. Canadian implementation legislation accordingly made the appropriate amendment to the Investment Canada Act. Because WTO and NAFTA rules are so comprehensive, the central and provincial governments had to change myriad existing laws.

NAFTA

Tariff reductions or the prohibition of import and export controls are straightforward examples of the kind of supraconstitutional limits on government that any trade treaty imposes. Reducing tariffs on agricultural products showed how the three NAFTA partners attempted to negotiate declining levels of defensive measures against each others' exports. Canada conceded zero tariffs in the foodstuffs that it produced most efficiently and retained the longest transition period for those that were most vulnerable to being overwhelmed by cheaper California, Florida, or Mexican produce.[5]

Detailed rules of origin were also required to distinguish products that qualified for the lower border tariffs from those that had insufficient North American content. Two American industries with great political clout in the negotiations not only improved their position vis-à-vis their continental rivals but gained greater protection against extra-continental competition. American clothing manufacturers protected themselves against Canadian imports of suits by an import quota on the number of suits made from foreign cloth. They also achieved a further plum by a rule specifying that textiles had to be woven from North American yarns to qualify for intra-continental tariff exemption. These provisions set limits on the Mexican and Canadian governments' ability to promote their own textile sectors.

Trade liberalization theory promotes lowering border barriers to let the market operate in the most efficient way to provide the cheapest goods to the consumer. In stark contradiction to this principle, a basic component of trade law aims at preventing the free flow of knowledge in the public domain. NAFTA and the WTO now constrain government efforts to make drug patents available for general manufacture, giving corporations monopoly rights over their 'intellectual property' so that they can profit from commodifying their knowledge. For instance, NAFTA's chapter on intellectual property forbids renting computer software in order to duplicate it. The Canadian Copyright Act was accordingly changed by section 55 (2) of the NAFTA Implementation Act.[6]

Whereas NAFTA's intellectual property regime guarantees corporations the right to exploit their knowledge, the treaty enjoins Canadian governments from benefiting from their natural endowment in cheap fuels. Its energy chapter forbids federal or provincial governments from pricing energy consumed by Canadian citizens or industries below its export price. Even in an energy supply crisis, Canada must share with the United States the same proportion of its energy production as it has done for the preceding three years. (Although Mexico is geopolitically weaker than Canada, it was less compliant on energy issues than Canada. It refused to accept this restriction in the exploitation of its prime natural resource.)

Canada had already given up under CUFTA most of the powers to regulate foreign investments that it had created under the Foreign Investment Review Agency (later renamed by the Mulroney government the Investment Canada Act).[7] Indirect takeovers – when another foreign company bought a Canadian subsidiary of a foreign company – were to be entirely exempted from review.

Government procurement contracts issued by federal departments and federally controlled state enterprises valued above U.S. $50,000 and construction contracts over U.S. $6.5 million could no longer be reserved for national bidders but had to be opened to bids from NAFTA companies. While this reduced the protection provided Canadian companies at home, it also opened up possibilities for Canadian transnational corporations (TNCs) such as Bombardier to bid for projects such as the Mexico City metro or public works projects in U.S. states that were previously out of bounds because of their 'Buy America' laws.

Entrenching neoconservatism at home by accepting Washington's desire to constrain Canadian governments' interventionist potential was only a secondary objective for Ottawa. Its main negotiating aim was to put limits on the harassment costs that the American government could impose on Canadian exporters by unilateral protectionist actions. Ottawa wanted exemption for Canada from American trade remedy sanctions. First, it wanted Washington to renounce anti-dumping actions as inappropriate within the free trade area. Second, a comprehensive subsidy code would defang U.S. countervail measures. Such a code would specify what kind of Canadian subsidies were unacceptable to the Americans (and so legitimate targets for countervailing duties), as opposed to what were acceptable. Canada completely failed in this objective in both agreements, which imposed negligible limits on U.S. trade law. Indeed, CUFTA acknowledged, in a standard clause that U.S. negotiators insert in commercial documents, Congress's constitutional right to pass new trade measures that could supersede the trade agreement. In supraconstitutionally constraining the peripheral states without equally constraining the continental hegemon, NAFTA made the two existing bilateral relationships more asymmetrical than they had been.

These changes to laws and regulations mandated by the WTO and NAFTA were supraconstitutional less because they had to be made automatically than because they were irreversible. Unlike the normal amendments to statutes made by sovereign legislatures, which can further amend or revoke their acts in response to changing domestic considerations, statutory amendments incorporating international trade norms can be validly amended only if the external regime changes its rules by international agreement. In this respect not only has the political order been changed by the amendments, but the legal order has been altered by Parliament's accepting legal and regulatory changes over which it loses sovereignty. This is what defenders of free trade meant when they described NAFTA as 'locking in' the neoconservatism currently practised in Ottawa. Even if more activist political parties were to win power, they would find their hands tied by these domestically implemented limits to which their predecessors had committed them.

WTO

Below its normative system, the WTO includes many specialized agreements, all intended to limit governments' capacity to restrain trade or to interfere with the investment decisions of transnational or domestic capital.

Some of these interdictions impede states that are dependent on exporting primary resources from taking measures to increase the local processing of raw materials. Preventing the sale abroad, say, of raw logs can be a policy tool for promoting the industrial development of a hinterland economy or for supporting community development in indigenous communities. Such *export controls*, which have been a basic tool of industrial development for staples-exporting economics, are banned as a quantitative restriction. While NAFTA and the WTO contain some exceptions allowing governments to pass laws in the public interest, states appealing to these provisions to justify trade-restricting environmental actions have typically found the exceptions to be interpreted very narrowly.

Technical barriers to trade (TBT) embrace environmental, health, food safety, and other regulatory standards. Measures in these fields must restrict trade as little as possible. Measures, commonly used to manage industrial processes on behalf of the public's need for such public goods as a sustainable environment and healthy food, are now subject to review if deemed to improperly restrict trade.

The foodstuff sector was brought within GATT's disciplines by two sets of rules. The WTO's Agreement on Agriculture expanded GATT's scope to include agricultural policy. Members committed themselves to transforming such quantitative restrictions as import quotas into tariffs, which they were then to reduce. Canada duly proceeded to 'tariffy' its protective regulations for farmers in central Canada. The WTO's Agreement on Sanitary and Phytosanitary Measures (SPS) required that governments have scientific evidence to justify imposing any food or health safety regulations controlling the import of agricultural products that are more restrictive than the standards established by the Codex Alimentarius – an international institution staffed by scientists and government officials. The SPS agreement gave the United States and Canada a legal weapon with which to contest the European Union's ban on importing North American beef that is raised with a growth hormone.

Canada's interests are unevenly affected by this new regime because of its two, geographically determined, types of agriculture. To the extent that its western provinces are exporters of grains and livestock, Canada can expect to benefit from these new rules, which will have supraconstitutional impact on other members by restraining the massive subsidies that the European Union, Japan and the United States offer their farmers. In contrast, farmers in central Canada, who supply a protected market of domestic consumers thanks to government-enforced marketing boards for eggs, milk, and poultry, will probably suffer from the required conversion of all quantitative restrictions into tariffs, which must then be gradually reduced.

Some WTO rules constraining member governments may work more in Ottawa's favour than in Washington's. When negotiating with Canada and Mexico, the United States refused to consider a subsidy code, which could have imposed some limits on its trade agencies' freedom to harass Canadian exporters by alleging that they have received unfair subsidies. Not gaining a subsidy code meant Mulroney failed to achieve the 'secure access' he had promised and vitiated the value of CUFTA and NAFTA for Canada as an equitable trade regime. Whereas these two agreements left Canada vulnerable to its power imbalance with the U.S.A., the WTO's subsidy text offsets this asymmetry. With the WTO's Agreement on Subsidies and Countervailing Measures, the United States has brought its countervail measures under international discipline. The WTO's specifications distinguish three types of industrial subsidies – acceptable ('green light' measures), unacceptable ('red light' measures), and contestable ('orange light' measures). In this instance the United States had to concur with other countries' (in particular the European Union's) notions of acceptable industrial development policies, which are generally closer to Canada's more interventionist practice. This reduces the vulnerability of Canadian exports to the kind of American harassment that can arbitrarily identify unfair subsidies and impose stiff, pre-emptive countervailing duties.

In sum, the WTO's many agreements contain two types of supraconstitutional limits on member governments. Positive, 'thou shalt' agreements *prescribe* how members must rewrite, for example, their laws on intellectual property. Negative, 'thou shalt not' agreements such as SPS and TBT *proscribe* a wide range of practices. When global trade scholars talk of the deep integration embraced by the WTO, they are referring to the intrusive quality of these rules, which dictate how governments should or should not act in realms where they had previously been sovereign.

Rights

As the corollary to limiting government, a state constitution establishes specific rights for its citizens, whether individual or collective.

NAFTA

The only 'citizens' whose rights in Canada were extended by continental governance are corporations based in the United States or Mexico, which received a powerful new defence against governments whose regulations might reduce their earnings.

Under previous international commercial law, a company whose business was hurt because of a foreign government's action had either to defend itself within that state's legal system or to prevail on its own government to launch a trade complaint through the GATT on its behalf. Transnational capital wanted to enjoy protection not just from outright nationalization but from normal regulatory actions of a state using its sovereign discretion within its own borders. NAFTA's major innovation in the service of corporate empowerment was to broaden the definition of investment (for instance, to include mortgages) and to extend investors' rights to include the capacity of a NAFTA firm – that is, a company headquartered in a partner state – to challenge a government's domestic legislation for jeopardizing its profitability.[8]

Article 1110 provides that no government may 'directly or indirectly expropriate or nationalize,' or take 'a measure tantamount to expropriation or nationalization' except for a 'public purpose,' on a 'non-discriminatory basis,' in accordance with 'due process of law and minimum standards of treatment' and on 'payment of compensation.'[9] While not appreciated at first by most observers, including the Canadian government officials who 'signed off' on the clause, this innovation has given NAFTA firms the power to challenge almost every regulatory action taken by federal, provincial, or municipal governments that might 'expropriate' their future earnings. This 'Chapter 11' prohibition of actions 'tantamount to expropriation' was tantamount to a new constitutional right for foreign corporations. Indeed, it has proven the most controversial of NAFTA's provisions, because it allows NAFTA firms to overturn the outcomes of national political debates on the desirable regulatory regime to secure the health and safety of the citizenry. (In the United States, a NAFTA firm would be a Canadian or Mexican company; in Mexico, an American or Canadian business.)

An illustrative case is Ottawa's debacle over cigarette packaging. In the mid-1990s the federal government decided to ban differentiated cigarette packaging as a natural extension of its prohibition on cigarette advertising. Although the tobacco industry claimed that *branding* served no other purpose than facilitating competition for existing smokers, the government maintained that it was targeted at 'lifestyle marketing' and thus promoted increased sales and smoking.[10] Misunderstanding the treaty that it had negotiated, the government had thought that NAFTA merely required it to respect the principle of national treatment. In other words, as long as it treated American and

Mexican tobacco companies the same as Canadian ones, the proposal was NAFTA-proof.[11] After lobbying efforts threatened to invoke Chapter 11's corporate rights against 'expropriation,' Ottawa officials became convinced they would lose a challenge and gave way. The movement to liberalize foreign investment rules had become a means to prevent government from regulating business.

When Canada's domestic constitution was amended in 1982 to incorporate a Charter of Rights and Freedoms, property rights were excluded on the grounds that they would excessively enhance corporate power. NAFTA's Chapter 11 has created property rights only for foreign corporations with implications that neither the government nor the public at first understood.[12] Local entrepreneurs, whose sales had been hurt by some new municipal by-law, would have to take their lumps. An American competitor could launch a suit for damages against the city in question because the value of its property had been 'expropriated.'[13] The potential effects of this provision are increased by the wide latitude given the notion of investor: an American or Mexican investor would have the right to sue about some government regulation merely when seeking to be an investor, even before actually making an investment.[14]

The corollary of the new disciplines that Chapter 11 imposed on governments was the new freedom it gave corporations. No longer could NAFTA states impose performance requirements on foreign investors in order, for instance, to achieve environmental goals or promote indigenous people's welfare. Beyond having to determine whether they could afford a measure or had enough public support for it, the federal and provincial governments now have to live with 'the most extensive rights and remedies for foreign investors ever set out in an international agreement.'[15]

Although corporations received new rights and opportunities, including temporary immigration of their key personnel for business purposes and although firms had greater freedom to locate where they wanted (and so unemploy those workers left behind when they closed branch operations), no balancing obligations were imposed on them. No continental-level institutions similar to those of the European Union had the clout to regulate, tax, or even monitor the newly created continental market that has proceeded to emerge.[16] Nor were Chapter 11's new corporate rights balanced by a provision to promote the public interest by protecting the environment or public health. To sum up, NAFTA empowered the continental market less by creating a new institutional structure for it than by reducing members capacities and by creating a means for capital to discipline governments that stood in its way.

WTO

In some respects the fit between NAFTA and the WTO is very close. First, the rights incorporated in the WTO are not for its members' citizens but for their corporations. Second, some of the rules are nearly identical. This is the case for the WTO agreement on Trade-Related Aspects of Intellectual Property Rights (TRIPs), adopted after years of sustained lobbying from the American information, entertainment, and pharmaceuticals sectors in concert with their European and Japanese counterparts. First written into the Uruguay Round's Dunkel draft, they were then incorporated, at U.S. insistence, in NAFTA's Chapter 17, which gave NAFTA firms new rights in Canada. Ultimately TRIPs became part of the WTO's GATS and now benefit firms from all the WTO's members.[17] This means that their disciplinary effect on the Canadian state is greater than was NAFTA's clauses in this area.

Adjudication

Norms, limits, and rights rapidly become dead letters without a judicial system to interpret the constitution's texts in the case of conflicts over their meaning. Whereas most of NAFTA's adjudicatory provisions are of little consequence, the WTO's most significant innovation – and the principal cause of its power as global governance – is its powerful judiciary.

NAFTA

A principal criticism of the old Canadian-American relationship was its lack of institutions that could mediate the disputes that erupted over each government's actions and claims by corporations or citizens that the other side had caused them damage. Trade liberalizers hoped to depoliticize these conflicts by creating dispute settlement institutions. In practice, the two trade agreements' judicial effect has not been to empower a continental level of governance. Rather it has endowed the corporate sector with greater muscle vis-à-vis the three territorial states. To understand this situation, we must distinguish between NAFTA's three main processes for settling disputes. The import of one is negligible (for trade disputes), that of another is substantial (for investor-state disputes), while the third is minor (for general disputes).

Trade Disputes

For Canadian promoters of free trade, far more important than reducing American tariffs was gaining 'secure access' to the U.S. market. But Washington had no interest in real trade freed of internal barriers. The American negotiators refused to grant exemptions for Canadian exporters from harassment by U.S. anti-dumping (AD) and countervailing duty (CVD) actions. Faced with the impossibility of achieving their prime objective, Canada's negotiators had focused on the second-best goal of an authoritative arbitration system to contain U.S. protectionism.[18]

Article 1902 allows each party the right to continue to apply its existing AD and CVD law to goods imported from the territory of any other party.[19] Retaining their sovereignty, Canada, the United States, and, later, Mexico avoided creating a permanent supranational institution. They simply agreed to cede appeals of their trade determinations to binational panels that could review the AD or CVD rulings made by one party against imports coming from another party's exporters. CUFTA's resulting Chapter 19 created an unusual tool for settling conflicts over AD and CVD actions. This mechanism, over which much ink has been spilled,[20] merely enabled a party to request the striking of an ad hoc panel to consider whether an AD or CVD ruling properly applied that country's trade law. If the panel found that the law had not been correctly interpreted, it would recommend to the Trade Commission that the decision be remanded for review.

Canada has not had a satisfactory experience in using Chapter 19 to appeal American trade determinations. In 1993, for instance, there were multiple remands in five cases, which led the panels to pass their deadlines significantly. Furthermore, problems have arisen over the lack of consistency in Chapter 19 panel decisions which have shown differing degrees of deference to national agency decisions. That Chapter 19 did not establish an effective, rules-based continental judicial order was demonstrated by the long-running dispute over softwood lumber, which failed to settle a high-tension Canadian-American conflict in either an expeditious or a rules-based manner. The long, drawn-out process whose roots go back to the 1970s was dealt with by power politics in the 1990s,[21] even though Canada won its case under a CUFTA panel.[22] Congress proceeded to amend the definition of subsidy so that the Canadians' short-term victory resulted in long-term defeat when the Americans launched another CVD action against the Canadian lumber exporters. Motivated by fear of future U.S. harassment over exports of softwood lumber – and since a Chapter 19 panel decision does not set a precedent that would constrain future legal manoeuvres by the American lumber lobby[23] – Canada agreed to U.S. demands for restrictions on its softwood exports to the United States.[24] The fight returned with the new millennium, making a mockery of NAFTA's so-called binding dispute settlement. Punishing countervailing and anti-dumping duties were levied on softwood exports from Canada, which found scant solace in NAFTA's Chapter 19.

The spectacle of foreign nationals passing judgment on the application of American law has seemed to some U.S. legislators an unacceptable infringement of congressional sovereignty. That some of these panels should have remanded U.S. trade determinations as improperly made became the source of further political outrage in Washington. Accordingly, when it came time to negotiate NAFTA, Congress demanded that the new settlement mechanism for Chapter 19 disputes be weakened. The roster for panels, which had been dominated by trade experts who tended to criticize the lax reasoning and arbitrary method in U.S. trade remedy determinations, was now to be weighted towards retired judges, who could be expected to express greater deference to American institutions. Procedures of the Extraordinary Challenge Committee (ECC) made it easier to challenge NAFTA panel decisions, facilitating U.S. appeals of rulings under Chapter 19 that turn out to be in Canada's favour.[25]

In American exporters' appeals under Chapter 19 against determinations by Canadian agencies (Revenue Canada or the Canadian International Trade Tribunal) on AD and CVD, Ottawa has 'won' and 'lost' almost equally. Under CUFTA, Canada won seven of the eleven U.S. challenges. It consistently won cases in which an agency levelled countervailing duties for injury caused by U.S. producers to the Canadian market. However, in panels involving the application of anti-dumping duties, Canada consistently lost challenges. Some panel determinations have been made more than once because an agency's non-compliance required the panel to be reconstituted at the plaintiffs' request.[26]

Although AD and CVD jurisprudence is highly technical, binational review has broader implications for the policy-making capacity of the federal government as well as for the behaviour of trade law administrators. Anticipating possible CVD actions being launched by Washington, policy makers in Canada have become cautious about the policies they create that may appear to offer subsidies to Canadian exporters. Canadian trade agencies have become more careful in the standards that they apply in determining AD or CVD out of concern for what panels may later decide.

The addition of continental participants to domestic review gives non-national actors some influence over domestic trade procedures. The result is that Chapter 19 panels have had a small supraconstitutional impact, altering the rules by which these bodies operate. For instance, Ottawa amended the standard of review it employed to include two new grounds for remanding agencies' determinations: when a tribunal acted (or failed to act) by reason of fraud or perjured evidence, and when it acted in any other way contrary to the law.[27] Thus some U.S. judicial norms have been imported through NAFTA into the standard of review for Canadian agencies.

Investor-State Disputes

The panel system set up by Chapter 19 to oversee trade remedies bureaucratized AD and CVD cases without depoliticizing the major cases. Chapter 11 has established a new zone of privatized adjudication which has politicized issues that would previously have escaped most public notice. Not only has it added to the Canadian constitution a new corporate property right which treats firms unequally depending on their nationality. It has introduced an existing arbitration mechanism designed to handle international corporate disputes, turning it into a device to constrain governmental capacity.

Cases initiated against a municipal, provincial, or federal government under the investor-state provisions of Chapter 11 are not heard before a Canadian court using Canadian jurisprudence. These 'investor-state' disputes go to arbitration before an international panel operating by rules established under the aegis of the World Bank or the United Nations for settling international disputes between transnational corporations.[28] Since each of these forums operates according to the norms of international commercial law, Chapter 11 actually transfers adjudication of disputes over government policies from the realm of national law to international commercial law, with several serious implications.

This process violates many values held dear in the common law tradition. Transparency is the first victim in this secret world of commercial arbitration. Proceedings are held in camera. The briefs that document the parties' pleadings and even the existence of a case may be kept secret if the parties so wish. The public may never learn what has happened or why, even though its government may have been forced to change its properly passed regulations as a result of this process.

Appeals from these rulings can take place only in the jurisdiction where the arbitrators declared their formal address. When the U.S. waste-disposal company Metalclad used Chapter 11 to attack the environmental order made by a Mexican village that had shut down its landfill site, the arbitrators, who met in Washington, ruled in the firm's favour. Because the tribunal had named Vancouver as its nominal address, the Mexican government's appeal had to invoke BC jurisprudence, adding yet another twist of legal strangeness.

Neutrality is the second legal value that falls by the wayside. The plaintiff investor has the right to appoint one of the three arbitrators, which is something like having one-third of the jury taking sides before hearing the evidence. This means that the defending government already faces a bench that is substantially weighted in favour of corporate rather than public values.

Judicial sovereignty is a third victim of this extraordinary addition to the Canadian legal order. A privatized process – whose rulings directly affect member-states' policies and institutions and bypass their public courts[29] – creates more supraconstitutional norms. The sociology of the panellists' selection makes it more likely that they will respond to the legal arguments privileging the norms of international commercial law. As the investor and the state each have the right to appoint one arbiter, and since the panel's chair is chosen by consensus, it is likely that there will be just one Canadian adjudicating suits launched against Canadian governments. This suggests that, when a norm of international corporate law comes into conflict with a Canadian legal standard, the latter is likely to be overridden. Since American corporate law tends to dominate international commercial law cases, conflicts between U.S. corporations and the Canadian state will inexorably cause U.S. legal definitions to infiltrate Canadian legal standards and force Canadian governments to operate as if American law on 'regulatory takings' applied to them. While some observers expected that Canadian, American, and Mexican jurisprudence would interpret 'expropriation' differently in each country,[30] it is generally acknowledged that panel findings will impose the U.S. interpretation instead of the other two signatories' legal notions.[31]

Chapter 11 disputes have a great potential for developing more supraconstitutional norms. For instance, NAFTA accepts government monopolies if they provide essential services to the public, but they must 'act solely in accordance with commercial considerations.'[32] But providing an essential public service may be uneconomic, requiring, for instance, subsidizing reasonably priced telephone or postal services in remote communities by charging higher rates in urban areas. Should a provincial government set up a crown corporation to build and maintain non-profit housing, a NAFTA corporation could argue that the public entity's failure to operate by commercial standards reduced its profits. A Chapter 11 arbitration could decide what was permissible action for a crown corporation, subject only to 'interpretations' offered by the NAFTA trade commission. The Canadian regulatory system thus becomes subject to judgment and correction by arbitrators who are not necessarily privy to the cultural and historical rationale for its practices and who are applying norms developed under the influence of the litigious and individualistic American legal culture to Canada's less litigious and less entrepreneurial public domain.

Ottawa's abandonment of its cigarette packaging policy and of several environmental regulations, which we look at in chapter 17, suggests that, under the supraconstitutional aegis of NAFTA's Chapter 11, the issue is no longer which order of government – federal or provincial – *should* initiate a regulation. It becomes whether either order of government *can* initiate such legislation at all.[33] Beyond questions surrounding this stunning and unacknowledged change in Canada's constitutional sovereignty and regulatory autonomy, these examples raise the spectre of a serious democratic deficit.

General Disputes
Access to continental justice under NAFTA varies according to subject and chapter. Only the federal government of Canada, Mexico, or the United States can initiate a Chapter 20 proceeding, although a third party may join the process when the matter has reached the panel stage in disputes involving environmental concerns.[34] Governments initiate Chapter 19 panels on behalf of grieving corporations. Foreign corporate actors can challenge domestic law under Chapter 11.[35] So, unless they are corporations, third parties are generally excluded from continental dispute settlement. Given that citizens and

non-governmental organizations (NGOs) can neither launch a complaint nor be involved until the matter reaches the panel stage, the public is effectively shut out of continental dispute settlement processes. The restriction of standing to corporate and governmental players necessarily skews the course of continental justice.

Through NAFTA's environmental and labour commissions, environmental organizations and trade unions enjoy some modest access to litigating in defence of their values, but these organizations are so tightly circumscribed that their presence does not begin to tip the balance of power away from governmental and corporate dominance. Apart from these symbolic genuflections in the direction of civil society, CUFTA and NAFTA's adjudicatory institutions overwhelmingly favour market forces.

CUFTA's Chapter 18 and NAFTA's derivative Chapter 20 provide for panels to be struck when member-states have been unable to resolve their differences over issues generated by these economic agreements. Although under Chapter 18 dispute settlement was initially expeditious,[36] some panel decisions caused more controversy than calm. One concerned the enforceability of putatively binding decisions. Despite a panel ruling in Canada's favour in the wheat case,[37] Washington responded to its loss by threatening to launch an investigation into Canadian wheat exports. Temporary closure was achieved only when political pressure from the United States caused the Canadian government to give way. Ottawa ultimately agreed to limit wheat exports to the United States during 1994/95 to 1.5 million tons, with certain exceptions.[38] Repeated rhetorical attacks by U.S. farmers on the Canadian wheat board as a public grain marketing agency and several investigations by the U.S.T.R. warn Canadian grain growers that no trade agreement can ultimately shelter them from relentless political pressure.

Chapter 18 raised a different problem in the case over Puerto Rico's obstructing the import of Quebec's long-life milk.[39] Essentially, the panel offered a compromise between the two governments' positions.[40] Since neither side felt that the process enforced the trade agreement's rules, the political dénouement decreased the legitimacy of dispute settlement under CUFTA. If legal norms are ignored and replaced by political deals, predicting the outcomes of disputes becomes more difficult and governments are less likely to risk using the process.[41]

Both the U.S. and Canadian governments have demonstrated their dissatisfaction by their decreasing use of Chapter 18 for resolving disputes – twice in the first year of CUFTA, but only three times in the next five years.[42] With Canada not receiving 'secure access' through Chapter 18 dispute settlement, Ottawa is forced back to the political bargaining table, but with a less powerful position than it had enjoyed before it signed CUFTA.

NAFTA's Chapter 20 (which weakened CUFTA's Chapter 18) manages to complicate dispute resolution without really removing it from continental power politics. It allowed for the adjudication of a broader range of issues,[43] but its alterations aggravated, rather than resolved, the main problems demonstrated by the old Chapter 18. The reformed process still does not prevent panels from delivering compromises. Nor does NAFTA make panel decisions under Chapter 20 binding: these rulings are merely recommendations to the NAFTA trade commission.

In the end, the three governments may feel that the submission of serious issues to continental dispute settlement is largely futile. If a case is going to end up in political bargaining, it runs the risk of inflaming, not depoliticizing Canadian-American conflicts. If continental dispute settlement degenerates into a shoving contest where might prevails over right, the concerned governments may choose instead the global dispute settlement system embodied in the WTO. With numerous members, a substantial subsidy code, and a more authoritative process for resolving conflicts, the WTO is better able to offset the asymmetric power relationship with the United States that CUFTA and NAFTA failed to mitigate.[44]

WTO

Without a means of adjudication, the stupendous expansion in the scope of the WTO's rules would have been as inconsequential as the International Labour Organization's dozens of conventions. The explanation for the WTO's importance lies in its dispute-settlement mechanisms, which are far stronger than those of either the old GATT or the new NAFTA. Panellists base rulings not on the contenders' own laws, as in NAFTA's Chapter 19, but on the international norms written into the WTO's texts and the international public law developed by prior GATT jurisprudence.

Also in contrast with NAFTA, panellists are not nationals to the dispute in question. This makes their decisions less liable to accusations of unfairness for reason of national bias, and hence more legitimate in the eyes of the international community. However, when a country loses a case, the foreign panellists' unfamiliarity with its cultural and societal specificity can seriously undermine the decision's legitimacy.

Strict time limits and appeal procedures were designed to forestall future U.S. use of its unilateral trade remedy legislation and so promised prompt, less politicized justice. However, 'less politicized' can also mean less responsive to the specific circumstances obtaining in each state.

The speed and effectiveness of the WTO's dispute settlement body give it authority but do not guarantee legitimacy. The behind-closed-doors secretiveness of its judicial process leaves the public ill-informed. Only territorial states have standing in this system, which excludes all but government representatives. This adds to civil society's frustration from being left outside a process that affects social interests such as the environment, cultural sectors, and labour.

Notwithstanding a formal lack of precedent-making capacity in the WTO's dispute settlement process, the logic of one panel's decision can be invoked in the argumentation placed by the contending parties before another panel. Given the permanence in office of the Appellate Body's (AB) members, their individual rulings are cumulating as a body of coherent, if not predictable trade law. The AB has regularly given a broad interpretation to rules inhibiting government policy that might limit trade. Since these judgments have tended to give a narrow interpretation to principles invoking 'legitimate domestic objectives' such as cultural diversity, public health, and environmental sustainability, they have further delegitimized the WTO in the eyes of NGOs working to promote non-economic causes. These groups have·learned that, in case after case, the goal of expanding trade trumps cultural and environmental protection. Even when international environmental agreements enshrine the objective of sustainability by seeking to control the trade of endangered species or hazardous substances, trade panels habitually rule against measures embodying such objectives in favour of promoting trade unhampered by moral or ecological concerns.

The sociology of dispute panels enhances the WTO's legalistic rigidity. Panellists adjudicating WTO disputes are either trade lawyers and professors of international law, who tend to stick very close to the letter of the WTO's texts that they are interpreting, or middle-level diplomats who take their cues from the secretariat's neoconservative legal staff. In either case, they know full well that their judgment will be appealed by the losing side and that the judges on the AB will be responding to highly refined legal reasoning.[45] Under these conditions, 'soft' arguments defending cultural autonomy or environmental sustainability hold little weight against the 'hard' logic of the WTO's rules.

While the WTO's norms, limits, and rights create new supraconstitutional principles for member-states to ingest, their practical meaning, as interpreted by the dispute settlement process, cannot be anticipated with any certainty. The AB memorably compared the concept of 'likeness' to 'an accordion, which may be stretched wide or squeezed tight as the case requires.' This arbitrariness in the WTO's judicial interpretation of its rules means that national policy makers can be sure only that they will never know what this supreme court of commercial law will decide until it rules on a trade dispute involving a specific WTO provision.[46]

Its initial bias towards dogmatic neoconservatism is not a *necessary* quality of the WTO's judicial system. Beyond the anticipated reaction of their professional colleagues, judges also have to consider the reactions of the general public when rendering their rulings. As the WTO's judgments reach deep inside members' regulatory systems, the panels may find themselves pressed by an emerging global public opinion to give greater heed to environmental, social, and cultural values in their decisions. In the Canadian government's case against France for banning the import of asbestos, the AB recognized the French public's health concerns as a valid conditioning factor in denying Ottawa's petition.

Whether national courts will unquestioningly accept the superiority of the WTO's rulings over their own constitutional norms also remains to be seen. Colombia's superior court has ruled that a WTO decision does not invalidate national law. The Mexican Supreme Court decreed in 2000 that the country's constitution was superior to international treaties. The fact that treaties properly negotiated and signed by the Mexican government made them automatically 'the supreme law of the land' – and so hierarchically superior to federal and local law – did not mean they could trump the constitution's own supra-legislative norms.[47] No case has yet been brought to Canada's Supreme Court to test whether a ruling by a global or continental dispute panel necessarily has precedence over a Canadian norm.[48] We must expect continuing clashes between these external and internal constitutional orders.

Enforcement

As with other trade treaties, NAFTA has no enforcement capacity other than the parties' sense of their long-term self-interest. If one member state does not comply with the judgments of dispute panels, it cannot expect its partners to continue to do so. In the background there remains the possible resort to economic muscle. Under North America's conditions of extreme asymmetry, the hegemon remains able to reject the trade agreements' rules and to impose its will, as it has done repeatedly in the long-standing disputes over Canadian softwood lumber and American split-run magazines.

Under GATT, a signatory state's failure to accord national treatment to some foreign good was unlikely to have very serious consequences because dispute settlement was a slow, diplomatic process in which a guilty defendant state could often escape retribution. Under the new liberalization agreements, an errant state is much more likely to be brought to 'justice' by a litigant partner state because dispute settlement rulings sanction retaliation by a successful plaintiff.

Once a signatory state's behaviour has been judged in violation of a WTO norm, it's supposed to change the offending provisions or pay compensation. The WTO has no police service capable of enforcing its dispute decisions, but it does mandate the winning litigant legitimately to make reprisals if the losing side does not comply. This retaliation can target any exports of the guilty state and can amount to the harm caused to the complainant. The global trade regime's enforcement muscle makes the WTO far more legitimate than CUFTA or NAFTA.[49]

Conclusion

When Ronald Reagan hailed CUFTA as North America's new 'economic constitution,' he was not showing signs of premature senility. Even if it did not define new institutions for the two countries, CUFTA did constrain the role of governments (if those of Canada rather than those of the United States). It did define rights for citizens (albeit those of TNCs rather than those of individuals). It did establish a judicial process (if only an appeal system accessible by the federal government and corporations but not by provinces or citizens). It was ratified by each government's duly passing the requisite implementing legislation. And it did allow for amendment and termination.

Much the same was said of NAFTA, mutatis mutandis. 'North America' now took on this true geographic sense by including Mexico. But the rule book of this new economic bloc had very different effects on its three members. With most of its new rules exporting U.S. norms and with its lack of a supranational institutional structure that could give Canada and Mexico voice at the continental level, it barely affected U.S. constitutional reality. For the two peripheral countries, NAFTA entered their constitutional makeup as external components, reconstitutionalizing both.[50] The previous, informally operating norms of continental coexistence had given way to elaborate, highly specific rules designed to bind governmental practices at the federal, provincial, and municipal levels.

Since political regimes are socially constructed, we can expect the robustness at these five levels of state activity to differ from each other and to change over time in an interrelated manner. If the federal level becomes weaker, provincial and local orders will probably become stronger. If the global becomes more authoritative, the continental will lose some of its dominance. If new norms on investment, cultural protection, or intellectual property rights are successfully developed under the WTO's aegis, the scope of its legal impact on government decisions would increase. If these efforts fail, and the regulation of these issues falls to continental or inter-continental agreements such as the negotiation of a hemispheric Free Trade Area of the Americas, then the latter would be proven ascendant. If hemispheric and continental governance falters, the national may regain lost clout.

This suggests that constitutionality, like statehood, is a matter of degree and power: some constitutional orders are more legitimate and authoritative than others. Indeed, the same external constitution's legitimacy may vary between members. Ottawa's acceptance of a WTO ruling is virtually automatic. By contrast, Washington's acceptance of the WTO's authority is conditional. When the European Union threatened to launch a dispute panel to challenge the Helms-Burton Act, the U.S. government made it clear that it considered this a matter of its national security, so it would boycott any legal proceedings. What was considered unconstitutional by the hegemon was accepted as supra-constitutional in the semi-periphery.

Establishing the importance of global governance and its impact on the Canadian legal order only takes us part way through our discussion. To weigh the significance of changes from without, we need to assess what changes to the Canadian political order have been made from within – the purpose of the next two chapters.

CHANGE FROM WITHIN

In trying to measure the structural impact of globalization on the
Canadian state, we need to find out what other forces have caused it to
change besides the shifts resulting from global governance that we saw
in chapter 4. Keeping our five-tiered governing structure in mind, we
now proceed to investigate recent changes that have come about in the
nature and redistribution of federal, provincial, and municipal power.
Some may be the product of endogenous pressures introduced during
the Mulroney-Chrétien regime, while other changes were caused by
institutions such as the courts which were inherited from the Diefenbaker-Pearson-Trudeau era. We look at these issues in chapter 5.

Constitutionally speaking, the country's municipalities are mere
pawns of their province, which can do with them what it wills.
Although they may be politically inferior as the third level of government, cities none the less constitute the most important locality for the
majority of the public. They provide the spaces where most global
forces are actually experienced. In chapter 6 we will see in a case study
how the complex interactions between globalization and neoconservatism impinge on the patterns of the municipal political economy.

5 The Federal State: Internal Trade and the Charter

After acknowledging that global governance has added two supraconstitu-tional layers to Canada's political order, we need to inquire whether globaliza-tion as constructed in the public mind by neoconservatism has also affected the structure and workings of Canada's three traditional political orders. Commentators speculate, for instance, that the devolution of power upwards to global and continental bodies reduces citizens' sense that national politics matter and so helps account for the decline in voter participation.[1] While the causal connections between globalization and electoral consciousness are intu-itively valid, they are virtually impossible to prove. Somewhat more amenable to evidence is identifying a link between Canada's new trade agreements and its institutional structure. Because the central reality of the political system is the federal-provincial relationship, this chapter explores the putative impact of the new global governance – along with its ideological corollary, neoconserva-tism – on federalism's basic trade-off between national integration and local autonomy.

The Fathers of Confederation intended to create a classic federal sys-tem with sovereign powers carefully allocated to either the provincial or the federal level in mainly exclusive, watertight compartments. But alarmed by the carnage of the American Civil War, which seemed to demonstrate the folly of a constitution endowing its constituent states with excessive autonomy, colonial leaders asked Westminster to endow the proposed dominion government with many instruments that, in the interests of constructing a coherent political system, empowered it to intrude in and prevail over the affairs of the federated colonies and any future provincial accessions.

The earliest external force to affect the power relationships within the new federation was the British judicial system. Although the British North America Act 1867 created a dominant central government, British lords sitting on the Judicial Committee of the Privy Council in London inverted the centralized system during the first seventy years of Confederation by supporting the provinces in jurisdictional disputes with the Dominion. In the aftermath of the Great Depression, the Second World War, and the bold prescriptions of the economist John Maynard Keynes, Canadian federalism had recentralized under an activist government committed to rapid industrialization. But as the provinces built up their own capacity to administer social policies and as their premiers demanded to be heard in federal decision making affecting their powers, a new cycle of decentralization set in.[2] By the time that the new trade regime was being negotiated in the mid-1980s, the provinces' constitutional powers and financial autonomy rivalled those of the German Länder and the Swiss cantons for ranking as constituents of the world's most economically decentralized federation.[3]

This chapter examines four phenomena that have altered the federal-provincial balance of power in the last two decades – trade liberalization, the emergence of global governance, the setting up of the federal-provincial Agreement on Internal Trade in 1995, and the patriation of the constitution with the entrenchment of the Charter of Rights and Freedoms in 1982.

Federal-Provincial Rebalancing under Trade Liberalization

Claims that globalism further exacerbates an already dangerous degree of decentralization in Canada are not entirely convincing.[4] One problem is the difficulty in distinguishing federal government actions motivated by ideological solidarity with the new continental and global governance regimes from those due to neoconservatism. Another is making sense of Ottawa's contradictory approach, which has alternated between trying to reinforce its authority and devolving its own powers.

Free trade and neoconservatism seemed to lock arms when Prime Minister Brian Mulroney resorted to the traditional technique of executive federalism to modify the constitution. His attempt to accommodate Quebec's demands (but also to respond to the anglophone premiers' pressure for more power) through the Meech Lake Accord period (1987–90) was fruitless. Mulroney then floated a heavily ideological proposal to make the constitutional changes required by his conception of free trade which involved granting Ottawa intervention-ist powers in order to discipline provincial protectionists into conform-ing with the new norms of global competitiveness. A related change would have reduced the Bank of Canada's mandate solely to control-ling prices.

An uproar ensued. Mulroney's overtly neoconservative attacks on the state's economic capacity were not popular with a public brought up on the Keynesian paradigm. Traditional conservatives rejected the proposed federal powers over the economic union as an illegitimate and unnecessary strengthening of the state over the market. Social democrats denounced the idea of diverting the Bank of Canada's mon-etary policy function from minding the general condition of the national economy into a single-track obsession with a market-centred watch on inflation.

Distinct from but connected to globalization are changes effected by governments when downsizing the state in order to liberate market forces. On the whole, federal downloading in Canada has increased the de facto power of the provinces, whose responses varied with their ideological position about their role vis-à-vis the market and with their level of affluence. Generally premiers have welcomed extra policy powers when the financial implications were neutral but have had mixed reactions when Ottawa's withdrawal has not had uniform fiscal effects. All provinces have protested when downloading consisted of contractions in transfer payments driven primarily by Ottawa's deficit-cutting imperative. When federal cuts have disproportionately favoured the have-not, equalization-receiving provinces, their better-off cousins have objected unashamedly.

Taking the opposite tack, the Charlottetown Accord of 1990 – the Mulroney government's last, best attempt to reach a constitutional agreement – proposed restoring to the provinces powers that were under their constitutional jurisdiction and that Ottawa had encroached on over the decades. In the October 1992 referendum, this weakening of the central government seemed inadequate to Quebec sovereigntists and excessive to federalists from coast to coast. The No verdict showed that changing the country's internal constitution through democratic processes was virtually impossible.

The rejection of constitutional measures to reduce federal power did not prevent federal politicians, even after Jean Chrétien and his Liber-als took power in 1993, from adjusting the federal-provincial balance of power by other means. When Chrétien's finance minister, Paul Martin, launched a crusade against the deficit as the government's overriding priority, cutting programs became a means of escaping federal responsibility for policies originally set in motion by Ottawa's use of its spending power during its activist, Keynesian phase. Following the Quebec referendum of 1995, which came within 50,000 votes of victory for the sovereigntists, the prime minister formalized more withdrawal by negotiating individual agreements with provinces, many of which assumed full working responsibility for labour-market training in return for certain financial considerations.

The confusing effects of globalization on the federal-provincial balance of power appear in trade policy, the area that one might assume to be most favourable to enhancing the central government. Even when negotiating trade agreements, Ottawa appears quite limited by the powers of constitutionally strong provincial governments. The extensive jurisdiction of provinces – broad over natural resources, transportation, education, and social policy; concurrent in agriculture and immigration; and partial in labour policy and the environment – meant that Ottawa could not do much more than speak on their behalf in international forums on these issues. Nevertheless the government of Canada is the one that ultimately signs the agreements. The provinces have not managed to achieve the guarantees that Germany's Länder got from the courts to reverse Berlin's commitments made in the course of international negotiations that alienated any of their powers.[5] Not even Quebec has achieved direct representation in the new regime of global governance.

Since the Canadian government can implement treaties only in areas of its own constitutional jurisdiction, provincial involvement has been necessary to realize more fully the general vision of liberalized trade. For this reason, Ottawa has encouraged increased provincial participation since the Tokyo Round of the GATT negotiations first brought such non-tariff barriers as industrial policy measures to the bargaining table.[6] While provincial influence over trade policy has increased, Canada's global and continental economic initiatives have been driven by federal leadership.[7] While many of the resulting supraconstitutional rules did reduce the federal state's competence, many of these restrictions applied equally to the provinces.

Beyond the difficulty involved in playing a game whose agenda is set by their federal rival, it is unclear how far the provinces can go in representing their interests abroad. Even though these governments may have considerable potential international activity in a globalizing world, practical budgetary constraints and the formal barriers to diplomatic recognition limit them in this ambition. If their bureaucratic capacity is inadequate to project their interests overseas, provinces need to rely on Ottawa to represent them in intergovernmental forums even in areas of provincial jurisdiction. Deficit-shrinking cutbacks of their quasi-embassies overseas and in the United States, not just by Ontario and Alberta but by Quebec, confirmed that neoconservatism limited provinces' capacity for direct participation in global affairs. The return of budgetary surpluses has emboldened Alberta, Ontario, and Quebec to open offices abroad again.

Given the potential for playing out domestic squabbles on the international stage, there is surprisingly little federal-provincial discord in this area beyond the perennial red-carpet jostling between Ottawa and Quebec City over the latter's diplomatic status. Indeed, provincial voices sang in surprising harmony as part of a federal chorus when 'Team Canada' sallied forth on federal-led trade missions in Asia, Latin America, or Europe. The 1994 inaugural tour saw nine premiers (sans Quebec's Jacques Parizeau) along with Prime Minister Chrétien promoting Canada in the Far East. This trade mission (the first Canadian visit there since Pierre Trudeau's last official trip to the region in 1982) combined the political expertise of senior international trade officials, the economic interests of provincial leaders, and the hopes of daring entrepreneurs. This first sortie proved so successful that teams later visited Latin America (1995), South and East Asia (1996), and South Korea, Thailand and the Philippines (1997 – *avec* the Quebec premier, Lucien Bouchard).[8]

Federal leadership in international trade policy may be accepted in principle, but it is flouted in practice. Provinces and cities find themselves forced to court foreign direct investment in the hope of attracting projects that generate tax revenues and jobs. Their resulting offers of subsidies and tax incentives – long-established instruments of regional strategies for industrial growth – often violate the formal rules laid out in supranational trade agreements. They are called to order only when an aggrieved foreign corporation provokes a trade dispute because of its complaint.[9] Provincial bidding wars that attempt to lure investors away from another jurisdiction, as well as regulations that require an investor to locate facilities in a province and impose other performance requirements as a condition of doing business, do more than violate the country's external commitments. They may also impede domestic commercial activity by erecting barriers to internal trade. A fragmented internal market may diminish provinces' competitiveness in their global bidding wars for new investment. Efforts to address this problem in the mid-1990s led to a startling innovation in Canada's internal economic architecture.

Global Governance and the Federal Balance of Power

Neither NAFTA nor the WTO directly determines the structure of its member states' political organs. But their intrusive norms, rights, and limits indirectly affect each state's institutions.

The government of Canada claims, for instance, that its trade and commerce power in Section 132 of the constitution gives it the power to implement trade agreements. Specifically, the NAFTA implementation act apparently defies the constitutional division of powers by claiming 'the right of Parliament to enact legislation to implement any provision of the Agreement.'[10] Federal paramountcy is enhanced by other aspects of trade liberalization. In the general disputes arising from NAFTA's provisions under its Chapter 20, only the government of Canada may launch a dispute panel and appear in its hearings, even when a provincial grievance or measure is the issue.[11] Similarly, only Ottawa may initiate a dispute under the supplementary environmental agreement. For provinces to have to rely on Ottawa to defend their interests at the continental and global levels of governance in areas where they enjoy constitutional sovereignty creates considerable potential for centralization.

Like CUFTA, NAFTA and the WTO set Canada up for the possibility of a severe constitutional impasse by including obligations that impinge on areas of provincial jurisdiction, even though the provinces did not sign the relevant agreement. Although the federal government consulted the provinces during its negotiations with Mexico and the United States, NAFTA's wider sweep and greater policy depth increase the effect on provincial powers by including significant fields of provincial jurisdiction.[12]

Provincial regulation of loan, mortgage, and trust companies and the security industry now comes under the aegis of NAFTA's Chapter 14 on financial services, which opens new doors for U.S. financial institutions to enter the Canadian market. The inclusion of services in NAFTA has further expanded the threat to provincial sovereignty. Since most services such as social security, education, and health care come under provincial jurisdiction, inclusion of government services within NAFTA's ambit constitutes a time bomb. Its transformative potential may take years to realize, as American service providers learn how to use NAFTA's corporate rights to challenge the public sector's dominance in the provinces' provision of social services.

Similarly, many of the WTO's norms also apply to sub-central governments. The agreement on Technical Barriers to Trade, for instance, requires that regulations protecting human and animal health and the environment respect national treatment, be non-discriminatory, and restrict trade no more than necessary – a criterion eminently suited to litigation by foreign corporations that feel aggrieved at a province's efforts to conserve its environment.[13] Some principles in the General Agreement on Trade in Services (GATS) are so vague that years may pass before we know how extensively they constrain provincial and municipal services – even before the Doha Round of WTO negotiations extends these GATS disciplines. Should the federal government agree to let education and health care come under the GATS rules on services, that commitment would bind the provincial constitutional order more than the federal.

A further uncertainty generated by global trade governance is the signatories' responsibility for their sub-central governments' conformity to its rules. NAFTA may have altered the country's delicate constitutional balance by obliging Ottawa to ensure the provinces' conformity to its provisions.[14] Not only is the government of Canada responsible before the other two parties for all actions of its own agencies, but CUFTA and NAFTA both commit it to taking 'all necessary measures' to ensure provincial compliance with their stipulations – a stronger requirement than the obligation to take 'reasonable measures' undertaken in the GATT.[15] But if a province defies one of these clauses, claiming it intrudes in an area of its jurisdiction, Ottawa has no constitutional authority to oblige its compliance.

In a hypothetical conflict between the United States (pressing Ottawa to force a province to honour a right that Washington believed it had won in NAFTA) and a province (claiming Ottawa had no jurisdiction for signing away that right), it is not clear how the Supreme Court of Canada would rule. It could declare the *Labour Conventions* case of 1937, which prevented the federal government from implementing treaties in areas of provincial jurisdiction, still to be valid. This would not prevent the United States from taking NAFTA-legitimated retaliatory moves against Ottawa, which would have no constitutional way to pass on the liability to the offending province. The Supreme Court could rule that, owing to the realities created by globalization, meeting NAFTA's obligations represented a 'national concern' and so could bring that area under federal jurisdiction. If the province lost such a case, Ottawa would gain the authority to compel provincial compliance. In this scenario, NAFTA would have restored to the Canadian constitution a federal power of disallowance that had fallen into disuse.

Such an eventuality is not idle speculation. Although this treaty provision has not been tested in a Canadian court, it has already entered NAFTA jurisprudence. In the case taken to arbitration under Chapter 11 by the California company Metalclad, Mexico was deemed responsible for ensuring its sub-central governments complied with NAFTA's rules.[16] This ruling suggests that, whatever constitutionalists might believe about Canada's decentralized federalism, the U.S. or other foreign governments will expect Ottawa to ensure provincial compliance to NAFTA or WTO norms.

NAFTA norms also create policy anomalies in interprovincial relations. The application of national treatment and investor-state conflict resolution to sub-central governments means that provinces, territories, and municipalities have to give NAFTA investors non-discriminatory treatment, whereas they were not required to accord 'provincial' treatment to Canadian investors from other provinces.

The Agreement on Internal Trade

Throughout the latter half of the twentieth century, federal officials maintained that the economy's balkanization posed a serious problem. Even in the 1940s, there were calls for better co-ordination of dominion-provincial relations in order to reap efficiency gains from the internal market.[17] This perennial complaint resurfaced in the 1970s through the Ontario Economic Council, but with little effect.[18] The new trade order brought this issue to a head when some of the rules incorporated in CUFTA, NAFTA, and the WTO renewed questions about provincial protectionism. Canadian entrepreneurs bewailed the fact that a province could discriminate against Canadian out-of-province firms, although 'national treatment' forbade it from discriminating against NAFTA businesses. NAFTA companies had rights to any government assistance offered to in-province companies, whereas firms from other provinces would continue to suffer discrimination under many province-building programs. Paradoxically, Canada's internal market was in this way less open than its external one.

Because a national 'economic union' increasingly seemed a prerequisite for international success, Ottawa started to promote a strong agreement to complement its external trade agenda.[19] For their part, the provinces started to realize – despite their common currency, their closely harmonized tax system, the absence of interprovincial tariffs, and their capital and labour mobility[20] – that NAFTA and the WTO were giving American, Mexican, and other foreigner competitors a more advantageous trading and investing environment in Canada than local firms.

When it made its historic pitch for continental free trade, the Macdonald Report of 1985 had also called for tackling the harmful economic effects of internal trade barriers.[21] The Mulroney government took the first part of this advice to heart but became so fixated on making a deal with the United States that it ignored internal trade liberalization. Although international competitive pressure made economic unity a high priority in theory, internal political pressure pushed domestic trade to the top of the federal-provincial agenda. The failure of Mulroney's mega-constitutional reform efforts in the early 1990s left a long list of intergovernmental policy issues to be resolved in some other, presumably non-constitutional ways. The ensuing negotiations encompassed many subjects, including labour, industrial, and cultural policies, along with the basic issue of federal-provincial relations. Once the protagonists' interest in the economic union was rekindled, they reconsidered the Macdonald Report's recommendation – to apply an international trade-negotiating model by pursuing an internal free trade agreement under the auspices of first ministers' conferences with the aid of a federal-provincial commission on the economic union.[22]

Ottawa had generated a dialogue on trade-policy with the provinces during the CUFTA, NAFTA, and Uruguay Round negotiations in order to secure their support for new rules that would fall within their jurisdiction. Because they knew that these agreements would affect them and that they would ultimately have to implement them, the provinces had developed considerable expertise in trade issues. This new fluency in the language of global commercial policy helped translate international trade norms into the discourse of intergovernmental relations within the country.

Concepts have consequences. In this case, the logic of trade liberalization shaped, as we see in this section, the negotiating process, the nature of the resulting rule book, and even the institutions of Canadian federalism.

The Negotiating Process

The first noteworthy aspect of the federal-provincial negotiations on the economic union, which began under Mulroney and finished under Chrétien, was its use of strict GATT-WTO negotiating protocols. Designed to facilitate discussions between highly competitive states, they now disciplined federal-provincial participants notorious for late-night, kitchen-table deal making and their openness to the media.

Besides adapting political practices from their global counterparts, the economic-policy negotiations had a more familiar pattern. Outcomes depended on political alliances made between key players. The pro-free trade Progressive Conservatives in Alberta and Manitoba, followed by the federal Liberals, tried to restrain the other provinces from demanding exemption from general market-liberalizing rules.[23] With the Bourassa government in Quebec trying to demonstrate that, in the shadow of the Charlottetown Accord's failure and in the run-up to the 1995 referendum, trade-based liberalization could work, the negotiations over an Agreement on Internal Trade marked a rare Canadian moment. Ottawa, Alberta, Manitoba, and Quebec took the same position in an intergovernmental battle. Because the provinces governed by the New Democratic Party (NDP) – British Columbia, Saskatchewan, and Ontario – wanted a series of sectoral agreements, they participated reluctantly, defending provincial diversity. The remaining governments played minor roles owing to their political weakness.

The introduction of such closed-door, trade-style negotiating conventions was a striking departure from the earlier, more informal patterns of executive federalism. From the outset, all parties agreed to adhere to stringent decision-making deadlines, a resolution reinforced by the then-imminent Quebec election. To facilitate communication, they created a consensus-building administrative organ – the Winnipeg-based Internal Trade Secretariat (ITS). Most remarkably, they brought in a neutral, third-party arbitrator in the person of Arthur Mauro.[24] Such formality had previously been absent from intergovernmental relations.

Rule Book

In 1994, provincial, territorial, and federal governments signed the Agreement on Internal Trade (AIT), which came into effect on July 1, 1995. Their objective was pure neoconservatism: an economic union enhanced through greater efficiency, accelerated productivity, and increased interprovincial commerce, which accounted for just over 20 per cent of Canada's gross domestic product at the time that it was enacted.[25] In typical trade treaty discourse, a preamble set forth objectives – increase competitiveness, encourage sustainable environmental development, and augment accountability. The text declared its intention 'to promote an open, efficient, and stable domestic market for long-term job creation, economic growth and stability,' as well as 'equal economic opportunity for Canadians.'[26]

These objectives were to be achieved through typical trade-treaty means. In the hope of stimulating market activity in the form of increased investment and factor mobility, new rules would constrain individual jurisdictions in their traditional use of policy instruments to promote local economic development. Provincial and territorial governments undertook to refrain from discriminating against another party's goods, services, persons, and investments, from restricting movement across provincial barriers, and from maintaining obstacles to internal trade. Further entrenching neoconservative globalism in their praxis, they agreed to 'provincial treatment' – guaranteeing that their policies would treat pan-Canadian goods, services, investments, and persons just as well as those from their own jurisdiction.

In the negotiation process, Ottawa pressed hard, but without much success, to have governmental standards harmonized with obligations in international trade agreements. It tried to have goods, services, and investment treated in an all-encompassing approach. It also wanted to include the same science-based approach for risk assessment and for sanitary standards that NAFTA and the WTO use. The provinces were aware that global trade governance was limiting the luxury of having ten different sets of technical standards – for example, for fluid milk – but they did not want new *national* standards to be *federal*, made-by-Ottawa standards.[27] In labour mobility, for instance, they resisted federal pressure for the kind of harmonized set of norms favoured by Washington in economic agreements. They preferred instead the European, subsidiarity-inspired approach of mutually recognizing each others' certification of professional qualifications.

Beyond the general rules aimed at reducing existing trade barriers, the AIT contained a set of specific obligations to harmonize regulations or reduce beggar-thy-neighbour competition in two types of policy fields that had long bedeviled federal-provincial relations. Horizontal or framework rules cutting across policy sectors dealt with investment (chapter 6), labour mobility (7), consumer-related measures and standards (8), and environmental protection (15). Vertical or economic sector rules covered agriculture and foodstuffs (chapter 9) and alcoholic beverages (10). Hybrids – processing of natural resources (11), energy (12), communications (13), and transportation (14) – were economic sectors that are also inputs for other production processes. The chapter on government procurement (5) was the longest, detailing the extent to which provinces may discriminate in favour of their own firms. In contrast, energy was the shortest, consisting of only one sentence, since no agreement could be reached.

Although the AIT shifted the federal-provincial dynamic in a government-constraining direction, its provisions excluded several key areas – notably, culture, financial services, regional economic development, taxation, national security, and measures pertaining to Aboriginal peoples.[28]

Institutions

Although the AIT's text claims that it does not alter the authority of Parliament and provincial legislatures, the object of the exercise was obviously to reconstitute the federal order by incorporating a regulatory regime within its framework.[29] Beyond the constitutional division of powers, which the courts interpret and enforce, the AIT created a new, if weakly institutionalized mode of federal governance. A new cabinet-level Committee on Internal Trade, which has met only irregularly, oversees the agreement's implementation and operation though hobbled by the need to achieve consensus before it can make decisions.[30]

Compared to other intergovernmental structures, the ITS was 'the first such body mandated exclusively for the purposes of managing the Canadian economic union.'[31] Through administering the AIT's provisions, formulating protocols to resolve immediate problems, such as the definition of 'wine,' documenting its parties' compliance, and presiding over negotiations on unresolved issues, such as energy, the ITS was to provide a new locus for making policy and rules.

Though intended to be a catalyst in harmonizing provincial standards, the Secretariat has a delicate role, taking its direction from thirteen jurisdictions. Given their weak support for internal trade integration, it kept a low profile.[32] Its documentation of annual reports and many other unfulfilled obligations signaled that some governments were not honouring their commitments.[33] Its own reporting on provincial foot-dragging was itself sluggish: it released its 1996–7 annual report in late 1998.

The impact of global governance on intergovernmental relations appears most clearly in the AIT's incorporation of a process for resolving disputes, which it imported from the toolbox of international trade law. Although this mechanism encourages consultation and mediation between opposing parties (which can include individuals), it may refer disputes to ad hoc panels of experts (rather than to a permanent tribunal or to a court) when such diplomacy fails. Borrowed from NAFTA,[34] this mechanism was born weak, because it did not allow claimants to pursue awards for damages, injunctions, sanctions, or even retaliation. Nor would panel determinations formally bind the disputing parties, whose compliance with rulings was to be voluntary. Thus the AIT's neoconservatizing impact on the federation may turn out to be more apparent than real. Its capacity to liberalize interprovincial trade would depend on political goodwill, and its ability to constrain provincial governments remains to be seen.[35]

What was seen in the first years has not been inspiring. In its effort to pressure Quebec to allow its construction industry to hire Ontario workers, Queen's Park declined to use the AIT's dispute-settlement process. Instead, it retaliated by unilaterally excluding Quebec construction workers from the province, deliberately breaking the agreement.[36] When Canuk Sales, a small BC company, came up against Ontario legislation making it illegal to sell products combining non-dairy with dairy oils, it was unable to persuade the BC government to initiate a dispute panel. Victoria considered the AIT's dispute process ineffective and too adversarial.[37]

The business press originally hailed the AIT as a historic breakthrough in containing excessive regulation by provincial governments. But actual experience has disappointed such hopes. After the initial stir over signing the deal, momentum to carry through on its commitments stalled in the face of powerful forces of inertia. Provincial protectionism lodged in procurement rules, policies on labour mobility, and trade regulations continued to present a stumbling block for industry. Even the agreement's novel incorporation of mandatory reporting measures to improve information flows between governments has failed to evoke action.

In addition, the implementation schedule set out in the text has been ignored, and the annual meetings scheduled between the provincial and federal trade ministers responsible for internal trade have not occurred. The Canadian Chamber of Commerce reported being told that AIT deadlines are not to be taken seriously and that 'they were put in for appearance's sake.'[38] Although energy ministers were supposed to have negotiated an energy chapter by July 1995, no chapter has emerged. Despite the fact that most provinces and territories, except British Columbia and Yukon, signed a follow-up agreement allowing out-of-province firms to bid on municipal, academic, school, and health care services, negotiations to implement this understanding fell two years behind schedule. Critical issues related to regional economic development programs remain unresolved. Hence, scepticism towards the AIT presents a considerable hurdle to its comprehensive implementation.

The AIT failed to shift outward-looking governments' attention inward. During a period when foreign trade issues, such as NAFTA and the WTO, dominated the public agenda, internal trade issues were largely ignored. Except in government procurement, the AIT has had minimal impact, amounting to little more than a symbolic gesture supporting the rhetoric that internal trade should be freer.

Trade data suggest that this agreement is far less significant than originally expected. Notably, the provinces' international trade grew in real terms by nearly 12 per cent annually between 1991 and 1996, while the corresponding interprovincial figure was less than 2 per cent.[39] From 74 per cent of Canada's international trade in 1992, interprovincial trade had fallen to 50 per cent by 1998.[40] This trend away from interprovincial commerce needs to be put against studies that have shown that provinces trade with each other far more than their market size and their distance from each other would lead one to expect.[41] In other words, regulatory differences among the provinces inhibit trade far less than experts generally assumed.

The negative, 'thou shalt not' provisions in the AIT that proscribe provincial protectionism will do little to promote interprovincial economic activity. To strengthen the Canadian economy as a national entity would require positive, 'thou shalt' incentives by governments that stimulate interprovincial trade and investment, but provinces have never been keen to take such steps. Their ability to develop a strategy for pan-Canadian integration has been paradoxically curtailed by NAFTA's anti-statist injunctions and by the WTO's more gradual, yet still government-unfriendly rules. But it was not the increasing dominance of global and continental regimes that prevented the federal state from pursuing integration within its own borders. More significant was the provinces' capacity – partially shielded as they are from the direct impact of trade liberalization – to defend their traditional turf from federal direction, even when Ottawa was acting as intermediary between the supranational and the subnational tiers. In this case at least, federalism trumped globalization, not the reverse.

In effect, the agreement struck a series of compromises between general rules and exceptions, between co-operation and competitiveness, at the subcentral level – in other words, between the economic unity required by neoconservative globalism and the provincial autonomy defended by federalism. The AIT embraced a qualified, but negative integrative approach – telling provinces what they were not to do – while providing plenty of exceptions and 'wiggle room' for them to continue promoting their own economic interests. Free-trade federalism did not envision positive policies that would encourage east-west economic development across Canada.

Thus, while the AIT has not transformed federalism, its rules about rules mark an early milestone in the policy community's ingestion of globalizing principles. It remains virtually invisible to the public because of the general silence about it in political discourse. Most members of the business community barely understand it. Those who are aware of its existence find it too complicated and functionally inaccessible. It enjoys very little credibility even among policymakers, who remain equivocal about its provisions and uncommitted to its application.[42] The Agreement on Internal Trade is admittedly only in its infancy. New rounds of negotiation may enhance its privileging of commercial, government-restraining values over environmental or social, government-enhancing functions.

The Charter and the Court

Besides the supraconstitutional weight of the new global governance on federal-provincial relations and the modest institutional change on internal trade generated by neoconservatism, a third historical force has acted to reconstruct Canadian governance, namely the continuing impact of judicial decisions. The process of judicial review, entrusted to the Supreme Court of Canada since 1949, helped in the Mulroney-Chrétien era to reconstitute aspects of the Canadian state from the inside. Since the judicial system is driven by the interpretations of judges, and since their values can change, the legal system can have an evolutionary effect. In our look at the third major force that has moulded the Canadian state under globalization, we need to observe the curious way in which the courts have reconstructed federalism under free trade. This is a genuine issue, since some observers have argued that the most significant force reshaping Canada's political institutions in the 1980s and 1990s came less from recent manifestations of globalization or from the influence of neoconservatism than from the workings of a primarily domestic factor – the judicial legacy entrenched in the Canadian constitution by Pierre Trudeau.[43]

The crucial factor in this argument was the Charter of Rights and Freedoms, which Trudeau managed to insert into the Canadian constitution in 1982 as part of his 'patriating' to Canada from Britain the power to amend the BNA Act. Federally appointed judges – this thesis maintains – have used the task of interpreting the Charter to wrest policy-making power from democratically elected and putatively sovereign federal and provincial legislators.[44] The Charter rearranged the machinery of government to the advantage of the courts but to the detriment of parliamentarians, making the Canadian system look more like the American, with its constitutionalized division of powers between the political and the juridical. In the process, it favoured the federal relative to the provincial governments and developed a new sense of political identity among Canadians who started to see themselves as rights-bearing citizens.[45] Although much of this argument is attractive, we need to nuance its stark contours with three preliminary qualifications.

Adopting the Charter was part of an international human rights movement. Far from being an exclusively indigenous force, Charter-based judicial activism was itself connected to global movements favouring entrenchment of individual rights. Early advocates of a Canadian bill of rights, such as a Senate committee in 1950, cited the United Nations Charter and the Universal Declaration of Human Rights in support of their position.[46] Thirty years later, civil libertarian and human rights organizations appeared before the Special Joint Committee of the Senate and of the House of Commons on the Constitution of Canada, stressing the need for Canada to implement the obligations that it had undertaken when it signed these international covenants.[47] More important, the influential legal advocate and law professor F.R. Scott and his intellectual disciple-turned-prime minister, Pierre Trudeau, also believed profoundly in the liberating value of such constitutionally binding documents as the American Bill of Rights and felt that a similar treatise could be successfully grafted onto Canada's federal, though parliamentary system.

The Charter was part of Trudeau's strategy to combat separatism. The Charter may have had an international genealogy, but it was intended to implement a domestic political agenda. It was a federalist instrument designed to thwart Quebec's independentist aspirations more than to combat the country's balkanization. Trudeau calculated that the Charter's minority language rights (insulated from any legislative override) and its rejection of special legal status for Quebec would dissuade neofederalists – that crucial 20 per cent of Quebecers who were neither unrepentant federalists nor hard-core separatists – from supporting their province's separation from Canada. It would also set up legal barriers to deter irredeemable sovereigntists from achieving their goal.[48]

The Charter was part of a federal agenda on province-building. Besides capping Trudeau's struggle with Quebec, the Charter would also provide an instrument for containing what Ottawa saw as aspirations of the other provinces for ever-greater autonomy. While strengthening rights for citizens would limit the powers of both provincial and federal governments, the Trudeau gamble had a subtler rationale. Since the Supreme Court's interpretation of a right would ultimately apply to all provinces and territories, its judgments would reinforce the expression of *nationally* harmonized, pan-Canadian values. And, to the extent that rights are politically popular, the assertion of any right by the Supreme Court would be a sly vindication of the federal over the provincial governments, which had mostly been hostile to Trudeau's constitutional initiative because they feared it would have a centralizing effect. Besides, once a rights discourse had taken root in the public's mind as the way in which it thought about *its* constitution, this attitude would undermine the provinces' historical dominance in the constitutional amending process.

The passage of time has not been particularly kind to Trudeau's

grand plan. Rather than beating back separatism, the Charter and constitutional patriation without Quebec's assent played some role in
aggravating it. Then, the Supreme Court turned out to be more neutral
than expected as an umpire refereeing the potential process of Quebec's secession. As for reinforcing Ottawa at the expense of the anglophone provinces, the balance of power seems to have remained
remarkably stable. When efforts were made to use the new amendment formulas to reallocate powers between the federal and provincial
governments, Canadian constitutionalism turned out to be paralysed.
Prime Minister Mulroney twice attempted to amend the constitution in
response to Quebec's demands by negotiating compromises among the
political elites first at Meech Lake in 1987 and then at Charlottetown in
1992. He was thwarted in both his attempts to get these accords ratified. The old system of executive federalism, in which decisions were
made by the prime minister and his provincial counterparts meeting in
private to make deals, had been trumped by manifestations of popular
distrust – a continuing fear in Quebec of an anglophone-dominated
federalism – and by a new, citizen-based constitutional assertiveness in
the rest of Canada.[49]

This failure to change the black letter of the constitution through a
process of formal amendment did not prevent the courts from altering
the country's institutional balance through their ongoing judgments,
as they had in the past. There is consensus on one point. All observers
agree that entrenching the Charter in 1982 constrained democratically
elected legislatures in favour of the judiciary. Experts disagree, however, in assessing the overall impact on federal, as opposed to provincial powers of some two decades' worth of Supreme Court decisions.

Those who see Trudeau's malign influence reaching from beyond
the grave can point to political and sociological factors. Generous federal funding for linguistic and other minorities to mount Charter-
based challenges of provincial legislation helped transfer final authority over language policy and other issues to the courts from the legislatures, which lost in the process their former policy sovereignty in these
areas. The anti-balkanization effect of the patriated constitution was
further enhanced by the fact that the men and women sitting on the
country's court of last appeal continued to be appointed by the federal
government. Since prime ministers usually elevate to the bench those
candidates who had shown support in their career for federalist as
opposed to provincialist values, the sociology of the court would sub-
tly contribute to national integration.[50] In these ways the politics of

rights would implicitly serve to strengthen the *Canadian* community, as opposed to provincial satrapies.

Without question, the Charter enhanced the judicial system's power over legislatures by vastly expanding the grounds on which it can review their legislation.[51] But offsetting this trend is the controversial 'notwithstanding' clause in Section 33, which Trudeau himself opposed because it gave legislatures the power to overturn Supreme Court judgments, if only for a limited period. One might have expected that this legislative override, on which the premiers insisted when negotiating with Trudeau the contents of the proposed Charter, would give the public some assurance that their elected parliamentarians had the ultimate de jure power to express the will of the people over the wishes of the non-elected judges.[52]

Paradoxically, both the extensive mobilization of social movements in the debates over constitutional patriation and the resultant shift of political discourse to issues of identity, community, and diversity generated a sense of popular sovereignty, which gave the constitution greater democratic legitimacy as a valued component of the public culture. The lofty esteem that the Charter rapidly achieved severely reduced in practice the capacity of provincial politicians to use the notwithstanding clause to defend their legislatures. Nevertheless, when a provincial government considered the Supreme Court to have thwarted its will, it could invoke the clause as a failsafe mechanism to defend provincial sovereignty. This happened in 1988, when the Supreme Court ruled that a Quebec law requiring exclusive use of French in commercial signs violated the right to freedom of expression guaranteed by the Charter's section 2b. Premier Robert Bourassa immediately invoked the Charter's *non obstante* clause to countermand what he felt was an unacceptable attack on the province's law to promote the use of French. Quebec's distinctiveness has also been preserved by the Charter's section 23, which leaves discretion over the language for the schooling of immigrants to the National Assembly.[53]

Through cases in which citizens challenged federal or provincial laws, alleging that their Charter-defined rights had been violated, the Supreme Court examined the constitutionality of many other laws, both federal and provincial. In so doing it necessarily took on policy-making functions previously the prerogative of elected legislatures. (This loss of their democratic mandate did not bother some politicians when they faced difficult social issues such as abortion. Pointing to the Supreme Court's rulings, they could pass the moral buck, telling voters

that their hands were tied.) Reacting to criticism that this judicializa-
tion of politics would politicize the judiciary, the court carried out an
exercise in self constraint. Establishing criteria in the *Oakes* case that in
effect curbed its own power to limit parliamentary sovereignty, the
court mitigated the worst fears that it was appropriating powers that
belonged to legislatures.[54] On balance, the Supreme Court's interpretation of the Charter has not significantly affected the legislatures' social
and economic powers.[55]

However restrained, the Supreme Court necessarily alters Canada's
political landscape as it proceeds to rule on the many cases involving
existing federal and provincial laws. Comparing cases where it has
declared statutes invalid reveals the federal, not the provincial level to
be more often the loser. From 1990 to 1997, it nullified twenty-one federal legislative acts as opposed to only nine provincial acts. Provincial
governments have been more successful than Ottawa in defending
their policies against Charter challenges. By this measure, fears that of
judicial review by a federalist court would weaken the provincial order
of government do not seem to have been borne out in practice.

Besides nullifying laws, the Supreme Court also validates them. In a
series of significant cases, it upheld many provincial powers – in 1986,
New Brunswick's Official Languages Act providing for using English
or French in court; the creation of linguistic school boards in Quebec;
and in 1987, the full funding of Catholic public schools in Ontario
against a Charter appeal, on the grounds that the Charter could not
trump an existing constitutional protection for Roman Catholics.[56]

Furthermore, the Supreme Court has sought to preserve the separate
sovereignties inherent in federalism. In case after case, it has developed a doctrine of federalism that explicitly invokes the importance of
preserving diversity among the provinces. The court has explicitly
accepted variations in policy from province to province and endorsed
flexibility in developing legislation – provided that it respects the basic
rights contained in the Charter.[57] If the universalistic nature of pan-
Canadian rights can coexist with the particularistic needs of different
provinces, fears of a centralizing juggernaut diminish. In sum, the
Charter-armed court has continued to respect provincial autonomy
and to forswear judicially imposed uniformity.[58]

In some highly publicized rulings concerning abortion and discrimination on the grounds of sexual orientation, the Supreme Court has
implicitly quashed provincial diversity. Its rulings in effect established
national standards for policies dealing with women's and homosexu-

als' rights.[59] Perhaps the most contested of these judgments was the 1998 *Vriend* case in Alberta, in which the Supreme Court read into the Charter's list of rights one of sexual orientation, which the Alberta legislature had deliberately omitted when passing the Individual Rights Protection Act. In this clear example of judicial policy making, opinion polls showed that the Alberta public massively approved the court's ruling – as was suggested by Premier Klein's reluctance to invoke the notwithstanding clause to overrule the judges.[60]

Even if the Supreme Court has shown quantitatively less deference towards federal than towards provincial laws in applying the Charter, it may still have shifted the balance of power away from the provinces when traditional concerns for national unity or new requirements of globalization persuade judges to favour federal predominance. As with the chilling effect of the supraconstitution's constraining provisions, the lawyers appointed in each government department to vet new regulations and laws for consistency with Charter provisions can powerfully inhibit government action.[61] This non-decision making cannot be measured empirically, but anecdotal evidence suggests it is a significant governmental reality.

In overturning many of the decentralizing rulings by the Judicial Committee of the Privy Council, the Supreme Court had already strengthened the central government's powers before the constitution's patriation in 1982.[62] The prime rationale used by the court to favour the government of Canada in a jurisdictional dispute with the provinces was the BNA Act's Section 91 description of the federal responsibility to make laws for the 'peace, order, and good government' (POGG) of the country. This notion was so broad that judicial review over the years had circumscribed it by developing some demanding criteria for invoking POGG. One of these required an emergency – some extraordinary peril to the nation – before Ottawa could justify extra power if only on a temporary basis. Using this rationale in 1976, the Supreme Court upheld the federal government's Anti-Inflation Act on the grounds that its national program to reduce inflation was dealing with an exceptional circumstance, even though Ottawa never formally declared an emergency.

In later rulings that leaned on a variety of principles, such as 'national concern,' the court reinforced this trend. In the *Crown Zellerbach* case in 1988, for instance, it deemed controlling pollution to be a national concern and so validated the federal Ocean Dumping Control Act. The court gave Ottawa the capacity to pre-empt provincial powers when it has 'occupied' a legislative field or acted in a case of provincial inability to deal with the problem under dispute. It endorsed the federal executive's power to spend conditionally – and so affect policy – in areas of provincial jurisdiction. It endorsed the federal government's use of its jurisdiction in criminal law for achieving public purposes such as improved health. Using this logic, it upheld the federal Canadian Environmental Protection Act over activities otherwise falling under Quebec's exclusive provincial jurisdiction.[63] It has also ex-panded the sway of the trade and commerce power over provincial legislation.[64]

The connection between the Supreme Court's thinking and neoconservative preferences for the primacy of market forces is evident in rulings about 'what,' in Justice LaForest's words, 'one would now call a common market.'[65] While in some cases the court gave Ottawa the means to implement national policies in order to bridge regional differences, the presence of globalization in the court's thinking is occasionally explicit, as in its recognizing the federal power to legislate under the trade and commerce clause with respect to enforcement of foreign judicial rulings in Canada.[66] As a noted authority on constitutional jurisprudence concluded, 'In this grouping of apparently scattered decisions, one can recognize the federalization of the jurisdiction necessary for the Canadian 'economic union' recommended by the Macdonald Commission – in short a constitutionalization of free trade's requirements.'[67]

Nothing in the court's practice is completely coherent. Despite its being dismissed by many Quebec sovereigntists as the biased guardian of Canadian centralization, the Supreme Court has been resolute in steering a careful course between the Scylla of national unity and the Charybdis of decentralization. When asked by the Chrétien government to decide whether Quebec had a right to secede, the court adopted a Solomon-like stance:[68] if in a referendum on sovereignty Quebecers should give a clear answer to a clear question, secession would be valid – provided that both Quebec and the rest of Canada negotiated in good faith the terms of secession, respecting the interests of such concerned parties as the Aboriginal nations, which would be affected by Canada's partition. In a typically self-limiting gesture, the court left it to the politicians to resolve what might constitute a clear answer to a clear question. Emboldened by this cue, Prime Minister Chrétien proceeded to tilt the playing field in the federal direction by passing a 'Clarity Law' that gave Parliament the right to decide whether a referendum question and the answer are sufficiently clear for it to authorize negotiations with a secessionist government.

The redefinition of Aboriginal nations' relationship with the federal and provincial governments is a further dimension of constitutional change that is being managed by the courts free of direct pressure from globalization and neoconservatism. Empowered by legislation pursuant to the BNA Act's mandate to manage the affairs of 'Indians,' the federal government had kept Native peoples under its tutelage for almost a hundred years. Starting in the 1950s, it gradually liberalized this shockingly discriminatory regime. As hydro and mineral development proceeded throughout the north, Native peoples began to press for recognition of their treaty rights to the lands containing these resources. The slow process of litigating land claims through the courts received a significant boost when the Charter of Rights and Freedoms included a clause recognizing Aboriginal rights.

Although the conferences on Native governance mandated by the constitutional agreement of 1981 were unfruitful, the courts have generally supported self-government as an Aboriginal right while once again leaving it to the politicians to define its practical content. The approval of a detailed treaty with the Nisga'a nation by Parliament and the BC legislature would create a regime of self-government in which the Nisga'a legislature's paramountcy in matters of culture and education is bitterly contested by many in the province's white population.[69] In a geographically more ambitious initiative, a new non-autonomous government called Nunavut has been created by federal statute for the eastern territory north of the Quebec and Labrador boundary. While the promotion of Aboriginal rights has taken on global dimensions – thanks in good part to the transnational activities of Canadian Native leaders – such reconstitutionalizing developments as those involving the Nisga'a and Nunavut result primarily from forces within the Canadian system. In this context, the politics of identity, sometimes equated with globalization, respond more to internal forces rooted deeply in the country's troubled relationship with its indigenous population than to external pressures.

In sum, changes in the balance of power between the federal and provincial tiers in the Mulroney-Chrétien era were filtered by Supreme Court judges applying the Charter of Rights and Freedoms which was the heritage of the more social-democratic Trudeau era. The Supreme Court has not become a hostage to minority groups achieving extreme liberal goals that they could never have won in representative politics.

The persistent arm-wrestling between the sovereign provincial and federal governments has been influenced but not redirected by the discourse of neoconservatism and by the exigencies of globalization. Canadian federalism continues to be driven by a dynamic rooted in disparate provincial governments struggling to work out with the government of Canada a constantly contested modus vivendi for their country.

If the federal government's ability to promote a vibrant economic union is limited by the rules of global governance and if the provinces' disinclination to endorse national economic programs is inherent in traditional federalism, uncertain prospects also characterize the situation at the bottom of the constitutional ladder. Canadian cities have felt the domino effect of downloading but have not been able to shed their increased responsibilities except by reducing the money, food, and shelter that they can offer their most destitute. Had devolved functional obligations been accompanied by the granting to municipalities of greater budgetary powers, residents and their organizations might have gained more capacity to finance and control their local destinies. At least in one celebrated case – Toronto, to whose fate we now turn – the reverse happened. The provincial government defied the preferences of the town dwellers, arbitrarily reconstitutionalizing their 'megacity' in a structure desired by neither ratepayers nor experts.

6 The Municipal State: Megacity and the Greater Toronto Area

In the late 1960s I shared the general unease then gripping Torontonians who worried about their city's contracting the contagious diseases that seemed to be killing its American counterparts. Racial violence, inter-ethnic tensions, drug abuse, poverty ghettos, the flight to suburbia, and eviscerated city centres were all signs of urban decline that we wanted to avoid.

The word 'globalization' was absent from our vocabulary. At the most, we talked about being Americanized by the influx of draft dodgers escaping the Vietnam war, a mainly beneficial influence. The mother of one of these refugees, who came to Toronto in 1968 with her family the day before her son was to be drafted, was writer Jane Jacobs, who had battled expressway construction in New York's Greenwich Village and had articulated a new consciousness of how the variegated fabric of urban communities was threatened by planners' homogenizing renewal schemes. She would stay on in Toronto to influence a whole generation of civic-minded Canadians.

That year I myself was stirred by Pierre Trudeau's vision of a participatory and just society as he campaigned to become leader of the federal Liberal Party. Within months I became involved with a group of progressive Liberals who wanted to enter Toronto's hitherto non-partisan municipal politics. An unanticipated complex of factors led to my being nominated by the fledgling municipal Liberal Party as its mayoralty candidate. A complete tyro in politics, I suddenly found myself fronting a novice party during the city's 1969 election campaign. Apart from the fire-next-time subtext of the American anti-model that haunted us, I had no thought that our city's destiny was other than in our own hands. If Toronto followed the American path, we had only ourselves to blame. Thirty-three years later, no municipal problem seemed disconnected from global forces.

Globalization and the City

The city is the level of government least linked in the public's consciousness to globalization. Whether as institutions or as locations, cities are simply taken for granted, visible more to tourists as collections of monuments than to citizens as political entities. We know that buying a pair of Nike sports shoes may involve us with the exploitation of child labour in India, but we have a hard time seeing the connection between traffic problems in our neighbourhood and the "G" word, which describes those great issues of international integration championed over the last two decades, for better or worse, by neoconservative politicians. For most people, city hall seems to occupy a petty administrative space concerned with construction permits and far removed from the big challenges facing humankind. Beyond this general presumption of cities' irrelevance to the broader discourse on public policy, it is particularly difficult to make sense of two conflicting statements related to this book's problematic. One has to do with cities being *global*. The other maintains that cities *compete*.

Cities have become global actors. One could posit that the global nature of cities is an extension of their ancient role as engines of economic activity. At their most primitive, towns grew up around markets exchanging food from the countryside for material necessities such as tools manufactured by artisans. As these trading centres grew into cities, they became the chief loci of political power and sites for worship, learning, and services such as money lending. As focal points for their immediate hinterland, they fostered webs of social interaction and developed institutions of judicial and political power. Their regional reach was determined by communications media and transportation technologies, whose evolution from papyrus to printing and from sail to steam made possible wider networks of exchange and interaction.

In cities nowadays we find the national economy's centres for both traditional manufacturing and for advanced services such as financial intermediation and consulting, telecommunications and new media. They act as Meccas for sports, entertainment, culture, and consequently tourism. They host the main institutions of advanced education, research, and health care. They provide hubs for all modes of transportation and so constitute dynamos for commerce, local and international. As concentrations of entrepreneurial energy, they house factories for production and the workforce that they require. These agglomerations

of a nation's citizenry provide the hearth for its politics, social movements, and identity formation. They attract migrants from the countryside and immigrants from other provinces and countries. And, of
course, they comprise gigantic markets for all the goods, services, information, and human capital that they produce and acquire. By this logic
concerning the evolutionary nature of cities, it would follow that, if
national economies have become globally interpenetrated, then cities
would, *ipso facto*, constitute an important component of globalization.

Another potent aspect of globalization involves the way in which
global images, processes, and structures take root in local social and
economic spaces. The arguments making these connections assert that
global phenomena find local expression within a powerful spatial context. If the proposed construction of an expressway threatens a neighbourhood, it is not just because the old values of community and local
identity are put in question but because the automobile, now a globally
produced consumer good, emits the gases that are depleting the ozone
layer and endangering the capacity of future generations all over the
planet to survive, whether or not they have roads and cars. The notion
of 'glocalization' captures the way that the various actions of government continually affect this global-local interface, whether by supporting or resisting globalizing impulses.

The computerized communications revolution putatively brought
an 'end to geography' through the capacity of e-mail, cell phones,
cheaper long-distance calls, and video-conferencing to conquer distance. The place and space of territoriality nevertheless remains a basic
ingredient of most social, economic, and political life. In the past, cities
acted as growth nodes and connectors to other cities and to the
regional hinterlands of their national economies. Leading cities such as
London, New York, and Tokyo now act as nodal points for the co-ordination of global capitalism, providing control centres within the international regime of accumulation and regulation.[1] Secondary cities,
such as Chicago and Mexico City, play an analogous connector role
acting as networks that provide cohesiveness to their continental
order.[2] Just as these transnational characteristics of cities have grown
naturally out of their local essence, the competitive tension that they
now experience with distant conurbations is an outgrowth of more pri-
meval rivalries.

As cities become global, they compete globally. We do not have much trouble accepting the idea that businesses compete. Some companies suc-

ceed. Others fail. And the winners' gains typically take place at the expense of the losers' losses. Nor is it difficult to comprehend how states originally competed geopolitically to establish dominance. With the end of the Cold War's ideological struggle, we have had to adjust to a new interpretation of competition between nations. States have had to abandon their previous, inward-facing concentration on national problems, as they learned that they too are competing economically for both financial and human capital.[3] They hope that investors will locate companies within their borders, bringing along their technologies, energy, and know-how. They hope that their highly trained citizens will remain at home and/or that hard-working immigrants will flock in to meet the resulting demand for workers.

While the government of Canada has been thinking and speaking this language of competition since the mid-1980s, the provinces took longer to realize that the urgent competitiveness engendered by globalization was also confronting them with a more direct rivalry from other subcentral players. It was not just that New Brunswick tried to attract back-office functions such as telemarketing from British Columbia. Representatives from Florida, Georgia, Illinois, Michigan, New York, and Ohio crossed the international border to set up Canadian offices, from which they tried to lure firms from Alberta or Quebec to what they claimed were warmer and more business-friendly climates.[4]

Globalization's relentless imperative does not stop at the provincial level, although it makes little apparent sense to say that Toronto is *competing* with Montreal or Buffalo. Obviously, the city cannot pick up and move east to Quebec or cross Lake Ontario to relocate in the state of New York. Of course, it has always been true that some cities rose in prominence, while others fell. The vibrant Renaissance city-state of Florence, where Michelangelo sculpted 'David' and Machiavelli wrote *The Prince*, slipped into decline when gold started to flow to Europe from the Americas and its ruling Medici family's Europe-wide banking operations stumbled. Not too far away, Venice's access to the sea gave it a source of riches from maritime trading that was connected to its neighbour's misfortunes and made it more powerful than London in far-off England. Aware that their future was clouded without maritime communications, the Florentines proceeded, in their quest for Mediterranean markets, to employ mercenary soldiers to conquer the cities of Lucca and Pisa that blocked their access to the sea down the River Arno.

So it is not at all new that cities have struggled within their regions for military and economic dominance. They have also long competed through the civic pride once manifested in great urban architecture. (Florentines were determined that their cathedral would be the biggest in Christendom and were triumphant when a local architect, Filippo Brunelleschi, managed to cap their *duomo*'s huge walls with the biggest dome ever built.) Now civic rivalry is expressed more commonly in sports encounters between teams of athletic mercenaries bearing the logos of city TV markets.

What globalization has added to this Darwinian mix is cities' vulnerability to the effects of the increasing cross-border competition that results from the liberalization of trade, investment, and services. If imports can displace their products, if their tradeable service jobs can be performed cheaper elsewhere, or if their corporate headquarters find faraway fields to be greener, their future is in jeopardy. With the displacement of standardized mass production by flexible, specialized, high-tech production, cities increasingly compete against each other as clusterings of business energy and technological innovation. Those metropolises that can demonstrate a dynamic synergy of specialization-cum-diversity in knowledge, sophistication in production capabilities, and leadership in enterprise are likely to experience success in producing wealth – at least until some other cities do even better in the twenty-first century art of urban seduction.

The question for this chapter revolves around how Canadian cities compete. We also want to know what this competition tells us about our larger subject – the interactive nestedness of the Canadian state structure. Looking mainly at Toronto, touted until recently as a great urban success story, we need to ask whether yesterday's triumph heralds tomorrow's disaster. To disentangle the various threads of a decidedly complex skein of factors, it is helpful to see Toronto's evolution as involving four stages: postwar Toronto under Fordism, particularly its gradual eclipse of Montreal; how its Keynesian success became unstuck in the 1980s; neoconservative restructuring in the late 1990s; and the future for a newly polarized and regionalized urban area.

Our consideration of the city's place in neoconservative globalism has to start with a basic startling disjunction in Canada's political economy. Cities may be the major sites of economic and social dynamism, but they are the lowest forms of political life in Canada. Although not everyone agrees that the problem is serious, no one contests the disconcerting fact that the municipalities languish at the bottom of the national power hierarchy. Local administration is constitutionally the pawn of higher levels of government, primarily provincial but also federal, which have been only too pleased to perpetuate their dominance. For better or for worse. *For better,* I argue, under the Keynesian and Fordist state; *for worse* under neoconservatism.

Toronto under the Fordist State (1945–1980)

The emergence of Toronto as Canada's dominant city took place under the continentalizing influences of the Fordist state, which helped Ontario's capital city surpass Montreal as the national economy's financial, manufacturing, and even transportational hub. Although it was not the target of specifically urban policies, Toronto benefited substantially from Ottawa's post-1945 development strategy, which sought American direct investment in resource exploitation for export and in manufacturing for the domestic market. Easily accessible by federally subsidized railways, by highways, and by federally built airports and well-equipped with physical amenities, Toronto became the location choice for the local head offices of most transnational corporations (TNCs). When the branch-plant car and truck industry ran into trouble, the federal government negotiated the Canada-U.S. Automotive Products Agreement (Auto Pact) of 1965, which integrated Toronto's hinterland into the American automobile market. Vehicle assembly plants in Oakville, Oshawa, and Windsor flourished, simultaneously boosting the local, highly efficient steel industry and a less efficient auto parts sector.

Other federal policies also helped Toronto overtake a Montreal already deprived by the St Lawrence Seaway after 1959 of its role as transshipment point for ocean-going vessels trading with central and western Canada. The Department of National Defence's equipment needs nourished such aerospace companies as de Havilland in Toronto and Pratt & Whitney in Montreal, generating groupings of high-value-adding activities. Federal contributions to housing assistance, medicare, and social security policies dramatically improved the quality of urban life everywhere. The Trudeau government's decision to keep broadcasting under Canadian ownership and to raise minimums of domestic content for radio and television stations particularly benefited Toronto, which generated the country's principal complex of English-language media activity. For similar reasons, Montreal developed around Radio Canada into the French-language media capital for francophone Canada. Protected as a regional monopoly by federal legislation, Bell Canada's headquarters remained in Montreal. On the way to becoming the country's largest nationally owned corporation, it renamed itself Bell Canada Enterprises (BCE) and spun off Northern Telecom as a subsidiary making switching equipment just outside Toronto, where it became the hub of a vibrant cluster.

Toronto's faster growth gave it momentum, pulling companies away from its bicultural rival. When major financial institutions – first, the Royal Bank and, later, the insurance company Sun Life and even the Bank of *Montreal* – moved their head office functions westward, they denied that their actions were a response to the Parti Québécois's linguistic nationalism of the late 1970s. But no one denied that Montreal lost a large part of its anglophone, and in particular its Jewish, population which emigrated westward to what they felt were politically safer sites. Also the preferred destination for a steady influx of immigrants, Toronto surpassed Montreal economically and demographically in that decade. With its snowballing growth creating cultural multiplier effects, it drew Buffalo – which had been expected to emerge hegemonic seven decades earlier, at the turn of the twentieth century[5] – within its cultural orbit, whether for its restaurants or its theatres, its professional sports, or its architectural services.[6]

The Ontario government's mid-century contributions to Toronto's rise supported the federal-led growth strategy. First came its benign institutional engineering targeted at modernizing municipal governance. Its Planning Act of 1946 empowered Ontario cities to develop official plans for directing local development under the watchful veto power of the Ontario Municipal Board. The same year, Queen's Park authorized construction of Toronto's first short subway line, which later grew to a seventy-kilometre network that has helped increase employment and residential concentration in the urban core, warding off blight and flight to the periphery. The keystone of the province's reconstitutionalizing intrusion came in 1953, when it federated the hub city of Toronto with its twelve surrounding boroughs into a two-tiered government called the Municipality of Metropolitan Toronto. The mission of 'Metro' was to preserve political values of participation and identity at the local level while fostering social equity and functional efficiency across the whole system. This institution of some one million people had the capacity to levy taxes, finance infrastructure, redistribute resources to weaker municipalities, disperse public housing facilities, offer social services, and develop effective public transit for the whole conurbation.[7] In the same decade, the Metropolitan Toronto and

Region Conservation Authority was established to preserve ravine systems and parkland as the regional watershed's lungs and recreational resource.

Metro Toronto also benefited from Ontario's general policies, such as its expansion of the university and college system in the 1960s, for which Ottawa paid half the cost. Although Ontario's long-reigning Progressive Conservative Party (1943–1985) was *conservative* in supporting a laissez-faire approach to economic development that paid no particular attention to the truncating effects of a branch-plant industrial structure, it was *progressive* in developing equity-based social programs for welfare and legal aid that set lower limits to tolerable social inequalities and forestalled the misery of urban ghettos.

While its two-tier structure let Metro manage efficiently such metropolis-wide functions as transit and police, the constituent municipalities were able to retain the participatory, if middle-class intimacy of local planning politics. The vitality of local democracy became dramatically evident in the 1970s, when Metro's central municipality, still called Toronto, responded to a double wave of citizen and post-materialist radicalism. This was a period of idealistic internationalism, in which Canadian cities twinned themselves to foreign counterparts or declared themselves nuclear-free zones. Under the direction of newly elected politicians leading a citizens' reform movement, planners were obliged to discard the modernist nostrums for city design that they had been busily applying – slum clearance, expressway construction, and unifunctional office tower redevelopment in the city centre. The middle-class activists who had won power in an albeit-unpowerful city hall were able to slow overdevelopment in the city core, defend residential neighbourhoods against destruction by high-rise apartment blocks, foster renovation of older districts, and, above all, persuade their provincial masters to halt construction of three expressways poised to lay waste wide swaths of the urban fabric.

The selfish concerns of local ratepayers' associations in the 1970s turned out to be consistent with the retheorizing of economic development by urban geographers in the 1980s. Good multicultural public schools and excellent hospitals, gourmet restaurants and high-end entertainment, along with amenities such as pleasant parks and efficient transit, functional neighbourhoods and safe streets – in short, a vibrant civic culture was recognized as crucial for attracting investors, whether domestic or foreign. The highly skilled professionals required by innovative corporations were increasingly demanding a superior quality of life. Municipal politicians were not consciously competing with other cities when turning into tangible urban forms the critical thinking of their famous immigrant urbanist, Jane Jacobs. If they had American cities in mind, it was not to keep up with them but to *avoid* following them down the path to decaying cores and racial-cum-class war. With quality of life gaining equal priority with infrastructure as a prerequisite for economic development, Metro Toronto suddenly found itself an admired model for city planners everywhere.

By this time, Toronto had become the country's headquarters for financial, insurance, real estate, and specialized business services, while remaining strong in traditional manufacturing. Helped, not hindered, by progressive local politics, Metro continued to grow alongside its surrounding municipalities which were together becoming known as the Greater Toronto Area. The GTA's plants accounted for half of Canada's chemicals production, 40 per cent of its aerospace sales, and 90 per cent of its metal, die, and mould shipments. It housed 80 per cent of the national economy's top legal partnerships and 90 per cent of its largest advertising agencies and accounting firms, and it boasted the country's greatest concentration of facilities for health research and higher education. Recovering from the 1980–1 recession, the GTA enjoyed annual growth rates in excess of 5 per cent between 1984 and 1988, while the unemployment rate shrank from 11 per cent in 1983 to 3 per cent in 1988, by which time the GTA was the leading economic region in Canada, comprising one-fifth of all its economic activity.[8] About 40 per cent of the top 500 firms operating in Canada had headquarters there, as did half of the country's top fifty foreign TNCs and forty-two of the fifty-six foreign banks.[9]

Paradoxically such data confirming Toronto's dominance in the Canadian economy by the beginning of the Mulroney-Chrétien era were not necessarily good news for those concerned about the city's future. For if Toronto's success was the product of a 'permeable Fordism'[10] with its branch-plant mass production economy and of a Keynesianism that had favoured Ontario's *national* role, the city had little cause for complacency.

Paradigm Shift: The 1980s

Metro's great successes bred problems that heralded its undoing. As the preferred destination of Canada's many immigrants, it had a swelling population that overflowed its political borders and strained its policy capacities.[11] Subdivisions sprang up in surrounding rural areas, which lacked the quality of planning, infrastructure, transit, and social services that Metro had been able to achieve within its boundaries. Initially ignored as a problem by provincial politicians, who shirked the responsibility inherent in their absolute power over their municipal wards, low-density suburbs proliferated beyond Metro's borders in an outer concentric semi-circle of sprawling, automobile-dependent municipalities with unco-ordinated transit and social services. The GTA had mushroomed from 2.1 million people in 1961 to 3.4 million in 1981.[12]

Queen's Park did not channel or regulate the demographic influx into the area around Metro that was to become known by its telephone area code: 905. Instead, it institutionalized the process of exurbanization by superimposing four upper-tier, indirectly elected regional governments over the twenty-four municipalities semicircling Metro. The disjuncture between the functional spaces energizing the region's economy and the territorial spaces of politics was becoming dangerous.

The federal government did little to resolve this issue. Since the Trudeauites had abandoned their experimental ministry of urban affairs, with its mission to engage with urban issues in the late 1970's, Ottawa had retreated to disengagement. In the late 1980s the federal Conservatives, whose leader and closest associates were committed Montrealers, seemed unaware of the consequences for the Canadian economy's golden goose of their aggressively continentalizing policies. The norm of national treatment for investment enshrined in the Canada-U.S. Free Trade Agreement (CUFTA) declared Canada's traditional measures of state-led economic development illegitimate. Tariff cuts opened the economy to more intense competitive pressure for customers and so for jobs. As CUFTA's critics had predicted, the discombobulating effects of free trade hit Toronto particularly hard. A deeper recession than that of 1980–1 aggravated the damage. Between 1989 and 1992, Toronto lost roughly one-tenth of its employment base. Over 180,000 jobs in the GTA disappeared – more than half the jobs lost in Canada during this period.[13] By 1992, the unemployment rate was 12 per cent, having more than tripled in three years.

This distress was not temporary. NAFTA and the WTO broadened and deepened free trade at the continental and global levels. Although they affected Canada as a whole, these agreements had a particularly disruptive effect on the GTA as hub of Canada's branch-plant, import-substitution economy. The removal of tariffs in previously protected industries, particularly labour-intensive ones such as food processing, clothing, electronics, and automotive parts, was a catalyst in promoting the large-scale corporate restructuring that led to plant closures, relocation southwards to the U.S. sunbelt or to Mexico, and overall continental rationalization of operations.[14] As well, the Bank of Canada's perversely high interest rates and the resulting overvalued Canadian dollar crippled exports from the GTA and increased the inflow of competing goods from abroad. Introduction of the federal Goods and Services Tax which replaced the manufacturing tax but seemed to hurt everyone, further aggravated the economic dislocation.

Toronto may have aspired in its late 1980s desperation to regain its footing and become, in the cliché of the moment, 'world class,' but its real fate depended on how it could operate as a North American city. However much municipal boosters carried on about being *globally* competitive, their actual terms of reference were *continental*. Now that the national economy's boundaries had been torn down by its new external constitution, the issue for Toronto had become how well and in what sense it could compete with rival North American cities – with Chicago, for example, as a second-tier financial centre or with Hollywood as a hive of film activity. And 'compete' meant getting jobs and investment for the GTA at the expense of the others. In this regard, its social assets were considerable. Its urban core had not become a disaster area needing emergency reconstruction. On the contrary, over half of the GTA's commercial construction in the late 1980s took place within the centre of the city of Toronto, whose physical endowments were shifting from providing factories for manufacturing to building office towers for services.[15]

On the economic side, the GTA's muscle was still impressive. North America's fifth-largest metropolitan region (after Mexico City, New York, Los Angeles, and Chicago), it ranked third after Detroit and Cleveland in its share of employment created by manufacturing. The GTA was second after New York in the portion of jobs produced by financial services[16] and had the continent's third-largest stock exchange and financial services sector (after New York and San Francisco).[17] Culturally, it was the second-largest centre for live, English-language theatre after New York and for film production after Los Angeles.[18] Though located north of the Great Lakes, its geography was nevertheless propitious. GTA plants were located within one day's truck drive of an area with U.S. $2 trillion in annual disposable income – as large a 'one-day's market' as Boston, New York City, or Detroit enjoyed.[19]

By 1996 the GTA held 4.7 million people, of whom 47 per cent were foreign born. (Its 911 telephone emergency service had a capacity to respond in 181 languages.) It had received 1.2 million new residents in the previous decade, half from abroad.[20] Beyond its population growth, the GTA's economy was unusually well balanced, strong in manufacturing, services, and the information economy. Its vibrant automotive sector had developed a superior capability in minivan production and had bred a sophisticated auto parts industry led by Magna International's technological pioneering. The GTA's suburban 'nerdistans' were vigorous in information and communications technology, with Nortel Networks and IBM (Canada) leading an advanced sector of software design and computing. Aerospace, led by Bombardier's de Havilland, was linked to thousands of the GTA's precision parts suppliers. Advanced machinery and production systems could supply high-end capital goods combining mechanical and electronics with robotics and automation.

Toronto was the country's banking capital and was richly endowed with business services, health research, and substantial educational institutions.[21] It fostered a busy cultural hive, producing books, television programming, music, live theatre, and professional sports. Its multimedia entertainment was globally active through supplying specialized material for Hollywood from its animation facilities. It outclassed by far both Montreal and Vancouver in the educational attainment of its working population.[22] One thousand foreign TNCs were situated in the GTA, making it the continent's third-largest site for these coveted prizes after New York and Chicago but (slightly) ahead of Los Angeles and San Francisco.[23]

The great concentration of power in provincial cabinets, which jealously guard their bailiwick – whether they lean to the left or to the right – has meant Ottawa's relations with municipal governments remained weak and indirect through the 1990s. Expanding trade has boosted the importance of the cities through which international commerce is organized, particularly Montreal, Toronto, and Vancouver. Harder to determine are the best methods available for the federal government to support these international cities.

Apart from establishing in 1978 a state agency for developing Toronto's harbour front, whose lands it controlled, Ottawa had abdicated any proactive role in the city. In refusing the application of four of Canada's five largest chartered banks to merge into two behemoths, it may have attempted to ensure Toronto's survival as a second-tier global financial centre. Taking the opposing view, the aspiring financial duopolists argued that, by rejecting the merger proposal, Ottawa was defending the banks' former *national* mission and so had jeopardized Toronto's future as a *continental* financial centre. Toronto's planners also publicly endorsed the bank mergers as a necessary response to globalization's demands. They maintained that, to become a 'world city,' the GTA needed the headquarters of at least one global financial player and hoped that the creation of two super-banks might produce this result.[24] More dangerous, as we will see in chapter 9, would be to allow foreign corporations to buy out the chartered banks and cannibalize their head offices, which provide enormous spinoff benefits for local business services, telecommunications, and information industries.

Although their immigration policies were forcing urban centres to cope with hundreds of thousands of low-income, high-maintenance newcomers, federal policymakers in the late 1990s were preoccupied more with their own problems than with those that they were causing the cities. Ottawa's response to its own financial crisis actually intensified the dilemmas experienced at the municipal level. It gave back powers to the provinces over labour training, forestry, energy, mining, and tourism in the 1990s largely to slough off its financial burdens and so reduce its budgetary deficit. This motive was particularly powerful in social assistance, whose costs grew in bad times, when tax revenues were lowest.

Accustomed to the sweet pleasures of power, the Ontario government readily accepted increases in its responsibilities but had a financial challenge of its own. Under the New Democratic Party (NDP) from 1990 to 1995 it had first increased its deficits in a defiant exercise of orthodox Keynesianism. When this pump priming failed to dislodge the recession or increase tax receipts, it attacked public services, imposing a 'social contract' to freeze or roll back salaries in the public sectors and in the quasi-public, municipalities, universities, schools, and hospitals, which all suffered increasingly from underfunding.

Local and regional governments in Ontario became the victims of economic uncertainty. In this crunch, adjacent municipalities competed with property tax rates to attract investors. Lacking efficient public transit, the GTA's outer semi-circle did not house the same concentration of new immigrants and poorer residents as did the core. (Average annual family income there was $66,000 in 1991, while in Metro it was $55,000.)[25] Not having to pay for the public amenities provided by Toronto's core, the adjacent exurbs vied with Metro and each other for new investment by flaunting their lower tax rates. Vaughan region, just north of Toronto, was the most blatant – it sponsored radio advertisements highlighting its low business property tax.[26] Local governments' inability to grapple with region-wide problems, combined with a slow and uneven economic recovery after 1992, prompted demands for action. There was a growing consensus that the GTA needed co-ordination of taxation and infrastructure investment.

In experiencing these problems of exurbanization, Canada was no different from almost all countries around the world, where spreading urban agglomerations were spilling over municipal boundaries and creating 'global region-cities' often with chaotic characteristics.[27] Metropolitan regions as economic spaces now commonly transcend the boundaries of municipalities and towns, of inner cores and suburbs, whose fortunes are completely interwoven. Foreign as well as domestic companies make decisions regarding investment in sites for production, distribution, and research based on the assets and qualities of the whole area. Furthermore, new technologies are accelerating information flows, cutting communications and transportation costs, moving economic growth centres, shifting population groups, and altering educational needs. This multidimensional change is undermining previous notions of scale economies, comparative advantage, and locational strategy.

The Fordist production of standardized goods had assumed economies of scale and so mass marketing of identical consumer products. 'Post-Fordist' processes tailored high-tech products to the specific needs of various customers. To stay competitive, companies had to keep abreast of the latest technological developments. Given the high costs of acquiring the requisite knowledge, firms found they had to achieve economies of scope by operating in networks with cognate companies that could share their knowledge and learn together. As proximity became a prerequisite, urban regions increasingly had to facilitate creative entrepreneurial clustering. For the Toronto area, beggar-thy-neighbour competition among its municipalities, degeneration of social services, and a lack of region-wide infrastructural development were undermining its overall capacity to offer the best location for a wide mix of desirable industries.

Late in its mandate, the NDP government turned to this new regional conundrum. In 1995, it asked Anne Golden, who had been active in such civic organizations as the Bureau of Municipal Research and the United Way, to direct a task force on regional governance in the GTA. Her masterly report presented a way to enhance the planning and governance capacity of the whole area. Of its fifty-one recommendations, the most noteworthy called for 'flexible service districts' to co-ordinate region-wide services and infrastructure investments, a uniform system of market-value property taxation, and a Metro-style structure for the 'commutershed.'

Had the province elected a Liberal government in 1995, as had been generally expected, the U.S.-driven economic resurgence of the late-1990s would quite naturally have brought the provincial budget back into balance. As a corollary, an indirectly elected GTA council would probably have extended the Metro model to the whole city-region. The upper-tier would have managed certain public goods, infrastructure, and services for the whole urban area, leaving the thirty existing municipal governments to deal with local needs.

The Neoconservative Counter-Revolution

This smooth evolution was not to be. Defeating the NDP and the Liberals in 1995, the Progressive Conservatives proceeded immediately to administer the harsh medicine they had promised, which they soon supplemented with even harsher surgery once they had taken Toronto's measure. First came Premier Mike Harris's general program, which had a province-wide scope with particular effects in Toronto. Then came his reconstruction of the city's political architecture.

Harris's 'Common Sense Revolution' (CSR) was more radically conservative than anything that Ontario had ever seen. Gaining power at the beginning of a cyclical upswing, Harris could keep his promise to cut personal income taxes by 30 per cent without reducing his government's revenues. He decimated many government ministries and programs, cut funds for social assistance across the province, and downloaded 20 per cent of its financing onto municipal shoulders.[28] Given the concentration of the poor in larger urban centres, these cuts had particular resonance in Metro's core. Homelessness became more visible as downtown sidewalks became cluttered with the destitute begging for spare change, and motorists at traffic lights were swarmed by unemployed youth vying to wash their windscreens for a loonie.

The Harris government's rejection of a *quality*-based emphasis on social policy in favour of a *competition*-motivated reduction of government spending constituted a politically shrewd but economically risky gamble. Shrewd was downloading to cities the onerous burden of financing public transit, social housing, and social welfare in return for their uploading some $2 billion of the costs of education to the provincial government.[29] By confusing the public about which level of government was responsible for specific policy deficiencies, this exercise in reallocating local services blunted political anger over reduced or cancelled programs. There seemed to be few electoral costs to the insufficient funding and poor coordination of programs that affected local governments. In any future recession, the financial obligation to provide welfare would fall not on the province but on the cities. There, dramatic cuts to the quantity and quality of services took place. Overburdened local administrations could not meet even basic needs for shelter which they now had to finance from municipal property taxes rather than from the province's more progressive general revenues. Municipalities became too fiscally desperate to maintain their social programs, let alone ensure a high quality of service, but this deterioration did not prevent Harris's being re-elected with an increased majority in 1999. Discriminating against Toronto had not hurt the Conservatives in its political bastion, the suburban '905' area.

Whether cutting taxes, rolling back the province's regulatory framework, reducing expenditures on infrastructure, and shrinking payments to welfare recipients made Ontario – and even more the GTA – more attractive to investors was unprovable. Formation of high quality human capital is the 'most important policy lever for economic development.'[30] Toronto had promoted its own development by setting high standards for public education, which it financed from its property taxes. The CSR platform had given no hint that Harris intended to impose order on the chaotic property assessment system, set educational tax rates for cities, and even impose uniform budgets on the province's public schools. This standardization forced Toronto's schools into rapid decline, because teaching highly diverse children has long been much more expensive than education in more socially homogeneous areas. The social polarization created by the deteriorating quality of public education is likely to prove severe as middle-class parents, encouraged by Ontario's new tax break for private schools, withdraw their children from public schools or move to the suburbs.

If provincial cutbacks in the staff and resources for enforcing environmental regulations worsen ambient conditions, the GTA's attractiveness as an investment site will decline – at least for those high-value-adding sectors whose employees demand a certain quality of urban life and environment. Letting roads, bridges, and sewers deteriorate and threatening the social safety net have serious implications for its longer-term economic prospects.[31] The reorganization of expenditure and revenue between the provincial and local levels is forcing municipalities to follow ideologically inspired but socially and even economically irrational diktats to accelerate the privatization of local government services such as electricity distribution and the supply and testing of water.

Flexible local responsiveness to diverse demographic needs seems to many urbanists the key to survival for healthy residential communities. Moving beyond the Common Sense Revolution – and even breaking his campaign promise to municipal leaders – Harris imposed uniform regional government on a number of the province's cities. He disregarded the Golden Report, along with the advice of leading independent experts who recommended amalgamating the administration of some services at the GTA level and warned that enlarging Torontonians' government would only produce diseconomies and increase political alienation.[32] Taking a scunner against the social-democratic mayor of Toronto, Barbara Hall, Harris borrowed a formula that Margaret Thatcher had used against a recalcitrant London County Council. He abolished the city. In January 1998 he forcibly incorporated it, along with Metro's other municipalities, in a single-tier 'megacity.' Harris left the surrounding '905' regional municipalities, which had given him his electoral majority, in control of their sprawling domains, unhindered by any supra-regional governing structure, apart from a non-elected, powerless, and short-lived Greater Toronto Services Board with minor advisory responsibilities. Unlike his immediate predecessors, the premier had shouldered the provincial government's constitutional authority, but he exercised this unfettered power in what seemed to many Toronto residents an unacceptable way.

Local opposition was fierce. Directly connected by its leadership with the reform movement of a quarter-century earlier and driven by a passionate concern to conserve and build on Toronto's social and cultural development, the anti-megacity movement raised cries of alarm. Anguished protests that amalgamation would jeopardize their city's hard-won civility sparked a grassroots campaign led by an internet-activated organization called Citizens for Local Democracy, which held numerous mass meetings and organized a march to celebrate the 1837 rebellion against the Family Compact, the colonial oligarchy.[33] A last-ditch legislative stalling ploy, in which the opposition parties introduced 13,000 amendments to the Conservatives' City of Toronto Act, failed to stop amalgamation.

The government, which had campaigned on a platform promoting 'direct democracy,' both ignored a non-binding referendum that showed 76 per cent of local citizens opposed and disregarded the limited public hearings that it reluctantly held on its proposed legislation.[34] Clarifying the value it accorded political representation, Queen's Park went on to pass the 'Fewer Municipal Politicians Act,' which eliminated 60 per cent of the city's councillors, reducing their ranks from 107 to 44.

This metropolitan region owed much of its past success to its *quality*-based development strategy. Since the GTA had no institutions and so no control of key policy levers such as taxation and education, it could not pursue such a strategy. Its prospects were linked to its remaining a centre – or a series of centres – of innovative activity that combined creative human talent with technological and organizational capacity in a wide range of products and production processes. Whether clusterings of interdependent economic activity blossomed in the Toronto region or occurred in other spaces depended in part on the amenities, facilities, and infrastructure available there compared to those offered elsewhere. The quality of the metropolis's policy-making process would help determine whether these locational attractions continue, improve, or degenerate. In amalgamating Metro Toronto, Queen's Park disregarded the historic contribution of local institutions to the GTA's economic success and left it unable to act for itself.

A key ingredient in the rebirth of a number of cities in the American 'rust belt' has been the public sector's role in creating private-public partnerships and setting up transportation and other services on a regional basis. Animated as it was by Mike Harris's small-town continentalism,[35] the CSR drove Ontario's cities in the opposite direction, forcing them by law or by budgetary limitations to contract out their services and sell off their assets. If dynamic industry networks should develop, this happy circumstance will not have occurred in response to the province's political leadership, which, in applying neoconservative solutions to the GTA, thumbed its nose at the region's rich social and political history. The 'one-size-fits-all' solution threatens Canada's most important economic dynamo with a rigid structure that will have difficulty responding to economic challenges. These transcend the capacity of the new 'megacity' which soon proved too big to deal with local community issues while too small to cope with the larger region's planning challenges.

The most visible symptom of the GTA's incipient economic and social decay was the desperation of its poorest and most vulnerable peoples. The Daily Food Bank,[36] and the Out of the Cold program expanded their efforts substantially in Toronto in the aftermath of the NDP's defeat, the Harris government's 20 per cent cut in welfare rates, and the resulting increase in its misery index. In response to worsening urban blight, municipal governments sponsored with growing frequency such initiatives as Toronto's Task Force on Homelessness. Of course, local programs that provide hostel space, food, and sleeping bags do nothing more than offer band-aid solutions for a structural problem. Local actors are powerless to address the root cause of homelessness – the collapse of the welfare state. Canada is the only G7 member without a national housing strategy. Mandating U.S. corporations to build prisons, appears to be the primary way in which neoconservative Ontario addresses the shelter needs of its most disadvantaged citizens. Since municipal governments across Canada have encountered similar downloading dilemmas, they have begun to meet biannually to share information, co-ordinate agendas, and attempt to present a unified, if vain, resistance to provincial and federal cutbacks.

Approaches to glocalization vary in their success rates. If unsuccessful, they may generate local responses that themselves become globalized. Neoconservative federal and provincial social policies have hurt the economically disadvantaged most severely. Attempting to fill the resulting void in the provision of social welfare and responding to Ontario's curtailment of Toronto's political process,[37] activist groups have taken initiatives to educate the citizenry. Despite some success, many citizens' organizations are frustrated by their lack of direct, legitimate access to social policy making. In many countries, urban grassroots dissatisfaction with influencing public policy only at its edges and with the enormity of its social and environmental problems has provoked some groups to organize regular, often illegal events that are now held in cities around the world and are co-ordinated through the internet.

While the anti-corporate Reclaim the Streets movement holds an annual Global Street Party to promote the pedestrianization of urban space, regular Critical Mass events draw attention to the socially and environmentally polluting effects of carbon-fuelled vehicles by swamping downtown cores periodically with large bike-riding processions that temporarily paralyse traffic. These happenings, co-ordinated across several countries, often occur on the same day in order to focus international attention on local struggles. By building these types of global-local alliances, civil society has been able to emphasize that cities everywhere are facing similar problems with pollution, urban sprawl, social polarization and inadequate provision of services for the poor.

The Future: Beyond Polarization?

The political conundrum cities face under globalization is the historical injustice that they have suffered at the hands of the nation state in recent centuries. Although always the prime generators of innovation, wealth, culture, and learning, they have experienced permanent oppression from the triumphant modern state, which has assumed constitutional sovereignty over all municipalities.

World city formation may be globally induced, but it is locally contingent on cultural, historical, and economic conditions as well as on governance structures. In the last quarter of the twentieth century, Toronto occupied a place of high distinction within North America as a model for big-city government. Despite the global economic shocks and crises of the 1970s, its two-tiered municipality assured it flexibility and responsiveness to local needs.[38] Since it avoided many of the pitfalls that befell U.S. cites – blight in the urban core, wholesale disinvestment by the middle class in favour of suburbia, and high rates of urban crime – Toronto earned an international reputation as the 'city that works.' This record in a Keynesian political economy was no guarantee of success under neoconservatism, particularly if politicians make the wrong responses to economic signals.

Whether Toronto is the example of a triumph on the way to failure remains unclear. Although globalization is a force driving local change, the policies pursued by the city and for the city are not predetermined. Local and regional authorities still have to respond to external forces, but policies imposed by the provincial – and potentially the federal – government will continue to be decisive. (The U.S. government's role in urban redevelopment is significantly greater than Ottawa's, even though in both countries federal authority over the city is weak.[39] Indeed, creative collaboration between the three levels of government and private enterprise is far more prevalent in the United States than in Canada.)[40]

Massive, Washington-led investment in infrastructure is spurring a renaissance in urban America. Since growth depends on individual entrepreneurial decisions to locate in one place versus another, many U.S. cities are becoming more attractive thanks to community development corporations that receive government support but remain locally controlled.[41] At a time when Toronto was facing increased competition from metropolitan revitalization south of the border, Ontario reduced the city's authority to raise taxes, and federal and provincial transfers declined.[42] In addition, Queen's Park saddled the city with extra welfare costs and the responsibility for capital improvements to the subway system, leaving it 'the most fiscally restrained of Canadian cities.'[43]

The Harris government's autocratic deeds made its new-think discourse on the city-region suspect. The government's strategic thinking unit, the Ontario Jobs and Investment Board, issued a mission statement that spoke of giving 'priority attention to the economic challenges and opportunities facing the Greater Toronto Area and Golden Horseshoe – Canada's only global scale city-region.'[44] It is true that the Harris government carried off one courageous feat. It levelled the regional playing field by harmonizing property tax assessment on the basis of current value. But in reducing Toronto's business tax rates for education to the provincial average and in allowing municipalities to increase taxes only on below-average rates, it condemned Toronto to financing all its revenue increases from residential property.[45] In rejecting the principle of democratic subsidiarity in favour of paternalistic centralization, Ontario's neoconservatism seemed disturbingly out of touch with the spirit and the needs of the times, which called for flexibility in both productive and political systems.[46]

Shaken by undeniable evidence of urban gridlock and planning chaos, Queen's Park moved, towards the end of Harris's premiership, to correct some of the problems that its excessive zeal had aggravated earlier. In the 2001 speech from the throne, it committed itself to 'smart growth,' suggesting that it would restore stronger land-use planning in the province. In the 2001 budget it created a SuperBuild Corporation to co-ordinate infrastructure spending, particularly in constructing university buildings and generating public-private partnerships. And later that year it even took back responsibility for public transit and committed several billion dollars to renovating the GTA's system.

The discrepancy between political-economic realities and institutional constraints on the local state is so patent that some federal politicians have made tentative noises about Ottawa's re-engaging with urban issues.[47] As part of courting the Toronto vote, the federal government joined Queen's Park to commit $500 million each to a tripartite redevelopment of the waterfront as part of the city's bid to win the summer Olympics of 2008. In their federal election platform in 2000, the Liberals promised a dialogue with the provinces and cities about their urban 'opportunities and challenges'[48] and they reiterated this undertaking in their speech from the throne in 2001, mentioning public transit infrastructure and affordable rental housing. For Montreal, the federal government already provided local coordination of federal programs through an officer with deputy-minister rank who makes visible the 'nestedness' of federal with provincial and municipal forms of state involvement.

Bolder and more visionary, some civic leaders have been testing out ideas of endowing Toronto with a form of constitutional status.[49] Objecting to being reduced to an observer role within the city he is supposed to govern, Mayor Mel Lastman called for provincial status for the region. This cry of distress seemed less significant than a contemporaneous but more thoughtful wave of urban progressivism, also inspired by Jane Jacobs's concern that Canada's 'larger, economically vibrant cities don't have the powers or resources they need to meet the challenges before them.'[50] A coalition of concerned citizens has proposed a charter to grant Toronto 'greater local autonomy to ensure the Region's continued prosperity and effective governance.' Aspiring to constitutional status analogous to that of Dutch cities and older city-states such as Hamburg and Singapore, this new localism both claims the restoration of historic rights and explicitly recognizes the multicentred reality of the future city-region. Implicitly suggested by this localist discourse is the potential for a defiant urban identity that could have powerfully disruptive political effects.

Toronto's urbanists may be in revolt, but their call to action is unlikely to bear fruit until either the province's ruling ideology changes or the courts consider municipal governments' claims to legitimate autonomy. Provincial change could occur if Ontario's neoconservatism rediscovered its professed distrust of big government by giving back to its cities the tax and policy autonomy to discharge the responsibilities that it has downloaded to them. Change could also come from the ballot box, should the city-region politically express its new identity as a diverse, complex community with both a national and a continental destiny. Electoral change in British Columbia in 2001 brought to the premier's office a former Vancouver mayor, Gordon Campbell, who quickly created a Community Charter Council to propose a new foundation for more autonomous and empowered municipal government.[51] But it verges on the utopian to posit the emergence of a solidaristic region-city identity when flexibility and temporary work under post-Fordism are breeding a culture of insecurity that undermines the formation of civic attachments, whether by managers or by workers.[52] Judicial support for applying subsidiarity to the political remapping of urban space in Canada seems just as unlikely.

Even though municipalities have been a component of government for centuries, courts in Canada have been extremely reluctant to apply to them the same standards of flexibility in their rulings that they have lavished on provincial governments. By convention, local governments have a historical claim to considerable autonomy, but attempts to gain recognition for their constitutional stature have failed, leaving them pawns in the hands of provincial politicians. The Supreme Court of Canada continues to reject the argument that there are historic conventions which should invest municipalities with some court-enforceable guarantees of constitutional autonomy.[53]

Having seen how globalizing forces from the outside and ideological, institutional, and domestic forces from the inside have reconstituted the framework of the Canadian state, we can now ask to what extent the resulting political system is able to perform the tasks that citizens expected of it by the late 1970s. These tasks cover a wide range of policies that I will divide into two broad categories – managing the economy and sustaining civil society. By the end of the twentieth century the state in advanced societies was directing or regulating every conceivable aspect of economic and societal life. In part II we look at four economic areas – macro-economic management, regulatory policy, trade and investment, and industrial policy. In part III we review five policy fields in which the Canadian state is nurturing society by providing social security, refereeing industrial relations, protecting the environment, supporting cultural development, and carrying out diplomatic relations with other states in the global system.

PART II

The Economy: Reframing the State's Functions

Having established the extent to which the framework of the Canadian state has been reconstituted from the outside by globalizing forces and from the inside by ideological, institutional, and indigenous forces, we can now ask to what extent the political system is able to fulfill the functions that citizens had grown to expect of it by the end of the 1970s. These tasks cover a wide range of policies that we can place into two groupings – social, cultural, environmental, and diplomatic, on the one hand, and the various roles engaging with the economy, on the other.

These economic functions are treated in four pairs:

- managing the level of taxes and flow of money in the macro-economy

7 The Taxing State: From Lord Keynes to Paul Martin
8 The Banking State and Global Financial Governance

- regulating activity in key sectors such as banking and telecommunications that are characterized by some kind of monopoly conditions in the oligopolistic economy

9 Financial Services: National Champions at Risk
10 Telecoms: from Regional Monopolies to Global Alliances

- affecting economic links with other economies via trade and investment policy in the external economy

11 The Trading State
12 The Investing State

- then industrial policies aimed at encouraging specific sectors in the microeconomy

13 The Residual State: Accommodation at the Federal Level
14 The Industrial State Goes Provincial

THE MACRO ECONOMY
AND THE MANAGERIAL STATE

7 The Taxing State:
From Lord Keynes to Paul Martin

The activist state was clearly what Lester Pearson's coterie of ministers and advisers in the 1960s – the economic nationalist Walter Gordon, the Fabian democrat Tom Kent, and the social welfare advocates Allan MacEachen and Paul Martin, Sr – believed that the Liberal Party had been elected to construct. Pierre Trudeau's writings display a related belief in equity-oriented social engineering as the proper role for the state that he subsequently came to lead.[1] He based his promise of a 'just society' on the modernist, yet liberal belief that, although government had no business in the bedrooms of the nation, state action was necessary if social justice was to prevail over the inequities caused by the laissez-faire attitudes of the economy's boardrooms.

By contrast, what made the Mulroney-Chrétien epoch *postmodern* was its scepticism that states can be rationally and purposefully run to achieve any specific ends. Neoconservatism exploited this systemic doubt about politics, insisting that, because government was more likely to present the problem than offer the solution, it had no business in the boardrooms of the nation. Social conservatives, whose moral agenda remained politically marginal outside Alberta, were not so sure about the nation's bedrooms, in whose activities they took a major interest because of their principled opposition to liberal positions on the 'family issues' concerning life's beginning (abortion), middle (same-sex marriage), and end (euthanasia).

We can see the degree to which the Keynesian vision in the economic domain had given way to the neoconservative model from the mid-1980s on in this 'paradigm shift'[2] in which:

- the long run prevailed over the short run as the policy focus
- controlling inflation trumped reducing unemployment as an immediate priority
- government was intended to steer, not row – that is, to establish framework policies, but not engage directly in micro-management, because an economy was thought to reach an optimal equilibrium through the play of market forces
- the supply side, as opposed to the demand side, of the economic equation was emphasized
- planning a budgetary deficit was rejected as an unacceptable policy tool

None of these characteristics in and of itself defined neoconservative economic policy, as traces of Keynesianism persisted. Nevertheless, the neoconservative vision tended to delegitimize the state's use of direct, short-term, demand-based, deficit-supported measures. Emphasizing structural, long-term, supply-side, fiscally balanced approaches, the neoconservative governors of the late 1980s and the 1990s had neither a capacity for nor an interest in day-to-day economic intervention.

In Canada, changes in macro-economic, trade, and industrial policy were closely connected. Under neoconservatism, these three fields shared a diminished concern with fine-tuning the demand side of the economy in favour of engineering permanent, structural solutions that would provide a framework within which market forces could be entrusted to make their own best decisions. As attention turned towards the threats and challenges of international competitiveness, the prime goal of public policy shifted from intensifying domestic demand and building up nationally owned corporate champions to expanding trade and attracting investment.[3]

This switch to a new paradigm was designed to repudiate two related policy systems. On the one hand, neoconservatism delegitimized the Fordist regime of accumulation, the labour-market arrangements through which capitalist accumulation functioned under conditions of mass production and productivity-centred collective bargaining with powerful trade unions. If the high wage levels achieved by the Fordist model lost their cachet as a means for supporting domestic demand, this was because doubts had undermined the credibility of Keynesianism – the institutional framework of macro-economic demand management that enabled Fordism to prosper. Manipulating demand by varying interest rates and stimulating demand through budgetary deficits became politically incorrect uses of monetary and fiscal policy. The Swedish high-wage, high-tech success story, so attractive to Canadians with a post-Keynesian mind-set,[4] was anathema to neoconservatives. They believed that high wages and low unemployment impaired the country's ability to compete internationally on the basis of low prices.

The focus on trade shifted the levels in our multi-tier model at which governance functions occurred. Control over industrial policy, for example, now resided at least as much in NAFTA's supraconstitutional thou-shalt-not policy commandments and the WTO's dense rule book as in the federal or provincial capitals. With the possibility of interventionist industrial policy curtailed from above by the norm of national treatment and with its value dismissed from within, we need to ask what room was left for macro-economic policies in the new order.[5]

For three decades after the Second World War, Ottawa's policy community believed that government could countervail the ups and downs of the business cycle, preventing the excesses of economic booms and forestalling the hardship caused by recessions. Tax policies made in the Department of Finance could directly affect how much money citizens had to spend. If consumer demand needed boosting in order to increase employment, the minister of finance was expected to plan for a budgetary deficit, in which the government received less from its taxes (which took money out of citizens' pockets) than it distributed on its social programs (which put money back in those pockets to be spent). It was assumed that, if consumer wants increased, business would invest more to increase its production of goods to satisfy that aggregate demand. Few at the time were bothered by the cumulative impact on the national debt of chronic deficit budgets.

While astutely adjusting these fiscal levers constituted the macro-economic magic that had made Lord Keynes the guru of postwar prosperity, policy thinking in the Department of Finance was only partly in the Cambridge economist's thrall. Long before the slogans of supply-side economics were made popular by Ronald Reagan in the United States, Ottawa practised them by working on the micro side of fiscal policy. Typically, it created exceptions or loopholes in its tax measures as incentives to stimulate business activity. These 'tax expenditures' were expanded greatly in the early 1970s by Finance Minister John Turner and his deputy, Simon Reisman, in their effort to keep the economy from recession. In the context of stable spending on social welfare though the 1970s, these tax cuts for business and higher-income taxpayers reduced federal revenues and became the direct source of Ottawa's structural deficits.[6]

By that time, Keynesianism had become associated with the notion that inflation and unemployment were inversely related: if one condition was high, the other would be low.[7] Since everyone agreed that unemployment was a social scourge, Keynesians became inured to a slow rise in the rate of inflation. However, the crisis of 'stagflation' in the 1970s – the coexistence of a stagnant economy, high inflation, and high unemployment – necessarily called into question this relationship and, with it, Keynesianism's credibility. It also prompted two important federal policy changes, which heralded the beginning of the end of the Keynesian era.[8] The imposition of the Anti-Inflation Program (AIP) by Finance Minister Donald Macdonald in 1975 and the attempt to restrict growth in federal spending signalled Ottawa's post-Keynesian effort to save the Keynesian mode of regulation from itself.

The AIP was designed to contain inflation without lowering the employment levels that continued to concern post-Keynesians. By controlling wages and prices directly, the federal government sought to reduce inflation without creating more unemployment.[9] In a difficult economic situation, Trudeau's Ottawa still felt that social justice required state action to protect citizens from economic dislocation.

One by-product of the international capital markets' new liberalization was the purchase of Canadian bonds by foreign financial funds. Another was the ease with which governments could borrow abroad to finance their budgetary deficits at home with short-term treasury bills. A third innovation was the rising power of the credit-rating agencies, on which international bond holders relied to gauge the risk that they incurred when deciding to invest in, say, a Canadian rather than an Argentinian bond. This internationalization of its debt put the federal government on the horns of the following dilemma. The severe recession of the early 1980s, continuing high unemployment levels, and a U.S.-generated spike in short-term interest rates caused government expenditures to rise relentlessly. But the federal government's revenues had plateaued in the 1970s because its tax expenditures had reduced levies on corporations, while 'indexing' income-tax brackets to the cost of living kept individuals' tax bills from rising with inflation.

The resulting deficits put both federal politicians and their provincial counterparts at the mercy of the credit-rating agencies, which assign a grade to the quality of all countries' corporate and governmental debt. An institution with a high grade can raise capital on the global market at a relatively low rate of interest. Should that grade fall, the interest on its borrowed funds automatically increases. As any teacher knows, grading is an essentially subjective process that depends on a prior set of values. Credit-rating agencies espoused the monetarist doctrine of budgetary balance, so they punished any government that committed the sins of chronic deficits and a high public debt. Canadian federal and provincial governments learned this simple lesson in international finance in the 1980s. Their recurring budgetary deficits had rapidly increased their debt loads. This profligacy caused Moody's and other agencies to downgrade their bonds. These reprimands created a vicious circle. The resulting higher interest rates increased the governments' deficits and caused bond ratings to be lowered further. Ultimately this pressure from the global capital market forced Canadian and provincial finance ministers to raise taxes and cut spending in order to eliminate their deficits. Neoconservatism in this instance was mediated by the workings of the private sector at the transnational level.

Notwithstanding the heavily ideological content of this kind of 'government by Moody's,' the rationale for countercyclical deficit financing remained alive and well after 1975. Until as late as 1984, federal budget documents defended deficit financing as an appropriate countercyclical response to the economy's poor performance. Underperformance was not yet understood to result from a gradual decline in both growth and productivity rates.[10]

Post-Keynesian thinking implied no reduction for the federal state's role in the economy. On the contrary, the AIP extended Ottawa's jurisdiction to price controls, a sphere with which it had little previous experience. Significantly, the courts legitimized this increased federal jurisdiction in the face of provincial protests.[11] The Trudeau government's intractability in its dealings with the provinces, its resistance to continental integration as manifested by the 'third option' for trade diversion, its creation of the Foreign Investment Review Agency to scrutinize new initiatives by transnational corporations, and its commitment to the interventionist National Energy Program showed that Ottawa refused to abdicate its role.

Though consistently defended by Trudeau and his government, the federal role was nevertheless challenged by province-building. This threat began in the 1960s in Ontario, as the Auto Pact expanded vehicle manufacturing there, and in Quebec, with its Quiet Revolution, and spread in the 1970s to the western provinces. Provincial governments were becoming more important economic actors, both in absolute terms and relative to the federal government.[12] The friction with business and the provinces caused by the Trudeauites' repeated interference in micro-level decisions created a generalized obloquy in the private sector, in some provincial capitals, and in the media over any policy that challenged corporate or provincial autonomy.

The resulting delegitimation of interventionist policy in the public consciousness by the early 1980s created political space for Brian Mulroney to shift towards a neoconservatism in which the state provided a context for private-sector growth without making decisions for it. Having campaigned in 1984 on restraint in government, the Tories deplored the deficit financing in which the Trudeau Liberals had indulged.[13] The official disavowal of a shattered Keynesian consensus was signalled shortly after the Progressive Conservatives took office by a white paper, *A New Direction for Canada – An Agenda for Economic Renewal*, which was to define the new government's economic doctrine.[14] It made little difference that this analysis had not originated in Mulroney's party. According to Douglas Peters, an economist working in the Department of Finance at the time, the paper had been written there in the summer of 1984 and would have been presented for the Liberals to adopt had John Turner won re-election. Finance Minister Michael Wilson and his Progressive Conservative colleagues 'accepted the document as is because they did not know what to do and had no ideas of their own.'[15] In sync with government thinking throughout the Anglo-American world, *A New Direction for Canada* rejected deficit financing as an appropriate response to cyclical economic underperformance. Budgetary deficits had now become reconceptualized as dangerously inflationary. Deficit reduction became a major part of the comprehensive reforms that the Mulroney government believed would restore competitiveness to the Canadian economy.

In the event, the Tories did not come close to attaining their deficit reduction goal because they had implemented other politically costly changes. Free trade, CUFTA-style, brutally exacerbated the impact of the 1990–1 world recession.[16] This economic slowdown actually engendered increased government spending (particularly in the form of unemployment insurance payments and increased debt-servicing charges caused by the Bank of Canada's deliberately ratcheting interest rates upwards) and yielded major reductions in tax revenue – and so a deficit that rose still higher. Procrastination in introducing the consumption tax known as the Goods and Services Tax (GST) made fiscal balance still more elusive.

The Mulroney government presented these structural reforms as necessitated by the forces of globalization, which had eroded Ottawa's capacity to control economic activity. An economy increasingly open to trade and capital flows frustrated Keynesian demand management because money put into voters' pockets would as likely increase demand for imported as for domestically produced goods. At the same time, supraconstitutional trade norms such as national treatment precluded post-Keynesian industrial policies that intervened on the supply side by providing help to restructure domestic corporations or economic sectors. Making a virtue out of necessity, Ottawa's neoconservatives argued that Canada *should* not be protected from ineluctable global change. Protectionism should be abandoned, and competitiveness embraced, so that Canada could fully engage in the unavoidable international economic struggle for survival. The GST exemplified this attitudinal shift: it liberated domestic producers from a manufactures sales tax that had harmed their competitive position internationally. A value-added tax, though regressive, was a lesser, and much preferred, evil.

Neoconservative restructuring and the alienation of jurisdiction upward to the global and continental governance regimes also had affected the movement of powers between the federal government and the state tiers above and below. As receipts from tariffs shrank, trade liberalization further impeded Ottawa's efforts to balance its budget. In hobbling the market's economic performance and raising the cost of servicing the debt, these structural policies prevented the government from reaching its goal of fiscal balance.

By the early 1990s the rising deficit was targeted as the problem rather than the safety valve. Worsened fiscal conditions became a crucial reason for the movement of state functions downward to lower levels in the multi-tier state. This dilemma caused Ottawa to make substantial cuts by stealth to its own social programs[17] and to offload some of its fiscal headaches by cutting transfers of funding for social policies, particularly to the 'have' provinces. In this way it shifted both deficits and more responsibility for social policy to the provincial tier, which in turn tried to pass its problems on to the municipalities. Casting off this policy power reduced the *size* of the federal state. Nevertheless, the GST and free trade required a federal state with enough muscle to face down both the protests of the electorate and objections from various provinces that suffered serious regional effects from these tough-love policies.

Despite these measures, which appeared drastic at the time, the social distress caused by high unemployment in the early 1990s was so severe that the gap between Ottawa's spending and its revenue was greater when the Mulroney government left office than when it took power. The recession of the early 1990s, and the very slow recovery that followed, accelerated a trend towards detaching the public from the Keynesian welfare state and the deficits that had come to support it. High unemployment, declining real incomes, and the shift of employment from unionized mass-production jobs to part-time and non-standard work undermined the sense of solidarity that had once generated public support for a more generous state. Instead, the combination of great personal economic stress in the general public and its sense that the welfare state benefited only bureaucrats and what neo-conservatives caricatured as extreme or ne'er-do-well 'special interests' elicited a turn inward for self-protection. In addition, there was a growing apprehension among the public that the welfare state would not survive to help people, even when they ultimately qualified for support.[18]

The restructuring of the manufacturing sector engendered by free trade – particularly in Ontario, where hundreds of firms closed and hundreds of thousands of permanent jobs were lost – was largely completed by the time the Progressive Conservatives were routed from office in 1993.[19] By that time, the GST had become an indispensable source of increasing revenue. Mulroney's completed measures, the public's acquiescence to them, and a final repudiation of Keynesian thinking meant that fiscal balance could become the dominant theme of the Liberal Party's tenure, once the Department of Finance had brought its new minister under ideological control.[20]

This was no small challenge, since the Liberals had worked hard in opposition to develop a post-Keynesian critique of neoconservatism. Supported by Douglas Peters's economic analysis, Paul Martin, Jr had played a major role in drafting his party's campaign platform, which attacked neoconservative monetarism, advocated a more intervention-ist industrial policy, and promised a restitution of federal cuts.[21] As minister of finance, Martin infused his first budget in 1994 with this approach, shifting spending from national defence to social programs and watching the economy grow by over 4 per cent. Shortly after-wards, his bureaucrats wore him down. Martin's 1995 and 1996 budgets made draconian cuts in government programs – and in economic growth, which fell to under 2 per cent.

The federal government could at least plan around a predictable level of underperformance (particularly high unemployment and low productivity), rather than having to cope with a deep recession. When interest rates started to fall after 1995, the Liberal government reaped a big reward in the form of a lightened debt-servicing burden. The public's gradually changing consciousness allowed deficit reduction to be credibly presented as a matter of the 'general' interest. In effect, the Progressive Conservatives had created the political conditions that let Jean Chrétien and his finance minister eradicate their deficit. Wide public support for the endeavour allowed program cutting to be done in the open rather than by stealth and gave the Liberals the electoral backing for a radical deficit reduction that had eluded Mulroney's grasp.

With his notorious 1995 budget, Paul Martin banished Keynesian notions from government rhetoric to an even greater extent than had his Tory predecessor. Deficit reduction was to be permanent, not confined simply to the upside of the business cycle.[22] Even if the minister of finance understood that fiscal retrenchment would contract demand and so could reduce growth or employment, he was not so foolish as to admit this out loud. Because the terms of political discourse had changed so far that the public no longer thought that cutting the deficit meant failing to stimulate the economy, Martin was able to pursue his new fiscal agenda. Besides, neoconservative theory did have an employment logic. Reducing their fiscal deficits would reduce governments' need to borrow, lessen demand for capital, and lower the cost of borrowing. The subsequent decline in interest rates would stimulate private, job-creating investment.

Policy of every stripe was filtered through its relationship to the government's budget-balancing priority. While Paul Martin's insistence on making prudent assumptions and keeping a contingency reserve certainly facilitated deficit reduction, his success in balancing the budget and then running surpluses was due to the prime minister's unflinching support, which made possible the Liberals' remarkably firm commitment to the goal even in the face of concerted provincial opposition to federal cuts of transfer payments. Ottawa's tenacity on the fiscal front had become electorally viable, brilliantly marketed, and administratively disciplined.

One interpretation of the relationship between the Liberals' fiscal performance and the role of the federal state argued that the government reluctantly cut programs to preserve its social policy power in the longer run. While the social and regulatory tapestry was torn by what were indeed neoconservative measures, Liberals presented this damage as a temporary, if necessary, response to the government's fiscal straits. Rising debt-interest payments squeezed out valuable program spending. Paying interest to foreign holders of Canadian bonds diverted public funds from stimulating the domestic economy. Only by balancing the federal government's books, these Liberals maintained, could they save and ultimately strengthen social programs. Once budgetary surpluses were achieved, it would be possible both to reduce tax burdens and to 'reinvest' in the social fabric. According to this view, fiscal retrenchment was a means to the higher social goal of embedding the Liberal vision of a secure society, which the government purported to hold dear.

This reasoning may have assuaged the guilt of some left Liberals, but the Chrétien regime's liberalism proved itself in practice to be distinctly more 'neo' than embedded. Official Ottawa had become much less sensitive to variations in economic conditions than it was even in the early 1990s. The rhetoric of budget documents now dismissed demand management as policy without economic value. Concerns about unemployment disappeared from policy-makers' discourse – although, when Statistics Canada uncorked bullish figures, the prime minister was not averse to claiming credit for the number of jobs that had been created on his watch. While the Liberal fiscal agenda was of primarily neoconservative stock, the justification of retrenchment as a mechanism to save social programs was certainly part of what animated the government's actions. Some of the cutting was manifestly reluctant. Once budgetary balance was achieved in 1997 and the government found itself awash in surplus funds, some 'reinvestment' in health and education did occur.

While federal fiscal policy did retain glimmerings of a social-democratic DNA, its main genetic glow was unreconstructedly neoconservative. The harshest fiscal retrenchment of any industrial country in the postwar era, federal spending fell over four years from 16 per cent to 10 per cent of gross domestic product (GDP) – the lowest level since the late 1930s.[23] Nor was Paul Martin's repudiation of Keynes conjunctural. After 1998, when his draconian program cutting had achieved a budget surplus, he stuck to his course by moving the goal posts to debt reduction. Even as the economy slowed in response to the U.S. economic decline of 2001, Martin insisted on accumulating huge surpluses to pay down the national debt and cut taxes. In 1996 the federal debt had risen to 71 per cent of GDP. The surpluses that Martin accumulated since 1998 had been so substantial that the Finance Department expected to have the debt ratio down to 47 per cent of GDP by 2003 – its level in 1985.[24] As long as debt reduction and tax cuts remained the dominant priority for both federal and provincial governments (which had also achieved record surpluses by the start of the millennium), there was little prospect for reviving the generous state.

Complementing the Finance Department's leading role in fiscal policy was the Bank of Canada's monetary policy functions, which buttressed the federal state's continuing dominance in macro-economic management.

8 The Banking State and Global Financial Governance

A separate currency is more than just a symbolic proxy for statehood; it is a primary tool of governments for managing their economy. In Canada's case this could already be seen in colonial times. As early as 1853 the Province of Canada decided to produce its own coinage. Before the end of the decade, it had rejected the British pound and adopted a decimal currency to facilitate trade with the United States. Fears of annexation notwithstanding, a Canadian 'dollar' was retained by the new Dominion as part of its project to build a nation-state based on an integrated market supported by a patriotic identity.[1] The issues surrounding monetary autonomy continue to enliven public debates a century and a half later.

A state bank to manage the state currency was a twentieth-century invention. After decades of experimentation with letting the Canadian dollar 'float' rather than having it convertible into gold at a fixed rate, Canada followed Britain in definitively abandoning the gold standard in 1931. From sizzling in the frying pan (under the gold standard, Canada had suffered from fluctuations of world commodity prices and international capital flows), it found itself badly burned by the fire (New York's financial markets controlled its interest rates, and the now-floating exchange rate determined the value of its dollar). It was in large part to achieve some monetary autonomy that the Conservative prime minister, R.B. Bennett, created a central bank in 1935. Nationalized by William Lyon Mackenzie King a short time later, the Bank of Canada became the government's banker and the monetary system's manager. It issued bank notes, managed the public debt, set the interest rates for the chartered banks, affected the supply of money in the economy, and intervened in foreign currency markets when trying to offset shifts in the dollar's exchange rate.

The Keynesian model reigning in the advanced capitalist countries for the first quarter-century after the Second World War viewed capital flows as a disruptive force, disequilibrating exchange rates and trade patterns and threatening the domestic political order. Within this nationally embedded international order, each state would continue to control capital movements across its borders, as it had during the war, in order to maintain the policy autonomy necessary for promoting social stability. In a regime established at Bretton Woods in 1944, each country would also fix its currency, but at a rate collectively determined by the new International Monetary Fund (IMF), which was to act as a global currency watchdog and troubleshooter should a balance-of-payments crisis get a national currency into trouble. Governments delegated to their central banks the task of managing their exchange rates in their external relations while managing interest rates and the money supply within their national economies.

At the same time as stagflation in the members of the Organization for Economic Cooperation and Development (OECD) started to undermine the Keynesian system's legitimacy from inside in the 1970s, a U.S.-led deregulation of capital controls was undermining the Bretton Woods system externally. Attracted to the American economy by its safe-haven stability, the dominance of the U.S. dollar, and the strength of its financial markets, mobile capital, Washington calculated, would flood in to the United States and so help finance its budgetary and trading deficits. Westminster believed that London's traditionally strong financial institutions would also benefit from capital mobility, so radically deregulated the City in its celebrated 'big bang' of 1986. In this classic example of regulatory competition, other governments found themselves obliged to follow the major players by relaxing their own controls over cross-border capital flows, lest their own increasingly footloose business decamp to the more attractive U.S. or British markets.

In this follow-the-leader process, all states lost at least one in their trio of policy instruments for Keynesian macro-economic management. Without control over their national *capital markets*, countries could no longer keep their currencies' *exchange rates* fixed unless they were willing to have *domestic interest rates* track international levels. Otherwise speculators would shift their assets elsewhere, driving down the exchange rate and making autonomous monetary policy impossible.

From the Bank of Canada to Government by Moody's

Canada had been an early Bretton Woods non-conformist because its peripheral position in North America already prevented it from maintaining the 'unholy Trinity' of simultaneously controlling capital movements, fixing its exchange rate, and maintaining an independent monetary policy. Its financial markets had been too integrated with New York's for it to control the movement of capital across its border, except during the years of mobilization for total war and their immediate aftermath. Unable to control capital movements, Canada had not been able to sustain a fixed rate for its dollar. As a result, it was the first to break out of the Bretton Woods system and let its dollar float again in 1950. In effect, the government had decided that it could no longer control its currency's international value through the instrument of its central bank.

This meant that, should speculators consider the Canadian dollar to be overvalued, they would sell Canadian stocks, bonds, or dollars on the open market and so cause the international value of the currency to fall. Only a marginal factor when facing the global market, the Bank of Canada could use its reserves of cash, gold, or foreign exchange to enter the market as well and, in buying back dollars, try to mitigate this kind of market swing.[2] Generally the Bank left exchange rates to look after themselves, while it tended to its chief preoccupation – macroeconomic fine-tuning.

Giving up the stability of a fixed exchange rate left the Bank of Canada free to concentrate on the countercyclical objective assigned to its monetary policy by Keynesian theory. While the Finance Department used its tax and spending instruments to augment (or reduce) consumer demand, the Bank could expand (or contract) the money supply. Its additional capacity to lower (or raise) interest rates would encourage (or discourage) consumers to increase consumption and investors to expand production. Beyond the immediate goal of taming the capitalist market's boom-bust roller-coaster, job creation was the ultimate objective of this Keynesian causal chain.

Canada was ahead of the deregulating pack in monetary policy terms in another way. It was the first OECD country to delink its central bank from government control. In 1961, tensions over economic policy between John Coyne, the bank's governor, and Prime Minister John Diefenbaker resulted in a major political crisis, the upshot of which was to remove Coyne from the Bank but leave his successors largely insulated from political control. Once appointed by the politicians in power, the governor became effectively independent of their direction, even though they remained ultimately responsible to the public for the Bank's behaviour.[3] Thus it was for conjunctural, rather than systemic, reasons that Canada's central bank achieved functional autonomy well before most of its counterparts.

This independence became another factor in loosening Keynesianism's hold in Canada. For the last decade of their era, while the Trudeauites were mounting a post-Keynesian defence of their interventionist state, the Bank of Canada was steadily pushing economic policy in another direction. Ahead of the pack once again, it was an earlier convert to Milton Friedman's attack on Keynesian theory than Washington's central bank, the Federal Reserve. Governor Gerald Bouey adopted a monetarist approach by introducing 'monetary gradualism' in 1975, well ahead of Paul Volcker's conversion at 'the Fed.'

There was a post-Keynesian touch to Bouey's monetarism. Out of concern for his policy's effect on employment, he rejected a harsh monetary contraction in favour of a steady reduction in the growth of the money supply.[4] Nevertheless, the Bank's new fixation on controlling inflation was clearly out of step with the Liberals' still-expansionary philosophy. Fighting inflation by constraining the supply of money pushed up interest rates, which the Bank deliberately raised lest the dollar fall and fuel inflation with higher import costs. Tight money and high interest rates directly obstructed what the government was trying to achieve. High interest rates raised the cost of borrowing for consumers, investors, and governments. Expensive money impeded Ottawa from gaining control over the petroleum industry through the National Energy Program or combatting high unemployment with repeated budgetary deficits.

Central bank autonomy presented the Liberals with a conundrum. If they tried to discipline Governor Bouey, the global currency market would punish them by attacking the Canadian dollar. In this way the Bank of Canada provided the institutional conduit introducing the monetarist thrust of global neoconservatism into the heart of the Canadian policy-making system.[5] And it did so in stubborn opposition to the programs of the democratically elected government.[6]

Whereas the monetarist Bank of Canada blocked the Trudeau Liberals' efforts, it complemented the Mulroney Conservatives' mission. When an inflexible apostle of price stability, the IMF-trained, British-born John Crow was appointed governor in 1987, the Bank became the messianic collaborator in the neoconservative counter-revolution. Crow's dedication to wiping out inflation – a policy known officially as 'price stability,' but more commonly as 'zero inflation'[7] – supported the government's own objectives in the late 1980s and early 1990s. The governor pushed relentlessly till short-term rates were 5 per cent above the U.S. level.[8] Denounced on the left and even by mainstream economists for precipitating a made-in-Canada recession, the Bank helped to discipline wages by reducing inflation-based demands for pay increases and by creating enough unemployment to undermine the bargaining position of the labour unions.

More recently, the Bank of Canada proved not to be completely autonomous. At the end of 1993, when it came time to renew John Crow's term, the new Liberal finance minister, Paul Martin, Jr, engaged him in tough negotiations over the Bank's inflation target. When Crow's objectives turned out to be too restrictive for Martin's slightly more expansionary taste, the finance minister appointed Crow's deputy in his place, because Gordon Thiessen was more amenable to a less punishing range for inflation.[9] This episode suggests that, with the appointment power still in its hands, the government of Canada had retained some capacity to harmonize the broad lines of the Bank's monetary policy with its own fiscal policy. It also indicates that the Canadian case is far from a pure example of the neoconservative state.

Canada's Role in Global Banking Governance

The globalized capital market has not just become free from control *by* governments; it exerts considerable control *over* those governments that depend on it for financing their operations, although its size and psyche make it far from rational as a force on the world stage. The volume of transborder capital movements has grown so fast and so far that figures cited to describe its flows are almost beyond comprehension. To report that international capital markets' financing activities went from $400 billion in 1990 to $1.8 trillion in 1997 may have little meaning for most citizens.[10] But the effects of the market's psychology have very great meaning indeed. Exaggerating the boom-bust phenomenon characteristic of national markets, long- and short-term capital has flooded into newly, and often immoderately deregulated, economies only to take flight when some problem, whether real or imagined, causes it to panic. Whether the victim of this footloose capital was Mexico in 1994 or Thailand in 1997 or Brazil in 2001 or Argentina in 2002, the resulting currency crises have had devastating effects in the target economy, decimating the income of its wage earners. Their repercussions have also been virulently contagious, affecting exchange rates and dislocating economies even in the healthiest of states.

Which brings us back to Canada. However balanced its books may be, it is no more immune to the moods of global capital traders than any other country. In the wake of the Asian crisis of 1997–8 the Canadian dollar fell to a historic low of 63.11 cents U.S. – after federal and provincial governments had already reduced their budgetary deficits to well below averages recorded by the industrialized members of the OECD. A chronically undervalued dollar, which depreciated by 25 per cent over the 1990s, is hardly a tribute to the rationality of a market that persists in ignoring not just Canadians' conformity to the dictates of fiscal probity, but the economy's minerals, forests, energy resources, water, safe cities, and well-educated, hard-working population. While some economists continue to offer reassurances that it is 'difficult to believe that market forces will not one day rediscover' Canada's attractive fundamentals,[11] others are resigning themselves to living with a sinking, rather than a floating, currency that could fall to 50 cents U.S.[12] The dollar's irrationally low value is a relatively benign example of the market's persistent misreading of Canada's economic fundamentals. More worrying for policy makers would be a further precipitous fall in the apprehension or aftermath of a successful referendum on Quebec's secession.

This sense of vulnerability to the capricious responses of an unregulated global financial world explains the energetic, rule-making role played by Canada in several international financial institutions. A prime means to buttress global currency stability is the Bank of Canada's participation in committees of the OECD and in the secretive monthly sessions of the Basel Committee on Banking Supervision within the Bank for International Settlement (BIS). This working group of gnomes sets voluntary standards for best practices of transparency and prudential supervision with the hope that better regulation for national banking systems and their more rigorous enforcement will reduce the possibility of national currency crises erupting and spreading around the world in chain reactions. In this case, international cooperation develops rules, such as the Core Principles for Effective Banking Supervision, which are then implemented by national banking supervisors, who require domestic banks to maintain specified levels of capital reserves against their outstanding loans. Global governance in this sector aims to strengthen the member-state. Accordingly, implementing the BIS's proposed regulatory reforms reinforced the monetary authority of the Canadian government and its oversight role over domestic financial institutions.[13]

A parallel indicator of Canada's backroom role in global monetary governance is its Finance Department's active contribution to the IMF and the World Bank. In these institutions, where its voting power is low, Ottawa has developed a solid reputation for contributing well-reasoned, progressive positions favouring more generous and respectful treatment of Third-World countries than Washington generally advocates. At the highly visible annual confabulations of the G7/G8 Economic Summit, Canada has argued with some success for debt relief for the most impoverished nations. This position is consistent with Finance Minister Paul Martin's advocating a reinvigorated international 'architecture' that strengthens Bretton Woods institutions.[14] At the G7/G8 Economic Summit in May 1998 he laid out a plan for an international body for financial surveillance that would provide a response team for new crises and a mechanism for peer review of regulatory regimes for national financial sectors.[15] His efforts hearken back to Canada's role in the creation of the postwar order and can be understood as moving authority up to the global level so as to buttress the federal state's capacity to achieve its domestic policy objectives. As Martin expressed this strategy, 'There is no greater threat to national sovereignty than the threat of financial crisis ... Canada's goal is to defend not only its own sovereignty, but also that of other nations so that all countries will be better placed to offer their citizens protection and stability.'[16]

Towards a Continental Currency?

Although the world currency market – with its high-tech, 24-hour-a-day, instant transmission of billions of dollars in funds – is the most extreme aspect of economic globalization, exchange-rate autonomy is touted as a prime instrument of national policy not only by the continental hegemon but by its two immediate neighbours. Bankers north of the 49th parallel and south of the Rio Grande concede that, as economic integration among the three countries continues to deepen – increasing pressure on the two peripheral countries to harmonize their industrial standards and their external tariffs up or down to U.S. levels – exchange rates can be expected to fluctuate less and long-term interest rates converge more. They concur that policies straying from orthodoxy will in any case be rapidly punished by globalized capital markets. Nevertheless, contrary to Ohmae's prognostication that globalization has made obsolete the traditional instruments of central banks,[17] North America's three sets of banking officials cling to their institutional freedom.

The autonomy case should not be taken too far. The fact that the Bank of Canada operates in a continental dollar zone dictates a high degree of convergence in monetary policy, following a consensus generated in Washington. The Bank of Mexico follows the U.S. lead in most important shifts of monetary policy, unless it wants to be even more conservative than the Fed. This suggests that there is already some kind of virtual continental governance in monetary policy based on autonomous institutions harmonized through close communications.

The revived debate about continental harmonization of currencies serves indirectly to affirm how crucial is the slight degree of freedom still enjoyed by the federal state. A few economists have argued for a North American Monetary Union (NAMU) that would fix the Canadian to the American dollar, emulating to some degree the European Monetary Union. Those favourable to fixing the dollar argue that Canada, with its highly diversified economy, does not need exchange-rate flexibility – an instrument too insensitive to respond to the differing needs within an economy characterized by enormous regional variations.[18]

Such 'fixers' believe that, because the locus of industrial policy is increasingly moving to the provincial and municipal levels, policy made locally will respond more appropriately to local conditions, including the geographically specific fall-out from general economic or political shocks. Other factors – including different government policies – could or should also come into play. Provincial jurisdictions can target many tools of micro-economic policy to stimulate an economic region or sector in distress. While NAFTA prohibits some policies (particularly those that discriminate against foreign-controlled corporations) and the WTO's subsidy code rules out others (particularly those targeted at export promotion or import substitution), high unemployment or low income can justify government intervention that the WTO would otherwise deem protectionist. Since fixers disparage exchange-rate flexibility, it follows that they see little point to the Bank of Canada, whose policy capacity they dismiss as negligible compared to the U.S. Federal Reserve Board, which would control a new NAMU.

The fixers' ideas are still seen as maverick views. A consensus among the experts considers a floating currency preferable to fixing exchange rate. These 'floaters' argue that a flexible exchange rate remains a valuable tool for a government trying to help its economy adjust to untoward supply and demand shocks, whether generated internally or externally. Floaters also contend currency elasticity affords a degree of policy independence that is not worth sacrificing in order to gain such relatively minor advantages offered by pegging as reduced transaction costs – savings on commissions paid for converting Canadian into American dollars. In their view, the Bank of Canada is a legitimate, important, and even indispensable shock absorber in an increasingly integrated global-cum-continental system that permits few other interventions by the state.

Everyone concedes that the Canadian system is closely interlocked with the American. Although their room for manoeuvre is limited, Bank of Canada officials insist their capacity for autonomy is effective precisely because the volume of North America's capital flows is so large that the Canadian section of the market is responsive to the interest-rate fine-tuning that the central bank can still practise. High Canadian-American capital mobility and easy asset substitutability mean that monetary policy can effectively, if indirectly, massage exchange rate levels by manipulating interest rates and affect the market's judgment about resulting price stability. Although the Canadian dollar's persistent undervaluation would seem to belie the Bank's effectiveness in this domain, it is this capacity for sophisticated monitoring and adjusting that would be lost to the national economy from currency union.

While capital markets may be responsive to fine-tuning by separate central banks, the political constituencies in North America are hardly likely to welcome the creation of a continental central bank. Unlike their European counterparts, the states of North America show little inclination to share sovereignty by participating in new supranational institutions. While Americans might tolerate Canada and Mexico's joining a U.S. dollar zone, it is hard to imagine their agreeing to grant their neighbours voting rights in the Federal Reserve Board. Given Argentina's disastrous romance with the U.S. dollar, it is equally improbable that Canada or Mexico would formally adopt the American dollar without gaining a voice in the management of the new continental currency. Having a seat on the Fed would yield Ottawa little influence but cost it the hundreds of millions it makes in 'seigniorage' – the money it pockets by printing currency.

Supporting the floaters' belief in the Bank of Canada's continuing power are those mainstream economists who complained in the early 1990s about the 'made-in-Canada' recession. They explicitly credited the Bank of Canada and its steely Governor Crow with having independently steered a route of monetary austerity more stringent and more prone to generate unemployment than that of the Federal Reserve Board.[19] These neoclassical analysts are joined in their defence of a floating Canadian dollar by more radical economists who consider currency autonomy to have helped insulate Canada from global market pressures and so maintain its relatively more generous social security system. Exchange-rate flexibility after 1970 played a crucial role in protecting the competitiveness of Canadian industry, despite the rise in its labour costs relative to the United States.[20]

Politically, too, the 1990s built strong latent support for currency autonomy. Had the Canadian dollar not fallen drastically following its initial post-free trade spike, CUFTA and NAFTA most probably would have caused far more long-lasting damage than they did. Canada's unwilled, irrational, but persistent devaluation sweetened the bitter pill of trade-induced restructuring by providing a far greater stimulus to exports and a far higher restraint on imports than the reduction of already low American and Canadian tariffs would have induced. Business organizations appreciate that the low dollar accounts for much new foreign direct investment in Canada. Labour unions, concur but are also sensitive to the fact that NAMU is promoted by people arguing it would increase pressure on workers to moderate wage demands.[21] Neither side of the management boundary is likely to favour fixing the Canadian dollar under these conditions.

In effect, bank, treasury, and finance officials in the three countries already form a continental chapter of the global fraternity of financial officials – reading the same books, thinking the same thoughts, convening in the same conferences,[22] and persuading their respective political masters and publics that low inflation achieved through tight monetary discipline should trump low unemployment as the number-one policy priority.

It may be that a middle-to-large power enjoys more influence on global monetary matters through its participation in these many-membered global institutions than it would in a three-member continental NAMU, in which its GDP represented but 8 per cent of the total continental product. While trilateral, continental integration driven from below by market forces proceeds apace in North America, its three members are willing to sacrifice exchange-rate stability in order to retain what for them is the greater good of autonomy in monetary policy. At the multilateral level, the central bank has become a transmission belt for redefining the Canadian state's relationship with the global economy. But as a participant in global financial governance, it reinforces its own role as a substantial organ of the federal state, which also acts through its Finance Department in international financial organizations. In its own financial institutions, the Canadian state still retains considerable strength both at the federal and at the global levels of governance.

The story of the Canadian state is somewhat different when it comes to regulating the private financial sector and telecommunications, where the state was once supreme but has retreated in considerable confusion.

THE OLIGOPOLISTIC ECONOMY
AND THE REGULATORY STATE

The Department of Finance concerned itself under Keynesianism with macroeconomic fine-tuning but restricted itself under neoliberalism to taxation matters. The government was also actively involved through its central bank in watching over its currency through managing the money supply and setting interest rates. Beyond trying to set the conditioning framework within which the economy operated, the Canadian state has played an active role in regulating particular industrial sectors that have been considered crucial to the economy's performance.

The shift in regulatory policy from the Diefenbaker-Pearson-Trudeau period to the Mulroney-Chrétien era can be monitored by comparing the approaches taken during these periods by the Department of Communication and the Canadian-Radio-Television and Telecommunications Commission to regulating the telephone industry. In the last twenty years the telecommunications sector has been transformed by interdependent factors ranging from changing business needs and tempestuous rates of technological innovation to emerging international trade regimes. These forces pushed the Canadian state to abandon its long-held doctrine that the telephone created a natural monopoly – which had therefore to be regulated – and to follow the American path towards deregulation as the means to promote corporate competition in the telecom industry. Continental and global policy norms came to exercise significant influence over decision makers within Canada, whose ultimate goal was to transfer power to the private sector. The outcome has meant momentous change in government's regulatory policies and in the structure and functions of the industry (chapter 10).

For financial services, the Department of Finance and other federal agencies have played an active part, with the Bank of Canada retaining a major role in the wings, and the provinces, a residual regulatory. It is the portentous changes in this central sector that chapter 9 shall now consider.

9 Financial Services: National Champions at Risk

Banks are central to states in a myriad of ways. Bank edifices are among the biggest and sometimes most beautiful buildings in a community, rural or urban, to which they help give identity. Bankers play central roles in the power elite of the same communities to which they provide several crucial functions. Banks mediate between savers and investors. They provide a mechanism that allows payments to be made between purchasers and sellers or between employers and employees. Banks generate employment both directly and indirectly through their use of many other services. And they contribute through charitable donations to local cultural life. (The financial services industry is actually the country's second-largest taxpayer, paying 9 per cent of all corporate taxes, and is the second-largest source of charitable donations, which total some $120 million.)[1] As we saw in chapter 8, a country's central bank manages the supply and price (interest rate) of the money that banks handle and helps maintain the whole economic system's integrity and stability.

Banks have been central, too, in Canadian history as one of its great success stories, tracing their roots to the financing needs of a staple-exporting economy and the policies of the nascent state. Granted charters by colonial administrators, commercial banks made fortunes for their owners by issuing bank notes and providing short-term credit for the relatively low-risk needs of the timber and wheat trade or for merchants importing necessities for settlers. The 'chartered' banks remained averse to assuming the long-term risks involved in taking equity shares in manufacturing, unlike banks, for example, in Germany. They had also been shielded by the colonial authorities, which repressed radical movements demanding the kind of community-based financing that, in the United States, led banks to be more responsive to local entrepreneurial initiative.[2] Budding Canadian industrialists were left to the tender mercies of the embryonic stock exchanges to find capital for industrial development.

By 1900, Canadian bankers had induced the Dominion government to diverge more drastically from the American model of state banking by allowing them to expand through mergers and achieve the economies of scale that resulted from establishing nation-wide branching networks. As a result, Canada's banking landscape in the twentieth century was dominated by a few large institutions that operated deposit-taking branches from coast to coast. By the beginning of the new millennium the financial system stood out as having survived domestic recessions and international turmoil.

The collapse of the capitalist economy following the stock market crash of 1929 caused the Canadian state to intervene more boldly than it had ever done before. The federal government's modern role in the financial services industry dates back to this shattering crisis, from which came the establishment in 1935 of a central bank, following recommendations made by the McMillan Commission.[3] Once the Bank of Canada appropriated some of the chartered banks' functions vis-à-vis money supply, the federal government became progressively more active in the regulation of the private sector's remaining activities.[4] To prevent the self dealing that had helped fuel a boom and then triggered the bust of 1929, government policies prohibited cross-ownership among the four major 'pillars' in financial services (banks, trusts, insurance companies, and investment brokers). By the time that the ideas of Lord Keynes had become conventional wisdom among the elites of the Atlantic world, Canada's financial-services sector was heavily regulated and rigidly segmented into these four watertight compartments.

Their legislated barriers did not prevent the four sectors from constantly lobbying government to maintain, adjust, or abandon them, depending on what served their interests. For example, the Bank Act of 1967 again broke from the American mould by eliminating the 6 per cent ceiling on loan rates. This allowed the chartered banks to expand their residential mortgage financing. At the same time, Parliament created the Canadian Deposit Insurance Corporation (CDIC) to protect depositors in all provinces except Quebec, which established its own insurance scheme.

Canada has directed its comparatively modest level of financial regulation – the United States had about ten times the number of inspectors, because American institutions were so much smaller and more numerous – at achieving a large number of objectives such as managing the money supply, maintaining an efficient payment system, protecting depositors against bank failure, supervising financial institutions' viability, and maintaining their competitiveness as well as efficiency.

Sometimes these aims have conflicted with each other. Providing the public efficient, low-cost banking services may require fostering competition. One of the 1967 Bank Act's objectives was to increase competition by encouraging new banks. The legislation was successful, but all the new banks went bankrupt. If introducing more competition turns out to mean urging foreign banks to enter the marketplace, this may undermine the Bank of Canada's capacity to effect a monetary policy. Making capital markets function smoothly for entrepreneurs may also suggest the need for more foreign banks competing to offer loans to small business. But protecting the chartered banks in the home market from excessive competition may be the most efficacious method that the state can use to encourage them to be *internationally* competitive risk takers.[5] Helping banks to compete globally may also require allowing them to merge, but mergers will reduce *internal* competition and jeopardize consumers' needs for good service (many branches) and good prices (low banking charges).

When the Keynesian state confronted these dilemmas, it favoured stability and safety over efficiency and competitiveness. In the banking sector, the half-dozen chartered banks operated as an exclusive club linked intimately to the federal government's central bank, which managed the money supply, and its Finance Department, which presided over the periodic rewriting of the crucial legislation for the pillars in its charge – the Bank Act, the Trust and Loans Act, the Insurance Company Act, and the Co-operative Credit Association Act. In its own boosterist rhetoric, the department seeks to achieve a 'legislative and regulatory environment in which the financial sector can meet and beat the challenges it faces, in which it can seize new opportunities and in which all Canadians can enjoy the benefits of a world-class financial system.'[6]

By the early 1960s, Canada's prudential public policy had created a lopsided banking relationship with the outside world. On the one hand, Canada's capital markets had been integrated within the U.S.

market centred in New York since the turn of the nineteenth century. Canadian insurance companies and banks had long operated transnationally, developing niches in the United States, the Caribbean, Latin America, and London. For all this openness, Canada's financial system had remained largely insulated from outside competition for both historical and political reasons, and so the chartered banks, along with the trusts and brokerages, were held widely and in Canadian hands. Foreign capital was solidly implanted only in the insurance industry.

During the Pearson years, Ottawa took a more defiant step to defend Canadian banks from foreign takeovers following a dramatic confrontation between Finance Minister Walter Gordon and Stillman Rockefeller, president of Citibank, who had wanted to buy control of Mercantile, a small Dutch bank's Canadian subsidiary. The Bank Act of 1967 prohibited foreign banks from operating agencies, branches, or subsidiaries in Canada.[7] Foreigners could not own more than 25 per cent of a Canadian bank. Nor could any individual own more than 10 per cent of a chartered bank. While foreign financial institutions did enter the Canadian economy under provincial jurisdiction, they could not aspire to compete at the retail level with the chartered banks, which had massive competitive advantages in having already invested in the physical bricks and mortar needed to run branch networks.

Nevertheless by the late 1970s, some one hundred foreign institutions had incorporated provincially as non-bank financial affiliates. Since these 'non-banks' were carrying on business outside the Bank Act, they were not required to maintain reserves with the Bank of Canada, giving them a 50- to 75-basis-point advantage over the Canadian-owned chartered banks in the corporate lending business.[8] Ottawa responded to this unexpected consequence by bringing foreign banks under 'Schedule B' of the Bank Act of 1980 and by making them participating members – along with the chartered, 'Schedule A' banks – in a new cheque-clearing system called the Canadian Payments Association, which had previously been self-managed by the Canadian Bankers Association.[9] Having unlocked the door to foreign banking, Ottawa made sure that it was kept barely ajar. Schedule B banks were limited in their growth potential by ceilings on their total assets and by having to be separately capitalized subsidiaries of existing foreign banks. Although Schedule B banks were not subject to the same 25 per cent maximum of foreign ownership as were the large, chartered banks, the new mechanism prevented them from competing equally with the Canadian-owned chartered banks.

New legislative amendments in 1980 permitted the Schedule A banks to diversify functionally by participating in leasing, venture capital, and mortgage loan companies. This let them position themselves to compete directly with Schedule B subsidiaries such as the Hong Kong Bank of Canada and Citibank and so ensured that banking remained predominantly Canadian.[10] Thanks in part to the massive number of mergers in the American and European banking industries, there were just forty-four foreign bank subsidiaries operating in Canada by 1998, with just 8 per cent market share, down from fifty-six in 1991. Only the Hong Kong Bank of Canada had an extensive branch network with a significant share of the market. By the late 1990s, these foreign banks still controlled only some 10 per cent of domestic assets.[11] By the early 1980s, when Keynesianism was perceptibly failing, Canada's banks were still few in number, large, profitable, efficient, and domestically controlled. This comfortable arrangement had proven a huge success. But many factors were jeopardizing their enviable situation.

Their centrality was no longer what it used to be. As the relentless process of corporate cannibalization through mergers and acquisitions continued, neither rural nor urban communities could be sure that *their* bank or trust company, stock broker or credit union, with which they had had a personal relationship, would still be there for them another year. As new information technologies allowed financial institutions to operate across longer distances, banks did not even need to be physically present in a given territory in order to operate there. The implication was that banks would not continue to provide the visual, social, or entrepreneurial backbone for individual communities' political economies.

Many other financial institutions could now play roles similar to banks. Brokerage houses could mediate between saving and investment by selling equities to the public and so raising capital for corporations. Insurance companies could offer investment opportunities to clients via mutual funds. Even the Bank of Canada was losing its ability to control the money market as non-Canadian banks responded to priorities of their home governments or head offices. Other state regulators who could not control financial institutions operating from abroad resorted to multilateral agreements in their continuing efforts to supervise the operations in their territory of nationally or foreign-owned banks' often high-risk operations.

In response to this changed conjuncture, the Canadian state reversed its role in banking. From a defensive, inward-looking posture, it shifted to a Janus-like stance that looked both outward, as it participated in making co-ordinated, multilateral agreements, and inward, as it implemented these commitments in the attempt to adjust its financial institutions to their new, globalized and competitive context.

Changing the Paradigm without Changing the Guard

With capital markets, production processes, and distribution systems becoming globalized, the Canadian chartered banks found that they had to reinforce their international operations if they were to support their corporate clients as they transnationalized. Besides, more and more banks were becoming international. An added incentive to favour foreign markets was the prospect of achieving higher returns and raising extra capital abroad. Already by 1980 non-traditional operations accounted for 19 per cent of chartered banks' revenue and were moving up to 50 per cent by the end of the century. The chartered banks invested billions of dollars to expand in the United States, with each one following a different strategy to develop a niche in this large market that was fragmented by each state regulating its own banks. They did not limit themselves to the United States. By 1992, 30 per cent of their assets were offshore – that is outside North America.[12] By 1999 they would be earning 40 per cent of their revenue from abroad.[13] All these efforts notwithstanding, they were actually losing position in the global pecking order. By 1982 the five largest banks had fallen to 17th (Royal), 30th (CIBC), 34th (Montreal), 45th (Scotiabank), and 59th (Toronto-Dominion).

Going global didn't mean that they were about to give up their home turf, where their dominance was challenged. Competing monetary instruments were eating into their deposit-taking operations. Because of the growth of money-market mutual funds, their share of total deposits had fallen from 80 per cent in the 1950s to 55 per cent by the late 1980s.[14] Facing competition on the domestic front from foreign credit-card services, small business lenders (such as Wells Fargo), virtual banks (such as ING), and even non-regulated entities (such as GE Capital), they agitated for legislative and regulatory changes that would let them pre-empt this competitive thrust and grow at home as well. Unless they could expand domestically, they argued, they would have inadequate resources with which to invest in the technologies necessary for survival.[15] They promised synergies if they could service all the needs of a corporate borrower, and they lobbied specifically for permission to underwrite securities so that they could then compete with 'universal' or 'full-service' investment banks abroad.

Federal and provincial officials responded to these domestic pressures within a consolidating international consensus in the epistemic community of high finance about the need for deregulation (removing barriers to allow foreign competition) and reregulation (increased prudential supervision to enhance systemic stability). At the same time they were also pushed by the actions of other states, which were trying to change their own financial systems in the hope of gaining a globally competitive edge. This explains why Canadian governments appear actually to have defied the putatively irreversible, state-shrinking logic of globalization and increased their regulatory and supervisory control over financial services.

The provinces, which regulate investment houses and share with Ottawa regulatory power over trust companies, were the first to move. Competing with each other at a time when Montreal was hoping to recapture from Toronto its dominance in the Canadian economy, Quebec and Ontario took steps on their own to restructure the securities sector under their jurisdiction.

The securities industry, which provides a market for corporate equity and debt, had been protected from ownership by Canadian banks or foreign investment banks. It, too, was an oligopoly, self-regulated, in this case, by the Investment Dealers Association of Canada. Despite their legislated separation, banks and investment dealers had been penetrating each others' core business areas, with brokerages offering interest on credit balances and banks competing directly for bond issues. Corporations were alarming the banks by making increased use of the capital markets instead of borrowing. Securities markets had *deepened* with the introduction of new products such as derivatives to allow hedging against risk.[16] Investment dealers needed larger amounts of capital in order successfully to operate in riskier world securities markets that had themselves *widened* with the deregulation that had taken place in New York and with London's 'big bang' deregulation of the City in 1986. The liberalization of these highly competitive systems put pressure on Canada's provinces – particularly Ontario and Quebec, which also housed important stock exchanges – to follow suit.

Under the aegis of Jacques Parizeau, first as Liberal bureaucrat then as Péquiste finance minister, Quebec had developed a desegmentation strategy to promote indigenous financial conglomerates on the universal banking model. It opened the floodgates in 1986 by permitting Scotiabank to set up its own securities subsidiary. Faced with the threat that the other chartered banks would establish brokerages in Quebec, Ontario hastily opened up its own securities legislation. In December 1986, Ontario suddenly allowed brokerages to be owned by foreigners as well as by banks and trust companies. Ottawa was swept along by this first wave of competitive deregulation. Coincident with Ontario, federal legislation allowed banks and federally chartered trust and life insurance companies to own securities firms.[17] Although foreign brokerages could now legally move into the Canadian market, the chartered banks effected a quick operation of defensive expansionism. Pre-empting their Wall Street competitors, five of the six chartered banks purchased the main securities dealers, while the TD Bank set up its own investment subsidiary. Within three years the 'big six' accounted for over 80 per cent of the country's corporate underwriting business.

In the wake of this 'desegmentation,' Ottawa moved to strengthen its prudential powers. In 1987 it merged the Office of the Inspector General of Banks with the Department of Insurance to form the Office of the Superintendent of Financial Institutions with enlarged responsibilities and powers for overseeing all federally chartered financial institutions. Its 'Standards for Sound Business and Financial Practices,' which have the force of law, cover such issues as liquidity, credit risks, and securities management. The CDIC's mandate was also expanded to promote sound practices among all insured firms, federal or provincial, that held deposits for customers.[18]

Hot on the heels of the liberalization of the securities industry, the late 1980s brought the banking industry its first international agreement that linked finance to trade. Constituting one of its most powerful economic sectors, Canada's banks could have been expected to make major gains in a Canadian-American free trade mega-deal. But the rush to deregulate the securities industry and allow foreign ownership of the brokerage houses deprived Ottawa's negotiators of bargaining power in this sector. With the chips already given away for nothing, the chartered banks had no chance of achieving the *reciprocity* they coveted with the United States. The right to operate in the United States in the same way as they did in Canada would have let them launch multi-state, multi-function banking operations in the American market. In the event, they were granted only *national treatment*, which meant they still remained constrained under the laws of the individual U.S. state in which they were located. Consequently, CUFTA's extension of national treatment to financial services did little to alter the position of Canadian banks within the United States while giving American banks significant concessions in Canada.

CUFTA's chapter on financial services exempted U.S.-owned Schedule B banks from the Bank Act's limits on the expansion of their domestic assets, gave them access to the formerly protected auto-leasing sector and the right to use Canadian ATM and INTERAC networks. These 'non-banks' would no longer require ministerial approval to open branches.[19] Nor would they be bound by the 25 per cent maximum foreign ownership applied to Canadian chartered banks. This concession did not represent an immediate gain for U.S. banks, because the 10 per cent rule protected the big six from any takeovers except by each other and ensured that banking in Canada would continue to be a cosy, highly concentrated, and extremely profitable oligopoly.

With the Bank Act of 1992, the federal government took further steps towards desegmentation in its response to moves made by other states in promoting their financial-services sector. Henceforth, any federally chartered financial institution could provide almost any financial service. Ottawa achieved this state of affairs primarily by allowing one type of institution to own a subsidiary in another financial field. The new legislation permitted financial institutions to diversify through new in-house business and subsidiaries while preserving their traditional core functions.[20] This reregulation allowed Schedule A (rechristened 'Schedule I') banks to enter the trust and insurance businesses, trusts to expand their commercial lending, and insurance companies to own a bank.

With the regulatory barriers between the four pillars disintegrating, Canadian banks, insurance companies, mutual funds, credit unions, trust companies, caisses populaires, and other financial service providers adopted a multitude of strategies aimed at securing their long-term growth in a transformed environment. These strategies included introduction of new services, increased use of new technologies, acquisitions across sectors, and mergers between competitors within the same sector. As a result, banks now own securities dealers, trust companies, and insurance companies – although they cannot distribute insurance products in their branches. The earth had moved, Canada's four-pillar architecture had collapsed, and the chartered banks emerged owning not just all the major brokerages but virtually all the trust companies as well.

From Continentalism to Globalism

Rules were changing at both the continental and the multilateral levels. By signing NAFTA, Canada extended to Mexican banks the benefits that U.S. banks obtained under CUFTA, but this concession had little impact on Canada's banking landscape. Although Canadian banks were permitted full access to Mexico's market under its Law on Credit Institutions, passed in 1995 to fulfill Mexico's supraconstitutional NAFTA obligations, only the Bank of Montreal and Scotiabank chose to enter that market aggressively.[21]

Canadian bankers' real gains in NAFTA came from their getting the American states bound by national treatment. More important is their being in a position to exploit U.S. deregulation when amendments to the Glass-Steagall Act removed the barriers between banks, securities, insurance, and trust companies. Supraconstitutional change and Washington's domestic reforms sparked massive investment south of the border by Canadian banks, which spent over $10 billion there in the first seven years after NAFTA.[22]

With the tripling of cross-border trade in financial services between 1985 and 1995, the WTO's General Agreement on Trade in Services (GATS) represented a first step towards bringing 95 per cent of global trade in financial services under the purview of powerfully liberalizing international rules. But because of banking's centrality to national economies, most states were reluctant to abandon their regulatory powers. As a result, a 'prudential carve-out' provided an exemption from GATS strictures for government measures taken to protect investors and deposit holders or to ensure the integrity and stability of the domestic financial system. The provision is so general that it partially protected countries wanting to limit foreign investors' access to their markets.[23] Dissatisfied with this impediment, the major banking powers pressed for further negotiations.

The WTO's resulting Financial Services Industry Agreement of December 1997, which contained specific commitments for opening their markets by its 102 signatories, presents another example of Canada's capacity to portray itself as a good world citizen opening its market to foreign competition, while actually protecting its own national champions. Giving voice to its WTO commitment to eliminate ceilings on foreign ownership of trusts and chartered banks, Parliament amended the Bank Act in 1997 to allow any large and experienced foreign banks to establish operations in Canada without having to set up separately capitalized subsidiaries. It also removed the requirement that non-NAFTA foreign-bank subsidiaries operating in Canada seek authorization before opening additional branch offices.[24]

Although NAFTA and the WTO established continental and global norms that created supraconstitutional direction of member states' financial services regulation, the federal government still exercised substantial autonomous control over Canada's industry. While these continental and global agreements created new rights for foreign financial transnational corporations, they did not immediately alter the relative weight in Canada of foreign banks. Their possibilities for expansion apparently remained limited because of the state's defensive and offensive measures on behalf of the chartered banks. Defensively, the latter enjoyed the continued protection of Schedule I's 10 per cent single-owner limit. Offensively, desegmentation had allowed them to expand in the domestic economy through the economies of scope achieved by acquiring trust and brokerage companies. By the mid-1990s they had regained their historic share of total deposits and had increased their share of the residential mortgage market to 55 per cent.[25]

While some of the proposed reforms (allowing credit unions to band together in a national network and giving insurance companies and brokerages access to the Canadian payments system) strengthened competition for them, the big banks were allowed to set up holding companies within which they could enjoy greater flexibility and competitiveness. For instance, if a bank operated an insurance firm within its holding company, the insurance operations would not be bound by the stricter rules governing banks' assets.

Ottawa's regulatory activity reflects a continuing effort to maintain a delicate balance. The federal government made a concerted effort to keep the banking sector profitable, stable, and dominant vis-à-vis its foreign competitors, while responding to seismic shifts in technology, international competition, and the corporate behaviour of the financial sectors. At the same time, it was sensitive to the public's concerns about availability of service, its price, and its strong preference for keeping the banks in Canadian hands. In this central economic sector, neither globalization nor neoconservatism had caused the state to collapse. Rather, it has redefined itself. A concrete example of the dilemmas of government policy in this field is offered by Toronto, which is a success story poised on the brink of possible failure.

Toronto's Banks

To give the abstract notion of banking some concrete meaning, we can shift our discussion from the policy level to the question of the banking sector's impact on the Greater Toronto Area (GTA), for whose economy its financial services have enormous importance.

The financial services' impact on Toronto's economic geography is symbolically obvious from its skyline: many of the tallest skyscrapers are bank buildings densely concentrated in the downtown core, whose cultural life they help sustain. For starters, they make the second-largest contribution (after manufacturing) to the region's GDP, and are its fifth-largest employer (after manufacturing, retail, hospitality and entertainment, and health and welfare).[26] Translated into aggregate numbers, financial services contribute 165,000 jobs and $12.2 billion per year to the regional economy. These jobs are mainly at the 'high end,' requiring strong qualifications, yielding high salaries, and providing considerable stability. Because of the large proportion of financial businesses with their headquarters in the GTA (75 per cent of Canadian banks and 70 per cent of Canadian insurance-companies), they offer the greatest managerial and entrepreneurial challenge for their personnel.

More important, the clustering of these company headquarters has generated a self-reinforcing circle of innovation, competition, and sophisticated skills, that generate new business development. This entrepreneurial creativity typically takes the form of spinoff ventures, in which financial services stimulate related economic sectors. In numbers, this means 158,000 other jobs and $8.6 billion per year in cluster benefits through the sector's demand for such necessities as telecommunications, software, and computer specialists. One in every five lawyers and accountants in the city, for instance, depends on the financial sector. These static figures do not transmit the dynamic quality of the financial services' impact. The GTA's financial services are the second-fastest-growing centre in North America after New York, giving it, at 9 per cent of all financial centres' GDP in North America, the third-highest concentration of financial services after New York (with 24 per cent) and San Francisco (10 per cent), but ahead of Chicago (8 per cent), and Philadelphia and Minneapolis (7 per cent each).

All these indicators make concrete the oft-heard statement that services in general and financial services in particular are one of the local economy's main drivers. This said, any euphoria must be quickly qualified by the problem of the region's high vulnerability to the loss of this golden-egg-laying goose. The problem lies in the fact that a large proportion of the work done in the GTA's financial services could be done elsewhere. In economists' terminology, these 'traded' services compete with firms in other regions or bring in new wealth by substituting for imports from outside the GTA.

Some 25 per cent of the GTA's industry – corporate finance, security and currency trading, equities research, mutual fund management – are *traded internationally*, meaning that they compete against similar services offered in New York, Chicago, and London, and so are vulnerable to foreign banks capturing the business. U.S. firms are aggressively tapping into the huge and lucrative Canadian mutual fund market. The giant New York investment bankers have set up shop in the heart of Toronto's financial district, where they already dominate the market for very large public offerings such as the IPOs of privatized crown corporations.

Another 30 per cent of Toronto's financial service operations – back-office support, head-office functions of domestic firms, insurance underwriting – are *traded nationally*, and hence vulnerable to relocation within Canada. This means that 55 per cent of the GTA's jobs in financial services could be performed elsewhere in the country, particularly as new technologies facilitate functional dispersion. New Brunswick has already attracted the back-office function of call centres. Calgary is energetically courting corporate headquarters.

Toronto's ability to maintain its status as a secondary international centre in the continental hierarchy will depend substantially on its capacity to retain head offices both of the chartered banks themselves and of their client corporations. To some extent it will hang on the dynamism of the Toronto Stock Exchange, still the second largest in North America after New York's. The gravitational threat of the American stock markets can be seen in the 217 Canadian firms whose shares are listed south of the border. While 23 per cent of Canadian firms were raising capital in the United States in 1990, more than twice as many were looking south just seven years later. As major corporations turn south for financing, Toronto must develop a distinctive continental niche on the model of Chicago's specialization in derivatives.

The future of Toronto's cluster of financial services will also be affected by related sectors – the software industry and telecommunications, to name the most crucial. Their fate in turn will depend on the quality of the region's physical, human, and social infrastructure and its public policy environment. It is the latter issue that is the most perplexing for Canadian governments.

For the public policy areas cited in its study of Toronto's financial services, the Boston Consulting Group recommended international promotion efforts, tax policy neutrality, university technical training, excellent transportation and fibre optics, and harmonizing of the regulatory regime both vertically (between the federal and the provincial governments) and horizontally (among the provinces). It did not mention the 10 per cent rule.

International institutions, foreign governments, and financial firms had been demanding reciprocal access to the Canadian market. In the legion of revisions to the Bank Act passed into law in 2001, Finance Minister Paul Martin gave way. Under his new legislation, an investor – meaning any global corporation – may now hold up to 30 per cent of a chartered bank's non-voting shares and 20 per cent of its voting shares. According to the accounting profession, holding 20 per cent of the voting stock of a widely held firm represents effective control over it.[27] Ottawa had opened the possibility of the big six's shifting from Canadian to foreign hands. With the 10 per cent limit removed, larger foreign competitors could swallow up the chartered banks. Whether these were American or overseas banks, Canada would lose its chartered banks' headquarters. Without major head offices in Toronto and Montreal, these financial centres would fall into decline, following the examples of Philadelphia and Los Angeles after the takeover of their banks.[28]

This spectre has been obscured by the more immediate spectacle of the chartered banks' turning their enormous appetite for mergers and acquisitions on themselves. In quick succession, the Royal Bank and the Bank of Montreal, then the CIBC and the TD, announced their decisions to merge. The prospect of these mega-mergers' impending transformation of Canada's banking system shook up the long-standing market-state relationship that has supported its historic success.

Merger Mania

After six decades of cosy rapport between the regulated and the regulator, the Department of Finance under globalization seemed to have turned its back on its long-time clients, showing a surprising capacity to withstand their pressure and obstruct their development. The Task Force on the Future of the Canadian Financial Services Sector favoured creating a more equal playing field between foreign and domestic banks by allowing the chartered banks to consolidate within a deregulated market.[29] Even in the face of data showing that Canada's banks had fast been losing ground compared to their international competitors despite a frenzy of mergers and acquisitions between 1993 and 1996, Ottawa refused to grant four of Canada's biggest six banks the right to merge.[30]

This was not just because of estimates that 1,000 of their 8,000 branches would close and 20,000 to 40,000 jobs would disappear.[31] Beyond the political pressure from voters concerned about these realities, the government had serious competitive concerns. Trust and mutual fund assets under these banks' management, combined with their own assets, would amount to about $1 trillion, which is greater than the Canadian GDP.[32] Provincial securities regulators would have had difficulty supervising a market underwriting stocks and bonds dominated by a duopoly. The federal government also had reason for concern about the two behemoth banks dominating the auction of its own bonds and treasury bills and about endangering the entire financial system should either of them get into trouble. Banks make blunders, particularly in taking international risks. The implications of bailing out a vast bank on the point of failing outweighed the banks' plea that they needed to be bigger to reap the economies of scale, offer their global clients one-stop services, and afford the investments in new technology they needed to compete internationally.

The old oligopoly's collusive relationship with the state had changed even though the five largest chartered banks accounted for 85 per cent of the banking sector's profits and 76 per cent of its domestic market share.[33] No longer did they receive government's unthinking support. By 1992 they had 30 per cent of their assets and 68 per cent of their bonds placed offshore. Canada in fact accounts for more global bond trading than the United States – 31 per cent in 1994, compared to 19 per cent by the United States.[34] Canadian banks had expanded aggressively in the United States, buying 'platforms' to develop their niches. The Bank of Montreal targeted the U.S. midwest as an untapped market, acquiring in 1984 Harris Bank of Chicago, whose base of operations is at the centre of the eight-state region that accounts for nearly half of Canada's trade with the United States. In planning to become a North American bank, it recognized 'that economic borders don't always line up with political borders, and that internal economies, like the Great Lakes regional economy, can be more cohesive than national economies.'[35] The TD Bank bought three discount brokerages, the Royal focused on wealth management, while CIBC acquired the investment bank Oppenheimer & Co. Non-conformist, Scotiabank has concentrated on retail and commercial banking in the Western hemisphere outside the United States.[36] The coincidence of interest between the two sets of players was no longer identical. Viewed from Ottawa, it was no longer obvious that they should be bailed out if one of them failed. The more the big banks follow high-risk strategies to increase their profits,[37] the more they threaten the national system's stability. Mutual deference was no longer the order of the day. Ottawa's interest in internal competition among banks counterbalanced its concerns about their external competitiveness.

The banks' loss of deference for Ottawa could be measured by their CEOs' not bothering to inform the minister of finance before announcing their decisions to merge. So powerful were they that they assumed Ottawa would sanction the deals. But the two mega-banks would have controlled 75 per cent of the chartered banks' assets – a level of concentration not approached in other developed economies.[38] Their planned efficiencies translated politically as the loss of jobs and the closing of branches in communities across the country. Their greater global competitiveness meant higher bank charges to generate higher profits.

One could observe Ottawa's loss of deference for the banks in the finance minister's anger at finding himself sandbagged by the proposed mergers, in the competition bureau's thorough investigation of their economic implications, and even in the Liberal caucus's Task Force on Financial Institutions which held its own hearings and issued a negative opinion on the venture. Ottawa's reform package released in June 1999 denied permission for banks to sell insurance or to offer direct automobile financing from their branches, even though the government's own task force recommended the previous autumn that they be allowed into those businesses.[39] Martin vetoed the merger.

Conclusion

The Canadian state has been engaged in a prolonged and precarious balancing act. The evolution of global governance in financial services shows that the federal government has redistributed its former sovereignty in domestic regulatory control through the international definition and co-ordination of rules governing national banking while strengthening, at the provinces' expense, its capacity for both prudential and competitive objectives. On the strength of these new, multilaterally established norms, states have instituted more formalized regulatory controls over the domestic market.

The extra strength acquired by Ottawa through this reregulation may be more apparent than real. Capital traverses borders much more easily than do financial institutions whose movements national regulations monitor and constrain. For instance, cross-border transactions in bonds and equities have escalated from 64 per cent of Canada's GDP in 1990 to 235 per cent in 1998.[40] Instruments of control may also be less effective: with current speed and volumes of capital flows, disclosure rules may work too slowly to be effective. The government of Canada has refused so far to abdicate its prerogative to regulate corporate conduct in an effort to balance considerations of monetary management, consumer protection, internal systemic stability, protection from market volatility, and domestic ownership. The Bank of Canada's influence over the money supply has become less effective because increasing numbers of the banks operating within Canadian territorial limits respond more to incentives coming from outside those borders than to its interest-rate signals.

All these caveats notwithstanding, Canada's banking system – 'one of the most efficient, stable, and competitive in the world'[41] – appears safe and sound. Service charges are one-third lower than in the United States, and interest-rate spreads are the lowest in the English-speaking world.[42] Even if its five champions have slipped further down the global totem poll to 49th (Royal), 51st (CIBC), 54th (Montreal), 58th (Scotiabank), and 69th (TD) in respective assets, they still rank 9th, 10th, 11th, 12th, and 13th in North America. They have made the Greater Toronto Area a textbook example of how home-based companies, protected and supported by appropriate public policies, can have a positive effect throughout the national economy and its societal environment.

Under globalizing pressures, it is not clear whether the federal state has jeop-ardized its own capacity to maintain control over competitive conditions in financial services. For the present, Ottawa remains very much in charge, but it may be poised to follow the pattern that it set in telecommunications, when it appropriated power from the provinces as a step towards conceding control of the industry to globally oriented, foreign-owned corporations.

10 Telecoms: From Regional Monopolies to Global Oligopolies

Where financial services supplied the veins and arteries carrying the economy's blood supply, the telegraph and telephone used to be understood as a society's nervous system. Without an ability to communicate, individuals cannot form a community, create a market, or generate its common culture. In mass industrial societies, the capacity to communicate over long distances enabled states to operate their political system, to maintain their social cohesion, to promote their economic development, and to cultivate a national identity. So crucial were communications to the nascent Dominion's hopes for political, social, economic, and cultural development that it followed the example of most European states in creating a postal service as a federal government monopoly to provide inexpensive – that is, heavily subsidized – mail delivery for all its citizens, urban or rural.[1]

With the advent of signal transmission over wire leading to the non-voiced telegraph and then the telephone, European states typically integrated these new communications capacities within their state-owned postal systems. The telephone was quickly understood to be a natural monopoly because it was more efficient for one entity to offer 'end-to-end' service, providing the handsets for the speaker, installing the wiring, controlling the switching equipment, and delivering the sounds to the listener's ear.[2] In the process, the monopoly would achieve economies of scale and so lower average costs.

Given its federal division of jurisdiction, Canada's situation diverged from Europe's in two important ways. Telephone corporations were established as regional, generally province-based, monopolies. With three exceptions, they were run privately; one was even foreign-owned. These 'common carriers' provided facilities for the transmission of non-voice data traffic (such as telegraph, stock market, and news wire services), but voiced telephone signals constituted the major part of their telecommunications business.[3]

Since monopolies can exploit their dominance to gouge the public by increasing prices and reducing services where costs are high, governments set up regulatory bodies to establish rules for phone companies' behaviour and to control prices on the services that they offered. Balancing the need for economic efficiency for business against the social equity consideration of cheap and equal access for all, a system of cross-subsidization emerged, with below-cost local phone charges in cities and relatively above-cost prices charged for long-distance calls, financing loss-making services to far-flung rural communities.

As complex and fragmented as Canada's phone system was for the bulk of the twentieth century, it was a phenomenal success, both socially and economically. By the time that Keynesianism reached its apogee, 98 per cent of Canadians had telephones, the second-highest degree of universality after Sweden.[4] The social policy goal of achieving universal, affordable access had produced significant economies of scale, despite the large investments needed for installing wires over huge distances. The costs for residential users were among the lowest in the world.[5]

Phone companies were big employers. As large corporations in a leading industry, they invested in technology and played an incubator role, spinning off related operations, the most successful being equipment manufacturing.[6] From 1945 to 1984, labour productivity in telecommunications grew at an average annual rate of 6 per cent.[7] By 1997 the industry employed 145,000 workers, had revenues of $18 billion per year, or 3 per cent of GDP, spent $180 million on research and development (R&D), and was still maintaining a rate of growth of 6 per cent.[8]

The industry consisted of eighty-one systems of enormously disparate size, sixteen of which earned more than 98 per cent of the industry's revenues. Federally regulated, but privately owned, Bell Canada was the largest, accounting with its networks in Ontario and Quebec for more than 55 per cent of industry-wide revenues.[9] It had attained this dominance thanks to ruthless business practices and aggressive lobbying, which had yielded extraordinary government-accorded privileges.[10] Legislative enactments conferred charter privileges on the Bell Telephone Company of Canada as early as 1880. Subsequent acquisitions of rival telephone systems by Bell and its affiliates, along with restrictive and predatory trade practices preventing new companies from entering the market, helped to forestall competition.

Given the high costs of establishing phone service to remote areas, the three prairie provinces created their own systems as public corporations, while the four Atlantic provinces regulated their private carriers. This left the federal government to regulate the two largest common carriers – the American-owned BC Tel and Bell Canada, which controlled Ontario and Quebec. To operate the phone companies' international connections, Ottawa created a publicly owned monopoly, which was to be known as Teleglobe, and had taken a 50 per cent equity stake in the railway companies' merged data-transmission company, CNCP Telecommunications. Once satellites were developed with the capacity to transmit voice signals, Ottawa set up another monopoly, Telesat, together with co-owners Spar (the satellite manufacturer) and Stentor (the consortium set up by the main regional phone companies) to operate this new part of the national communications system.

Shifts of Paradigm and Power

The days of this superficially stable paradigm were numbered. Technological, economic, and political forces were at work both within and south of its borders that would quickly transform Canada's self-contained set of protected and regulated national champions. In order to cater more directly to business needs, the old system was shifted towards a market run along American norms, which were written into international agreements. In the process, many power shifts occurred. The provinces lost constitutional control to Ottawa. Within the federal government, the industry's nationally focused regulators were shoved aside by politicians and bureaucrats bent on moving away from monopoly regulation to the new American model of telecom competition, which they helped write into the continental and global levels of governance.[11] In the process, consumers' groups, trade unions, and provincial politicians lost voice to a resurgent business community. The public sector shrank to the benefit of the private sector, whose players became junior partners within an emerging world oligopoly of transnational telecom giants unconstrained by any global competition policy.

During the Trudeau era, this sea change from a monopoly-based system to one driven by corporate competition was set in motion by technological developments mediated by new regulatory ideas. First of all, new technologies undermined the rationale for treating telephony as a monopoly. Microwaves, satellites, and fibre optics revolutionized the capacity and cut the cost for transmitting data. It was no longer obvious why long-distance charges should subsidize local rates. Digitization eliminated the distinction between voice and data transmission. Developments in computer hardware and its software applications created saleable new services such as videoconferencing. Recognizing the convergence that was linking broadcasting, telecommunications, and computerized information technologies, Ottawa moved its telephony regulators in 1976 from the Canadian Transport Commission (which had set phone rates since the railways pioneered long-distance telegraph and telephone lines alongside their tracks) to the radio and TV broadcast regulator now renamed the Canadian Radio-television *and Telecommunications* Commission (CRTC).

What principles should guide this reconstituted CRTC formed a crucial question. A large part of the answer came from the introduction of competition by rapidly transformed U.S. telecommunications regulation. Over a number of years, court challenges and regulatory changes by the U.S. Federal Communications Commission (FCC) had permitted large corporations to exploit new microwave-transmission technology for their internal long-distance needs. Competitors of AT&T, such as MCI and Sprint, had been empowered to use their own facilities to offer private microwave service to any customers. 'Enhanced' or 'resale' services such as electronic stock brokering and videoconferencing facilitated by new, computerized data-processing and switching equipment were authorized to use AT&T's public long-distance facilities. And customers were allowed to attach their own phones, fax, or answering machines to the common carrier's line, breaking its 'end-to-end' monopoly.[12]

Temporarily following in the FCC's pro-competitive footsteps in 1979, the CRTC allowed CNCP Telecommunications to interconnect its private voice and data lines to the local networks of Bell Canada. The next year it let customers attach their own equipment to BC Tel and Bell Canada's systems, to the cheers of the Consumers' Association of Canada (CAC). 'Competition in the terminal equipment market,' it said, 'will result in increased innovation and efficiency and ultimately lower prices and better quality products.'[13] This was a significant change for Bell, since its end-to-end monopoly had let its in-house equipment manufacturer, Northern Telecom, develop in the protected market provided by Bell's consumers, who had till then rented their telephones or fax and answering machines from the common carrier.[14]

In 1984 the government authorized duopoly competition in cellular telephones.[15] The CRTC went on to endorse the U.S. position on enhanced services, such as voice-mail, electronic stock trading, and videoconferencing, as well as allowing the resale and sharing of basic phone service, whether local or long distance.[16]

This embrace of the American competition model was interrupted after another U.S. deregulatory move – the divestiture of AT&T on anti-trust grounds in 1984 – caused disruption and price increases in the marketplace. Ottawa reverted to favouring Bell's monopoly, which was again able to prevent virtually any rival independents from entering the market. Rather than inviting competitors into the industry, government in the late 1980s focused on how best to keep them out. With federal regulators marching in step with their provincial counterparts and supported politically by trade unions (which feared job losses) and consumers' advocates (who feared price increases in local markets), the rest of the business community reluctantly kept to itself its desire for a more competitive system, with lower long-distance costs and more services.

Facing the application by CNCP to compete directly with Bell in long-distance service[17] and threatened externally by reduced U.S. long-distance prices, Bell proposed in 1984 a scheme of rate rebalancing, whereby its long-distance prices would be slashed if local rates could be more than doubled.[18] The CAC, which had favoured increased competition as a means of reducing prices, now urged the maintenance of monopoly, bringing in the fiery Ralph Nader to describe the disaster of American-style competition.[19] Responding to the CAC and the provinces, the CRTC rejected both CNCP's request and Bell's pre-emptive rebalancing scheme. Cross-subsidization was to continue to keep consumers' costs down, even if it kept up long distance costs for business. As the minister of communications, Marcel Masse, put it, Canada was to be safeguarded against the *'déreglementation brutale'* of the American model.[20]

As late as 1988, the Department of Communications (DOC), which had responsibility for both culture and the broadcasting system that would create and transmit it, still called for shoring up the country's regional monopolies in long-distance transmission. Its discussion paper proposed that the DOC assume licensing power 'for the construction and operation of any telecommunications transmission facility that crosses provincial or international boundaries.'[21] Would-be competitors would face formidable barriers in attaining their required authorization. Admitting a strong predilection against competition in transmission, the DOC declared that 'open entry to the telecommunications markets by many carriers could well result in unnecessary duplication of costly facilities, threats to socially desirable cross-subsidies, and service disruptions resulting from the failure of new entrants.'[22]

Whatever state regulators may have wanted, the phone industry was feeling major pressure from the United States, where market-driven deregulation of long-distance traffic had produced astounding effects.[23] By the late 1980s, a phone call from Detroit to San Francisco cost 30 cents a minute, compared to 68 cents for a call from Toronto to Vancouver, the same distance.[24] This difference presented a competitive disadvantage for large Canadian businesses, which claimed that telecommunications constituted a significant share of their costs. The chartered banks, for instance, spent $470 million annually on telecommunications services. The Royal Bank alone spent $100 million.[25]

Living next door to Nirvana, Canada found itself facing a revolt of business users, who were coping with severe pricing pressure from foreign competitors. Business believed that domestic deregulation would bring down costs, improve service, and get it access to foreign information systems. Since 300 of the largest corporations in Canada account for about 40 per cent of the telecom companies' long-distance billings, they started to lobby for competition to bring down prices. Prominent Canadian industry groups complaining about the situation included the Business Council on National Issues, the Canadian Banking Association, the Canadian Business Telecommunications Alliance (representing 340 companies with $4 billion in annual telecom expenditures), the Communications Competition Coalition (representing forty of the largest corporations), and the Information Technology Association of Canada (which represents an industry with $15 billion per year in revenue).[26] They insisted either that they be allowed to reroute their calls through the United States or that they obtain competitive rates in Canada.

With this lobbying power brought to bear, the Mulroney government's thinking soon changed. As competition moved to the forefront of Ottawa's agenda, the CRTC's posture shifted again. Now wanting to deregulate the telecommunications market, it let the companies influence its regulatory, pricing, and network-design decisions.[27]

Emboldened by the CRTC's second change of heart and defying the DOC's hostility to competition, CNCP filed another application in 1989 seeking to provide long-distance message service in competition with the telephone companies. Communications Minister Masse's declaration that his department was investigating the possibility of allowing open competition in the long-distance telephone industry signalled that the days of Bell's monopoly, along with its now-tattered doctrine of natural monopoly, were numbered.[28]

While interested groups were concentrating their lobbying power on telecom policy, three related developments were helping to set aside the monopoly model and harmonize the government's approach to telecommunications with its general neoconservatism. The first two factors had to do with Canadian telecommunications companies pushing to become increasingly integrated in the U.S. market both as manufacturers of telecommunications goods and as purveyors of telecommunications services. By the late 1980s, 37 per cent of total domestic telecom equipment manufacturing was exported. In 1986, 62 per cent of those exports went to the United States, amounting to $781 million and 13 per cent of U.S. imports of telecommunications equipment.[29] When Nortel was bidding for U.S. government contracts, its American competitors complained of unfair competition, arguing that Northern Telecom had benefited from the sheltered market provided in Canada by its parent corporation, Bell Canada. Domestic deregulation thus became a demand made on the Canadian government by its own national champion, as it was determinedly transforming itself into a mainly American company.

Similar pressure arose from privatization. The Alberta government sold Alberta Government Telephones, which became Telus. Meanwhile the Mulroney government offered its 54 per cent share in Telesat to Spar and Stentor, the consortium of Canadian common carriers. It also sold off its wholly owned overseas carrier, Teleglobe, which ended up under BCE's control.[30] Under Bell's profit-maximizing direction, Teleglobe started looking abroad for markets. In the United States, its prospects were stymied by the doctrine of reciprocity. Washington strategically used the desire by foreign telecom companies for access to the U.S. market by requiring 'reciprocal' access for U.S. business to their home telephone markets. In this way Bell, the product of a century of monopoly regulation, discovered its own interest in deregulation as the domestic price that it had to pay if it wanted to go global – meaning go American.

Beyond turning Canadian companies into surrogates for its pressure to open the Canadian market to American telecom companies, the U.S. government made its demand directly. Exploiting the Conservative government's urgent desire for an all-inclusive trade agreement, Washington pressed its case on two fronts. Formerly, telecommunications had been touched by trade considerations only in the import and export of telecommunications equipment. Canadian duties on U.S. products ranged from 6 to 17 per cent, resulting in a 3 to 7 per cent price advantage for Canadian manufacturers selling in their own market.[31] In signing CUFTA, both Canada and the U.S. agreed to eliminate tariffs on such telecommunications goods as telephones, key systems, large switching systems, fibre-optic and coaxial cables, and other transmission equipment. Although tariffs were originally scheduled to be phased out gradually over five years, Simon Reisman, Mulroney's chief negotiator, convinced Canada to speed up tariff removal on some major products. Not surprisingly, AT&T was pleased with the tariff aspects of the Agreement, commenting that the tariff treatment of telecommunications hardware was 'the most positive element introduced in the agreement.'[32]

This reaction was short-sighted. CUFTA's most positive element for long-term goals concerned telecommunications *services* not *manufacturing*. As we have seen above, the Americans' negotiation agenda went far beyond trade in goods and tariff barriers. Powerful telecommunications corporations such as AT&T had learned how to operate successfully in a largely deregulated U.S. market. They wanted to exploit this know-how in other economies, which were still run as domestic monopolies closed to foreign investment. Washington planned to move foreign governments' policies towards its own free-enterprise model by universalizing American norms into the General Agreement on Tariffs and Trade (GATT) so that all member countries would deregulate their public-sector service industries and open them up to foreign competition.

Signalling Canada's role in its global strategy, the United States insisted that CUFTA cover services for the first time in a trade treaty[33] and held out for telecommunications to be included in this category. This step was more significant as precedent than as practice. Traditional telecom policies were 'grandfathered,' and nothing in CUFTA disallowed either country from maintaining, authorizing, or designating 'monopolies' for the provision of 'basic' telecommunications facilities or services. In addition, each country was permitted to mandate the use of its own basic telecommunications network for internal telephone traffic as well as for any phone traffic originating or terminating in that country.[34]

The first significant change was Canada's agreement to guarantee national treatment for American corporations offering 'enhanced' services[35] and computer services. This meant that provincial and federal governments had to accord a U.S. investor – that is, a corporation such as AT&T – the same concessions that they gave a domestic firm such as CNCP, Cantel, or Rogers. In the late 1980s, 'enhanced' and computer services represented only a small part of the telecommunications market. But they constituted the crucially important growth element in modern telecommunications services, because the demand for manipulated information was increasing rapidly. With their already established pre-eminence, American firms stood to gain from the application of the national treatment principle in Canada.

While an agreement for completely liberalized trade that included basic services was not reached, Canada had irrevocably removed the telecommunications industry from its regulatory cocoon and introduced it to a process of continuing international trade and investment negotiations. Reframed by this context, telecommunications policy was no longer the exclusive domain of the CRTC and the DOC. It had become an issue over which other departments – Finance, Consumer and Corporate Affairs, Industry, and Foreign Affairs and International Trade – had claims to influence policy. And it would now be subject to rules negotiated between the United States and the European Union, with which Canada would be constrained to agree.

Although CUFTA's national treatment rule did not apply to basic telecommunications, another clause affected traditional domestic regulation by requiring state monopolies to operate on commercial principles. This could make CRTC-sanctioned cross-subsidization of telephone rates vulnerable to American corporations' claiming a violation of their rights achieved in CUFTA on the grounds that cross-subsidization was anti-competitive. This argument gave another cudgel to those attacking the CRTC's monopoly approach.

Another factor pushing in the same direction was constitutional. In a landmark judgment, the Supreme Court of Canada[36] ruled that the federal government enjoyed jurisdiction over telecommunications. In *Alberta Government Telephones v. the CRTC* (1989), AGT had argued that it was a local undertaking under Section 92 (10) of the Constitution Act, 1982, because it had all its physical facilities and subscribers in Alberta. Chief Justice Dickson, however, ruled that these criteria were inadequate to determine whether an undertaking was merely local in nature. He believed that there was an indivisibility in telecommunications that made even a provincially owned carrier the proper concern of a federal regulator.[37] The judgment held that all interconnecting telephone companies, no matter how small, were subject only to federal authority. As an interprovincial undertaking, AGT thus came under the regulatory jurisdiction of the CRTC.[38]

As a result of this decision, the privately owned, but provincially regulated Atlantic region telecommunications companies were placed under CRTC jurisdiction. AGT and SaskTel were ultimately privatized, while Manitoba Telephone Service (MTS) was brought under the CRTC's aegis by a direct deal between Ottawa and Winnipeg. Even though the provinces had legitimate claims to regulate local rates and terms of service, policies affecting interprovincial services had to be made at the federal level.[39] All of the larger carriers that made up Stentor were subject to exclusive federal jurisdiction. In sum, no matter how big or small the carrier was, it was subject only to federal authority.[40]

Empowered with complete jurisdiction over telecommunications by the courts and freed of provincial interference, Ottawa was able to force the industry out of its closed, monopolistic market into an openly competitive one. If the federal government controlled interconnection, it could introduce competition on a uniform basis across the country and pursue its new telecommunications agenda in the emerging international regulatory context.[41]

Competition Prevails

Until the early 1990s, the CRTC neither fully endorsed the virtues of competition nor acknowledged the inherent limits of regulation.[42] Bending to the pressures coming from business, the federal cabinet, and other departments, it accepted the argument that rapid technological change, competitive U.S. rates, and CUFTA's new requirements had invalidated the natural-monopoly rationale of regulation. The CRTC embraced the logic of competition. Notwithstanding the 'inconclusive nature of the evidence,' it first stripped Bell Canada and other established carriers of their monopoly in long-distance telephone voice service.[43] It permitted CNCP (rebaptized Unitel) and others to enter this large and growing market via 'facilities-based competition.'[44] In 1994, the CRTC went even further, removing all legal barriers to entry into local telephony.[45] By 1998, Canada was ahead of the United States in opening local telephony for competition.[46]

This rejection of monopoly in favour of competition as a means to other ends was no accident. It corresponded to a shift within the federal government of structure, function, and idea. Institutionally, the DOC's cultural policy division was split from its telecommunications division, which moved into the Department of Industry. This marked the end of the Canadian state's seeing telecommunications as a tool of social and cultural policy with economic ramifications. Instead, telecom questions were henceforth an integral part of increasing the general efficiency of what was becoming an information-based economy. Beyond that, Ottawa wanted to give special support to an industry that had nearly tripled its share of GDP since 1970. The needs of business were to prevail over those of culture.

To ensure that the CRTC remained converted to competition, the Conservative government introduced new legislation in 1992. Articulating a national policy sensitive to conditions of rapid technological change, the Telecommunications Act of 1993 gave the minister and cabinet exceptional discretionary power not just to rescind the CRTC's regulatory decisions but to issue it directives on matters of broad policy, national security, and international telecommunications policy.[47] By authorizing the CRTC to exclude labour unions, consumers' associations, and other groups of civil society, the new legislation signalled to a regulation-focused CRTC that the market-centred government had assumed ultimate policy control in this field.[48]

As a result, the bias of government regulation shifted from defending the monopoly positions of the regional common carriers to entrenching a corporate-driven strategy to undermine their dominance. Whereas the regional carriers still had to provide universal service, their competitors could compete only where they wanted to – in the lucrative urban markets.[49] Under this double standard, the original vision of universal, lowest-cost service became untenable. As with private medical services in the United States, competing telecom corporations spend lavishly on advertising in order to defend or increase their market share, with customers paying the ultimate bill for the resulting competition-induced inefficiency and chaos.

The main principles incorporated in NAFTA further restricted the possibility of cross-subsidizing private and public services and limited the range of new telecommunications technologies that could be governed by the principle of universality and so respond to the public interest.[50] NAFTA defined enhanced services more extensively, further circumscribing government control over the grandfathered basic services. Telecommunications had become more explicitly governed by the trade norms of most favoured nation, national treatment, and transparency.

Since other governments in the GATT Uruguay Round were still not willing to surrender state control of their basic telecom services, negotiating an agreement that would incorporate American demands had to be postponed beyond the WTO's founding as part of finalizing its new General Agreement on Trade in Services (GATS). The writing was on the wall: telecommunications policy was to be defined within an overarching framework of global investment and competition norms. No longer would it be driven by social, cultural, and economic factors articulated through domestic political struggle.

The subsequent GATS Agreement on Basic Telecommunications was the ultimate step by Washington to export what U.S. Trade Ambassador Charlene Barshevsky called the 'American values of free competition, fair rules, and effective enforcement to global telecom service providers.'[51] On February 15, 1997, members of the WTO concluded complex negotiations on basic telecommunications services, in which the signatories committed themselves to the goals of allowing market access for facilities-based competition, permitting foreign ownership of telecom facilities, and instituting pro-competitive regulatory policies. The world's previously untouchable telecom monopolies had turned out to be touchable after all. This agreement fundamentally changed the international regulatory regime by accelerating the elimination of national borders across the globe, by promoting the liberalization of national telecommunication markets, and by encouraging the transformation of state telecoms into global conglomerates.

Member countries undertook to eliminate anti-competitive conduct by their domestic monopolies and to negotiate further liberalization of their basic services.[52] U.S. companies would now be able to interconnect with foreign networks at prices no longer skewed by cross-subsidization.[53] Beyond accepting general norms that would govern their domestic regulatory policy, signatory states made individual bindings that specified the degree to which they would open their markets to foreign competition, allow overseas companies to buy stakes in domestic companies, and abide by common rules on fair competition in their telecommunications markets.[54]

Canada agreed to the telecom liberalization that was already under consideration domestically,[55] but put up some resistance against American pressure to allow majority foreign ownership. Ottawa was concerned that, with telephone companies able to deliver video programming, foreign ownership would sabotage the CRTC's efforts to retain some control over broadcasting content. Ultimately it promised to end Telesat's monopoly on fixed satellite services by 2000, to raise the limit on foreign investment in telecom companies to 33 per cent, and to liberalize international routing arrangements.

These developments helped change the regional landscape of telecommunications in Canada.[56] Its four Atlantic telephone companies merged to create AtlantiCo, a regional player, which hoped to be strong enough to fend off new competitors. The deal led to a merger of equals between Bruncor of Saint John, Maritime Telegraph and Telephone of Halifax, NewTel Enterprises of St John's, and Island Telecom of Charlottetown. However, Bell Canada acquired a controlling interest in AtlantiCo, took over MTS, and signed a co-operation agreement with SaskTel. Meanwhile, Telus merged with BC Tel, reducing U.S.-based GTE's ownership of the new company to less than 30 per cent.

With the market deregulated, Canadian-controlled firms faced the traditional entrepreneurial dilemma: if they couldn't beat their gigantic foreign competitors on their home turf, they had to join them at whatever terms they could negotiate. These terms were clearly affected by remaining regulatory provisions that define permissible levels of foreign ownership. Anticipating the new competitive environment established by CUFTA and NAFTA, U.S. carriers expanded northwards, where they were welcomed by Canadian companies seeking to make 'strategic alliances' with global networks having deep pockets and advanced technology. In 1993, Unitel obtained $150 million from AT&T for technological development in exchange for the maximum 20 per cent equity share in the company then allowed by federal legislation. Following a restructuring two years later, AT&T emerged with 33 per cent of the voting stock. With the banks holding 50 per cent of Unitel's stock, AT&T was in actual control, as was signalled by its 'rebranding' as AT&T Canada Long Distance. AT&T was realizing its strategy of incorporating Canada into its seamless and global marketing of information services from wired to wireless and from programming to consulting, passing through its telephone-based translation service in 140 languages.[57]

Stentor concluded a deal with MCI for technology purchases and development flowing both ways. In August 1993, Sprint and CallNet Enterprises signed a $60-million agreement to share technology and services, giving Sprint 25 per cent ownership of Callnet.[58] Limits on foreign ownership seemed merely symbolic, since most of the new boards of directors consisted of American executives. This suggests a triple segue. Control over the Canadian telecommunications industry first shifted from the provincial level to the federal government, which moved control to the private sector, where in turn control shifted from Canadian to American hands.

In 1999, Bell Canada struck what turned out to be a temporary $5.1-billion deal to sell a 20 per cent stake to the giant Ameritech Corp., which gained two seats on Bell's ten-member board, the right to appoint Bell's chief financial officer, access to Bell's network and services, and a 21.5 per cent stake in Teleglobe, the former crown sold to Bell by the Mulroney government, giving Ameritech part ownership in the doomed international carrier. In June 2002, Bell reversed course and decided to buy back full control. AT&T, which owned 31 per cent of AT&T Canada, announced a $4.9-billion merger with Metronet Communications Corp. of Calgary.[59] Although these first steps towards the continental consolidation of the telecommunications industry suggested that it wouldn't be long before Ottawa's rules on foreign ownership collapsed, the Telecommunications Act of 1993 was explicitly designed to 'promote the ownership and control of Canadian carriers by Canadians' and to 'strengthen the cultural, social, political, and economic fabric of Canada.'[60]

The convergence of computers with television is the next major evolution in telecommunications services and has momentous implications for broadcasting policy.[61] Microsoft's $600-million investment in Rogers, announced on July 12, 1999 was aimed at delivering interactive television services to Rogers' 2.3 million cable subscribers across the country. The venture would enable customers to obtain access to services such as internet and e-mail through their television sets. British Telecom and AT&T's subsequent purchase of a major block of Rogers's equity confirmed the trend to the denationalization of the Canadian industry as it endeavours to survive. As a global oligopoly emerged from the ceaseless amalgamation process, the Canadian telecommunications sector, which was once the country's nervous system, was morphing into a subcontinental informational infrastructure for a globalized information economy.

These mergers showed that telecommunications was only tenuously defined by national frontiers or controlled by the Canadian state. As regulators lose control, national firms seek to survive by striking deals with corporations anywhere in the world. Radical though these changes may be, little public concern was expressed about their implications for Canada's political economy. Opinions expressed in the media revolved around gaining access to better, cheaper, faster phone service with the very latest technological developments in mobile phone and e-mail capacity.[62] Rather than relying on state regulators and worrying about what was best for the national interest, Canadians were simply looking to the market to bring them competitively priced products and the most up-to-date telecom services. In thus accepting the benevolence of the invisible hand, Canadians were also condoning their state's loss of capacity to defend what many did want to retain – a vibrant, made-in-Canada cultural life to offset their bombardment by U.S. entertainment, which the now deregulated telecommunications system was bringing them in ever-greater volumes – an issue to which we will return in chapter 20.

Before we proceed to the Canadian state's capacity to sustain its cultural integrity, we need to tackle a number of other issues, the first of which is its involvement in the new ethos of promoting global trade and investment. The resulting continental market integration has definite implications for all government policies aimed at promoting economic, social, and cultural development.

THE EXTERNAL ECONOMY AND THE INTERNATIONALIZING STATE

Governors have always been concerned about trade with other jurisdictions. For all their inward-looking preoccupation with controlling their own economies' functions, Keynesian governments devoted considerable diplomatic capital to negotiating the reduction of commercial barriers at the Geneva-based General Agreement on Tariffs and Trade. Their logic was simple: commerce could be profitable for companies and yield benefits to the political economy as a whole. Although much of our text so far has been about trade agreements, chapter 11 reviews the Canadian state's commitment to trade policy.

Imperial states also fostered overseas investment, particularly in their peripheries. As a long-time exporter of staple commodities and site for foreign capital investment, Canada has had a direct interest in the prices, commercial flows, and investment capital available in the world market. With its own companies becoming more mobile and more interconnected across national boundaries, the government of Canada has become actively engaged in making new rules both for global commerce and for global investment – rules that have become supraconstitutional elements of its own legal order. Chapter 12 will open up government policies towards incoming foreign direct investment and outgoing Canadian direct investment abroad.

11 The Trading State

In the repertoire of the neoconservative state, trade policy is a doubly difficult instrument to use. For one thing, trade policy is not made by a territorial government on its own. It is negotiated with other states playing a game in which each tries to minimize the concessions it makes to its partners while at the same time maximizing the gains it wrings from them. While the resultant treaties become part of international commercial law, signatories (particularly less powerful ones) can never be certain that the commitments made are going to be honoured (particularly by the more powerful ones). The second problem is that negotiators cannot be sure how the new rules will actually affect their own society. They are generally inspired by the deductive logic of trade theorists arguing with blackboard-perfect certainty on the basis of the often quite unrealistic assumptions on which their models rely. But the real world of trade politics and business behaviour makes it impossible to anticipate the consequences for an economy of any agreement. Despite these problems, trade agreements have constituted the primary mechanism, alongside monetary and fiscal discipline, through which the neoconservative state has attempted to promote economic development.

The grand rationale in the 1980s for solving the Canadian economy's two related problems – sluggish productivity growth and inadequate efficiency – was to subject it as a whole to the disciplines of international competition. Forced to be more efficient or go under, national firms that survived the tough test would have opportunities to expand into foreign markets to which the new rules would give them greater access. While not a fully proactive approach, using trade policy in lieu of an industrial strategy was more than a merely negative, reactive

approach.[1] It was a non-invasive, but covert way to precipitate industrial restructuring without the need for any overt action beyond signing economic agreements.

Trade policy is also distinguished from macroeconomic policy in the
neoconservative toolbox by its dual action. The state imposes limits on
itself as the internal *quid* in return for which a government achieves an
external *quo*. As we saw in chapter 4, the federal government's implementation of CUFTA, NAFTA, and the WTO indicated its desire to create both continental and global modes of regulation that prevented its
partner states, in increasingly continentalized and globalized regimes
of accumulation, from restricting Canadian exports.

Fourteen years after CUFTA, eight years after NAFTA, seven years
after the WTO, and five years after the Canada-Chile Free Trade Agreement of 1997 came into force, Canadian citizens could expect to have
some idea about the economic effects of what free traders and anti-free
traders alike predicted would transform the Canadian economy.
Strangely, it is difficult to make a coherent and reliable assessment of
the Mulroney-Chrétien gamble. At the turn of the millennium, citizens
were swamped with economic information of all kinds, but it is doubtful whether these daily doses of data allowed interested observers to
determine if free trade had delivered its promised salvation.

Even when a trend can be determined and a difference with comparable countries' behaviour observed, statistics are unlikely to indicate
the phenomenon's cause. An economic result is generally the product
of many forces, and the impact of different external factors is almost
impossible to isolate. The devastating effect on Canada's industry of a
global recession, which set in only a few months after CUFTA, was
hard to distinguish from managerial decisions to restructure in
response to the trade agreement. And these decisions themselves may
have been affected by the already strong trend pushing companies
towards continental restructuring. The effect of free trade was further
obscured by concurrent policy changes inside the economy. For
instance, John Crow at the Bank of Canada started a campaign to wrestle inflation to the ground shortly after CUFTA was implemented. Jacking up interest rates and boosting the value of the Canadian dollar
made it much harder for firms to cope with the impact of decreased
demand and increased competition from imports, so that employment,
personal incomes, and the growth rate were all grievously affected.
When the Bank reversed its monetary policy and the dollar fell, the
economy started to grow again.

Even if we were sure that tariff reduction had caused unemployment to increase in a certain sector – the clothing industry, for example – it may still be inappropriate to blame *North American* free trade, since the tariff reductions mandated by the WTO would soon have forced Canada to reduce the industry's level of border protection in any case. It is impossible, of course, to know what would have happened without tariff reduction, *ceteris paribus*, as economists argue. But other things are not equal. The pace of technological change also affects employment and the job market, but in ways that are difficult to pinpoint when so many other variables are in play. Corporate management's obsessions with downsizing and 'deskilling,' merging and restructuring, which had major effects on employment levels in some industries, might have swept through the business world irrespective of trade liberalization.

Should intrepid citizens persist, they are likely to come to two conflicting conclusions. On the one hand, reliable data show that Canadian trade figures have increased substantially during the new trade era, faster even than under the Keynesian dispensation. On the other hand, there are serious grounds for doubting whether this story of increased trade flows has translated into the stellar economic performance that was expected.

Trade Performance

Economic liberalization has indeed coincided with a strong increase in Canada's merchandise trade, which grew 12 per cent per year for the twelve-year period 1987–99 from $290 billion to $694 billion.[2] This expansion represented a further increase in the Canadian economy's commercial openness: exports plus imports as a proportion of gross domestic product (GDP) rose from 52 per cent in 1987 to 54 per cent in 1992 and to 74 per cent in 2000.[3]

If the purpose of free trade was to reverse the Trudeau government's 'Third Option' strategy, which had tried in vain to direct the Canadian economy away from what was thought at the time to be a dangerously excessive dependence on the American market, it was successful. From 1950 until 1971, Canadian-American trade as a proportion of total Canadian trade had increased from 67 per cent to 70 per cent.[4] Even under the Third Option, North American economic integration had kept growing, with the Canadian-U.S. trade proportion rising to 73 per cent by 1987.[5] After the official inauguration of continental free trade in

1989, Canadian trade dependence on the United States intensified, as intended. The U.S. share in Canadian imports grew from 70 per cent in 1988 to 77 per cent in 1998, and U.S. dominance as Canada's sole significant market became even more overwhelming: the proportion of Canadian exports going to the U.S. market grew from 73 per cent in 1988 to 86 per cent in 1999.[6]

That the free trade agreements had some role in this expansion can be inferred by distinguishing sectors that had no duties from those whose tariffs were cut by free trade. Many sectors were not directly affected by trade liberalization since tariffs were already negligible or non-existent. Tariff cuts explain the increased trade in heavily protected industries.[7] For the years 1988-95, the growth of Canadian exports to the United States for products that had been liberalized was over twice as high (139 per cent) as for products that were already liberalized (65 per cent).[8] Export dependence on staples had declined in some areas (pulp, newsprint, lumber) but increased in others (electricity, wood-fabricated materials, and specialized papers).[9]

Canada's historic inability to export manufactured end products has been gradually mitigated. End products, which made up only 8 per cent of Canadian exports in 1960, had increased their share to 41 per cent by 1988. Under trade liberalization, this trend continued, with the figure rising to 48 per cent by 1996.[10] Beyond an expansion in its trade surplus in auto parts and cars, Canada's chronic trade deficit in end products declined markedly in such technology-intensive sectors as industrial machinery, office equipment, telecommunications, precision equipment, and aircraft.[11] For the five years of liberalized trade when the exchange rate for the Canadian dollar was stable (1991–6), the trade deficit for non-auto manufactured end products fell by almost one half.[12]

As was predicted, Canadian imports also rose most where tariff cuts were greatest. Formerly high-tariff sectors saw imports rise 81 per cent in the first seven years of free trade.[13] Certainly the third of the manufacturing sector with the highest tariff protection suffered the greatest losses. The growth of Canadian imports from the United States for the years 1988–95 for products that had been liberalized was 102 per cent, compared to 38 per cent for products that were already trading freely.[14]

CUFTA's encouragement of U.S.-led continental corporate consolidation increased cross-border trade within industries (intra-industry) and within corporations (intra-corporate trade). By 1993, 38 per cent of Canadian imports from the United States were intra-corporate shipments. 90 per cent of these were within American TNCs. By the same year 45 per cent of Canadian exports to the U.S. were within firms, 82 per cent of which were American.

Unlike other advanced and rich economies, Canada remained a net importer of services and highly manufactured goods. It has relied on its resources for many reasons. Although U.S. tariffs no longer inhibit Canadian exports of finished goods, CUFTA prevented Canada exploiting its comparative advantage in cheap petroleum as an industrial input. Because imported components make up so much of Canadian manufactured exports, resource exports add more value to the economy, dollar for dollar. These high-volume – although low value-added – staple exports finance a chronic current-account deficit caused by the outflow of dividends, royalties, interest on the public debt owned abroad, and charges for consulting and technology that TNC parents levy on their branch plants. Foreign-controlled TNCs' propensity to import is thrice that of their domestic competitors and accounts for 51 per cent of all merchandise imports. (Whereas foreign-controlled firms are net importers, domestic firms are net exporters.)[15] In the high-tech industries – electronics, computers, pharmaceuticals – where world trade has grown over the last decades, Canada has serious trade deficits, although these are diminishing in telecommunications equipment and aircraft.[16] Whereas the second National Policy sought foreign capital in order to substitute local production for imports, FDI now actually generates imports by subsidiaries from the parent corporate structure. These intra-corporate imports substitute for the goods and services that local firms could otherwise supply and so may inhibit the development of a mutually supporting local economy.

Foreign-controlled firms' export propensity is over twice that of domestic firms and accounts for 44 per cent of all merchandise exports. In sum, both Canada and the United States have increased their propensity to import from one another.[17] Increased FDI creates increased trade, particularly in the transportation equipment, electrical and electronic products, chemicals and textiles, and machinery and equipment industries that make up the bulk of the high-tech, high-value-added sectors of Canada's manufacturing. Because of their industrial dominance, foreign-controlled TNCs account for three-quarters of Canada's manufactured exports – a figure that rises to 94 per cent for transportation equipment, thanks to the Auto Pact, and falls to two-thirds for other, secondary manufacturing.[18] Set against these sales figures are the TNCs' massive imports. Even when the transportation sector's huge imports were set aside, foreign firms accounted for 80 per cent of manufacturing imports in 1987.

At the same time as Canada's manufacturing sector declined, its services sector grew, though less vigorously than in many countries belonging to the Organization for Economic Co-operation and Development (OECD). And as the service sector expanded, so did the growth within the OECD of cross-border trade in such services as tourism, banking operations, media sales, software, and consultancy. Surprisingly, the expansion of two-way services trade with the United States actually declined sharply under free trade, in the case both of imports and of exports. In contrast, Canada's trade in services with other countries increased.[19]

In the short term, a rapid increase in imports was understandable. The Canadian dollar appreciated 16 per cent from U.S. $0.75 to U.S. $0.87 in the first four years under CUFTA, making foreign goods much cheaper than they had been in 1987. But then the exchange rate slipped rapidly, with the Canadian dollar falling 23 per cent – 20 cents – from its 1991 peak. At U.S. $0.63 in 2002, it had fallen 16 per cent from its 1987 level. This currency devaluation constituted a greater barrier to imports than most of the previous tariffs and an equivalent stimulus to import substitution. The fact that imports expanded so rapidly suggested that much more was going on than simple tariff reduction. Corporate restructuring was an obvious factor in cases such as Gillette, which closed its Montreal factory as soon as the 1988 election ensured CUFTA's passage in order to supply the Canadian razor market from its plant in Boston. Within transnational corporations, cross-border trade increased substantially, particularly in assembly operations in which ultimate exports depend on importing intermediary inputs.

The business press and most government officials exult when they report increases in trade, clearly believing that growing commerce is the talisman of progress and prosperity – a.k.a. better economic performance. More trade, they imply, is synonymous with faster productivity growth, more and better jobs, better wages and salaries, and therefore a higher standard of living, because greater openness induces a more rapid diffusion of new technology. We need to review the basic indicators to see whether free trade achieved the promised result of boosting growth, closing the persistent productivity gap with the United States, and generating higher value-added jobs. It is now clear that the economic bonanza that free trade was expected to produce did not materialize. In most respects the economy's performance during the first decade lived under trade liberalization was even worse than during the preceding decade, whose dismal indicators had sparked the belief that trade liberalization was Canada's elixir.

Economic Performance

One of the main forces impelling Canadian politicians to take Donald Macdonald's recommended 'leap of faith' into free trade, was the alarming decline in the economy's growth rate. Compared to the economy's expansion by 5.3 per cent per year in the 1960s and the substantial annual record of 3.6 per cent from 1973 to 1979, growth in the early 1980s had slowed down to 2.9 per cent.[20] However, economic growth for 1988–97 under 'free trade' slowed still further. Shackled by a Bank of Canada-induced recession, the economy grew during this decade at a rate of only 2.0 per cent.[21]

Far from generating a renaissance, trade liberalization witnessed a further decline in Canada's economic position. With the newly industrializing countries expanding at impressive paces, Canada's share of global GDP fell during this period from 2.9 per cent (1980–89) to 1.8 per cent (1990–9). Having stood seventh (after Italy) in the world hierarchy of economies measured by GDP,[22] Canada was displaced by China and Brazil and fell to ninth place, just ahead of Spain. To consider the factors involved in this slowdown, we need to look first at Canada's productivity results and then at its record of employment and income.

Productivity

The advocates of trade liberalization argued persuasively in the mid-1980s that free trade would stimulate lagging Canadian manufacturing productivity to rise to American levels. The cold shower of increased competition would force Canadian firms to adopt new technology quickly or fail. As they produced goods for a larger market, they would achieve greater economies of scale. Ultimately, their increased efficiency and productivity would lead to rising incomes for Canadian workers.

Alas, in the years after Canada inaugurated free trade with such fanfare, the growth of labour productivity in manufacturing did not even keep up with American productivity growth. In fact the gap widened under free trade. Within the context of a worldwide productivity slow-down that began in the 1970s, the information about Canada's productivity gap with the United States is particularly disputed. Andrew Sharpe, director of the Centre for the Study of Living Standards, has shown that, prior to 1977, productivity in Canadian manufacturing had been about 90 per cent of the U.S. level. At the end of the 1990s, Canadian productivity trailed U.S. levels by 15 per cent and accounted for more than 80 per cent of the difference between per capita incomes in the two countries. All G7 members suffered from a productivity gap with the United States, but only Canada fell further behind. Between 1991 and 1996, Canadian plants raised their output per hour worked by 12 per cent, while their American competitors pulled off an 18 per cent increase. By 1996, Canada's global productivity position had actually deteriorated from second place among G7 countries in 1976 to fifth.[23]

The continuing lag in Canadian productivity probably has a good deal to do with the dominance of foreign corporations in the manufacturing industries. Foreign firms perform 67 per cent less research and development (R&D) than domestic firms – spending 1.2 per cent of their revenue on research, compared to 2 per cent by Canadian-owned firms. This discrepancy is understandable, since branch plants typically import their technology, restricting their local R&D to research about how to adapt a company's products to local marketing tastes. There are variations, of course – from pharmaceuticals, which are 86 per cent foreign owned but have R&D intensities as high as domestic firms, to the auto industry, where foreign firms spend 0.2 per cent of sales on research, compared to 2.2 per cent by domestic companies.[24]

FDI has had no discernible effect on productivity levels in machinery and equipment, electrical and electronic products, transportation, and communication.[25] Its greatest, but still minimal, impact has been in the energy industry, where a 1 per cent increase in FDI reduces total cost of production by 0.5 per cent *in the long run*. The equivalent figure for the finance and insurance industries is a mere 0.16 per cent.[26] Partisans of FDI argue that it improves total factor productivity, on the assumption that, when more efficient TNCs displace domestic firms, they pay less for the foreign technology than its value.[27] In this optic, the economy's performance could worsen if Canada doesn't meet the challenge of increasing global competition for FDI by continuing to cut taxes, make labour markets more flexible, and reduce regulation.[28] This argument does little to assuage the concerns of sceptics who believe that FDI condemns Canada to second-rate technological status because TNCs typically concentrate R&D functions near the head office in the home, not in the host economy.

Some mainstream research lends support to the sceptics. According to Steven Globerman, the efficiency benefits of FDI to the host economy tend to be overestimated. In many cases, the host government lures FDI by offering subsidies that exceed its expected net benefits.[29] Furthermore, the costs of acquiring the TNCs' superior technology may be excessive, since head offices may overcharge their branch plants through royalty and management fees that are arbitrarily priced to increase profits of the corporation in the home economy and decrease taxes owed to the host government.

Indeed, slippery accounting practices may themselves explain the putative differences in productivity rates between Canadian and American corporations. If a foreign firm wants to shelter its profits offshore, it can do so by nominally importing its products from its Canadian branch via a Caribbean tax haven at deflated prices and exporting to the same branch at inflated prices. Such transfer pricing – whose existence is well known but little documented – reduces the branch plant's reported taxable income and exaggerates the costs of production of untold numbers of subsidiaries. This debate is unresolvable, since Canada does not require foreign TNCs to disclose enough data on their pricing policies to produce an accurate productivity profile. In an era known for its concern for stakeholders' rights, the Canadian public – which has a huge stake in the foreign-controlled sector of the economy – is left permanently in the dark, its rights in this matter disregarded.

Foreign firms have registered some improvements since the early 1980s. Their R&D expenditures increased by 40 per cent from 1980 to 1993, suggesting that they are exploiting Canada's well-educated labour force and its lower R&D costs. The trade deficit by foreign-controlled businesses in technology acquired through licences and patents has shrunk by half. Technology trade by domestic firms remained in surplus, thanks to their increasing R&D expenditures by 200 per cent from 1980 to 1993.

The economist Daniel Trefler at the University of Toronto has challenged this gloom by insisting that Canadian and U.S. productivity indicators measure different phenomena. He has shown that Canada's manufacturing productivity (redefined as total factor productivity) has grown since 1988 at the compound rate of 0.6 per cent per year, *closing* the gap with U.S. productivity by 0.56 per cent per year.[30] This may be a reassuring figure in the light of most other authorities, who insist on the continuing fall in Canadian productivity. However, free trade gets distinctly lower marks when Trefler shows us his data in their historical perspective. The growth of labour productivity was 50 per cent *higher* (0.9 per cent per year) in the immediate pre-free trade period of post-Keynesianism (1980–8) and 150 per cent higher (1.5 per cent per year) in the Keynesian years (1961–80).[31]

Trade liberalization's role in this poor economic performance is still under debate. Economists from the labour movement have attributed job losses directly to free trade. Business economists have pointed out that over the period 1970–88, manufacturing's share in Canada's total employment had already experienced a steady fall – from 22 per cent to 17 per cent. They do not, however, claim that free trade reversed this trend. By 1993 this index had fallen to 14.5 per cent.[32]

Both sides of this debate can agree with two propositions. First, the increased economies of scale, the easier marketing conditions, and the greater efficiencies gained from corporate restructuring anticipated from economic integration were not achieved and did not translate into a new lease on life for Canadian manufacturing, although eventually a recovery did occur. From its 1988 level, manufacturing production had fallen 10 per cent by 1991; by 1998 it had risen 21 per cent from its free-trade benchmark. Second, the data reveal a bitter tradeoff between those who won by benefiting from long-run efficiency gains and those who lost by suffering the immediate adjustment costs of eliminated jobs and closed plants.

Employment

Employment levels, incomes, and gender differences can give us a good measure of workers' well-being. Working Canadians' experience in the 1990s justified their union leaders' opposition to free trade, which was as devastating in the traditional smokestack economy as they had feared. By 1995, economic liberalization had imposed severe adjustment costs on manufacturing, which accounted for 20 per cent of the economy and 15 per cent of its employees when free trade was introduced and lost 400,000 employees, or 17 per cent of its 1988 workforce. The most highly protected sectors provided most of these losses and experienced the largest reductions in output as well as the most establishments shut down.[33] In the economy as a whole, wages and the

number of jobs declined among the lower-skilled, the rate and duration of unemployment rose, and the participation rate by both the
youngest and the oldest in the labour force declined.[34]

The annual rate of job creation, which had been 2 per cent for the
1980s, fell to 1 per cent in the 1990s.[35] During the first twelve years of
free-trade, the economy generated full-time jobs at the average rate of
116,000 per year for the first eight years, 135,000 a year in the late
1990s, and 52,000 part-time jobs per annum.[36] In response to these less-
than-stellar figures, neoconservatives asserted that trade liberalization
is about the long run, not the short. Over time, they argued, abolishing
protection would stimulate more efficient and competitive enterprise.
In some sectors, such as the wine and furniture industries, this does
seem to have occurred. Niagara and BC wines are now served in the
best local restaurants.

The furniture industry offers succour to both friends of free trade
and its foes. For critics of free trade, the sector was paradigmatic. Having enjoyed considerable tariff protection, it suffered a substantial
shock from CUFTA. U.S. producers' share of the Canadian market rose
from 20 per cent to over 50 per cent from 1988 to 1995. The number of
establishments in Canada fell by one-third and employment by one-
quarter. Imports from the United States tripled. Giving heart to trade
liberalizers, the surviving Canadian firms restructured and doubled
their exports in the same period. Niche furniture suppliers were now
able to market their products across the continent. Critics responded,
however, that this minor success after major failure came thanks, in
good measure, to the favourable exchange rate.[37]

Official unemployment is a measure of those who report that they
are seeking work. It is increased by the numbers of youths and women
who enter the labour market and reduced by those who actually find
work or give up their search for a job. Unemployment rates averaged
5.0 per cent from 1960 to 1973, rising to 7.2 per cent for 1974 to 1979.[38]
Job losses induced by free trade combined with the deep recession of
the early 1990s to aggravate unemployment, which had remained
high, at an average of 9.3 per cent, between 1980 and 1989. As officially
recorded, unemployment then rose to 9.7 per cent for the period 1990–
9.[39] By the new millennium, general levels of unemployment were falling, and by the first quarter of 2000 they had reached 6.8 per cent, the
lowest figure since 1974.[40] Hitching itself ever closer to the U.S. economic star seemed finally to have paid off. The mild American recession of 2001–2 did not alter this picture.

Income

The proponents of trade liberalization maintained that an 'open trade policy was necessary to prevent the country's average incomes from falling behind those of competitors with more open economies.'[41] Despite the extreme openness of its economy and despite the steady, GATT-led increase of trade liberalization since 1945, growth in Canadian per capita income had trended down – along with that of most advanced countries. In the Keynesian period from 1960 to 1979 Canada's income per capita had grown by an average of 3.4 per cent per year (just under the figure for G7 countries of 3.6 per cent). During the post-Keynesian years 1979–89, Canadian per capita income grew by an average of 1.8 per cent per year – well below the G7's 2.6 per cent. Trade liberalization patently failed to reverse this trend. From 1989 to 1996, per capita income in Canada actually *declined* at an annual average rate of 0.1 per cent, while the G7 figure *grew*, if sluggishly, at 1 per cent per year. Given that Canadians had one of the G7's most open economies, their faith in free trade had proven ill-founded.

In sum, real wages had stagnated. Women's earnings increased on average 1 per cent per year 1989–98, while men's grew at a virtually invisible 0.1 per cent yearly.[42] (However much trade unions were losing clout, wage increases in collective agreements increased from 0.9 per cent in 1995 to 2.0 per cent in 1999).[43] Free trade had not changed earnings except for lowering the wages of non-production workers.[44]

Women were still more likely to work in part-time, lower-paid, non-unionized jobs compared with men, who tended to have full-time, higher-paid, unionized jobs. These differences were significant, as part-time and/or non-unionized workers generally earned less than full-time and/or unionized workers doing the same work.[45] Moreover, despite claims that there were more women in non-traditional female occupations, such as the managerial, administrative, professional, and technical fields, where the number of women occupying positions had increased relative to men, many of these women held jobs in small enterprises and had junior positions, with low pay and security. Similarly, despite fewer men filling the ranks of senior managers and other senior officials, women did not replace them. There were lower levels of female growth in management positions relative to male losses; the fewer female senior managers earned an average $40,633 per year compared to $71,349 for men; and only one in five management positions held by women was full time.

Women continued to predominate in the insecure and low-paid cler-
ical, service, and sales occupations, which in 1998 accounted for two-
thirds of growth in female employment[46] and for 32 per cent of total
female employment, up from 31 per cent in 1989.[47] This group also lost
EI protection faster than men, because more women worked part time
and re-entered the labour force more often if they had children. Moreover, raising the minimum number of hours required to qualify for EI
meant that those women who worked part time and on a temporary
basis could not accumulate enough hours in a year to qualify.[48] Still,
the distribution of female earnings changed marginally, with fewer
women earning in the lower end and more earning in the higher end.
In 1997, 32 per cent of the female workforce earned below $10,000 per
year (compared to 34 per cent in 1989); 7 per cent $40,000–$50,000 (versus 6 per cent in 1989), and 4 per cent $50,000–$60,000 (as opposed to 2
per cent in 1989).

If the wage gap between men and women was decreasing under
neoconservatism, it was a result of men's deteriorating status, rather
than women's improvement. Men's wages fell significantly in the
wake of free trade, when the manufacturing sector was restructured
and many senior-level managerial jobs disappeared. The largest
decline in the wage gap occurred among those with less than eight
years of education – those most likely to work in the primary and manufacturing industries, where many unionized jobs for men turned into
part-time work.

Contrary to the claims of supporters of free trade, gains in productivity did not boost wages to the extent forecast. Wages have grown
significantly more slowly in the manufacturing sector, vis-à-vis
productivity, than in other industries.[49] Workers' personal disposable
income grew by an average of 3.0 per cent annually between 1973 and
1981, by 1.1 per cent per year 1981–9, and by *minus* 0.3 per cent per
annum 1989–99.[50] On average, real wages have been stagnant, while
the social wage has fallen. If trade liberalizers have fought for the
hearts and minds of ordinary Canadians, greater well-being has won
over very few.

Since the United States provides the measure for most indicators of
economic success, a further ground for concern among trade liberalizers must be the disparity in wage and salary levels between the two
economies. Free trade was meant to ratchet Canadian living standards
up to American levels. But wage rates for U.S. production workers are
14 per cent higher, whereas U.S. management and professional salaries

are 38 per cent higher than those in Canada.[51] Whatever the cause of this continuing problem, free trade – with its increased economic inter-dependence and accompanying flows of investment – did not achieve a reduction of the gap. It saw the gap grow.

National Disintegration

Increasing continental economic integration bears a cost: it aggravates federal disintegration in Canada. Confederation constitutionalized the east-west orientation of an economy built on the watersheds and river systems that made possible the fur, timber, and wheat trades with Europe. The young Dominion's National Policy aimed to create a more coherent economy, in which central Canada supplied the eastern and western provinces with manufactured products in return for their resources. North-south commercial intercourse has long been under-mining what many economists in any case dismissed as an artificial, politically created economy doomed to inefficiency and backwardness.

Whether Canada's inefficient political economy, with its more egali-tarian notions of regional redistribution, plays a valuable role for its population as an alternative to the more efficient, but more unequal society to the south is a matter of values and judgment. But it is a mat-ter of fact that, under the acceleration of north-south commerce, east-west economic ties have weakened. While merchandise exports to the U.S. grew at 9 per cent per annum and GDP grew at the yearly rate of 1.2 per cent through the recession and recovery years of 1989–96, inter-provincial shipments contracted. Interprovincial trade, which matched exports to the United States in 1989, had fallen to half the volume of U.S. exports by 1996.[52] Except for Prince Edward Island, the American market is a more sizeable export site for every province than is the Canadian market.

Equally important in this decline in interprovincial trade is the increase in imports. Growing merchandise imports have displaced domestic flows of durable consumer goods and processed foodstuffs.[53] Such a dramatic change in commercial flows helps explain a funda-mental decline in the pan-Canadian attitude of Ontario, which used to favour Ottawa's redistribution of its wealth to the poorer provinces, because these in turn bought central Canadian products with their equalization payments. A sharp decline of trade with the eastern and western provinces has produced as a corollary Queen's Park's increas-ingly selfish demand for its 'fair share' from federalism. Starting with

Bob Rae's objections in the early 1990s to the Mulroney government's capping its transfers to the have provinces, the once notable Ontario-Ottawa axis has become disconnected.

Notwithstanding the Macdonald Report's assurances, free trade has not reduced inequalities within the federation. On the contrary regional variations in export success vis-à-vis the United States have increased disparities within the federation. The western provinces have been the main beneficiaries of Canada's growth in exports, whereas the Atlantic provinces' share of Canadian exports has declined.[54]

If Ontario has become more parochial in its attempt to extract benefits from federalism, it has also become more global in joining federal efforts at trade promotion. Premiers' participation in Team Canada trade missions, is reconstituting the federation in global salesmanship. The primary objectives espoused by Team Canada (made up of government leaders and CEOs of outward-oriented firms) are to raise Canada's profile in targeted countries and to advise businesses on how to adapt their practices to the unique features of these markets. Since Canada is internationally respected for its integrity, a Canadian firm with aspirations abroad gains some advantage – according to official rhetoric – if it is equated with these values.[55] The government presence on trade missions attempts to transfer this legitimacy to the firms trying to gain access to a particular market.

Canada's trade mission to strengthen economic relations with Israel and Gaza in February 1999 illustrates the theory of this approach, but also its potentially embarrassing futility. International Trade Minister Sergio Marchi was accompanied to the Middle East by forty corporate executives, including two from Bombardier. Palestinian representatives hoped that goodwill towards Canada for its role as a champion for refugee rights would foster better investment relations and provide Canadian firms with the opportunity to participate in the infrastructure development projected in Gaza.[56] The Palestinian trade mission was also expected to give Canada international diplomatic leverage. As the trade minister argued, a Canadian economic presence there could modestly help bolster peace in the region.[57] In this way, the Team Canada strategy sought to draw domestic business closer into the crafting of foreign trade policy by making it an instrument of Canada's effort to ensure prosperity, security, and the projection abroad of Canadian values. Palestine's subsequent descent into chaos reminds us of the yawning gap between wishful thinking in Ottawa and the intractable reality in many areas where Canada naïvely hopes to expand its commercial links. In the aftermath of cementing its fusion in the North American economy through NAFTA, Canada's share of global trade is falling and is ever more concentrated on the United States' market.

If free trade had not provided the Canadian economy with a magic potion to correct all its blemishes and launch it on its way to fame and fortune, perhaps this was because NAFTA and the WTO were less about liberalizing the conditions for international trade than about liberalizing the conditions for international investment.

12 The Investing State

Economists agree that while trade may drive economic growth, investment does drive economic growth. But they don't agree on what best drives investment, let alone on whether the state should be in the driver's seat or the passenger's. Ever since the collapse of communism, those who insist that only the state should make the economy's investments and operate the resulting publicly owned enterprises have been discredited. At the other extreme, libertarians believe that, because the state is inherently inefficient, if not inevitably corrupt, the market should be left entirely to its own devices: individual capitalists should make all the investments plus, of course, own and operate all enterprise. In the mainstream, economists agree that, while the market is the most efficient allocator of resources in principle, political action should be taken when it fails in practice. If, for instance, market forces create a price-gouging monopoly, or pollute the environment, or fail to develop the culture, or provide poor telephone and mail service to rural communities, then government should step in as entrepreneur or regulator or tax collector or lawmaker to achieve the common good. There have been enough such market failures in Canada that its governments have become active investors and participants in the economy – even though socialists have never controlled the federal government and only a small proportion of provincial governments have been run even by moderate social democrats.

Responding to the market's failure to create or sustain socially important activities, such as efficient power generation, accessible public transportation, and national radio broadcasting, Canada's federal, provincial, and municipal governments have become directly involved in economic activities through the institutional form of crown corporations. At first, the development of a mixed economy – part private, part public – took place at the instigation of and to serve the interests of Canadian capitalists. It was because railway entrepre-

neurs were going bankrupt that the conservative government of Robert Bor-den saved their bacon by purchasing their failing companies and turning them into the publicly owned Canadian National Railways (CNR). At the begin-ning of the twentieth century Ontario's business community wanted secure sources of cheap electricity. Because it could not manage the necessary large investments, it sought the provincial government's financial muscle to create a public electricity-generating corporation, Ontario Hydro.

But ownership connotes control. And control of assets by some affects the profit-making potential of others. As the capitalist class grew in wealth and established international alliances over the decades, it started to covet these government enterprises. By the end of the Trudeau era the federal government owned 67 parent companies with 128 subsidiaries boasting assets worth $50 billion. The bulk of these entities were managed by crown corporations that acted as financial intermediaries extending government-supplied credit for public housing (Central Mortgage and Housing), agricultural development (Farm Credit Corporation), or export promotion (Export Development Corpo-ration, or EDC). Public enterprises also played a substantial role producing goods and services for sale. Nineteen of Canada's top 500 industrial firms were federal crown corporations, while thirteen belonged to provincial govern-ments. Petro-Canada alone had fifty wholly owned subsidiaries, $4 billion in assets, and 6,000 employees. In addition, Ottawa's controlling interest in the Canada Development Corporation (CDC) gave it a portfolio of 100 companies worth another $8 billion.[1]

This direct involvement in the economy by the Canadian state led neo-conservatives in the mid-1980s to call for a radical reduction of what they claimed had become a gargantuan public sector that distorted capital markets, spoiled workers, wasted tax dollars, and interfered with the liberating forces of competition. The vast pension funds and mushrooming mutual funds took up the cause, demanding a privati-zation that would commodify economically viable chunks of the pub-lic domain and so make available profitable assets that they could include in their portfolios. Potential entrepreneurs manoeuvred to gain control. Merger-and-acquisition specialists and stock brokers salivated at the expectation of the huge commissions involved.

Following many years of effort by its Ministry of State for Privatiza-tion, the Mulroney government removed itself as a competitor from aerospace and biotechnology, air travel and rail transport, the telecom-munications and petroleum sectors, and manufacturing munitions. While the scale of privatization was impressive, this disinvestment policy was less libertarian than the Progressive Conservatives tried to make it appear. For one thing, the federal government was left with eight wholly owned and sixteen partly owned companies in *The Financial Post 500*. For another, some of the 'privatizations' were simply shifts of control to other public sectors or provincially owned crowns. Northern Canada Power Corporation became two crown corporations owned by the Yukon and Northwest Territories governments. Eldorado Nuclear Ltd, North America's largest uranium producer, remained 100 per cent state-owned, but by a provincial government via the Saskatchewan Mining Development Corporation. The overseas telecom company, Teleglobe Canada, was sold to a company that was itself a consortium of largely state-owned entities, including the Canadian Broadcasting Corporation, Ontario Hydro, and Quebec's Caisses de Dépot.[2]

Whether by design or by inadvertence, federal and provincial disinvestment policies actually reduced competition and strengthened monopolistic tendencies in a number of economic sectors. Developing globally competitive 'national champions' may have fallen out of favour as the discredited, allegedly self-defeating policy legacy of the Trudeau years, but the Quebec transportation equipment manufacturer Bombardier rose from 69th position on Canada's corporate ladder in 1984 to 32nd in 1992 thanks in large measure to acquiring from government at bargain prices the aircraft companies Canadair and de Havilland and Ontario's mass transit company, Urban Transit Development Corporation. Canadian Pacific and Bell Canada Enterprises each strengthened their market dominance (fifth and first, respectively, in the top 500) by picking up parts of CNR as it divested itself of trucking, hotels, and telecom holdings.[3]

Even with its role as public entrepreneur considerably reduced, government still affected private-sector investment in many ways, but chiefly through its tax policies, whose carrots and sticks influence investment decisions. Limits on the proportion of pension funds that can be invested abroad help channel Canadian savings into domestic enterprise. Tax credits for money spent on research and development (R&D) prod business to invest in producing innovative technology – or at least to claim to be doing so.

In addition to acting as a fail-safe entrepreneur and guiding hand, Canadian governments have inhibited undesirable kinds of investment. They passed laws to regulate oligopolies such as the chartered banks, as we saw above in chapter 9, and established agencies to monitor monopoly sectors, such as telephones, as we saw in chapter 10. In addition, they legislated to prevent non-nationals from gaining control in specific industries. In order to secure ownership by Canadians in certain sectors deemed key to the well-being of the economy (banks, insurance companies) or its culture (newspapers, broadcasting), they have legislated to limit the proportion that foreign investors can own and so control. Even when putatively launching its venerable crown corporations on the free market's unruly seas, the Mulroney government set limits on the amount that foreign investors could hold in Air Canada (25 per cent) and Eldorado Nuclear (20 per cent).

Beyond shielding this limited number of privileged safe havens, Canadian politicians and their civil servants have been mostly unconcerned about the nationality of corporate assets, particularly if it was American. After the Second World War, the United States became the largest single supplier of direct investment capital to the world. Adjusting the model pioneered by the first National Policy of 1879, Prime Minister Mackenzie King's dominant economic minister, C.D. Howe, refined a second national policy in the decade following 1945. He wanted to attract U.S. investment for two main reasons – to develop Canada's resources (and market them in the United States) and to set up import-substituting, job-creating factories for which it would provide capital and technology. So successful was this policy that Canada became an example to the world as archetypical host economy for transnational corporations (TNCs), which dominated, when they did not monopolize, most of its advanced industrial and resource-extracting sectors.

The Canadian economy was so attractive that it became the premier location for American foreign investment. By 1950, American capital constituted more than 86 per cent of the total foreign direct investment (FDI) in the country. At that time, the United Kingdom was the only other major source of FDI in Canada, with but a 12 per cent share.[4] In the late 1960s, anger about the U.S. war in Vietnam and an accompanying wave of university-led idealism, which surged through the country, revived latent nationalist feelings. The issue became foreign (read 'American') control of the economy. This groundswell pushed the federal government to sponsor ground-breaking research that documented how FDI had created a 'branch-plant economy' whose enterprises were inefficient, miniature replicas of their parent U.S. firms (Watkins Report, 1968). When aggregated over thousands of companies, the effect of FDI was to truncate the entrepreneurial and innovative capacities of the domestic economy (Gray Report, 1972).

Unconvinced by this evidence, the economic mainstream still insisted that the nationality of capital did not affect its performance and that FDI brought positive benefits to the economy in the form of new technology, new capital, new jobs, and the latest in managerial expertise. Unpersuaded, in turn, by these assurances, an aroused public opinion worried that U.S. corporations had secured a debilitating stranglehold over the economy. Such concerns pushed a reluctant Trudeau government to take three initiatives in the mid-1970s. It set up the CDC as a holding company to repatriate ownership of selected TNCs. It established Petro-Canada as a crown corporation to play an entrepreneurial role in the oil and gas industry. And, most relevant to our concerns in this chaper, it created the Foreign Investment Review Agency (FIRA) to screen incoming FDI in order to reduce the debilitating effects and negotiate greater benefits from proposed new foreign investments and takeovers of Canadian corporations.

Whether because FIRA's screening function was thought to be turning away potential investors or because Canada's growth prospects were lower than other countries', business lobbyists and mainstream economists by the early 1980s were expressing concerns that Canada's attractiveness as an investment location was declining and that, far from getting too much FDI, it was not getting enough. Canada should no longer strive for what they believed was in any case a quixotic economic autonomy. Taking FDI to be both a measure of and a means to boost an economy's competitiveness, the business class argued it had to compete for its share of global investment if it was to benefit from the strategic alliances with leading-edge firms in other countries that could stimulate the innovation and niche-market penetration that it saw as the keys to success in the new information economy. The alternative, for this school of thought, was to fall further behind in the international struggle for survival. The issue was not market failure but government failure. In this optic, they felt that the role of the state was to get out of the way and let the world's entrepreneurs exercise their magic. Cut it back, and they will come.

This return to courting foreign investment did not simply represent a nostalgic reversion to the second National Policy. In C.D. Howe's era, investment *displaced* trade because a factory installed abroad replaced exports to that market. In the economy of the mid-1980s, investment was seen to *create* trade because a production facility established abroad would manufacture only part of a TNC's total production process. Supplying that facility with components and receiving back what it produced to incorporate in the firm's global operation necessarily increased inter-nation trade.[5] Because firms need to achieve economies of scale – larger sales, which require longer production runs, which in turn reduce their average costs – to amòrtize the high R&D costs required to innovate, 'trade issues,' as Susan Strange and John Stopford have written, 'are increasingly and inextricably bound up with FDI and the behaviour of the multinationals.'[6] So if trade and investment are complementary, and if flows of FDI have been increasing at more than twice the rate of growth of foreign trade,[7] then investment policy had to be rethought in order to support trade policy.

Thanks to this logic, removing the government's regulatory power over foreign investment became the government of Canada's wedge issue in its push for trade liberalization. Even before taking its continental trade initiative, the Mulroney government shifted Canada's FDI regime towards greater deregulation as part of its effort to declare the country 'open for business.' In 1985 it passed the Investment Canada Act , which rechristened FIRA as the Investment Canada Agency (ICA) and substantially streamlined the investment review process, moving it from generalized controls on investment to specified restrictions on foreign takeovers in the vulnerable industries of energy and culture. A mandatory review of new foreign investment proposals was necessary only if they exceeded $5 million. FIRA had transmogrified from an agency vetting investors' proposals critically into ICA, whose job was to promote Canada as a prime investment site.

In this promotional function, ICA had competition. Mexico's rejection of its former import-substitution strategy in favour of neoconservatism focused on attracting foreign investment that would exploit the comparative advantage of its low labour costs and close proximity to the U.S. market. Many American states set up offices in Toronto and elsewhere in Canada to lure Canadian firms south. When European or Japanese TNCs went shopping to decide where to locate a new North American plant, they found U.S. states outbidding each other and Canadian provinces in offering packages of subsidies, tax exemptions, and serviced land to lure perhaps the new Mercedes Benz sports utility vehicle plant or Siemens's proposed electronics operation.[8]

The New Investment Regime

The strengthening connection between the flow of commerce and the flux of capital made it increasingly difficult to keep rules treating foreign capital separate from norms governing trade. This became clear for all to see when the Conservatives proposed negotiating the terms for freer trade and found that the United States would not talk unless what it considered Canada's excessively restrictive investment practices were put on the table and negotiated away. Under the resulting CUFTA, national treatment, which had previously applied only to goods under GATT, was extended to investment. Having resisted international pressure to take this step for years, Ottawa quietly capitulated, its retreat concealed by the bilateral agreement's myriad other provisions. National treatment for investment required Canadian governments to offer American corporations the same benefits and subsidies that they offered Canadian business. CUFTA curtailed ICA's mandate to monitor U.S. investment by introducing two more giant changes. Any future indirect takeover – the purchase of one TNC's Canadian branch plant by another foreign-controlled company – was to be exempted from review. The minimum corporate size for ICA screenings was also to rise from $5 million to $150 million, ensuring that the bulk of mergers and acquisitions by foreign corporations would now take place free of government oversight.

As advanced capitalist economies, both signatories of CUFTA shared a consensus on how investors should be treated, so they felt it unnecessary to sign a comprehensive investment treaty. Because it did not provide any special mechanisms for settling disputes between U.S.-controlled companies and the Canadian state, CUFTA was considered a 'weak' agreement.[9] This situation soon changed. NAFTA broadened the Canada-U.S. investment regime to include Mexico and deepened its normative system. Incorporating a Third-World neighbour in a process of accelerated economic integration impelled Washington to insist on the same strong, 'high-standard' judicial protections against 'expropriation' that were embedded in the countless bilateral investment treaties it had signed with developing countries. Canada was reluctant to be bound by this investor-state mechanism, but Mexico insisted this was a deal breaker, and Ottawa caved in on this issue.[10]

Accordingly, Chapter 11's provisions for investor-state disputes represented a high-water mark for the favourable treatment of foreign investment in the countries of the Organization for Economic Cooperation and Development (OECD). It was the only provision in any of the world's major trade agreements that permitted private investors to take First-World governments to binding arbitration. This innovation in investment policy, which has given foreign firms the power to challenge almost any regulatory action that might 'expropriate' their future earnings, poses a major threat to Canadian governments' autonomy. As the legal scholar David Schneiderman observed, 'Canadians no longer will be discussing which level of government can initiate which economic regulation. In many instances, Canadians will now be discussing whether either level of government can initiate such legislation at all.'[11]

Chapter 11's investment provisions retained the tough standards for national treatment and the right of establishment found in CUFTA, supplementing them with a more specific and transparent set of exceptions. It also broadened the definition of investment to give rights even to investors *contemplating* an investment. It also detailed a more exhaustive and stringent ban than did CUFTA on performance requirements that federal or provincial governments could impose on American or Mexican investors as a condition for their operating in Canada.

Although the agreements on Trade Related Investment Measures, on Trade in Services (GATS), and on Trade-Related Intellectual Property Rights in the 1994 texts establishing the World Trade Organization (WTO) fell short of the protection provided investors under NAFTA, they caused substantial changes in Canada's treatment of foreign investment from outside North America. WTO adherence required Canada to extend most-favoured-nation and national treatment to services investment under the GATS. Thus the same protections available to U.S. and Mexican investors under NAFTA – except for investor-state arbitration – have been made available to all WTO members. In implementing its commitments, Canada extended liberalized treatment across the board to investors trading in both goods and services, in order to avoid disputes over the differentiation of the two modes of commerce. Essentially, 'in implementing the WTO Act Canada has virtually disabled the ICA.'[12]

The Effects of the New Investment Regime

Free traders predicted that NAFTA would make the American economy itself more competitive. Although Canada started with a far larger stock of U.S. FDI than Mexico (hosting 2,000, or 12 per cent of American TNCs' foreign affiliates, compared to Mexico's 1 per cent),[13] Mexican leaders argued that NAFTA would help their country become a more attractive investment platform for foreign investors seeking a North American base for their penetration of the U.S. market. Canadian supporters of liberalization predicted massive increases in high-tech FDI, while critics expected foreign investment to expand in the resources sector but shrink in manufacturing.[14]

Notwithstanding its enhanced continental integration, North America has actually lost ground in the struggle to attract new FDI. From a 44 per cent share of global FDI in the period 1984–8, NAFTA countries' share of the pie fell drastically to 26 per cent in 1994–5. Continental free trade had failed to make North America relatively more attractive for investors. Within the context of this overall decline, Mexico appeared to be winning and Canada losing the bid to become more attractive to foreign investors. The average growth rate of FDI in Mexico jumped from 3.7 per cent during the five years preceding NAFTA to 11.4 per cent during the five years following.[15] Rising to second place after China as FDI site among developing economies, Mexico's share of incoming FDI increased 50 per cent from 2 to 3 per cent of world FDI inflows, while Canada's share declined by 25 per cent, from 4 to 3 per cent.[16] From receiving 37 per cent of North America's FDI in 1980, Canada's share had sunk to 14.5 per cent in 1997.[17]

Contrary to predictions by both trade proponents and their critics, rates of incoming FDI fell. In absolute terms, Canada's stock of FDI did increase, but not as fast as expected. In Canada, FDI grew at the annual rate of 9.5 per cent over the first ten years of trade liberalization, from $123 billion in 1989 to $240 billion in 1999.[18] This was *slower* than in the ten years before free trade (1978–88), when FDI grew from $50 billion to $114.5 billion – an annual rate of 12.9 per cent.[19] Even though its growth rate was higher in the decade before free trade, FDI's relative size in the Canadian economy had fallen then – from 20.7 per cent of GDP to 18.9 per cent.[20] In other words, the degree of foreign control was declining. Under free trade, by contrast, the ratio of FDI to GNP grew from 19 per cent to 24.5 per cent.[21] When measured in assets, the proportion of the Canadian economy under foreign control rose under free trade from 21 per cent in 1988 to 22.4 per cent in 1997.[22]

At the same time that it was becoming more foreign controlled, the Canadian economy seemed to be becoming less dominated by American capital. The U.S. share of Canadian FDI declined steadily from 87 per cent in 1950 and 83 per cent in 1960 to 71 per cent in 1987. The quasi-nationalist policies of the Trudeau government were thought to have been responsible for this relative decline, but the Mulroney government's adoption of free trade did not immediately reverse the trend. The American share of FDI in Canada fell to 64 per cent by 1991, as Mexico attracted larger volumes of U.S. investment.[23]

American dominance in Canadian investment began to revive in the 1990s. Mexico received more U.S. FDI than Canada – but only between 1988 and 1991.[24] In 1999 Canada was the second-largest recipient of U.S. FDI after Britain, receiving 16 per cent of all American foreign investment.[25] (Mexico came tenth after Britain, Canada, the Netherlands, Switzerland, Germany, Japan, Bermuda, Brazil, and France.[26] From 1993 to 1999, the U.S. share in Canada's overall FDI stock increased 8 per centage points from 64 per cent to 72.2 per cent, while the European Union's (EU) share of Canadian FDI declined by two points and Japan's by one point.[27]

It is one thing to read these bare figures. It is another to decipher their significance. Have these inflows of FDI reinforced Canada's old pattern of hewer of wood, drawer of water, or have they pushed it into the new information economy? Have they sucked promising Canadian enterprises into the maw of global conglomerates, or have they given Canadian managers access to transnational innovation networks? Despite the fundamental importance to Canadian society of this hotly contested, decades-long debate over the virtues and vices of FDI, the Canadian government expends little effort on gathering the basic information needed to resolve it. For instance, it does not require foreign-owned corporations that are private to report the kind of data that would allow its scholars, its citizens, or its decision makers to know in what ways they are bolstering or sapping the economy. As part of their NAFTA restructuring, many TNCs have bought back their publicly listed shares in order to 'go private' and so avoid accountability.

We have, for instance, no reliable information that would describe directly the impact of free trade investment patterns on head-office jobs. Indirectly, if we take management and professional employment (MPE) as a proxy for the better-paid jobs generated at corporate headquarters, we can infer that trade liberalization has not yielded the better jobs that were promised. In 1971, Canadian MPE was 39 per cent of production employment in the manufacturing sector. By 1996 it had fallen to 33 per cent, even though production employment – the blue-collar jobs in manufacturing – had risen. By contrast, U.S. MPE grew in the same period from 35 per cent to 53 per cent of production workers. This greater proportion of top manufacturing jobs in the United States suggests to the business economist Myron Gordon that the extensive U.S. investment in Canada explains the decline in the Canadian proportion of better jobs, because the parent firms keep the managerial, professional, and R&D positions in the home office.[28]

Corroboration of this view comes from the fact that almost all FDI comes in the form of takeovers of existing firms rather than the establishment of new businesses.[29] Proponents of trade liberalization claim that 60 per cent of this inbound investment has acquired technology-intensive firms, which automatically obtained needed capital and broadened the collaborative networks through which they will be able to grow. Critics can lament the same figures on the grounds that the local economy is deprived of the benefits that should come from the self-reinforcing regional clusters that normally evolve when small and medium-sized (SME) firms generate synergies and help each other grow. When a promising high-tech SME is acquired by a foreign TNC, it may be closed down and moved to the corporate headquarters. Even if it remains in Canada as a component that gets integrated into a new transnational corporate framework, its head office responsibilities are denationalized and it will typically purchase more of its needed inputs from the parent company or its suppliers and so become disconnected from the local economy.

The cumulative impact of head office hollowing is to move some sectors from a condition of truncation to one of acute anemia. The chemical industry illustrates this trend, as the business economist Isaiah Litvak points out: 'Largely U.S. dominated, the Canadian subsidiary offices of the major U.S. TNCs have virtually disappeared or, as in the case of the two heavyweights – Dow and Dupont – have become mere shadows of what they used to be.'[30]

The end result is a Canadian investment policy under trade liberalization that can be compared to polliwog breeding. A generous tax regime to favour R&D, universal public hospital and doctor insurance, high-quality public education, excellent infrastructure: these are the conditions put in place to promote entrepreneurial breeding. Beyond these framework measures, government does little to manage the growth process, let alone protect the successful progeny from predators. The frogs' eggs hatch into polliwogs (trained workers). The most-entrepreneurial polliwogs evolve into frogs (SMEs). FIRA was designed to forestall foreign TNCs from swallowing the young Canadian frogs as they matured. CUFTA and NAFTA's castration of Investment Canada certainly makes life more dangerous for frogs. There is virtually nothing that Canadian governments can legally do under the new continental and global investment rules to stave off foreign aquisitors.

Suggestive evidence shedding light on this phenomenon comes from comparing the R&D performance of Toronto and Montreal. Although Toronto is Canada's major manufacturing centre, its national share of R&D has remained stuck at 26 per cent, whereas Montreal's increased between 1986 and 1995 from 19 to 24 per cent. The number of its R&D establishments nearly doubled in this period, while those in Toronto increased by under one-third. Montreal benefited from local, provincial, and federal institutional support in nurturing and support- ing small firms' networking. Ontario never developed coherent devel- opment policies to promote head offices and forestall the process that has sucked successful small innovative firms into large foreign corpo- rations, continually undermining the municipality's capacity to develop local high-tech clustering.[31]

Strong intra-corporate networks on the continental scale with mar- kets mainly outside Canada militate against the development of strong inter-corporate links at the local level, because foreign firms have little interest in developing close supply connections within the local econ- omy. Domestic firms, by contrast, are more inclined to find local sources for their needs and so enter more readily into collaborative connections with their suppliers.[32] As described by Michael Porter, the lack of domestic champions means that 'Canada reaps fewer direct and indirect advantages from the presence of these industries than would otherwise be the case.'[33]

Montreal, with smaller amounts of FDI, but an active venture-capital banker in the form of the Quebec government's Caisse de Dépôt, has generated many more R&D-performing firms. Toronto's smaller popu- lation of SMEs reflects the merger and acquisition activity of foreign firms, which search for targets of all sizes. As could have been expected, foreign firms account for half the plants in Toronto employ- ing 1,000 or more workers. More surprising, they represent 44 per cent of those with 10–49 employees.[34] A vicious circle seems to have devel- oped. Without a burgeoning local innovation economy, start-ups find it harder to get venture capital and other local supports that encourage self-sustained growth. As a consequence, they seek to sell out as a safer route to growth. The circle continues, with half of Toronto's technol- ogy-intensive industrial economy tied to foreign TNCs.

Significance for Corporate Governance

Following decades of high FDI and years of substantial Canadian direct investment abroad (CDIA), Canada's corporate structure was already highly integrated with the American economy well before the advent of 'free' trade. The typical subsidiaries of a TNC with a U.S. head office were miniature replicas of their parent. Canadian branch plants had their own head offices, which, however truncated in function, in turn created a local multiplier effect by generating demand for professional services such as investment and legal counsel, accounting, advertising, office design, software, and associated types of consulting – all high paying work that generated its own economic spinoffs in the local economy for culture, restaurants, and even nannies. There was considerable variation in the autonomy of Canadian subsidiaries, which were in the main publicly held national companies. With local executives and boards of directors, a majority of whom were required by federal law to be Canadian citizens, they generally played a positive role in their host communities, to whose voluntary sector they contributed corporate charitable donations.

The impact of the new supraconstitutional norms on investment has been to insulate corporations against pressure from any of the governments involved. At the same time it erased national borders from corporate consciousness, presenting TNCs with the prospect of reorganizing production for a single continental market of nearly 400 million consumers. As a result, CUFTA provided a 'powerful stimulus to cross-border reorganization and rationalization,' while NAFTA was 'an even more powerful driver of change in corporate goals and structures.'[35]

There is no single template that can capture all corporate responses to continentalism. Corporations respond in different ways to new technology as well as to new waves of de or reregulation. They reshape their production processes in response to different corporate cultures, which produce a range of solutions for their basic organizational dilemma of balancing central control against unit autonomy. In the case of branch plants, we can observe a spectrum of business responses between two extremes.

At the negative pole, the corporation shuts down its low-output, high-cost branch operation, which had sheltered behind protection and import-substitution policies of various kinds, closes its Canadian head office, and relocates management, production, and marketing functions, along with the associated jobs, to its U.S. headquarters, leaving a mere warehousing operation to distribute American-made goods in the Canadian market.[36] In these cases, the impact on the local economy is directly measurable in the vacant office space, empty high-end restaurants, and struggling advertising, accounting, and legal firms.

Demand for these professionals' services is repatriated to rival conglomerates, whose head offices are next door to those of the global corporations, for whom they can provide one-stop legal or consulting
services.

At the positive pole, the Canadian subsidiary restructures to compete within the widened, continental economic space of its TNC's production network, bidding for mandates to develop new products
within the firm's integrated, global operations.[37] Where this occurs,
parent TNCs restructure their subsidiaries to produce a narrower
range of products for their whole market, be this the continent or the
world. A mid-1990s sample of U.S. firms in Canada found that half had
some such mandate.[38]

Typically, these remaining subsidiaries have been reconstituted as
private, wholly owned entities with reduced autonomy, a downgraded
head office, and a shrunken executive, whose job is to respond to global demands, not to local markets. Public shares have been bought
back and the companies delisted from Canadian stock exchanges. Of
115 leading subsidiaries assessed in the late-1990's, 55 were already
privately held in 1985. Ten years later, 45 per cent had disappeared,
and 84 per cent of the remainder had gone private.[39] The effect of this
'hollowing out' has been pervasive.

The stock exchanges have been particularly affected by the vacuuming up of shares available for trading. They themselves are losing their
autonomy. Following belated efforts to consolidate them, the country's
several exchanges now seem headed for integration as regional extensions of the various New York exchanges, with NASDAQ taking the
lead in connecting with the Montreal Stock Exchange. The attrition of
Canadian capital market institutions is aided by the rapid takeover
noted above of rising, high-tech SMEs.

The ultimate shape of corporate responses to NAFTA is unclear. We
can concur that U.S. TNCs have restructured to create a truly continental architecture. It is easy to believe that mergers and acquisitions have
driven growth of foreign ownership as well as higher levels of industry concentration.[40] We can agree that the continentalization of capital
will lead to higher levels of intra-firm exchange and so higher levels of
trade between NAFTA's three partners. We know that the average size
of the top American companies is over twice that of Canadian firms in
most industries.[41] What we cannot tell is whether the takeover of a
promising young Canadian company will lead to its operations being
closed down and its personnel relocated to Silicon Valley, California, or

to their being expanded in Kanata, Ontario. Nor can we tell whether successful transnational growth by a domestically owned company will lead to its headquarters and research facilities' expanding in Canada or to their moving closer to the continent's commercial centre of gravity.

As numerous expert observers keep telling us, North America is consolidating as one of the three economic regions that, along with Europe and Asia, make up the global Triad. Within this triadic system, we also know that the Canadian industrial structure is moving towards a knowledge-intensive, high-technology position offering better-paying jobs, albeit from a small base.[42] But we still cannot be sure what fate the new corporate models have in store for those living north of the Canadian-American border. Juan Palacios of Guadalajara University has written of North America's international division of function. With the large differentials in wage rates and labour supply between Mexico and its neighbours to the north, 'the headquarters and high-end functions of major TNCs are typically located in the United States, while the bulk of their manufacturing operations are deployed in Mexico.'[43] Cross-border production platforms that are geographically organized on a regional basis are not likely to keep jobs in Canada.

Canadian Direct Investment Abroad

In the first two decades following the Second World War, only minor initiatives were taken by the federal government to aid Canadian businesses with operations abroad. Promoting Canadian direct investment abroad (CDIA) seemed irrelevant to Canada's place in the world and ran counter to the inward-looking stance of a nationalism that decried investment abroad as the exporter of Canadian jobs.[44] The Export Credits Insurance Corporation (ECIC), a crown agency established in 1945 to insure Canadian exports in the event of foreign buyers' not paying their bills, promoted sales abroad rather than direct investment, since exporting commodities was thought to stimulate job creation at home. CDIA was negligible in comparison with U.S. FDI in Canada, which was a hotter policy issue. Since it was uncommon for Canadian-owned firms to invest abroad at all, policies towards CDIA were ad hoc and reactive prior to 1967, when Canada contributed only one dollar to the total world stock of FDI for every sixteen dollars invested by the United States.[45] That year, a government statement instructed officials 'to assist Canadian businessmen' in locating foreign investment opportunities and notifying them when these appeared to be consistent with the overall national interest.[46]

During the peak years of nationalist concern about foreign investment, a lonely voice had proposed a different approach to the issue: rather than expending its political energies in controlling foreign investment, Canada should encourage its own domestic corporations to grow transnationally. Alastair Gillespie was considered something of a maverick for espousing this position in the mid-1970s as minister at Industry, Trade and Commerce in the Trudeau government. Why, he was asked, would Canadians want their firms to export jobs by moving away? How could they be expected to compete abroad when they could barely hold their own as they struggled for space in their own market against foreign transnationals? Gillespie was raising this issue at the very moment when Canadian corporations, in response to GATT-mandated declines in tariffs, were indeed finding their position in their home market increasingly threatened. Many decided that, if they were to survive at home, they had to expand their operations abroad and go global, or at least continental. Higher profitability and faster capital accumulation rates in the United States and Britain provided a further, more positive inducement for them to seek markets beyond their home base.

As CDIA began to involve more Canadian nationals and Canadian dollars, the Trudeau government passed legislation that ushered in an active public-sector interest in CDIA. Ottawa attempted to encourage and protect Canadian-based business ventures abroad when it became clear that they could achieve success there. In 1969, it set up the Export Development Corporation, on the model of the ECIC before it, to insure Canadian firms against the political risks incurred by operating abroad, including investment in politically unstable, Third World economies. Added to the insurance program for exports was a provision to help finance the sale of Canadian-made capital goods to the subsidiaries of Canadian-based TNCs overseas. Insurance eligibility was determined by the nature, the size, and the area of the investment, its economic benefit, and the host government's formal permission for the Canadian firm to set up a subsidiary and to repatriate capital and earnings.[47] Implicit in the EDC's mandate was the recognition that host governments had some regulatory authority over investment conditions and that the transnational firm was not completely autonomous in its operations. The federal government wanted to stand behind its own nationals' investments abroad but was also interested in monitoring those investments.

In 1970, Ottawa's aid-dispensing department, the Canadian International Development Agency (CIDA), set up a Business and Industry Division to encourage Canadian investment in developing countries and provided grants for this purpose. Although the federal government was beginning to warm to CDIA, these incentive programs did not of themselves produce its expansion.[48] More influential factors were competitive pressures at home, overall advances in trade liberalization, the relatively small size of the Canadian economy, and the consequent desire of Canadian firms to penetrate non-traditional markets.

These changes helped prove Gillespie prophetic. In one of those ironies so common to public policy, FIRA, which symbolized the concerns of a *host* economy on the receiving end of TNCs' branch-plant operations, came into being at the very moment in Canada's history when its economic character was starting to shift. For the first time in 1975, the flow of domestic corporations' investment abroad exceeded the inflow of foreign TNCs' capital. In addition to its role as host economy, Canada was becoming a *home* economy.

As Canadian corporations accelerated their investments abroad, they pressed Ottawa to negotiate better guarantees for them. Given that CDIA was shifting away from the United States and towards non-OECD countries, primarily in Asia and Latin America (which accounted for 22 per cent of total CDIA by 1997),[49] Ottawa's trade officialdom became concerned about protecting the interests of Canadian investors against mistreatment by host governments in the Third World, which currently accounts for upwards of 30 per cent of CDIA. Federal policy makers, who had been largely sceptical about nationalist concerns, adjusted their approach to embrace both sides of the new phenomenon. Expanding Canada's international economic policy beyond its traditional emphasis on exports, they actively pursued the strengthening of investment rules, both bilaterally and multilaterally. Application of the rules of CUFTA, NAFTA, and the WTO to these agreements' other signatories expressed the government's determination in the Mulroney-Chrétien era to support its exporters by encouraging trade liberalization and to protect its investors on the continent and all over the world by securing such principles as national treatment and settlement of investor-state disputes in its commercial partners' legal regimes.

Now thinking of Canada more as a home than as a host for foreign investment, Ottawa's trade officials welcomed the tough rules that the United States wanted to impose on the world. It was not their responsibility to worry that more rights were given to and fewer obligations were imposed on foreign than to domestic investors. The government of Canada went on to sign twenty-four bilateral investment agreements with weaker countries, to incorporate investment clauses in its 1997 trade agreement with Chile, and to declare its interest in greater trade and investment linkages with Eastern Europe. As well, it worked multilaterally on the WTO's agreement on Trade-Related Investment Measures (TRIMs) and then at the OECD to draft the notorious Multilateral Agreement on Investment (MAI), which was ultimately aborted in the face of objections around the world, led and orchestrated by Canadian non-governmental organizations.[50]

Industry Canada initiated the Canadian International Business Strategy (CIBS) in October 1995 to help business expand markets abroad and stimulate job creation at home, while promoting a partnership between all three levels of government and the private sector.[51] Though the crux of CIBS was export promotion, Industry Canada did address CDIA. The strategy's investment development prong supports the growth of Canadian firms abroad through international investment partnerships and joint ventures. Widening investment ties beyond traditional (read 'American') markets to gain a foothold in emerging economies is also a federal priority, as is strengthening the international norms that govern FDI and anti-competitive behaviour.[52] CIDA's Industrial Co-operation Program offers funding to assist Canadian-based firms to invest in, rather than export to, the rapidly growing economies of Brazil, Singapore, and Indonesia – and of Mexico, where, in the wake of NAFTA, 5 per cent of CDIA is now located.

A continuing higher growth rate of CDIA relative to incoming FDI led to the cumulative stock of the former's approaching, then surpassing, the size of the latter. By 1991, total FDI in Canada was $132 billion, while CDIA was $94 billion.[53] The ratio of FDI to CDIA had shifted from 4.7:1 in 1975 to 1.2:1 in 1995.[54] By year-end 1999, CDIA amounted to $257 billion, compared to $240 billion of FDI in Canada.[55] This steady growth of CDIA has transformed Canada's investment picture from a branch-plant to a more balanced economy, which has developed a stock of directly controlled investments abroad greater than the stock of FDI at home. In 2001, Canada attracted $43 billion in foreign direct investment, while Canadian direct investment abroad reached $57 billion.

Geographical distribution of CDIA reflects both traditional patterns and emerging shifts. The North American continent remains the primary focus, housing about half of total Canadian investment stock abroad. NAFTA's provisions on national treatment; its guarantees on cross-border flows of capital, including profits, interest, dividends, and fees; and its dispute-settlement mechanism, which enables a private firm to bring a case against an offending government on its own behalf: have created a legal framework that reassures Canadian entre-preneurs and managers abroad, whether in a developed (U.S.) or a developing (Mexican) economy.

Given all this protective armament, it is surprising that so much CDIA has moved outside North America. CUFTA did not initially increase the concentration of Canadian investment in the United States. While maintaining its role as the primary site for Canadian investment, the United States saw its share of CDIA decline from 64 per cent in 1988 to 58 per cent in 1991, a period when the EU and Japan were increasing their shares.[56] This may reflect Canadian firms' greater ease in serving the U.S. market by exporting from Canada.[57] It also reflects the greater propensity of Canadian firms to conclude technical alliances with European partners in information technology (Nortel), transportation equipment (Bombardier), and biotechnology.[58]

While non-OECD countries received only 13.7 per cent of CDIA from 1982 to 1989, their proportion increased to 30.7 per cent from 1990 to 1997.[59] Barbados trails behind only the United States and Britain as the most common destination for CDIA, accounting for $14.3 billion worth of the total $240 billion that Canada invested in foreign assets by 1999.[60] Latin America and the Asia-Pacific region are parts of the developing world that are of emerging interest to Canadian firms and to the Canadian government, as demonstrated by trade missions to these markets.

In terms of sectoral distribution, resources and resource-based man-ufacturing, including the energy, metallic minerals, and metal products industries, still reflect the economy's historic *comparative* advantage and account for 40 per cent of CDIA. Financial services and technol-ogy-intensive industries, such as the transportation equipment, chemi-cals, and electronic equipment industries, which reflect the country's newer *competitive* advantage, have been increasing their share in CDIA, with financial services accounting for 30 per cent by 1996.[61] In general, CDIA sets up horizontal linkages, with Canadian firms investing in industries in which they have established their expertise.[62]

The economic benefits accruing from CDIA to the Canadian econ-omy have increased over time as foreign branch-plant participation in it diminished. (An investment abroad by a foreign-owned subsidiary located in Alberta is counted as *Canadian*.) Its growth, which lasted throughout the 1970s, coincided with its increase in the hands of Canadian business persons. Canadian control of CDIA reached 84 per cent in 1980, up from an unimpressive 64 per cent in 1965, when it was made up predominantly of investment by American-owned Canadian subsidiaries.[63] As CDIA became more Canadian in origin, it helped improve Canada's current accounts. Income receipts from direct investment, including management fees, royalties, profits, and other intra-firm payments, have in recent years come into better balance with payments on FDI that leave Canada. CDIA receipts were equal to 63 per cent of FDI outflows between 1986 and 1992, up from only 25 per cent between 1970 and 1975.[64] In 1997, that ratio stood at 103 per cent, and it jumped to over 110 per cent in 1998. Between 1991 and 1997, net outflows of CDIA averaged $6.3 billion per year and then reached $18 billion in 1997. The total stock of CDIA soared from $200 billion in 1997 to $240 billion in 1998, setting a record net outflow in one year of $40 billion.[65] Earnings from CDIA amounted to $16 billion in 1998, some 2 per cent of Canada's gross national product.[66] Cross-border mergers and acquisitions have given Canada as a whole a more visible presence abroad. In 1997, Canadian firms acquired $24.7 billion worth of foreign-owned assets at home and abroad. This figure paled in comparison to the $40.7 billion worth of foreign holdings absorbed the following year, when 265 of the 403 firms taken over by Canadians were American-owned.[67]

In principle, CDIA strengthens the Canadian economy by providing it with revenue and competitive advantage. Although Canada does not tax income earned abroad from direct investment, it does tax headquarters operations. If the Canadian parent provides a service to a foreign subsidiary and levies a management fee on this service, this constitutes part of the parent's income and is therefore subject to Canadian taxation.[68] Canadian-based firms improve Canada's overall competitive position by consolidating trade links between Canada and its trading partners. Canadian TNCs' participation in joint ventures and strategic alliances with up-and-coming SMEs stimulates vertical linkages at home, creating opportunities for these smaller firms to engage in more at-home expansion. Through this spillover effect, the benefits of CDIA trickle down to local firms with a high growth potential by way of technology absorption, capital exploitation, and service providing.[69] SMEs contribute to economic growth and job creation because they foster dynamic innovation. It is this innovative capacity that contributes to productivity gains, increases domestic standards of living, and fosters the creation of a new generation of Canadian-based TNCs.[70]

While CDIA is generally celebrated as evidence of Canada's perhaps belated adaptation to the new economy, in practice it can have a darker side. The Canadian government's original trade policy objective when negotiating free trade in the mid-1980s was to exempt domestic exporters from the unilateral, unpredictable, and arbitrary effects of U.S. trade laws. One striking consequence of Washington's refusal to oblige its neighbour in this regard emerged in the Canadian steel industry. Though highly efficient, Canadian steel makers were prevented from increasing their share of the U.S. market because of their systematic harassment by anti-dumping actions launched against them by their less efficient American competitors. Faced with a partially closed border and the high legal costs of fighting endless trade-remedy cases in Washington, Canadian steel companies drew their own conclusions from Ottawa's failure to achieve genuinely free trade. They proceeded to make all their new start-up investments in the U.S.. As a result, further increases in Canadian-owned steel producers' productivity and employment have accrued via CDIA to the benefit of American, not Canadian, workers. Demonstrating a further complexity in the North American integration story, the greater participation by Canadian steel firms in the U.S. industry has helped deflect Washington's protectionist energy. Its massive safeguard actions in 2002 against foreign steel exempted Canada and Mexico.

Nor does CDIA necessarily translate into good job news for the average Canadian in other sectors. Thanks to intense competition based on costs, quality, variety, and service, the growth of jobs in outward-oriented firms has been significantly lower than it has been in domestically oriented firms in the free trade years. In the long run, the employment effects of CDIA are expected to be neutral, although the quality of employment should be higher in the head-office jobs.[71] As CDIA activity increases, more managerial jobs at the head-office level are created in Canada, with higher wage-earning potential. More value is added as R&D is pursued there, while the firm exploits the host country's labour pool. Ultimately, domestic firms' capacity to establish operations abroad should increase their ability to partner with foreign companies and raise their own technological abilities.

Whether CDIA's creating employment abroad jeopardizes jobs and technology in Canada remains an open question. Nortel Networks –

Canada's largest high-tech company before its collapse in the 2001 meltdown of the dot com sector – argued that it would not have been a globally competitive player had it remained exclusively within the Canadian market, and Canada would have benefited less from Nortel's operations than it did. Although Nortel's official head office is in Canada, where only twenty-eight of the company's top 400 executives worked at the turn of the century, its international headquarters and some major R&D functions are located in the United States. Canada was still able to extract benefits from Nortel's operations, despite the firm's high degree of transnationality. At its peak it employed several thousand Ontarians in R&D mainly at its central lab in Ottawa.[72] Sales in American and other markets financed research programs in Ottawa and Toronto and allowed Nortel to invest millions in education and skills training. It contributed $6.6 million in post-secondary research programs at Canadian universities, half located in Ontario. In partnership with the Ontario government's Access to Opportunities Program, its private investment combined with public-sector contributions to promote enrolment in the computer engineering programs that were meant to correct a skills shortage holding the Canadian economy back in knowledge-based competitiveness.

Even to stay competitive at home, successful Canadian firms have to 'go global,' which generally means locating substantial facilities in the United States. Once U.S. operations exceed sales in Canada, the American subsidiary typically acquires greater decision-making powers than the parent. Increasingly, Canadian TNCs are locating their North American headquarters in the U.S.A. whose nationals they appoint to executive and board positions. With more than half of its sales in 2000 going to U.S. customers, the Saskatchewan steel company, Ipsco, moved its operational headquarters to Illinois.[73]

Complementing and reinforcing these trends, the most aggressive Canadian firms are listing their stocks on American exchanges (over 200 were interlisted in 1999) and reporting their results in U.S. dollars (as did one quarter of the Toronto Stock Exchange's top hundred companies in 1999). These Canadian TNCs with a major presence in the American market participate more actively in American business associations where they can defend their interests. As a result, less strategic planning is done in Canada. And as corporate Canada depatriates itself, domestic governments lose their capacity to persuade it to expand at home.[74]

MacMillan Bloedel, the BC lumber giant, took this process one step further.[75] While it is common for a Canadian head office to supply R&D while acquiring its labour supply from the host country, Mac-Millan Bloedel moved much of its highly skilled operations to the United States, leaving low-skilled jobs behind in British Columbia. It used R&D carried out at home to establish, and service, these production facilities abroad. The takeover of MacMillan Bloedel by the American paper manufacturer Weyerhaueser Co. marked the logical conclusion of this trajectory to becoming an American-owned subsidiary and relocating its best jobs out of the national economy.

These data suggest an uncomfortable hypothesis. The effects of direct investment abroad are not symmetrical for small countries whose best jobs are drawn by the gravitational pull to the big country. This asymmetry is reinforced by the hegemon's dominance of the capital markets. As Canadian firms use U.S. rather than Canadian capital markets to expand their operations, they help keep the American dollar overvalued and the Canadian currency undervalued.[76]

Canadian companies have always made attractive targets for foreign purchase, but the depressed value of the Canadian dollar has induced a spate of takeovers of flagship companies that has worried even the leaders of the Canadian corporate elite who pushed for freer trade and investment rules in the first place. When MacMillan Bloedel was taken over and when Ottawa announced that it would scrap foreign-ownership limits on Petro-Canada shares while it waits for a chance to sell its stake in the company,[77] Donald Macdonald worried in public about foreign investment while admitting that he did not know what to do about the problem.[78] When Nova Chemicals, the one major Canadian controlled chemical company, moved its senior executive team to Pittsburgh, Peter Lougheed, mortal foe of the Trudeau government's nationalistic energy policy when premier of Alberta and later leading apologist for CUFTA, bewailed the loss, saying his province should have prevented the management shift.[79] Even the Business Council on National Issues, which masterminded the switch to free trade, has expressed alarm at its impact on corporate Canada.

As long as the trend towards the production and distribution of goods and services on a transnational basis continues on its globalizing course, all enterprise is becoming footloose. Firms will presumably become more denationalized as governments lose control over their national champions. And corporations will become even more multinationalized as they respond simultaneously to many governments and various levels of regulation. The Canadian economy will become ever more entangled in these corporate systems that cross its national borders, and its national sovereignty will continue to diminish.[80]

This does not mean that we have reached a stateless economy. States are intensifying their cross-border competition as they woo investors.[81] Business in Canada will continue to lobby for trade policies that reduce foreign (U.S.) protectionism. Big companies – Alcan, Du Pont, General Electric, General Motors, Noranda, Nortel – will press for policies that help them exploit their specific advantages and gain increased efficiencies. Some firms, such as breweries which have been protected by agricultural marketing boards, will plead to remain exempt from free trade.[82]

The implications of these developments for the distribution of power between market players and the Canadian state are complex. If a hallmark of globalization is the transnationalization of capital at the expense of state power, Canadian transnational corporate autonomy should have expanded at the same time as the federal government lost control over both domestic and foreign firms. Growing Canadian business presence in the global economy has allowed Canadian TNCs to become more distinct centres of power. Paradoxically, their relationship with the Canadian state has become more intense, not more distant. Public sector-private sector co-operation in formulating trade and investment policy has replaced the autonomous approach to economic management that characterized the Diefenbaker-Pearson-Trudeau era, when business was decidedly unwelcome in the boardrooms of the state. In managing Canada's trade dispute with Brazil over subsidies for aerospace exports, Bombardier became the conductor directing how the Canadian government, as orchestra, followed its score.

Prime Minister Chrétien's regular presence, accompanied by trade officials and top Canadian executives, at the Davos World Economic Forum symbolizes this privileged position of business in government.[83] Participation at the forum, which is attended by Fortune 500 executives and world leaders, gives Canada a stage on which to enhance its profile as a site for inward investment and an opportunity to negotiate deals for Canadian firms abroad. These cosy events increase Canadian-based TNCs' opportunity to influence government trade and investment policy, thereby shifting some degree of policy-making power to the TNC. The top Canadian-based TNCs test international waters, then return to lobby through their business interest groups for lower taxes and increased public funding for R&D, education, and training.

A partial shift of power from the federal to the provincial governments, which also undertake international initiatives to promote their companies, has also occurred, albeit with federal support. Among the Canadian officials accompanying Chrétien to Davos in 1999, for instance, were the premier of Manitoba, the deputy premier of Quebec, and the economic development minister of Ontario who were trying to boost their provinces as attractive sites for FDI.[84] Through Team Canada trade missions, the federal government seeks to promote international business by combining provincial with public and private-sector expertise and by seeking new markets to broaden Canada's investment destinations beyond the United States.

As a foreign firm operating in another NAFTA member, a Canadian TNC has a right to challenge domestic laws and decisions that violate its rights to intellectual property, right to invest, and right to market its products.[85] The Loewen Group launched the first Chapter 11 case in the United States.[86] This Canadian-based funeral conglomerate was found liable under Mississippi state law for using 'fraudulent and malicious business practices' to drive out local competition and for breaching previous contracts that granted exclusivity in that geographical area to a local funeral company. Loewen claimed that it was discriminated against and that the Mississippi civil justice system attempted to seize its assets without compensation in violation of NAFTA's Chapter 11.

Given Loewen's financial straits, a second Canadian Chapter 11 case may have greater significance in determining whether NAFTA has bolstered Canadian TNCs' position in the U.S. market. Methanex, the Vancouver-based methanol producer, is seeking restitution from the U.S. government for California's outlawing the gasoline additive MTBE. The ban is being defended on environmental and health protection grounds. California argues that MTBE, an end product of methanol, contaminates ground water and is linked to some cancers.[87] Methanex is using NAFTA's Chapter 11, which can nullify U.S. state or federal law if it amounts to expropriation – depriving a Canadian or Mexican firm of property, ownership, the right to market and sell its product, and the right to earn profit. The case is strikingly similar to the Ethyl Corporation's successful attack on Ottawa's ban of the gasoline additive MMT. Methanex argues that there is no scientific evidence to substantiate the ban of MTBE and wants to be compensated for potential losses of profit and market.

These decisions to take legal action defying American or Mexican legislation indicate that Canadian TNCs are participating in a semi-privatized continental governance. As a NAFTA member, Canada implicitly recognizes that Canadian firms with North American operations are their own legitimate centres of power. But in the light of several successful Chapter 11 challenges to its own legislation, the Canadian government pressed for a return to the NAFTA negotiating table to limit the scope and use of article 1110's expropriation language in such delicate areas of public interest.[88] American reluctance to open this issue could dissipate if Loewen and Methanex win their cases. If Ottawa succeeds in its renegotiation campaign, some of the TNCs' new power would return to the three states.

The continuing globalization of business through FDI and CDIA has produced both horizontal and vertical power shifts within Canada. The federal government has shed some of its policy-making power to accommodate Canadian TNCs and provincial leaders who are developing global interests. A coalition approach to trade and investment policy that embraces all levels of public- and private-sector expertise has emerged, resulting in an international business strategy that seeks to create opportunities for Canadian foreign investment.

Bringing business formally into the making of trade and investment policy by way of the CIBS and Team Canada creates a new role for market players within the state's councils. But empowering business politically has not guaranteed greater success than it experienced under the Keynesian state. After thirteen years of wrenching debates, cold showers, and leaps of faith under CUFTA, Canada had simply maintained its previous share of the U.S. market. It had not increased its market presence in the important American high-tech centres of Boston, California, and the Pacific northwest.[89]

Some authorities maintain that in the era of globalization governments cannot direct their economies' resources because they cannot control where and how international production takes place. They have only the negative power to distort, manage, and disrupt trade.[90] If they adopt this position, citizens of Canada will have to accept that their governments can do little more than look to the quality of their infrastructure and hope for the best.

But there is another view, less impressed by the apparent self-liberation of the corporation from the state. This position observes that nation-states still produce policies, albeit some more effectively than others. We saw in chapters 7 and 8 that they still try to manage the economy's macro functions with fiscal and monetary tools. Although the transnationalization of capital reflected in the explosion of FDI has diminished the power of states to control economic developments, governments still try to alter the competitive position of their businesses for the better on the assumption that this will redound to the benefit of all. These policies try to target specific sectors of the economy for encouragement and support and, in the case of economies suffering from excessive dependence, may aim to restore a balance between foreign and national producers. It is to these formerly leading, currently challenged functions of the Canadian state that we now turn our attention.

THE MICROECONOMY AND
THE INTERVENTIONIST STATE

'Interventionist' carries a strongly pejorative connatation in neo-conservative discourse, expressing the judgment by believers in self-regulating markets that the post-Keynesian state had become too involved in micro-managing Canada's industrial sectors, whether in the east-coast fishery or the prairie transportation system. With the Mulroney Conservatives adopting this position in their reaction against the Trudeau heritage, the government of Canada proceeded to negotiate in the trade liberalization agreements we have already analyzed the supraconstitutional norms that limited its powers to direct corporate activity. The provinces rapidly filled the industrial policy vacuum created by the federal government. Ontario was a case in point, as we shall see in chapter 14. While the federal government retained an active interest in the well-being of sectors such as automobiles, pharmaceuticals, and software, it found its ability to promote their interests severely restricted by the new global and continental rules. Accommodating their needs at the margin, not directing them to fundamental restructuring, became Ottawa's stance vis-à-vis industrial clients as its own functions became increasingly residual (chapter 13).

13 The Residual State: Accommodation at the Federal Level

In the late 1960s, most central Canadians wanting to boost the economy out of its dependent, branch-plant torpor looked to the federal government to devise the appropriate solutions. However, the weightiest advice that the prime minister, Pierre Trudeau, received in those days came from mainstream economists at the Bank of Canada, the Department of Finance, and the Economic Council of Canada, or from advisers convened in his own Prime Minister's Office who agreed with his scepticism about the value of Ottawa's intervening actively in the marketplace. This orthodox counsel held that Ottawa should restrain itself to the fine-tuning prescribed by Keynesian theory. If policy changes were to be made, they should support the forces of continental integration rather than bolster the structure of the national economy.

This blithe continentalism was shattered on August 15, 1971, when U.S. President Richard Nixon exploded the assumptions on which Canada's special relationship with the American economy had been based. In response, the Trudeau government's Third Option explicitly recommended adopting a coherent industrial strategy designed to reduce the country's economic dependence on and vulnerability to the American behemoth. 'Industrial strategy' was code for a more vigorous role for the state in shaping the economy by, for instance, negotiating more active trading relationships with Europe and Japan and by pressing foreign investors to increase the benefits that Canada received from their corporate activities.

Responding to the need for more adventurous policy thinking, the Liberal government officially sponsored another, more activist centre of policy advice. Distant though it was from the centre of Ottawa's policy firmament, the Science Council of Canada produced studies urging a more proactive approach to increasing the productivity of an economy in which foreign-controlled investment had truncated innovative capacities. Generic policies could

*strengthen industrial performance by boosting research and improving Cana-
dian-owned businesses' capacity to absorb new technology. In the academy,
comparative analysis of industrial success stories such as Sweden, West Germany, and Japan added scholarly substance to those urging the federal government to promote entrepreneurial champions.*

*For all the talk about industrial strategy, Ottawa in the 1970s achieved lit-
tle in the face of stonewalling by sceptical, neoclassical economists entrenched
in the Department of Finance and also the Department of Industry, Trade and
Commerce, whose mandate it was to support manufacturing interests.
Another external shock – the world petroleum crisis of 1979, which redoubled
the price of oil – and the election of a re-energized Liberal Party in 1980 led
Ottawa to define a powerful, comprehensive, and far-reaching strategy, if only
for one industry. The grandiose National Energy Program (NEP) of 1980 to
repatriate control over the oil and gas sectors was Ottawa's most ambitious
attempt ever to transform a staple industry oriented towards exports into a
sector redesigned to exploit Canada's comparative advantage in cheap energy
and boost industrial development. Former critics, who had long bewailed
Trudeau's economic timidity, now applauded him for his courage in defying
the U.S. and Alberta governments on behalf of this mega-policy. Their excitement was short-lived. World oil prices soon started falling, so that the financial premise underlying this experiment in grand industrial policy proved
faulty.*

*As they staggered from one failing economic sector (east-coast fisheries) to
another (prairie agriculture) in the aftermath of a debilitating recession in the
early 1980s, the Trudeauites also had to confront sporadic crises such as the
threatened bankruptcy of several large employers. Ottawa propped up the
Canadian subsidiary of Chrysler and the crown corporation Canadair with
public cash. The Liberals' Science Council-endorsed approach to promoting
home-based enterprise was on the ropes. Tainted by these bail-outs and the
NEP's spectacular failure, Trudeauite post-Keynesianism was condemned as
regressive, firm-based, and protectionist by business leaders who had no doubt
that Margaret Thatcher was right: there was no alternative to neoconservative
liberalization. Industrial strategy was dead.*

It was not Brian Mulroney's arrival in office in 1984 that made federal
intervention in the national market unacceptable. His first chief policy
adviser, Charles Macmillan, believed that the secret of the Japanese
economy's great success in the previous decade lay in Tokyo's dirigiste
role in influencing private-sector strategic planning. By extension,

Ottawa should also nourish a hands-on leadership role with industry. It was only after being in power for a year, when the Conservative prime minister seemed to be steering with no compass, that he was seduced by the radical policy agenda offered by Donald Macdonald in his royal commission report of 1985.

Making trade liberalization the centre-piece of federal economic policy was both an explicit repudiation of post-Keynesian industrial policy and an implicit – and negative – framework industrial strategy of its own. The idea was clear and Darwinian. Firms should be weaned from the government's teat and forced to be competitive on pain of extinction. Once it bought into the new paradigm, the government took pride in negotiating international rules that, as supraconstitutional norms, were to replace and even prohibit the Canadian state's old ways of affecting the nature of the economic game. When CUFTA and NAFTA extended the norm of national treatment to investment, they obliged governments in Canada to give up policies favouring domestic firms in their struggle with their more powerful foreign competitors. Although the Mulroney government steadily withdrew from making microeconomic policy, it was not clear whether continental governance necessarily deprived Ottawa of any legitimate role in industrial promotion. This is the issue that we now need to address, because still another school of thought began to articulate a new rationale for government action.

As part of a general effort to 'reinvent' government and cure it of its formerly spendthrift ways, discourse among most of the political elite by the mid-1990s contended that what used to be microeconomic – firm- or sector-centred – industrial policy should now focus on 'investing' in infrastructure to attract footloose capital to locate in Canada. For an information-based economy in which the laurels go to those who innovate, government's role should move towards 'investing in innovation,' by increasing the supply of highly trained knowledge workers.[1] Depending on its inclination, such a reinvented role for the state in skills training could provide Ottawa with a rationale for reasserting its role in training. Alternatively, it could be a reason for abandoning this sphere to the tender mercies of the provinces.

Elected with a comfortable majority in 1993 partly on the strength of a reactivated industrial policy plank formulated by their finance critic Paul Martin, Jr, Jean Chrétien's Liberals seemed bent on redeploying Ottawa's support for industrial development. But once Martin had been converted to his Finance Department officials' faith in budgetary probity, and once Chrétien grasped the federalists' near-loss in the 1995 Quebec referendum, a deficit-shrinking, national unity-obsessed Ottawa was only too pleased to get out of labour training and let the provinces pick up the slack – the subject of chapter 16. The Liberals actually accelerated Ottawa's withdrawal from its costly industrial policies because they gave top priority to reducing their inherited deficit. The resulting program cuts radically restricted the use of federal funds to enhance either innovation or productivity, as described below.

As the Liberals continued the Tory retreat, Ottawa's capacity for economic development became increasingly residual, as we can see by looking at three cases: an established, Fordist sector (auto production); an industry directly affected by global governance (medical drugs); and a high-profile facet of the new information economy (software). This approach reveals the niche that the residual central state has attempted to carve out for itself in promoting what it is pleased to call an innovation economy.

The Auto Industry

The Canadian auto industry presents a special case for studying free trade's consequences because of its prior history of virtually complete continental integration under U.S. ownership and control. Canada's largest manufacturing sector, it produces roughly 25 per cent of all Canadian exports[2] – one-third of Canadian exports to the United States[3] – and provides direct employment for 180,000 Canadians,[4] and as many 'spin-off' jobs. In 1998, Canada's total export of all automotive products amounted to $78 billion, and the industry enjoyed a trade surplus of $11 billion.[5]

From the introduction of the assembly line in 1913, the industry has been characterized by branch-plant production. In the interwar period, miniature-replica plants produced the same models as their American parents in Detroit for tariff-protected, local consumption and for the large export market in Commonwealth countries made possible by the old imperial preference rules. Apart from its tariff policy, the Canadian state adopted a largely passive stance until the early 1960s, when crisis struck an industry that had failed to recapture the export markets lost during the Second World War. Between 1955 and 1960, imports of cars and parts from outside North America had tripled, while exports had dropped catastrophically, leaving Canada with a $389 million trade deficit in auto products.[6] With production and employment falling, the federally commissioned Bladen Report called in 1963 for waiving the duty on the import of selected parts, provided that the auto companies increased their exports accordingly. Rather than impose the countervailing duties that the U.S. congress demanded in retaliation for what it denounced as an export subsidy, President Lyndon Johnson preferred negotiating a structural solution with Ottawa, Detroit, and the branch plants.

The resulting Canada-U.S. Automotive Products Agreement (Auto Pact) of 1965 transformed a nationally organized, tariff-protected industry into a continentally rationalized industry that guaranteed a minimum level of Canadian production in U.S.-owned assembly plants, albeit at the expense of the highly paid R&D and managerial jobs remaining at the U.S. headquarters.[7] The agreement changed the two countries' tariff structure to allow conditional free trade in auto products. Through negotiated letters of understanding with the 'Big Four' – American Motor Co., Chrysler, Ford, and General Motors (GM) – Ottawa gave their Canadian-based manufacturers the right to import components and vehicles duty-free from anywhere in the world on condition that they respect two safeguards designed to maintain Canada's share of total continental production. First, a Canadian-content rule required that 50 per cent of each vehicle assembled in Canada be made in Canada. Second, a market-share rule stipulated that at least one car was to be produced in Canada for every car sold in Canada. The Auto Pact stimulated a tremendous increase in trade between the two countries (it rose over nineteen-fold between 1964 and 1977, to $20 billion).[8] The Americans, who placed no restrictions on vehicle imports, considered the safeguards a temporary measure and rejected the Canadian claim to their long-term validity.

The safeguards established an incentive to manufacturers to open parts-production plants in Canada rather than in the United States. Not only would the safeguards enable the Canadian-based parts producers to benefit from Big Four contracts, they protected Canadian production for the continental market and helped to sustain growth within the Canadian industry throughout the 1980s.

Seven Asian 'transplants' set up assembly plants to take advantage of the Auto Pact's Canadian content rule. By 1985, the new Japanese plants accounted for one-fifth of total continental production,[9] and had introduced more efficient production techniques to the Canadian auto industry, characterized by 'just in time' delivery systems, which reduced inventories by requiring precisely timed delivery of parts to the auto assemblers. By 1998, Toyota's Ontario plant had doubled the capacity of its Corolla assembly line[10] and was the second most productive car plant in North America.[11] Canadian-based Japanese manufacturers now set the standard against which production efficiency was compared in the North American auto industry. The Big Three (after Chrysler's acquisition of American Motors) in the United States and Canada found themselves forced to adopt these transplants' methods in order to sustain their share of the continental market. This pressure led by the end of the decade to four Japanese-American joint ventures operating in North America, of which one, CAMI (GM/Suzuki), was in Canada.[12]

The 'Big Three' persuaded Washington to adopt a particularly tough position when negotiating CUFTA. Although Ottawa wanted to protect its Japanese transplants, the Americans argued that the Canadian-content rule undermined their competitive position by letting the transplant use Ontario as a base for penetrating their market. CUFTA's automobile chapter effectively withdrew the Japanese transplants' privileged position within the North American market. CUFTA divided the Canadian auto industry into two classes of producers: those that retained their Auto Pact status, including the Big Three, Volvo, and CAMI, and those that could not achieve such status. Only the Big Three, Volvo, and CAMI could import parts and vehicles into Canada duty-free from any country, whereas the Japanese transplants and any new producer operating in Canada would have to pay a duty on all imports from countries other than the United States.[13]

The more restrictive rules of origin were designed to give the Asian transplants an incentive to relocate to the United States where they could export vehicles to Canada at a lower cost under the new rule. But a Japanese exodus from Ontario did not occur because the province's infrastructure remained unmatched in either the United States or Mexico. At least five major factors – history (the intangible cultural patterns developed over the decades in a long-established auto sector), geography (the clustering of parts producers in close proximity to manufacturers), physical infrastructure (including well-kept roads and highways), human infrastructure (especially government-supplied universal medical care),[14] and human resources (a skilled labour force developed from colleges that provide specialized education) – contributed to central Canada's attractiveness for the long term as an investment area vis-à-vis its southern competitors.

NAFTA's auto provisions showed again that the Big Three called the shots on North American auto production, which were to be further integrated on an expanded continental basis. In the face of Ottawa's attempt to maintain Canada as a production area, Washington dictated that North America was to be the reference area. As a result, Canada lost its status as a designated region within the continental industry. This meant that assemblers and parts producers in all three countries would no longer have to source a specific quantity of components in Canada in order to gain duty-free access to the continental market from Canada. All parts could be bought in Mexico if the assembler so desired. The new rule of origin would have little effect on Canadian parts producers, which could still supply the transplants as 'North American' suppliers. The Auto Pact's discrimination in favour of North American content was still in place. The Japanese transplants, which were previously allowed to import parts duty-free from cheap sources abroad, now had to meet an even higher North American requirement (62.5 per cent) under NAFTA than under the CUFTA rule. Turning North America into a 'regional zone of preference'[15] made Mexico a desirable investment area for parts and assembly production. Indeed, in the years after NAFTA was signed, Mexico became the second-largest exporter in parts production to Canada, after the United States.[16]

Mexico's Automotive Decrees, designed by the government of Carlos Salinas de Gortieri in 1989 to attract high-quality, capital-intensive manufacturing operations to Mexico by lowering import and investment barriers,[17] were to be phased out over a ten-year period. This gave the Big Three, Nissan, and Volkswagen, which had already established manufacturing in Mexico, a privileged chance to restructure their operations in the face of incoming assemblers.[18] By muscling Washington, the existing manufacturers succeeded in keeping Mexico for themselves and the transplants out, if only temporarily.

Yet both Mexico and Canada benefited from U.S. continental protectionism. Mexico improved the conditions for its already-robust, foreign-dominated manufacturing base and profited from new joint ventures between Canadian and Mexican parts producers, who gained lucrative Big Three contracts in Mexico. While some Canadian parts producers moved to Mexico, where wages were one-tenth the Canadian level, most stayed in Canada, where product quality and cost standards remained higher and more reliable.

Although the NAFTA rules represented a definite loss for the Japanese transplants, whose managers would have to wait up to ten years before they could set up plants in Mexico, they had little overall effect on the Canadian auto industry, which continued to thrive. The Canadian-based Big Three were already meeting the higher North American-content requirement before it became mandatory under NAFTA. So were the transplants, which continued to outperform the Big Three in Canada, thanks to just-in-time techniques. Moreover, Canadian negotiators achieved their goal of open access to the Mexican market – any North American manufacturer can either launch a parts production company in Mexico and be considered a 'national supplier of parts,' or invest up to 100 per cent in indigenous auto parts companies after five years.[19]

While the Canadian state proved weak in negotiating power, it nevertheless demonstrated its capacity to create competitively advantageous conditions. State-financed unemployment insurance and universal hospital and doctor care contributed to Canada's desirability for present and potential auto investors, along with another factor for which the government did not claim credit – a favourable exchange rate which translated into a 30 per cent advantage in labour costs over the United States. Lower payroll taxes also bolstered Canada's competitive advantage.[20] The proximity of parts producers to assemblers within a relatively small geographical area serviced by well-maintained highways sustained Canada's attractiveness vis-à-vis Mexico, where many roads remain inadequate, driving conditions precarious, and distances between suppliers and assemblers considerable – a crucial consideration for just-in-time production.

Although relatively little enterprise shifted out of the country (some parts producers did pack their bags and move to the Mexican maquiladoras, but many stayed behind to service auto assemblers), civil society lost ground. Mexico's authoritarian work environment, its lack of union autonomy, and its lower labour costs threatened the quantity and quality of Canadian jobs at a time when Canadian auto workers' greatest concern remained employment security. Indeed, between 1990 and 1992, 15,100 Canadian jobs in motor vehicles and equipment evaporated as manufacturers struggled to narrow the growing productivity gap with the United States.[21] Positions were lost when plants moved to the Mexican maquiladoras or the. U.S. southwest where so-called 'right-to-work' states constrained unions' ability to organize. Working conditions in Ontario deteriorated when companies threatened to follow this trend unless employees made various concessions. Even the Big Three increased out-sourcing to independent parts producers and pressed for shorter collective bargaining agreements.[22] The corporations' ability to leverage their position against Canadian civil society is a testament to a continental system that protects business rights before those of workers.

Canadian labour demonstrated remarkable strength within the North American auto industry despite this pressure. After they split off from their American parent union, the United Auto Workers (UAW), in 1985, the Canadian Auto Workers (CAW) actually helped maintain Canada's competitive position within the auto sector. To the surprise of its critics, a mature and healthy, if confrontational labour-management relationship contributed to Canada's positive environment for investors by enhancing a well-educated workforce's commitment to its jobs.[23] The 1996 collective bargaining round between GM and the CAW brought about significant improvements to benefits: reduced hours, gains in wages, cost-of-living adjustments, and income security, plus limits on the corporation's ability to out-source work.[24] The CAW managed to extract these gains from the Big Three at a time when managers were searching for new ways to increase productive capacity and improve efficiency. In return, the Big Three gained high labour discipline and productivity.

In a genuflection to the forces of market deregulation, the federal government dismantled the Auto Pact beginning in July 2000. In response to a Japanese complaint, the WTO's Dispute Settlement Body ruled that the Auto Pact broke various international trade rules. Though a victory for European and Japanese auto producers, who gained more equal access to the North American market, it was unlikely to have much effect on Canadian producers of auto parts which were still able to source parts in Mexico for the continental market. According to the ruling, the Big Three would have to pay the same 6.1 per cent tariff on all car imports as the North American-based Japanese and European manufacturers, thus creating a 'level playing field' between Canadian, American, European, and Japanese auto manufacturers. While prices for luxury cars imported by the Big Three would be affected, any cars produced within North America would still be sold duty-free because of NAFTA.[25]

Despite the increased American dominance of the industry offered by the North American content rule, free trade did not diminish the Canadian share of the North American market. Indeed, between 1988 and 1995, Canada's share of North American auto production rose from 17 per cent to 18 per cent, while the U.S. share fell from 80 per cent to 78 per cent. (Mexico's share of auto production rose from 3 per cent to 4 per cent.[26]) Although it is dwarfed by its southern neighbour's capacity, Canada's increase demonstrated its relative strength as a medium-sized player within the continental regime at a time when the U.S. plants were downsizing. The effects of free trade on Canada were mitigated by the nature of the industry's organization. Continental rationalization had been the model of production for three decades and already, prior to free trade, had led the Canadian-based Big Three to produce 80 per cent of their cars for American consumption and only 20 per cent for Canada.[27] Investors continued to choose Canada as a positive climate in which to set up and expand operations. Honda and Toyota, as well as the jointly administered transplants, expanded their plants in Ontario in the mid-1990s. Canada proved itself a competitive and successful production and investment site under free trade, given a long expansion of the U.S. economy. Declining work standards throughout North America and increasing calls for efficiency in the workplace rendered the federal and Ontario governments only indirectly effective monitors of their biggest manufacturing sector. The greatest challenge facing Canadian-based manufacturers, government officials, and the CAW was to continue to defend the growth of their industry against these threats as Mexico's auto industry became fully integrated into a truly continental trading and investing regime.

In sum, both CUFTA and NAFTA exerted substantial, though contradictory effects on the Canadian automobile industry, reducing its protections but strengthening its competitive position. Trade liberalization also complicated the relationship between the various levels of the Canadian state. In 1989, CUFTA took over from the bilateral 1965 auto agreement as the sector's 'constitution' providing the U.S.-dictated mode of regulation for managing the largely American-owned Canada-U.S. automobile industry. Five years later, the U.S. oligopoly managed with NAFTA to rewrite the rule book for the continental automobile economy and give itself a preferred position. Invoking the superior authority of global governance, the Japanese and European producers exploited the WTO's rules to challenge the discriminatory vestiges still existing in the Auto Pact. Once its negotiating was done, the federal government was left with virtually no role in the continuing saga of the auto industry. The role for the government of Ontario, the chief site for vehicle production, remained indirect: maintain the quality of the physical and social infrastructure, and provide training for human resources. Continentalization also linked the Canadian state in a delicate, co-operative/competitive relationship with its southern neighbours. As the Canadian auto industry became increasingly integrated in continental production platforms, Canadian-based Big Three plant managers lost some bargaining power to the CAW, which in turn lost ground vis-à-vis the Mexican labour market.

Pharmaceuticals and Intellectual Property Rights

Vehicle production is so prototypical of the mass production of consumer goods where profits are related to economies of scale that it gave a name – Fordism – to the industrial era for which Keynesianism was the counterpart mode of state regulation. Concentrated in giant, continentally based corporations, it had international policy implications centred on the provisions about tariffs, rules of origin, and investment found in the original Auto Pact and later in NAFTA. A different economic logic characterizes another globally oligopolistic industry. Medical drugs are extremely expensive to develop but ridiculously cheap to produce. Global profitability – and so survival – for the pharmaceutical giants depend on their being able to capture the profits from their branded drugs.

The United States, the European Union (EU), and Japan account for roughly 75 per cent of the world's pharmaceutical market and undertake 90 per cent of all drug-related research and development (R&D) activity.[28] As ownership of transnational pharmaceutical firms became concentrated in the hegemonic economies, these firms pressed for a strong international legal regime to protect their sales from competition. Because patents provide firms with a legal monopoly to exploit their products' financial potential, intellectual property law plays a key role in brand-name pharmaceutical firms' growth strategy.

Prior to the entrenchment of intellectual property protection in the WTO's agreement on Trade Related Aspects of Intellectual Property Rights (TRIPs), patent systems varied substantially from state to state. At one end of the spectrum, the strict U.S. patent regime provided seventeen years of protection for both products and processes. After 1994 this increased to twenty years' protection. At the other extreme were the no-patents-for-medicine regimes of countries such as Brazil and Argentina.[29] The majority of patent systems fell somewhere in between. They employed a variety of mechanisms designed to promote the availability of affordable drugs and to foster domestic, pharmaceutical-related R&D and manufacturing activity, which included varying the length of patent terms, legislating compulsory licences requiring licensees to manufacture or import patent-protected products, limiting what could be patented (product or process), establishing work-the-patent requirements, or having price controls on patented products.[30]

Canadian patent law has a considerable history of distinguishing pharmaceutical products from other manufactured products. The Patent Act was amended in 1923 to allow domestic firms to manufacture patented pharmaceutical products in Canada under compulsory licences, which cut into brand-name drug firms' profits during the basic, seventeen-year patent term for their medicines. Since the primary intention of this act was to stimulate Canadian pharmaceutical manufacturing and to encourage competitive pricing, it gave weak protection to drug patent holders. However, its success was limited because the Canadian market lacked enough depth to warrant the economies of large-scale production necessary to support manufacturing facilities.[31] Between 1923 and 1969 only forty-nine compulsory licences were applied for, and of these, only twenty-two were granted.[32]

The issue of pharmaceutical patents was reopened in 1958 when the Department of Justice initiated an investigation by the Restrictive Trade Commission into allegations of anti-competitive conduct by pharmaceutical firms.[33] The resulting report noted that drug prices within Canada were among the highest in the industrialized world.[34] Because the Patent Act of 1923 could not ensure that medicines were made available to the public at the lowest possible cost while still giving due rewards to their inventors, the report called for the abolition of all patents on pharmaceutical products. Although this recommendation was never acted on, the Royal Commission on Health Services and the Hartly Report[35] in the mid-1960s confirmed that Canadians paid disproportionately high prices for medications but made the less radical proposal that compulsory licences include the importation of generic versions of brand-name drugs. The Pharmaceutical Manufacturers' Association of Canada (PMAC), which represented the transnationals' subsidiaries in Canada, mounted a costly campaign against this idea.[36] The failure of this lobbying was marked in 1969 when the Trudeau government amended the Patent Act to allow firms to import generic pharmaceutical products manufactured abroad. The implementation of this amendment – section 41(4) – was delayed by a year while a large U.S.-based pharmaceutical firm, American Home Products, unsuccessfully challenged its validity in the Canadian courts.[37]

Since one repercussion of this amendment was that medicines would no longer have to be manufactured in Canada, it was highly controversial. Brand-name pharmaceutical firms continued to fight the importation of generic drugs by appealing in the courts forty-three of the sixty-nine compulsory licences issued. Because it was cheaper to import generic drugs than to manufacture them in Canada, the generic import industry flourished. From 1970 to 1978, the majority of the 142 compulsory licences issued on forty-seven prescription drugs were imported from U.S. manufacturers.[38] Prices for generic drugs were usually more than 20 per cent below those of their brand name equivalents. Provincial legislation requiring pharmacists to fill prescriptions with the generic equivalents of higher-priced patented medicines when available guaranteed a large market to holders of compulsory licences. The expansion of provincial drug plans to cover elderly and low-income individuals increased the demand for these generics. Attempts by certain multinational drug firms to undermine generic firms with letters to doctors that called into question the quality of generic drugs backfired, because most recipients regarded these letters as a blatantly manipulative marketing ploy.

While the inclusion of section 41(4) encouraged lower prices through the greater availability of generic drugs, it had a significant impact on Canadian pharmaceutical R&D and manufacturing activity. Many pharmaceutical firms moved their research facilities from Canada to the United States. For instance, Smith, Kline & French closed its R&D facility in Quebec, and Abbot moved its Montreal operations to Chicago. As well, Hoffman-LaRoche, Warner Lambert-Parke Davis, Merck-Frosst, and Syntex publicly announced (in a move obviously calculated to garner public support) that they had aborted their plans to open R&D facilities in Canada.[39] While between 1963 and 1969 the annual growth rate of pharmaceutical R&D activity had been 18 per cent, it shrank to 7 per cent between 1970 and 1977.[40]

Since pharmaceutical manufacturers are concentrated in the Montreal area, the PMAC focused its lobbying activity throughout the 1970s and early 1980s on Quebec's Liberal caucus in Parliament, promising more investment in Quebec if compulsory licensing was abolished.[41] This political pressure, supported by the well-documented decrease in R&D activity, eventually paid off. The powerful caucus's sympathetic attitude was reflected in a 1983 red paper from the Department of Consumer and Corporate Affairs that put forward proposals to modify compulsory licensing in ways favourable to patent-holding firms.[42] The minister, André Ouellet, who was also deputy head and whip of Quebec's Liberal caucus, called for a rebalancing of the 1969 policy on compulsory licences in order to stimulate pharmaceutical R&D activity. The three proposed ways to change the Patent Act were: initiating variable royalty rates for compulsory licensees that reflected the level of R&D activity they carried out in Canada; giving compulsory licence exceptions to firms that gave market and price commitments; and giving patent-holding firms market exclusivity for a specified number of years at the beginning of their patent term.[43] With caucus and industry pressure to re-examine compulsory pharmaceutical licensing and a federal election imminent, the Liberal government attempted to defuse the issue by referring the question to an inquiry headed by a University of Toronto economist, Harry Eastman.

In addition to examining the market performance and research activity of pharmaceutical firms operating in Canada, the Eastman Commission was asked to make recommendations concerning pharmaceutical patent protection and compulsory licences. Despite the PMAC's claims to the contrary, the Eastman Report found that pharmaceutical firms had continued to be highly profitable after the introduction of section 41(4).[44] Moreover, the profitability of multinational firms was higher in Canada than in most industrialized countries. Eastman calculated that transnational firms had lost only 3.1 per cent of the Canadian market to generic firms, which took in only 14 per cent of the total revenue of the Canadian market. Nevertheless, compulsory licences saved consumers $211 million in 1983 alone. Upjohn and Syntex had themselves established generic manufacturing subsidiaries – Kenral and Syncare, respectively – that directly competed with the parent firm's expired-patent products. Because Eastman found the compulsory licensing system to be working well, he recommended only minor changes – a four-year period of market exclusivity would provide a sufficient profit incentive to encourage patent-holding firms to introduce new drugs to the Canadian market.

By the time the Eastman Report appeared in 1985, the political tides had changed substantially. Canada was on the point of abdicating its power to tailor its laws to its own needs in favour of a continental and then global regime of intellectual property rights. The Diefenbaker-Pearson-Trudeau system, which had carved out a partially national approach to offset the price gouging that made public health care increasingly expensive, was under attack. The Mulroney Conservatives' urgent desire for a free trade deal exposed them to intense political pressure from Washington. Although they consistently denied that intellectual property was on the bilateral negotiating table, substantial evidence indicated the contrary. One of the top items on the U.S. agenda at the March 1985 'Shamrock Summit' in Quebec City between Ronald Reagan and Brian Mulroney was Canada's drug patent legislation.

Washington's impatience with Canada at the time was reflected in the U.S. Trade Representative's annual report for 1985 which listed Canada's drug legislation as a 'trade irritant.' Linda McQuaig quoted Bill Merkin, the U.S. deputy chief trade negotiator, as saying:

> Ottawa didn't want it [intellectual property] to be in the free trade negotiations. They didn't want to *appear* to be negotiating that away as part of the free trade agreement. Whatever changes they were going to make, they wanted them to be *viewed* as 'in Canada's interest' ... It was a high priority for us. We were not above flagging the issue [to the Canadian negotiators] for the success of the overall negotiations.[45]

Hence, in return for the Americans' signing on to the free trade agreement, the Progressive Conservatives introduced the Patent Act amendment, Bill C-22, in November 1986. To accommodate the interests of brand-name drug firms, the bill drastically overhauled the Canadian patent system. It delayed the issuing of compulsory licences to manufacture by seven years and similar licences to import by ten. In order to encourage brand-name firms to expand their Canadian manufacturing operations, the government agreed to extend the seven-year grace period before a compulsory licence (to manufacture) was issued if a firm secured a domestically produced supply of that drug. Since Bill C-22 reduced competition in the drug market, the Patented Medicine Prices Review Board, an independent, quasi-judicial body, was created to ensure that the prices of human and veterinary drugs sold in Canada did not become exorbitant.

In several important ways, the changes made under Bill C-22 brought Canada's patent system in line with the American one. The most startling change was the new 'first-to-file' rule. Washington's refusal to accept the international 'first-to-invent' norm had made it a pariah state within the global intellectual property community, which believed that the first-to-file rule constituted a discriminating trade barrier that gave an advantage to American firms. Bill C-22's introduction of the first-to-file rule constituted an astonishing breach by Canada of its earlier international solidarity.

Another important provision of this amendment was the creation of product patents rather than process patents for medicine. Process patents provide a weaker form of protection because they allow competitors to introduce the same drug if they can find another way to manufacture it. Because Canada granted patents only for the process used to manufacture a drug and not for the drug compound itself, transnational firms had pressed for change. By providing patent protection to the product, regardless of the process used, by extending the patent protection period, and by moving to a first-to-file system, the harmonization of Canada's patent law with the United States skewed it further to benefit U.S. drug firms.

Because of Bill C-22's highly controversial nature, the Liberal-dominated Senate stalled its passage for several months. While many senators suggested that delaying the introduction of generic drugs would result in higher costs to private insurers and consumers, several also cast doubt on the ability of the price control board to ensure that the prices of new drugs would remain reasonable. Provincial governments were also alarmed because this legislation would increase their health care system's operating costs.[46] In addition to intense U.S. governmental pressure, the PMAC offered the government a further enticement to amend the Patent Act by offering a conditional commitment to raise its Canadian R&D-to-sales ratio to 8 per cent by 1991 and 10 per cent by 1996.[47] Senators were sceptical that the brand-name firms would meet these undertakings and noted that the bill did not contain any enforcement provisions. In actual practice, PMAC member companies appear to have exceeded their stated R & D goals. In January 2001, Ottawa released an independent audit that found these firms had achieved an R&D-to-sales ratio of 12.5 per cent.[48]

Canada made further commitments to strengthen its patent regime under NAFTA and the General Agreement on Tariffs and Trade (GATT). To implement these obligations, Bill C-91, passed in February 1993, revoked the compulsory licence scheme that had enabled the Canadian generic industry to thrive. Patent-holding firms were now guaranteed market exclusivity for the entire patent term. Moreover, Bill C-91 extended the period of patent protection to twenty years from the date that the last patent pertaining to a drug had expired. Pharmaceutical firms exploit this clause by filing multiple patents on a drug at different dates, effectively extending their patent's market exclusivity.[49] This tactic delays generic firms from entering the market after the expiration of a patent by provoking groundless, expensive, and time-consuming lawsuits. Bill C-91 also set out procedures for those contesting the validity of patents to delay generic firms, pending resolution, for up to thirty months. Estimates of the increase of drug costs to Canadian consumers resulting from the passage of Bill C-91 were as high as $9.4 billion over the ensuing twenty-year period.[50]

Notwithstanding its series of victories in Ottawa, Washington remained on the offensive. In 1999, it challenged Canada's pharmaceutical patent system at the WTO. In a statement on April 30, 1999, U.S. Trade Representative Charlene Barshefsky claimed that the current patent term was not in compliance with Canada's obligations under TRIPs.[51] The issue related to the length of the patent term, which on October 1, 1989 was extended from seventeen years from date of grant of patent to a term of twenty years from date of application for patents. Patents applied for prior to this date still had the old seventeen-year term, but Washington argued that the regular term of twenty years should be extended retroactively to these patents.[52]

The EU also challenged Canada's patent system at the WTO, alleging that Bill C-91's 'Bolar provisions' were incompatible with Canada's trade obligations under TRIPs. Bolar provisions provide specific exemptions from patent infringement to allow a generic manufacturer to do the product R&D required to gain manufacturing approval prior to the expiration of the patent term. The Canadian provisions allowed manufacturers to stockpile their medicines for up to six months, ensuring that generic drugs were ready to ship as soon as the patent expired. Besides Canada, the United States, Israel, and Australia employ Bolar-style provisions. In 2000, Ottawa lost both the EU and U.S. challenges at the WTO, forcing it to amend its Patent Act in favour of brand-name drug firms once again.[53] Since generic drugs cost approximately 50 per cent less than their branded equivalents, these changes increased health care costs, upsetting health groups, seniors' organizations, and, of course, the generic drug manufacturers.

Intellectual property protection (IPP) was presented in this debate as the legal shield needed to ensure that inventors can collect the fruits of their creative genius. In the domain of pharmaceutical patents, the economic super powers established an international IPP regime to defend a global transnational corporate (TNC) oligopoly against the forces of competition. As experienced in Canada, this trade liberalization amounted to the U.S. state's using bilateral pressure (CUFTA), trilateral negotiations (NAFTA), and a multilateral forum (the WTO) to force the Canadian state to abandon a policy experiment that had given its citizens some relief from monopoly pricing.[54]

Neoclassical theory predicts that unhindered competition between manufacturers of a drug should result after its patent term has expired. However, pharmaceutical firms employ a variety of tactics to circumvent anti-trust laws and perpetuate their monopolies. In more than one case, patent-holding drug firms have attempted to acquire generic firms that produce the same drug in order to control the entire market. Patent-holding firms also try to monopolize a market by pre-emptively introducing their own generic version of a drug prior to the expiration of a patent. For example, one month before the expiration of Upjohn Company's tranquillizer Xanax, it introduced its own generic version of the drug. As a result, even after new competitors entered the market, Upjohn was able to maintain a 90 per cent share for this drug.

Although this section has focused on pharmaceuticals to illustrate the impact of new global trade norms, it would be a mistake to infer that the great powers' success in commodifying intellectual property rights at the global level is significant only for their drug companies. IPP also creates the legal regime allowing the biotechnology giants to transform the world's agriculture by creating, copyrighting, and commercializing new forms of plant life. It is also central to the growth capacity of information technology firms, enabling, as we see in the next section, such giants as Microsoft to expand their hegemony.

Software

Ensuring the availability of adequate information technology (IT) has become a high priority for nearly all governments and industries around the world in response to the economy's increasing dependence on information processing. The backbone of the IT industry is software and computer technologies, whose sales grew from less than $1 billion in the late 1970s to $15.3 billion by 1998. The Canadian software sector was tied closely to and dwarfed by its American cousin, of which it was about one-twentieth the size.[55] Some 91 per cent of the firms were privately owned 'micro-businesses' with fewer than ten employees and annual revenues of less than $250,000. They targeted niche markets and were typically unprofitable.[56] The top five corporations were large and, with the exception of Ottawa-based Corel, U.S.-owned. They were highly profitable as a group and generated more than half of the sector's revenue.

Generally, Canadian software firms develop new products with an eye on the continental market. While 97 per cent of Canadian software products companies sell at least some of their software products in Canada, 73 per cent export to the United States.[57] They are headquartered in Montreal, Toronto, and Ottawa-Carleton, sustained by multifarious links with funding sources. In Ottawa-Carleton, for instance, they connect with the key player fostering regional innovation system – the Ottawa Centre for Research and Innovation – which in turn receives funds from the local municipality, numerous corporate sponsors, the province, and the federal government.

As in the United States, the software sector in Canada has grown consistently, even during the 1991–3 recession. U.S. dominance has been secured by American firms selling direct to the Canadian market and by high levels of consolidation through mergers, acquisitions, and strategic alliances set up by the market leaders – IBM, Microsoft and Novell.[58] Given Canada's familiar role as farm club, many successful domestic firms have been acquired by large American software companies: Alias by Silicon Graphics Inc., Delrina by Symantec Corporation, Softimage and Zoom-it by Microsoft. American supremacy in the Canadian software market has been facilitated by geographical proximity, cultural similarities, and the elimination of the government's capacity to screen foreign takeovers.

Since Canadian software firms are necessarily niche market players, what industry standards there are, how open they are, and who controls them are key issues that affect their competitiveness. Corel offers business and graphics products made for various operating platforms. Smaller firms do not have the resources to create versions of their programs adapted to several different operating systems. They program for one or two operating systems in the hope that they will grow in popularity. In graphics and media-oriented operating systems, software companies face an even more acute standards problem because of the fragmentation inherent in the early stages of an emerging technology. Apple, Dobi, Media 100, SEI Alias Wavefront, Windows 95, Windows 98, Windows NT, and Windows 2000/ME are just some of the incompatible platforms currently competing to become the industry standard. Although compatibility of standards is a central issue for many Canadian firms, Ottawa follows Washington's example (with the possible exception of its anti-trust case against Microsoft) in choosing to leave the issue unaddressed.

A significant *trade* issue that affects the software sector is intellectual property protection (IPP) across international boundaries. Because the 'Asian Tigers,' the rapidly industrializing economies of Taiwan, Singapore, Hong Kong and South Korea, threatened the United States' technological hegemony by pirating the U.S. rights-holders' property, Washington sought to bypass the World Intellectual Property Organization, whose agenda was controlled by less developed nations. Arguing that the poorer states' lack of international IPP created 'unfair competition' by allowing theft of its firms' intellectual property, the United States shifted intergovernmental discourse towards the creation of an international IPP regime that commodified information and controlled its flows. Since widespread disregard of intellectual property rights decreases the attractiveness of investment and growth in technology-intensive industries such as software and pharmaceuticals, the GATT Uruguay Round's agreement on TRIPs became a U.S. policy tool to protect and promote its global technological dominance.

Changes to the international IPP regime pushed through by the United States ipso facto reinforce the hegemony of its software giants in the Canadian market. Microsoft, which has a massive legal capacity, is far more likely to pursue patent infringements than the majority of small and medium-sized Canadian software companies for whom exorbitant legal costs make protecting their intellectual property rights in a new product unfeasible. Some Canadian firms have sought patents solely to make themselves more attractive for U.S. takeover offers rather than to be able to defend their intellectual property in court.

Despite the success of their software industry, Americans worry that they might follow the same path as the home electronics and automotive industries, whose early global leadership was lost to foreign competitors.[59] For this reason, Washington has supplemented its aggressive advocacy of multilateral and continental IPP agreements such as TRIPs and NAFTA's Chapter 17 with unilateral measures. Its Super 301 legislation stipulated that the Special 301 review committee must annually review the IPP, trade, and industrial-development policies of its trading partners. This committee reviews whether U.S. right-holders' intellectual property privileges have been adequately protected, while investigating whether foreign governments have given special IPP privileges to their domestic firms. Industrial policies of China, India, and Ireland that target the software industry have already come under significant scrutiny from this committee. Although the aggressive use of the Super 301 underscored the high priority that Washington placed on software, it was doubtful that it would be used against the Canadian software industry, since federal and provincial support for it has been indirect, piecemeal, and above all weak.

Local, regional, provincial, and federal microeconomic policies aimed at the software industry influence it mainly at the edges. Successful initiatives by the National Research Council (NRC) and certain universities aim to help specific firms, not to boost the industry as a whole. When the Canadian government sought to address industry-wide problems, it met with only limited success. For example, when there was a lack of qualified software developers, Canada's several respected, university-level computer science programs were unable to meet the labour demand. This shortage was aggravated by computer science graduates being enticed to the U.S. by higher wages. In response to petitioning from the Information Technology Association of Canada – the chief IT lobby group – the federal government began accelerating the immigration of foreign IT workers. Some provinces, including Ontario, responded to this labour shortage by increasing funding to university-level computer science programs, an indirect subsidy to the software industry that reduced its need to spend on training. Despite these measures, the IT labour shortage problem continued to worsen until the 'dot.com' meltdown of 2000. Another indication of the Canadian state's limited policy impact on the industry is the fact that, despite a generous program of R&D tax incentives, Canadian software firms consistently spend less on R&D than their American counterparts.[60]

The Canadian state is under indirect pressure to reshape its software industry by following the American lead in promoting the convergence of computer, telephone, television, wireless, and data broadcast systems. Since these services are likely to be increasingly combined and delivered together over unitary systems, further mergers, acquisitions, and strategic alliances between software and telecommunications firms are inevitable.

The combination of this further consolidation with the hegemonic control already exerted over the Canadian software industry by U.S. interests, suggests that government will become ever less able to influence the direction and shape of its information-intensive economy except at the local level, where the provision of amenities can be a critical factor determining the location decisions of footloose corporations. The indirect influence of municipal government on the future of the software industry finds an intriguing parallel in the indirect role that Ottawa has played in supporting what is now known as the 'knowledge–based economy.'

Knowledge and Innovation Policy

With education falling squarely within the provinces' constitutional jurisdiction, the government of Canada has long had an ambivalent attitude to its promotion. To the extent that Ottawa worries about its budgets, it is relieved to be free of responsibility for financing schools and universities from sea to sea. But when it has compared Canada's economic prospects with those of other states, it has understandably become concerned when provincial finances proved inadequate to sustain the educational base required for a knowledge-based economy.

Drawing a distinction between education and research, the federal government has paid attention to promoting science and technology since the Dominion's early days. Reflecting the young economy's rural preponderance, it first assumed agricultural research as a federal responsibility in the nineteenth century. Sir John A. Macdonald set up a network of experimental farms by act of Parliament in 1888 to help farmers improve their soil, crops, and livestock. Expanded into every province, these research stations operated on the assumption that new knowledge was a public good to be made available at no charge for farmers – the hardy Marquis strain of early ripening wheat being the first and most famous example. Sir Robert Borden set up the National Research Council (NRC) in 1916 to support studies in the physical sciences. Under Louis St Laurent Ottawa founded the Canada Council in 1957 to promote development in the arts and humanities. Pierre Trudeau's governments set up the Medical Research Council (1969), the Social Sciences and Humanities Research Council of Canada (1977), and the Natural Sciences and Engineering Research Council (1978) to support academic research in these domains.

Ottawa's original concern for supporting research led it naturally to an involvement with higher education when it became clear that the provinces' restricted financial base had become a bottleneck. The grants for universities that were initiated under St Laurent evolved into a 50–50 cost-sharing agreement signed by Lester Pearson with the provinces in 1967.[61] With their ensuing massive expansion of universities and colleges costing provinces only 50 cents on the dollar, Ottawa found itself saddled with rising financial obligations over which it had no control and for which provincial politicians took most of the credit. In 1977 Pierre Trudeau negotiated Established Program Funding (EPF) with the provincial premiers, who received block grants to be used at their discretion for funding health care or post-secondary institutions. EPF began a twenty-year federal retreat from funding higher education, which consequently lost a great deal of financial support. Provincial politicians, who had become used to federal burden sharing, proved reluctant to pay all the bills for tertiary education, which yielded fewer votes than supporting health care.

With their economies' prospects increasingly dependent on the competitiveness of their knowledge-based sectors, governments around the world intensified their support for research to generate innovation that their entrepreneurs could exploit globally. Ottawa fully embraced an innovation-led growth strategy only when the advent of free trade gave signals that policy-makers had to change their ways. As we have already seen, various norms in international trade law inhibited the continued use of subsidy programs targetted to remedying specific industrial deficiencies. The general principle of national treatment, for instance, explicitly prevented governments from favouring domestic enterprises with subsidies. (Canadians discovered the WTO's bite when the Brazilian government successfully challenged Ottawa's Technology Partnerships at the WTO as an unfair subsidy to Bombardier's regional jet planes.) Trade liberalization's outlawing of such long-standing government practices augmented the vulnerability of national economies to international competition, causing policy-makers to seek other avenues to support their economies.

Since funding for research was GATT-proof as long as it was generally available to all sectors and not directed specifically to increasing exports, it was perhaps no accident that 1987 was a banner year for industrial funding. That year's federal budget paper, *Securing Economic Renewal*,[62] offered smaller firms a generous, refundable R&D tax credit. As well, Ottawa committed itself to an additional $4 billion in direct expenditures on science and technology. It set up the National Advisory Board on Science and Technology in order to improve Canada's international competitive position.

Pouring public funds into programs dedicated to innovation gave the federal government high visibility and squared another political circle. With the spasmodic exception of Quebec, the provinces did not object to Ottawa's allocating more funds for research, provided that it kept out of their education policy. Indeed, Ottawa paid the provinces the ultimate compliment by policy plagiarism. Brian Mulroney's government copied the Ontario Centres of Excellence Program set up by David Peterson's Liberals when it launched its own National Centres of Excellence in 1989.

But escalating deficits forced Ottawa to scale back its commitments both to research and to higher education. When Paul Martin folded EPF into the Canada Health and Social Transfer (CHST) in 1995, he removed the ambiguity surrounding responsibility for higher education. The CHST marked Ottawa's final retreat from sustained participation in university funding, whose support by government declined 25 per cent in the 1980s and 1990s. (Mythologies notwithstanding, U.S. governments are relatively generous, providing $30,000 per student – $8,000 more than the Canadian figure).[63]

Once its deficit had been eliminated, Ottawa reaffirmed its interest in supporting research. In 1997 it established the Canada Foundation for Innovation to support major research projects in partnerships with universities. In 1999 the Canadian Institutes for Health Research were set up with funding that doubled the Medical Research Council's budget. Paul Martin's budget of 2000 launched the Canada Research Chairs program to stem the brain drain of skilled researchers to the United States by funding 2,000 junior and senior professorships. Committing substantial sums to research and innovation represents one of the principal instruments for economic intervention in the neoconservative policy paradigm, which is geared to creating competitive advantage in a knowledge-based global economy.[64]

In addition to these programs, claims under the federal Science, Research and Experimental Development tax credit amount to $1.3 billion annually. In total, the federal government estimated that it funded 22 per cent (or about $3.3 billion worth) of all Canadian R&D in 1998–9[65] and projected a steady rise in spending for the subsequent three budgets.

By attracting and linking partners from industry, government laboratories, local business, and educational institutions through technology centres, research parks, technology incubators, and virtual networks for developing entrepreneurship, these policies aim to foster innovative, highly competitive new firms. For instance, the NRC's mandate is to promote technological diffusion through establishing linkages between firms, helping them to reduce research costs, and providing strategic information on science trends and emerging technologies. The NRC provides capital and support services to new ventures through its Industrial Research Assistance Program,[66] which supports unproven technologies until they reach the point of commercialization by aiding companies in developing appropriate links with external sources of technology or technical assistance and providing partial start-up funding. The NRC has a second and sometimes conflicting task of ensuring that industry meets regulatory standards, which puts it in the difficult position of being expected to build relationships of trust with the business community, while simultaneously being charged with policing the same industry.[67]

Government partnering of this kind has encouraged educational institutions, private business organizations, and a handful of large, high-tech firms to create or extend incubator initiatives. University research laboratories conduct basic research that adds to the repository of fundamental knowledge and in turn provides the basic science for applied R&D activity. Academe has always been the technological driver of industry in the United States, where high-profile universities such as the Massachusetts Institute of Technology, Harvard, and Berkeley have benefited from decades of federal defence and industrial spending and consequently have a long tradition of fostering high-technology, spin-off firms. Canadian universities' more recent interest in fostering closer relations with industry is in part a response to decreases in public funding. They are searching for new sources of income through licensing intellectual property rights and setting up business alliances. The University of Waterloo's celebrated Technology Transfer and Licensing Office allows professors and graduate students to sell their intellectual property for equity in the resulting venture.

Federal as well as provincial spending increasingly targeted the promotion of innovation by small and medium-sized companies. A related urban development was the emergence of entrepreneurship-support organizations in the private sector aimed at start-up firms. Often sponsored by local business and municipal governments, they offer services that include counselling on how to start an enterprise, training and education programs, mentorship opportunities, and extensive networking services. For instance, the Ottawa-Carleton Research Institute, a private, non-profit organization, runs an Entrepreneurship Centre that fosters a regional system of innovation. These organizations have ties with the government and para-government research centres, the two local universities, and several R&D-intensive telecommunications and defence-related firms.

Just as the former sharp distinctions between municipal, regional, provincial, and federal governments' approaches to industrial development are being blurred, so is the distinction between initiatives undertaken by the public and private sectors, since governments, universities, business associations, and large corporations are implementing similar types of incubator policies in the quest for the entrepreneurial pot of gold now called innovation.

Considering where Canadian companies started at the beginning of the high-tech revolution, their present level of personnel competence and research capacity is remarkable. Yet innovative start-ups remain hampered by insufficient sources of venture capital when compared to the abundance available for new American entrepreneurs. A few large high-tech corporations such as Ottawa's Newbridge and Brampton's battered Nortel have had their own incubator policies, spinning off an existing division, making an external entity an affiliate, and/or creating new firms through internal mechanisms. Such initiatives offer parent firms an opportunity to foster potential affiliates, increase the technological capacities of local, specialized industrial agglomerations, and generate revenue when the parent retains an ownership share in the start-up. As businesses advance, governments have retreated in offering capital to high-risk candidates.

Another change in the policy climate raised questions about the value of Ottawa's role in industrial policy. In the putatively new, knowledge-based economy, management gurus insisted, government should no longer be a hierarchically superior organization trying to control the market from the top of a vertical relationship. Instead, it should become a 'heterarchically' articulated agency nourishing a horizontal, information-sharing, and morale- boosting relationship with the private sector.[68] Such rethinking emphasized the economy's move away from Fordist, mass-production assembly plants towards more specialized and dynamic clusterings of very flexible, knowledge-based firms with a less permanent, less structured workforce. If under this optic, government should not be declaring one-size-fits-all policies from the political centre, decentralized federalism has a new economic logic and provincial activism in industrial policy a new rationale. We now turn to Ontario to see how this logic played itself out under neoconservatism.

14 The Industrial State Goes Provincial[1]

For nationalists in the late 1960s, the Ontario government was more the cause of the Canadian economy's addiction to branch plant dependence than its cure. The Progressive Conservative (PC) Party had governed the province since 1943 and seemed perfectly positioned to remain in power for ever: the opposition vote was nicely split between a social-democratic New Democratic Party (NDP) on its left and an ineffectual Liberal Party on its right. PC thinking amounted to little more than maintaining the physical infrastructure, providing schooling and social services, and hoping that the invisible hand – especially if it involved an American car assembled by Chrysler, Ford, or GM under the Auto Pact – would create enough jobs to keep the public happy and prosperous. Otherwise, industrial strategy was Ottawa's business.

By the late 1980s, all this had changed. Continental governance in the form of CUFTA's restrictions nixed the Canadian state's powers to discriminate in favour of home-owned enterprise and to impose performance requirements on foreign investments in the hope of improving the benefits that they produced. Neoconservative thinking declared such industrial policy wasteful and futile. The coup de grâce for federal interventionism was deficit cutting, which forced Ottawa policymakers – whatever their ideological bent – to cut back support programs aimed at promoting economic activity. This federal withdrawal created a policy vacuum that the provinces were not reluctant to fill. Three governments succeeded the Ontario Conservatives when their luck finally ran out in 1985 – Liberal (1985–90), NDP (1990–5), and a new type of Tory (1995–).

Progressive Conservative Ontario, to 1985

However logical the provincial level might be for making industrial policy in such a vast, regionally diverse country as Canada, even the mighty subcentral government of Ontario had initially played a largely passive role in the formulation and execution of policies aimed at economic development. During the post-Second World War construction of the Fordist and Keynesian system, Queen's Park restricted itself to massive infrastructural investments in building roads, extending free public schooling to the community-college level, and upgrading the electrification generated and distributed by its public utility, Ontario Hydro. As the 1960s unfolded, Ontario under Premier John Robarts became more involved in managing economic issues. With the emerging fiscal crisis of the state in the 1970s, Premier Bill Davis started to expand the province's macro- and micro-economic policy capacity in an effort to respond to regional needs not adequately met by the federal government.

At the tail end of four post-war decades of province building, Ontario had developed a sophisticated, highly competent, and extensive government system that responded to the needs of an industrial economy structured generally along Fordist lines which mirrored in many respects the Keynesian state constructed over the same period at the federal level. The parallel was not coincidental. The working alliance between a usually Liberal government in Ottawa and a PC one in Toronto had provided the core axis for Canadian politics since 1945. Ontario's Tories supported the federal Liberals' constitutional and industrial-strategy policies. In return, the federal Grits, whose political bastion was central Canada, supported Ontario's special economic position by bolstering the country's financial and manufacturing dynamo, often at the expense of other provinces in the west or the Maritimes.[2]

This second National Policy posited Ontario as the main beneficiary of Confederation, as had the first. In reality, its economy (like that of the country's other regions) was becoming integrated more with the United States than with any other province. In recognition of this change, Ontario, in the 1970s, established quasi-diplomatic offices in the United States, and the premier carefully nurtured his relationship with the governors of the neighbouring Great Lakes states in order to fend off the occasional bout of protectionism that threatened the smooth flow of Ontario's exports to the south. When, for example, Washington imposed steel quotas on Canada, Davis rallied the Great Lakes state governors to support his province's case in the U.S. capital.

That Ontario's approach to economic policy mimicked Ottawa's was apparent in parallel developments at each level. Within each government tension existed. The more cautious, macro-focused economists in the provincial Treasury (or the federal Finance Department) preferred framework policies aimed at getting the economic fundamentals right. In contrast, more interventionist, micro-centred policy-makers represented the needs and aspirations of small and medium-sized enterprise (SMEs) in the provincial Ministry of Industry and Trade[3] (or the federal Department of Industry, Trade and Commerce).

This was the era in which to be in government was to spend money. It may be true that the federal tax system concealed the most substantial aid for business through such devices as capital-cost and depreciation allowances. But, if the provincial government was in the mood for doing things for people, how better to accomplish this than by offering money to business for job creation? In particular, the Industry Ministry lent itself to the aspirations of such ambitious politicians as Frank Miller and Larry Grossman, who amplified their visibility by trumpeting programs for business development. The decentralized Ontario Development Corporation (ODC), with its offices strategically placed in the province's major centres, was a substantial source of 'last-resort' lending for entrepreneurs unable to borrow from the chartered banks.

Liberalism Embraces High-tech, 1985–1990

Although Liberal leader David Peterson defeated a PC government to become Premier of Ontario (1985–90), his ideas were less a repudiation of the former regime than an affirmation of continuity with its spirit. Continuity certainly characterized his constitutional dossier in which he supported Prime Minister Mulroney's initiatives aimed at reforming the federal system – occasionally at the cost of Ontario's immediate interests. Peterson even volunteered to reduce Ontario's representation in the Senate in order to achieve a consensus with his more assertive fellow premiers.

Continuity at Queen's Park did not guarantee continuity in Ottawa. Peterson's self-abnegation failed to engender federal support for Ontario. A gap developed between the premier in his first, minority mandate (1985–7), supported and pushed by the left-leaning NDP, and Mulroney's explicitly right-leaning government of Canada. Where Ottawa was emphasizing the national debt, though not actually managing to reduce its $30 billion deficits, Toronto was revelling in a six-year-long economic recovery and took the decidedly non-Keynesian approach of spending rather than taxing to counter the boom.

More seriously, Ottawa's plans for free trade were threatening to destroy the branch-plant economy that supported Ontario's employment and wealth. The Mulroney government negotiated the Canada-United States Free Trade Agreement (CUFTA) in open defiance of Queen's Park's apprehensions.[4] Federal trade officials traditionally scorned their provincial counterparts, who were not steeped in the arcana of the General Agreement on Tariffs and Trade (GATT), and Mulroney's belligerent chief trade negotiator, Simon Reisman, thoroughly alienated Ontario civil servants during the negotiations.

As the province most reliant on the American economy – its exports to the United States were by then double its sales to the rest of the country[5] – Ontario might have been expected to support Ottawa's trade initiative. But the 1965 Auto Pact covered most of its exports. U.S. branch plants provided hundreds of thousands of jobs and had prospered under the shelter of Canada's tariff-based import substitution. Free trade threatened trade-union supporters, who had prospered in this dependent regime of capital accumulation. The closing down of many factories in CUFTA's wake, exacerbated by a recession, spelled disaster for the province's industrial structure. In intensifying restructuring pressures, free trade administered a profound shock from which Ontario took a long time to recover because the Mulroney government refused to deliver the adjustment policies that it had promised as the federal *quid* for the free trade *quo*.

Beyond this economic concern – which was hotly contested by economists, Progressive Conservatives, and business lobbyists – lay a political issue. Mulroney had been attempting to decentralize in order to please his ill-assorted allies: Quebecers, who supported free trade because it would undermine Canada's central government, and Albertans, who sought to increase provincial control over areas viewed as crucial to their well-being. But for other subcentral governments CUFTA was a significant intrusion into their jurisdiction.[6] Although the provinces had neither negotiated nor signed CUFTA, it would affect their autonomy and constrain their decision making.

It was politically expedient for Ontario to chastise the federal government for undermining its economy, but thoughtful insiders around Peterson saw that the provincial economy was in trouble with or without CUFTA. Whether foreign-owned or national, Canadian capital had been going continental, if not global, for a decade. The tariff reductions required by Canada's participation in the Tokyo Round of GATT negotiations (1973–9) had already increased foreign competition. This constituted a threat not just to Ontario's branch-plant sector, which by definition had little innovative capacity, but also to the low-value-added and staple-export sectors and even to the auto-parts and car-assembly plants.

In Ontario, continentalists maintained from the 1960s that all was for the best as long as foreign investment poured into the economy, while nationalists bewailed the debilitating effects of foreign control on managerial initiative and technological innovation, as well as on the Canadian capital market and the balance of payments. Federal actions in the 1970s to correct the economy's dependence on staple exports and to promote a more mature industrial economy were limited and grudging, constrained by the orthodox concerns of the Department of Finance. The resource-exporting, capital-importing provinces – Ontario very much included – supported this anti-nationalism. David Peterson tried to change this debate by transcending it. He dissolved the Ontario Economic Council and established the Premier's Council of expert advisers from business, labour, and various communities to review economic needs and offer the government strategic policy advice.

In the aftermath of Trudeau's failure to develop an effective industrial strategy and Mulroney's conversion to free trade, the Premier's Council developed a new analysis. Unlike previous left-wing advice to the federal government, its proposed strategy centred not on constraining foreign investment but on encouraging it to develop alongside Canadian capital. The objective was to promote higher-value-added manufacturing in high-growth industries. Who owned firms was secondary to whether they used the highest possible levels of technology, innovated by carrying out research and development (R&D), manufactured their products for the world market, and increased domestic capacity. The province had to accept the impending demise of tariff shelters.

Queen's Park also needed to abandon its politically inspired proclivity for propping up slow-growth regions. Instead, the council maintained, it should bolster indigenous firms enjoying fair prospects for building 'home-based' transnational corporations (TNCs) that concentrated their planning, product development, marketing, and manufacturing in Canada. Tax incentives would increase R&D. Greater use of government purchasing would build industry infrastructure and worker-ownership incentives. The council was speaking the language of activist government but steering the economy towards enterprise committed to technological innovation. Dollars should not be spent on direct job creation. Jobs would result if wealth were created. If companies restructured to produce more goods with fewer employees, they would shed jobs; if they then competed successfully, they would end up employing more workers. As the Council suggested in its first report, *Competing in the New Global Economy*, provincial policy should foster businesses, both small and large, by building the human capital, science, and technology infrastructure needed to compete in foreign markets.[7]

Anticipating this advice, the Peterson government established in 1986 a Technology Fund, to which it allocated $1 billion over a ten-year period to encourage the private sector to set up partnerships with research institutions. Other incentives included the R&D Super Allowance, the Industry Research Program, and the creation of seven Centres of Excellence. Worker-ownership incentives never got off the ground and the bureaucracy blocked greater use of government purchasing to improve industry infrastructure. By making international competition the key to both higher wages and a better standard of living for Ontario's workers, the Peterson government was first in the province's history to address the province's global interdependence and the 'knowledge revolution.'[8]

Apart from such sectors as land development, steel making, and food processing, which had a specific interest in provincial policy, business had traditionally ignored a provincial government with little involvement in industrial policy. Even taxes, regulations, and other measures aroused scant interest among entrepreneurs. During the four long decades of PC rule, social relations between the business community and the province had never been as intimate as those in 'Québec, Inc.' The circulation of American managers in an economy dominated by branch plants did not allow consolidation of a stable corporate elite that could interlock with government in meshed career patterns. No political-industrial complex emerged because Ontario never developed Quebec-style involvement in supplying credit, management expertise, and public participation in the economy and never offered the same level of financial incentives to its entrepreneurs. Symptomatically, business concentrated on lobbying federal politicians.

Although Peterson sought to involve business, along with labour and community representatives, in his Premier's Council, this participation did not change the private sector's relationship with the province. Business even found the Peterson government unreliable. Not only had it opposed the free trade agreement; it brought in new and far more restrictive environmental regulations that management found offensive and crippling.

Yet the political conditions for launching a province-based industrial strategy were propitious. The Peterson government was supported for its first two years by an NDP that shared the activist biases of the Premier's Council. At the same time the federal government was moving out of microeconomic management thanks to its neoconservative belief in the 'invisible hand.' Continental integration was further eroding federal powers, opening political space for a more assertive provincial role. But with the double whammy of free trade-induced plant closings and the Bank of Canada's jacking up of interest rates to rein in provincial spending, especially in Ontario, the provincial economy went into its worst spin in decades just as the New Democrats in the summer of 1990 surprised themselves and the country by winning power.

Experiments in Social Democracy, 1990–1995

The tumultuous five years of Premier Bob Rae's government saw as much discontinuity as continuity with those of his predecessors. In Ontario's predominant external relationship, the one with Ottawa, constitutional politics remained as active under Rae as under Peterson, but with a significant difference. The NDP premier asserted Ontario's position in the months leading up to the Charlottetown Agreement of 1992, insisting on seating Aboriginal leaders at the negotiating table and on including a social contract that I will discuss in chapter 15.[9] Like his Liberal predecessor, Rae faced a federal government committed to a different political constituency, one that was located outside Ontario. More conflict was brewing.

For his part, Prime Minister Mulroney stepped up the confrontation that he had provoked with Ontario over CUFTA by reneging on Ottawa's fiscal commitments. He capped the growth of Canada Assistance Plan payments to Ontario, when a deep recession was already creating social distress in the province that hosted the most generally destitute immigrants. In response, Ontario had to spend even more as its revenues fell dramatically.[10]

Queen's Park's resulting outrage did not translate into equivalent anger over Ottawa's pursuit of a second round of continental trade liberalization. Rae and his ministers evinced the same ambivalence towards free trade as had the Peterson government – opposing it in their rhetoric and doing little to obstruct it in practice. They felt that the province lacked the means to act against free trade. They sponsored a cross-province series of public hearings on NAFTA[11] and even affirmed that they would challenge NAFTA's constitutionality in the courts – a threat on which they did not deliver.

Provincial officials had a less arduous experience with NAFTA's negotiation than with CUFTA's. The new federal negotiator, John Weekes, included them as much as Simon Reisman had excluded them. Even if provincial autonomy would be circumscribed in the future, they felt exempted in the present. During the final stages of the GATT's Uruguay Round, Ottawa actively consulted the Rae government, particularly on agricultural matters. International trade rules were being rewritten not under Washington's unilateral dominance, as with CUFTA, but in the multilateral context of give and take among governments, many of which shared Ontario's propensity for activism. As a result, NDP Ontario's response to its new global and continental constitutions was more accepting and better informed. As the premier put it, 'It is clear that on a great many issues Ontario and Canada will have to adjust our policies to take our membership in NAFTA, GATT, and the World Trade Organization more fully into account.'[12]

In one example, the NDP broke its electoral commitment to introduce public auto insurance. For years as an opposition party it had demanded rationalization through socialization of this fragmented, inefficient, high-cost sector. When elected in Manitoba, Saskatchewan, and British Columbia, NDP governments had duly implemented public insurance. Once installed in Queen's Park, the New Democrats realized that the car-insurance industry was many times bigger in Ontario than it was in the west. The greater efficiency from merging many companies and subsidiaries would have reduced premiums but destroyed a few thousand jobs. The NDP decided not to keep its promise for several such reasons, including CUFTA's strictures on public monopolies. American insurance companies with Canadian head offices in Ontario would have filed colossal claims for compensation on the grounds of expropriation of future revenues.[13]

Even though NAFTA went further than CUFTA in restricting provincial autonomy, Ontario found the trade agreement less of a millstone than it had feared. This was partly because the government could no longer afford to do what it might have liked. The concern, for instance, that provisions on national treatment would prevent it from discriminating in favour of Canadian-owned enterprise had become moot. The

Ontario government was so financially strapped that a costly proactive industrial strategy had become infeasible.

Even NAFTA's obligation that sub-central governments report all policies that contravened its provisions turned out to be inoperative. Ontario made a big effort not only to co-ordinate its own ministries but took the lead in working with other provinces to list the many measures that would be in violation of NAFTA's various chapters. Some U.S. state governments, with their lower capacity for policy analysis, proved incapable of mounting such an exercise; others simply refused to conform with an agreement that they hadn't signed. After many jurisdictions missed the deadline of January 1996 and a new deadline of March, mutual, bilateral agreement killed the exercise. All existing non-conforming provincial and state measures that did not conform to NAFTA's new rules were simply grandfathered.[14] No longer was it a case of 'list it or lose it.'

Despite the expectation that deepening continental integration would foster an increased role abroad for sub-central governments, Ontario renounced its prior engagement with the outside world. Peterson had set up formal co-operation with the dynamic 'four motors' of Europe – Baden Wurtemberg, Catalonia, Lombardy, and Rhônes-Alpes – and Rae actively pursued this transregional relationship until 1993, when the four motors shifted the focus of their intergovernmental activities to Brussels.[15] The NDP premier attended the world economic forum at Davos each year, participating in its informal regional caucus. He was also very active in the Council of Great Lakes Governors and signed a document proposing an industrial strategy for the transborder super-region. Despite the premier's personal involvement in Ontario's international relations, his government's bureaucratic involvement was low and falling. In 1993, Ontario closed down its seventeen offices abroad, set up over the decades to represent commercial interests in major U.S. cities and overseas, to give retired senior politicians a perch, and to provide the premier with photo opportunities. Intensified globalization was forcing the province to pull in its horns and – contrary to prophecies about the emerging regional state – become at least temporarily more insular.[16]

Like the Liberals before them, the NDP concluded that CUFTA and NAFTA did not oblige the provinces to do anything in particular. The issue became how to forge new tools to achieve old objectives without running up against the new constraints. Disengaging from the outside world did not mean denying globalization. The Rae government became more serious about developing a coherent, proactive industrial policy than its predecessor. The personnel and institutional framework shifted. The Premier's Council lost its pre-eminence to the cabinet office, which brought in experts from academe. Inspired by the latest literature on economic development, the NDP refined the main analytical lines established by the Liberals.

From its first throne speech on November 19, 1990, the government sought to work with labour and business to create education and training partnerships. Economic development would focus on investment in infrastructure to create a learning society and on working with the private sector to develop higher technology through R&D partnerships.[17] In 1992, with the province deep in a desperate recession, the government still forged ahead by publishing its *Industrial Policy Framework for Ontario* – a reworked industrial strategy intended, in the words of one civil servant, 'to be NAFTA-proof as well as effective.' Following in the steps of the Premier's Council, this document envisaged a tariff-free world where government would no longer legally subsidize firms even if it could afford to. 'Old-think' was jettisoned: industrial strategy would no longer be a blueprint for government to create jobs by spending money, particularly on vulnerable industries. 'New-think' meant that the document was a framework, a reformulation of government's role as a catalyst to help industry compete and to facilitate business's own creation of higher-value-added jobs. Ontario's future competitive advantage lay in the skills and brains of its people, not in the rocks and logs of its hinterland. Government would invest in people through the education system, training programs, and a 'smart' infrastructure that provided superior transportation links and centres of communication, where high-tech firms could cluster and communicate with researchers in the university system.[18]

Taking a leaf from the Harvard professor Michael Porter's copybook, Ontario would upgrade its competitive fundamentals, its capacity for innovation, its technological capability, its skills, its home-based companies. It would foster technological capacity at service centres for innovation and productivity. Public investment would go into technological infrastructure to link the private sector with universities. Whether out of fear of NAFTA or in response to the new way of thinking, the industry ministry repackaged a proposed make-work program, which would have appeared to be subsidizing jobs, as subsidies for training. Government training programs offered by JobsOntario would now enhance skills. Technology funding would stimulate the adoption of new techniques. An investment development office would provide advice, so that promising small firms, ready for 'take-off,' would not flounder. These local companies would be supported as 'innovative growth firms.'

With this policy framework, New Democratic Ontario was declaring both that it would withdraw from activity that overlapped with the federal government (supporting Ontario's trade objectives abroad) and that it would move further into industrial policy, where Ottawa's involvement was declining (addressing specific sectors' structural problems). But for all its rhetorical commitment to advanced thinking on economic frameworks , the recession forced the government back to the old habits of rescuing troubled companies to save jobs. Saving the lumber mill at Spruce Falls and the Algoma Steel plant, and restructuring de Havilland to help it survive in a fiercely competitive aerospace market attested to both an NDP-style capitalism that emphasized employee stock ownership and to the premier's hands-on political practice, which contradicted his government's policy rhetoric. Rae became enthusiastically involved in resolving corporate crises – injecting provincial resources through the Ontario Development Corporation or Ontario Hydro, soliciting federal support, and personally brokering management-labour agreements – to prevent companies from closing down.[19]

With CUFTA and the recession driving firms out of business or out of the province, Queen's Park became an active lender of last resort, providing, for example, interest subsidies through the ODC's Office for Industrial Assistance and its Manufacturing Recovery Program. Between 1989 and 1995, 108 such deals were struck with individual firms, and Ontario put more money into direct job support than the federal government in this period. Even several years later, 104 of these investments were thought to have succeeded.[20] For a putatively anti-business government, the NDP in power spent huge amounts of time and money on courting and cajoling capital.

While handouts to keep businesses afloat were decidedly old-think, establishing sector partnerships was just as clearly new-think. The Sector Partnership Fund (SPF) was a venture designed to keep business talking to government and to fight the free-trade induced flight of capital. Financed by a modest $25 million a year, the SPF was intended to help industries make themselves more competitive. Out went the old notion of picking winners or supporting losers. The emphasis was now on encouraging large companies and small producers from the same sector to get together and, by responding to the carrot of some government seed money, to develop a labour-management consensus on their industry's chief needs. The government hoped that this three-phase process – holding discussions, forming a secretariat to develop a work plan, and launching the project with the government's blessing – would develop informal networks among participants, leading to greater trust and more potential for innovative, serendipitous learning within the sector.

With a refundable R&D tax credit in the 1995 budget and the SPF's spawning a new Ontario Centre for Environmental Technology Advancement, the NDP had put its industrial strategy in place.[21] Of the twenty-five sectors that experimented with a new labour-management and inter-enterprise discourse, a few survived, particularly those with less established firms that benefited from the learning process. But for all its efforts to adjust to the WTO and NAFTA and for all its diligence in engaging business in a creative dialogue, the NDP's days were numbered. Businessmen were ready to take a government hand-out, of course, but they were not willing to support a government that called itself socialist and, worse, actually passed legislation expanding labour's rights to organize. The NDP's introduction of labour legislation promised to hurt their bottom line. However much frantic private-sector pressures watered down the bill, the law, which enhanced trade unions' power, stuck in the craw of the business community. Still, the days of capital's alienation in Ontario were numbered.

Neoconservatism's 'Common Sense,' 1995–

With the election of 1995, it was as if the invisible hand had waved its magic wand and the corporate community's wildest fantasies had been realized. Mike Harris brought to power a caucus committed to getting government off the backs of business, liberating the market from regulation, and promoting economic development by replacing targeted industrial policies with across-the-board tax cuts.

It was easy at first to dismiss the new government as made up of know-nothing, vindictive, anti-intellectual politicians who despised their own civil service and would be bound to self-destruct. Whatever their personal limitations – and as a group they appeared the least urbane and least educated cabinet in memory – the Harris team represented an important sociological reality, the growing prominence of a small-business, petty-bourgeois, non-metropolitan constituency that had embraced the values of U.S. libertarian populism. This class's belief in individual hard work and 'tough love' combined with its suspicion of activist government and hatred of big labour to form a congenial political partnership with the interests of big business. Harris had been hand-picked by senior Bay Street figures, and his transition to power was masterminded by former deputy ministers of earlier Conservative governments. It was no coincidence that the Toronto business community expressed a mix of relief and delight when this godsend appeared from out of the blue to take over the government at Queen's Park.

Form was not necessarily content. Whether the regime represented a paradigm shift so soon after the Peterson-Rae transformation would become clear only through its policies and actions, some of which declared less difference from than similarity with the previous decade.

Change was the message on national unity questions when Prime Minister Chrétien pleaded, after the 1995 referendum, to entrench 'distinct society' status and a veto for Quebec in the constitution Harris said no. Rather than offering up Ontario's powers for the sake of federal-provincial reconciliation, he wanted further powers through decentralization. But in eschewing national unity and becoming avowedly provincialist, Harris was merely harmonizing his constitutional views with the economic side of the province's deteriorating relationship with Ottawa, which had become very bitter. Although he was the first Ontario premier fully to support free trade and although his own anti-government agenda ran parallel with Ottawa's cutting social benefits to reduce the deficit, Harris echoed Bob Rae's earlier demand for a 'fair share' of federal grants to the provinces. After further cuts in 1995, the provincial Conservatives became openly confrontational.[22] By the time of the 1998 budget, blaming Ottawa had become a mantra.[23]

Although he joined in bashing a neoconservative Ottawa, the premier chose common sense over revolution in his relations with the other provinces. While Ontario had a trade deficit with the rest of the world, it had a surplus with the rest of Canada. And in the crude competition to attract investment in order to create jobs, Harris continued to offer generous tax credits for film production. Like his predecessors, he formed a close working relationship with the premier of Quebec, then Lucien Bouchard. The two provinces negotiated agreements on the fair distribution of labour and on government procurement. And like his fellow premiers, he was reluctant to give up protectionist measures such as occupational standards that restricted workers' interprovincial mobility unless all provinces agreed to disarm collectively.

Nor was much shift observable in Ontario's relations with the rest of the world. Difference was salient more at the level of personality than of program. Bob Rae had revelled in his constitutional statesmanship and loved representing Ontario abroad. But apart from joining the heads-of-government Team Canada trade missions, Harris was disinclined to nurture international connections through personal diplomacy. He participated only spasmodically and reluctantly in the network of Great Lakes governors with whom relations withered.

Unlike Peterson, Rae, and their 'policy wonks,' the authors of the Common Sense Revolution had no political-economy analysis of globalization. Trade officials reported no change in mandate for trade negotiations. NAFTA and the WTO were simply the context in which Ontario must operate – external forces completely beyond influence by the province. Neoconservative Ontario addressed its problems exclusively as a matter of internal rather than of external policy and action.

While the Harris team might not give much thought to Ontario's role in the rest of the world, it worried about what the rest of the world thought about Ontario. It commissioned two major studies to provide this information, complementing federal reports. Goldfarb Consultants interviewed executives responsible for foreign investment decisions in 409 large corporations in the United States, the United Kingdom, Japan, and Germany to gauge their attitude to Ontario. The study found disconcertingly little knowledge about Ontario, particularly outside North America, where the United States was the overwhelming first choice for investing. While views of the province tended to be positive as a place 'open for business,' it was seen as a 'high tax' regime.[24]

Harris's Red Tape Commission published *Responsible and Responsive Regulation for Ontario* in May 1996. An outgoing deputy minister interviewed several hundred corporations and business associations in Ontario in 1998, and prepared a report, *Removing Barriers to Doing Business in Ontario*. The two documents gave a clear message, both negative and positive. Existing legislation was too intrusive; enforcement of environmental regulations was a problem; payroll taxes were too high; Ontario Hydro rates were uncompetitive. Business managers wanted a stable government that could tell them where they would be in ten years, with a tax system and regulatory regime that would remain the same. In short, government should create a permanently predictable environment, friendly to investment.

This was advice that the new government hardly needed to hear. Well before the reports came in, it had started to implement its campaign promise of a 'revolution.' In its throne speech of September 1995 it promised to dismantle the previous government's 'red tape' by repealing the Employment Equity Act, reforming the Workers Compensation Board and cutting its premiums, dismantling the Planning and Development Reform Act, abolishing corporate filing fees, freezing Hydro rates, repealing labour legislation, and introducing mandatory training programs for welfare recipients. Taxes were too high, government spent too much, and the private sector needed to be unshackled.[25] 'Get out of the way and they will come' was the implicit approach to attracting foreign investment and retaining domestic enterprise.

Demonstrating a consistency that confounded its civil servants and shocked even some of its business friends, the Conservative government scrapped most of its old industrial-policy tools. It abolished every program generated from the Premier's Council except its Centres for Excellence. It closed down the ODC. It scrapped the Ventures Program and the Pre-venture Technological Assistance Program. On the grounds that entrepreneurs should make rational decisions on the basis of economic fundamentals, it terminated grants to business. It even stopped the traditional game of offering incentives to foreign investors playing Ontario off against other potential locations. Business was not to be bribed to locate in Ontario, whether with forgivable loans or with capital cost reductions. In all, the government closed down thirty-two programs offering direct assistance in one form or another. As its social-policy agenda and as a signal to business that Ontario was business-friendly, it did away with Bill 40's labour legislation; Bill 91, the Agricultural Labour Relations Act; and the Advocacy Act. The message was clear: government had cut back its own interventionist capabilities and limited spending in order to reduce the deficit.[26] As proof, it drastically truncated the Ministry of Economic Development, Trade and Tourism, cutting its budget by more than 50 per cent and firing half of its personnel.

In good part, this was necessity that dressed up as virtue. The province was under such tremendous fiscal pressure that the Ministry of Finance insisted it could no longer afford its microeconomic development policies. The central ministry had been saying this in the past.

Now the word came from the premier himself. But to claim that financial imperatives dictated this policy shift is not to deny that such imperatives are ideologically determined. The belief in the premier's office was that grants were either ineffective, because they did not create many jobs, or unfair, because they went to some companies and not others. The market, not government, should evaluate investment projects, so the ODC's assessment machinery was dispensed with. Entitlements create dependence, so tax incentives, programs for SMEs, filling gaps in the market, and correcting structural imperfections were tasks that government could do less well than the market itself. The market, not the provincial state, would now remedy market failure.

There was considerable slippage between ideology and execution. Even the 1996 budget, which delivered the tough actions promised in the finance minister's 1995 fiscal and economic statements, showed traces of Liberal-NDP new think when it referred approvingly to the 'strategic alliance' in animation production between Sheridan College and the Disney Corporation. The $20 million promised for 'Telecommunications Access Partnerships,' to engage 'entrepreneurs, sectors and communities in improving Ontario's competitivenesss through advanced telecommunications applications and infrastructure,' was a continuation of the NDP's Ontario Network Infrastructure Program.[27]

Encouraging sectoral partnerships with modest sums was a secondary strategy. The Harris regime's favoured recipe for economic development was tax reduction. The most salient tax change was the loudly promised 30 per cent reduction in the personal income tax, which was part of the government's economic development strategy. As the finance minister never tired of intoning in his Reaganite litany, 'The best job creation program is a tax cut.'[28] Curiously, the policy had a partly Keynesian character: by increasing consumer spending, tax relief for individuals was to generate economic growth. Less visible to the general public were fiscal changes responding to business demands. First came the slashing of existing provisions, particularly payroll taxes. More interesting because less transparent were the many tax expenditures in the form of tax credits, which gave financial benefits to companies without appearing to interfere in the economy: the Ontario business-research institute tax credit; the co-operative education tax credit; the exemption on the retail sales tax for R&D equipment; and tax credits for acquiring intellectual property or foreign technology. By targeting other tax credits to specific sectors such as the provincial film industry and computer animation, the government was readopting the post-Keynesian industrial policy of picking winners.

Beyond keeping intact some significant policies, the Harris team in its third year quietly endorsed government intervention in the market to generate private-public partnerships. Even though it was still a long way from its zero-deficit goal, Ontario's 1997 budget, *Investing in Our Future*, was replete with old-style spending programs, including incentives to enterprise. While it officially repudiated bribing business, it retained and even enhanced substantial incentive programs. Support continued for enterprise centres giving advice to small business on planning, marketing, and business strategy – another indication that industrial strategy old-think had not been fully eradicated. The same inference could be drawn from the budget's incentives which encouraged banks to lend to SMEs and provided investment funds for small businesses, loans to help unemployed youths start businesses, labour-sponsored investment funds, and a program for rural jobs. A tax expenditure worth $30 million replaced the $3-million University Research Incentive Fund killed in 1995.

A wandering Ontarian who had left the province in 1995 and returned in time to peruse the government's 1997 budget papers could have been excused for thinking that little had changed in the province's industrial strategy. Innovation in knowledge and technology-based industries and support for clustering high-tech companies to facilitate inter-firm learning were at the heart of the Peterson-Rae discourse.[29] Citing Ontario as the second-most-competitive jurisdiction in the Organization for Economic Cooperation and Development for R&D, the 1997 budget encouraged innovation to 'help ensure the province could continue to attract global investments.'[30] The budget papers concentrated on 'innovative growth firms,' a hallmark of the Rae period.[31] Economic development bureaucrats still concentrated on identifying the 5,000 to 6,000 SMEs that employed from ten to two hundred people and that were keen to adopt new technology so that it could help them to resolve their growing problems as they moved from small to medium size. In economic policy, the government showed more common sense than revolution. A focus on SMEs was covertly nationalist, in line with the Peterson-Rae consensus – and NAFTA-proof. Small enterprises are almost entirely created by Canadian entrepreneurs although a SME stimulation policy that is not complemented by protection against foreign takeovers means that the successes cannot be guaranteed to remain home-based.

Reiterating the new-think view that future success depended on encouraging the knowledge-based economy, the 1997 budget expressed its commitment to supplying a skilled workforce to help make its technologically advanced industries globally competitive. It allocated $500 million over a ten-year period to the R&D Challenge Fund to complement the federal Canadian Foundation for Innovation. Designed to lever partnerships between business and universities or other research-oriented institutions, the fund was intended to produce $3 billion in investment partnerships. Seven smaller tax measures, taken together, would increase R&D support by $100 million a year. The Research and Development Tax Incentive provided deductions for qualifying R&D performed in Ontario. The Ontario Business Research Institute Tax Credit, the Ontario New Technology Tax Incentive, and the Telecommunications Access Partnerships were to provide skilled labour for areas such as auto parts, metal working, and new media.

Ontario's 1998 budget and accompanying papers singled out the need to develop technology-based skills. Modelling the proposal on the 1997 R&D Challenge Fund, it levered a relatively small provincial contribution of $150 million over three years to lever large commitments by universities and the private sector into partnership deals that targeted four sectors (auto parts, telecommunications, metalworking, and new media). The Access to Opportunities Program was to double the number of university students in computer science and high-tech engineering programs.[32]

Promoting Ontario's attractiveness by lobbying for investment had deep roots in the provincial government's culture. Harris's Tories kept alive the NDP's state-of-the-art facility for marketing the province's charms to foreign investors. The Ontario Investment Service offered sophisticated databases along with sales people who took clients to already serviced 'greenfield sites' and explained the various requirements for establishing businesses in the province.[33] Besides fashioning an investment-friendly environment by eliminating policies oriented towards social or economic justice, the government emphasized marketing itself as a brand. Market Ontario received resources for trumpeting the province's virtues.[34] It bought an advertising supplement in *Site Magazine* to change Ontario's image among investors abroad from that of a high-cost, unionized, socialist mess to that of a hospitable province run by business-savvy politicians.

In sum, the Ontario government's efforts in industrial policy-making under four governing parties in two decades had an improvised character whose success was hard to document. When observed from the point of view of economic policy, the Common Sense Revolution seemed to be more correction than crash. If there had been a paradigm shift in strategic thinking about the economy, it had started well before, with Ontario's response to trade liberalization in the 1980s. In the context of his predecessors' record in power, Mike Harris had stumbled along dogmatically, but inconsistently, under the looming but generally ignored shadow of globalization.

For all their good intentions, there was a quality of smoke and mirrors about claims of federal and provincial finance ministers that they were meeting the new education and research needs of the knowledge-based economy. Canada's productivity growth kept declining. However many recycled R&D programs were announced to foster innovation, Canada's spending on R&D remained below the OECD average. Actual expenditures on post-secondary education also contradicted official rhetoric about preparing Canadians to work in an information economy. Closely linked with the more obviously economic policy questions that we have examined in this section are the more 'civil' areas considered in Part III – social, labour, environmental, cultural, and foreign policy – each of which is directly affected, but in varying ways, by neoconservatism within and globalization without.

PART III

The Society:
The Contradictions of Neoconservatism

Having first looked at the more political and institutional impacts of globalization and neoconservatism on the Canadian state in Part I, we turned in Part II to consider the effects that these two forces have had on the state's economic functions.

We now come to a number of policy areas that are concerned primarily with non-economic issues. Part III will try to identify the ways in which globalization and neoconservatism have changed governmental capacity in five fields that affect the nature of Canadian society as a whole.

- the state's ability to create a civil society that educates its young, cares for its sick, provides for its disabled or unemployed, and looks after its elderly (chapter 15)
- the state's involvement in writing the rules that govern the conditions of work and the way that workers organize their contracts with employers (chapter 16)
- government's role in controlling pollution and other types of environmental degradation (chapter 17)
- government's efforts to generate cultural activities that enable its communities to communicate with themselves and each other (chapter 18)
- government's traditional role in representing the country's interests with foreign powers and participating in international organizations and decision-making (chapter 19)

15 The Civil State:
Social Policies under Strain

In the early years of the Trudeau era, I was a policy activist in the ranks of the Liberal Party, whose well-meaning, public-spirited members believed that continually reinforcing an ever-broader social safety net was the way to achieve the Just Society that Pierre Trudeau as party leader had himself held up to Canadians as a vision for the country.

In my ignorance, I looked to the federal government to improve the social condition of Canadians, not to my province. Although it had constitutional jurisdiction over matters of welfare, I expected little from Ontario's ruling Progressive Conservative Party because of its close ties with the business community and its ideology, which favoured equality of opportunity for citizens rather than equality of their actual well-being.

However idealistically we militated for stronger measures, Canadians from my post-Depression generation of pre-boomers had good reason to be proud of the network of social policies that had developed following the Second World War. Certainly there were still problems after twenty-five years of halting evolution. Notwithstanding Trudeau's charismatic call for social justice, pockets of poverty still persisted in urban areas and indigenous communities when he retired in 1984, ten years after I had abandoned his party out of disillusionment. Income inequality had proven stubbornly resistant to change. Dentistry, eye care, drug costs, and home care remained uncovered by the public sector.

By the end of the Diefenbaker-Pearson-Trudeau era, a complex but integrated web of federal and provincial policies provided substantial income security against disability, poverty, unemployment, and old age, as well as medical and hospital care for most procedures for the whole public. The mix of public-and private-service provision had proven both equitable and effective. Basic indicators of health showed the Canadian system to have produced better results at lower costs than the U.S. system. Life expectancy was 1.9 years longer in Canada, where the infant mortality rate ran 28 per cent below the American level. Canadian hospitals provided 55 per cent more beds per capita than their U.S. counterparts, but the health sector as a whole was much more efficient. It consumed much less of the economy's resources – 8.6 per cent of Canadian gross domestic product (GDP) versus 12.2 per cent of U.S. GDP.[1]

Few observers disputed that the lion's share of the credit for this success went to the enlightened evolution of federal and provincial policies under the aegis of the Keynesian welfare state. It is understandable, then, that the simultaneous arrival in the late 1980s of trade treaties and domestic neoconservatism was greeted with alarm even by the boomers and Generation X for whom public education, welfare, and health services formed a defining part of their national identity. Critics warned that threats from without and within would destroy this comparatively generous social security system. The combination of the new globalism's external constraints with internal ideological attacks on what was caricatured as excessively generous social assistance, excessively rigid labour market policies, and excessively costly health care, all created by excessively interventionist governments, would, it was feared, wreck a great public policy achievement.

Forced by Circumstance?

It was obvious to anyone accosted by beggars on the streets of Canadian cities that much of the social security system had been cut back during the last two decades of the century. Soup kitchens for the hungry did not exist in 1980. At the millennium, there were more than two thousand across the country. Less obvious was the role played by globalization in this decay. Even domestic neoconservatives, who made the policy changes that we examine below, deserve only part of the blame (or credit) for directing the Canadian state's retreat from welfare to workfare. To the extent that they *wilfully* cut back the role of government in providing public services because they believed in a society shaped by the private sector, neoconservatives were the authors of their own destiny. But to the extent that they *reluctantly* reduced funding for social policies because of their budgetary constraints, they had little choice but to cope with a situation created for them by their pre-decessors in power.

My aim in the first part of this chapter is to disentangle these three factors of external constraint, domestic volition, and financial necessity. We then explore the efforts by both federal and provincial governments to reconstitute the framework for Canada's 'social union.' Finally, we return to the question of global governance to look at what international developments are likely to impinge on public provision of social, health, and educational 'services' in Canada.

Initial responsibility for the decline of Canada's social security system must be attributed to the faulty fiscal foundations laid by the welfare state's advocates who constructed it. Conventional wisdom has it that Pierre Trudeau became recklessly generous with taxpayers' money when he was in office. In fact, once unemployment insurance had been enriched and then cut back, spending on social programs during the 1970s remained steady. What really changed was the Trudeau government's supply-side tax cuts in that period, which reduced the growth in revenue that it needed to pay for the rising costs of ongoing social programs. The Trudeauites' incapacity to control the resulting deficit was dramatized by their retreat from Finance Minister Allan MacEachen's proposed budget reforms of 1981, which would have closed the many loopholes and ended the tax expenditures that they had created.

The Liberals' failure to deal with the deficit by raising revenue necessitated cutting back their spending on programs whose costs were tied to inflation. In 1982 they reduced the annual increase of benefits to 6 per cent for one year and 5 per cent for the second. This '6 and 5' deindexation of benefit rates launched a fifteen-year period of increasingly severe restrictions on spending growth that largely transformed Canada's social safety net. It also signalled the Department of Finance's assertion of control over the Department of Health and Welfare, whose minister and civil servants were putatively responsible for making social policy. Concealed from public view by the strictures of budget secrecy was the political castration of the organizations representing those who provided and those who received social policy programs. Driven by the urgency of deficit reduction, those in power considered democratic practices to be a luxury that Canadian society could no longer afford.

Of course, federal politicians were not the only players in this drama. Provincial governments under Keynesianism's thrall turned

out to be equally enthusiastic on the spending side and equally diffi-
dent about raising the taxes necessary to pay for programs. After all,
borrowing abroad provided an apparently painless way to run budgetary deficits that were doctrinally acceptable. The doctrine was the
notion attributed to John Maynard Keynes that budgetary deficits
were a desirable method for stimulating the economy when it was
depressed. But the lord of Cambridge economists had not sanctioned
chronic deficits. He had assumed that technocrats would balance deficits with surpluses over the course of the business cycle, not anticipating how difficult it would be for flesh-and-blood politicians to raise
taxes, even in prosperous times. In Ontario in the booming mid-1980s,
for instance, Liberal Treasurer Robert Nixon had increased spending
more than taxes, thereby bequeathing his successors a runaway deficit.

As the midwife of trade liberalization in this period, Brian Mulroney
has been elevated to the status of prime enemy of Canada's social security system. This is not an entirely fair charge. Pierre Trudeau's immediate successor, John Turner, had already sounded the tocsin on the
unsustainable level of the government's budgetary deficit under conditions when much of the country's rapidly growing debt was held
abroad and Canada led all G7 nations in its net foreign indebtedness.[2]
Since foreigners responded to national credit risk assessments made by
such major bond-rating agencies as Moody's, Canada could not continue deficit financing without paying a huge penalty in higher interest
rates. To this extent, globalization in the shape of the integrated world
capital market created a 'government by Moody's' in which pronouncements by business investment houses prevented Canadian governments from running chronic deficits. Given that no political party
was willing to increase taxation enough to balance Ottawa's books, it
was the heavy budgetary legacy that they received when taking power
that forced Mulroney and his finance minister, Michael Wilson, to
restrain their spending on social programs. Had Turner remained in
power, he would have had to face the same music. How and by how
much was an open question to be decided by the politicians who did
hold power.

For the Tories first mandate, Wilson certainly toyed with making
radical cuts to universal programs, but a vociferous reaction from civil
society in the form of powerful pensioners' organizations caused the
government to retreat from its proposed frontal attack on the welfare
state's structure. Instead, it adopted a strategy of cutting back by
stealth. Rather than announcing policy in Parliament, Wilson intro-

duced far-reaching changes through arcane, misleadingly worded
amendments in his budgets that camouflaged regressive changes as
exercises in equity and presented tax increases as tax cuts.[3] By partially
deindexing tax brackets and the growth of social programs he began to
save billions of dollars in expenditures and to generate billions in new
revenue.

It was the worsening of social conditions induced by continentalization that pushed the Mulroney government to adopt the harsh measures from which it had desisted earlier. While economists debated
how to distinguish the employment effects of CUFTA from those of
globally induced recession, governments had to respond to the social
policy consequences of permanent job losses by over half a million
workers. Such a huge increase in unemployment automatically raised
government expenditures on social assistance and simultaneously
reduced government revenues from income tax. Desperate to reduce
its deficit, the Department of Finance recommended tougher measures
to lower the social safety net just when it was most needed. In 1990,
Wilson capped the growth in Canada Assistance Program (CAP) transfers to the three richest provinces: Alberta, British Columbia, and
Ontario. Family Allowances for parents of young children were abolished, and other universal programs such as Old Age Security benefits
for the elderly were truncated. Wilson's 1990 budget announced
expenditure reductions averaging $8.5 billion for the next five years.
As a result, the federal share of health funding shrank to 30 per cent.
The promise to introduce a national child care program was shelved.[4]
Despite these efforts, the government's welfare expenditures did not
decline. Even after Ottawa introduced a controversial new Goods and
Services Tax (GST), the federal deficit remained above $30 billion.

The Tories' annihilating defeat in the 1993 election did not bring an
end to Ottawa's attack on social spending, even though the victorious
Liberals had won power having promised not just to restore social welfare but to enrich it with a national child care program. Jean Chrétien
found himself as prime minister in a transformed political landscape,
with the Progressive Conservatives and the New Democrats both
reduced to rumps, having lost their standing as parties in the House of
Commons. Although the Bloc Québécois as official opposition leaned
to the left, Lucien Bouchard's tireless separatism caused the government to dismiss his criticisms on social-policy. At the same time that
Parliament's traditional voices for social justice had been muted, Canada's extreme right had arrived in full bray, with Preston Manning

breathing down Bouchard's back as he jockeyed to become leader of the opposition. In this new political conjuncture, the Liberal Party behaved true to form. It continued to straddle the ideological centre, while moving to neutralize its main challenge. Among the 220 seats outside Quebec, Reform and the PCs held 53 and had run second in another 141 ridings.[5] Rather than moving to the left to co-opt its ideas and ward off the threat of a collapsing social democracy, it nimbly moved to the right to borrow its ideas and defuse the threat of an ascending neoconservatism.

With the voices arguing the case for social justice out of earshot, the Liberal government became even more draconian than its Conservative predecessor. Declaring deficit reduction to be the government's overriding priority, Finance Minister Paul Martin prevailed where even the more ideologically neoconservative Wilson had failed to deliver. Building on his predecessors' efforts and profiting in particular from the cash flow generated by the unpopular GST,[6] Martin in his 1995 budget escalated the attack on the deficit by cutting cash transfers to the provinces by one third and raising taxes.[7] He ended Established Program Funding for health care and post-secondary education and the CAP for social services. Much reduced funding through the new Canada Health and Social Transfer (CHST) and the loosening of Old Age Security in 1996 caused the provinces radically to scale back their welfare programs unhampered by the federally imposed standards that had once been the quid pro quo for federally provided funds.

Given the historical ambivalence of the Liberal Party of Canada, there were two ways to interpret the Chrétien government's single-minded drive to eliminate its deficit. Social democrats in the cabinet argued that regaining fiscal health was the sine qua non of being able to resume liberalism's commitment to social equity. Belt-tightening behaviour by the New Democrats in Regina and the Parti Québécois in Quebec City during the 1990s confirmed that social democracy had to live within its means under globalization. But another interpretation saw the Liberal Party's turning neoconservative less from expediency than from conviction. Officials in the leading government departments interacting with foreign states had adopted as theirs the gospel of trade liberalization and had convinced their political masters that what was good for globalizing business was good for Canada.

To determine to what degree the Liberal government was a reluctant deficit cutter or a wilful neoconservative, it may help to consider its finance minister, whose own personal ambivalence was both genetically and professionally constructed. In his first political phase, as finance critic in opposition, Paul Martin, Jr, the businessman-turned-politician, didn't hesitate to identify himself with the social policy achievements of his father. Paul Martin, Sr, had been one of the most progressive Liberal ministers throughout the postwar era, having already championed national health insurance in the St Laurent government. In his 1990 leadership campaign, Paul Martin, Jr, had downplayed his business-liberal credentials in favour of his welfare-liberal support for maintaining the social safety net. The Liberals' 1993 campaign platform, for which Chrétien had made Martin co-author, spoke a prudent economic language but also adopted a generous approach to social security, promising a national child care program. A daily morning telephone conversation between father in Windsor and son in Ottawa doubtless helped keep Martin *fils* mindful of his ideological heritage.[8]

It would be psychologically simplistic to think that the death of Martin *père* caused the future finance minister's defence of social security to collapse. Nevertheless, the passing of Paul Martin, Sr, in 1992, can symbolize for us the son's move from the apologetic to the exultant deficit cutter who ultimately boasted that he had reduced government spending to its 1951 level.[9] Martin's full conversion can be dated with some precision. His 1994 budget still contained traces of Keynesian rhetoric about the harm done to the economy by budget cuts.[10] Strongly influenced by Finance officials and business Liberals,[11] his 1995 budget spoke a qualitatively different language.

His script did not lack for global prompting. Just weeks before Martin unveiled his 1995 budget, the *Wall Street Journal* warned that 'if dramatic action is not taken ... Canada could hit the debt wall ... and have to call in the International Monetary Fund.' Just days before budget night, Moody's did indeed put the government of Canada on a 'credit watch.' Whatever a debt wall might be, and however unlikely was the prospect of IMF intervention, these orchestrated messages from both the daily bible of neoconservative globalism and the watchdog of the global capital market were just what Martin needed to make what he would himself call the most radical reduction in government since postwar demobilization.[12]

Martin's born-again zeal can be measured by the size and fate of his ultimate surplus. Had the finance minister wanted to cut only the minimum necessary to balance his books, he would have eased his restraints as the booming U.S. economy revived growth in Canada. In the event, he maintained his spending strictures in order to overshoot his zero-deficit target. Far from using his huge surplus to restore the programs that had been cut, he applied it to the next two items on the neoconservative agenda – tax cuts and debt reduction.

Ottawa could only establish the framework for undoing the welfare state. Since most social policies lay within provincial jurisdiction, their actual redefinition had to be carried out at the subcentral level. Most clearly of all the provinces, Ontario demonstrated in its politics the same distinction between a reluctant response to globalization-induced pressures (with the NDP) and a proactive desire to shrink the state (with the Harris Conservatives). As we have seen, the NDP under Bob Rae won power in 1990, just in time to cope with the worst recession since the 1930s, aggravated by Ottawa's partisan attack on Ontario. (The cap on CAP, which saved the government of Canada $10 billion between 1990 and 1995, deprived Ontario of $8.2 billion in transfers from Ottawa.[13]) The NDP responded by administering a classic Keynesian stimulus, enriching social policy benefits in the spirit of equity and in the hope of stabilizing the economy. With 1.4 million men and women receiving enhanced social assistance at the same time as Ottawa was cutting back its transfer payments, the provincial deficit escalated.[14] The economy had become so integrated continentally that citizens' welfare-financed spending was likely to 'leak' – creating demand for goods made outside as much as inside the province.

Thanks to free trade, factories closed by companies moving to the sunbelt states in the American southwest or to the Mexican maquiladoras did not reopen when the recession abated. With Keynesian responses unable to work, unemployment remained stubbornly high. Seeing the provincial debt relentlessly expanding, Premier Rae was persuaded to take a tough-love approach to his spending problem. Facing down furious resistance from his allies in the labour unions, he imposed what he called a 'social contract' that froze wages for employees in the government and para-public MUSH sectors (municipalities, universities, schools, and hospitals).

Ontario's reluctant neoconservatism was not aberrant. Until the mid-1990s, all the provinces had responded to the recession by cutting back their social programs less aggressively than had the American states. Where their U.S. counterparts had lowered benefits for single parents with dependants by 5.5 per cent, the provinces had cut them an average of 1 per cent.[15] Had the unpopular Rae government been defeated by the Liberal Party under its leader, Lynn McLeod – as opinion polls had generally predicted – this civil response to the recession by the Ontario state would likely have continued. The economic revival of the late 1990s would probably have permitted McLeod to sustain a marginally tightened welfare system along the social-democratic lines laid out by her party's Social Assistance Review Committee of 1988.

But McLeod's error-struck election campaign handed power in 1995 to the Progressive Conservative (PC) leader, Mike Harris, whose Common Sense Revolution proceeded to give neoconservative social policies a distinctly Thatcherite toughness. The CSR changed the definition and treatment of welfare. No more would welfare be for everybody in need. It was to be reserved – after rolling back benefit rates – for the deserving poor, those who were unable to work for reasons of age or infirmity. Henceforth, the able-bodied were to work or get trained for work for their welfare payments, even if they were single mothers and even if unemployment rates remained high. An era of paternalist conservatism had dawned, although it had not become as ruthless as it was south of the border, where assistance was being withdrawn entirely from employables and singles without dependants.

The Social Union Framework Agreement

Actions provoke reactions. The obsession of trade liberalization proponents with economic competitiveness at the expense of solidaristic considerations elicited calls by its critics to formulate a more explicit social strategy.[16] But reactions themselves trigger further responses. The ensuing wide-ranging debate extended free-trade federalism beyond the confines of economic policy and the Agreement on Internal Trade (AIT), which we examined in chapter 5. As broader issues were raised, the traditional tensions of the federal-provincial power struggle resurfaced, with Chrétien's Ottawa attempting to dominate a contest in which poor provinces tried to rein in the rich, while a sovereignty-bent Quebec premier was distrusted by all. In the context set by globalization pressures impinging from outside and neoconservative voices pressing for change from the inside, a new federal-provincial agreement codified for the first time a set of rules for intergovernmental behaviour in social policy. This reconstitution of an important policy function represented a significant stage in the development of Canadian fiscal federalism.[17]

At stake were the rules governing how Ottawa would continue to employ its spending power in maintaining or creating social policies for which the Constitution Act had unambiguously made the provinces entirely responsible. Over the previous half-century, Ottawa had used its superior financial resources to take a number of initiatives, typically proposing to pay half the cost for a province if it joined in creating enti- tlement programs for its residents such as health care, provided it met certain standards that would ensure the policy was consistent across the country. When budgetary constraints caused Ottawa unilaterally to cut back its participation in these programs, the provinces protested against arbitrary changes to conventions of federal-provincial collabo- ration. On the financial level, they demanded restoration of federal funding, release from the imposition of pan-Canadian standards, or some combination of these remedies. Some pressed for a binding agree- ment that would discipline the federal government's proclivity to make changes without warning in its financial commitments, changes that disrupted and endangered the provinces' capacity to sustain their local welfare state, to which their voters felt they had a right.

Liberal thinking, which had triumphed in the nineteenth century in industrializing societies, had viewed the state in a largely negative light. Under this optic, for which the American Bill of Rights had iconic status, citizens were to be protected from abuse by state power. By the mid-twentieth century, liberalism had evolved, endowing the state with a more benign, positive responsibility. According to this more social-democratic approach, citizens should have more than legal rights. They had social and economic rights to security from the depre- dations of ill health, unemployment, old age, and poverty.

By the early 1990s the impetus for a 'social union' in Canada came from left-leaning politicians wanting to insulate the achievements of the Keynesian welfare state from the onslaught of neoconservatism. In 1991 the Ontario NDP government moved this project forward with its groundbreaking discussion paper, *A Canadian Social Charter*, which called for the entrenchment of social rights in a legally strong docu- ment that could empower citizens to sue governments for not deliver- ing their entitlements. Although the social charter proposal contained in the Charlottetown Accord was non-justiciable and therefore weak, its inclusion in the first ministers' constitutional reform package was nevertheless of consequence. It represented a recognition by the coun- try's political elite that the public wanted the state to guarantee such diverse objectives as public health care and education, full employ- ment, and a reasonable standard of living.

The popular rejection of the Charlottetown Accord in 1992 and the sovereigntists' near-win in the 1995 referendum decisively terminated decades of exhausting constitutional debate. Henceforth, there would be no discussion about the pros and cons of constitutionally entrenching anything, let alone controversial positive claims on government munificence. In the aftermath of these shocks, political consensus focused on negotiated, piecemeal federal disentanglement as an alternative solution to Canada's continuing national unity crisis. A close reading of how Chrétien interpreted his promises made during the 1995 referendum campaign also suggests that, even under the twin pressures of separatism and fiscal restraint, the federal government had a strategy to renew the federation that would modify but maintain Ottawa's relevance.[18] Two results of these promises were a House of Commons resolution in late 1995 to recognize Quebec as a distinct society and a federal law requiring Quebec's consent before Ottawa would concur in most constitutional amendments.

Beyond these two symbolic gestures, the Chrétien Liberals focused their attention on withdrawal, prudently targeting items already assigned to provincial jurisdiction in the Constitution Act of 1867 that Quebecers strongly valued: health, welfare, and education. Shifting administrative responsibility back to the provinces for specific policies was doubly attractive because it reduced Ottawa's spending obligations and required no further constitutional amendments that might reopen a Pandora's box.

Disentanglement also fitted nicely into neoconservative governing norms. Downloading Ottawa's spending obligations to the provinces would accommodate the Finance Department's deficit-cutting agenda. Working out new federal-provincial arrangements – for instance, in job training – would show that the federal government was forging partnerships collaboratively rather than imposing its will coercively. Such collaboration responded to the theories of the new public management, in which government should steer rather than row. It could still claim to be setting the policy framework while getting out of providing services itself.[19]

Disentanglement also worked politically, because, consistent with the rationale for Meech Lake and Charlottetown, it allowed Quebec's demands to be approached in a symmetrical way, tying them to interprovincial equality.[20] With the PCs and NDP in federal eclipse following the 1993 election, the ascendant Reform Party leader Preston Manning agreed with the Liberals that Ottawa's abdication of policy responsibility was a solution to the national unity crisis, while Lucien Bouchard favoured it as a step towards achieving Quebec's sovereignty.[21] Popular with the richer provincial governments, federal withdrawal from social spending also enjoyed strong support from business spokespeople, who reckoned that it would reduce the size of the public sector, which could then become a candidate for gradual privatization, as state capacity for welfare provision faltered and its popularity among the middle class subsided.

As proof of its good intentions in this domain, the federal government announced in the 1996 Speech from the Throne that it would no longer use its spending power to create new shared-cost programs in areas of exclusive provincial jurisdiction without the consent of a majority of the provinces. Those not consenting would be compensated if they operated an equivalent or comparable initiative – a backhanded example of the spending power. The provincial premiers picked up this cue in their subsequent annual conferences in Jasper (1996) and St Andrews (1997). By the time of their 1998 conference in Saskatoon, the political impetus to formalize an agreement with Ottawa on social policy had gained enough momentum that the premiers could make a formal proposal. This included demands:

• for an opt-out clause for new or modified pan-Canadian social programs giving a province full compensation if it offered its own program in that field
• for a formula governing federal expenditures in fields under provincial jurisdiction
• for an impartial procedure for settling disputes
• for the federal government to initiate no new social spending programs without prior consent from a majority of provinces[22]

From this policy statement there followed secretive negotiations – adjourned briefly while Lucien Bouchard successfully fought for re-election in Quebec – with the federal government arguing for the equality of all citizens and their mobility across the country, as well as a transparency for social policy spending that provided accountability to the voters. The lack of transparency in these discussions was bitterly criticized as being undemocratic by the Canadians for a Real Social Union, which included such leaders of non-governmental organizations as the chair of the Council of Canadians, Maude Barlow.

Within the negotiating loop, the federal Liberals portrayed these talks as their response to the national unity crisis. At the same time, the two richest, Progressive Conservative provinces (Ontario and Alberta) seized on this opportunity to rebalance federal-provincial powers in their favour, while the NDP-led provinces (British Columbia, Saskatchewan, and Manitoba) and the Atlantic provinces manoeuvred to preserve a central role for Ottawa. Distrusted by its interlocutors, Quebec kept a cautious distance. Flush with his newly achieved budgetary surplus, Prime Minister Chrétien offered a restoration of transfer payments to their pre-1995 level and a new equalization formula. Still battling with budgetary deficits, the anglophone premiers rose to the bait and signed a Social Union Framework Agreement (SUFA) on February 4, 1999 without Quebec. An angry Lucien Bouchard denounced this three-year administrative agreement as an affront to him personally and to all Quebecers collectively.

The anglophone premiers' and Chrétien's willingness to move ahead with the agreement *sans* Québec left them vulnerable to the charge of what the Quebec Liberal Party's former leader Claude Ryan called a third instance of abandoning their francophone counterpart.[23] Eighteen years earlier, seven premiers had abandoned their commitment to solidarity with René Lévesque in opposing Pierre Trudeau's project to patriate the British North America Act. At that time, Chrétien and Trudeau were accused of presiding over a 'night of the long knives' – November 5–6, 1981, when they had fashioned, without Quebec's participation, the deal that paved the way for patriation.[24] In the Meech Lake process, two provinces reneged on their commitments. Although SUFA conformed to the thrust of the Saskatoon accord, it could become another symbol of Quebec's alienation from English Canada in a future referendum, turning it into a rallying point for independence.

Two completely different interpretations assessed SUFA's significance for Quebec. On the whole, those sympathetic to Quebec's aspirations for autonomy saw it as 'the death knell of an asymmetrical Canada.'[25] Alain Noël considered Quebec City to have been marginalized, for

the federal and provincial governments did not genuinely seek the approval either of the Quebec government or even the official opposition in the National Assembly ... Canada now marches on as if Quebec did not exist or did not matter. The Social Union Framework Agreement is a case in point. As with the constitution, Quebec will be bound by an agreement it did not demand and did not approve. No matter how the Quebec government uses the situation to act autonomously, the outcome has more to do with domination than with freedom.[26]

Seen through the eyes of federalists, Quebec had carried off a coup. Despite not signing the accord, Quebec would probably receive whatever benefits flowed from this agreement without having undertaken the obligations that bind the other provinces. In the event of a failed or indefinitely postponed referendum, SUFA could ironically become the prototype for that very asymmetrical federalism that Trudeau and Chrétien had each opposed for so long. As Roger Gibbins put it,

> The Prime Minister has achieved for Quebec what the majority of Quebec nationalists have sought for the past thirty years – a distinct position within the Canadian federal system in which Quebec is not a province like the others but rather has the de facto status of a separate national community, dealing one-on-one with the government of Canada ... Quebec maintains its autonomy, is able to block constitutional change, and is able to use its political leverage in Ottawa to ensure that no financial costs are imposed ... The Prime Minister may have delivered on the ultimate paradox: an independent Quebec within a strong Canada.[27]

Seen from the outside at least, Quebec under free-trade federalism looks increasingly like other ethnically distinct subcentral governments such as Catalonia and Scotland, which are in a postmodern, globalizing phase that connects them more directly to the outside world at the same time as they are less integrated in their federal system.

In SUFA, all provinces (except Quebec) committed themselves to the principles of treating citizens from the other provinces equally, providing access to essential social programs and services of reasonably comparable quality, and ensuring adequate, affordable, stable, and sustainable funding for social programs. To do this, they would improve public accountability, transparency, and – most pressing for the federal government – labour mobility. They would endeavour to work collaboratively to avoid and resolve intergovernmental disputes. They would ensure reciprocal notice and consultation prior to the implementation of any major changes in social policy or programs that would 'substantially' affect one or more governments.

Perhaps most important for the anglophone provinces, the agreement went further than Meech Lake in circumscribing Ottawa's power to intervene in social policy by initiating jointly funded programs. The government of Canada agreed to consult its provincial partners at least one year prior to making any major change in social transfers. This provision was specifically drafted to prevent Ottawa from unilaterally cutting provincial transfers as it had done in its infamous 1995 budget. But in defining Ottawa's long-contested spending power, the anglophone premiers formally accepted and so legitimized its ability to intervene in exclusive provincial domains.[28]

While the federal government could not initiate any new joint programs without the consent of a majority of the provinces, concurrence by the six smallest provinces, though arithmetically a majority, would represent the approval of just 15 per cent of the country's population. In short, the agreement left Ottawa considerable leeway in direct social spending. Although it could not use its spending power without warning, it could still make direct transfers to individual citizens if it provided three months' notice – a politically negligible constraint. This was an important, if circumscribed, political gain for Ottawa as it withdrew from the costly fields of social assistance and universal programs in favour of boutique policies that allowed it to use its now formally legitimized spending power to provide individuals with support, for example, in child care or university education.[29]

Despite SUFA's putatively binding nature, it was clear that the federal government still envisioned an autonomous, if altered, role for itself. Although the Chrétien government had already promised to withdraw from labour market training, forestry, mining, and recreation, it still wanted to be the lead player in reinvigorating the economic and social union. Despite provisions on notice and consultation, SUFA did not prevent Ottawa from transferring money directly to Canadians in areas of de facto shared jurisdiction. Indeed, it formally recognized such use of the federal spending power. Ottawa proceeded to introduce the Millennium Scholarship Fund, the Canada Foundation for Innovation, and the Canada Research Chairs, a federally funded program to stem the brain drain by endowing universities across the country with some 2,000 professorships. These three unilateral initiatives affected education, an area of provincial jurisdiction, and gave Ottawa a substantial role in resetting policy priorities affecting universities.

The agreement also imposed performance monitoring on the provinces, which committed themselves to being transparent and accountable in their use of federal funds and to giving Ottawa public credit for its role in jointly funded programs. However, SUFA did not specify the means to attain its principles, aims, and modalities. Nor did it give clear deadlines for compliance.

The issue of mobility overlapped most clearly with the needs of the economic union. Indeed, the discourse of trade liberalization could be heard in the provision eliminating 'any residency-based policies or practices which constrain access to post-secondary education, training, health and social services and social assistance unless they can be demonstrated to be reasonable and consistent with the principles of the Social Union Framework.'[30] Governments agreed to eliminate all obstacles to mobility in three years. Furthermore, all parties would ensure full compliance with the AIT's mobility provisions by July 1, 2001. However, sanctions for non-compliance were weak. Provinces were required to do little more than provide justification for policies that discriminated in favour of their own residents. Nonetheless supporters of SUFA argued that it would make medicare coverage and educational qualifications more portable.

The agreement had parallels to and connections with the logic of continental trade liberalization. It extended the reach of free trade federalism by encouraging the use of a dispute settlement mechanism – albeit non-binding, as with the AIT – to resolve conflicts in areas of shared jurisdiction. Neoconservative globalization may have been SUFA's father, but social democracy was its mother, as one could see in its invitation to citizens to appeal unfair practices by either level of government and to complain if dissatisfied.

Negotiation of the two broad federal-provincial agreements on internal trade and the social union, which followed the failure of constitutional politics, signalled a return to Ottawa-led executive federalism. It allowed Canada's political elites – those 'eleven men in suits' made infamous during the debate on the Meech Lake Accord – to circumvent the public's rejection of neoconservative constitutionalism in the Charlottetown referendum. In this light, the AIT and SUFA become surreptitious, quasi-constitutional repackagings of selected elements from Meech Lake and Charlottetown. Earlier constitutional debates about negative and positive rights had become negotiations over negative integration (removing barriers to trade in the federal order) and positive integration (promoting equalization of provincial programs). Whether phrased in trade-based or rights-based language, the dynamic between the two agreements linked the continuing tensions of Canadian federalism (between the politics of fiscal restraint, policy retrenchment, and social justice) with the new constraints created by trade liberalization (whether its specific limitations on government initiatives or the transnational elites' consensus on neoconservative values).

Beyond linking federalism to continentalization, these intergovernmental approaches to managing federal-provincial interdependence revealed several attributes of neoconservative governance. The two agreements' reliance on closed-door negotiations, whose outcomes were rubber stamped by legislative assemblies, shielded from public consultation and scrutiny the discussion of such central issues as national standards.[31] Despite lip-service to the contrary, the failure to lodge transparency and accountability in these agreements threatened to widen the democratic deficit already inherent in the Canadian policy process.

Prior to these negotiations, critics warned that social programs would be further hurt and that any remaining national standards embedded in them would be undermined.[32] Many provinces did indeed leap onto the social union bandwagon because it could increase provincial autonomy in social welfare and loosen such standards as nation-wide equal access. In any new policy, for instance, 'Each provincial and territorial government will determine the detailed program design and mix best suited to its own needs and circumstances to meet the agreed objectives.'[33] *National* standards need no longer be *federal* standards. Instead, provincial governments and Ottawa have agreed to set standards by consensus – probably at the lowest common denominator. Since such autonomy gives provinces a greater say in setting their own standards, the more conservative provinces will probably push for the lowest and most flexible guidelines that they can get. Moreover, provincial input may make the crafting of standards democratically unaccountable. Although SUFA will ease federal-provincial tensions, critics argue that Canadians could pay a high price. The quality of social programs could worsen as national standards disintegrate and regional disparities grow.

SUFA's defenders responded that, should voters clearly want universal services maintained in the public domain, the agreement's open-ended, general, and hortatory quality could allow the provinces to respond, with Ottawa, to such pressure. The National Child Benefit of 1997 was one harbinger of such innovation under free-trade federalism with a collaborative face.[34] Since SUFA redefined not only the boundary between the federal and the provincial, but between the public and the private sectors,[35] it became a blank canvas for a continuing complex process of struggle and contestation.[36] If Ottawa had surplus funds to distribute, its spending power in areas of provincial jurisdiction, now accepted by the anglophone premiers even if only six provinces concur, might give it the lead once again in determining provincial priorities – at least outside Quebec.

Ottawa pulled off a federal-provincial Health Accord in September 2000, which included Quebec, by agreeing to restore some of the funds cut during the previous decade. It signalled a provisional truce while the fate of the financially stressed health care system was debated within the context of a federal and provincial fiscal imbalance.[37]

To sum up the argument so far in this chapter, the legacy of the Diefenbaker-Pearson-Trudeau era was a relatively generous, comprehensive social security system that had been enriched even as late as the early 1980s when the Liberals recommitted Canada to a high-standard, single-tier public health system. Unhappily, it was inadequately funded. Globalized capital markets mediated by the bond-rating agencies forced federal and provincial governments to break the addiction to deficit financing they had developed because of their inadequate revenues. Federal responses to this external pressure varied from reluctant to wilful spending cuts that were premised on at least partial restoration pending economic recovery. Provincial responses varied from reluctant restraint by NDP governments in Saskatchewan and British Columbia or the Parti Québécois to Ontario's in-your-face neoconservative attack on the needs-based rationale for social welfare programs. We then looked at how the Social Union Framework Agreement legitimated Ottawa's spending role and implicitly acknowledged Quebec's asymmetrical position. Absent so far from this causal picture is any significant role played by global governance in determining national social policy.

Services, Social Policy, and Global Governance

As Canadians contemplated the new millennium, their earlier fears that globalization or continentalism would force the proud Canadian social security system to harmonize to some lower American standard had eased. The deterioration in welfare programs in response to globalization had been made by decision makers in Canada according to their fiscal constraints or ideological imperatives.[38] But external pressures are likely to increase for two related reasons. First, the existing normative structure of the global trade regime sets the stage for privatizing such service functions still delivered by government as the provision of education and health care. Second, the multilateral agenda for the negotiation of new trade norms includes more constricting 'disciplines' on public policy that will enlarge the field for the private provision by transnational corporations (TNCs) of services hitherto supplied by the state. We will briefly address these two issues by looking at the WTO's treatment of services in its texts and at its agenda for future negotiations.

Public-sector activities providing health care, education, or mail delivery and supplying electricity or water have something in common with private-sector activities such as wholesaling and retailing, the travel industry, hotels, pension fund management, and telecommunications. Whether offered for the public good or for private profit, both kinds of activity are considered 'services' in the arcane discourse of trade law. We know that much of the past century's political energy went into the struggle over which activities should be left to private initiative and how much responsibility government should assume. In the first case, individuals as consumers pay for what they want or can afford. In the second, individuals as citizens receive benefits, which are financed sometimes by taxes and sometimes by user fees.

We have already seen that the public-private divide is a moveable frontier. When we recognize that global corporate interests are involved in providing services such as fast food (McDonald's), entertainment (Disney), credit cards (American Express), health care (Pfizer), travel (United Airlines), and software (Microsoft), it immediately becomes understandable that transnational private interests can come into bitter conflict with national governments. A public corporation in oil or broadcasting or transportation or schooling or health care can occupy economic space that a foreign company may covet, along with the profits that could come with it.

When trade rules covered only goods, as was the case under the GATT, then conflicts between a host government and foreign corporations that provided services were handled within that state's political processes. European states tended to favour national over non-national service providers and in many sectors, such as water, telephone, post, electric power, and transportation, favoured public over private service provision. If the new regimes of continental and global economic governance heralded significant shrinking effects for the state, it was in large part because *services* were included for the first time within their new, supraconstitutional constraints on government actions.

The first commercial treaty to include services was the Canada-United States Free Trade Agreement. Part of the political uproar precipitated in Canada by the debate over CUFTA focused on its putative threat to the social provision of health and education. The immediate cause of this fear was the neoconservative hostility to the welfare state espoused by the Reagan administration, which had insisted that the accord cover services. CUFTA's Chapter 14, in fact, addressed services, but the agreement's immediate impact on Canadian social policy was negligible. For the first half-decade under free trade, differences between American and Canadian policies increased in health and public assistance. The common switch from universal family allowances to income-targeted child benefits was due to ideological convergence, not continentalism, while the convergence in pension policies resulted from fiscal cutbacks.[39]

In the longer term, including health-care management in the appendix of services 'covered' by CUFTA was expected to boost the expansion of U.S. health insurance and hospital management corporations in Canada.[40] Whether this presaged an eventual privatization of public health despite public resistance was not clear, particularly when the preamble stating that *'tout en laissant aux Parties la latitude voulue pour protéger l'intérêt public'* seemed to guarantee Canadian governments' freedom to sustain their welfare state.[41]

In the negotiation of NAFTA, Washington was under so much pressure from its pharmaceutical and phone companies that it focused more on intellectual property rights and telecommunications services than on attacking its neighbours' social policy capacities.[42]

The leading TNCs operating in American health and education industries had long been frustrated by their inability to expand abroad. The WTO's General Agreement on Trade in Services (GATS) of 1995 marked a double success in the U.S. strategy to commercialize the potentially enormous markets represented by the public sectors in all other countries. First, it applied broad principles that had been developed to govern trade in goods, such as the 'most-favoured nation' discipline over governmental measures. Then it listed the 'commitments' made by each signatory state to have specific services covered by more restrictive norms such as national treatment. It was understood that those sectors omitted from each state's offer (and any exceptions that modified any state's commitments) would be subjected to increased limitations following subsequent negotiations, which, as part of the WTO's built-in agenda, started up in February 2000.[43]

Initial cases have shown that WTO jurists are interpreting GATS obligations very expansively. Their early judgments will encourage challenges to an almost unlimited range of government measures. If successful for TNCs, these disputes will accelerate the commercialization of public services around the world. As the WTO panel on the U.S. dispute with the European Union over bananas concluded, 'In principle, no measures are excluded a priori from the scope of the GATS.'[44] Whether its purpose be child care or distance education, environmental or consumer protection, promoting labour standards or fair competition, any governmental measure that modifies the conditions of competition for foreign firms relating to service provision is subject to corporate challenge as a violation of the WTO's services rules.

GATS's extraordinary intrusiveness can be seen in the way that its broadest norms cover all government measures, even in services where the government has declined to make specific commitments to liberalize. For instance, Canada did not make commitments to open up public health care to foreign investors. However, national treatment requires that, once Alberta allows any health-care provider to offer for-profit hospital services, it must allow any foreign health-care provider to operate on the same terms. And, once any foreign health-care provider is allowed to operate, then most-favoured nation requires that every other 'like' foreign health-care provider must 'immediately and unconditionally' be allowed entry. And because most-favoured nation rights are 'bound' – that is, irreversible – should Alberta in this example withdraw for-profit hospital providers' right to operate, then Canada as the signatory state would be liable to retaliation from the government of the deprived foreign company.[45]

GATS does not only apply to the *trade* in services, such as their 'cross-border supply' (i.e., by phone, mail, or fax). It also covers government measures affecting the three other modes of service delivery. 'Consumption abroad' of services would cover foreign students studying in Canada, for whom NT would require equal access to government financial aid. 'Commercial presence' for service providers dispenses foreign firms from the need to incorporate subsidiaries in a host country where it wants to win contracts for hospital management or offer courses. Requiring that a foreign business school offering its degrees to Canadian nationals conform to provincial certification procedures might be ruled illegal. 'Presence of natural persons' would permit an education or hospital corporation to bring its personnel into the country on a temporary basis to provide a teaching or surgery 'ser-

vice' regardless of the training standards set by a province's professional associations. GATS is expansive, finally, in covering not just
measures taken by governments but those of state entities and even
organizations mandated by governments.

Apart from the member-states' lists of exempted areas, the only and
quite limited exception to GATS's disciplinary effect is a government
service provided neither on a commercial basis nor in competition
with other service suppliers.[46] Since the supply of most education,
health, and social services involves a mix of private and public delivery, these policy areas – though considered by most Canadians to be
the prime responsibility of their state – are probably not protected by
this exception. 'Probably,' because it is too early for the massive areas
of uncertainty created by this far-reaching, yet largely untried agreement to have been resolved. Until more disputes are settled through
the interpretations handed down by WTO panels and its appellate
body, much of GATS's significance remains contingent on the aggres-
siveness of TNCs in pushing to exploit their new rights in the countries
that they have targeted for expansion. This contingency on foreign corporate litigiousness is itself dependent on how panellists and the WTO
appellate body proceed to interpret the many grey areas lurking in the
text. The overlapping spheres of exceptions and commitments multi-
ply this uncertainty. If Canada listed no limitations when it committed
its data-processing and database services to the full application of
GATS rules, a government measure to require that personal educational information not be exploited for commercial purposes might be
challengeable, even though Canada did not list education among its
scheduled commitments.[47]

If the Doha Round of global (WTO) talks or the hemispheric negotiation on a Free Trade Area of the Americas (FTAA) endorses a more
intrusive set of proposed rules on services, governments may be for-
bidden from maintaining 'monopolies' that traditionally deliver publicly financed programs to citizens. In his annual report for 2000, the
WTO's controversial director-general, Mike Moore, confirmed which
way the global winds are blowing. Confirming the purpose of the
GATS agreement is to 'bind, reduce, or eliminate impediments to the
supply of services by foreign providers,' he noted that ten states which
have recently joined GATT have made commitments in health, education, and social services.[48] If foreign capital ultimately wins the legal
right to sue governments for not giving it free rein to commodify their
social security systems, then global governance – as opposed to global-

ization – will indeed spell the end of publicly provided social security as Canadians have known it. Social policy, which has been a domain where the primary boundary for political contestation was between the federal and the provincial states, could become one in which the political war zone becomes a transborder conflict between the federal and provincial public spheres on one side and a panoply of transnational corporate sectors on the other.

As a semi-peripheral country, Canada plays both rule taker and rule maker in developing global governance. As potential rule maker in the hemispheric negotiations of an FTAA, it has pushed its thirty-odd interlocutors to expand the coverage of trade rules to include public health and educational services, because it claims that there are opportunities abroad awaiting Canadians with health management and educational expertise who could enter foreign health and educational markets. In its guise as rule taker, however, it professed to its concerned citizens at home that nothing in the FTAA would jeopardize Canadian provinces' capacity to sustain their public health and education systems.[49] Given the gap between Ottawa officials' past professions of certainty about the meaning of the trade agreements they have signed and the actual consequences for public policy, these assurances could hardly be taken seriously. In two decades, Canada has moved from a set of universal policies providing benefits as a matter of right to a more precarious mix of constantly shifting targeted benefits, for which citizens may or may not qualify. The next wave of social policy change may well come from the supraconstitutional pressures of stronger global governance.

The interaction between globalization and social policy is a two-way street. On the one hand, we have seen that globalization has harmed welfare provision in reducing the state's capacity to tax (because of competition among governments to offer TNCs low taxes) and to spend on programs for the public's benefit (because capital markets no longer tolerate an indebted government's running budgetary deficits). But threats by the mobility of transnational capital to the quality of social programs can also strengthen the demands of the national policy constituency. Much depends on the strength of democratic politics. Seniors' organizations deterred the Mulroney government from its initial attack on old-age pensions. Organized labour is a vocal force resisting the reduction of the social wage, but its protests have become less effective as membership has declined, capital has become more mobile, and governments have moved to the right. Feminist organizations have also supported family, redistributive, and equity policies, but government cutbacks to funding for women's organizations have eroded the feminist voice in public policy.[50] Despite some political marginalization of these advocacy forces, mass opinion remains clearly in favour of the public provision of social services. This political reality suggests that, as neoconservatives supported by globalism erode the welfare state, the struggle to redefine Canada's distinctive mix of private and public provision is far from over.

If the social commons consists of the shared public supports that generate a community's cohesion, and if the social security system is the foundation for this societal resource, then the public quality of a country's schools and hospitals, along with their egalitarian policies become crucial ingredients in its development. Wealthier states are not necessarily healthier states. Societies with greater income equality have greater health equality. High levels of inequality and social exclusion reduce well-being and life expectancy. Social policy affects all aspects of a society's quality of life. For this reason, maintaining a vibrant social commons is an aspect of good economic policy. By the same logic, social policy that increases disparities by aggravating inequalities of class, status, or income also replaces the social commons' mutually reinforcing dynamic of inclusion with the spiralling destructiveness of alienation and social exclusion. Some social barriers are of course endemic in the workplace, which divides employers from those who work for them. The role of the state in the crucial relationship of workers to capitalists is our next subject for inquiry.

16 The Working State: Labour Relations under Stress

Noma Industries Ltd of Toronto is an electronics and auto parts manufacturer which, in the wake of NAFTA, set up three plants in Mexico between 1994 and 1998. In explaining the company's locational strategy, Noma's chief financial officer illustrated how free trade is commodifying labour in North America: 'For us it is the access to the lower labour rates and to be able to get our products back to our U.S. customer base in one or two days. When you look at the all-inclusive costs, there are still significant advantages to operating in Mexico versus elsewhere in North America. Mexican wages are a sixth of those for comparable jobs in the southwestern United States.'[1]

Labour and the State

Before exploring NAFTA's impact on the situation of Canadian workers, we need to understand the three principal areas – working conditions, industrial relations, and job creation – in which the state has addressed labour in order to regulate the unequal relationship between capital and labour.

Governments define for employers minimal levels for working conditions and create entitlements to such rights as pension schemes and advance notice before being laid off. Governments also protect the right to bargain by setting the framework within which employees negotiate their contracts with management. Finally, governments intervene in the marketplace when they establish policies aimed directly at creating jobs or more indirectly affecting the supply of labour power to various sectors of the economy.

These three types of interaction are closely related. For example, if governments fail to create jobs, higher unemployment makes business more reluctant to concede better labour contracts. Other types of public policy can affect the labour market as well: if the Bank of Canada raises interest rates to curb inflation any resulting rise in unemployment helps business resist wage increases. In order to assess the impacts of globalization and neoconservatism on labour market policies, we first need to see how these three dimensions interacted in the modern Keynesian state.

Working Conditions

From the Middle Ages, when rulers decreed the conditions of work recommended by craft guilds until the dawn of capitalism, a leitmotif in the evolution of the state was its tendency to respond repressively to the needs of 'servants' by concurring with the demands of their 'masters,' as these laws put it. When steam technology allowed entrepreneurs in the nineteenth century to mechanize and expand the scale of their manufacturing, an underclass of workers emerged – whether from the marginal farms in the old world or from the immigrant ships in the new – to sell their labour for cash.

During the early stages of capitalism, housing, social, and working conditions for the emerging proletariat were as degrading as any that Charles Dickens described in his most vivid passages. Socialist ideas began to spread visions of alternative utopias to the exploitation of some humans by others. The British Parliament began to ameliorate the worst abuses of the industrial revolution in the 1830s by legislation to protect the most vulnerable – notably women and children. It was only later in the century, when the swelling ranks of the proletariat voiced their needs through mass action and through their superior numbers at the ballot box to which they gradually gained access, that Westminster repealed legislation treating as criminals workers who tried to organize unions. Late-nineteenth-century liberals addressed capitalism's social ills, expanding workers' rights to health, work, and security.

With its staples-based, export-led economy balanced by the National Policy's import-substituting industrialization, the young Dominion followed the British hegemon's model with its reluctant response to the human misery created by industrialization. Constrained by fiscal and constitutional limits to their capacities, federal and provincial governments and municipal administrations instituted over the twentieth century a cumulatively more comprehensive body of employment law. Typically, improved benefits were first negotiated by some unions, then legislated as general rules by progressive provincial governments such as Saskatchewan, before being adopted in federal laws. By the 1970s an extensive and detailed regulatory system had established workplace conditions that impinged substantially on employers' autonomy by specifying, among other things, the length of the working day, the quality of sanitation and safety in the workplace, and paid vacations.

These regulations placed few demands on the public purse, but once Keynesian ideas provided an economic rationale for a redistributive public policy, the regulatory state also became a spending state. To offset the flagrant inadequacy of money wages in meeting workers' needs for housing, education, medical care, job security, or dignified retirement, governments started providing, then radically improving, housing subsidies, secondary and postsecondary schooling, public health facilities, job insurance, accident compensation, and old-age pensions. With the provinces too financially strapped to satisfy the social needs for which the British North America Act made them responsible, a constitutional amendment passed in 1940 allowed Ottawa to institute unemployment insurance (UI) for the whole country. As the citizenry came to consider these policies to be its social right and demanded an adequate 'social wage,' governments shifted towards activism. This meant a legislated minimum for wages, an annual vacation paid by the employer, public compensation in case of industrial accidents, and basic financial support to cover ill health, unemployment, and retirement.

Many of the legislative changes made in the Diefenbaker-Pearson-Trudeau era consolidated these worker-welfare programs. Provinces entrenched human rights in anti-discrimination legislation. The social wage reached its federal apogee with the enrichment of UI in 1971. Thereafter it entered a confusing period of contestation, with UI being gradually retrenched while benefits increased for the retired and those with the lowest incomes. But as the Liberals started to wrestle with their budget deficit in the early 1980s, it became clear that benefits had hit a ceiling.

On the threshhold of the Mulroney-Chrétien era, the Canadian working class was already on the defensive. As protection by tariffs fell steadily with successive reductions under the General Agreement on Tariffs and Trade (GATT), Canadian business came under pressure from those international competitors whose workforces enjoyed a less generous social wage and a less protective labour code. The resulting managerial drive towards greater competitiveness through higher efficiency started to reshape the Canadian labour market. Establishing more efficient enterprises meant flattening hierarchical structures within corporations, reducing the number of managers, and 'shedding' workers as 'lean,' automated production techniques reduced the labour content in manufacturing.[2] Employers 'outsourced' work to smaller firms which used non-unionized labour and strove to contain the costs of their remaining employees.[3]

Although labour standards were to improve in some areas, such as wage parity for women and parental leave, management was not willing any longer to tolerate governments being 'soft' on workers. Automation and computerization had changed the nature of work so greatly that business strongly objected to the government's continuing role as rule-maker and umpire in an industrial relations scene that had changed radically. Getting government (selectively) off their backs became a popular refrain among Canadian business leaders. Although they didn't want rid of socialized public health, which gave them an advantage over their American competitors, they felt constricted by other rules written for the Fordist system of mass production.

Industrial Relations

Embedded in the notion of a 'civil' state is that of a 'civil society' directed by and for citizens who articulate their interests by participating in multifarious associations as they develop their personal identities and express their social solidarities. One of the most universal of these many identities is constructed by the conditions under which citizens work and by which they organize themselves as workers. The way governments have managed conflicts between employers (with their associations on the one hand) and employees (with their unions on the other) has provided a continuing subplot in the conflictual history of the modern state.

Canada's working class had been exposed to global and continental influences from its earliest days. As mining and manufacturing expanded in the young Dominion, the organizing energy and socialist angers of immigrant British workers set the tone for their first nineteenth-century labour organizations. But the border was as open towards the rising industrial power to the south as it was towards the motherland across the Atlantic. American union leaders sent organizers north to protect themselves against competition from rival, more radical unions in the Dominion. They quickly realized that recruiting new members increased their bargaining power as well as their income.[4] In 1902 Samuel Gompers's American Federation of Labor (AFL) gained control of Canada's Trades and Labour Congress and, with it, 90 per cent of the country's labour movement.[5]

Well before the personally ambitious and ideologically ambivalent Mackenzie King was appointed deputy minister by Prime Minister Wilfrid Laurier in 1907 and charged with setting up the Dominion's first Department of Labour, the Canadian state had been involved in industrial relations. Unions of workers, which were originally considered seditious, had been given legal protection in the 1870s. King pioneered a technique of appointing conciliation boards in industrial disputes to force employers to sit down with labour and accept their recommendations. His successful conciliation technique was borrowed by the U.S. industrialist John D. Rockefeller, Jr, and found its way – as an acknowledged adoption of Canadian practice – into inter-war American legislation on collective bargaining. This cross-border influence then reversed direction when, in 1937, strikers at General Motors in Oshawa, Ontario, invited Local 222 of the United Auto Workers (UAW) from the militant Congress of Industrial Organizations (CIO) to take over their organizing efforts.[6] American labour had moved north hand in hand with American capital to dominate Canada's industrial system.

Only when labour militancy in the country's war industries forced his hand did King as prime minister finally turn into policy his ideas about civilizing Industry in the name of Humanity.[7] In 1944 a cabinet order adopted American labour law 'holus-bolus' by imposing a collective bargaining system on both labour and management.[8] Taking his lead as well from innovations in Ontario, Saskatchewan, and Quebec, King wrote a commitment to state-regulated industrial relations into the 1945 Speech from the Throne. He had finally determined to rewrite the rules for industrial relations for Fordist capitalism. In his idealized thinking, government would be the honest broker monitoring the certification of trade unions and providing mediation services for labour–management disputes over employment contracts. In 1946 Justice Ivan Rand of the Supreme Court of Canada made a famous recommendation in an industrial dispute between Ford and the UAW: the company should automatically 'check off' the UAW's dues from its employees' pay. Collective bargaining and the Rand check-off formula, which was subsequently inserted in provincial legislation, consecrated the Fordist compromise between capital's need to employ a disciplined workforce and workers' desires to share through wage increases in the fruits of their labours. It was on this bargain between labour and capital that the Keynesian state was to be constructed.

Decentralized in hundreds of separate bargaining units, fragmented among rival union centrals, divided by ideological differences, balkanized by region and language, and lacking the discipline a strong labour party could have provided, the Canadian union movement was fractured. Ideological control of Canada's trade and industrial unions by the American leadership of the AFL and CIO had severely inhibited labour's participation in Canadian politics for the first half of the twentieth century, blunting its potential to influence social reform. The AFL's rapprochement with the CIO in the United States during the 1950s permitted their northern dependencies to unite under the umbrella of the Canadian Labour Congress (CLC). Now Canadian unions could formally integrate with the New Democratic Party (NDP), created in 1961 out of the floundering, once-socialist Co-operative Commonwealth Federation. Since the postwar doubling of real income under Fordism had tempered industrial workers' consciousness of belonging to an oppressed class, and because Canadians polarized more along regional, linguistic, and religious than along class lines, this political initiative came too late substantially to affect labour legislation in Keynesianism's remaining years.

More significant in the late 1960s was federal legislation that, taking its cue from Saskatchewan in the 1940s and from Quebec in the wake of its Quiet Revolution, enabled civil servants to strike. The resulting large public-service unions helped Canada defy the remorseless trend of trade union decline in the United States. In the same period between the early 1960s and the early 1980s, when the American movement lost ground by 10 per cent, the Canadian unionization rate increased from 30 to 40 per cent of the non-agricultural labour force. American-controlled unions' membership fell from 70 to 35 per cent of the Canadian labour movement.

However well organized, Canadian labour was not strong enough to prevent a weakening of its economic muscle by legislatures and courts. It protested, but it could not stop the Trudeau Liberals from introducing wage controls in their anti-inflation program of 1975 and again in the '6 and 5' policy brouhaha of 1982, when they temporarily abolished the right to strike for workers in federally controlled industries. The recession of the early 1980s, the withdrawal of strike rights from workers in provincial government services deemed 'essential,' and the persistence of high levels of unemployment further diminished labour's bargaining power.

Even once-upon-a-time labour sympathizer Pierre Trudeau's hardwon Charter of Rights failed to reverse the Canadian courts' longstanding antipathy to the special rights of organized labour. As a result, court cases failed to offset the growing capacity of business and the state to curtail union power. Not satisfied that unions were weak enough, management and business-friendly economists called for greater 'labour flexibility,' which meant loosening constraints on companies' freedom to alter such working conditions as extending the work week without paying overtime rates. Business was also concerned about government's direct involvement in the labour market.

Job Creation

Ever since Jean Talon shipped the *filles du roy* to Quebec to marry the first *habitants* and populate the new colony, the Canadian state had developed many kinds of policies aimed at improving or expanding the labour market, whether based on attracting immigrants, on exploiting natives to supply the fur trade, or on establishing institutions of education to produce properly trained workers for the economy. Under laissez-faire thinking, government had left the market to look after itself. But in the Great Depression employment levels fell so low that the massed ranks of the unemployed threatened the capitalist order. The resulting widespread malaise of the 1930s popularized ideologies on the left and the right that looked to the state as the agency to create jobs for the jobless.

It was as this time that the English liberal economist John Maynard Keynes worked out his famous formula to save capitalism from communism or fascism while only moderately activating the state's economic powers. In Canada, Ottawa's mobilization of the economy during the Second World War proved that state-owned and -directed enterprise could indeed create work for everyone. Encouraged by the then widely accepted Keynesian belief in the possibilty of full employment, federal and provincial governments from the 1950s on experimented with increasingly activist job creation programs, some of which we have already looked at under the rubric of industrial policy in chapter 13 and 14.

Institutionally significant for labour market policy in the Trudeau government was the Department of Manpower and Immigration with its mandate to furnish the Canadian labour force with appropriate skills and training. In the Adult Occupational and Training Act, Ottawa undertook to finance training for industrial needs. Throughout the 1970s, innovative programs such as the Local Initiatives Program and Opportunities for Youth reached more sectors of the job market and stimulated a greater variety of training methods.

International Governance and Canadian Labour

With this background in mind, we can now consider the effects of trade liberalization and neoconservatism on this complex situation for both unionized and unorganized labour, bearing in mind that over two-thirds of the workforce are not protected by any union. We have already seen how the Mulroney-Chrétien repudiation of Keynesian thinking and its related European model of capitalism entailed rejecting industrial strategies aimed at job creation in favour of U.S.-style thinking. Free trade was expected automatically to increase the supply of high value-added jobs without governments' having to micro-manage individual sectors of the economy. But free trade would also affect government capacity in the labour market (job training), working conditions (employment standards), and industrial relations themselves. To ascertain how these policy spheres were affected, we next assess the impact of the new global governance regimes created to manage the new system. We then identify domestic neoconservatism's contribution to reordering the labour scene. Finally we see to what extent the well-being of Canada's working people has changed under the new paradigm – for better or for worse.

Global Governance

While violent demonstrations during such high-profile global meetings as the G7/G8 economic summit in Genoa in 2001 reflected widespread concerns about the deterioration of working conditions around the world, traditional international bodies have had difficulty addressing labour issues effectively. Since its creation alongside the League of Nations in 1919 to counteract the global influence of Bolshevism, the International Labour Organization (ILO) has led a troubled existence. Post-1945 difficulties with the communist bloc were compounded by its tripartite, labour-management-government constitution, which impeded consensus. Although large numbers of states have signed many of its 183 conventions – defining fundamental norms for working conditions (e.g. the rights of children) and industrial relations (freedom of association) – many of these have been boycotted by the United States.[9]

In sharp contrast with the WTO's rules, which can be effectively enforced as we saw in chapter 4, the ILO's conventions contained no mechanism to ensure adherence to the principles they endorse. Under the ILO's charter, for instance, unsatisfactory national implementation of an adopted convention can trigger the creation of a commission of inquiry, which can make suggestions in its report. If a state refuses to accept a commission's censure, the general board of the ILO can only recommend 'such action as it may deem wise and expedient to secure compliance.' In plain language, the ILO relies on moral suasion and peer pressure to achieve compliance with its labour standards. Since states need not fear any type of tangible retribution for their inaction, ILO norms are effective only in countries whose civil society is already strong enough to insist on their observance.[10]

The United Nations has proven no more effective than the ILO. Attempts in the 1990s to create enforceable international labour standards came to naught, and there has been little support for using the GATT as a lever for upholding such norms. Governments of developing countries particularly fear they would lose the competitive advantage they garner from labourers working in poor conditions for meagre wages if they were forced to comply with tough standards defined by the Organization for Economic Cooperation and Development (OECD) or even the ILO.[11]

The issue will not go away. When unionists in the North belatedly became conscious of globalization's threat to their membership, they started to demand that their governments attach labour clauses to any new trade agreements in order to end 'social dumping' by countries with low wage costs and poor working conditions. When it looked as though new anti-labour rules were being negotiated at the OECD as the Multilateral Agreement on Investment, Canadian labour took a lead in building the transnational coalition of non-governmental organizations (NGOs) that orchestrated worldwide demands to abort the negotiations. Unions increased their activity in the ILO, urging the international community to enhance its powers and dealing with new issues such as working conditions and industrial relations for temporary and part-time workers. Following his presidency of the Canadian Auto Workers (CAW) and then of the CLC, Bob White became an active NGO spokesman at the OECD on behalf of the Canadian labour movement.

Continental Governance

Below the global level, the effectiveness of continental agreements for labour standards varies from moderate to negligible. The European Union and NAFTA offer an example of each. The EU responded to its national labour movements' concerns that a 'race to the bottom' set off by market-liberating deregulation would undermine their hard-won rights.

Norms generated by the European Commision in Brussels to affect national policies sought to prevent labour from being treated merely as a marketable commodity. Various directives based on the idea of a continental social contract were designed to raise standards for working conditions of the 'social partners' in the poorer member-states to the level of the richer. The EU had considerable success because it moved beyond simply declaring a level field. Establishing high standards below which no country should fall and providing substantial social and structural funds, it actually helped the more indigent countries raise their practices towards the level of the more affluent.[12]

In contrast to the slow process of European amalgamation, in which considerable care had been taken to protect labour market policies, the tight deadlines imposed by the U.S. Congress's 'fast track' authority for trade negotiations forced the pace and reduced the transparency of CUFTA's negotiating processes. Fearing co-optation by a business-biased government, the CLC refused the token seat at the consulting table offered it by Prime Minister Mulroney in 1986. Even if its position had been voiced within Ottawa's consultation process, it is highly unlikely that the bilateral trade and investment deal would have addressed industrial relations and blunted the Canadian labour movement's opposition.

The subsequent negotiation of NAFTA provoked further controversy, as American labour leaders joined their Canadian colleagues in predicting a race to the bottom as business moved plants and jobs to Mexico to exploit its lower wages. Trade liberalization did not unite workers of the world; it made them compete. Beyond increased unemployment, American unions feared that closer integration with the low-wage Mexican economy would exacerbate trends that were already moving jobs to anti-union states. Their campaign against the agreement was politically effective enough to induce Governor Bill Clinton, when running for the U.S. presidency, to call for extra negotiations on the social dimension of free trade.[13]

Following Clinton's election, Mexico refused to reopen the NAFTA document. Under strong pressure from Washington, President Carlos Salinas de Gortari finally accepted 'side agreements' on labour as well as on environmental issues, on the condition that they not further impinge on Mexico's national sovereignty or allow recourse to trade sanctions.[14]

The resulting North American Agreement on Labour Co-operation (NAALC) mouthed the language of strong and comprehensive labour rights spoken by the European Social Charter of 1989. Sensitive to the individual circumstances of the three states involved, the negotiators agreed on wording that assumed NAFTA would foster a larger labour market (by creating 'new employment opportunities'), would 'improve working conditions and living standards,' and would enhance industrial relations ('protect, enhance and enforce basic worker rights') within the continent.[15]

Whereas the European Community's member-states had been obliged to implement the provisions of the 1989 charter, the NAALC did not require adjustment of national legislation to ensure compliance with its eleven principles.[16] Nor did its principles establish minimum standards for domestic law, since it simply assumed that each country's laws embraced high standards.[17] In committing each country only to enforce its own laws, it achieved the Americans' objective. The AFL-CIO had believed that if Mexico's impressive labour legislation were actually implemented, then its working conditions and trade union rights would rise towards U.S. standards. The danger to American jobs of social dumping by Mexican firms' unfairly exploiting cheaper labour would supposedly then recede.

Like the ILO's conventions, the NAALC's declaration of eleven labour rights was only as significant as the mechanism enforcing them. In fact, the side agreement specified that none of the eight standards prescribing trade union rights was enforceable through dispute settlement.[18] It only provided for enforcement of three technical labour standards – labour protection for youths or children, health and safety, and minimum wages.[19] Worse, complaints about these three trade sanctionable norms had to identify *continual* failure by a member government to enforce its domestic labour laws. If a trade-related infringement were proven, NAFTA benefits could be withheld from the offending government. There was no provision in the NAALC allowing a judgment to be enforced against an individual employer. (In contrast, European citizens can bring their employers before the European Court of Justice if they are not satisfied with the outcome of legal proceedings at the national level.)

If violations of any of the side agreement's other eight principles is proven, the offending employer and government only suffer from the bad press they receive in the investigation process. In this respect, labour unions correctly felt that the NAALC structure was not designed to protect labour from the negative impacts of trade liberalization. It merely constituted a U.S. effort – albeit an ineffectual one – to prevent Mexico from using its labour force as a competitive tool against it.

In 1994, the NAALC established its Commission on Labour Cooperation (NAALC CLC) in Dallas as the executive responsible for the accord's overall implementation. Each country set up a National Administrative Office (NAO) to investigate breaches of the accord. According to the NAALC CLC, these institutions have busied themselves mainly with increasing communications with their counterparts in order to create a better understanding of each other's policies and to define their role.

Dispute resolution under the NAALC requires that a citizen or group – typically a trade union – with a grievance about practices in another NAFTA country file a complaint with its own NAO. The subsequent process involves an investigation, ministerial consultations, recommendations, and ultimately creation of an Evaluation Committee of Experts. If the ECE still cannot resolve the complaint and if it involves the three trade sanctionable norms, penalties may be applied to the offending state.[20] This process is so convoluted that so far no dispute has reached the ECE stage.

Debate about the side agreement started with a claim that the NAALC was a 'breakthrough' for labour rights advocates – a 'unique accomplishment of the governments of Canada, Mexico, and the United States' – and an admonition that 'scorn directed at the process reflects more impatience than analysis.'[21] Indeed, the three NAOs did adopt a relatively liberal view of their jurisdictions. The U.S. NAO has been the most active and aggressive, having reviewed fifteen cases between 1994 and 2000, of which thirteen involved labour issues in

Mexico, two in Canada. In six of these it held public informational meetings that resulted in forceful criticisms of workers' inadequate rights to organize collectively and moved to the level of ministerial consultations.[22] In six of the fifteen cases the NAO absolved the defending party; the other three complaints were withdrawn.

Mexico's NAO has been more ambivalent. On the one hand, it strongly criticized aggressive U.S. reviews of Mexican practices. On the other hand, it has supported the complaints of Mexican migrants about the abuses that they have suffered, particularly apple pickers in Washington state. The Canadian NAO has had the least to do, handling only one substantive case.[23]

Canadian unions initially dismissed the NAALC. Only peripherally involved in the activities of the trilateral NAALC CLC, they initiated a complaint to their national NAO regarding the health and safety of a plant in Mexico City.[24] Observing the political ground to be gained from supporting complaints about Mexican labour practices, the CLC has become more active, helping to orchestrate sophisticated, media-focused complaints along with the AFL-CIO and with Mexico's independent National Union of Workers.

By signing the labour side agreement, Ottawa brought the federally controlled industries of banking, transportation, and telecommunications, which employ one-tenth of the Canadian labour force, under the NAALC. Only those provinces and territories that opted in were bound by the accord. As of 2002, only Alberta, Manitoba, Prince Edward Island, and Quebec had ratified NAALC.[25]

Because the Canadian workplace was not the object of American concern, it was less affected by the NAALC's enforcement provisions. If Canada breached one of the three sanctionable principles, it could be penalized only with fines. NAALC involvement in Canadian industrial relations has consequently been minor. One case shamed the Quebec government into prohibiting plant closings motivated by opposition to unions. In a second case, the threat to file a NAALC action against Alberta moved the government to abandon its proposed plan to privatize the enforcement of health and safety standards.[26] In 1998, postal workers' unions in all three countries jointly filed a petition under NAALC about Canada Post's refusal to negotiate with rural route mail couriers, but the trinational initiative came to naught.

Even if more Canadian cases did come before the NAOs, they would not likely improve the situation of domestic labour unions or resolve any labour disputes. Unlike dispute settlement in the EU's supranational court, domestic NAO's administer NAFTA's labour disputes and are themselves creatures of the governments they are supposed to be investigating. Thus the NAOs' broad interpretations of their jurisdiction could easily be reversed if the three governments take a less accommodating stance towards complaints about violations of labour rights.[27]

As a manifestation of continental governance, the NAALC CLC has had some of its intended impact on Mexico, where members of independent unions challenging the government-controlled unions have found material and moral support in their U.S. and Canadian counterparts and in the publicity resulting from the dispute process. Transnational collaboration between trade unions has also increased. As Canadian and American unionists tried to defeat NAFTA, they developed close connections with each other, as well as with Mexican labour groups, especially those which were independent of the government-controlled unions.[28] However, great differences still separate the three labour movements, making it premature to talk of a continentalization 'from below' strengthening labour in North America to an equivalent degree that continentalization 'from above' has strengthened continental capital.

Continental Restructuring and Labour

Economists supporting NAFTA argued that free trade would stimulate an automatic increase in Canadian employment and living standards. They also anticipated that any jobs lost from the closure of uncompetitive firms would be offset by increases in productivity and high-end work, but they did not promise more jobs or more job security. Canadian manufacturers would achieve greater economies of scale in their high-value-added facilities and become more competitive by using Mexico's low-cost labour for their production plants.[29]

As tariff barriers fell, Canadian businesses did become subject to more competition from the south. They reacted by pressing the federal and provincial governments to lighten or lift regulations of working conditions and industrial relations. Its helping to release transnational corporations (TNCs) from high labour standards shows NAFTA's primary, though indirect, impact on Canadian labour. By cutting back national modes of regulation – at least in Canada and Mexico – but not replacing them with enforceable continental regulations, NAFTA created space for freer capital accumulation on a continental basis.

Industrial Relations

Labour has become a competitive tool in a continentally integrated market, in which NAFTA increased corporations' ability to insulate themselves from trade-union pressures. The CLC documented many bargaining situations where 'companies make it clear that production and new investments can be shifted if rates of return do not match those in the U.S. or Mexico.'[30] To the extent that it constitutionalizes a new regime of capital accumulation in which labour has lost bargaining power, NAFTA has entrenched, rather than mitigated, the phenomenon of social dumping.

NAFTA also acts to aggravate social divisions within its peripheral members by discriminating between high- and low-paid labour. American unions' fear that Mexican immigrants would drive down U.S. wages led to North American economic integration denying mobility to most workers. In response to the needs of continental TNCs to have key personnel move unhindered within their corporate domain, NAFTA allows corporate executives, managers, and skilled workers to move among a company's affiliates. In addition, professional workers in a specified list of occupations can obtain renewable 'temporary' work permits on proof of citizenship. From 2,677 Canadian temporary professional workers migrating to the United States in 1989, the flow had increased to 26,987 by 1996.[31] Beyond facilitating the 'brain drain,' this mobility enhances the market value of those who already earn the most. This is just one of the ways in which NAFTA increases class divisions within Canada.

Working Conditions

Once thought crucial to running an economy based on Fordist methods, high labour standards have come to be viewed as costly rigidities imposing unnecessary and anti-competitive expenditures on both government and business. Competing with less regulated economies, businesses announced that they could no longer survive under Canadian labour regulations (which raised their costs) and industrial relations rules (which empowered unions to bargain for more benefits). Quite the opposite: they needed to cut costs by using labour more 'flexibly' and becoming more efficient. Canadian policy makers (and much of the public at large) have generally condoned this argument for lowering labour norms.

Beyond pushing down domestic labour standards, governments are undermining previous methods of mitigating social and gendered inequalities. As Canada competes against the United States and Mexico for investments, it has become less able to tax corporations in order to fund national expenditures that maintain a social wage. Most provinces had significantly cut social assistance schemes since 1992, as we saw in chapter 15.[32] The NAALC does not provide any means for redressing these inequalities or offsetting the erosion of labour's position. NAFTA rules ensure the market's effectiveness as the most powerful stratifier of labour and social relations and obstruct any equalizing redistribution of the gains derived from continentalization. In sum, the Commission on Labour Cooperation cannot offset the asymmetry caused by capital's great increase of power and by increasing labour insecurity in North America.

Domestic Neoconservativism and Labour

Federal and provincial policies addressing labour under neoconservativism have been confused. While most reject government intervention in the marketplace, as do the free trade agreements, others have continued in a Fordist direction. Complaining of competitive pressure from low-wage jurisdictions, managers demanded that government rebalance the labour-management relationship in their favour by lightening the load of work standards and diluting such collective bargaining rights as regulations facilitating union organizing drives.

Industrial jobs continued to fall steadily, while new employment in Canada was increasingly in service sectors and non-standard forms of employment – for example, temporary and part-time workers, who do not have the same minimum standards that protect full-time workers. Temps are not easy to organize and so enjoy fewer fringe benefits and less job security. According to Statistics Canada, temporary employment made up 5 per cent of the total workforce in 1991. The proportion had increased to 11.6 per cent by 1996,[33] when part-time workers earned only two-thirds as much as full timers. Less than 20 per cent received benefits.

Policy-makers were understandably torn. On the one hand, many agreed with the Business Council on National Issues that, if they were to bring foreign investment to Canada and prevent or postpone plant closings and mass layoffs, they must create 'competitive' regulatory conditions – i.e., norms that lowered the costs of employing workers.

On the other hand, policy-makers knew that developing a high-value-added, knowledge-based economy depended on offering investors a skilled labour force and a high-quality social infrastructure, for which a generous social wage was necessary.[34] When leaning in this direction, they agreed with labour unions and voters who wanted better, not worse, labour standards to counteract globalization's threats to their job security.

Job Creation

Mulroney's team responded to market demands by moving from emphasis on the social wage to concentration on labour market support. Following its *Canadian Jobs Strategy* paper in 1984, Ottawa started 'offloading' responsibility for job training to employers and employees on the grounds that the programs developed under Trudeau had not provided the trainees with the skills that they needed to keep them fully employed.

The government used UI funds to support private-sector employers who hired and trained unemployed people, with the goal of improving their long-term prospects. In the event, the employee-trainees gained few skills: 20 per cent were placed in jobs where they could not acquire transferable skills. They worked in doughnut shops and pizza parlours, grocery and variety stores. Although the scheme also created positions that required more skills, it mainly provided many major national franchisers with cheap, subsidized labour.[35]

Because of their constitutional jurisdiction over labour in most industries, the provinces have always played a large role in Canada's labour market. Their importance increased when fiscal straits blocked the Chrétien Liberals' plans to boost training for job-related skills.[36] They had laid out their active labour market plan, inspired by an OECD job study, in the 1994 paper *Agenda: Jobs and Growth*, but deficit-reduction measures led them to return responsibility for many labour programs to the provinces. As a result, their monetary commitment to training was 11 per cent lower in 1999–2000 than when they came to power in 1993–4.

Following a series of intergovernmental agreements, most provinces assumed administrative control – albeit with a reduced budget – over labour training programs, such as providing wage subsidies to employers who took on new workers and supporting the incomes of beneficiaries who started their own businesses.[37] Alberta, Manitoba,

New Brunswick, Saskatchewan, and Quebec welcomed this gain in power, although they had to promise not to reduce spending while administering the funds.[38] British Columbia, Newfoundland, Nova Scotia, and Prince Edward Island elected to have Ottawa continue adminstering the measures while gaining some say in disbursing funds. As of 2002, only Ontario did not have an agreement with Ottawa.[39] Except for their offering more arguments to those who bewail the incoherence of Canadian federalism, these shifts have not had noticeably positive results. The programs had no clear strategy specifying what skills they would impart, who would provide them, and who would receive benefits. Nor did they help already marginalized workers.

Working Conditions

In 1989 the Mulroney government ceased federal contributions to UI, thereby adopting the American model, which relies entirely on employers' and employees' premiums. Finance Minister Paul Martin went far beyond the relatively modest reductions of UI coverage made by his Tory predecessor to savage the Unemployment Insurance Fund, once the central pillar of the Pearson-Trudeau social security system. He reduced premiums paid by employers and employees, cut the value of benefits, shortened the duration of payments (from a maximum of fifty weeks to forty-five), and tightened eligibility requirements.[40]

In 1996 Martin renamed the program 'Employment Insurance (EI)' to emphasize the government's desire to reduce disincentives to work and develop an active labour market, systematically raising the bar facing the unemployed. The new 'hours system' doubled and even tripled the time some people had to work in order to qualify for benefits. The minimum for those already in the workforce rose from 240 to 560 hours for most of Canada. For new entrants and re-entrants (such as young mothers returning to the labour force), the number of hours required for eligibility tripled, from 300 to 910. These tightened eligibility rules were designed to reduce claimants' access to benefits. Indeed, the proportion of unemployed Canadians receiving benefits fell from 74 per cent in 1989 to 36 per cent in 1999.[41] Those who did qualify received reduced payments for a shorter period. No longer a citizen's social right in a generous state, insurance against loss of livelihood had become a reluctant concession from a punitive state.

Even a social democratic finance minister would probably have been forced to tighten labour market policy. But the EI fund's burgeoning annual surplus of contributions by employers and employees over payments to the unemployed showed that its tightening went much further than strict budgetary needs required. This surplus also led Martin into a temptation he could not resist. He started taking billions of dollars a year from this surplus to pay down the government's operating deficit. As he acknowledged in a August, 1999 letter to the city of Prince Albert, Saskatchewan, 'EI surpluses of the last several years have helped us to eliminate the fiscal deficit. In fact, without the annual EI surpluses, the federal government would be back in deficit.'[42] The minister had adopted as his own the neoconservative line that 'labour market inflexibility' harmed the economy's competitiveness. In plain English, if workers enjoyed too much security from the threat of redundancy, they could not be forced into the less-secure, lower-paying jobs that would increase the corporate sector's capacity to compete on the basis of lower costs.

The Chrétien government continued the divestiture of federal responsibility by turning back all remaining responsibility for training to the provinces. It did not, however, provide enough funding to maintain previous levels of support. Responsibility for training employees fell increasingly to the private sector – an expensive burden for firms wanting to win markets by following the high-skill rather than the low-wage strategy. They needed well-trained employees if they were to produce innovative products and services. Without government support for wage subsidies and training, managers had difficulty improving the design and quality of their products.

Despite Ottawa's reduction of the social wage's EI component, its redistributive tax policies continued to mitigate income disparities across the country. Under a progressive system of income-tax, low-earning Canadians paid very little and benefited from public services worth thousands of dollars per person per year.[43] Those middle-class taxpayers who comprised the majority of the workforce paid a relatively low proportion of their earnings in income taxes. Despite years of program cuts, all but the richest fifth of Canadians still got more back from government than they paid in.

Industrial Relations

In the Fordist era, all provinces' labour laws embodied very similar principles. As neoconservative pressures increased, the provincial governments displayed more diversity. The highly politicized changes to

Ontario's labour laws over the years highlight the contrasting ideological interpretations of the government's proper role in industrial relations. When the NDP won power in 1990, it revamped labour legislation, which had remained essentially unchanged for fifteen years. The growth since the mid-1970s of a largely non-unionized service sector and its characteristically smaller workplaces resulted in a significant portion of the labour force being ineffectively protected. Existing laws had been designed for large-scale manufacturing and standard employment relationships. Following prolonged and bitter complaints by the government's business enemies, who claimed they had been only minimally consulted, and vigorous lobbying by their union friends, the New Democrats introduced strong anti-scab measures, expedited hearings about unfair labour practices, and facilitated collective bargaining and union certification. Bolstered by these legal supports, labour unions increased their organizing efforts and succeeded in raising certification, with the United Steelworkers notably managing to organize security guards.[44]

When the Conservative Mike Harris swept into office in 1995, one of his first acts was to wipe out the NDP's changes.[45] In opposition, the Tories' attack on Bill 40 had been particularly vocal for its discouraging impact on investment just when competitive pressure from less-regulated U.S. states was intensifying. Their own Bill 7 was intended to rectify the perception that Ontario labour legislation was hostile to business. They abolished the employment equity legislation, which was designed to have the labour force reflect the public's racial and gender profile. They weakened the Liberals' legislation on pay equity, which assured women pay of equal value to that of men in similar jobs. And they rescinded expedited hearings into unfair labour practices. These provisions, which limited unions' ability to function, made Ontario's labour market policies resemble Alberta's. The government's priority was to attract foreign capital, not to protect labour. Shortly after the giant U.S. retailer Wal-Mart set up shop in the late 1990s, the Ontario Labour Board ruled that the company's labour practices during a certification drive were unfair. When the OLB ordered the union's certification as a remedy, the Tories promptly amended the Labour Relations Act to deprive the board of the power to take such action.

While these statutory changes showed that the Common Sense Revolution had set Ontario on a decidedly neoconservative course, the most visible evidence of Mike Harris's antagonistic approach to labour was his treatment of public-sector workers. Because of city government amalgamations, municipal unions found their collective agreements were invalidated. The province targeted teachers for particularly aggressive attacks, insisting on dividing principals from their staff, dictating working conditions, and introducing testing of teachers.

The Parti Québécois also had to bow in the 1990s to neoconservative practices, but it remained closer to continental Europe's corporatist model by integrating the labour movement in formal consultations with business over government policies. Its labour policies continued to offset the asymmetrical power relationship between employers and workers in a market economy. Thanks to the strong public service union movement, which has persisted since the Quiet Revolution, Quebec's state workers could still bargain in a common front. Although the government was now less willing to make concessions, even the police and hospital workers could still go on strike. Under an NDP government, Saskatchewan also cut spending in health care and education but remained social democratic in its labour legislation.

External pressures from the globalization of competition and new ideological currents were not the only reasons that organized labour ran into trouble in post-Fordist times. A factor of continuity from the Keynesian era was the Supreme Court of Canada's long-standing conservatism. The negotiations that produced Pierre Trudeau's precious Charter of Rights and Freedoms had not entrenched the right to strike.[46] Even though the Charter specifically identified the liberal freedom of association as a fundamental right, the Supreme Court made a series of pronouncements in 1987 that gutted this principle for the workplace.[47] 'Freedom of association is a freedom belonging to the individual and not to the group formed through its exercise,' wrote Justice Gerald LeDain in the *Alberta Reference Case* that year.[48] In effect, freedom of association did not protect the right to strike as a legitimate means of defending workers' or unions' interests.

Unions kept going to court and they kept losing in court. The Nova Scotia Nurses Union against decertification (1989); the International Longshoremen's Union against back-to-work orders (1990); the Nova Scotia Teachers' Union against public-sector wage freezes (1993): all lost their cases that the constitution protected bargaining rights. The Supreme Court concluded that collective bargaining rights were not fundamental enough to merit protection by the Charter.[49] In supporting the autonomy of the economic sphere from government or judicial intervention, the court resisted the social-democratic thrust that had produced the Charter and rejected the argument that workers need to associate in order to overcome their individual vulnerability vis-à-vis capital.

Both provincial and federal governments flirted with the idea of enacting openly restrictive labour legislation. Canada's largest public-sector unions – including the Canadian Union of Public Employees, the National Union of Provincial Government Employees, and the Public Service Alliance of Canada – decried such initiatives. Touting anti-union legislation as effective tools of regional development, the business-friendly National Citizens' Coalition lobbied governments to enact similar laws to those in Alabama, Tennessee, and Texas, where 'right-to-work' legislation weakens union security and inhibits unions' defence of their members' interests.[50]

Declining rates of unionization indicated business success in defusing organized labour's efforts. The labour movement in Canada as a whole appeared to be weakening. Canada's union density had stagnated since the late 1970s and fallen since 1992 because of layoffs, closures, and 'downsizing' in unionized workplaces. New employment opportunities were shifting to service industries and small business, where workers are more difficult to organize,[51] where employers want 'flexibility' in hiring and firing and fear their loss of competitiveness when unions negotiate wages and benefits. Even in sectors where they were still active, unions have protected their members only moderately well.

In 1990, 72 per cent of all public- and private-sector agreements in Canada covering 500 or more employees provided no protection against inflation. Furthermore, 48 per cent of such agreements required no advance notice of lay offs to employees. As of 1997, under one-third of all Canadian workers belonged to a union; 42 per cent of these unionized employees worked in the public sector. Thus less than 20 per cent of working people belonged to private-sector labour unions.[52] These unimpressive figures were nevertheless better than those for the United States, where only 15 per cent of the *total* labour force was unionized.

Bucking these unfavourable trends, organized labour achieved significant gains in one traditional and one new field under neoconservatism. Canadian auto workers have shown their capacity to swim against the current of continentalization. In 1985 they declared their institutional autonomy from their parent union in Detroit, the UAW.

Rejecting the American leadership's insistence on making concessions, the CAW went on to practise a militancy in their negotiations with the Big Three auto makers that brought its members such successes as stronger protection against lay offs and financial support for the post-secondary education of workers' children.

Despite the general lack of protection that unions were able to achieve for their members in an era of trade liberalization, they also made gains in the relatively new field of female labour. Women were better represented than ever in unions, which offer members higher wages and more standard forms of work opportunities. Unionization rates in Canada were now comparable for men and for women, with 34 per cent of men unionized compared to 32 per cent of women.[53] Unions also offered benefits to part-time workers, who in 1997 earned 94 per cent of the hourly wage of a full-time unionized worker, compared to a non-unionized part-time worker's earning only 76 per cent as much as a non-unionized full-time worker.[54]

Strengthened female participation in industrial relations improved working conditions for women. Clauses inserted in collective bargaining agreements during this neoconservative epoch sought to protect women in particular. In 1998, 28 per cent of workers covered by major collective agreements in Canada had access to a provision calling for equal pay for work of equal value, compared to just 5 per cent in 1985. And half of workers covered by major collective agreements had the protection of a clause against sexual harassment – more than double the level of 1985.[55]

Regulating labour is a century-old practice for the industrial state. Regulating environmental conditions became important only when Keynesianism was poised to decline. While labour forced itself onto the governmental agenda in the late 1870s, it took until the 1970s for the environment to achieve the same political salience. Whereas labour relations touch many people, only a minority of the workforce belongs to a trade union, making it easy for governments to turn against 'big labour.' Since all citizens must breathe the air, walk under the sun, and drink the water, the environment generates conflicts that are more difficult to dismiss.

Workers' consciousness arises spontaneously from the employment condition and centres on the local. Once aroused, environmental consciousness tends to the global, because solutions cannot work unless most countries abide by them. Where labour issues are relatively simple (what dollar figure per hour, what length of paid holidays), environmental issues are hugely complex, requiring high levels of scientific expertise to identify danger and causality (what caused depletion of the ozone layer and is it reversible?) While the state addressed both sets of issues as products of industrial capitalism, chapter 17 explores whether that neoconservatism has more difficulty abandoning the environmental than the labour achievements of the Keynesian state.

17 The (Un)sustainable State: Deregulating the Environment

After a recent conference at the University of Chile, I tried out my elementary Spanish on the taxi driver who was taking me to the airport by making an off-hand remark about the smog that was covering Santiago. This reference to the darkened sky caused him to erupt in a rage '¡Contaminación!' he exclaimed, shaking his fist at the invisible forces responsible for the pollution. His young daughter, he told me, had contracted debilitating asthma from the effects of the galloping industrialization in Chile whose effluents the state had failed to regulate. Clearly, environmental concerns were no longer confined to the 'tree huggers' that neoconservatives had been denigrating for years. Environmentalism had become embedded in the consciousness of ordinary people trying to survive in the mega-cities spawned by globalization.

Whether contamination – the Spanish word resonates more powerfully than our milder-sounding pollution – can be contained does not seem in doubt as a technical question. Having a clean environment appears to depend more on the will and capacity of governments to control – whether within their territories or between them – those economic forces that jeopardize the earth's sustainability. This ultimately comes down to resolving tensions between citizens' demand for clean-up and their willingness to foot the bill. How globalization and its neoconservative collaborators impinge on humankind's survival is a complex issue that we need to unravel step by step. First we will see how the Keynesian state came very late to environmental regulation. Then we will follow the path of neoconservative policy changes at the federal and provincial levels. Finally we can come to grips with what global governance adds to (or subtracts from) the challenge of keeping the planet livable.

In Canada, the most recent indicator of the state's civility is the capacity of federal, provincial, and municipal governments to monitor, regulate, and even reverse processes that damage the natural environment, whether on land, in the water, or in the air. In contrast with social or labour policy, which, after a halting evolution through the twentieth century, had reached its apogee in the Fordist state following the Second World War, environmental sustainability became a legitimate concern of Canadian governments only in the Trudeau era. While this policy field came into its own just when Keynesianism was starting to decline, its increasingly universal quality, and the corresponding increase in global ecological consciousness, have continued to put pressure on states to deal with the problem. However, a growing green consciousness among the general population has come up against a stiffened greenback consciousness among business groups who resist paying the costs of cleaning up the damage that their corporations cause.

Understanding the connection between environmental issues and globalization starts with individual behaviour. London residents burning dirty coal created a smog that was dangerous to the health of all those breathing the air in England's capital. Cottagers without sewage treatment contaminated their once-pristine lakes in Canada. The development of clean-burning coal and strict regulations requiring its use transformed London's air. Environmentally clean toilets improved vacation-area lakes markedly. Without feasible remedies, adequate state regulatory capacity, and a popular consensus that collective behaviour must change, problems caused by people remain unresolvable.

Within post-industrial North America, efforts to contain environmental degradation also confront corporate interests in the marketplace. Regulating business behaviour imposes costs on firms that create the problem – whether these 'externalities' are experienced locally or beyond. In the end, consumers pay these costs in the form of higher prices.

Air pollution was once a local issue engaging the attention of municipal politicians, who would prefer to have polluters purify their discharges. But if a local community could not prevail on its industrialists to 'internalize' the externalities that they were creating, it was generally not averse to letting them displace the problem. Of course, the remedy – building taller smokestacks to carry toxic waste into the atmosphere or discharging dangerous chemicals into the city's sewer system – only created regional problems, such as acid rain or the circulation of toxic substances in the whole watershed.

Relentless pressures for economic expansion in both the North and the South intensified pollution to the point that such continental problems became global environmental concerns. By the mid-1980s, stratospheric issues (atmospheric warming and depletion of the ozone layer) and more traditional conservation problems (the destruction of forests and the extinction of endangered species) had joined the mix as threats to the earth's capacity to sustain plant and animal life.

A number of dramatic international conferences addressed this agenda with passion and rallied the ecologically conscious to the cause of saving humanity from itself. The most important way-stations along the tortuous road to convincing all governments to regulate their economies' behaviour in the interests of rescuing planet earth bore the names of the cities where the negotiations were held. 'Stockholm' (1972) made the environment a legitimate concern for governments and led to the United Nations Environmental Program (UNEP). 'Montreal' (1987) put together the first agreement to set target dates for reducing emissions of chemicals known to be depleting the ozone layer. 'Rio' (1992) – the 'Earth Summit' – grappled with a convention on climate change. 'Kyoto' (1997) produced a protocol for emission reductions to slow global warming.

Although these accords seemed to mark triumphs for the future of the planet, their successes were more apparent than real. In contrast to territorial governments, which have to reconcile clashes between conflicting principles and policies, global governance has evolved on the basis of specialized functions, each with its separate institution. If the norms of one regime contradict those of another, they clash when they come into effect. Just as local environmentalists confront local polluters, so global environmentalism clashes with global commercial governance in philosophy and policy. Trade expansion imposes costs on the environment, because increased economic activity strains the earth's reproductive capacities by promoting consumption of traded goods, depleting natural resources, and burning more fossil fuels when goods are transported. Eco-logic contradicts trade logic. An environmentalist's sought-after regulatory measure becomes a trade barrier to an exporter. But before we address how globalization has affected the Canadian state's environmental functions, we need to see how these functions developed.

For their first millennia on earth, human beings feared and revered the natural. It is only in the last two centuries that technology has made it possible to reverse this power relationship, turning humans into masters who are able to destroy their habitat rather than simply live as its vulnerable tenants. The destruction caused by William Blake's 'dark satanic mills' was locally generated, but in his time governments preferred not to think about human suffering, let alone nature's torments. Indeed the first awareness of industrialism's threat to nature went hand in hand with the growth of consciousness about social distress. Just as the first labour laws were negative (Thou shalt not employ children in the mines!), the first governmental responses to environmental consciousness were defensive. They protected nature from the depredations of industrialism by establishing parks that would save the flora and fauna.

Such environmentalism in Canada goes back to the Banff National Park created in 1885, but the origins of the modern regulatory state really lie in early public health legislation that empowered municipalities to deal with local causes of illness such as water and air pollution. Ontario passed its first public health act in the 1880s. But Canada's serious regulatory engagement with the (North American) environment began in the 1960's and intensified in the next two decades, as we see in the first section of this chapter. The impact of neoconservatism on environmental regulation, particularly in the 1990s, is the subject of the second section; and the third deals with the impact of global governance.

A Tardy State

Since 1962, when Rachel Carson's book *Silent Spring* first aroused public concern about the spread of toxins through waterways and prevailing winds, consciousness has waxed and waned about pollution as a threat to nature and so to human health. Periods of regulatory intensity have fluctuated with these shifting waves of public concern.

In Canada, environmentalism became evident as a new force only in the late 1960s, when the country's first politically effective green wave created unprecedented public concern. Universities established programs in environmental studies, whose graduates filled the ranks of an ecological community rooted in a new, technologically sophisticated environmental science and animated a new breed of citizens' groups.

Pollution Probe, a University of Toronto group founded in 1969, made a legal and scientific case for radical policy reform. A Vancouver group, Greenpeace, formed the next year, linked ecological consciousness with a Quaker-inspired, non-violent, resistance bearing witness to nuclear proliferation. It developed an in-your-face style of stunt-making to dramatize its causes and became in the process the world's most effective environmental non-governmental organization (ENGO), eventually winning the Nobel Peace Prize. Striking a responsive chord in a citizenry willing to donate money and/or time, these ecological zealots publicized their issues for the media, lobbied governments, and infiltrated political parties.

With this green wave cresting at a time of an ebullient state still inspired by a social-democratic faith in activism, Canadian politicians proved eager to respond. Undaunted by their congenital tension over constitutional turf, both federal and provincial governments occupied the inviting field. Invoking its jurisdiction over interprovincial and international trade, navigation and shipping, fisheries, criminal law, and the ownership of federal lands, Ottawa eagerly stepped in to create a regulatory framework. Buoyed by Pierre Trudeau's deep love of nature, the Liberals created a new department, Environment Canada (1970), amended the Canada Shipping Act (to cover oil discharges) and the Fisheries Act (discharges harmful to fish in all bodies of Canadian water), and introduced the 1970 Canada Water Act (water quality standards) and the 1971 Clean Air Act (ambient air quality objectives). By the mid-1970s, when the first green wave was abating, the federal government had enshrined elaborate marine safety standards in the Arctic Waters Pollution Prevention Act, (designed to assert Canadian sovereignty over the North-West Passage), and the Ocean Dumping Control Act, (fulfilled the government's obligations under the London Convention on ocean dumping). Equivalent ecotoxicity restrictions had been decreed in the Pesticides Control Products and the Environmental Contaminants Acts in which Ottawa played a supportive role to the provinces.

As Ottawa developed national standards on environmental quality and industrial discharges, the provinces addressed economic activities within the extensive domains of their own primary jurisdiction – agriculture, forestry, mining, and hydro-electric generation. Following a process of 'uploading' in which they had taken back responsibility for public health from their municipalities, they signed a series of federal-provincial accords to implement their own standards and incorporate the federal ones through parallel laws and institutions. Ontario, for example, created a Ministry of the Environment in 1971 and passed a set of pollution-control laws including the Ontario Water Resources Act, the Environmental Protection Act, and the Ontario Environmental

Assessment Act.[1] All provinces passed similar water and air pollution acts requiring enterprises to obtain permits before they could discharge contaminants, and then only on specific grounds.

If Rachel Carson's toxins could travel long distances within a country, they could travel even further between countries, especially when *national* frontiers were not *natural* frontiers. In these cases action within a country's borders could not resolve its problems. For Canada, sharing so many water basins and river systems with the United States and subject to prevailing winds carrying particle-laden air across the international border, transnational pollution raised a continental problem.

Continental Building Blocks

In the early nineteenth century, the boundary between the United States and British North America had been maintained by military and diplomatic means, with war and negotiations dividing the land mass and allocating the waters where fishermen from both sides could ply their trade. By the early twentieth century, much of the two countries' dealings had shifted to coping with common problems and rival interests in border-region watersheds. The Boundary Waters Treaty (negotiated between London, for Canada, and Washington) established the International Joint Commission on Seaway Boundaries (IJC), which has managed common problems in shared rivers and lakes since 1912.

By the late 1960s, excessive nutrients were producing algae that were killing fish and other creatures in Lakes Erie and Ontario, and a coalition of provinces and states were pressing their respective federal governments to negotiate a bilateral accord to resuscitate the lakes and the St Lawrence River. Although implementation of the resulting Great Lakes Water Quality Agreement (1972) was halting, discovery of carcinogens and other toxins led to a renewed agreement in 1979. Slowly, the lakes' water was brought back from death under the IJC's supervision. U.S. cities had a strong self-interest in clean water and could see the direct relationship between their clean-up efforts and higher water quality, even if they had to spend more than their Canadian counterparts.

Such happy symmetry did not characterize the next major border issue, which suddenly arose in the early 1980s, when the airborne transmission of sulphur dioxide, nitrogen oxide, and other toxins – popularly known as acid rain – was discovered to be 'killing' lakes in Ontario and Quebec. Once ecologists proved that the prevailing winds were 'exporting' sulphur dioxide and nitrogen oxide across the Canadian-American boundary to acidify Ontario's aquatic ecosystem, air pollution became a binational issue. Salvation for the large tourist industry, which depended on the fish and fun that these lakes provided, hung on two largely intractable factors. Ontario evidently had to clear up its own sources of contamination: Inco's nickel smelter in Sudbury was North America's largest generator of airborne pollutants. But this was not enough. However clean Ontario's industry might be, its lakes would die, since half of the province's acid deposition was made-in-the-U.S.A. Because domestic governmental action could not deal with the issue, Canadian environmental activists went transnational. Forming the Canadian Coalition against Acid Rain, they became the first major citizens' group to lobby for congressional action in Washington, alongside the Canadian embassy.

Despite Ottawa's unprecedented efforts to press Washington, and Canadian environmentalists direct lobbying on Capitol Hill, companies that burned coal to generate electricity in the Ohio Valley had enough political clout to resist regulators' efforts to clean them up. But when New York residents found dying lakes in their Adirondack Mountains and joined the Canadian environmentalists' cause, Congress started seriously to address toughening its air quality standards. And when Montana and North Dakota, downwind from Alberta and Saskatchewan, joined Vermont and Maine in worrying about air pollution from Canada, Congress urged a reluctant Republican administration to negotiate with Canada. Ottawa had learned that any reduction in the cross-border flow of U.S. contaminants would result less from its diplomacy than from Congress's actions.[2] Indeed, environmental issues fell so low on the agenda that when the next major bilateral negotiating round proposed a formal continental trade regime in 1986, it was virtually ignored.

Neoconservative Responses to the Regulatory State

Free Trade

When, in the autumn of 1987, Canadian trade officials first presented the results of their trade negotiations with Washington, they claimed that, because CUFTA did not include clauses on the environment, it had no ecological implications. Ecologists, however, pointed out three problems – two general and one specific. First, CUFTA had a *bias towards growth.* Given its philosophical support for economic expansion and its hostility to government regulation, trade liberalization would intensify economic growth. This pressure would further impede the country's rather reluctant efforts to achieve ecologically sustainable growth.

Second, it aimed to stimulate *resource depletion.* Fostering unsustainable development was CUFTA's subtext as manifested in some of its significant provisions, both positive and negative. These were clearest in the energy chapter, which embodied the American desire to accelerate the delivery of Canada's non-renewable petroleum reserves at the lowest possible prices. Despite strong U.S. animus against foreign governments' industrial subsidies, CUFTA explicitly permitted Canadian governments to subsidize the discovery and development of oil and natural gas reserves without having to fear countervailing tariffs against the resulting exports of cheap energy to the United States.

Equally revelatory was the chapter's negative pressure on regulations. Ottawa was prohibited from taking conservation measures that would impede the flow of energy exports to the United States as it had done following the global energy of 1973 and 1979. Even in conditions of another crisis in energy supply, Canada undertook to share with the United States the same proportion of its energy production as it had been delivering, on average, over the preceding three years. (Although Mexico is geopolitically weaker than Canada, it was less compliant on energy matters when negotiating NAFTA. It refused to accept a similar restriction of the government's constitutionally entrenched monopoly control over its primary natural resource and source of comparative advantage.) Furthermore, trade agreements encourage corporations to challenge high standards and so create pressure to harmonize regulations down to a lowest common denominator.

Finally, continental free trade provided a *legal route to water diversion.* Both despite and because of its great abundance, water has a powerful place in the Canadian imagination. During the first debate on free trade in the late 1980s, water became the subject of much rival hypothesizing. Government spokespersons affirmed that nothing in CUFTA except for tariff elimination applied to the export of surface or ground water. In the subsequent NAFTA debate, Canada attempted to counteract the new treaty's supraconstitutional power by stating in its implementation legislation that nothing in NAFTA except tariff elimination applied to trade in surface or ground water. While this might have been Ottawa's fond hope, legal experts doubted that such assertions would affect a tribunal's interpretation of foreign investors' rights, should Canadian measures to prevent export of water be challenged.[3]

Environmentalists claimed that CUFTA actually deprived the state of its capacity to protect Canada's water, by not specifically exempting it from the disciplines concerning national treatment and market access for goods. On the contrary, water appeared in the agreement's appendix defining the meaning of tradeable 'goods.' This suggested that its export could no longer be legally prevented. Although the government's own review of NAFTA's environmental side deal maintained that Canada's Federal Water Policy of 1987 safeguarded national bodies of water,[4] some experts in international trade warned that tariff item 22.01 included water in river systems.[5] Others warned that, as with energy, so in water, CUFTA would oblige Canada to guarantee perpetual and proportional provision to the United States as soon as it started to export bulk supplies.[6]

Defying Neoconservatism

By the time that Keynesianism was on the ropes in the 1980s, the environmental movement was merely pausing for breath. Canadian governments may have been moving towards a neoconservative paradigm, but the cumulating evidence of growing global environmental problems – such as climate change, stratospheric ozone depletion, desertification, and deforestation – energized a second green wave, which in turn prompted concomitant government activism. Between 1988 and 1993, the federal and provincial governments launched a number of legislative and spending initiatives, despite their leaders' desperate efforts to rein in escalating budgetary deficits.

New federal legislation on Mulroney's watch featured two advances. The Canadian Environmental Protection Act (CEPA) of 1988 heralded an enhanced federal role in setting and enforcing standards. Stricter regulations covered fields as diverse as discharges from pulp and paper mills, manufacture and disposal of toxic chemicals such as PCBs, and emission of CFCs, discharges which deplete ozone. The Canadian Environmental Assessment Act of 1990 created a quasi-judicial process that made sustainable development a fundamental objective and funded some input by citizens' groups. In *Attorney General of Canada v. Hydro Quebec*(1997), the Supreme Court of Canada confirmed that federal jurisdiction over criminal law allowed it to intervene in Quebec's bailiwick to regulate toxic substances under CEPA.[7]

Lucien Bouchard, Mulroney's environmental minister for a brief, if tempestuous period, decided to exploit this jurisdictional opening. In 1990 (shortly before separating from the Conservative party in a rage and founding the sovereigntist Bloc Québécois),[8] Bouchard announced a dramatic Green Plan, which would spend $3 billion in five years on over one hundred policy initiatives to clean up air, water, and land as far north as the Arctic. The plan would foster global environmental security, environmentally responsible decision-making, ecological stewardship, and preparation for environmental emergencies. Environmentalists charged that the plan leaned too much towards educational and informational initiatives instead of imposing costs on polluting industries.[9] The Green Plan nonetheless represented an ambitious effort to promote sustainable development across government departments and economic sectors.

Responding both to the public's revived concerns and Ottawa's renewed activism, Ontario led its provincial counterparts towards environmental radicalism under the Liberal premiership of David Peterson (1985–90). Beyond applying environmental assessments more extensively, the Liberals introduced new regulations on water and air pollution along with policies on solid or hazardous wastes. Queen's Park set up new advisory groups such as the Ontario Roundtable on the Environment and the Economy in 1989 and established new programs on waste reduction and recycling. The succeeding New Democrats kept up the Liberal momentum with an Environmental Bill of Rights and a Crown Forest Sustainability Act in the early 1990s. They tightened regulations on water pollution, reformed land-use planning, and introduced subsidies to encourage green communities and green industries.

Another series of judicial rulings supported Ottawa's assertion of environmental leadership. In the *Crown Zellerbach* case of 1988, the Supreme Court of Canada upheld the federal government's environmental authority. The ruling recognized the federal capacity to legislate on the environment under the 'national concern' interpretation of the Peace, Order, and Good Government (POGG) power, particularly if it had committed itself by international treaty.[10] The court read into its 'national dimensions' principle a version of subsidiarity, giving jurisdiction to Ottawa in cases where provincial inability to deal effectively with intraprovincial matters could have adverse effects beyond its borders.[11] In *Friends of the Oldman River Society v. Canada* (1992), the Supreme Court expanded federal jurisdiction based on both POGG and more specific heads of power, such as fisheries and navigation.[12]

Ironically, just as the court was substantially expanding Ottawa's environmental authority, the federal government was pursuing a four-part program to cut back its own environmental capacity.

- It embarked on a process of budget-cutting that reduced its ability to enforce existing statutes.
- It initiated a devolution of environmental responsibilities to the provinces, which some felt was tantamount to achieving 'a de facto constitutional amendment.'[13]
- It pursued deregulation, which it called 'building a more innovative economy.'
- It continued negotiating NAFTA and the WTO's supraconstitutional provisions, which limited its capacity to protect and nurture such public goods as a clean environment.

The institutional means for the federal government's devolution of environmental responsibilities to the provinces was the intergovernmental Canadian Council of Ministers of the Environment (CCME). At first, the two levels of government had been willing to work co-operatively on the environment and share responsibilities, even accepting some overlap. In 1990, for example, the ministers of the environment signed a Statement on Interjurisdictional Co-operation, and in 1991 they agreed to a statement of environmental assessment principles intended to promote consistency and co-ordination in their environmental assessments.

But in 1993, the shift was more definitively executed. The brief Conservative government of Prime Minister Kim Campbell expressed an interest in reducing federal involvement in environmental protection. The transfer of federal decision-making power to the CCME meant decisions would be made by consensus, with Ottawa as just one of thirteen governments (including ten provinces and two territories) represented and voting.[14] The same year, the CCME made environmental harmonization its top priority.

Succumbing to Neoconservatism

The environmental neoconservatism that Kim Campbell tentatively initiated, Jean Chrétien and Paul Martin surreptitiously delivered. Their government, which won the booby prize for 'the weakest environmental record of any federal government in four decades,'[15] was responding to two principal motivations. First, there was Martin's deficit-cutting imperative. Although the Conservatives had already reduced the Green Plan's initial budget and postponed much of its proposed action, the Liberal government terminated the plan entirely in early 1995, when less than 30 per cent of the originally budgeted $3 billion had been spent.[16] Following two program reviews, it cut the Department of Environment's budget by almost a third (from $737 million in 1995–6 to $503 million in 1997–8), and its staff by a quarter (1,400 of 5,700).[17]

Chrétien complemented Martin's truncating Ottawa's environmental *capacity* with a comprehensive devolution of its *responsibilities* to further the cause of national unity. Following the near-loss of the 1995 Quebec referendum on sovereignty, the prime minister determined to prove his flexibility to vacillating Quebecers and so reduce irritants in federal-provincial relations by withdrawing from jointly occupied fields. Along with getting rid of Ottawa's role in job training, he launched a harmonization initiative in environmental policy. Facing down strong opposition from environmentalists and the House of Commons Standing Committee on the Environment, which wanted to preserve a competitive federalism with a meaningful federal role, Ottawa negotiated at the CCME a Canada-wide accord, which was signed in 1998.[18]

Environmentalists had several reasons to view the accord as the opening shot in a competitive race to the bottom.[19] First, consensual decision making at the CCME gave each participating government an effective veto over environmental initiatives, thus tending to produce 'lowest common denominator' standards. The CCME's proposed standards on climate change reflected the positions of Alberta and Ontario, the provinces most resistant to taking action. The subagreement on Canada-wide standards also allowed for departures from uniform discharge standards, which would have promoted consistency across the country. Instead, ambient environmental standards would result in a patchwork of standards so that some provinces might become pollution havens.[20] In addition, the accord allowed for variable and inconsistent implementation, including voluntary rather than mandatory approaches.[21]

In a textbook case of neoconservative administrative reform, environmental harmonization was, about 'rationalization,' or disentanglement, in which the two orders of government divided up the state's functions. In sharp contrast to the previous periods, when Ottawa alternated between unilateral activism and close partnership with the provinces, the Canada-wide accord seemed intended for governments *not* to work together.[22] Since the provinces ended up with most of the environmental responsibilities at a time when they too were cutting back their budgets, resolving supposed regulatory *overlap* risked creating regulatory gaps or *'underlap'* due to decreased provincial capacity.[23]

The drive to cut the costs to business of environmental regulation also facilitated drastic policy changes. The rise of neoconservative ideas in government reflected the growing influence of the business sector. Its policy preferences carried the day at a time when the environment ranked low among the public's priorities.

Submissions to the CCME by the mining, pulp and paper, chemical, electrical, and other industrial associations sought voluntary initiatives, site-specific ambient standards (rather than national discharge standards), and provincial predominance in environmental assessment, standards, and inspections.[24]

The environmental consequences reflected this new balance of political power. Undermining Canada's implementation of the Kyoto Protocol on reducing emissions of greenhouse gas, Canada's fossil-fuel industry achieved a Voluntary Challenge and Registry (VCR) program as the country's main response to Kyoto. Although the VCR was launched in 1995, emissions grew by more than 10 per cent by 2000.[25]

Environmentalists remained committed to an activist federal state where intergovernmental competition would produce higher, rather than lower, levels of regulatory protection.[26] In their view, the checks and balances of shared jurisdiction led to positive results. By the same token, a shift of responsibilities to the provinces increased the risks of 'regulatory capture' by powerful local resource industries and encouraged jurisdictions to compete for business by weakening their environmental laws. Activists deplored the democratic deficit created when the CCME made public policy through a version of executive federalism unaccountable to either federal or provincial voters. The resulting policy framework reflected the preferences of industry rather than those of citizen-based ENGOs.[27] We can see this reversal under neoconservatism, from government's heeding environmentalists to favouring business, most clearly in Ontario, which typified trends in all provinces but British Columbia in the late 1990s.

Ontario: From Environmental Leader to Pollution Haven

At the same time as the federal government was withdrawing from environmental protection and offloading its responsibilities and costs to the provinces, a parallel development took place in Ontario, but with more dramatic consequences. Unlike Jean Chrétien, who, in the tradition of his party, ran for election on the centre left only to govern on the centre right, Mike Harris had not prevaricated. His Common Sense Revolution of 1995 was explicitly aimed at overturning the activist state. His government proceeded dramatically to erode Queen's Park's environmental capacity and unleash an even more fateful process of 'disentanglement' between the province and its municipalities.

The dismantling of Ontario's once-proud and competent environmental ministry proceeded under an ideological fervour unseen in the province's history. Having vied for leadership with the federal government in setting environmental standards, the province had developed a strong scientific capacity to set, implement, monitor, and enforce them. Under Harris's direction, Ontario now took the lead in dispersing this capacity and undermining these standards. By the late 1990s, it had become one of North America's major recipients of hazardous waste. Remarkably, from 1997 to 1999, the Ontario government was not even interested in being notified by the federal government of any toxic shipments to the province.[28] A pollution haven, it was also publicly ranked year after year by NAFTA's Commission for Environmental Co-operation (CEC) as the second-worst polluter north of the Rio Grande – after then-Governor George W. Bush's Texas.

How it achieved this distinction is a cautionary tale. On assuming power, the Harris government launched a four-pronged program of downsizing, deregulation, devolution, and privatization.

Downsizing. The Harris government immediately cut staff at the Ministry of Environment by more than 40 per cent. From 2,430 in 1994, the Ministry's staff fell to 1,277 by 1999.[29] Its budget was cut in half. In constant dollars (taking inflation into account), its 2000 budget was actually below the level of 1971, when an earlier Tory government created it.[30] Its staff and budgetary cuts led to a major loss in its ability to set environmental standards, report on and respond to chemical spills, implement environmental policies, and monitor and enforce standards.

Complementing the shrinking of budget and staff was an institutional downsizing. In September 1995, the government eliminated a host of independent advisory boards and multi-stakeholder committees, including the Advisory Committee on Environmental Standards, the Environmental Assessment Advisory Committee, and the Ontario Round Table on the Environment and Economy. It closed or amalgamated a number of district offices and suboffices. It laid off abatement officers, technical support staff, junior investigators and managers and administrators.

The consequences of the cuts were immediately apparent in the ministry's capacity to enforce its regulations. In 1999, it issued an internal priority-setting document, *Operations Division Delivery Strategies*, which told government inspectors to ignore pollution complaints related to 'illegal dumping of sewage from pleasure boats, many pesticide infractions, foul-tasting drinking water, littering, poorly functioning commercial-recycling programs, and the stench from manure spreading' in order to save ministry resources and focus on other, *more serious* threats to the environment and human health.[31]

Deregulation. At the same time as the government was defunding and destaffing the ministry, a deregulatory drive aimed at reducing or eliminating environmental, labour, and health safeguards was launched. The assumption was that such regulations were 'red tape' that unnecessarily hindered business. In addition, the Tories set up a Red Tape Review Commission composed of nine Conservative MPPs, a secretariat attached to the Cabinet Committee on Regulations, and an External Advisory Committee comprised of business representatives. The commission reviewed all seventy-eight regulations under Ontario's environmental statutes, many of which were weakened as a result. In 1996, the commission developed a 'Less Paper/More Jobs' test in which all proposed new regulations and programs would undergo a cost-benefit evaluation, making it one of the first jurisdictions in Canada with such a requirement.[32] In effect, the commission created a regulatory freeze in which bureaucrats in the ministry were afraid to propose new regulations and face the wrath of what a Tory pamphlet proudly called the Red Tape 'attack dog.' All of the province's major environmental laws were weakened, except the Environmental Bill of Rights.

Devolution. As the federal government had done with the provinces, Ontario launched its disentanglement with municipal governments in order both to eliminate shared jurisdiction and financing and to transfer to them those responsibilities that it did not keep and did not offload to the private sector. In May 1996, it set up a 'Who Does What' panel, chaired by former Toronto mayor David Crombie, which recommended that the province terminate funding for municipal sewer and water infrastructure, ownership of which it would transfer to the municipalities. Accordingly, in 1996 the government also fatefully downloaded to municipalities the responsibility for testing drinking water. Queen's Park also closed three of the ministry's four regional water-testing laboratories, in London, Kingston, and Thunder Bay. These facilities were, in the words of one of their former microbiologists, 'the heart of the MOE. And what the government did is cut out the heart of the Ministry of the Environment.'[33]

Privatization. Finally, the province moved to industry self-regulation, essentially privatizing government functions. Privatizing water testing was highly controversial. It appeared out of the blue (municipalities had eight weeks' notice) as a cost-saving measure based on neither consultation with municipalities nor analysis of its effects on water safety.[34] The government transferred regulatory responsibilities to the aggregate, commercial fishing, baiting, sport hunting, and fur industries and increased self-monitoring and self-management of the forestry and mining sectors operating on Crown lands.[35]

While deficit cutting and national unity drove the federal government's harmonization initiative, ideology accounted for the even more aggressive behaviour of the Harris government, which recast the provincial state's role in protecting public goods.[36] Not content with increased reliance on the free market, it actually provided major subsidies for resource-extracting and polluting industries, which it encouraged not to internalize the costs of their pollution and to extract public resources on Crown lands.

Compared to the 1970s and 1980s, when environmental transparency and participation had increased markedly, it was the democratic deficit that increased in the 1990s. The Canada-wide accord had been reached through a fast-tracked process of executive federalism without national public consultations. As the prime federal-provincial policy-making institution in environmental matters, the CCME was less accountable than the federal or most provincial governments. But the deficit was most blatant in nominally populist Ontario, where the Harris government systematically reduced public input and access to information while setting up a closed, clientelist relationship with the once-regulated industries as it moved them towards self-regulation and self-monitoring of reporting.

Emblematic of the toll taken by the neoconservative anti-environmental agenda was the Walkerton disaster. In May 2000, seven people died and more than 2,400 became severely ill from a deadly strain of E. coli that had leached into the town's drinking supplies from a nearby cattle farm's excremental waste. Apart from confirming the incompetence and negligence of the local water utility's personnel, the public inquiry learned from more than a million government documents and witnesses testimony that Harris's cabinet had turned a blind eye to the approaching disaster, if not wilfully creating it. The government had chosen to ignore a strongly worded warning from the Environment Ministry 'business plan' that the proposed severe cuts to its staff and budget 'increased the risk to human health and the environment.' It had focused instead on developing a communications plan to deflect public concern.

Although the ministry's professional staff feared for its clientele, the general public, its political leadership had been more interested in enforcing the party line. Two consecutive environment ministers ignored pleas from the Ministry of Health for an enforceable regulation (rather than an unenforceable guideline) that would require private labs to inform the local medical officer of health and the Environment Ministry of any problems with water quality. In the event, the private lab that tested Walkerton's water refused to notify public authorities of health risks, citing 'client confidentiality.' That the Common Sense Revolution had given economic growth priority over community health was clear from its acts. It had invited bigger factory farms by passing 'right-to-farm' legislation, which restricted local municipalities' ability to regulate farmers disposal of the resulting manure.[37] When the unapologetic, evasive, and aloof premier submitted to a five-and-a-half-hour cross-examination at the Walkerton inquiry, his Revolution went on trial. Harris's remarkable display of dissembling, evasion, rationalization, inconsistency, and hair-splitting recalled President Clinton's infamous parsing of the word 'is.'[38]

The Third Level: Municipal Fallout

One year after the Walkerton tragedy sent shock waves across the country, the lethal pathogen Cryptosporidium broke out in North Battleford, Saskatchewan, killing one person and making 100 people ill. At the annual meeting of the Federation of Canadian Municipalities in May 2001, the top two issues were water and public transit, in that order. Municipal leaders called for assistance for water infrastructure and for national safe water standards. In Newfoundland, boil-the-water advisories were issued in about half of the province's water systems. Seventy-nine Aboriginal communities (about 12 per cent of the country's total) had water systems that posed a potential health risk. While the prime minister chose to claim that the issue was one of provincial jurisdiction, Liberal Senator Jerry Grafstein put forward a bill that would amend the Food and Drug Act to address water safety. The real reasons for federal reluctance seemed to be a combination of the Chrétien government's national unity strategy and its neoconservative preference for cost-cutting and government shrinking.

The newly amalgamated city of Toronto had a number of concerns in addition to water. Urban sprawl on its outer edges was eating up agricultural land and the Oak Ridges Moraine – the source of its water. Smog alerts had become a regular summer occurrence, with respiratory illnesses increasing among the elderly and the very young. Toronto also fretted about the province's having downloaded responsibility for delivering a host of programs without providing sufficient resources. In particular, the province cancelled financial support for the delivery of sewer and water services (saving it $140 million per year) and public transit ($720 million per year). It also transferred testing of drinking water, regulation of septic systems, and management of conservation lands to the municipal governments and conservation authorities. Toronto estimated that provincial downloading would cost the city a total of $3.7 billion between 1998 and 2010.[39]

Despite, or perhaps because of, these provincial assaults on its finances and its health, Toronto generated higher levels of environmental activism. In 2000 an ad hoc, province-wide coalition of environmentalists, Aboriginal peoples, and councillors prevented Toronto from transporting its waste by train to be dumped in the disused Adams' Mine in northern Ontario. In June 2001, the city adopted a radical – but expensive – program of waste reuse, composting, and recycling, which would have residents separate dry and wet waste.[40]

Global Governance

Given this self-inflicted truncation of the Canadian state's environmental capacity, the neoconservative counterrevolution hardly needed help from the outside. Help was forthcoming nevertheless. Despite their ecologically correct wording, both continental and global trade agreements were to prove antipathetic to the cause of environmental sustainability.

Two-faced Continentalism: Defending and Attacking Sustainability

At first reading, there was good reason to agree with NAFTA's negotiators who claimed it to be the first international agreement frankly trying to reconcile trade and environmental issues.[41] In its preamble, the signatory states committed themselves to pursue their economic goals in a manner consistent with environmental protection and conservation, to encourage practices that led to sustainable development, and to strengthen the development and enforcement of environmental laws and regulations.[42]

To its credit, NAFTA's main text did make environmentally correct noises. It confirmed each party's right to choose its own level of environmental protection in areas concerning human, animal, or plant life within its own jurisdiction. Each was admonished against lowering health, safety, or environmental standards in order to attract foreign investment. Chapter 20's general dispute process allowed for incorporating environmental concerns into the adjudication of trade conflicts. Most important, it was the first trade agreement to recognize the juridical primacy of three existing international environmental agreements. This was taken to mean that, should a conflict arise between a member's economic obligations under NAFTA and its commitments on trade in endangered species, on the ozone layer, and on hazardous waste, the latter would take precedence over the former.

Another innovation was imposed by the Clinton administration, which, in responding to concerns expressed by its environmental supporters, had insisted that a North American Agreement on Environmental Co-operation be added to the treaty. The NAAEC's mission was to empower citizens in helping achieve sustainable development by promoting the continent-wide adoption of best environmental practices. The NAAEC's Commission for Environmental Co-operation (CEC) institutionally connected ecological questions to trade issues at the continental level. NAFTA's most substantial and best-financed institution, it had a mandate to reconcile controlling protectionism with sustainable development. In one of its public information functions, the CEC annually published a report card on government performance. Because of their anger at its success in supporting ecologists' goals, the three member-states took steps to hobble the nominally supranational and independent body. For all its mechanisms for inserting citizens and scientists in continental environmental issues, the CEC's capacity for empowering citizens appears to have wilted. This failure of reality to meet expectations was deepened by the revelation of Chapter 11's true potential to empower foreign corporations and castrate democratic governments. The CEC's citizen complaint process was intended to counterbalance Chapter 11, but, according to Mark Winfield, 'the Canadian and Mexican governments tried to kill it as soon as it showed some promise.'[43]

Trade advocates insisted that defining water as a tradeable commodity under NAFTA did little to limit Canada's ability to determine levels for bulk water exploitation and sales. They disagreed with the alarmist suggestion that 'once the tap is turned on it cannot be turned off.' The only obligation that Canada took on in handling water exports was to respect the treaty's non-discrimination provisions. Continental free trade did not give other NAFTA members the authority to force Canada to keep any tap turned on.[44] In this view, trade liberalization might restrict some policy instruments but would not detract from a government's ability to set its own policy goals. Consequently, it did not prevent the Canadian government from enforcing or even strengthening measures to protect the environment. This optimism took no account of the extraordinary power of NAFTA's Chapter 11 to negate such putative policy autonomy.

In November 1998, the California-based Sun Belt Water Inc. filed a notice of intent to arbitrate a claim under NAFTA's Chapter 11 against the BC government for refusing to expand its existing licence to ship fresh water by tanker and then imposing a moratorium on all new or expanded licences. In its notice of intent, Sun Belt claimed $220 million in damages, arguing under the national treatment rule (Article 1102) that British Columbia had given preferential treatment to its Canadian partner. A year later, in its October 1999 notice of demand for arbitration, the California company raised its bill for damages to between $1.5 billion and $10 billion, claiming its long-term lost profits to have been expropriated (Article 1110). It also invoked Article 1105 to allege that British Columbia had breached 'minimum international standards' – a norm of potentially great malleability – for treating a foreign investor.[45]

With the case in abeyance, Canadian governments' ability to manage their fresh water systems in ways that they deem environmentally responsible remained under a cloud. This case of suspended legal animation also lent retroactive weight to charges made by trade critics in the early 1990s. At the height of the trade and environment debate,[46] they asserted not only that NAFTA would have disastrous implications for resource depletion and environmental degradation, but that it would limit the ability of all levels of government to use regulatory tools to mitigate environmental externalities.[47]

Illustrative of Chapter 11's anti-regulatory impact was the federal government's abandonment of its attempt to eliminate the use of the gasoline additive MMT. Ethyl Corporation of Virginia, producer of this octane-enhancing chemical, had been unable to persuade Washington to request a dispute panel under Chapter 20, NAFTA's regular process for resolving conflict between governments. Since the U.S. Environmental Protection Agency had since 1977 banned MMT as a dangerous neurotoxin, Washington was unwilling to expend political capital on contesting Canada's right to ban trade in the same substance. Using Chapter 11's provision on investor-state disputes, Ethyl was able to bypass its government's reluctance to fight on its behalf. It put forward a claim that Ottawa's legislated ban on the fuel additive had cost it U.S.$250 million in lost business and future profits.[48]

Ottawa had made a doubly unfortunate decision in choosing a trade policy instrument to achieve its environmental goal. First, it became embroiled in a federal-provincial dispute when Alberta and Saskatchewan challenged the means that Ottawa had used to achieve its objective. The two prairie governments argued that a federal ban on interprovincial trade of MMT violated the provisions of the Agreement on Internal Trade (AIT). This was in itself a telling example of how the country's supraconstitution affected the workings of its existing, internal constitution (described in chapter 4), introducing norms of international trade into the workings of federal-provincial relations. When it lost its case at the AIT, Ottawa backed down before the American company to which it agreed to pay U.S.$13 million in damages and to issue an apology.[49] (Ethyl subsequently used this settlement for its global marketing strategy, proclaiming its product to be safe because the government of Canada had declared it acceptable.)

The MMT case revealed how Canadian environmental policy, once thought to be the purview of the sovereign legislature, has been taken hostage by continental governance. Under the supraconstitutional aegis of Chapter 11, the issue is no longer the classic Canadian question of *which* level of government – federal or provincial – can initiate an environmental regulation. The issue now became *whether any* level of government could initiate such legislation if it jeopardizes the interests of a foreign company.[50] Far from the polluter's paying to rectify the externalities that it caused, Chapter 11's expropriation clause led to the polluter's being paid to keep on polluting.

A second piece of federal environmental legislation was invalidated in another Chapter 11 arbitration that had even more devastating implications. When Ottawa banned the export of PCB waste, it thought that it was conforming with three of its international environmental commitments – the Basel Convention on the Control of Transboundary Movement of Hazardous Wastes and Their Disposal, the Canada-U.S. Agreement Concerning the Transboundary Movement of Hazardous Wastes, and NAFTA's Article 104, which proclaims the primacy of the international environmental treaties. Nevertheless, S.D. Myers, an American waste-disposal company with all its facilities in the United States, triggered an arbitration. In a flight of stupefying legal logic, the arbitrators deemed the Canadian ban to have violated Article 1102 on national treatment and Article 1105 on minimum international standards – on the aberrant grounds that it discriminated against a facility *in the United States*. National treatment apparently now meant continental treatment. The tribunal added to its exercise in judicial innovation by ruling that Canada was not authorized to institute a ban on the export of hazardous waste. If Ottawa's application for judicial review of this ruling were to fail, the sway of the investor-state dispute process would have been dramatically expanded at the expense of NAFTA's alleged friendliness towards sustainable development.

The democratic deficit accompanying NAFTA's legal deficit concerns the organized role of citizens. Unless they are corporations, third parties are generally excluded from continental environmental disputes. Given that citizens and their non-governmental organizations can neither launch a complaint nor be involved until the matter reaches the panel stage, the public is effectively shut out of the various dispute-settlement processes of continental governance.

In the MMT affair, Ethyl claimed that the Canadian federal government could not provide 'convincing evidence that MMT puts toxic levels of manganese into the air.'[51] Had qualified ENGOs been allowed to provide the missing scientific information, the final outcome might have been different. The restriction of standing in dispute settlement under NAFTA to corporate and governmental players further skews the course of continental environmental justice.

The Canadian Environmental Law Association (CELA) claimed that NAFTA's general bias against state activism would disable the policy tools that governments had available to favour the environment. By committing itself to NAFTA, CELA maintained, Canada abdicated its right to implement or strengthen policies that promote green industries, counter depletion of non-renewable resources, or advocate internalization of environmental costs.[52] There is, of course, another view. Institutional optimists maintain that, despite its slow start, NAFTA has proven itself environmentally sensitive and demonstrated some characteristics of a supranational regime. It has prevented some disputes, encouraged transparency, improved sanitary and phytosanitary standards, and achieved regulatory convergence not by encouraging a race to the bottom but by setting high standards for the transportation of dangerous goods and pesticides.[53] Continental governance is not the only level where the environment-versus-economy glass can be seen to be either half empty or half full.

The Clash of Multilateral Regimes: Commerce versus the Environment

Multilateral environmental agreements, of which there are more than 300, try to *convince*.[54] Rules for global commerce have been developed to *coerce*. Ontario's attempt in the 1980s to require that all beer be sold in recyclable bottles sparked accusations of protectionism from angry American breweries (which sold their ale in cans) and resulted in an adverse ruling by a GATT panel.[55] Then, when Ottawa attempted to protect the BC salmon fishery against American overfishing, Washington initiated another case against Canada in Geneva. The GATT panel ruled that the Canadian conservation measure, which fostered local processing by BC fish plants, was excessively protectionist.

These judgments at the global level have become just as politically explosive as continental rulings. Heated rhetoric expresses clashing ideological positions. Charges of protectionism are hurled by corporations when they allege that environmental regulations are a smokescreen to shelter inefficient domestic producers against more competitive global rivals. Equally outraged, environmentalists see ruthless corporations jeopardizing the very survival of humankind through their irresponsible exploitation of global trade norms.

Energized by these value-based confrontations, ENGOs have become a significant transnational force, often taking direct action to frustrate dangerous activities by governments or companies. The prototype for the postmodern ENGO, Greenpeace, is able to mobilize a transnational coalition of counterelites against particular domestic targets, ranging from the BC practice of clearcut logging to Newfoundland's seal harvesting.[56] By moving into global and continental forums, these ENGOs are invoking a supranational consciousness that is linking trade questions to environmental issues.

Much of the popular anger at the WTO is the product of clashes with trade norms that environmentalists consistently lost. In the tuna-dolphin case, the U.S. legislation to ban the import of tuna caught using nets that killed dolphins, was declared in violation of GATT. U.S. environmentalists were equally appalled when legislation to ban the import of shrimp caught by methods that killed off sea turtles was judged illegal by the WTO's dispute process. The new trade regime has exacerbated the long-standing tension between the economy and the environment by changing the balance of power among international regimes. While conforming to environmental norms remains largely voluntary, the WTO has greatly strengthened the enforcement of commercial conventions.[57]

The transnational qualities of environmental politics clearly transcend the scope of the territorial state, but federal-provincial politics still determines collective intergovernmental action – as the disappointing follow-through from the Rio and Kyoto environmental summits confirmed. Most provinces have declined to sign the North American Agreement on Environmental Co-operation, lest it bind them with further obligations. As for the Liberal government in Ottawa, its ecologically correct discourse is belied by its reluctance to implement the commitments that it made at Kyoto in 1997 to combat global warming. Ottawa seemed without shame in taking a case to the WTO against France for its ban on importing Canadian asbestos, a carcinogen whose domestic use in insulation Canada bans. When the U.S. administration withdrew from Kyoto, Ottawa's vain attempt to weaken the subsequent successor treaty revealed how much it was equally in thrall to the energy industry.

Conclusion: Trade Liberalization and Neoconservatism

It is impossible to measure with precision the respective effects of home-grown neoconservatism, NAFTA, and the WTO on the domestic environment. In the case of the neoconservative government of Ontario, a radical reduction in the budgetary resources devoted to monitoring and enforcing environmental protection was clearly driven by neoconservative ideology, not by the new norms of continental or global governance. The lack of commitment by the government in Queen's Park, combined with Ottawa's tendency to offload its environmental responsibilities, significantly raised pollution levels in the province – a fact that the partially defanged CEC has publicized every year.[58] The CEC's monitoring has not been enough to offset the indirect effects of neoconservatism – the deliberate degradation of federal and provincial monitoring and enforcement of environmental regulations in order to stimulate economic growth in a less regulated market.

Yet there are limits that restrict neoconservative governments' abdication of the environmental responsibilities taken on by their social-democratic predecessors. The continual reporting of meteorological data warning of daily ozone levels in the air and E.coli counts in the water have made citizens acutely conscious of the health hazards created by unregulated pollution. Medical data about skin, lung, breast, and prostate cancer rates emphasize the connection between people's health and the ambient environment. Politicians are surely conscious that, if popular awareness of globalization's environmental consequences can produce organized protests against global meetings, it can just as easily rebound against themselves.

Furthermore, there are still forces of liberal continuity at work that bolster the federal government's power in other dimensions. The Supreme Court's consistent support of Ottawa's power in federal-provincial fights over jurisdiction in environmental assessment has compensated for some of the powers lost to the market and continental governance through NAFTA's Chapter 11.

Even if there were no pressure coming from the voters to keep their air, water, and land cleaned of health hazards, the demands of economic growth paradoxically also counteract the push for environmental deregulation. If a locality no longer offers knowledge workers attractive amenities, which include a liveable environment, new investment will not locate there, and existing enterprises will not remain. Only such extreme versions of the present ruling paradigm as Thatcherism and Harris's Common Sense Revolution can disregard the environment. However hypocritically, even the Harris government at least needed to *appear* to be nature-friendly.

Beyond sustaining the environment, the civil state is involved in sustaining the identity and cohesion of its citizenry. For a country as vulnerable as Canada is to global cultural influences, this is no easy task, as we see in the next chapter.

18 The Cultured State: Broadcasting and Magazines

In the summer of 1959, on my way to study politics and economics at Oxford, I spent a week in Norway at an international students' seminar sponsored by NATO. During a recreational excursion one afternoon, as our ferry approached a dock at the end of a picture-post-card fjord, one of the African students went into a cold fury. Seeing Shell Oil's familiar yellow scallop sign suspended above the fuel pumps on the wharf, he was overwhelmed with anger over the economic exploitation and cultural imperialism against which his generation was struggling. At the age of twenty-one and with a prime interest in Soviet politics, my Cold War views didn't leave much room for thoughts of Western imperialism. Okot B'tek went on to become a major and politically influential East African poet, but it was nearly a decade before I could relate my nascent concern about the precarious condition of Canadian culture to the larger issues his anger etched in my mind that day.

The state has been involved in promoting and controlling what we now call culture for as long as politicians have wielded coercive force to buttress their authority. Emperors learned how to put on gladiatorial spectacles in Rome's colosseum – the second half of the famous 'bread and circuses' formula for repressing dissent and generating acquiescence. When England was emerging from Rome's spiritual monopoly, John Wycliffe was persecuted for translating the Bible from Latin into the vernacular. The church knew its authority would be threatened if the faithful could read – and so interpret – the scriptures for themselves. Later, absolute monarchs, as patrons, kept a close watch on culture's double function. They would patronize a playwright who entertained the public and glorified their reign but punish him if his plays questioned their authority or even made fun of the system on which it was based. The neoclassical public buildings designed for Washington at the end of the nineteenth century showed culture's *positive* power by proclaiming the proud American republic's imperial mission through their architectural forms. Joseph Goebbels, the Nazi minister of popular enlightenment and inventor of mass propaganda, expressed the *negative* potential of art to society as he famously said, 'When someone says "culture," I reach for my gun.'

Rather than using bullets and concentration camps, liberal governments rely on regulations and subsidies, but they have an even bigger stake in the role of culture than their totalitarian counterparts. Without an all-powerful sovereign or a dictator to enforce social cohesion, a community's ability to sustain itself depends on its capacity to nurture the shared values, beliefs, behaviour, memories, and symbols that generate its collective identity.[1] If a state's survival hangs on its citizens' constructing a common culture, we can understand why its leaders still demonstrate the age-old ambivalence, trying both to sustain what supports their official values and to restrain what subverts them.

The General Conundrums of Cultural Policy in Canada

This double burden has been more difficult for the Canadian state to bear than has been the case in Europe. There, many linguistically distinct ethnicities took on state forms after centuries of military conflict and institutional evolution that forged a political entity – and with it a *national* identity – out of their disparate components. As a settler colony whose government was constructed de novo, British North America had to reverse this progression from cultural to political identity. Born as an imperially constructed state, its challenge was to create a national identity for its population. Given that Canada started out encompassing two linguistic nationalities that – 'warring in the bosom of a single state,' as Lord Durham reported in 1838 – were too distinct to blend.[2] The difficulty involved in developing even a binational identity was exacerbated when immigrants from other nations in Europe, then Asia, the Middle East, the Americas, and Africa flocked in, and when the originally marginalized Native peoples also found their voice.

In addition to the need shared by all white-settler states, to generate *internal* cultural cohesion from multiple ingredients, Canada faced an *external* cultural threat. It had a love-hate relationship with the only force that could stop it from creating a culturally cohesive political nationality. As Anthony Smith observed in 1980,

> Canada has always been obliged to struggle to maintain a thriving indigenous culture because of the proximity of the United States with its enormous output of information and entertainment. To all intents and purposes, Canada has been treated as part of a large North American market for films, television programmes, and other media products ... No country in the world probably is more completely committed to the practice of free flow in its culture and no country is more completely its victim.[3]

More than most democracies, which also bolster and protect their cultures,[4] Canada has spent enormous energy building communications systems. From portages to canals, from railways to airlines, from phone lines to fibre-optic cables, from broadcast towers to satellite transmission: linking Canada's vast territory has always been a top priority for its governments. At the same time as they worked for economic growth and military security, Canadian politicians have also faced difficult questions of political development. If a trans*continental* railway from east to west was essential to building the nation, would trans*border* rail lines running from British Columbia to California, from the prairie provinces to the U.S. midwest, from Montreal to New York, or from Halifax to Boston contribute to breaking it? If direct-to-home satellite transmission could beam hundreds of channels from around the world into their homes, would Canadians lose their fragile sense of community?

Having invested so compulsively in these communications systems, Canada fortuitously produced two of the world's leading communications theorists, who helped us comprehend their significance. Harold Innis argued that, through the course of human history, each medium of communication – whether tablets or papyrus or print – had a 'bias' favouring a particular system of political and economic power.[5] Thus the twentieth-century technologies of radio, film, and television could extend an empire's reach without requiring the imperial power to exert direct political control. Marshall McLuhan perceived each medium as affecting the individual's nervous system in a particular way, so that new media created new modes of consciousness, reshaping society in the process.[6] If information systems wired the whole world together, we would all become members of a 'global village.' McLuhan was presaging cultural globalization before the internet made instant intercon-nection of everyone on the planet obvious to all.

Three Major Issues

Alerted by these media theorists, other commentators asked about the political consequences of 99 per cent of Canadian households having a TV set and a radio. Was the *medium* the message, or did the real issue involve the *content* of the message that the technology transmitted? Did it matter that the average Canadian spends the equivalent of nine years in a lifetime watching television? Should citizens be concerned that, by age twelve, Canadian children have spent less time in school classrooms than the 12,000 hours they have been glued to TV sets watching mostly American programs?[7] Determining whether it mat-tered depended on what cultural content this programming transmit-ted. The content problem itself begged a prior question about what ideological values a nation's culture should validate. And the whole abstract discussion about culture was premised on there being actual politically generated mechanisms available for nourishing and defend-ing it. These three issues have all been hotly contested subjects in Can-ada.

Cultural Content

If Canadians have not spent much time worrying about the values embedded in American TV, it is because Canada's battle lines on cul-tural issues have been typically drawn on linguistic grounds. In 1968, René Lévesque founded his Parti Québécois, championing French as the cultural vehicle to promote Quebec's political liberation. In the same year, Pierre Trudeau came to federal power, denying that Que-becers as a collectivity had a distinct culture. For him, language was an individual's, not a community's, business. Endorsing the idea of bilin-gualism (as the individual right of all citizens from coast to coast), he rejected that of biculturalism (which might have legitimized his sepa-ratist enemies' claimed need for sovereignty to promote their distinct, linguistically defined community).

Neither bilingualism nor biculturalism could satisfactorily describe the underpinnings of cultural policy in the Keynesian state, since nei-ther in Quebec nor in the rest of Canada did the population have a homogeneous identity. Multiculturalism, which the federal Liberals adopted as their mantra in 1971, proclaimed, in a defiant gesture of prematurely post-modernist self-contradiction, that a unifying national identity was to be found in demographic diversity. Even this inclusion of new ethnicities proved too limiting. With the evolution of a Charter-based rights consciousness, cross-cutting social groupings have superimposed gender, sexual orientation, and other characteristics as self-conceptions that vie with territorial or ethnic identities.

Ideological Values

Below this metapolitical level of debate, intense differences have characterized Canadians' discussion of what to do about the various forms of expression that give their culture (whether defined territorially, ethnically, or otherwise) its particular content. These ideological battles have been situated along two main axes – nationality and ownership.

Given the overwhelming presence within Canada of American cultural goods, worries have waxed and waned about the nationality of professors teaching Canadian (or Quebec) students, the nationality of Canadian (or Quebec) books' authors, the domestic ownership of publishing houses, the domestic content of the music broadcast over Canadian (or Quebec) radio stations, the lack of Canadian (or Quebec) films in Canadian (or Quebec) cinemas, even which nation controls professional hockey or baseball teams. The common assumption is that a political community must constantly reproduce a common consciousness and that an excessive presence of foreign – that is, American (or Anglo-Canadian) – cultural products will denationalize Canadians' (or Quebecers') consciousness and so unglue their political cohesion.

In extreme cases, when the cultural production of one nationality dominates the cultural consumption of another, assimilation will ensue, jeopardizing the political survival of the dominated community – as the descendants of Franco-Ontarians in Windsor or Acadians in Louisiana can attest. Fear of cultural assimilation was the essential concern of Canadian nationalists following the First World War and again in the aftermath of the Second World War, when the cross-border flood of American books in Canadian bookstores, of American stories over the newswires, of American magazines on the newstands, and of American films in the cinemas provoked renewed calls for government to establish defences against U.S. cultural invasion. Patriots concerned about preserving their community's distinctness and cohesion pressed politicians for protection. So did entrepreneurs struggling to compete for access to their own market without the benefit of their American competitors' massive economies of scale. As Grattan O'Leary, a conservative journalist, put it in 1961,

> The United States has ... the world's most penetrating and effective apparatus for the transmission of ideas. Canada, more than any other country, is naked to that force, exposed unceasingly to a vast network of communications which reaches to every corner of our land; American words, images and print – the good, the bad, the indifferent – batter unrelentingly at our eyes and ears.[8]

Related to this nationalist anxiety about the Americanization of Canada (or the anglicization of Quebec) is fear that the profit motive driving private enterprise, combined with the high costs of production in a geographically vast but lightly populated market, inevitably leads to U.S. ownership of Canada's profit-making entertainment sectors and therefore control of its consciousness. By contrast, under state or domestic ownership, cultural processes can be maintained as long as the public supports using the tax system to allocate sufficient resources for their sustenance.

In a country whose population often wants more access to the hegemon's culture than to its own and in cultural industries where foreign corporations often have more political clout than their Canadian competitors, government policy becomes self-contradictory. For instance, when the larger cities were wired for cable, intense pressure from the cable industry caused Ottawa to allow them to carry the three main private American TV networks – ABC, CBS, and NBC – plus the Public Broadcasting System. Having ensured universal diffusion of U.S. broadcasts, it then required the cable companies to carry CBC, local channels, and provincial services. In the periphery of the cultural hegemon, the state accelerates its population's assimilation into the dominant culture with one hand and tries to buttress domestic creation with the other.

Mechanisms

A national culture is not a fixed entity displayed behind glass in museums. It is a dynamic phenomenon that, to survive, must not just be constantly reproduced with new creations building on its heritage. It must also be continuously diffused and absorbed. To understand this dynamic, we have to comprehend the various roles that capitalism plays in industrializing a culture as it mass produces and distributes cultural 'products' for citizens to 'consume.' Books and broadcasting, music and magazines, film and football: every cultural 'industry' has a political economy based on five interdependent facets.

- Goods. Each cultural sphere ultimately produces a specific kind of cultural good (a book or radio program, a song or periodical, a movie or game).
- Creators. Each kind of cultural good is produced by a particular kind of creator – authors, film makers, musicians, athletes – all with their own unique professional characteristics.
- Institutions. To produce their goods, these cultural creators require special types of institutions (universities; broadcast, recording, or film studios; publishing houses; sports programs) in which to carry on their profession.
- Distribution Networks. Once produced, their works have to be distributed through distinct networks (bookstores and movie chains, airwaves or coaxial cable, school systems or sports leagues).
- Clientele. Finally a cultural industry's economic survival and cultural effect depend on the patronage of their clientele. If citizens don't buy and read the books that have been written, edited, printed, and distributed, the publishing industry will fail economically and have no impact culturally. And if Canadian or Quebec movies cannot be exhibited because Hollywood controls the exhibition channels, Canadian and Quebec cinema will not counteract the reproduction of the hegemon's identity.

In a culturally penetrated society such as Canada's, problems abound for each of these five facets, as these examples suggest.

- Goods. If textbooks used in the schools are produced by U.S. publishers, will children learn more about U.S. society than about their own?
- Creators. If professors teaching university students about Canada are not citizens of the country, can they convey a valid understanding of its problems?
- Institutions. Since independent Canadian publishers publish more Canadian authors than do those run from New York, is it in the public interest to support artisanal, Canadian-owned houses?

- Distribution. If newsstands make more money by giving greater prominence to U.S. than to Canadian magazines, should they be required to give Canadian periodicals equal access to their public?
- Clientele. If the 'free market' systematically inculcates Canadian citizens with American cultural symbols, should public money be spent to 'brand' Canadian symbols into the collective consciousness?

Each of these facets of every cultural industry has become the object of public policy to some degree, at some point, and with greater or lesser success. In the process, the federal and provincial states have developed a continuing and highly complex involvement with the country's cultural economy.

Two Solitudes

Given the specific characteristics of each industry's political economy, government policies to promote and protect specific cultural sectors have been highly diverse. In some cases the state plays patron and subsidizes the art form – for instance, through helping publishers finance their authors' book promotion efforts. In others, the public is left to choose whatever entertainment it wants to pay for, movies being the prime example. In a middle zone, governments leave the private sector free to produce and distribute cultural products but play a regulatory role in requiring guaranteed access for Canadian creative talent to their market, as with music broadcast over the radio. When the free market completely fails to provide the public with the necessary means of communication, the state may set up institutions for cultural reproduction such as universities, which transmit values and encourage new thinking.

Following the 1951 report of the Royal Commission on National Development in the Arts, Letters and Sciences (Massey Commission), which sounded the alarm about the sorry condition of all the cultural media in Canada and about the dangers that American movies, television, and periodicals represented for the country's survival, a period of cultural policy proliferation began. Ottawa's cultural policy in this Keynesian period demonstrated the classic duality of state involvement with the arts.

On the positive side, the federal government provided institutional or regulatory support for two types of function. First, it founded the Canada Council to help creatively endowed men and women devote

their talents to artistic production. Incentives were also offered entrepreneurs to orient cultural reproduction and distribution networks to
deliver Canadian-made goods to the interested public. Canadian publishers were nurtured with subsidies to help a small, but feisty book
industry establish a toehold in a mainly American-dominated market.
(Proprietorial requirements had long made foreign ownership of newspapers uneconomical.)

On the negative side, cultural policy had huge problems with sub-
version – in Canada's case, from the United States. When supporting
national development in elite, loss-making art forms, such as theatre,
ballet, and opera, where no major American corporate entities were
threatened, the only constraint on policy was the generosity of the government and the size of its purse. But when challenging U.S. dominance in a profitable, mass-entertainment industry, policy makers
faced a dangerous, zero-sum game. To make room for a Canadian cultural industry to emerge or grow, they would have to reduce the space
occupied by the existing American industry, whose wrath would
expose Canada to U.S. sanctions.

Years of efforts by federal politicians and civil servants to create
more exposure for Canadian films in Canadian moviehouses (where
they typically enjoy 1 to 3 per cent of screen time) had come to naught
because of Hollywood's corporate-cum-political hegemony. Any sign
that its monopoly might be shaken or its bottom line jeopardized by
some Canadian legislation would typically generate objections from
domestic agents of the U.S. industry and threats from Washington of
such massive retaliation on behalf of its lucrative movie business that
Ottawa always backed down.

Unlike English Canada's cultural travails, Quebec's experience has
been a spectacular success. In part this is thanks to language and language policy. That 85 per cent of Quebecers use French as their mother
tongue explains in part how, as in continental Europe, language provides a substantial barrier against Americanization. But the fact that
French is so strong was not genetically determined. Without French
ancestry, of course, there would be no French spoken in Quebec, but
the use of French was in decline at mid-century, so that even Montreal
had to be 'reconquered.'[9] Actions taken by Robert Bourassa's Liberals
in 1974 (Bill 22) and by René Lévesque Péquistes' in 1977 (Bill 101)
enforced the predominant use of French in schools and the workplace.

Ironically, the *épanouissement* of francophone culture in Quebec was
stimulated by the turf war between Ottawa and the provincial govern-

ment. At the same time as Quebec was legislating the use of French, Ottawa competed for the loyalty of Quebecers by offering them substantial patronage of the arts. Radio Canada, the Office national du Film, the Conseil des Arts, and Telefilm Canada are but four of the major conduits for federal support of Quebec's artistic creators, the goods they produce, the institutions where they can work, their distribution networks, and their public. For its part, the provincial government has used public policy to achieve related goals, such as the public television network TV Québec, subsidies for artists and scholarly research, and support for book distribution, through requiring public schools to spend their book budgets in local bookstores.

The figures tell this success story. Domestic French-language television programs have 60 per cent of Quebec's market share – 75 per cent among francophones. (Domestic Canadian programs in English have 25–30 per cent of the anglophone market.) Domestic francophone cultural goods have 95 per cent of Quebec's French-language newspaper market, 75 per cent of the French-language magazine market, and 50 per cent of music broadcast on the radio.[10]

Despite Quebec's greater protection from cultural assimilation, three further factors, which are by now familiar to readers of this text, have emerged since the early 1980s to affect the state's capacity to foster cultural cohesion in the rest of Canada:

Global trade governance. Rules adopted by treaty to break down state barriers to trade and investment clashed with norms favouring the preservation of national cultural diversity. We will shortly see how the WTO's resolution of disputes, rooted in this tension, has invalidated significant laws and regulations made by Canadian governments.

Neoconservatism. When Margaret Thatcher denied the existence of society, she challenged the raison d'être of cultural policies everywhere. For if only individuals exist, while communities have no reality, there is no reason for the state to influence its citizens' cultural choices and behaviour. By demoting cultural activity to the status of just another industry, neoconservatism denied the socio-political functions of culture and reduced the policy problem to concerns for market-based tests of efficiency and consumer sovereignty.[11]

Technology. A third force bedevilling public policies was the arrival of communications innovations which defy the regulatory capacity of governments. Radio and then TV broadcasting were problems in earlier decades. More recently, satellite technology, computerization, the internet, and, soon, the convergence of all three allow both domestic and foreign entrepreneurs to escape the reach of state regulators.

To give this discussion concrete content, we will look at two major cultural industries – broadcasting and magazines – each of whose recent dilemmas sheds a different light on these contested issues.

Broadcasting

Radio gives us the clearest example of a state-led model in Canadian cultural policy. With an overwhelming penetration rate by the late 1920s, Canadians families who could afford a radio consumed a diet of largely American radio programming. Concern about the public's growing absorption of American popular culture was reinforced by the obstacles that had developed to broadcasting equivalent Canadian material. Privately owned Canadian stations, which had gone on the air when the public bought radio sets, favoured a laissez-faire approach to business. In practice, government's hands-off stance allowed them to become local transmitters for the programming provided by such U.S. networks as the Columbia Broadcasting System, which treated its affiliates north of the border as part of its American market. With the private sector controlling content and transmission, state intervention seemed the only viable way to gain access for Canadian voices to their own air waves.[12]

The rationale for state intervention in cultural activities was developed in the royal commission struck by the Liberal government of W.L. Mackenzie King in 1928. The resulting Aird Report recognized that, to regain cultural sovereignty and to link Canadians from east to west to north, Canada should establish a state presence in radio.[13] One ground for *regulatory* control lay in the limited number of radio frequencies, which constituted a scarce natural resource. But it was the small, uneconomic size of the domestic market which justified shifting production in broadcasting from private to public *ownership*. With this analysis the Aird Report established a public philosophy for government-owned and -regulated broadcasting that prevailed for the next three decades and was expressed as late as 1986 by the Mulroney government's Caplan-Sauvageot commission.[14]

This rationale for state *ownership* was closely linked to the intellectual basis for the *national* dimension of the debate, which was articulated by the prominent activist Graham Spry. Mobilizing support from a vast, pan-Canadian coalition stretching from provincial governments, through farmers' organizations, to the chartered banks, he argued that, without a publicly controlled broadcasting system, Canadians would be exposed exclusively to the commercialized content produced by the American radio networks. For him, the issue boiled down to a simple choice: the state versus the United States. Britannia might rule the waves, he asked, but should Columbia rule the airwaves?

The new Conservative government's answer was to establish a Canadian Broadcasting Corporation (CBC) modelled on the British Broadcasting Corporation. As R.B. Bennett put it to Parliament, 'This country must be assured of complete control of broadcasting from Canadian sources, free from foreign interference or influence.'[15] The CBC became the central electronic institution of cultural *reproduction*, where broadcasters could create programming, and as well as a *distribution* network for delivering to the public its made-in-Canada-by-Canadians-for-Canadians news, public affairs, music, drama, sports, and entertainment programs. In its halcyon days through the 1940s and 1950s, the CBC helped consolidate a national consciousness among anglophones as its French-Canadian arm, Radio Canada, did for francophones. At the same time it nurtured infant communities of writers, composers, playwrights, musicians, actors, and broadcast technicians.

The technology enabling the broadcast of images and the arrival of U.S. commercial television in the early 1950s revived the national debate over Canada's cultural survival. When the CBC moved into TV programming, the private broadcasters cried foul. Once licensed by the Progressive Conservative government of John Diefenbaker, private television stations duly became conduits for beaming American programming to Canadian audiences, who were captivated by the more entertaining production values of the richer American networks. Responding to this concern, the Trudeau government introduced a Broadcasting Act in 1968 to mandate the Canadian Radio-Television Commission (CRTC) to supervise and control the broadcasting system, both radio and television, both public and private.[16] Through regulations and provisions imposed when allocating broadcasting licences, the CRTC became a proxy for the state in all of its broadcasting activities, with substantial consequences for many cultural industries.

Television, Foreign Ownership, and Free Trade

One of the CRTC's most consequential regulatory powers was its authority to limit foreign ownership of Canadian broadcasters. Armed with a cabinet directive in 1969, the CRTC restricted broadcast licences to those firms with at least 80 per cent Canadian ownership and/or board membership.[17]

In the 1970s, the federal government expanded its regulatory efforts in broadcasting. To protect the revenue base of television's private sector, Bill C-58 amended Section 19 of the Income Tax Act to disallow firms deducting from their taxes the costs of advertising on foreign (in practice, U.S.-border) television stations.[18] To strengthen the cable industry, the CRTC further enabled its members to 'simulcast' – that is, to rebroadcast American programs without charge while deleting their commercials and replacing them with Canadian ads. Both simulcasting and the eliminated tax deductions were strenuously resisted by the U.S.-border TV broadcasters, who lost revenues from Canadian advertisers.

Despite the best efforts of Congress to retaliate and of the U.S. administration to threaten, the Trudeau government held the line on this issue, but with debatable results. Two decades' worth of protection for the economic base of the Canadian television market consolidated two private networks. Both Global and CTV broadcast some Canadian content shows licensed from independent Canadian producers, who in turn received financing from the Canadian Television Fund and from Telefilm Canada. Apart from national news shows, they rebroadcast mainly American programming, which nourished a nationally based, if increasingly foreign-owned, advertising sector.

In negotiating CUFTA, the Mulroney government willingly gave up much of the space created through protective regulations for Canadian cultural industries. CUFTA's Article 2006, for instance, required Canadian cable companies to pay royalties for the use of U.S. broadcast signals they had previously taken off the air gratis. For a neoconservative, this was simply a matter of eliminating government-created distortions in certain economic sectors.

But the cultural autonomy of the Canadian state faced its greatest challenge with CUFTA's starkly self-contradictory and deeply duplicitous Article 2005. In its first paragraph, this much-touted 'cultural exemption' stated that culture was exempt from the agreement's provisions and so allowed Mulroney to claim he had safeguarded Ottawa's ability to develop new cultural policies. Two factors made this victory hollow. The simple act of an economic treaty's mentioning culture – even in order to exempt it from the treaty's provisions – established the premise that culture is an industrial sector subject to the potential discipline of trade rules. NAFTA's Article 2107 entrenched this premise by providing the first extensive definition of cultural industries in trade law.

The second degree of hollowness came in the alleged exemption's second paragraph. Article 2005(2) bluntly negated the concession contained in 2005(1). 'Notwithstanding any other provision of this Agreement,' began this second clause, which permitted Washington to claim victory, because henceforth it could retaliate by taking measures 'of equivalent commercial effect' in any field it pleased against any new Canadian cultural policy that might hurt the interests of an American corporation.[19] In a single sentence, issue linkage – long taboo in U.S.-Canadian conflicts – became a legitimate means with which the hegemon could discipline its northern neighbour. Far from being exempt, culture had been directly targeted by CUFTA.

How far Ottawa's capacity to promote Canadian cultural development had been hamstrung by CUFTA was illustrated by the dispute over Country Music Television (CMT), a U.S.-owned channel that the CRTC had authorized the cable companies to offer their subscribers in 1984 but only and until a directly competitive Canadian channel was licensed. After operating undisturbed for eleven years, the American specialty network was enraged by the commission's decision in January 1995 to give a licence to the Canadian-owned New Country Network and so bump CMT from Canadian cable TV.[20]

After an unsuccessful appeal to the Federal Court of Canada and the Supreme Court, CMT induced the U.S. government to file a Section 301 complaint threatening retaliation. Washington's rumoured retaliatory targets were exports of maple syrup, bacon, fur coats, and phonograph records in addition to Teleglobe, Canada's supplier of international telecommunications; 'Muchmusic,' a Canadian music video channel carried on DirecTV's American satellite service; and Cineplex Odeon, which had extensive U.S. holdings.[21] U.S. Trade Representative Mickey Kantor made no secret that it would cost the Canadian entertainment industry billions of dollars more than CMT's estimated value.[22] This linkage of a dispute in the TV sector with a miscellany of other economic relationships was legitimate under CUFTA's Article 2005(2), although its excessive scope directly contravened the stipulation that the retaliation be of '*equivalent* commercial effect.' Still, Canada could do little because Article 2005(2) was not covered by CUFTA's general dispute resolution process.

The dispute's dénouement was as problematic as the threatened retaliation. The day Kantor was to announce his retaliation plan, the two rival companies formed a joint venture. Although CMT took only a 20 per cent equity interest, in conformity with the CRTC's limits on foreign ownership, the American company's de facto control was suggested by the new company's name – CMT Canada.[23] While continental governance had partially disabled the CRTC from managing the air waves as a scarce resource, the multi-channel universe did not stop the CRTC's content quota from requiring CMT Canada's 'narrowcasting' to showcase more Canadian artists than before.[24]

Radio, Cancon, and Recorded Music

As controversial as foreign ownership limits in television, content regulations for radio require broadcasters to include a certain proportion of Canadian material in their programming.[25] While 'Cancon' has done little to stem the flood of US TV programming, it has proven a largely successful policy for promoting Canadian pop musicians.

Canada's record industry owed its original development to an import tariff that Ottawa imposed in the 1920s on all foreign recordings. This typical infant industry strategy created a domestic market for records and allowed it certain economies of scale. Once importing American-made records became unprofitable, branch plants were established to supply the Canadian market from behind the tariff. Canada's recording business became a miniature replica of the U.S. industry. Each major transnational firm established record-pressing operations ('production') in Canada, while simultaneously creating coast-to-coast sales networks to market their products.[26]

While the tariff helped develop a Canadian market for recorded music in general, it did not create a market for music made by Canadians.[27] In the 1960s, such Canadian material accounted for only 4 to 7 per cent of all music played on radio.[28] Declaring that domestic talent should be heard on Canadian airwaves, the CRTC laid down minimum levels of Canadian music for radio.[29] These 'Canadian content' rules made radio a promotional springboard in Canadian homes by playing recordings that listeners would not otherwise have wanted to purchase. By 1986, Cancon levels had risen to 30 per cent for AM stations – still the dominant means of transmission at that time – and between 10 and 30 per cent for FM stations.

With such significant requirements for Canadian music, disk jockeys demanded a greater variety of local artists to play. Accordingly, the record 'labels' began to produce more albums by Canadian acts. The resulting increase in air time gave these artists more exposure, which in turn stimulated record sales for local talent and further strengthened the industry. Ottawa's import tariff and regulatory policy had created a virtuous, but vulnerable, circle of viability for Canadian music.

Expansion in the numbers of Canadian musicians had fostered the growth of the 'indie' market – characterized by the independent label recording the independent artist. Through a successful blend of talent and marketing, formerly independent groups such as the Barenaked Ladies, Hayden, and Wild Strawberries achieved local commercial success and eventually attracted the attention of the transnationals. The contractual negotiating leverage enjoyed by many independent Canadian artists, who had proven themselves commercially viable, consolidated Canadian music on the continental stage. The negligible start-up costs for musical groups and solo artists assured an abundant pool of promising musicians to sustain the industry in the face of continentalizing pressure.

From the 1960s to the 1980s, a division of labour characterized the Canadian industry. Domestic record labels 'produced' – that is, signed acts and made the master tapes – for some 90 per cent of Canadian-content recordings. While originating only one out of every ten Canadian albums, the transnationals actually 'released' – that is, distribute in retail outlets – a substantial majority of the domestic labels' production. The indies retained their copyright to the music that they recorded, ensuring them a continuing cash flow from Cancon-stimulated broadcast royalties. But to offset the industry's general decline in revenues in the late 1970s, the major transnational labels began taking a stronger interest in recording Canada's music.[30] Thanks as well to undertakings made to Investment Canada following indirect takeovers of TNCs, their share of the Canadian industry was growing by the 1980s to the detriment of local firms.[31] Trade liberalization would further jeopardize the indies' already tenuous position.

Whether the Diefenbaker-Pearson-Trudeau era's success in fostering a market for Canadian music could be sustained under continentalism remained an open question. On the one hand and surprisingly, protectionist measures such as Cancon regulations for music have been strengthened rather than weakened. In CUFTA's aftermath, a 30 per cent Canadian music quota became the requirement for both AM and FM radio stations. Under NAFTA, these levels rose again – to 35 per cent Canadian music for English-language stations and 65 per cent French-language content for francophone stations.[32] Evidently, these violations of national treatment have not caused the U.S. labels sufficient financial concerns to precipitate a legal challenge. This passivity may reflect the greater gains that the transnational corporations won elsewhere in the new continental norms, particularly by eliminating the tariff on recordings. The net result is their aggressive competition with the independent labels for Canadian artists.

Magazines and the WTO

Though less pervasive in its diffusion and less immediately powerful in its impact than television or radio, the printed word remains an impressively potent cultural medium in the global village. Compared to the millions of people hooked on TV, books achieve only modest circulation figures. Nevertheless, the values that they express can affect social identities and policies as their ideas ricochet through personal and public channels of communication. Mass-distribution newspapers have a shelf life of only a few hours, but they provide citizens with vital information about their locality and their world and play a central role in creating and sustaining community consciousness.

In between the slowly produced tome and the daily printed broadsheet, weekly and monthly magazines serve both national and niche roles. Trades, professions, avocations, and social interests are all maintained by the regular appearance of their specialized magazines, while general-interest periodicals provide a continuing forum for sustaining – or subverting – a collective psyche. Their impact is potentially high because 70 per cent of Canadians read them.[33] The history of magazines under the Diefenbaker-Pearson-Trudeau state appeared to show Ottawa's ability to create a niche for domestic cultural production. Then global governance made Canada safe once again for suffocation by American cultural expression.

Creating a Niche

Survival problems for Canadian periodicals in the face of American competition have presented a continuing policy conundrum. Nationally produced magazines had been granted special postal rates since the 1920s, but their position was still parlous at mid-century, when U.S. magazines commanded 80 per cent of the Canadian market. American-controlled distribution companies made it difficult for Canadian publishers to gain access to their own newsstands, which were filled with imported U.S. magazines.[34] Worse, the Canadian editions of *Time Magazine*, *Reader's Digest*, and *Sélections du Reader's Digest*, whose branch plants had recycled the editorial content provided by their American parent companies since the 1940s, together captured 40 per cent of the advertising revenues for the country's general-interest magazines. Most of the advertising dollars on which Canadian magazines depended were sucked up by their 'split-run' competitors who, having amortized their production costs from sales in their huge home market, could sell heavily discounted advertising in Canada. As a result, their would-be Canadian competitors, who had to produce all their editorial content from scratch, could not survive if they matched these rates.

A public inquiry commissioned by the Diefenbaker government considered the reuse of American content in these 'Canadian' editions to be dumping. In other words, the split-run competitors unfairly undercut the advertising rates of genuinely Canadian magazines. In 1961, the O'Leary Commission recommended vigorous government intervention to generate a healthy national magazine industry on the grounds that 'it is largely left to our periodical press, to our magazines big and little, to make a conscious appeal to the nation, to try to interpret Canada to all Canadians, to bring a sense of oneness to our scattered communities.'[35]

When the Pearson government moved in 1965 to abolish split-run editions of U.S. magazines from the Canadian market, it resorted to both a trade policy mechanism and a tax device. First, Finance Minister Walter Gordon amended the Customs Act with tariff code 9958 to prohibit the importing of American magazines that contained advertising directed primarily at the Canadian market. Then, he amended the Income Tax Act with section 19 to disallow corporations deducting from their taxes the costs of advertising in foreign periodicals.

Following an aggressive lobbying campaign orchestrated by the U.S. Department of State that threatened to abort the ongoing negotiation of a bilateral Auto Pact, Ottawa exempted the two branch plants, *Time* and *Digest*, from the tax measure. Two fat foxes had been given a key to the chicken coop.[36] Protected against competition from other U.S. periodicals by tariff item 9958, *Time* and *Digest* actually expanded their share of Canadian advertising revenues in consumer magazines to 56 per cent by 1969.

In 1974, the Trudeau government introduced Bill C-58 to disallow *Time* and *Digest's* exemption. Advertising in all non-Canadian magazines became a non-deductible expense, though *Digest's* powerful lobbying resulted in its continuing to publish its English and French editions in Montreal. *Time* closed its Canadian edition, but, with Ottawa turning a blind eye to its evading tariff item 9958, it sent its American editorial content by microfilm to Montreal, where it continued printing. It even increased its revenues by cutting its advertising rates to compensate for their no longer being tax-deductible.[37]

Hegemon Illustrated

The success of these half-cocked policies was greater than could have been expected. By 1987, only one of the twelve largest-circulation magazines sold in Canada was U.S.-owned. *Maclean's*, which had moved from monthly to bi-monthly to weekly publication, had twice *Time's* circulation. By 1993, the Canadian magazine industry accounted for 68 per cent of circulation in Canada.[38] But it remained vulnerable. Its total revenues in 1992 were $850 million, with $17 million in exports to the United States and a profit margin of 2.5 per cent. In contrast, the U.S. industry generated $22 billion in revenues, with $624 million of exports to Canada, and earned a 12 per cent profit.[39]

While these returns would have been sensationally good in Canada, they were alarming to Wall Street, which observed that the U.S. magazine industry's share of the American advertising market had shown no growth for a decade. The agreed remedy was to buttress sales abroad.[40] In this spirit, Time Warner decided to launch *Sports Illustrated Canada* (*SIC*) as a new split-run venture printed in Richmond Hill, Ontario, and obtained Ottawa's blessing by submitting its business plan to the Investment Canada Agency, which approved the proposal, deeming it consistent with its mandate to encourage foreign investment.[41] ICA had not bothered to consult the Department of Communications, which had responsibility for cultural policy.

The Canadian magazine industry panicked, and with cause. It feared that *SIC* would create a precedent, inviting a flood of some 120 more split-run magazines into the consumer and business trade markets. The competition of magazines with higher production values but lower ad rates would effectively destroy the Canadian industry by vacuuming up its advertising revenue base.[42] But when the Canadian Magazine Publishers Association pressed Ottawa to invoke tariff item

9958, Revenue Canada demurred. Because *SIC* was going to send its editorial copy by satellite to a printing plant in Richmond Hill, there would be no magazines physically crossing the border that could legally be interdicted by customs agents. Time Warner had successfully violated the spirit though not the letter of the Canadian law.

Responding to a task force report it commissioned in the spring of 1993 to review the problem of split-run magazines[43] and smarting from its defeat over Country Music Television, the Chrétien government took an uncharacteristically radical step. Bill C-103 levied a prohibitive, 80 per cent excise tax on the value of the advertising revenue contained in every issue of a split-run magazine. Furthermore, *SIC* was not to be granted an exemption. The Ottawa cultural policy community believed that this new legislation was compatible with the WTO's new global trade rules. Because it applied to any magazine, whether Canadian- or American-owned, that had less than 80 per cent Canadian content, it did not violate the principle of national treatment. And because Canada had not committed itself to include advertising under the General Agreement on Trade in Services, this tax on advertising would be sheltered from attack through GATS.

Washington knew better. Given CUFTA's grandfathering of existing cultural policies, it decided to attack by taking the global route in order to get a judgment in Geneva. The U.S. hoped that the WTO's brand-new dispute adjudication would strike down cultural protectionism in Canada, setting a precedent for policy in cultural trade for the whole world. Following the ritual first step of requesting in March 1996 'consultations' with Ottawa, which refused to withdraw its legislation, the Americans formally requested that the WTO establish a panel to resolve their grievance. In making their case in September, they contested not just Canada's new excise tax, but its old tariff code 9958, and, while they were at it, the magazine industry's ancient postal subsidies. The argumentation on each of these issues was complex and highly legalistic. The panel largely accepted the American position. When Canada appealed, the WTO's Appellate Body (AB) revised the decision and managed in its June 1997 findings to make things worse for Canada.

Ottawa had lost on all three fronts – tariff item 9958, the excise tax, and postal subsidies. The AB judged *tariff item 9958* to be inconsistent with Article XI:1 of the GATT 1994, which prohibits the quantitative restriction of imports. The panel had flatly rejected Canada's claim that it was admissible under Article XX(d), which allows trade measures necessary to secure compliance with other legitimate policies – in this case, preservation of a Canadian magazine industry. The U.S. position that the tariff gave Canadian magazine publishers a monopoly over advertising revenue and so a competitive advantage over imported foreign magazines had prevailed.

The issue about the prohibitive *excise tax* focused on whether American split-run magazines should be considered products that were 'like' Canadian magazines and so requiring national treatment. In vain, Ottawa's lawyers advanced the cultural defence. They argued that, because it is intended 'for intellectual consumption as opposed to physical use ... the intellectual content of a cultural good such as a magazine must be considered its prime characteristic ... Editorial material developed for the Canadian market reflects a Canadian perspective and contains specific information of interest to Canadians. The content is *qualitatively* different from editorial material copied from foreign publications.'[44] A split-run magazine was in its cultural essence not like a Canadian magazine. Futhermore, Canada claimed that, since advertising was a service and since Canada had not committed advertising to be covered by the GATS, it was perfectly free to tax advertising in split-run magazines without the WTO's having a say in the matter: it was not bound to provide national treatment in advertising services.

Wrong on both counts, said the AB: 'A periodical is a good comprised of two components: editorial content and advertising content. Both components can be viewed as having service attributes, but they combine to form a physical product – the periodical itself.'[45] Hence national treatment under GATT, if not under GATS, applied, and to Canada's disadvantage. Although the AB accepted Canada's argument that split-run and Canadian magazines were not 'like products,' it ruled that they were 'directly competitive or substitutable.' Canada's whole argument against split-run editions as unfair competition for local periodicals was used against it. Graphically demonstrating the blindness of trade norms to cultural concerns, the AB opined that American and Canadian magazines had to be given national treatment *because* they compete: 'newsmagazines, like *Time*, *Time Canada*, and *Maclean's* are directly competitive or substitutable in spite of the 'Canadian' content of *Maclean's*.'

Canada's *postal subsidies* lost on two grounds. The preferential scheme of postal rates, which gave greater discounts to Canadian than to foreign magazines, contravened the national treatment principle enshrined in GATT's Article III:4, requiring competitive opportunities for imported products no less favourable than for domestic goods. Then, thanks to a subsidy agreement with the Department of Canadian Heritage's Publications Assistance Program, Canada Post gave a better rate to Canadian than to foreign magazines. Although GATT's Article III:8(b) permits state subsidies, the AB ruled that the subsidy would in this case have to be a direct transfer of funds to the publishers, not a reduced postal rate.

The logic of commodification had prevailed over the logic of culture. Whatever the community-enriching values expressed by a cultural work, it was henceforth to be treated under global governance as a freely tradeable 'product,' whose commercial features were more significant than the ideas and cultural messages that it contained. Permissible cultural policy, as prescribed in Geneva, was henceforth reduced to direct cash subsidies to producers. This was a very blunt – and even dangerous – instrument, given the need for arm's-length relationships between the state and cultural producers and given the stigma attached to subsidies in neoconservative discourse.

The Americans' hat trick in Geneva was a crushing victory that made a mockery of the Mulroney government's boast in 1988 to have exempted culture from the disciplines of free trade. There is no indication that Mulroney's negotiators fought to exempt culture from the new rules being worked out in the Uruguay Round whose result the Chrétien team endorsed by signing on to the WTO with alacrity. As for Washington, it had accepted in 1987 the mix of tariff, tax, and postal subsidies that constituted Ottawa's policy of reserving Canadian advertising revenue for Canadian periodicals by agreeing to grandfather Canada's cultural policies. C-103's new excise tax had simply been designed to maintain this policy in the face of its evasion through Time Warner's exploiting a new technology. Nine years later, Washington had brilliantly exploited the WTO's fledgling judicial process to destroy this same magazine policy. Simultaneously it had fired a warning shot around the world – without having to make a single bargaining concession of its own. 'There is absolutely no doubt,' concluded the cultural policy scholar Ted Magder, ' that the WTO decision is the most dramatic single blow ever leveled against Canadian cultural policy.'[46]

Picking Up the Pieces

Ottawa's response was as devious as it was doomed. Before the House of Commons removed all its offending magazine policy measures on

October 17, 1998, Heritage Minister Sheila Copps tabled Bill C-55, which would have made it a criminal offence for split-run editions to accept Canadian advertising. The 'Foreign Publishers Advertising Services Act' was designed to address the Appellate Body's ruling by presenting the action as a pure services issue exempt from GATS and to force the United States, if it persisted, to start a new trade dispute. Tactically, it would thereby gain a couple of years' reprieve for the beleaguered Canadian magazine industry. By this action, Ottawa's trade community showed once again that it was too clever by half.

Washington was not amused by such cleverness. Rather than returning to Geneva with a complaint against Canada, it simply used the cover of NAFTA's 'notwithstanding' clause, 2005(2), to threaten retaliation against Ottawa for robbing it of what the WTO had awarded. It proposed to target $1 billion of Canadian sales in the United States, including steel exported from cultural minister Sheila Copps's own city of Hamilton.[47]

With Canadian steelmakers angrily telling Ottawa not to jeopardize their interests for the sake of Maclean-Hunter, the results were not long in doubt. Frosty negotiations between the neighbouring capitals began as Bill C-55 proceeded through Parliament's legislative process. As had been expected, the Chrétien government folded under the American pressure. What had not been anticipated was Ottawa's agreeing to turn the offending legislation into a law that implemented the U.S. magazine industry's agenda for Canada. Split-run magazines with no Canadian content would now be able to market up to 18 per cent of their advertising space to Canadian clients, who would be eligible for a 50 per cent tax deduction. The final Washington-Ottawa agreement also opened up the prospect of American-controlled alliances that let U.S. magazines take a 49 per cent ownership share in Canadian publishers.[48]

Not only had Canada played 'rule taker' in accepting nullification of its magazine policy by trade judges applying U.S.-made global rules. It had gone on to be 'rule maker' in a perverse way. Ottawa had turned Washington's demands on behalf of its publishing giants into domestic legislation that made its market safer for American than for Canadian publishers.

CUFTA had given a thumbs-up to established cultural policies that kept some limited spaces in the Canadian economy for nationally owned entities producing locally made cultural content. But Time Warner had cleverly used new satellite technology, and Washington had cleverly used the new WTO judiciary, to undo what it had previously, if reluctantly, accepted. Reaching back into Canadian political history, the supranational judges in Geneva had declared cultural policies democratically legislated years – even decades – earlier to be illegal in terms of the new global trade supraconstitution. And when Ottawa tried to achieve the same end of preserving a free zone for Canadian publishers in their own market by proposing new legislation that responded to the Geneva judges' interpretation of the WTO's terms, Washington switched from a legalistic, rules-based approach to a bullying, power-based mode. Disregarding NAFTA's paragraph 2005(2), which stipulated that retaliatory measures had to be 'of equivalent commercial effect,' it had threatened such massive punishment that it quickly forced Ottawa to its knees.

The lesson about trade rules, culture, and American behaviour seemed clear. When the global or continental rules worked for it, Washington made sure that they were applied to the letter. When they didn't, it resorted to the threat of force, bringing to mind Henry Kissinger's contention that, in its essence, globalization was just another word for Americanization.

Conclusion: Resistance Is Not Futile

This chapter has examined broadcasting and magazines. Had we looked at book publishing and film, we would have had further examples of state-assisted efforts to push back the American behemoth in order to create space for an always-precarious and chronically limited Canadian cultural production. In our quest to assess the impact of globalization in the era of neoconservatism, the prime force of continuity in cultural policy is the U.S. entertainment industry's unrelenting defence of every inch of the Canadian turf that it has occupied while pressing to move into any space still eluding it. The prime change is Washington's brilliant tactical exploitation of the new trade regimes – whether continental, global, or both in combo – to support its biggest export industry after aerospace and defence. This change is significant but not transformational. The hegemon has not given up the use of force when it does not achieve its desired results through playing by the rules.

For Canada as dependent and penetrated periphery, the difference between a Keynesian and a neoconservative paradigm was less dramatic in the cultural field than one might have expected. Neither the

Diefenbaker, nor the Pearson, nor the Trudeau governments had been entirely convinced that cultural integrity was sufficiently important to be worth provoking Washington's wrath. Even when U.S. interests were not directly affected, Ottawa showed only a modest commitment to cultural concerns. Compared to the much more culturally aware countries of continental Europe, whose languages already provided powerful built-in protections against Americanization, Canadian governmental support for the arts appeared niggardly, even in its most generous moments.

Since Liberal cultural policies relied largely on an economic, job-creating rationale, neoconservatives had little fault to find with what they inherited. Furthermore, their very success in creating jobs and attracting tourist dollars gave a burgeoning cultural community considerable clout. Initial attempts to shrink cultural funding provoked substantial resistance, particularly in Quebec. Although Progressive Conservative party militants favoured privatizing the CBC or abolishing the Canada Council, such libertarian actions were never seriously considered by the Mulroney government. Its successor arguably did far more damage to the CBC by its draconian cuts to its budget.

In Ontario, home-grown neoconservatism showed its colours in savage cutbacks for the cultural sector that defied globalization's imperative to nurture the local. Whereas courting TNCs requires offering them culturally vibrant locations that satisfy the demands of skilled employees for a high quality of life, the province's Common Sense Revolution treated the cultural and even the sports sectors as unnecessary and useless luxuries unworthy of sustained government support.

The story is far from over. The convergence of computer and communications technologies will make it even more difficult for the state to retain a protected economic space for its cultural producers in the electronic media. Both the internet and satellites are border-erasing technologies that provide individuals virtually unlimited global access and represent a formidable challenge to the regulatory power of government. The CRTC has already declared that it will not try to regulate the internet. GATS-driven liberalization of telecommunications will facilitate the creation of global multimedia oligopolies with little concern for preserving either national cultural integrity or domestic corporate ownership. While competition rules may have some regulatory effect on transnational mergers and alliances among television, print, satellite, and internet companies, cultural policy seems destined to diminishing salience.

The contradictions continue. While threatened domestically as never before, Canadian artists are enjoying unprecedented success abroad. Shania Twain and Céline Dion are global stars. The Cirque du Soleil has become a burgeoning transnational purveyor of spectacles, with headquarters still in Quebec City. Three decades of government measures to develop a commercially successful feature film industry have borne few fruits. But these efforts have installed in Montreal, Toronto, and Vancouver a vibrant film industry servicing Hollywood's insatiable demand for 'product.' These cities have screenwriters, actors, costume and set designers, camera operators, and sound engineers; editing facilities, recording studios, special effects expertise, and computerized animation; and clusters of small production companies. They can compete for business as production sites on the basis of high technical skills and exchange rate-induced low costs.[49] While the products of 'Hollywood north' are in some sense Canadian, streetscapes are shot to simulate Chicago or New York in order to satisfy the tastes of the largest global market, that of American viewers. These 'runaway' productions are far from satisfying movie workers in Hollywood, who blame Canada for unfairly stealing jobs from them.

While Canada plays periphery to the American hyperpower, it also remains an intermediate power of some substance on the world stage. With the WTO castrating its magazine policy and threatening its autonomy in all cultural fields, Ottawa has turned to building an international coalition to have the global rules changed. Frustrated in Geneva, the irrepressible Sheila Copps became an international activist. She took the lead in forming an International Network on Cultural Policy to promote co-operation among like-minded countries, including France, which also wants to sustain its national culture in the face of growing Americanization.[50]

Even domestically, with national treatment forcing officials to abandon ownership-based policies, efforts are being made to rethink cultural policy. To the extent that creating room for Canadian content occurs at the expense of U.S. control over that space, cultural policy operates in a zero-sum game with American corporate interests, which demand compensation or U.S. retaliation if their earnings are 'expropriated.' Instead, the economist Daniel Schwanen advocated extending norms on Canadian content from broadcasting to other media. Legislating quotas for domestic content could ensure that, whoever owns the publishers, there will be nationally produced books on the chains' shelves and Canadian stories on the newsstands.[51]

The Canadian state, which has never doubted the need for excellent communications systems, has always been uncertain about whether and how to affect the cultural content of what those systems communicate.[52] This irresolution reflects Canada's active connivance in its own economic dependence. American dominance is challenged only tangentially because many Canadians do not strongly oppose it.[53] Such inconstancy demonstrates the basic tension between preferences in industrial policy to increase jobs and production in Canada and priorities in cultural policy to replace foreign with Canadian cultural content. The state may be on the defensive in the face of neoconservative globalism, but in the cultural industries central to its processes of identity formation, it is not dead yet.

Nor is diplomacy a dead art. But the limits to Canadian foreign policy autonomy have been drawn as tightly under an American-led global war against terrorism as are the possibilities for autonomous cultural expression within a Time-Warner-led global campaign for market dominance.

19 The Diplomatic State: Lockstep under Hegemonic Dominance

As a newly hired lecturer at the University of Toronto in the mid-1960s, I was as middle-of-the-road internationally and as conservative domestically as my Tory parents. But the senseless and devastating war in Vietnam alienated me and legions of my contemporaries, from the American myths on which we had grown up. When Prime Minister Lester Pearson became mired in what seemed to be a satellitic compliance with the United States's disastrous imperial overreach, I joined some academic friends to write him a letter protesting Canada's exports of military equipment that supported the American war effort. Pearson replied that Canada could not afford to lose the thousands of jobs that were at stake.

We were shocked that for a statesman who had been awarded a Nobel peace prize for mediating British-French hostilities with Egypt through middle-power peacekeeping, pragmatism dictated that narrow economic interests should prevail over what seemed like elementary diplomatic wisdom. Our reaction was to reflect in print on what should be the shape of An Independent Foreign Policy for Canada? *– the title of the resulting book I edited that argued Canada should not automatically adopt identical positions to those of the United States on such issues as the first use of nuclear weapons and the diplomatic isolation of the People's Republic of China.*[1]

However justifiable our positions may have been in ethical terms, they certainly revealed how little I knew about the political economy of Canadian diplomacy. As an undergraduate in Toronto I had studied French, Russian, and history. At Oxford the economics and politics to which I was exposed taught me next to nothing about the realities of the Cold War. When I specialized as a doctoral student in Paris, I focused on the Soviet Union's impact on India. Back in Canada, where I redirected my research and teaching interests to the Canadian-American relationship, it took me another several years to learn the geopolitical-economic realities of Canada's position in the attic of North America.

In the late 1930s, when the hitherto unthinkable threat to North America from Nazi Germany and imperial Japan was becoming thinkable, the elected leaders of the United States and Canada set the template for the way they would cope with common security threats. In a speech in Kingston, Ontario, on August 18, 1938, Franklin Delano Roosevelt declared that his country 'would not stand idly by' if Canada were attacked. Two days later, William Lyon Mackenzie King responded with his own declaration from the sleepy town of Woodbridge, Ontario, to the effect that 'enemy forces should not be able to pursue their way either by land, sea or air to the United States across Canadian territory.'

Thus defined as a willing American protectorate, Canada's military relationship with the United States passed through various phases – most notably, active economic and later military co-operation during the final four years of the Second World War. Mobilization for that total war made it easy for the two countries to move towards more complete military and economic integration during the Cold War that followed. Blending Canada into a single military system was institutionally effected by the Permanent Joint Board of Defence (PJBD) and the North American Air Defence Command (NORAD). After the Pentagon indirectly aborted Canada's production of the Avro Arrow – a military aircraft far superior to any American plane on the drawing board – Washington helped resolve the resulting crisis in the Canadian aerospace industry by signing the Defence Production Sharing Agreements, which allowed Canadian-based firms to bid on Pentagon contracts.

For the next four decades, Canadian governments endorsed successive strategic doctrines on nuclear retaliation issued by the Pentagon in response to new circumstances and adopted new technologies using constantly improved missiles and satellites. Canadians may have been uncomfortable living under the flight path of bombers and missiles that might be shot down in any U.S.-USSR exchange. None the less, most of them were squarely on the American side in the Cold War, and they accepted the calculus of permanent risk of total annihilation.

A number of understandings completed this picture of happy continental co-operation. If Canadians didn't want the Americans taking over their airspace, they had to practise the policy of 'defence against help' – do it to the Pentagon's satisfaction, or have the job done for them. Eager to oblige, the Canadian armed forces lobbied for equipment to participate within U.S.-defined parameters. In order to produce the requisite weapon systems using leading-edge technology, Ottawa negotiated with U.S. contractors to offset the huge costs by sourcing and producing many of their components in Canada.

Another subtext in the dyad's dialogue was American leaders pressing a cost-conscious Ottawa to spend more on weapons. Canadian prime ministers periodically returned the compliment, counselling moderation on their more aggressive American counterparts. Pearson experienced the dangers inherent in offering unsolicited advice to the hegemon when early in 1965, during a speech at Temple University, he suggested a pause in U.S. bombing of North Vietnam to encourage Hanoi to negotiate a peace treaty.[2] President Lyndon Johnson was so enraged that he summoned his Canadian counterpart to the presidential retreat at Camp David on April 3, 1965. Taking Pearson out on the verandah, Johnson shook him by the lapels and shouted in his face, 'Don't piss on my carpet!'

The moral was clear. Washington was deaf to Canada's voice when it believed its vital interests to be at stake. Ottawa's vaunted 'special relationship,' which generally exempted Canadians from damaging U.S. measures against foreign competitors, was premised on a 'quiet diplomacy' that forbade public expressions of divergent views such as those Pearson had ventured.

Trudeau's Variations in Diplomatic Autonomy

When Pierre Trudeau succeeded Pearson at 24 Sussex Drive in 1968, he shared some of these positions, though not out of anti-Americanism. For Canada's self-defined rationalist prime minister, foreign policy autonomy was a matter not of economics over politics but, as he liked to put it, of reason over passion. In his view, the Canadian fear of offending the hegemon next door was part of an attitudinal problem located in its diplomats' excessive involvement with the excitement of high politics and their consequent disconnection from more mundane realities at home. No longer should the Department of External Affairs expend so much energy trying to impress the major powers. It should direct its diplomatic efforts at a hard-nosed defence of Canada's national interests.

In the review of Pearsonian diplomacy that the new prime minister caused External Affairs to produce,[3] he pushed his bureaucrats to reappraise Canada's emphasis on supporting U.S. leadership in the Cold War, as compared to other priorities. Circumstances had changed. After a decade of détente, Canada had, of course, to support a U.S.-defined approach to *international peace and security*, but it had other interests to pursue. It needed *economic prosperity* to build the Just Society that Trudeau had envisioned during his leadership campaign. And – most important to him, given the mounting threat of separatism in Quebec, which had been key to his electoral success – the country had to defend its *national unity*.

It could pursue only one of these three objectives free of American constraint. As code for combating separatism, *national unity* in foreign policy meant counteracting Gaullist support for Quebec's campaign to achieve international recognition. Since Washington was also concerned about French intervention in Quebec, which it considered its own backyard, and because it had its own problems with France's obstreperousness, the U.S. State Department did not get in the way of the national unity component of Trudeau's foreign policy.

Trudeau did find, as had his eminent predecessor, that he was boxed in when his views on how to enhance *international peace and security* were out of step with Washington's. The Pentagon vigorously resisted his encouraging détente between the Soviet Union and the West by reducing the Canadian garrison in Europe and by proposing the denuclearization of the North Atlantic Treaty Organization (NATO).[4]

Even when Ottawa's view of the international system coincided with U.S. perceptions, the exercise of Canada's diplomatic autonomy could cause friction. Trudeau's principled determination formally to recognize the People's Republic as China's legitimate government earned him President Richard Nixon's personal opprobrium. Nixon called the prime minister an 'asshole' not because he thought Canadian policy wrong-headed but because the prime minister and his secretary of state for external affairs, Mitchell Sharp, had upstaged the United States by managing the trick in October 1970, just one ping-pong ball's bounce ahead of Nixon and his national security adviser, Henry Kissinger.

Although partisan congruence between a Democratic Johnson and a Liberal Pearson had not prevented conflict between the two, ideological difference could further aggravate political tensions. When the White House was occupied by a conservative Republican while the

Prime Minister's Office was held by a liberal Liberal, confrontations over both bilateral and multilateral issues were likely to be more acute than when the two heads of government shared a common public philosophy. This was the case in the early 1970s, when personal pique jeopardized the other facet of Trudeau's diplomatic vision, *economic prosperity*.[5] On August 15, 1971, President Richard Nixon came within an inch of turning the screws even tighter on Canada by abrogating the Auto Pact.

A backward glance over the main features of Canadian foreign policy in the late Keynesian era showed a middle power of some international substance.[6] On *national unity* it had successfully contained the effects of Gaullist support for international recognition of Quebec. In the early 1980s, under the socialist president François Mitterrand, Paris finally normalized relations with Ottawa.[7]

Regarding *international peace and security*, its diplomats' intellectual contributions earned Canada a significant role in multilateral affairs as a member of the G7 and many other international organizations. Like his predecessor, Trudeau developed gravitas as a senior, experienced, and skilled head of government who intervened with verve, if not always with success, in the great issues of the Commonwealth, the Francophonie, the Third World, and the Cold War. With East-West tensions escalating in 1983, Trudeau had argued against the sabre-rattling of Margaret Thatcher and Ronald Reagan, who were sharpening their rhetoric against a still-dangerously nuclear, even 'evil,' Soviet Union.[8] Whatever Reagan's displeasure about Trudeau's peace initiative or his Third World advocacy, nobody shook him by the lapels, and he had not kowtowed to those 'pipsqueaks in the Pentagon' who derided his concerns about the accidental triggering of a global holocaust.

In Canada's pursuit of its own *economic interests*, the bilateral relationship remained central. Efforts under the 'Third Option' in the late 1970s to diversify by expanding economic relations with Europe and Japan bore no significant fruit.[9] Tensions with Washington escalated when Trudeau espoused energy nationalism just as his friend and confidant, the Democrat Jimmy Carter lost the White House to Ronald Reagan and his neoconservative Republicans. Although the Trudeau Liberals did not directly bend to the Reaganites' (and Alberta's) insistence that they axe the National Energy Program of 1980, the collapse of world petroleum prices sounded its death knell in 1982.

Foreign policy thinking throughout the whole Diefenbaker-Pearson-Trudeau era had been dominated by the ideas of the Western diplomatic mainstream, which saw Canada's role as a self-effacing adjunct to a benign American mission in the world. Sniping from the academic sidelines, Canadian nationalists had questioned the benevolence of a hegemon run amok and urged a noisy diplomacy to resist its dangerously misguided policies. The foreign policy trajectories of Lester Pearson and Pierre Trudeau largely reflected the diplomatic corps' response to an evolving balance of forces within the East-West confrontation. Only on selected high-profile issues such as China and nuclear arms did Trudeau intervene to give Canadian diplomacy his personal touch. In sum, Canada's interests abroad were defined by the Department of External Affairs, with occasional tweaking from the Prime Minister's Office.

Room for Manoeuvre within Continental Integration: The Mulroney Years

The interplay between internal and external forces of change and, within these categories, between idea- and interest-driven pressures, should have been clear in the mid-1980s for three reasons. Brian Mulroney came to power in 1984 with a dismissive critique of Trudeau's alleged anti-Americanism and promised to restore the special Canada-U.S. relationship from the St Laurent and Pearson eras. As the head of a self-defined conservative party, he next negotiated agreements on trade liberalization that introduced supraconstitutional constraints on economic policy makers. The third factor was the collapse of the Soviet bloc which transformed the basic paradigm of post-1945 international relations. Despite these new and powerful impulses for change, Canadian foreign policy showed marked continuity with its recent past.

While leader of the opposition, Mulroney had taken every opportunity to belittle Trudeau's handling of Canadian-American relations. In his 1984 election campaign he vowed to 'refurbish' that relationship. Canada would not criticize U.S. policy, as Trudeau had done so gratuitously, but give it the 'benefit of the doubt.' Once in office, Mulroney flaunted his warm personal contacts with Ronald Reagan, based on their common ideology. To restore Canada's special relationship, he speedily dismantled what remained of the Foreign Investment Review Agency and the National Energy Program. Within a year he rejected the Third Option, declaring his intention to pursue the once-preposterous second option – greater economic integration within the American system.

Mulroney's benefit-of-the-doubt approach to U.S. initiatives found expression in vocal support for Reagan's Strategic Defense Initiative (a.k.a. Star Wars) and the U.S. bombing of Libya in 1986.[10] Ingratiating himself with Reagan's successor, Mulroney loudly approved the invasion of Panama by President George H.W. Bush in 1989, despatching warships and jet bombers from Canada's depleted armed forces to join the president's Gulf War against Saddam Hussein in 1991.

In military affairs, Mulroney's cabinet proved more Catholic than the Pope, approving the Department of National Defence's bellicose White Paper, *Challenge and Commitment*, which declared Canada had to contribute more troops to the West's fight for freedom and democracy against tyranny and communism.[11] In tune with an ever-hawkish Pentagon, but out of step with a White House bent on co-operation with the Kremlin, the missile-rattling document appeared just in time for the Berlin Wall to fall and the Cold War to implode.

Despite his seemingly subservient foreign policy, Mulroney was not as supine as his opponents alleged.[12] He distanced Canada from Washington on the Strategic Arms Limitation Treaty and even on some policies concerning Central America to which the Reagan administration was deeply committed. The Progressive Conservative government was notably more resistant to Washington's Cuba policy than the Liberals had been. Its Foreign Extraterritorial Measures Act in 1984 made it illegal for firms operating in Canada to comply with U.S. laws that attempted to prevent foreign corporations from dealing with Fidel Castro's Cuba.[13]

Mulroney's responses to South Africa were also tougher in practice than his predecessor's good-words-but-few-deeds approach. Apartheid had three characteristics that offered a perfect opportunity for Mulroney to demonstrate his diplomatic autonomy. For one thing, because economic sanctions against Pretoria would have little impact on U.S. economic well-being, they did not threaten significant American interests. Equally, sanctions would hurt few Canadian companies, so the economic costs to Canada were low – although they had been too high for the Trudeau government to accept. Lastly, to denounce institutionalized racism far away on another continent was a moral issue conveniently suited to Canadians' fondness for the evocation of noble values and had a high level of political support. Canadian sanctions against apartheid displeased Reagan and angered Margaret Thatcher, Mulroney's other ideological role model.[14] Still, apart from the danger of being brained by a handbag at No. 10 Downing Street,

Mulroney showed that he could adopt a mildly independent stance without suffering reprisals.

Mulroney's capacity for limited autonomy within the American imperium emerged from the fact that the leaders of the U.S. and Canada shared similar worldviews. Although the keystone of this foreign policy was recreating Pearson's special relationship, the practice of quiet diplomacy in the 1980s and 1990s would have required more self-restraint than the boy from Baie Comeau could command. For its part, Washington was not inclined to offer Ottawa the exemptionalism – making exceptions to U.S. international economic policies – that would have contradicted CUFTA's mission of imposing strict rules on Canada.[15] A new relationship had been established, to be sure, but it was special in a different sense. U.S. hegemony was exercised not through unwritten conventions but through a formal document.

The question raised by free trade was whether institutionalizing the periphery-hegemon relationship would diminish or enhance Canada's diplomatic independence. In his influential report recommending continental free trade, Donald Macdonald urged not just the possibility but the necessity of greater autonomy.

> Given the high degree of global uncertainty that this Commission has identified, it is important that Canadians understand both the privileged position we occupy on this planet and the human imperative this places on Canada to provide leadership in those areas of critical concern to the world, where our nation has a capacity to provide that leadership. *Commissioners recommend that as a matter of high priority, Canada pursue a more activist foreign policy* based on the concept that Canada now occupies a more responsible position as one of the *principal powers.*[16]

To nationalists, it appeared blatantly contradictory for Macdonald to push for all-out economic integration with the world's superpower in one chapter and then advocate a more 'activist' foreign policy for Canada in another. They argued that such political independence could be built only on the foundation of economic independence.

Complicating this long-standing debate was the end of the Cold War. Even if Canada had been reined in by NAFTA, a formalized system of governance operating by strict, U.S.-made norms, didn't the new freedom created by the Soviet collapse allow Canada to pursue Macdonald's 'more activist foreign policy'? In this optic, the rearticulated balance of global forces released Canada from its role as territorial buffer between the two superpowers. In principle, it freed Canada of the major restraint, the need for NATO solidarity in the East-West struggle. No longer captive to NORAD, Ottawa would not have to be driven by the Pentagon's strategic views.

Room for Manoeuvre within Global Governance:
The Chrétien Years

The Mulroney government's preoccupation with negotiating trade liberalization both continentally with NAFTA and globally with the GATT left it little energy with which to test the limits of its new geopolitical freedom before the American voters ousted George Bush in 1992 and the Canadian electorate demolished the Conservatives in 1993. This apparent sea change masked a basic continuity. Jean Chrétien was, practically speaking, as conservative as Mulroney, and Bill Clinton was to the right of most of his fellow Democrats. In short, the changing of the guards in Washington and Ottawa set the scene for another harmonious relationship between two right-of-centre governments keen on globalization.

Though anxious to distance himself from Mulroney's reputation as an American lapdog, Jean Chrétien, as the little guy from Quebec's resource hinterland, was comfortable with continentalism. Unobtrusively, he set about developing a collegial rapport with the U.S. president based on repeated encounters at summits and long walks together along the quiet fairways of their countries' greenest golf courses. Their mutual accommodation established the context for Ottawa's redefinition of its foreign policy in the post-Cold War era.

Rethinking Foreign Policy

The Liberals set out to review their foreign policy options in the time-honoured fashion of new governments. The difference this time lay in the partial privatization of Canada's international relations industry and the new strength of the public's input.

'Privatization' is usually about business takeovers of public corporations. The privatization of Canadian foreign policy consisted of private foundations' contributing funds for the study of certain international issues and offering the resulting reports as recommendations to government. The Montreal-based CRB Foundation, whose largesse derived from the Bronfman family's liquor fortune, adopted the Arab-

Israeli conflict. The Toronto-based Walter and Duncan Gordon Charitable Foundation invested over $1 million in the development of an Arctic Council. The same foundation got the jump on the Liberals' official review by funding the Canada 21 Council, a hand-picked group from the internationalist wings of the two mainline parties. Orchestrated by Tom Axworthy, Pierre Trudeau's last and most progressive principal secretary, the council hoped through its report, by Janice Stein and Pierre Pettigrew, to set the agenda for the debate on defence.[17]

Internationally oriented non-governmental organizations (NGOs), quietly active for a long time, had lost their deference towards elite opinion and felt entitled to extensive consultations with governments. The umbrella Canadian Council for International Cooperation (CCIC) had responsibly represented the humanitarian and development community for many years. A newly concocted National Forum on Canada's International Relations attended by 130 participants as well as a hundred parliamentarians and government officials heard briefs from the CCIC and received Canada 21's report, which it put on the internet as the prelude to the parliamentary phase of the process.

Given Chrétien's insistence that NAFTA was not up for debate, the House of Commons Standing Committee on Foreign Affairs and International Trade dealt with relatively uncontroversial issues in the years after the treaty was signed. It consulted the people who had drafted the National Forum Report, heard testimony from about 500 witnesses, received nearly 700 other reports, and commissioned expert papers on security, trade, aid, and culture.[18] It then boiled down what it had heard and read, producing yet another report, so that the Department of Foreign Affairs and International Trade (DFAIT) could, finally, draft a response to the parliamentary review.

Having promised in their election Red Book to democratize foreign policy, the Liberals had created a *process* more significant than its *product*. Genuflecting before the familiar trinity of peace, prosperity, and national unity, DFAIT's *Canada in the World* proposed a poorly thought-out three-pillared model for Canadian diplomacy reminiscent of Pearson's internationalism.

Pillar 1 ('the promotion of prosperity and employment') characterized the Canadian-American relationship as that of two 'sovereign partners, *acting as equals*.' It even had the brass to use Third-Option language about diversifying the country's trade relations without apparently understanding how a half-century's relentless trend to trade integration with the U.S. economy had been made irreversible by NAFTA.[19] Nor did the government care to admit that Canada's economic muscle was puny. In 1992, the Canadian gross domestic product (GDP) was $629 billion – relatively low compared to its fellow G7 members, with Italy and Brittain at $1,030 billion, Germany at $1,502 billion, and the United States at an overwhelming $6,406 billion. The rise of various developing economies had diminished Canada's relative importance. But the threatened loss of membership in the great power club seemed to stimulate, rather than to diminish, Canadian efforts to participate in a global governance for which its diplomatic culture as a mid-sized, federal, binational power gave it a historical predilection.

Pillar 3 ('the projection of Canadian values and culture') was an uncomfortable mix of the familiar and the fantastic. Familiar was the insistence on human rights and democratic governance as values to be defended abroad. Fantastic was extending Canada's culture abroad which, for the first time in an official statement of diplomatic strategy, was presented as a way to promote Canadian values, develop national identity, and further national interests.[20] But DFAIT resisted this stance. Though a key source of identity and a valuable commodity in the information age (as described in chapter 18), Canadian culture lacked the corporate might to compete globally with the American entertainment industry. Diplomats thought that projecting National Film Board movies in Canadian embassies abroad was 'soft and squishy' work, which hardly counted as a source of power abroad. With the department stiffly resisting the culturalization of Canadian foreign policy, the cultural pillar was never erected.[21]

Pillar 2 ('the protection of our security, within a stable global framework') proposed a more promising foundation for a Liberal foreign policy than the other two because it recognized that the world had changed since 1989. No great power conflict existed to necessitate regional security measures. Of the 108 post-Cold War armed conflicts, 101 were fought *within* rather than *between* states. In contrast to inter-bloc nuclear war, the issue was how to respond to these intra-state conventional wars by peace*building* rather than peace*keeping*.[22] This reformulation of Canada's strategic interest broadened the conception of security from participation within NATO and NORAD to embrace new, more complex political realities. Although the rise of terrorism was flagged, it was only on a par with international crime and trafficking in drugs, people, and arms. The point made by Pillar 2 was that global security had shifted its focus from the sovereignty of states to the safety and protection of people.[23]

Conceptually weak though the first and third pillars were, the idea of a 'human security' agenda proved no more robust for André Ouellet, the francophone minister of external affairs. He had been given this prestigious position in recognition of his seniority in the Liberal Party's Quebec wing. Ouellet had dutifully presided over the foreign policy review but had shown no inclination to use its conclusions for defending security interests with any particular brio. His passivity did not prevent his colleagues from elbowing their way into his domain.

Oh, What a Fishy War

On March 9, 1995, Canadian authorities charged the captain of a Spanish trawler with illegal fishing in international waters. After a maritime chase ended with shots being fired across her bow, the *Estai* had been towed to St John's harbour, where an investigation led by Brian Tobin, federal minister of fisheries and oceans, found it to be using illegal small-mesh nets. It transpired that 79 per cent of the trawler's catch – double the allowable limit – was undersized, according to the standards set by the Northwest Atlantic Fisheries Organization (NAFO).[24] In the minister's view, the Spanish fishing fleet was undermining the Canadian government's own limits on total allowable catch, designed to reverse the stock exhaustion that had devastated the Atlantic provinces' economies.

While Canada argued that it was enforcing NAFO regulations, the European Union viewed such use of force at sea to be an outright violation of international law. A born populist with the requisite histrionic skills for stirring the public's passions, Tobin was impatient with diplomacy. He wanted confrontation.[25] When negotiations in Brussels to resolve the impasse broke down, Chrétien, with Tobin and the ministers of defence, foreign affairs, and justice, ordered federal fisheries officers to arrest more Spanish trawlers in the disputed waters. A frigate and a destroyer were dispatched to the Grand Banks to back up six fisheries-patrol vessels and coast guard ships already in the area.[26] Since it was 1995 and not 1495, when Spain was a great sea power, Canada could stand firm on resource preservation against a country which could not retaliate militarily and on an issue that stood far beyond the U.S. national interest.

The glorious little Turbot War would foreshadow other independent, if less chauvinistic, Canadian forays into international diplomacy once DFAIT had articulated a 'human security' doctrine with global scope.

A Local Politician Goes Global

When Paul Martin's relentless budget cutting showed there was no possibility for the kind of liberal social policy reform that Lloyd Axworthy was championing as Minister of Human Resources Development, Chrétien gave his loyal ally a political plum. Replacing Ouellet in 1996 with the stubborn activist from Winnipeg was a surprising move by a prime minister not noted for taking risks.

The eldest son of United Church parents, Axworthy had done graduate work on foreign relations in the 1960s at Princeton, where the great internationalist Woodrow Wilson had once presided and where the American civil rights movement and protests against the Vietnam War radicalized the young Canadian. After a remarkable career as a grassroots community politician in a generally business-oriented party, Axworthy's appointment to DFAIT finally put him in a position where he could activate his international idealism.

Axworthy quickly applied to foreign affairs a personal style that he had developed in other departments, using outside experts and mobilizing community pressure to counteract the instinctive resistance of naturally conservative civil servants.[27] To offset a professional bureaucracy that had converted to neoconservative orthodoxy, he cultivated the NGO and academic communities in Canada to build independent political and informational support which allowed him to force the process of innovation within his new institutional environment.[28] When he created a Centre for Foreign Policy Development in 1995 'dedicated to ensuring that the voice of Canadians will be heard,' he was belatedly fulfilling a Liberal campaign promise from 1993.[29] But he was also arming himself with political resources to make an end run around his own department.

Axworthy was operating under a further constraint specific to neoconservatism – fiscal austerity. DFAIT's budget had been cut ten times since 1988–9, and cumulative cuts amounted to $292 million.[30] Years of fiscal shrinking were paralysing the department. Extensive staff cuts and long pay freezes had increased work pressure while reducing financial incentives, all with a devastating impact on professional morale.[31] In this situation Axworthy had a choice between conducting a minimal but economical foreign policy and inventing new ways to pursue an activist foreign policy on the cheap.[32]

Opting for activism, he declared Canada 'well-placed to succeed as a leader in a world where 'soft power' [the ability to convince rather than to coerce] is increasingly important,' thanks to the growing role played by new information technologies in international affairs.[33] Canada, he wrote,

> is one of the most wired nations in the world ... because we are a high-tech, human-resource rich nation accustomed to functioning in a bilingual, multicultural environment ... Even more important, underlying these [capacities] is a set of profoundly attractive values: democracy, bilingualism, multiculturalism, tolerance and respect for diversity, the rule of law, a market economy tempered by unifying social programmes, and flexible federalism.[34]

In an extraordinary display of persuasive power Axworthy proceeded to put together a coalition of regionally diverse and economically disparate states to crystallize their common interest. His multilateral effort culminated in 122 states signing in 1997 the Anti-Personnel Mine Ban Convention 'to eliminate the manufacture, use and export of anti-personnel landmines.'[35] Although the military heavy hitters such as China, Russia, and – most significant – the United States chose to participate only as observers, the other powers presented a remarkable show of unity. It was the most rapidly ratified treaty of its kind, achieved in less than fourteen months, and its success seemed to show that the end of the Cold War had indeed eroded many traditional constraints on Canadian praxis.[36]

The newly minted statesman presented a curious paradox. He reduced globalization's democratic deficit in the most elitist of all public policy fields by raising levels of citizen participation higher than they had ever been. As a grassroots politician, he was in his element developing a transnational network of NGOs that helped negotiate the text and even mobilize public opinion abroad to press other governments to sign.[37] The obverse of Pearsonian quiet diplomacy, this Ottawa Process, as Axworthy's diplomatic whirlwind was called, was energized by a partnership with domestic civil society groups and international allies,[38] which exposed policy to the test of publicity as it was being developed.[39]

Admirers claimed that the Ottawa Process created a model for a different way to make Canadian foreign policy. At first blush, the arguments favouring this kind of populist foreign policy were compelling. Opening up the negotiating process made it more transparent and involved individuals and organizations from outside DFAIT who had knowledge, expertise and passion in human rights, peacebuilding, and international development – qualities that the Department might lack and which gave the outsiders a legitimate interest in its policy pursuits.

Canadians seeking an association with international civil society and expressing concern for foreign problems through their involvement with NGOs had felt unrepresented by a government focused on narrow economic interests. Involving them in the policy-making process helped the government compensate for its inability to represent them and for its lack of connection with the transnational component of civil society. Open policy making also helped inform the public on a topic traditionally left to elites. By making government more meaningful for the *governed*, increased participation can also reinforce the policy decisions of the *governors*. In this way Canadian foreign policy practitioners bolstered their capacity to resist falling too easily into 'a comfortable acceptance of U.S. positions.'[40]

The secret to Axworthy's success in pursuing a human security agenda was his careful selection of niches in the international environment. Focusing on where and how Canada could be effective outside the zone of American control was the antithesis of Pearson's predilection for great power diplomacy in order to affect it from the side lines. ('Canada is important, but not important enough,' Pearson is supposed to have lamented, reflecting this nose-pressed-against-the-window desire to play in the big boys' game.) Finding niches was Axworthy's way to satisfy Canadians' need to feel significant on the world stage as a country with a distinct moral purpose. Whether Canada pushed the United States onto the paths of righteousness became a secondary issue.

Axworthy's enthusiasm for the International Criminal Court (ICC) underlined his interest in low-cost, high-visibility, symbolic initiatives. Canada chaired the preparatory commission for over two years, providing financial assistance for poorer countries to participate and leading the final vote, which was 120 to 7 in favour of its adoption.[41] The groundbreaking ICC statute treated war crimes on an individual rather than on a state basis while extending jurisdiction to crimes committed in internal conflicts,[42] thus shifting global governance in a direction important to a middle power.

Beyond anti-personnel mines and the ICC came small arms control, the rights of the child,[43] and the Hemispheric Dialogue Group on Drugs and Human Security in the Americas – Canada's choices to achieve the most results with the fewest resources. Their pursuit also connected the second pillar (which broadened the understanding of defence from military to *human* security) with a truncated third pillar (which trumpeted the promotion of Canadian values abroad sans the hawking of Canadian culture).

While many observers gave Axworthy credit for making a positive mark on the world stage with very meagre resources, his critics came down hard on his performance. The Ottawa *Citizen* headlined Kim Nossal's critique of his record 'Foreign Policy for Wimps.'[44] Osler Hampson and Dean Oliver denigrated 'the yawning contradictions' of a 'pulpit diplomacy' that was 'penny-wise, loonie-foolish' and revealed a 'distressing gap between the alluring promise of the new diplomacy, evoked so enthusiastically (and dogmatically) by the foreign minister, and the prospects for its success.'[45]

Denis Stairs dismissed a foreign policy forced into niche diplomacy and fuelled on soft power as mere voluntarism, a cosmetic cover-up:

> Canada's *real* foreign policy – the foreign policy grounded in deeply rooted constituency interests, the foreign policy that drives out other foreign policies whenever those other policies get in the way, the foreign policy to which domestic political imperatives ultimately apply – is Canada's economic foreign policy. And that is not the foreign policy with which the Minister of Foreign Affairs routinely deals.[46]

Stairs's elegant critique identified the underlying reality of foreign policy under continental integration. As Chrétien's first minister of international trade, Roy MacLaren, had unabashedly declared, 'Foreign policy *is* trade policy.' Given integration within an American system in which Ottawa primarily played the role of rule taker, the question, as posed by the Macdonald Commission, was whether Canada's trade preoccupation prevented it from widening its international commitments and expanding its global partnerships in order to become rule maker with like-minded political partners.

The tension between the low road of Canada's economic interests and the high road of its humanitarian values had been institutionalized under Trudeau in 1982, when he 'economized' Canadian diplomacy by shifting the trade commissioners from Industry, Trade and Commerce to External Affairs. By 1985, when the Mulroney government opted for free trade negotiations with Washington, this small band of trade-policy interlopers achieved ideational dominance within their new home. When the Chrétien Liberals rechristened it the Department of Foreign Affairs *and International Trade*, they were formally recognizing its schizophrenic essence.

It was widely understood, when the prime minister offered the left-wing nationalist Axworthy this plum, that he was not to reopen the wounds of the NAFTA debate. Ministers of international trade, whether Roy MacLaren (1994–6), Sergio Marchi (1996–9), or Pierre Petti-grew (1999–), would negotiate ever-more-intrusive economic agreements undisturbed by Axworthy's deeply felt reservations about trade liberalization. He was to find his niches elsewhere. He could pull an occasional feather from the American eagle's tail. But any resulting contretemps with the United States had to be on the high road of multi-lateralism, not on the low roads along which the continental political economy travelled.

Canada's reaction was swift, vocal, and decidedly negative to the passage of the U.S. Helms-Burton Act, which established sanctions against foreign companies dealing with Cuban assets seized from Americans during Castro's revolution. Since a number of Canadian corporations such as Sherritt International, which mined nickel for processing in its Saskatchewan smelters, did business profitably with Cuban corporations, Helms-Burton meant that their executives could be jailed as criminals should they set foot on U.S. soil.[47] Along with the European Union, Canada vigorously protested the extra-territoriality of this statute. ·

There were two main reasons for the surprisingly low cost of such insubordination. To start with, there was the ideological congruence between the two countries' leaderships. Canada's reservations about Helms-Burton were shared by President Clinton, forced by Congress to be its reluctant executor. Far from playing diplomatic renegade, Axworthy was compatible with the thinking of Third Way leaders such as Britain's Tony Blair, France's Lionel Jospin, Germany's Gerhard Schroeder, and Italy's Giuliano Amato.

Clinton's doctrine of Democratic Enlargement held many of the same truths to be self-evident as Axworthy's notions on human security. The U.S. president often favoured embracing the logic of globalization, by which he meant 'that everything, from the strength of our economy to the safety of our cities, to the health of our people, depends on events not only within our own borders, but half the world away.'[48] For Clinton, it was best to take a wide view of the national interest and look at international affairs more in terms of how the

United States could contribute to the international interest. This mode of thinking was definitely in tune with Axworthy's.

Trade liberalization paradoxically provided the second reason why Axworthy enjoyed a degree of freedom in carving out a distinctive role for Canadian foreign policy. The new economic regime set commonly accepted and impartially enforced rules. For Canadian foreign policy, the more relations were governed by rules, the less susceptible Canada was to finger twisting by an unhappy hegemon. When, for instance, Axworthy suggested denuclearizing NATO's forces, critics feared that Washington would retaliate at such lèse-majesté. But economic sanctions taken by Washington against Canada, which were not legitimated by the supraconstitutional norms in NAFTA or the WTO, would be overturned by the dispute panels that Ottawa would request under these organizations' aegis. In short, the institutionalization of the Canadian-American relationship gave Ottawa a security blanket permitting it some autonomy in its foreign policy.[49]

Beyond the conjunctural (congruity between the Canadian and American political leadership) and the institutional (economic integration based on rules) there has long been a multilateral element in Canada's foreign policy strategy vis-à-vis the United States. Canadian diplomats have traditionally preferred international sites for dealing with Washington other than on bilateral issues. During the Cold War, NATO was not just a military shield in Ottawa's view, but a forum in which Canada could air positions critical of American views with the likelihood that they would be supported by other alliance members. But as NATO's strategic importance deflated with the collapse of communism, so did much of its political utility to Canada.

In the light of Canada's loss of leverage through NATO, a revived United Nations provided the basic focus for its multilateral actions. For this reason, *Canada in the World* paid special attention to this venerable experiment in global governance, making a four-fold pledge – to strengthen the UN's capacity for preventive action; to conduct a review of the organization's activities so that it reflected a broader definition of global security; to improve the functioning of its decision-making bodies; and to help put it on a sound financial basis.[50] Canada's proposal for a rapid-reaction force to respond more quickly to crises and conflicts received broad support at the UN Security Council, and the initiative was implemented.

The 1990s also saw the European Community expand its membership and consolidate its diplomatic behaviour under the Single Europe

Act to form a European Union based in part on a common foreign and security policy. Whereas Canada was used to sustaining fruitful diplomatic relations with 'like-minded' countries such as Holland and Sweden, it found that these former allies' priority for achieving a European consensus on international issues deprived it of valuable interlocutors.

Getting squeezed out of its historic intimacy with Europe pushed Canada to reassess its equally historic disregard for the Latin zones of the Western Hemisphere. Occupying its long-empty seat in the Organization of American States (OAS) in the late 1980s had given Canada a common point of reference with the countries of Latin America. Since each government's foreign policy had to be formulated with a keen eye on the United States, their interaction in the OAS gave them strength in numbers. Despite a substantial cultural divide, Canada's instincts for multilateralism proved beneficial.

Axworthy was instrumental in coordinating reactions against the Helms-Burton Act in 1996 and isolating Washington, though to little effect.[51] A Canadian resolution at the OAS to condemn Helms-Burton gained near-unanimous support: only the United States opposed it. Latin Americans came to distinguish the Canadian variety of gringo from the Yankee. It was no accident that the OAS invited Axworthy in June 2000 to serve on the two-person inquiry into electoral abuse in Peru that preceded President Alberto Fujimori's flight from office. Ottawa's expanding ties with a number of countries in Latin America – especially its new, NAFTA-based relationship with Mexico – became useful minor assets to broaden its room for manoeuvre. Canada also participated actively in the pre-negotiations for the Free Trade Area of the Americas launched by the Miami Declaration of 1994 as an extension of CUFTA and NAFTA. If successfully negotiated, the FTAA would further limit Canadian sovereignty while increasing the federal state's role in hemispheric affairs.

If soft power offered Canada only limited prospects for developing a major new presence in South and Central America, hard power was even less promising. Canada's economic relations with the region remain minor, in both investment and trade. If NAFTA had not forced Ottawa to give Mexico special attention, its economic interests in that country would not have been reason enough in themselves.

Largesse looked no more useful for increasing hemispheric influence. In the Diefenbaker-Pearson-Trudeau years, Canadian aid to Third World countries focused first on the Commonwealth and then, with the fight against Gaullist support for Quebec separatism, francophone Africa. Official development assistance (ODA) had risen from 0.23 per cent of GDP in 1964 to 0.5 per cent in 1974 but fallen back to 0.48 per cent in 1984.[52] Continual budget whittling cut ODA to 0.43 per cent in 1994 and to a paltry 0.28 per cent by the end of the decade.[53] Canada could not declare 'freedom from fear' for all peoples as a foreign policy goal and pose as a new source of aid for struggling countries[54] when its real expenditures on aid had fallen by almost 50 per cent in less than a decade,[55] and when the foreign minister had not integrated reduction of poverty and international equity into his advocacy of human security.[56]

This decline of generosity had created a credibility gap about Canada's commitments. With aid money spread thinly over many long-time clients, dispensing development assistance was not a credible option for building Canadian influence in the Latin world. Even when Canada took a lead in North-South economic relations in response to various Christian NGOs' Jubilee movement, which demanded forgiveness of the poorest countries' debts, the initiative would benefit African rather that Latin countries.[57]

Furthermore, Canada's actual behaviour revealed values that were closer to those of other rich, English-speaking countries than to those of struggling Latin American nations. Most notably, its zealous advocacy of a neoconservative economic agenda often made Ottawa appear more an advocate of Washington's stances than a counterweight to them.

Life after Lloyd

Whether Lloyd Axworthy's contested achievements survive him will depend both on personalities and on geopolitics. Chances appeared slim in the aftermath of his retirement from politics in August 2000, when John Manley, Chrétien's long-serving minister of industry, replaced him as foreign minister. Manley's deep interests in economic policy bore no relationship to Axworthy's human security agenda.[58] Saying that 'bland works,' the new minister signalled his desire to return to pragmatic, quiet diplomacy that was deferential to Washington's desires.[59] This leadership change in DFAIT fortuitously aligned Canadian diplomacy with the more significant leadership change in the White House, where George W. Bush showed no inclination to continue a Clintonesque, neo-Wilsonian foreign policy.

The election of a Republican U.S. president and the eighteen-month tenure of a conservative foreign minister in Ottawa did not erase popular support for a human security agenda. Opinion polls consistently find that Canadians are passionate about world affairs. Far from being parochial, they have generous convictions about most international issues. It may be in response to this sentiment that Manley expressed reservations about the U.S. proposal to build a nuclear missile shield that would weaponize an already militarized space.[60] Nor was it accidental that the prime minister intervened to ensure that Canada kept its distance from the Bush administration's rejection in 2001 of the Kyoto protocol on environmental warming; he instructed his negotiators to sign on to the successor agreement negotiated in Brussels in the face of Washington's continuing boycott. The luxury of cultivating such small differences came to an end on September 11, 2001, when the world's geopolitical contours were redrawn.

Defence against Terror

Suddenly Ottawa reverted to the Cold War template of a global struggle between the forces of light and those of an evil, if invisible, empire. The stunning catastrophe suffered directly by New York and the Pentagon dragged Canada, which had been languishing far off the Bush administration's cognitive horizon, back to being centrally located on the U.S. defence perimeter.

At the level of *strategy*, Ottawa endorsed the Bush administration's analysis of Islamic terrorism as a world threat. Prime Minister Chrétien immediately seconded Bush's declaration of total war against terrorism and offered Canada's armed forces to support its first phase. But replacing the Soviet Union with al-Qaeda changed not just the nature but the location of the combat. Terrorism was a threat to be fought not only abroad but at home. No longer the air space between the USSR and the United States, Canada had become a territorial buffer for U.S. homeland defence against infiltration by fanatical enemies. The implications were grave. If Washington defined its front line of defence as a Fortress America by blockading its territorial boundaries along the 49th parallel, Canada's NAFTA-integrated economy would collapse.

Ottawa's practical military and security responses to the Americans' extreme reaction after September 11 were driven as much by economic self-interest as Pearson's had been in the Vietnam War. It needed the U.S. to feel that the traffic of goods and people across its Canadian border was safe. The decision to put 750 Canadian soldiers under U.S.

command in Afghanistan was something other than symbolic of Canada's good standing in the multilateral alliance. Ottawa chose not to offer its expertise in peacebuilding, which concentrates on reconstructing a civil society from the devastation of war. In volunteering to do Washington's dirty or – as it turned out when four Canadian soldiers were killed by an American bomb – deadly work in the mopping-up phase after its high-tech bombing war, the Chrétien government sent an unmistakable signal that Canada was fully on side, fully trustworthy.

More to the point, the federal government proceeded to strengthen Canada's internal defences against terrorism, not just to its own satisfaction but to that of its edgy neighbour. It knew Washington must feel its security was not jeopardized at its northern border crossing points, or in Canada's airports from which agents of *jihad* could fly into the United States, or at its seaports from which miniaturized weapons of mass destruction might be transshipped, or even in its embassies abroad where visas could be issued to potentially hostile immigrants.

The known infiltration of terrorist networks through all liberal capitalist societies required not so much new policies as tightening a number of existing laws and putting more state resources behind their implementation. Ottawa accordingly moved on a wide variety of fronts:

- controlling the flow of funds through legitimate financial institutions to suspect networks
- reinforcing the security of potential targets for economic sabotage and social disruption
- improving background checks on immigration applicants made by the visa office in Canadian embassies
- securing Canadian airports, now an integral part of the United States's, and every other country's, defence perimeter
- making intelligence gathering more reliable in obtaining advance warnings that can abort attempted strikes

With the significant exception of Bill C-36, which provided a definition of terrorism absent from the Immigration Act and greatly strengthened police powers to the considerable dismay of civil liberties and ethnic groups, all of these areas were already addressed by federal and/or provincial legislation, regulations, or agencies, many of which implemented Canada's obligations spelled out in treaties Ottawa helped negotiate. While one might have expected Ottawa to resist spending as much as the U.S. government would want, Paul Martin's autumn budget allocated eight billion dollars over five years to various initiatives on infrastructure and high-tech surveillance to make the border smarter and safer for both goods and people.

Globalization of interdependence had transnationalized domestic security. Canada's defence perimeter now extended to every international airport in every other country from which potential terrorists could fly – presenting themselves perhaps as refugees who had lost or destroyed their documents, as immigrants, or even as tourists. Defence against terrorism therefore required a generalized sharing of data among national intelligence services, which used the latest technologies for trying to recognize dangerous individuals and then tracking their movements.

Measures announced to satisfy the government's two audiences – its own electorate and Washington – raised the perennial question of Canadian sovereignty. Certainly, if Ottawa negotiated its entry as junior partner into a continental homeland defence it would forgo sovereignty, as it had in NORAD and NAFTA, in return for a security and economic payoff. If the Canadian public wanted the same heightened security as Uncle Sam, its loss of sovereignty would not entail a sacrifice of autonomy.

Whatever the sober reality of Canadian-American compatibility in internal security, a congenitally misinformed Congress, alarmed by panicky media figures – whose ideas in turn come from too-smart-by-half pundits, themselves chronically ignorant about Canada – could be expected to generate continual turbulence about the security of the U.S. perimeter. Richard Holbrooke, Bill Clinton's ambassador to the United Nations, had once referred to Canada as 'a Club Med for terrorists.' Senator Hillary Clinton publicly stated that the terrorists came to the United States through Canada. The gripping TV series on presidential politics, 'The West Wing,' even referred in one episode to terrorists crossing a non-existent Ontario-Vermont border.

Within the context of an understandable but dangerous over-reaction around these issues, the U.S. ambassador to Canada voiced words of calm and reason. Paul Cellucci saw the issue as one of mutual confidence. Canadian standards for accepting desirable immigrants and procedures for dispatching dangerous applicants could be the same as, or different from, American practices, so long as they were effective. In intense discussions through the autumn of 2001, Canadian officials explained their practices to their predictably overbearing U.S. colleagues. The results were a thirty-point Action Plan for Creating a Secure and Smart Border, signed in Ottawa in November with U.S. Attorney General John Ashcroft, and December's Joint Statement of Co-operation on Border Security and Regional Migration Issues. Both agreements specified detailed measures for the two governments to take in the short and long terms.

The Supreme Court of Canada's unanimous ruling in January 2002 to allow the deportation of an Iranian assassin on the grounds of national security helped make Ottawa's case in Washington that it offered no safe haven for terrorists. Chrétien reinforced this message when he hived off the security functions from DFAIT for John Manley, who had been point man on bilateral security relations since September. By replacing Manley early in 2002 with Bill Graham and making him deputy prime minister with enhanced managerial responsibility, Chrétien gave maximum authority to the politician in whom the Bush administration had the greatest trust.

This appointment also indicated that Canada had moved back into lockstep with Washington. Henceforth Canada would respond quietly and on a piecemeal basis to American demands for harmonization on selected policy fronts. In the main, this would involve one small, low-profile issue at a time, such as extending the U.S. presence in Canadian departure points from immigration officers in airports to customs officials in seaports. These smaller integrative steps would be punctuated with the occasional giant stride forward in the process, such as insertion of Canadian soldiers under U.S. command in Afghanistan, where they would have to violate the Geneva Convention on Prisoners of War, which Washington decided to ignore by refusing to regard its captives as legitimate soldiers. Subsuming Canada's military forces within the U.S. Northern Command would lock the Canadian army and navy into a junior position similar to the Royal Canadian Air Force's in NORAD, though Chrétien's immediate reaction was to scotch the idea.

As Mexico and Canada struggled to be included within the U.S. anti-terrorist defence zone, business spoke loud and clear within the councils of all three governments, repeating a standard message about keeping goods and people flowing across borders. NAFTA itself had nothing to offer by way of institutions or processes that could aid continental decision-making – it convened no trilateral summit or emergency meeting of its Trade Commission. Clarified in crisis, governance in post-catastrophe North America turned out to reinforce, not replace, the double dyad of U.S.-Canada and U.S.-Mexico relations, confirming that an uncorrected asymmetrical bilateralism leaves Washington with enhanced control over its minor partners.

Conclusion

Canada's lurch from Lloyd Axworthy's human security agenda towards a globally networked, continentally implemented anti-terrorist state was sudden, but not necessarily permanent. By mid-2002, the Bush White House was already having difficulty maintaining the political solidarity at home necessary to shift public spending from welfare to warfare. Though it had succeeded surprisingly well in the first stage of its war on al-Qaeda, it could not continue as well for a second stage, when Israel-Palestine bloodshed broke the tenuous Arab coalition Washington had assembled. Mere intelligence advisories of further terrorist acts could not indefinitely maintain the mix of paranoia and patriotism needed to support a state of permanent alert against the unknown. If reason forced Americans to accept less than 100 per cent security, Canada would regain some degree of international freedom.

Were the causes of anti-American *jihads* to be addressed, the international system would again present a variety of opportunities suited to middle-sized countries capable of seeking out these niches. These policy options create choices for Canadian foreign policy even in conditions of economic integration. Whether this scenario becomes again the basis of Canadian foreign policy depends on whether civil society continues to be cultivated as a source of soft power to create both external and internal change.[61] Once the American war on terror subsides, Canada could again pursue an activist foreign policy in multilateral, if not in bilateral, relations under continuing U.S. hegemony – if its various leaders in the PMO and DFAIT, notably its unproven new foreign minister, Bill Graham, feel so inclined. But if the Middle East continues to be a war zone, Canada will continue to function as subordinate to the American commander.

After September 11, 2001, middle power Canada remained a hybrid – part American satellite constrained by its extreme economic vulnerability and part humanitarian activist. Ottawa has both a seat at the table with the economic giants and a voice among like-minded states: excellent qualifications for soft-

power leadership by a federal state. An unusual player on the world stage, with many characteristics of a 'principal power,'[62] Canada is neither strong enough to be a great power nor weak enough to be a small one. Its dependent assimilation in myriad American systems – from homeland defence to software technology, from corporate financing to professional sports – has made it less autonomous than it would have been without its several thousand kilometres of undefendable frontier. Pluralistic and multicultural, federal and unmilitaristic, highly developed in the latest technologies of communication and comfortable with the politics of identity, Canada is, in John Katzenstein's words, 'the first post-modern state par excellence.'[63] Whether it can reconcile post-modernity with democratic values of autonomy and self-determination is what we need to consider in our conclusion.

20 The Post-Globalist State: and the Democratic Deficit

If Canada has indeed evolved into the first postmodern state, my physicist friend's insistent question – 'Stephen, will Canada survive?' – has turned out to have deeper roots and more complex interconnections than he could have realized when he asked it. Its roots are deep because Canada's survival has been in doubt ever since the American Revolution drew a boundary separating a British from a republican North America. U.S. expansionism has constantly, if not always wilfully, put this border in question. A sense of imminent extinction became acute as soon as the colonies to the south declared their independence from George III and invited their northern neighbours into their new union. If the siren song of life, liberty, and the pursuit of happiness didn't seduce the habitants, the rebels felt that military muscle might help convince them. American troops came close to persuasion at musket point when they seized Montreal in November 1775. But their revolutionary zeal proved no match for the Canadian climate. As the American general Benedict Arnold unsuccessfully laid siege to Quebec City in the months that followed, he absorbed a lesson about the hazards of winter warfare that Napoleon would learn in his invasion of Russia in 1812.

That year political annihilation threatened British North America once again. The U.S. government declared war on Britain and sent its cocky cavalry to liberate Upper Canada. To Congress's astonishment the invading armies were repulsed in decisive battles thanks to British troops, local militia, Native warriors, and a woman called Laura Secord.

By the time the British colonies had been federated into the Dominion of Canada, the survival question had shifted from the military to the socioeconomic plane. In a provocative thesis published in 1907 as *The*

Americanization of Canada, the brilliant American journalist Samuel Moffett argued that the long, open border between a rising imperial power and a benighted colony, most of whose scattered population spoke English, created an intricate web of dependence that must lead to Canada's absorption by the more democratic, more virile, more prosperous, more technologically advanced United States. 'English-speaking Canadians protest that they will never become Americans,' he wrote in his concluding sentence, but 'they are already Americans without knowing it.'[1]

Moffett identified cultural, technological, sociological, and political factors that heralded Canada's ever-increasing integration into the American political economy. Within twenty years and a world war of his book's publication, Canadian governments could not even control the radio waves over which programming was beamed to their citizens. Within another decade, virtually the whole labour movement had become subordinated to either the American Federation of Labor or the more militant Congress for Industrial Organizations. Ten more years and a second world war saw Hollywood with a hammerlock on the public's creative imagination. Twenty years further along, as we saw in chapter 19, it seemed doubtful that Canada could have its own foreign policy, let alone its own border.

Moffett himself showed an inkling that his argument could prove wrong-headed when he noted that Canadians were stirred by a curious and retrogressive albeit 'growing spirit of nationality, which is striving passionately to make Canada a self-sufficing entity, free from dependence either upon the old sovereign power across the sea, or the gigantic neighbor next door.'[2] Looking back over the tumultuous century since he published his daring analysis, it is clear that this sense of national identity is what turned each economic, social, or cultural challenge into an assertion of autonomy. The federal state intervened to establish control over the radio waves. Trade unionists themselves grew tired of paying dues to 'international' organizations that were insensitive to their more militant demands. Hollywood's monopoly over Canadian screens was never broken, but radio regulation by Ottawa extended into public television, which did give Canadians some space to generate their identity and express their 'growing spirit of nationality.'

Circumstances have changed from period to period, but every generation faced and overcame one aspect or another of the survival question until the onset of globalization abroad and neoconservatism at home. In his social-democratic despair, my friend wondered whether these two phenomena had finally broken down Canada's capacity to survive. As we have seen, conditions of increased interdependence with the outside world were not new, even if the label of globalization made them appear novel. What was different about Canada's survival problem at the end of the twentieth century was its elite's abandonment of that 'spirit of nationality' which had guided its predecessors for two centuries. Neoconservative thinking, which espouses minimalist government and maximalist commercial opening to the world market, seemed to reject the historically normal, state-centred political response to the country's problems.

My friend's existential query was not whether the geographical *space* now known as 'Canada' would remain on the map, but whether the political, juridical, economic, societal, and cultural *entity* we call Canada would continue to exist in a sufficiently distinct way. Now that we have reached the end of this book's long journey, we can reframe the survival question more meaningfully by imagining a situation in which a new party coming to power – whether leaning to the left or favouring the right – would be forced by the supraconstitution to implement globally or continentally harmonized policies imposed by bodies over which it had no suasion. In this case the state would have lost its democratic raison d'être. If elections had no impact on outcomes, it would be hard for politicians to justify their existence. The Canadian state might still employ functionaries to perform certain operations for its citizens – collecting taxes at externally established levels and spending them in prescribed ways to maintain peace and order, if not good government. But it would do this without meaningful political debate between socialists and free marketeers or between nationalists and continentalists about how best to further the national interest. In the absence of political testosterone, the state could legitimately be considered castrated, a harem keeper for its global and continental masters, but without any vital fluids to call its own.

Such internationally determined impotence appears no more absurd than did Moffett's Yankee-annexationist vision of a hundred years ago. Because Canada's shift from relative autonomy to substantial incapacity had been noticeable enough to distress my scientist friend and countless others, it is easy to imagine a governance for Canadians that has been effectively neutered, whether for structural or for ideological reasons.

Structural Incapacity

The prime instrument of Canada's reconstitution through global governance was the CUFTA-NAFTA combo which Brian Mulroney's government negotiated and Jean Chrétien implemented on behalf of their business backers. Unlike Ottawa, Washington was interested less in real free trade than in settling its score with a liberal Canada that had shown unacceptable levels of autonomy under Diefenbaker, Pearson, and Trudeau. CUFTA and NAFTA did more than foreclose certain policies in energy, agriculture, economic development, and culture. As a supraconstitution, it imposed new institutions and norms, which, in the case of North American investors' ability to sue Canadian governments under NAFTA's Chapter 11, created a sinister forum of judicial decision-making in secret. Beyond affronting the norms of fairness, transparency, and equality embedded in the Canadian legal tradition, the radical empowerment of foreign NAFTA corporations chilled governmental policy-making to the point of deep freeze, particularly in environmental matters.

Trying to retrieve some of their failures in negotiating CUFTA, Canadian trade officials pushed in the Uruguay Round of GATT negotiations for more independent and authoritative dispute settlement. While precipitating the creation of a more muscular World Trade Organization, they helped create an affront of a different sort. The WTO's commitment to erase government regulation in the name of the free market trumped other values, such as environmental sustainability, better labour conditions, and human rights. The WTO increased the property rights of stateless capital while decreasing the social rights of state-bound citizens. In the galaxy of multilateral organizations, the WTO consolidated the asymmetry that gave international financial institutions preponderant power over all the others.

Even if its rules less egregiously favoured transnational corporations (TNCs) than did NAFTA's, the WTO also tightened the screws on the Canadian state. Unlike earlier epochs, when foreign threats to Canadian power were resisted, Canadian leaders implicitly connived with the supraconstitution's invalidation of government policies when they accepted trade rulings as *force majeure*. It suited Paul Martin to insist that Moody's credit-rating concerns obliged him to cut the deficit. With the exception of Heritage Minister Sheila Copps, Ottawa politicians appeared quite comfortable with the WTO's forcing them to abandon the magazine industry and to allow drug prices to escalate. Such invocations of external constraints strengthened neoconservative politicians in their concerted efforts to amputate their own governments' limbs and atrophy its muscles.

Beyond incorporating itself into continental and global governance structures which have truncated its capacity to interfere with TNCs, the government of Canada restructured its own powers to accommodate provincial demands. During the Chrétien years, particularly following the federalists' near-loss of Quebec's 1995 referendum, Ottawa evacuated areas of provincial jurisdiction that it had occupied during the Keynesian era. It even partially vacated such fields as the environment and telecommunications, over which the Supreme Court had awarded it jurisdiction. This federal retreat was partly an attempt to defuse sovereigntist energy by promoting Quebec as a distinct state within Canada.[3] As well, a perceived fiscal crisis – a large budgetary deficit, combined with an escalating public debt – put the government at the mercy of the international bond-rating agencies and investment houses.

Ideological Disjunction

To some extent the self-mutilation was neither forced nor reluctant, but ideologically determined. Inspired by an international consensus grouped around neoconservative ideas, federal leaders were joined by their provincial counterparts as they competed to do less. They negotiated an intergovernmental accord explicitly modelled on international trade agreements. The Agreement on Internal Trade had more to do with imposing handcuffs on their own policy capacity than on stimulating interprovincial trade, which continued its downward trend. Only Prince Edward Island sold more to its fellow provinces than it exported abroad. The Social Union Framework Agreement had more to do with constraining Ottawa from using its spending power to distort local priorities than with improving the provinces' social policies.

Neoconservative prescriptions had a further disempowering impact by propagating a related philosophy of government administration known as the New Public Management (NPM). Turning citizens into customers, public services into products, and policy goals into measurable outcomes, NPM applied a bottom-line, business-aping approach to the art and science of governing.[4] Mouthing slogans about 'cutting out the fat' and 'doing better for less,' neoconservative leaders at both levels cut back spending without showing much concern for the impact of their actions on the public service. Ottawa eliminated 45,000 of the federal government's 225,000 positions. Queen's Park cut the staff of its economic development ministry in half. Campaigns with vague labels such as 'Public Service 2000' were launched to improve the use of human resources in government. Senior management was supposed to operate according to business plans and become more accountable. Pressed to produce more with less money, civil servants burned out or left the public to join the private sector, where they would enjoy higher salaries and more creative work challenges. As a result, government staffing shifted from career civil servants to younger, non-permanent, less skilled, less experienced individuals working in an insecure environment for uncompetitive wages.[5]

Neoconservatism, which created conditions that fed on themselves, could not have been imposed if it hadn't reflected some significant value changes in society. Efforts by politicians across the country to stigmatize welfare recipients as not deserving of public support resonated among middle- and lower-income earners struggling to make ends meet in non-traditional jobs unprotected by labour contracts. The public generally felt that the social safety net should not be a hammock for the indolent. If public values had shifted away from deficit spending and collective responsibility for human suffering, it became easier for governments to practise fiscal prudence, blame the poor for their poverty, and shift the costs of care giving from the public health system to individual – typically female – caregivers. Buoyed by these sentiments, the neoconservative state might not be entirely hollowed out, but it had learned to be tough. In Ontario, it could cut back allowances for single mothers and could punish a pregnant woman who had bent the welfare rules by putting her under house arrest.

The public uproar over this abandoned woman's tragic death and the prolonged consternation over seven people who died from drinking improperly tested water in the Ontario town of Walkerton spoke to an ambivalence in the public's mind. Below an intolerance for budgetary deficits and welfare recipients ran a continuing commitment to an activist state. Opinion research confirmed a yawning gap between the anti-government attitudes of economic, media, and political elites and the pro-government views of the general public.[6] Faced with a choice between tax cuts and continuing government spending on social programs, respondents repeatedly preferred to continue investments in the public provision of services. If a liberal public was ruled by a neoconservative governing caste, it is not surprising that a high level of distrust was the result.

The fact that voters distrust politicians does not necessarily indicate a failure of democracy. On the contrary, it may reflect a knowledgeable public's revulsion at its elites' misleading discourse. Brian Mulroney promised 'Jobs, jobs, jobs' when overselling the virtues of CUFTA in 1988, but he refused to implement the adjustment assistance programs the Macdonald Report had recommended and that he had promised to relieve the unemployment that free trade engendered.

Public scepticism about politics is not simply a matter of unkept political promises – a phenomenon as old as election campaigns. There were reasons to take issue in the mid-1960s with Lester Pearson's economic defence of military sales that supported Washington's war in Vietnam. There were reasons to be offended in the mid-1970s by Pierre Trudeau's language, which could be as arrogant towards western farmers as it was elegant, and as insulting to Quebecers as it was logical. But Canadian political discourse in the Keynesian era did tend towards direct discussion of political choices. Pearson acknowledged thousands of industrial jobs to be the price of compromising a peacekeeping principle. Whether government should market prairie wheat was a real question that Trudeau posed to the agricultural sector. The cases for and against sovereignty for Quebec were hotly debated, often in carefully researched and finely argued detail.

Discourse in the Mulroney-Chrétien era is different, because neoconservatism won power under false pretences. Its practice has been to profess one set of values on the campaign trail and implement another when in government. Brian Mulroney and Michael Wilson strongly criticized free trade when campaigning for the leadership of their party in 1983 and were silent about the issue when they defeated the Liberals in 1984. Mulroney claimed that he would guard social programs as a 'sacred trust,' even as his government was stealthily reducing them. Never receiving a clear federal mandate – even when campaigning in the 1988 election during what became a near-referendum on free trade, the Conservatives won 57 per cent of the seats in the House of Commons with only 43 per cent of the vote – neoconservatism won power thanks to massive business support. It remained in control through a practice of systematic deception even when it changed its label. When Jean Chrétien campaigned against Kim Campbell in 1993, he was a critic of NAFTA. Once he became prime minister, he endorsed free trade following a transparently meaningless face-saving exchange of notes with President Clinton. He won three successive elections posing as a left-leaning Liberal, although his governments cut back the social wage more than his Conservative predecessor had.

Politicians have always manipulated information to suit their needs, but when an ideological civil war is in process – and trade liberalizers proudly described themselves as warriors in their cause[7] – official discourse becomes pathologically addicted to doublespeak. Selectively 'spinning' information became a way of life for neoconservatives who were compelled to front policies that had manifestly failed to perform as well as those that they displaced. They massaged data to suggest that free trade was an unqualified success, although its performance proved inferior to its predecessors'. They told citizens that they were better off, even though their real income had not grown; that services had improved, when they had been cut; that teaching was better, despite expanded class sizes; and that hospitals were more efficient, even if emergency rooms were more crowded. They peddled tax breaks favouring the upper and middle classes as relief for the ordinary Joe. They cast inequality-increasing deregulation in populist rhetoric. Citing abuses by the few, neoconservatives cut back welfare supports for the many. Claiming that the magic of the free market would benefit the consumer, they allowed market monopolies to raise prices and enrich their corporate backers.

Unlike the all-class support that Keynesianism enjoyed for decades, Canadian neoconservatism failed to develop a societal consensus. On the contrary, its deceptive style generated deeper alienation from the political process and provoked greater social polarization. The Mulroney government's communications strategy for selling the first free trade agreement was to withhold as much information as possible – on the correct assumption that the more the public learned, the less it would like the deal. The Chrétien government's approach to the Multilateral Agreement on Investment was also to conceal information on its negotiating position. When the public did find out that the MAI would extend the power of foreign investors to sue governments along the lines of NAFTA's infamous Chapter 11, a storm of protest caused the government to backtrack. This polarization generated public attitudes both sceptical about politicians and hostile to neoconservatism. As the opinion surveyor Frank Graves found in 2000, 'on virtually every indicator and test we examine, the neoconservative wave – always overstated in terms of public support – is in collapse.'[8]

If neoconservatism is on the brink of decline – and the election of Canada's third extreme-right provincial government (after Alberta and Ontario) in British Columbia in 2001 suggested that this was far from a foregone conclusion – we must be careful to avoid facile thinking about the alternatives. The pendulum is a common but misleading image, since history cannot allow politics literally to turn the clock back to earlier times. The 1960s social-democratic welfare state does not offer a viable model, since transnationalized globalization would not be compatible with a Fordist, mass-production, secure-employment regime of accumulation on which the Keynesian superstructure was built.

A Post-globalist Problematic

Whether or not neoconservatism is about to bow off the stage, we can clarify our understanding of the Canadian state's potential for survival if we speculate on the kind of strategy and approaches that post-globalist politicians might use if they come to power having rejected the nostrums of the past two decades and having promised to exploit the state's potential to provide the public with the services that it desires. In this exercise in counterfactual thinking the basic distinction is between powers lost irretrievably and powers merely left unused. In other words, did the Canadian state under neoconservatism act castrated because it had lost its vital parts or only because its leaders behaved as if it had?

This question was answered in part by state actions around the world following the catastrophe of September 11, 2001. However neoconservative they might be, governments with Washington in the lead showed they could flex their regulatory muscles to rebuild infrastructure, revive visa controls, reconstruct intelligence services, re-establish border barriers, and even regain control over the global capital market by increasing vigilance over funds that might flow to terrorist groups.

Two features of this recent state building are pertinent to our concern. On the one hand, the general thrust of the measures countered the formerly sacrosanct doctrine that all actions should lead towards ever-increasing economic liberalization. Multiplying the numbers of customs inspectors and requiring detailed manifests describing the contents of all containers shipped on the high seas would slow international trade. Setting up pre-clearance of trucks at their loading point and equipping them with transponders that would allow their continuous surveillance would raise the cost to TNCs of doing border-crossing business. In short, if raison d'état required it, globalization could lose its priority.

On the other hand, effective global action requires determined leadership from the global hegemon. Tax havens are a competitive technique exploited enthusiastically by U.S. corporations, as has become clear in the revelations of the scandal-ridden energy giant, Enron's hundreds of offshore corporate shells. Closing off this device for massive corporate tax evasion would require a greater commitment from Washington than simply targeting al-Qaeda's flows of funding, but is no more difficult.

The point that September 11 makes for our analysis is that the general autonomy of TNCs, whether foreign- or Canadian-owned, cannot be reversed by the Canadian state on its own. Failing concerted, U.S.-led global action, companies that have become mobile can be persuaded to re-locate or to remain only if the conditions are right for them. But 'right' is subjectively determined.

A Canadian post-globalist state could resolve to compete on the basis of high quality, rather than low costs. It might reject the Bank of Canada's exchange-rate policy, which gives Canadian producers a powerful export subsidy and reduces their need to compete on the basis of research, development, and innovation. A dollar that floated up to what is thought to be its true value would raise the wealth of all Canadians and reduce the cost of imports. Competing on the basis of quality would necessitate large public expenditures to rebuild an infrastructure that had degenerated because of the false economies inflicted by two decades of single-minded budget cutting. A quality-based economic strategy finally would require highly skilled personnel able to carry out demanding work tasks. Two decades of declining support for public schools and universities would have to be reversed. Nothing in such a strategy of improving the physical and human infrastructure would be beyond the capacities of the Canadian state under its new supraconstitution – assuming it makes no more concessions to the General Agreement on Trade in Services that would force the gradual privatization of its public services. But it would require the public's understanding the link between individual taxes and the collective good and so tolerating higher taxes to pay for a reinvigorated public sector.

'Build it and they will come' is too passive an approach to satisfy liberal post-globalists who would need to adopt a more proactive stance towards business. Since attaining environmental sustainability would be high on post-globalists' priority list, their policies would aim to force firms to pay the social costs created by their polluting activities. Getting tough on polluters would risk provoking a flight of capital to pollution havens, just as raising the minimum wage to improve working conditions might trigger an exodus of companies to the U.S. sun-belt or the Mexican maquiladoras. This race-to-the-bottom threat can be dealt with only by other states and by continental, hemispheric, and global governance also adopting post-globalist values. Just as the terrorism crisis gave a universal fillip to the police state, it will take a breakthrough among global elites' concern for international human, social, and labour rights to induce a universal resurgence of the social state.

States need markets to generate wealth that they can tax and redistribute to the public. But markets also need states to provide the legal system and the coercive power for enforcing contracts and resolving commercial disputes. The question becomes: 'Which state does the market need?' The post-globalist state would be no more capable than its neoconservative predecessor of regulating transnational capital on its own. Even if corporations liberated themselves from a particular government's influence by moving elsewhere, states could co-operate to set global rules for TNCs to follow everywhere and could participate in continental, hemispheric, and global governance to achieve the regulation and develop the kind of legal security that transnational capital needs.

In some of its once-important facets, the state's loss of power over the market appears irreversible. Technology has changed so radically that governments seem to have lost their capacity to regulate some sectors such as telecommunications or new media such as the internet. This is an issue of will. With sufficient concern about terrorism, Canadians tolerate their government's giving itself the power to monitor e-mail. In financial services, prudential needs for surveillance are so great that a combination of global governance and national implementation has crystallized. Where the neoconservative state has already sold off crown corporations, it is unrealistic to expect post-globalists to commit billions of dollars to buy them back. Once national companies have been taken over or have formed alliances with foreign transnationals, there would be little a post-globalist regime could do on its own. It would have to try co-operating with its peers in forging a worldwide competition policy that could regulate or break up the kind of price-gouging global oligopoly that has developed in a number of industrial sectors. But unless the United States and the European Union, the major economies harbouring these global giants, agree on the same approach, chances for such a regulatory advance are minimal.

Monitoring and controlling foreign direct investors' behaviour in the economy are capacities that a post-globalist state might well want to retrieve. Its prospects for doing so would be slim, because Canadian-based TNCs would resist regulations that could cause problems for them in other economies. Opposition from the United States would probably be even more negative than it was against the Trudeau government's Foreign Investment Review Agency. Returning to FIRA-type performance requirements would involve undoing central chapters in NAFTA and even the WTO's agreement on Trade-Related Investment Measures, on which Washington insisted in the 1990s. Realizing that no governing party would want deliberately to stir up such a hornet's nest is a way of establishing how much it would need to achieve a broad consensus among like-minded governments collectively to seek a rebalancing of skewed rules.

There is one part of NAFTA that a post-globalist government might be willing to violate on the clear understanding that there might be costs to pay. Chapter 11's investor-state dispute mechanism is so egregiously offensive to Canada's constitutional norms that its supraconstitutional status could be targeted for defiance. Consider an American corporation having won its case in a secret arbitration against a Canadian government's health regulation supporting a municipal ban of pesticides on lawns that had been legally enacted with solid popular support. Ottawa's considered decision to ignore the tribunal's ruling would certainly prod the victorious plaintiff to complain in Washington. Whether the U.S. government would consider it worth trying to force Canada to comply would depend on the political conjuncture. Much would depend on the strength of Canadian opinion and the importance of the policy in question to both governments.

If Canada had the courage to signal its displeasure with a continental norm whose implications it had not foreseen when it originally negotiated the treaty, it would lend support to the global project of rebalancing the WTO's controversial asymmetries. Dejudicializing the legal processes of the WTO's dispute process would reduce the anti-government bias of this rule-bound organization.[9] Rewriting the constitutions of the WTO, the International Labour Organization (ILO), and the many significant environmental regimes to give these normative systems more symmetry is an equally important task facing the world community. A post-globalist Canadian government concerned about environmental sustainability and social cohesion could use its position in these regimes to further this goal.

As part of their strategy of achieving greater fairness and balance in the international system, post-globalists would need to address two other problems that have long aggravated Canada, as well as many other countries. The United States attacks foreign government policies that subsidize exports to the American market at the same time as it gives its own producers massive subsidies. When it then demands access to foreign markets, domestic producers there are put at a colossal disadvantage. Mexican sugar producers are driven off their land, unable to compete with American high-fructose corn syrup because the vast subsidies received by U.S. corn farmers translate into below-cost prices for their produce in tariff-free Mexico. The hegemon's double standard has to be controlled lest it undermine the legitimacy of global governance.

A second running sore is the U.S. refusal to abandon its trade protection laws even within a so-called free trade area. As we have seen, congressional support for U.S. harassment of Canadian exporters is so severe a problem that Canadian steel makers have installed their newest production facilities across the border. Canada has had little success fighting Washington on its own, but the hemispheric negotiations for a Free Trade Area of the Americas provide an opportunity for it to develop in conjunction with Brazil a coalition that is disinclined to let Washington continue to extract concessions from other countries without giving any in return.

Canadian relations with Brazil had been extremely tense because of the two countries' trade dispute over export subsidies for their regional jetplane manufacturers, Bombardier and Embraer. The two countries will continue to be competitors in the American and other markets, but they could also share common goals, particularly if civil society groups from each country were to participate in their foreign policy making. Canadian environmental, humanitarian, labour, and human rights non-governmental organizations (NGOs) have set up active networks continentally, globally, and in the hemisphere, where they have connected with their Brazilian counterparts. The broader the agenda becomes and the more these NGOs are involved, the more complex becomes any international policy effort. Developing alliances with U.S. civil society to counterbalance American protectionist interests is crucial to any post-globalism project designed to displace the neoconservative consensus.

In building coalitions to put pressure on the United States to abandon its trade remedy system, a post-globalist government in Canada need not be anti-American. But it would have to evaluate the effects of two decades of a trade policy aimed at maximum integration of the Canadian economy into the American system, even though so-called free trade did little to rein in U.S. economic nationalism. Canadian exports of softwood lumber continued to suffer crippling countervailing duties. Canadian grain growers experienced continual harassment by U.S. farmers. Well before September 11, 2001, the Canadian-American border was an uncertain political barrier. While it disappeared for certain highly paid professionals and employees of TNCs, it remained in place for working people and was a checkpoint for customs officials to determine whether goods qualified for duty-free entry. In the aftermath of the attacks on New York and Washington, a panicked U.S. Congress sought to build up the barricades against terrorists slipping in from Canada.

The simple act of imagining what a post-globalist agenda would look like has suggested that the Canadian state as reconstituted by neoconservatism is not hapless, hopeless, or helpless. It has been severely and irretrievably weakened in some important respects. But it would not lack resources in its effort both unilaterally and multilaterally to remedy some of the worst mistakes made in the mid-1990s, when the continental and global trade governance regimes were designed.

Building a Post-globalist Canada

In carrying out this counterfactual exercise of imagining an alternative to neoconservatism in order to estimate the survival capacities of the Canadian state, we need also to speculate about the conditions – political, governmental, constitutional, economic, and social – for this scenario to be realistically conceivable.

Political

The most salient feature of neoconservatism's political economy is the increase in both the power of the corporation over national political systems and its autonomy from their control. For post-globalist government to restore a better balance between business, government, and society, electoral reform would be a first requisite. Prohibiting corporate and labour union contributions to political parties along the lines of the successful Quebec model would make politicians somewhat less beholden to business and somewhat more responsive to citizens. A related change would be needed in the media. For post-globalist discourse to receive fair treatment in newspaper, radio, and television reporting, the extraordinary degree of concentration and convergence in the Canadian media would need to be addressed.

If politics is to drive economics (rather than the reverse) and if the public is to instruct political elites (rather than the political elites imposing their preferences on the public), the institutional prerequisite for a post-globalist Canada would be reforms that offset the dictatorship that the prime minister[10] and premiers enjoy within the parliamentary system. Funding political parties adequately so that they can engage in sustained research and policy development could raise the level of political discourse and help the rank and file challenge its leadership's monopoly on expertise. Restructuring the electoral system could ensure that majorities formed governments (instead of a minority of voters producing a majority of seats for the winning party as is presently the case). Redesigning public subsidies so that political parties are discouraged from relying in their election strategies on simplistic and misleading TV commercials could increase the intellectual integrity of democratic discourse.

What makes elite expertise impervious to challenge by citizens is its control over information. Neoconservatism's new public management saw laws on freedom of information as a costly burden. Accordingly, prices for data were set at a level high enough to raise revenue and discourage citizens' inquiries. One might have thought that the internet would resolve this problem, with its instant access to mountains of data. In practice, information was commodified. Statistics Canada, for instance, charges some $3 per data series paid in advance – a significant disincentive for people looking for information without knowing whether it will contain what they want. As for governmental sites such as Industry Canada's 'Strategis' web page, they too operate on a user-pay principle, making 'freedom of information' an oxymoron. Federal, provincial, and municipal governments' record-keeping on issues of public policy has also eroded, as bureaucratic responsibilities have been contracted out to the private sector.[11]

Even when paid for and received, government information is often meaningless. Canadian statistics rarely have enough chronological depth to permit informed conclusions about economic performance over time. When old data are found, they are often not comparable to more recent figures because of variations in the value of the Canadian dollar or changes in an indicator's definition. Unemployment levels

were so high in the late 1980s that Statistics Canada came under political pressure to redefine the way in which it calculated this indicator.
This change brought the unemployment figures down by about 20 per
cent, so that recent data have a downward bias compared to those for
earlier years.

What the unsuspecting citizen cannot know is that similar changes
may have distorted such commonly used measures of economic or
social well-being as productivity rates or the cost of living. All this
makes the gap between information and knowledge dismayingly
wide. Public information under post-globalism would need to be reso-
cialized and data banks made 'user friendly' so that citizens can obtain
reliable data.

Governmental

Information also became a scarce resource *within* government under
neoconservatism, which let the state's own human infrastructure
degenerate. The policy-making and strategic-thinking capacity of federal departments sank so low that the Privy Council Office set up a
Policy Research Secretariat, which sought resources from the academic
community via the Social Sciences and Humanities Research Council.
A laborious process to identify the main trends facing government
engaged several dozen scholars for several years. Whether the resulting studies helped civil servants reorder their priorities was doubtful.

A post-globalist paradigm premised on a more effective governmental apparatus would have to address problems of public servants'
morale and salaries. With employees at the International Monetary
Fund earning from two to three times more than their Canadian counterparts, it is clear that any attempt to re-create a civil service of high
calibre would be costly.[12]

Regular policy making in government could also be reformed. Neoconservatives practised a closed, monopolistic governance as they
slashed social programs by stealth with no mandate, no consultation,
and no bargaining with 'stakeholders' on whom they imposed policies
by fiat.[13] This would not be acceptable under a new, more democratic
paradigm. Policies would need to be developed in a consultative manner, with position papers circulated for discussion within the policy
community, debates of the issues in public forums, and continual revision of the ideas under political leadership until an acceptable consensus is reached.

Task forces that bring together all the interested parties in an industry or sector or policy community can generate meaningful participation in public policy.[14] This technique was used by neoconservatives to devolve policy authority from public regulators to a self-regulating private sector. Industry associations were entrusted with the judge-and-jury task of setting standards for corporate behaviour and monitoring their own observance on a voluntary basis. A post-globalist scenario could re-empower public regulators and enhance citizens' participation to bring the often-opposing interests of civil society and market forces into a better equilibrium.

Given the constraints facing the state as it attempts to provide services to citizens from severely reduced budgets, the federal government has explored ways to increase citizens' engagement in the 'third sector' of voluntary, charitable, and athletic organizations. The resulting Voluntary Sector Initiative (VSI) received a $90-million budget for five years to increase the sector's involvement in policy making and service delivery.[15] VSI is part of the reconfiguration of the neoconservative state in which government as service provider has diminished significantly. Post-globalists should reconsider the co-optation of citizen groups, the manipulation of public opinion, and the accountability and representativeness of NGOs receiving public funding in order to achieve more balanced partnerships with the third sector.

Constitutional

The single most crucial desideratum for reform of Canada's internal constitution beyond securing Quebec's and Aboriginals' special status is the eternal question of empowering the municipality. Although cities produce the bulk of the economy's wealth, they are burdened with increased responsibilities – for beaches and transportation, ambulance and emergency services, air and water quality, social housing and emergency shelters – by their provincial overlords, who have simultaneously undermined their tax base. Collectively, Canadian cities posted a deficit of $443 million in 2000 – a radical change from their $2.5-billion surplus in 1999. The deterioration was mainly in Ontario, where municipal spending exceeded revenue by $889 million in 2000 because of provincial downloading unaccompanied by transfers of adequate revenues.[16] For cities to remain liveable with more responsibilities and fewer transfers they would need their power reconstituted, perhaps by intergovernmental agreements to devolve power along the lines proposed by the Liberal government elected in British Columbia in 2001.

Unlikely though a constitutional revision in favour of cities may be, changing their status through the judgments of the Supreme Court is almost as improbable. Still, the justices have to keep their eyes peeled to trends in public values. If a consensus ever developed for re-empowering municipal government, the court might finally decide to shift the constitutional goal posts. Of even greater urgency is the need to test the constitutionality of such supraconstitutional norms as foreign investors' NAFTA-granted right to sue Canadian governments for measures tantamount to expropriation. The court could help remove a dagger stuck in the ribs of the Canadian state by declaring the measure incompatible with the Canadian legal order's own charter of rights.

Economic

Neoconservatism gave the market great deference and tried to apply business techniques to make government more efficient. Post-globalist politicians would want business to be run with more concern for the public good. They would be less uncritical of the market, conscious that it often fails to perform as theory dictates. Given that the bulk of the economy's production is directed towards satisfying its own needs, post-globalists would worry less about expanding trade and concentrate more on satisfying internal economic needs.

Although the transnationalization of capital diminishes the power of states to control economic events, post-globalists would use the state to alter the competitive conditions for capital.[17] Conscious too of the denationalization of their own TNCs, they would attempt to supplement the old dialogue with their 'national champions' to convince them not to move their production, research, or head-office operations out of the country with a multilateral framework to combat transnational corporate blackmail over tax cutting.

Post-globalists would also want foreign policy to be consistent with, not contradictory to, international economic policy. If it abandoned the goal of maximum conformity to Washington's whims, Canada could play its diplomatic hand among the middle powers with which it has long curried good relations, rallying them on crucial issues to support its efforts to press the United States to undo its protectionist policies.

Societal

There would be two polar extremes to a post-globalist social agenda. Rather than adopting neoconservatism's hostile stance towards its organized citizenry, post-globalists would encourage the active participation of civil society. NGOs, trade unions, and environmental groups, which were enraged at having been duped about and excluded from the negotiation of NAFTA and the WTO, know they lost badly during that long decade of global governance building. They want the rules rebalanced so that the interests of labour, the environment, and human justice receive equal weight to those of business.

While disempowered by their governments, some have re-empowered themselves with their colleagues both nationally and transnationally. They make the trek to far-off cities to manifest their views at considerable risk of suffering bodily harm from security forces trained to violate these globally minded citizens' basic rights of free association and expression. Many have developed sophisticated transnational networks that extend the reach of Canadian civil society. They already work creatively with officials to strengthen the Canadian state's involvement in global governance. Measures to empower civil society could include arm's-length public funding for NGOs that are democratic in their structures and keep open membership and funding records. Public funds would help them build better links to their community. Strict transparency rules would bolster their legitimacy in the political system.

At the other end of the social spectrum from the hyperactive are the dispossessed, the excluded, and the insecure. A post-globalist agenda would give high priority to restoring social cohesion. Income redistribution and other forms of support would aim to incorporate these marginal citizens in programs to build community solidarities. Such an approach would aim to build trust and strengthen social capital throughout a society in which cultural, ethnic, religious, and linguistic cleavages are more significant than class divisions.[18]

Post-globalists would have to accept that a brain drain will continue, since wannabes will always be pulled south by the U.S. system's gravitational force. Unlike neoconservatives, however, they would not use this pseudo-crisis to cut taxes and take further steps to Americanize their society. Rather, they would put their energies into reversing the trend to increased social inequality and a deteriorating public sector.

Not only would they feel it was worth creating a kinder, gentler, more just society for Canadian citizens. They would also consider a high quality of life across the country to be a valuable competitive tool for spawning new enterprises, reversing the flow of talent, and keeping existing entrepreneurs. Rather than trying to become more American than the United States, Canadian post-globalists would respond to their own public's aspiration to re-establish a more equitable society boasting better public services, such as efficient, universal health care and high-quality, free public education.

Given that Canadians aspire to communicate with the various communities to which they belong, a post-globalist social agenda would encourage Canadian cultural expression, with 'Canadian' defined very broadly to include all the ethnic groups that have established communities in the country. A land of minorities, its many diversities would be the unifying identity appropriate to a postmodern society that also interacts with diasporas around the world.

Summing Up

This whole discussion of a counterfactual, post-globalist Canada suggests that the Canadian state has substantial unused capacity. While its external supraconstitution has both constrained aspects of the Canadian state and opened up avenues for activity abroad, our review suggests that homegrown neoconservatism accounts for the greatest changes since the era presided over by Diefenbaker, Pearson, and Trudeau. Unique to the present period is the state elites' adoption of a value system antipathetic to the values of the general public. With political leadership seeming to have turned its back on its predecessors' sense of national purpose, the survival of a recognizable Canada appears to be jeopardized.

Beleaguered though we have found the Canadian state to be under neoconservatism, we saw that it could hardly extinguish itself. Propped up between the municipal and provincial state levels below it and the continental and global state tiers above, the government of Canada is unable to collapse. It stays in place by playing the intermediary, which feeds off and is kept alive by its collaborative and contested relations with the other levels of governance. If the U.S. interpretation of NAFTA's provisions threatens the regulatory regime engendered by the Canadian Wheat Board, then Canada will invoke and adapt the WTO's rules to help ensure its own survival. Seeing the state in its multi-tiered configuration shows us that, even while some of its internal functions disintegrate and reallocate, the federal tier remains operational and legitimate *because of* its interactions with the other state levels and with the societal organizations and markets to which it has lost functions.

It is wishful thinking to suggest that neoconservatism is exhausting its potential. Gordon Campbell has driven the attack on the provincial state further in British Columbia than his role model, Mike Harris, did in Ontario. Coexisting uneasily with neoconservatism is a resurgence of what Moffett called Canadians' 'spirit of nationality.' There is a basic self-awareness driving popular discourse among Canadians that they constitute a distinct society. Hence the popularity of an 'I am Canadian' beer ad proclaiming the pride of a young Canadian in the difference between himself and Americans. If this rekindling of nationalist sentiment is a reaction to a disturbing sense that North American integration has obliterated too much of Canada's political culture,[19] it could, once again, cause the Canadian state to re-energize as it travels along the long, bumpy road of surviving on the American periphery.

If we can personify American political, economic, and cultural power with the familiar moniker 'Uncle Sam,' we can also imagine a Canadian state acting from the municipal through the provincial to the federal, as well as in continental and global, tiers of governance to reaffirm the needs of the 'us.' In many ways Samuel Moffett's caustic conclusion is still valid: Canadians are in many respects already Americans without knowing it. As with Mexicans, however, Canadians want to preserve and promote what is valuable, not to say superior, in their heritage. Rather than proposing yet another big idea to achieve still further leaps of integration with the United States on the dubious assumption that erasing the economic border will magically increase the standard of living, the Canadian state needs to recommit itself to its historic task of strengthening its own democracy.

Notes

1. Not Whether, but Which Canada Will Survive

1 Gordon Smith and Daniel Wolfish, eds., *Who Is Afraid of the State? Canada in a World of Multiple Centres of Power* (Toronto: University of Toronto Press, 2001).
2 Eric Helleiner, 'From Bretton Woods to Global Finance: A World Turned Upside Down,' in Richard Stubbs and Geoffrey R.D. Underhill, eds., *Political Economy and the Changing Global Order* (London: MacMillan, 1994), 163–75.
3 Jagdish Bhagwati, 'Bhagwati on Trade: Fast Track to Nowhere,' *Economist* (October 18, 1997), 21–3; and Kenichi Ohmae, *The End of the Nation State* (New York: Free Press, 1995).
4 'Our central argument is that the neo-liberal agenda threatens the continued existence of Canada' (12). 'In Canada ... there is real doubt that the country will survive long into the twenty-first century' (18). Stephen McBride and John Shields, *Dismantling a Nation: The Transition to Corporate Rule in Canada*, 2nd ed. (Halifax: Fernwood, 1997).
5 William Watson, *Globalization and the Meaning of Canadian Life* (Toronto: University of Toronto Press, 1998), 253.

2. The Peripheral State: Globalization and Continentalism

1 Gordon Laxer, *Open for Business* (Toronto: Oxford University Press, 1989).
2 Andrew Jackson, *Falling Behind: The State of Working Canada, 2000* (Ottawa: Canadian Centre for Policy Alternatives, 2000), 13.
3 Gordon Stewart, 'A Special Contiguous Country Economic Regime: America's Canadian Policy,' *Diplomatic History* 6, no. 4 (fall 1982), 339–57.
4 Because the following broad analysis builds on research that I have

previously published, I will not repeat the extensive referencing, which can be found in Stephen Clarkson and Christina McCall, *Trudeau and Our Times. Volume 2: The Heroic Delusion* (Toronto: McClelland and Stewart, 1994), chaps. 2 and 3; 'Continentalism: The Conceptual Challenge for Canadian Social Science,' *The John Porter Memorial Lectures: 1984–1987* (Toronto: Canadian Sociology and Anthropology Association, 1988), 23–43; *Canada and the Reagan Challenge: Crisis and Adjustment, 1981–85*, 2nd ed. (Toronto: James Lorimer, 1985), chaps. 1 and 2.

 5 The Supreme Court of Canada's 1981 judgment on the patriation of the British North America Act established three conditions for a convention to be constitutional. First, the relevant behaviour should be constantly repeated. Next, both parties should feel bound by the constraint. Lastly, there should be some principled rationale for the rule.

 6 Livingston T. Merchant and A.D.P. Heeney, 'Canada and the United States – Principles of Partnership,' *Department of State Bulletin* (August 2, 1965).

 7 John Redekop, 'A Reinterpretation of Canadian-American Relations,' *Canadian Journal of Political Science* 9, no. 2 (June 1976), 227–43.

 8 Kim Richard Nossal, 'Congress and Canada,' in Robert A. Pastor and Rafael Fernandez de Castro, eds., *The Controversial Pivot: The U.S. Congress and North America* (Washington, DC: Brookings Press, 1998), 50–69.

 9 Author's interview (Sept. 7, 1989) with Philip Trezise, a retired senior officer of the U.S. State Department, who had been in charge of the department's Canadian desk during the 1970s.

10 Stephen Clarkson, *Canada and the Reagan Challenge: Crisis and Adjustment, 1981–85*, 2nd ed. (Toronto: James Lorimer, 1985).

11 Ibid., 57–81.

12 Greg J. Inwood, *Nationalism versus Continentalism: Ideology in the Mirror of the Macdonald Royal Commission* (Toronto: University of Toronto Press, forthcoming).

13 Brian Tomlin and Bruce Doern, *Faith and Fear: The Free Trade Story* (Toronto: Stoddart, 1991), 34.

14 Maxwell A. Cameron and Brian W. Tomlin, *The Making of NAFTA: How the Deal Was Done* (Ithaca, NY: Cornell University Press, 2000).

15 Wolfgang Streeck suggests a similar hypothesis for the member states of the European Union, arguing they compensated for what they had lost in internal sovereignty by what they gained in their intergovernmental bargaining in the EU's institutions – even if decision-making deadlocks and democratic deficits at the continental level of governance are high prices to pay for this exchange. 'Public Power beyond the Nation-State: The Case of the European Community,' in Robert Boyer and Daniel Drache, eds., *States against Markets: The Limits of Globalization* (London: Routledge, 1996), 299–315.

3. Continental and Global Governance

1 Stephen Blank, Stephen Krajewski, and Henry S. Yu, 'U.S. Firms in North America: Redefining Structure and Strategy,' *North American Outlook* 5, no. 2 (Feb. 1995).

2 Stephen Clarkson, 'The Canada-United States Trade Commission,' in Duncan Cameron, ed., *The Free Trade Deal* (Toronto: Lorimer, 1988), 26–45, 255.

3 For instance, the Free Trade Commission could decide as weighty a matter as the security of a party's social welfare system from attack by a NAFTA investor by clarifying the meaning of such key phrases in the agreement as the exemption from investor-state suits of social services that are 'established or maintained for a public purpose.' NAFTA Article 1101 (4), Barry Appleton, *Navigating NAFTA: A Concise User's Guide to the North American Free Trade Agreement* (Toronto: Carswell, 1994), 88.

4 Commission for Environmental Cooperation, *NAFTA's Institutions: The Environmental Potential and Performance of the NAFTA Free Trade Commission and Related Bodies* (Montreal: CEC, 1997). In May 2001 George Bush, Jean Chrétien, and Vicente Fox set up a group to study continental energy trade: Barrie McKenna, 'Klein to Deliver Sales Pitch to Cheney,' *Globe and Mail* (June 14, 2001), A12.

5 Rafael Fernández de Castro and Claudia Ibargüen, 'Las instituciones del TLCAN: una evaluación a los cinco años,' in Beatriz Leycegui y Rafael Fernández de Castro, eds., *Socios naturales? Cinco años del Tratado de Libre Comercio de América del Norte* (Mexico City: ITAM, 2000), 486.

6 Ibid., 515–32.

7 Stephen Clarkson, 'The Joy of Flux: What the European Monetary Union Can Learn from North America's Experience with National Currency Autonomy,' in Colin Crouch, ed., *After the Euro: Shaping Institutions for Governance in the Wake of European Monetary Union* (Oxford: Oxford University Press, 1999).

8 W.D. Coleman and Tony Porter, 'Regulating International Banking and Securities: Emerging Co-operation among National Authorities,' in Richard Stubbs and Geoffrey Underhill, eds., *International Political Economy* (Toronto: McClelland and Stewart, 1993), 190–203.

9 John H. Jackson, *The World Trading System: Law and Policy of International Economic Relations* 2nd. ed., (Cambridge, Mass.: MIT Press, 1997), 32.

10 Philippe Le Prestre, 'International Convention Secretariats and Canada's Role in Future Environmental Governance,' in Gordon Smith and Daniel Wolfish, eds., *Who Is Afraid of the State? Canada in a World of Multiple Centres of Power* (Toronto: University of Toronto Press, 2001), 230.

11 Jeffrey Schott and Jayashree Watal, 'Decision-Making in the WTO,' *International Economics Policy Briefs* (Washington, DC: Institute for International Economics, March 2000), 3.
12 Sylvia Ostry, *Getting to First: The Post-Cold War Trading System* (Chicago: University of Chicago Press, 1999).
13 Gilbert R. Winham, 'International Trade Policy in a Globalizing Economy,' *International Journal* 51, no. 4 (autumn 1996), 638–50.
14 Michael Hart, *Fifty Years of Canadian Tradecraft: Canada at the GATT, 1947–1997* (Ottawa: Centre for Trade Policy and Law, 1998), 191.
15 Some observers doubt whether officials representing dozens of Third World countries understood the significance of the documents that they were signing. Nor did Canadian negotiators of NAFTA and the WTO foresee how far judgments applying the new economic rules to trade disputes would go in overturning legitimate government policies such as the Auto Pact and the EU's banana regime: Scott Sinclair and Jim Grieshaber-Otto, *Sorting Out the GATS Debate: A Critical Guide to WTO and OECD Claims* (Ottawa: Canadian Centre for Policy Alternatives, 2002), 34.
16 Although NGOs and the French government feared that the OECD's document was going too far, the U.S. Congress would probably have rejected the MAI because it did not go far enough in strengthening TNCs' rights abroad.

4. NAFTA and WTO as Supraconstitution

1 When a UN committee censured the government of Ontario for not extending to all religious schools the state funding that it gives Catholic public schools, it was challenging a key element of the 1867 confederal bargain that guaranteed Roman Catholics in the provinces the preservation of their educational system.
2 Scott Sinclair, *GATS: How the World Trade Organization's New 'Services' Negotiations Threaten Democracy* (Ottawa: Canadian Centre for Policy Alternatives, 2000), 44.
3 Ibid., 45.
4 Ibid., 53.
5 Thomas Grennes, 'Toward a More Open Agriculture in North America,' in Steven Globerman and Michael Walker, eds., *Assessing NAFTA: A Trinational Analysis* (Vancouver: Fraser Institute, 1993), 148–71.
6 Barry Appleton, *Navigating NAFTA: A Concise User's Guide to North American Free Trade Agreement* (Toronto: Carswell, 1994), 126.
7 North American Free Trade Agreement, Article 1106.

8 Richard C. Levin and Susan Erickson Marin, 'NAFTA Chapter 11: Investment and Investment Disputes,' *NAFTA: Law and Business Review of the Americas* 83, no. 2 (summer 1996), 90.

9 NAFTA, Article 1110.

10 Susan Goodeve, 'Canada Commits to Trade Liberalization,' in Peter Haydan and Jeffrey Burns, eds., *Foreign Investment in Canada* (Scarborough: Carswell, 1996), 280–6.

11 David Schneiderman, 'NAFTA's Takings Rule: American Constitutionalism Comes to Canada,' *University of Toronto Law Journal* 46 (1996), 499–537.

12 Ibid., 536.

13 Of course, Canadian firms operating in the United States and Mexico would benefit from this right to attack American or Mexican regulations that they allege 'expropriated' their property.

14 NAFTA, article 1138. An example occurred in 1993, when newly elected Liberal Prime Minister Jean Chrétien kept his campaign promise to cancel the former Conservative government's contract to privatize the Toronto airport. Since the U.S. company Lockheed was a partner in the consortium planning to take over the airport, it used the threat of a Chapter 11 suit to force Ottawa to pay substantial compensation for foregone profits on an investment that it had not even made.

15 Howard Mann, *Assessing the Impact of NAFTA on Environmental Law and Management Processes*, Working Paper, First North American Symposium on Understanding the Linkages between Trade and Environment (autumn 2000), 29.

16 Stephen Blank and Stephen Krajewski, 'U.S. Firms in North America: Redefining Structure and Strategy,' *North American Outlook* 5, no. 2 (Feb. 1995).

17 Christopher Kent, 'The Uruguay Round GATT, TRIPS Agreement and Chapter 17 of the NAFTA: A New Era in International Patent Protection,' *Canadian Intellectual Property Review* 10, no. 3 (1994), 711–33.

18 Canada, The Canada-U.S. Free Trade Agreement Synopsis, 1987, 1.

19 L. Trakman, *Dispute Settlement under the NAFTA* (New York: Transnational Publishers, 1997), 277.

20 William J. Davey, Beatriz Leycegui, William B.P. Robson, and Dahlia Stein, eds., *Trading Punches: Trade Remedy Law and Disputes under NAFTA* (Mexico City: ITAM; Toronto: C.D. Howe Institute; Washington, DC: NPA, 1995).

21 Charles Doran, 'Trade Dispute Resolution "On Trial": Softwood Lumber,' *International Journal* 51, no. 4 (autumn 1996), 712.

22 Robert Howse, 'Settling Trade Remedy Disputes: When the WTO Forum Is Better than the NAFTA,' *C.D. Howe Institute Commentary* 111 (June 1998), 14.

23 Robert E. Burke and Brian F. Walsh, 'NAFTA Binational Panel Review –

Should It Be Continued, Eliminated or Substantially Changed?' *Brooklyn Journal of International Law* 20, no. 3 (1995), 560.

24 Doran, 'Trade Dispute Resolution,' 718.

25 Howse, 'Settling Trade Remedy Disputes,' 9.

26 CDA-91-1904-02. Certain beer originating in or exported from the United States by G. Heilman Brewing Company, Inc., Pabst Brewing Company, and the Stroh Brewery Company for use or consumption in British Columbia.

27 Subsection 18.1(4) of the Federal Court Act amendment provides that the Canadian International Trade Tribunal's decisions will be reviewed on these grounds.

28 Chapter 11 disputes are governed and administered by one of three multilateral conventions: the International Convention on the Settlement of Investment Disputes between States and Nationals of other States (ICSID); the Additional Facility Rules of ICSID (provided that either the disputing party or the party of the investor, but not both, is a party to the ICSID convention); or the arbitrarion rules of the United Nations Commission on International Trade Law (UNCITRAL). Gary N. Horlick and F. Amanda DeBusk, 'Dispute Resolution under NAFTA,' *Journal of International Arbitration* 10 (March 1993), 52.

29 In the Metalclad case, the tribunal ruled that the local municipality had exceeded its constitutional authority – a judgment that hitherto only the judges of the Supreme Court of Mexico had the power to make. Mann, 'Assessing the Impact of NAFTA,' 31.

30 Richard Dearden, 'Arbitration of Expropriation Disputes between an Investor and the State under the North American Free Trade Agreement,' *Journal of World Trade* 29, no. 1 (Feb. 1995), 127.

31 'The term "expropriation" includes, but is not limited to, any abrogation, repudiation, or impairment by a foreign government of its own contract with an investor with respect to a project, where such abrogation, repudiation or impairment is not caused by the investor's own fault or misconduct, and materially adversely affects the continued operation of the project.' United States Foreign Assistance Act of 1969, section 238, cited in Richard C. Levin and Susan Erickson Marin, 'NAFTA Chapter 11: Investment and Investment Disputes,' *NAFTA: Law and Business Review of the Americas* 83, no. 2 (1996), 97.

32 Article 1502 (3) (b) cited in Appleton, *Navigating NAFTA*, 114.

33 Schneiderman, 'NAFTA's Takings Rule,' 535.

34 Article 2013. See J. Holbein and D. Musch, *NAFTA : Final Text, Summary, Legislative History and Implementation Directory* (New York: Oceana, 1994), 480.

35 L. Trakman, *Dispute Settlement*, 7.

36 William J. Davey, *Pine and Swine* (Ottawa: Centre for Trade Policy and Law, 1996), 65.

37 CDA-92-1807-01, Interpretation of Canada's Compliance with Article 701.3 with respect to Durum Wheat Sales.

38 Davey, *Pine and Swine*, 56.

39 *Puerto Rican Restrictions on Ultra-High Temperature (UHT) Milk Case.*

40 Davey, *Pine and Swine*, 61–2.

41 David S. Huntington, 'Settling Disputes under the North American Free Trade Agreement,' *Harvard International Law Journal* 34 (spring 1993), 418.

42 Davey, *Pine and Swine*, 71.

43 The procedures found in Chapter 20 apply to the areas dealt with in the agreement's various chapters – National Treatment and Market Access for Goods (Chapter 3), Rules of Origin (4), Customs Procedures (5), Energy and Basic Petrochemicals (6), Agriculture and Sanitary and Phytosanitary Measures (7), Emergency Action (8), Standards-Related Measures (9), Government Procedures (10), Investment (11), Cross-Border Trade in Services (12), Telecommunications (13), Financial Services (14), Competition Policy, Monopolies, and State Enterprises (15), Temporary Entry for Business Persons (16), and Intellectual Property (17) – but only where the actual or proposed measures themselves are inconsistent with the provisions in NAFTA. Trakman, *Dispute Settlement*, 5.

44 Howse, 'Settling Trade Remedy Disputes.'

45 Joseph Weiler, University of Toronto, Faculty of Law, paper; and Robert Howse, personal communication.

46 Robert Howse and Donald Regan, 'The Product/Process Distinction: An Illusory Basis for Disciplining "Unilateralism" in Trade Policy,' *European Journal International Law* 11, no. 2 (2000), 268.

47 Amparo en revisión 1475/98: Sindicato nacional de controladores de tránsito aereo, 76: 'international treaties are situated on a second level immediately *below* the Fundamental Law [the constitution] but above federal and local law' (my translation and emphasis).

48 'WTO decisions generate international governmental rights/obligations but not necessarily for judicial arms of government at the national level.' Communication from Howard Mann, trade lawyer, to the author, January 2001.

49 Robert Howse, 'The Canadian Generic Medicines Panel: A Dangerous Precedent in Dangerous Times,' *Journal of World Intellectual Property* 3, no. 4 (July, 2000), 493–508.

50 Stephen Clarkson, 'Reform from Without versus Reform from Within:

NAFTA and the WTO's Role in Transforming Mexico's Economic System,' in Joseph S. Tulchin and Andrew D. Selee, eds., *Mexico's Politics and Society in Transition* (Boulder: Lynne Rienner, 2002).

5. The Federal State: Internal Trade and the Charter

1 Jeffrey Simpson, 'I Told You So: Canadians Are Not Voting,' *Globe and Mail* (Dec. 4, 2000), A17.
2 Peter H. Russell, *Constitutional Odyssey: Can Canadians Become a Sovereign People?* 2nd ed. (Toronto: University of Toronto Press, 1993), 228–35.
3 Whether Canada gets top (or bottom) marks as the most decentralized federation going remains a topic for debate among specialists. That it is still a leading candidate was claimed by Jacques Parizeau on February 28, 1999: 'Canadian federalism is about the most decentralized in the world, along with Switzerland.' Cited by Stéphane Dion, *Intergovernmental Relations within Federations: Contextual Differences and Universal Principles* (Ottawa: Privy Council Office, October 6, 1999), 1. Some who pay attention more to legal than to economic indicators consider the federal system to be centralized to the point of being almost unitary: Andrée Lajoie, 'Égalité et asymétrie dans le fédéralisme canadien,' in A.M. Le Pourhiet, dir., *Libertés et égalités locales* (Marseilles: Presses universitaires d'Aix-Marseilles, Economica, 1999), 325–40.
4 Richard Simeon develops this argument about globalization's surprisingly minor impact on federal-provincial relations in 'Globalization and Canadian Federalism,' paper presented at a conference 'Impact of Global and Regional Integration on Federal-Provincial Systems,' Ottawa, Dec. 8, 2000.
5 Thomas Hueglin, 'Globalization without Citizens: A Critique of Reinicke's Global Public Policy' unpublished paper, Wilfrid Laurier University, 1999, 8.
6 On the role of provinces in trade issues, see Douglas M. Brown, 'The Federal-Provincial Consultation Process,' in Peter M. Leslie and Ronald L. Watts, eds., *Canada: The State of the Federation 1987–88* (Kingston: Institute of Intergovernmental Relations, Queen's University, 1988), 77–93; 'Canadian Federalism and Trade Policy: The Uruguay Round Agenda,' in Ronald L. Watts and Douglas M. Brown, eds., *Canada: The State of the Federation 1989* (Kingston: Institute of Intergovernmental Relations, Queen's University, 1989), 211–35; and 'The Evolving Role of the Provinces in Canadian Trade Policy,' in Douglas M. Brown and Murray G. Smith, eds., *Canadian Federalism: Meeting Global Economic Challenges?* (Kingston: Institute of Intergovernmental Relations, Queen's University, 1991), 81–128.
7 Ian Robinson argues that CUFTA and NAFTA are centralizing in their

effects. See 'NAFTA, the Side-Deals, and Canadian Federalism: Constitutional Reform by Other Means?' in Ronald L. Watts and Douglas M. Brown, eds., *Canada: The State of the Federation 1993* (Kingston: Institute of Intergovernmental Relations, Queen's University, 1993); and 'Trade Policy, Globalization, and the Future of Canadian Federalism,' in François Rocher and Miriam Smith, eds., *New Trends in Canadian Federalism* (Peterborough: Broadview Press, 1995).

8 Claire Turenne Sjolander, 'International Trade as a Foreign Policy: "Anything for a Buck,"' in Gene Swimmer, ed., *How Ottawa Spends 1997–98: Seeing Red: A Liberal Report Card* (Ottawa: Carleton University Press, 1997), 118.

9 Peter Morici, 'Resolving the North American Subsidies War,' *Canadian-American Public Policy*, 27 (Sept. 1996), 1–34.

10 NAFTA Implementation Act, section 9.

11 Barry Appleton, *Navigating NAFTA : A Concise User's Guide to the North American Free Trade Agreement* (Scarborough: Carswell 1994), 145.

12 Unlike CUFTA, in which every *affected* issue was listed in the text, NAFTA has much broader effect by listing only *excepted* areas that are not covered in a given sector. Ibid.

13 Stephen McBride, *Paradigm Shift: Globalization and the Canadian State* (Halifax: Fernwood, 2001), 116.

14 Mark Gold and David Leyton-Brown, *Trade-offs on Free Trade: The Canada–U.S. Free Trade Agreement* (Toronto: Carswell, 1988), 131–59.

15 NAFTA, Article 105: 'The parties shall ensure that all necessary measures are taken in order to give effect to the provisions of this Agreement including their observance ... by state, *provincial and local governments*' (emphasis added). See Andrew Petter, 'Free Trade and the Provinces,' in ibid., 141–7.

16 International Institute for Sustainable Development, *Private Rights, Public Problems: A Guide to NAFTA's Controversial Chapter on Investor Rights* (Winnipeg: International Institute for Sustainable Development, 2001), 1–53.

17 Rowell-Sirois Commission, *Report of the Royal Commission on Dominion-Provincial Relations* (Ottawa: King's Printer, 1940).

18 A.E. Safarian identified various ways that interprovincial trade barriers cost the Canadian economy in *Ten Markets or One?* (Toronto: Ontario Economic Council, 1980). Specific statistics on the impact of such barriers are not available; however, John Whalley has argued that costs are quite small. See John Whalley, 'Induced Distortions of Interprovincial Activity,' in M.J. Trebilock et al., eds., *Federalism and the Canadian Economic Union* (Paris: OECD, 1983), 161–200. Whalley uses a static trade model, which does not allow for economies of scale or the effects of innovation. His study notes that a dynamic model would probably demonstrate greater costs.

19 Internal Trade Secretariat, *Brief History of Efforts to Enhance Internal Trade in Canada* (Ottawa: Internal Trade Secretariat, Industry Canada, 1994).
20 Micheal J. Trebilcock and Rambod Behboodi, 'The Canadian Agreement on Internal Trade: Retrospect and Propects,' in Micheal J. Trebilcock and Daniel Schwanen, eds. *Getting There: An Assessment of the Agreement on Internal Trade* (Toronto: C.D. Howe Institute, 1995), 21.
21 Royal Commission on the Economic Union and Development Prospects for Canada (Macdonald Commission), *Report, Vol. 1* (Ottawa: Minister of Supply and Services, 1985), 138.
22 G. Bruce Doern and Mark MacDonald, *Free Trade Federalism: Negotiating the Canadian Agreement on Internal Trade* (Toronto: University of Toronto Press, 1999), 41.
23 Ibid., 89.
24 Ibid., 31.
25 Global Economies Ltd., 'Interprovincial Trade: Engine for Economic Growth' (paper prepared for the Canadian Chamber of Commerce and the Chambre de Commerce du Québec, May 17, 1995).
26 Industry Canada. *Agreement on Internal Trade*, http://strategis.ic.gc.ca/SSG/il00022e.html
27 G. Bruce Doern, 'Rules about Rules? The Canadian Internal Trade Agreement and Cross-Jurisdictional Influences,' in G. Bruce Doern et al., eds., *Changing the Rules: Canadian Regulatory Regimes and Institutions* (Toronto: University of Toronto Press, 1999), 324–9.
28 Daniel Schwanen, 'Overview and Key Policy Issues,' in Trebilcock and Schwanen, *Getting There*, 7.
29 Doern, 'Rules about Rules?' 233.
30 Robert H. Knox, *It Can Work If We Want It To: Canada's Agreement on Internal Trade* (Vancouver: Certified General Accountants Association of Canada, 2001), 7.
31 Mark R. MacDonald, 'The Agreement on Internal Trade: Trade-Offs for Economic Union and Federalism,' in Herman Bakvis and Grace Skogstad, eds., *Canadian Federalism: Performance, Effectiveness, and Legitimacy* (Toronto: Oxford University Press, 2002), 138.
32 Patrick Grady and Kathleen MacMillan, *An Analysis of Interprovincial Trade Flows from 1984 to 1996* (Ottawa: Industry Canada, Feb. 26, 1998). See http://strategis.ic.gc.ca/
33 Knox, 'It Can Work If We Want It To,' 8.
34 Robert Howse, 'Between Anarchy and the Rule of Law: Dispute Settlement and Related Implementation Issues in the Agreement on Internal Trade,' in Trebilcock and Schwanen, eds., *Getting There*, 171.

35 Kathrine Swinton, 'Law, Politics, and the Enforcement of the Agreement on Internal Trade' in ibid., 196–209.
36 Knox, 'It Can Work If We Want It To,' 10.
37 Ibid., 11.
38 Keith G. Banting, 'Federalism, Social Reform, and Spending Power,' *Canadian Public Policy* 14 (Sept. 1988), 581.
39 Grady and MacMillan, *Analysis*.
40 Figures by Robert Knox quoted in Ian Jack, 'Canada Chasing Foreign Trade at Expense of Domestic Deal,' *National Post* (May 22, 2001).
41 John Helliwell, 'Canada's National Economy: There's More to It Than You Thought,' in Harvey Lazar and Tom McIntosh, eds., *How Canadians Connect. Canada: The State of the Federation, 1998/99* (Kingston: Institute of Intergovernmental Relations, 1999), 87–100.
42 Knox, 'It Can Work If We Want It To,' 16.
43 F.L. Morton and Rainer Knopff, *The Charter Revolution and the Court Party* (Peterborough, Ont.: Broadview, 2000).
44 Christopher P. Manfredi, *Judicial Power and the Charter – Canada and the Paradox of Liberal Constitutionalism*, 2nd ed. (Toronto: Oxford University Press, 2001).
45 Alan C. Cairns, *Disruptions: Constitutional Struggles from the Charter to Meech Lake* (Toronto: McClelland and Stewart, 1991), 111.
46 Alan C. Cairns, *Charter versus Federalism: The Dilemmas of Constitutional Reform* (Montreal: McGill-Queen's University Press, 1992), 18.
47 Ibid., 29.
48 Russell, *Constitutional Odyssey*, 111.
49 Alan C. Cairns, *Charter versus Federalism*, 4.
50 F.L. Morton, 'The Effects of the Charter of Rights on Canadian Federalism,' *Publius* 25, no. 3 (summer 1995), 173–5.
51 Peter Hogg, *Constitutional Law of Canada* (Scarborough: Thompson, 1998), 635.
52 Henri Brun, 'The Canadian Charter of Rights and Freedoms as an Instrument of Social Development,' in Clare F. Beckton and A. Wayne MacKay, eds., *The Courts and the Charter* (Toronto: University of Toronto Press, 1985), 6.
53 James B. Kelly, 'Reconciling Rights and Federalism during Review of the Charter of Rights and Freedoms: The Supreme Court of Canada and the Centralization Thesis, 1982 to 1999,' *Canadian Journal of Political Science* 34, no. 2 (June 2001), 329.
54 This showed how judicial interpretation kept adjusting the constitution. For a discussion of the Oakes test's criteria for accepting a law's limitation

of a Charter right: Peter H. Russell, Rainer Knopff, and Ted Morton, *Federalism and the Charter* (Ottawa: Carleton University Press, 1993), 452–74. The proposed government action had to be clearly prescribed in law, a pressing and substantial concern, and important enough to override a constitutional right. Furthermore, the means chosen by the government had to be proportional to its objective, be minimally intrusive, and not be disproportionately severe. Hogg, *Constitutional Law of Canada*, 700–11.

55 Peter H. Russell, 'Canadian Constraints on Judicializatioin from Without,' *International Political Science Review* 15 (1994), 173 quoted in Kelly, 'Reconciling Rights and Federalism,' 334.

56 Kelly, 'Reconciling Rights and Federalism,' 339–40.

57 Ibid., 341–6.

58 James B. Kelly, 'Charter Activism and Canadian Federalism: Rebalancing Liberal Constitutionalism in Canada, 1982 to 1997,' PhD dissertation, McGill University, 1998, 287, 319.

59 Manfredi, *Judicial Power and the Charter*.

60 Ibid., 3.

61 Morton and Knopff, *The Charter Revolution*, 107–28.

62 Andrée Lajoie, Pierrette Mulazzi, and Michèle Gamache, 'Les idées politiques au Québec et le droit constitutionnel canadien,' in Andrée Lajoie et Ivan Bernier, dirs., *La Cour suprême du Canada comme agent de changement politique*, Études, Commission (Macdonald) royale sur l'union économique et les perspectives de développement du Canada, vol. 47 (Ottawa: Approvisionnements et services Canada, 1986), 1–110.

63 *R. C. Hydro-Québec*, (1997) 3 S.C.R. 213, cited in Jean Leclair, 'The Contribution of the Supreme Court of Canada to the Construction of National Identity,' unpublished paper, Université de Montréal, 2000, 22.

64 *General Motors v. City National Leasing*, (1989) 1 S.C.R. 657, in Leclerc, 'The Contribution of the Supreme Court,' 15.

65 *Black v. Law Society of Alberta*, (1989) 1 S.C.R. 591, in ibid., 11.

66 *Hunt v. T&N pic.*, (1993) 4 S.C.R. 289, 322, in ibid., 12.

67 My translation from Lajoie, 'L'égalité et asymétrie,' 325–40.

68 Andrée Lajoie, 'The Double and Inextricable Role of the Supreme Court of Canada,' *Canada Watch* 7 (1999), 14–15.

69 Terry Glavin, 'Canada's Native Peoples Fight for Self-government on Many Fronts,' *Federations* 1, no. 1 (Nov. 2000).

6. The Municipal State: Megacity and the Greater Toronto Area

1 Saskia Sassen, *The Global City: New York, London, Tokyo* (Princeton, NJ: Princeton University Press, 1991).

2 Allen J. Scott et al., 'Global City-Regions,' in Mila Freire and Richard Stren, eds., *The Challenge of Urban Government: Policies and Practices* (Washington, DC: World Bank Institute; Toronto: Centre for Urban and Community Studies, 2001), 11, and Thomas J. Courchene, 'Glocalization: The Regional/International Interface,' *Canadian Journal of Regional Science* 18, no. 1 (spring 1995), 1–20.

3 Michael Porter, *The Competitive Advantage of Nations* (New York: Free Press, 1990).

4 In the first half of the 1990s Michigan persuaded 150 businesses from the GTA to relocate there. Greater Toronto Area Task Force (Golden Task Force), *Greater Toronto: Report of the Task Force* (Toronto: Queen's Printer, 1996), chap. 2.

5 Samuel Moffett, *The Americanization of Canada*, 2nd ed. first pub. 1907 (Toronto: University of Toronto Press, 1972), 67.

6 The Toronto architect Raymond Moriyama won Buffalo's competition to redesign the urban core.

7 Larry S. Bourne, 'Designing a Metropolitan Region: The Lessons and Lost Opportunities of the Toronto Experience,' in Freire and Stren, eds., *The Challenge of Urban Government: Policies*, 32.

8 Municipality of Metropolitan Toronto, *Demographic Changes within the Municipality of Metropolitan Toronto* (Toronto: Municipality of Metropolitan Toronto, 1989), 110, and Graham Todd, '"Going Global" in the Semi-Periphery: World Cities as Political Projects. The Case of Toronto,' in Paul L. Knox and Peter J. Taylor, eds., *World Cities in a World-System* (Cambridge: Cambridge University Press, 1999), 197.

9 Meric Gertler, 'The Economic Context of Restructuring in the Toronto Region: Sources of Change and Implications,' paper read at Kyoto University–University of Toronto Symposium for Mutual Understanding of Japan and Canada, at Kyoto University, Kyoto, Feb. 15–16, quoted in Betsy Donald, *Economic Change and City Region Governance: The Case of Toronto*, doctoral dissertation, University of Toronto, 1999, 110.

10 Jane Jenson, '"Different" but Not "Exceptional": Canada's Permeable Fordism,' *Canadian Review of Sociology and Anthropology* 26, no. 1 (1989), 69–94.

11 In the 1980s, Toronto received 32 per cent of the newcomers to Canada, which was taking in immigrants at the rate of 1 per cent of the population per year – more than twice the rate of the United States or Australia. Todd, '"Going Global,"' 203.

12 In 1981, the population of Halton (0.3 million), Peel (0.5 million), York (0.3 million), and Durham (0.3 million) amounted to two-thirds of Metro's 2.1 million. By 1996 the figures had risen to 0.3 million, 0.9 million, 0.6 million, and 0.5 million, respectively, to make the '905' exurbia virtually equal to

Metro's 2.4 million residents. Bourne, 'Designing a Metropolitan Region,' 30.

13 Donald, *Economic Change and City Region Governance*, 111.

14 Meric Gertler, 'The Economic Context of Restructuring in the Toronto Region.'

15 In 1989, commercial construction in the GTA (which has 20 per cent of the country's population) represented over 40 per cent of Canada's investment in construction. Todd, 'Going Global in the Semi-Periphery,' 205.

16 Golden Task Force, chap. 2.

17 Thomas J. Courchene, 'Ontario as a North American Region State, Toronto as a Global City-Region: Responding to the NAFTA Challenge,' in Freire and Stren, eds., *The Challenge of Urban Government*, 175.

18 Ibid., 165.

19 Ibid., 165.

20 Between 1986 and 1996, 390,000 people moved into the GTA from elsewhere in the country, 575,000 came from outside the country, 255,000 more residents were born than died, and 590,000 moved away. Bourne, 'Designing a Metropolitan Region,' 38.

21 Meric S. Gertler, 'Self-Determination for Toronto: What Are the Economic Conditions and Do They Exist?' in Mary W. Rowe, ed., *Toronto: Considering Self-Government* (Owen Sound: Ginger Press, 2000), 33.

22 Census data from 1996 revealed that, where 24 per cent of Montreal's population over 24 years of age had a university education, Vancouver's figure was 29 per Cent, and Toronto's was 35 per cent. Peter Karl Kresl and Pierre-Paul Proulx, 'Montreal's Place in the North American Economy,' *American Review of Canadian Studies* 30, no. 3 (autumn 2000), 303.

23 Of Canada's 148 largest corporate headquarters, fifty-three were in Toronto, thirty-four in Montreal, twenty-two in Calgary, eighteen in Vancouver, and twenty-one in the rest of the country. Data for 1997 from *The Financial Post 500* (Toronto, 1998) cited in Kresl and Proulx, 'Montreal's Place,' 297. North American comparison: Golden Task Force, chap. 2.

24 Michael Valpy, 'What Will It Take to Light the Fire?' *Globe and Mail* (April 3, 1999), A11.

25 Gwyndaf Williams, 'Institutional Capacity and Metropolitan Governance: The Greater Toronto Area' *Cities* 16, no. 3 (1999), 174.

26 Donald, *Economic Change and City Region Governance*, 111. A phone call to Vaughan used to elicit the message, 'Vaughan, the city above Toronto.'

27 Scott et al., 'Global City-Regions,' 12.

28 Anne Golden, 'What Ontario's Disentanglement Plan Means for Toronto,' *Globe and Mail* (May 15, 1997), A29.

29 In public transit, the provincial government withdrew subsidies for both capital costs and day-to-day operations: Jennifer Lewington, 'TTC No Longer Model for US, Conference Told,' *Globe and Mail* (June 14, 2001), A20. It used to pay 75 per cent of the TTC's capital costs and 50 per cent of its operating costs and funded social housing to the tune of $232 million annually for 95,000 social housing units.

30 Gertler, *Self-determination*, 11. More generally, Robert Putnam's longitudinal study explains northern Italy's phenomenal economic performance in terms of the strength of values such as trust in its civic political culture. See Robert D. Putnam, *Making Democracy Work: Civic Traditions in Modern Italy* (Princeton, NJ: Princeton University Press, 1993).

31 Donald, *Economic Change and City Region Governance*, 199.

32 'Single governing councils and large organizations are simply incapable of dealing with the diverse range of issues that governments must deal with in urban areas. The diversity of metropolitan areas requires close links to citizens and the ability to handle a wide variety of activities on a small scale.' Robert L. Bish, 'Local Government Amalgamations: Discredited Nineteenth-Century Ideals Alive in the Twenty-first,' *C.D. Howe Institute Commentary* 150 (March 2001), 1.

33 Julie-Anne Boudreau, *The MegaCity Saga: Democracy and Citizenship in This Global Age* (Montreal: Black Rose, 2000).

34 Of 548 deputations, 80 per cent argued against amalgamation. Beth Moore Milroy et al., 'Who Says Toronto Is a "Good" City?' in Caroline Andrew, Pat Armstrong, and Andrée Lapierre, eds., *Les villes mondiales: y a-t-il une place pour le Canada? World-Class Cities: Can Canada Play?* (Ottawa: Presses de l'Université d'Ottawa, 1999), 171.

35 A term coined by Richard Stren.

36 Founded in 1984, this agency has seen users increase from 329,000 in 1989 to over 700,000 in 1998, and the percentage of people without food on one or two days of the week has risen from 10 per cent in 1987 to 41 per cent in 1998. Jane Gadd, 'Foodbank Lashes Out on 15th Anniversary,' *Globe and Mail* (Feb. 25, 1999).

37 Having cut the number of Metro representatives from 107 to 58 through amalgamation, the province then reduced the directly elected councillors to the megacity council from 58 to 44.

38 Andrew Sancton, 'Globalization and City-Region Governance,' *Policy Options* 20, no. 9 (Nov. 1999), 54–8.

39 Richard Simeon, 'Canada and the United States: Lessons from the North American Experience,' in Karen Knop, Sylvia Ostry, Richard Simeon, and Katherine Swinton, eds., *Rethinking Federalism: Citizens, Markets, and Gov-*

ernments in a Changing World (Vancouver: University of British Columbia Press, 1995), 251.

40 Marc Weiss, 'Metropolitan Economic Strategy: How Urban Regions Innovate and Prosper in the Global Marketplace,' *Global Outlook* (Washington, DC: Woodrow Wilson International Center, Jan. 2001), 8–12.

41 Paul S. Grogan and Tony Proscio, *Comeback Cities: A Blueprint for Urban Neighborhood Revival* (New York: Westview, 2000).

42 Joseph Berridge, 'There's No Need to Sit and Wait for a Handout,' *Globe and Mail* (June 7, 1999). In September 1996, *Fortune 500* named Toronto the top city outside the United States as a place for doing business. By 2000, Toronto had lost its top spot in *Fortune*'s ranking.

43 Courchene, 'Ontario as a North American Region State,' 183.

44 Ontario Jobs and Investment Board, *A Road Map to Prosperity: An Economic Plan for Jobs in the 21st Century* (Toronto, 1999), cited in Courchene, 'Ontario as a North American Region-State,' 169.

45 John Bossons, 'How to Turn Toronto into a Business Ghost Town,' *Globe and Mail* (Feb. 9, 1998), A21.

46 Ontario's cut-it-back-and-they-will-come approach to investors makes an instructive contrast with Quebec's. Montreal, having lost its primacy, has, with sustained provincial support, put in place a development strategy that encourages high-value-added enterprise in information technology.

47 John Barber, 'David Collenette's Toronto: By Land, Air, and Sea,' *Globe and Mail* (July 7, 2000), A17.

48 Liberal Party of Canada, *Opportunity for All: The Liberal Plan for the Future of Canada* (Ottawa: Liberal Party of Canada, 2000), 26.

49 John Lorinc, 'The Decline and Fall of Great Canadian Cities,' *Saturday Night* (March 17, 2001), 41.

50 John Sewell, *Local Self-government Bulletin*, 15 (April 2001), selfgovt-l@list.web.net

51 Ibid., 19 (Sept. 24, 2001), and www.legis.gov.bc.ca

52 Richard Sennett, 'La civilisation urbaine remodelé par la flexibilité,' *Le monde diplomatique* (Feb. 2001), 24.

53 Supreme Court of Canada's ruling on the *Alberta School Boards* case, Oct. 6, 2000. See http://www.localselfgovt.org

7. The Taxing State: From Lord Keynes to Paul Martin

1 Stephen Clarkson and Christina McCall, *Trudeau and Our Times. Volume 2: The Heroic Delusion* (Toronto: McClelland and Stewart, 1994), 339–40.

2 Stephen McBride, *Paradigm Shift: Globalization and the Canadian State* (Halifax: Fernwood, 2001).
3 Daniel Drache, 'Globalization: Is There Anything to Fear?' unpublished manuscript, Robarts Centre, York University, Toronto, 1998.
4 Wallace Clement and Rianne Mahon, eds., *Swedish Social Democracy: A Model in Transition* (Toronto: Canadian Scholars' Press, 1994).
5 The argument in this section borrows heavily from Timothy Lewis, *In the Long Run, We're All Dead: The Canadian Turn to Fiscal Restraint* (Vancouver: University of British Columbia Press, forthcoming).
6 H. Mimoto and P. Cross, 'The Growth of the Federal Debt,' *Canadian Economic Observer* (June 1991), 1–3.
7 The direct tradeoff between unemployment and inflation was not a strict application of Keynesian theory. Known as the Phillips curve, it was an empirical observation that countries with higher inflation rates had lower unemployment rates, and vice-versa. Given that Keynesians' concern for unemployment was greater than their fear of inflation, the curve helped sanction efforts to 'buy' lower unemployment at the price of higher inflation.
8 See Robert M. Campbell, *Grand Illusions: The Politics of the Keynesian Experience in Canada, 1945–75* (Peterborough: Broadview, 1987), 6; David A. Wolfe, 'The Rise and Demise of the Keynesian Era in Canada, 1930–1982,' in *Readings in Canadian Social History*, 5 (Toronto: McClelland and Stewart, 1984), 71–2.
9 The economic thinking underlying the Anti-Inflation Program is explained in Department of Finance, *Canada's Recent Inflation Experience* (Ottawa: Department of Finance, Nov. 1978).
10 For more on Canada's postwar Keynesianism, the forces that unravelled it, and the policies that replaced it, see Robert Campbell in Leslie Pal, ed., *How Ottawa Spends* (Toronto: Oxford University Press, 1999). Keeping the growth of federal spending within the GNP growth trend was explicitly argued to be consistent with deficit spending in a down year: when growth was beneath the previous trend, spending at the trend level that year would be stimulative. Donald S. Macdonald, *Budget Speech* (Ottawa: Department of Finance, May 25, 1976), 21.
11 *Anti-Inflation Reference*, (1976) 2 SCR, 373.
12 The federal government nonetheless sought to direct the provinces towards policies that were consistent with its economic philosophy. In 1973, Finance Minister John Turner used his budget speech to try to persuade provinces that they too had responsibilities for countercyclical demand management.

John N. Turner, *Budget Speech* (Ottawa: Department of Finance, Feb. 19, 1973), 20.

13 See Peter Aucoin, 'Organizational Change in the Management of Canadian Government: From Rational Management to Brokerage Politics,' *Canadian Journal of Political Science* 19, no. 1 (March 1986), 3–27, 17; and Donald J. Savoie, *The Politics of Public Spending in Canada* (Toronto: University of Toronto Press, 1990), 163.

14 Michael Wilson, *A New Direction for Canada: An Agenda for Economic Renewal* (Canada: Department of Finance, Nov. 1984).

15 Communication to the author from Douglas Peters, Sept. 15, 2001. In 1984, Peters was Clifford Clark Visiting Economist in the Department of Finance; he was subsequently secretary of state for international financial institutions (1993–7).

16 Duncan Cameron, 'Introduction,' in Duncan Cameron and Mel Watkins, eds., *Canada under Free Trade* (Toronto: James Lorimer, 1993), xiv–xv.

17 Ken Battle and Sherri Torjman, *Federal Social Programs: Setting the Record Straight* (Ottawa: Caledon Institute for Social Policy, spring 1993).

18 Edward Greenspon and Anthony Wilson-Smith, *Double Vision: The Inside Story of the Liberals in Power* (Toronto: Doubleday, 1996), 349–50.

19 Dan Trefler, 'No Pain, No Gain: Lessons from the Canada–United States Free Trade Agreement,' unpublished paper, University of Toronto, 1999.

20 The conversion of Paul Martin, Jr, to the new fiscal orthodoxy is described graphically in Greenspon and Wilson-Smith, *Double Vision*.

21 Liberal Party of Canada, *Creating Opportunity* (Ottawa: Liberal Party of Canada, 1993).

22 Paul Martin, *Budget Speech* (Canada: Department of Finance, March 6, 1996), 8.

23 Bruce Campbell, 'False Promise: Canada in the Free Trade Era,' Economic Policy Institute Briefing Paper (2001), 27.

24 Bruce Little, 'Remarkable Progress Cutting Federal Debt,' *Globe and Mail* (May 21, 2001), B7.

8. The Banking State and Global Financial Governance

1 Nova Scotia retained its sterling standard till 1871. For this history see Eric Helleiner, 'Free Trade and North American Monetary Relations: Back to the Future?' in Wallace Clement and Leah Vosko, eds., *Changing Canada: Political Economy as Transformation* (Montreal: McGill-Queen's University Press, forthcoming).

2 The Canadian dollar was fixed again from 1962 to 1970.
3 Following the Coyne affair, the Bank of Canada Act was clarified to give the government ultimate responsibility for monetary policy. If disagreement between the two institutions persisted, the finance minister had the right to issue a formal policy directive to the Bank. E.P. Neufeld and A.J. Thomson, 'The Bank of Canada,' *The Canadian Encyclopedia* (Edmonton: Hurtig, 1985).
4 See Gerald K. Bouey, 'Remarks by Gerald K. Bouey, Governor of the Bank of Canada,' *Bank of Canada Review* (Ottawa: Bank of Canada, Oct. 1975), 28; and 'Statement by Gerald K. Bouey, Governor of the Bank of Canada,' *Bank of Canada Review* (Ottawa: Bank of Canada, Nov. 1975), 4.
5 Global monetarism has been defined as 'an international regime centred on nationally-specific but internationally coordinated policies to control the growth rates of money.' André C. Drainville, 'Monetarism in Canada and the World Economy,' *Studies in Political Economy* 46 (spring 1995), 16.
6 Of course, the Trudeau government was not a homogeneous entity. Some ministers were truly angry at Bouey. Others were happy to be able to blame the Bank for the tough anti-inflation measures that they were unwilling to endorse in public, while the most conservative agreed entirely with monetarism in both theory and practice.
7 The governor of the Bank of Canada argued in 1987 that the Bank should direct itself to the goal of price stability. John W. Crow, 'The Bank of Canada and Its Objectives,' *Bank of Canada Review* (April 1987), 21–2.
8 Bruce Campbell, 'False Promise: Canada in the Free Trade Era,' in Richard P. Chaykowski, ed., *Globalization and the Canadian Economy: The Implications for Labour Markets, Society and the State* (Kingston: Queen's University, School of Policy Studies, 2001), 164–5.
9 Conversation with John Crow at the Munk Centre for International Studies, Dec. 1, 2000.
10 Roy Culpepper, 'Financial Fragility, Capital Controls and Economic Policy,' in Brian K. MacLean, ed., *Out of Control: Canada in an Unstable Financial World* (Toronto: Lorimer, 1999), 112.
11 Stephen Poloz, 'Undervalued Loonie Is Bound to Rebound,' *Globe and Mail* (Aug. 8, 2001), B6.
12 Jeffrey Rubin, 'Hands-off Approach Punishing the Loonie,' *Globe and Mail* (Aug. 9, 2001), B8.
13 W.D. Coleman and Tony Porter, 'Regulating International Banking and Securities: Emerging Co-operation among National Authorities,' in Richard Stubbs and Geoffrey Underhill, eds., *International Political Economy* (Toronto: McClelland and Stewart, 1993), 190–203.
14 For some exposition on Canada's vision for the future of international

economic institutions, see Department of Finance, *The Economic and Fiscal Update: Strong Economy and Secure Society* (Ottawa: Department of Finance, Oct. 14, 1998), 9.

15 Michael J. Trebilcock and Robert Howse, *The Regulation of International Trade*, 2nd ed. (New York: Routledge, 1998), 44.

16 Paul Martin, 'The International Financial Architecture: The Rule of Law,' speech to the Canadian Institute for Advanced Legal Studies (July 12, 1999).

17 'As the workings of genuinely global capital markets dwarf their ability to control exchange rates or protect their currency, nation states have become inescapably vulnerable to the discipline imposed by economic choices made elsewhere by people and institutions over which they have no practical control.' Kenichi Ohmae, *The End of the Nation State* (New York: Free Press, 1995), 12.

18 Richard G. Harris, *Exchange Rates and International Competitiveness of the Canadian Economy* (Ottawa: Economic Council of Canada, 1992).

19 George M. von Furstenberg, 'Monetary Union: Still Coming in Europe and North America?' *Challenge* 39, no. 4 (July-Aug. 1996), 34–40.

20 Letter dated June 9, 1997, to the author from Jim Stanford, economist at the Canadian Auto Workers, as cited in Stephen Clarkson, 'The Joy of Flux: What Europe May Learn from North America's Preference for National Currency Sovereignty,' in Colin Crouch, ed., *After the Euro: Shaping Institutions for Governance in the Wake of European Monetary Union* (Oxford: Oxford University Press, 2000), 150.

21 Thomas J. Courchene and Richard G. Harris. 'From Fixing to Monetary Union: Options for North American Currency Integration,' *C.D. Howe Institute Commentary* 127 (June 1999), 28.

22 On the sociology of this technique of developing a neoconservative consensus for the global community of bankers through conferences, see Drainville, 'Monetarism in Canada,' 18–19.

9. Financial Services: National Champions at Risk

1 Boston Consulting Group (BCG), 'Financial Services at the Crossroads: The Current and Potential Role of Financial Services in the Greater Toronto Area,' mimeo, Toronto, Jan. 1997, 8.

2 Gordon Laxer, *Open for Business* (Toronto: Oxford University Press, 1989).

3 George S. Watts and Thomas Rymes, ed., *The Bank of Canada: Origins and Early History* (Ottawa: Carleton University Press, 1993), 3.

4 Ibid., 6.

5 A.B. Jamieson, *Chartered Banking in Canada* (Toronto: Ryerson Press, 1953), 102.

6 Department of Finance Canada website, http://www.fin.gc.ca/

7 H.H. Binhammer, *Money, Banking, and the Canadian Financial System*, 4th ed. (Toronto: Methuen, 1982), 100.

8 John Harman, 'Working the Corners,' *Canadian Banker* 103, no. 3 (May/June, 1996), 24.

9 Charles Freedman, 'The Canadian Banking System,' Bank of Canada Technical Report No. 81' (Ottawa, March 1998).

10 Binhammer, *Money, Banking and the Canadian Financial System*, 100.

11 McKinsey and Company, *The Changing Landscape for Canadian Financial Services: New Forces, New Competitors, New Choices*, Report Prepared for the Task Force on the Future of the Canadian Financial Services Sector, 1998, Exhibit 7–10.

12 This 30 per cent figure for Canadian financial institutions was almost triple the 11 per cent international exposure of their rival American banks. William D. Coleman and Tony Porter, 'Banking and Securities Policy,' in G. Bruce Doern, Leslie A. Pal, and Brian W. Tomlin, eds., *Border Crossings: The Internationalism of Canadian Public Policy* (Don Mills, Ont.: Oxford University Press, 1996), 59.

13 Christopher J. Mailander, *Reshaping North American Banking: The Transforming Effects of Regional Market and Policy Shifts* (Washington, DC: Center for Strategic and Internaitonal Studies, 1999), 26.

14 Douglas D. Peters and Arthur W. Donner, 'Bank Mergers: The Public Policy Challenge,' paper presented to Sixth Annual Policy Conference, Laurentian University Sudbury, Ont., Sept. 1998, 3; they draw on Freedman, 'The Canadian Banking System.'

15 Whereas the three biggest Canadian banks spent $1.6 billion a year on technology, American banks of the same size spent U.S.$5 billion. Les Whittington, *The Banks: The Ongoing Battle for Control of Canada's Richest Business* (Toronto: Stoddart, 1999), 37.

16 Coleman and Porter, 'Banking and Securities Policy,' 70.

17 Michael Andrews, *The Canadian Securities Industry: A Decade of Transition*, Report 68–91 for the Conference Board of Canada, March 1991, 2.

18 Coleman and Porter, 'Banking and Securities Policy,' 72.

19 Debra P. Steger, *A Concise Guide to the Canada-United States Free Trade Agreement* (Agincourt: Carswell, 1988), 59.

20 Thomas J. Courchene and Edwin H. Neave, *Reforming the Canadian Financial Sector: Canada in Global Perspective*, John Deutsch Institute for the Study of Economic Policy, No. 34 (Kingston, 1997), 250.

21 http://142.43.226.103?MEXICOLA/me...580852565B4005C65C/?Open Document, 1.

22 Karen Howlett, 'Royal Buys U.S. Bank Centura,' *Globe and Mail* (Jan. 27, 2001), B1.

23 Michael J. Trebilcock and Robert Howse, *The Regulation of International Trade*, 2nd ed. (New York: Routledge, 1998), 40.

24 Department of Finance Canada website, http://www.fin.gc.ca/

25 Peters and Donner, 'Bank Mergers,' 4.

26 All data for this section come from BCG, *Financial Services at the Crossroads*, unless otherwise noted.

27 David W. Peters and Douglas D. Peters, 'Reforming Canada's Financial Services Sector: What Needs to Follow from Bill C8,' *Canadian Public Policy* (Dec. 2001), 509: 'A move to twenty per cent merely raises the *possibility* of control while maintaining the *fiction* of being widely-held.'

28 Arthur W. Donner and Douglas D. Peters, 'Public Policy Challenges of Bank Mergers and the MacKay Task Force Report,' Report Prepared for House of Commons Standing Committee on Finance (Ottawa, Nov. 6, 1998), 3.

29 Editorial, 'A Vision Worth Banking,' *Globe and Mail* (Sept. 16, 1998), A 16.

30 Growth as measured by the market capitalization of the top six banks. McKinsey and Co., *The Changing Landscape for Canadian Financial Services*, Exhibit 2–6.

31 Peters and Donner, 'Bank Mergers,' 7.

32 Ibid., 22.

33 *MacKay Report on the Future of the Canadian Financial Services Sector*, 'Report of the Task Force' (Sept. 1998), 63–5.

34 Coleman and Porter, 'Banking and Securities Policy,' 59.

35 Speech by Allan G. McNally, vice-chairman and CEO, Harris Bankcorp Inc., Toronto, May 25, 1994.

36 Mailander, *Reshaping North American Banking*, 27.

37 Bob Jenness, 'Canadian Banking, Macroeconomic Policy, and Regulation of International Finance,' in Brian MacLean, ed., *Out of Control: Canada in an Unstable Financial World* (Ottawa: Canadian Centre for Policy Alternatives, 1999), 194.

38 Ibid., 194.

39 Shawn McCarthey, 'Bank Reform Opposition Has Powerful Friends' *Globe and Mail* (June 25, 1999), B1.

40 Jenness, 'Canadian Banking,' 192.

41 Mailander, *Reshaping North American Banking*, 4, 5, 28.

42 Peters and Donner, 'Bank Mergers,' 24.

10. Telecoms: From Regional Monopolies to Global Oligopolies

1 Robert M. Campbell, *The Politics of the Post : Canada's Postal System from Public Service to Privatization* (Peterborough, Ont.: Broadview Press, 1994).

2 When more than one entity offered competing services, social chaos ensued, as Carlos Fuentes reminds us in *The Years of Laura Diaz* (New York: Farrer, Strauss: 2000). Mexico City had two rival phone systems, which complicated general communications, even though, the novel maintains, it facilitated extramarital trysts.

3 Canada, *Telecommunications in Canada* (Ottawa: Consumer and Corporate Affairs Canada, 1981), 10.

4 Richard J. Schultz, 'Winning and Losing: The Consumers' Association of Canada and the Telecommunications Regulatory System, 1973–1993,' in G. Bruce Doern et al., eds., *Changing the Rules: Canadian Regulatory Regimes and Institutions* (Toronto: University of Toronto Press, 1999), 192.

5 Dwayne Winseck, 'Power Shift? Towards a Political Economy of Canadian Telecommunications and Regulation,' *Canadian Journal of Communication* 20, no. 1 (winter 1995), 97.

6 Although it constituted only 2 per cent of the global telecom market by 1992, Canada's industry boasted revenues that year of $21 billion, or 3 per cent of GDP, employed 125,000 workers, accounted for the largest (24 per cent of total) R&D of any industry, and was growing at 8.6 per cent per annum. Winseck, 'Power Shift?' 95.

7 Jeffrey Keefe and Rosemary Batt, 'United States,' in Harry Katz, ed., *Telecommunications: Restructuring Work and Employment Relations Worldwide* (Ithaca, NY: ILR Press, 1997), 36.

8 Philip Somerville, presentation, Centre for International Studies, University of Toronto, Jan. 15, 1997.

9 Robert E. Babe, *Telecommunications in Canada: Technology, Industry, and Government* (Toronto: University of Toronto Press, 1990), 29.

10 Ibid., 189.

11 Joseph D'Cruz and Alan Rugman, 'Business Network Theory and the Canadian Telecommunications Industry,' in W.T. Standury, ed., *Perspectives on the New Economics and Regulation of Telecommunications* (Ottawa: Renouf, 1996), 63.

12 Richard J. Schultz and Mark R. Brawley, 'Telecommunications Policy,' in G. Bruce Doern, Leslie A. Pal, and Brian W. Tomlin, eds., *Border Crossings: The Internationalization of Canadian Public Policy* (Toronto: Oxford University Press, 1996), 87–9.

13 Schultz, 'Winning and Losing,' 191.
14 Schultz and Brawley, 'Telecommunications Policy,' 93.
15 W.G. Waters II and W.T. Stanbury, 'Deregulation, Pressures for Re-regula-
   tion, and Regulatory Shifts: The Case of Telecommunications and Transportation,' in G. Bruce Doern, et al., eds. *Changing the Rules: Canadian Regulatory Regimes and Institutions* (Toronto: University of Toronto Press, 1999),
   151.
16 Schultz and Brawley, 'Telecommunications Policy,' 96.
17 For many years, Canadian National and Canadian Pacific had competed directly in telecom. In the 1940s, however, the two telegraph
   companies started amalgamating services, choosing to co-operate rather
   than compete. By 1980, their co-operation culminated in a partnership,
   CNCP Telecommunications, jointly owned by Canadian National Railway Company and Canadian Pacific Limited. In 1988, CNCP was sold
   as Unitel Communications Inc. to Rogers Communications, a major provider of cable TV and other communications services in Canada. Babe,
   Telecommunications in Canada, 188. AT&T's connection to Rogers helped
   move telecom from regulated national cartel towards deregulated global
   oligopoly.
18 Ibid., 125.
19 Schultz, 'Winning and Losing,' 193.
20 Schultz and Brawley, 'Telecommunications Policy,' 98.
21 Ibid., 134.
22 Babe, *Telecommunications in Canada*, 134.
23 D'Cruz and Rugman, 'Business Network Theory,' 63.
24 George Harvey, 'Benefits of Competition,' *Canadian Telecommunications:
   Regulation and Competition* (Mississauga, Ont.: Insight, 1989), 5.
25 The claim that big business spends 5 per cent of total expenditures appears
   misleading. A federal-provincial task force on long-distance competition
   found that telecom represented only 0.7 per cent of business costs. Winseck,
   'Power Shift?' 96, 98.
26 Ibid., 89.
27 Ibid., 89.
28 Ibid., 135.
29 By the early 1990s, Canadian imports of telecom equipment from the
   United States amounted to $694 million, or 57 per cent, of Canadian
   imports in that sector, but Canada accounted for only 11 per cent of U.S.
   exports. Hudson N. Janisch, 'The Canada-U.S. FTA: Telecom and Regional
   Free Trade,' working paper, 1992, 6.
30 As a result of these efforts, the share of the Canadian telecom market under

private ownership rose from 68 in 1981 to 81 per cent in 1994. Winseck, 'Power Shift?' 95.

31 Janisch, 'The Canada-U.S. FTA,' 14.

32 Ibid., 7.

33 Hudson N. Janisch, 'Canadian Telecommunications in a Free Trade Era,' working paper, 1998, 1.

34 Janisch, 'The Canada-U.S. FTA,' 12.

35 'Enhanced' or 'value-added' services are those that offer more than the simple transmission of information, such as computer-processing applications that act on the format or content of a customer's transmitted information; that provide a customer with additional, different, or restructured information; or that involve customers' interaction with stored information. They include data-access arrangements, radio paging, telegraph, 911 service, home shopping, banking, storing and forwarding voice mail, and electronic mail service. Janisch, 'NAFTA: Definitions,' working paper, 1988, 23.

36 *Alberta Government Telephones v. Canada (Canadian Radio-television and Tele-communications* Commission), [1989] 2 SCR 225; *Téléphone Guèvremont Inc. v. Quebec* (Régie des télécommunications), [1994] 1 SCR 878.

37 Salvatore Mirandola, 'Towards a Principled Allocation of Powers over Tele-communications,' *Media and Communications Law Review* 3 (1993), 332.

38 Ibid., 330.

39 Janisch, 'Canadian Telecommunications in a Free Trade Era,' 35.

40 W.T. Stanbury, 'Editor's Introduction,' in W.T. Stanbury, ed., *Perspectives on the New Economics and Regulation of Telecommunications* (Ottawa: Renouf, 1996), 7.

41 Ibid., 7.

42 Hudson Janisch, 'International Influence on Communications Policy in Canada,' in Dale Orr and Thomas A. Wilson, eds., *The Electronic Village: Policy Issues of the Information Economy* (Toronto: C.D. Howe Institute, 1999), 61.

43 Telecom Decision 92–12, 'Competition in the Provision of Public Long Distance Voice Telephone Services and Related Resale and Sharing Issues,' cited in Winseck, 'Power Shift?' 99.

44 W.T. Stanbury, 'Chronology of Canadian Telecommunications: January 1992 to January 1996,' in Stanbury, ed., *Perspectives on the New Economics*, 288.

45 Telecom Decision 94–19, 'Review of Regulatory Framework,' cited in Stanbury, 'Chronology,' 312.

46 Waters and Stanbury, 'Deregulation,' 152.

47 Gerald Heckman, 'Ownership and Control in the Canadian Telecommuni-

cations Industry: The Case of Strategic Alliances,' *Canadian Business Law Journal* 29 (1998), 137.

48 'While labour unions and these other groups make valuable contributions to the regulatory proceedings ... the new telecom legislation allows the CRTC to exclude them from regulatory hearings.' Winseck, 'Power Shift?' 90.

49 Edward Comor, 'The Department of Communications under the Free Trade Regime,' *Canadian Journal of Communication* 16, no. 2 (1991), 249, and Winseck, 'Power Shift?' 100.

50 Winseck, 'Power Shift?' 85.

51 http://www.ustr.gov/agreements/telecom/barshevsky.htm/

52 Schultz and Brawley, 'Telecommunications Policy,' 104.

53 J. Gregory Sidak, *Foreign Investment in American Telecommunications* (Chicago: University of Chicago Press, 1997), 371.

54 Jong-Geun Oh, 'Global Strategic Alliances,' *Telecommunications Policy* 20, no. 9 (Nov. 1996), 715.

55 Hudson Janisch, 'International Influence on Communications Policy in Canada,' 70.

56 Interview with Professor Hudson Janisch, Nov. 5, 2001.

57 James Meenan, CEO of AT&T, Centre for International Studies, University of Toronto, April 30, 1997.

58 D'Cruz and Rugman, 'Business Network Theory,' 71.

59 Tyler Hamilton, 'Bell Deal Signals End of National Telecom Focus,' *Globe and Mail* (March 25, 1999), B7.

60 Richard J. Schultz, 'Still Standing: The CRTC, 1976–1996,' in G. Bruce Doern et al., eds., *Changing the Rules: Canadian Regulatory Regimes and Institutions* (Toronto: University of Toronto Press, 1999), 52.

61 Robert Cribb, 'Boot Up Your TV: That's the Future as Microsoft Buys into Rogers Cable,' *Toronto Star* (July 13, 1999), A1, 12.

62 Terence Corcoran, 'First the Canadarm, Now Bell Canada,' *Financial Post* (March 25, 1999), F1.

11. The Trading State

1 On the distinction between 'reactive' and 'anticipatory' industrial policies, see Michael M. Atkinson and William D. Coleman, *The State, Business, and Industrial Change in Canada* (Toronto: University of Toronto Press, 1989), 23–7.

2 Trade data: www.chass.utoronto.ca/datalib/cansim label D23103

3 Biz/ed Business and Economics Service for Students, http://www.bized.ac.uk/cgi-bin/stats

4 B.R. Mitchell, *International Historical Statistics – The Americas 1750–1993* (Abingdon: Nuffield Press, 1998), E2, G70-83, and G57-69.
5 Ibid.
6 *Trade Update 2000, First Annual Report on Canada's State of Trade*, 2nd ed. (Ottawa: Department of Foreign Affairs and International Trade, 2000), 7.
7 Daniel Trefler, *The Long and Short of the Canada-U.S. Free Trade Agreement* (Ottawa: Industry Canada, 1999), 28.
8 Daniel Schwanen, 'Trading Up: The Impact of Increased Continental Integration on Trade, Investment, and Jobs in Canada,' *C.D. Howe Institute Commentary* 89 (March 1997), Tables A-1 and A-2, 25.
9 John N.H. Britton, 'Is the Impact of the North American Trade Agreements Zero? The Canadian Case,' *Canadian Journal of Regional Science* 21, no. 2 (summer 1998), 167–96.
10 Ibid., 181.
11 Ibid., 182.
12 Ibid., 182. Trade deficit here is measured as a proportion of exports.
13 Trefler, *The Long and Short of the Canada-U.S. Free Trade Agreement*, 26.
14 Schwanen, 'Trading Up,' Tables 2, 8.
15 Richard A. Cameron, *Intrafirm Trade of Canadian-Based Foreign Transnational Companies*, Industry Canada Working Paper No. 26 (Ottawa, Dec. 1998), 8, 11. The average degree of export orientation of foreign-controlled firms in 1990–2 was 19.6 per cent, while the import orientation was 21.7 per cent. The figures for domestic firms were 9.0 per cent and 7.4 per cent, respectively.
16 John N.H. Britton, 'Does Nationality Still Matter? The New Competition and the Foreign Ownership Question Revisited,' in Trevor J. Barnes and Merie S. Gertler, eds., *The New Industrial Geography: Regions, Regulations and Institutions* (London: Routledge, 1999), 239.
17 Niosi, 'Foreign Direct Investment in Canada,' 374.
18 Britton, 'Does Nationality Still Matter?' 243.
19 Schwanen, 'Trading Up,' 13.
20 Organization for Economic Co-operation and Development, *OECD Historical Statistics. 1960–97* (Paris: OECD Publications, 1999), Table 3.1, p. 50.
21 Organization for Economic Co-operation and Development, *OECD Economic Survey 1998–9* (Paris: OECD Publications, 2000), Table A3.
22 The GDP figures for these countries in 2001 in billions of U.S. dollars: Italy $1,099, China $820, Brazil $960, Canada $1038, and Spain $559. The International Monetary Fund, *IMF Financial Statistics*, on the University of Toronto's Computing in the Humanities and Social Sciences website, http://datacentre.chass.utoronto.ca/cgi-bin/imf

23 Andrei Sulzenko and James Kalwarowsky, 'A Policy Challenge for a Higher Standard of Living,' *Isuma* 1, no. 1 (spring 2000), 126.
24 In the auto industry, which adapts foreign technology, productivity is essentially the same in Canada as in the United States. Communication by Daniel Schwanen to the author, March 1, 2002.
25 Surendra Gera, Wulong Gu, and Frank Lee, *Foreign Direct Investment and Productivity Growth: The Canadian Host-Country Experience*, (Ottawa: Industry Canada, 1999), 19.
26 Ibid., 19.
27 Steven Globerman, *Implications of Foreign Ownership Restrictions for the Canadian Economy – A Sectoral Analysis* (Ottawa: Industry Canada, 1999), 3–4.
28 Cameron, *Intrafirm Trade*, 34.
29 Steven Globerman, *Canadian Government Policies toward Inward FDI* (Ottawa: Industry Canada, 1998), 8.
30 Trefler, *The Long and Short of the Canada-U.S. Free Trade Agreement*, 21, 24.
31 Ibid., Figure 1, 4.
32 Schwanen, 'Trading Up,' 20.
33 Daniel Trefler, *The Long and Short of the Canada-U.S. Free Trade Agreement*, 19.
34 Schwanen, 'Trading Up,' 19.
35 Statistics Canada, 'Canada Labour Force Characteristics: Monthly Unadjusted Employment (Full-time and Part-time) Age 15+,' *Canadian Socio-Economic Information Management System (CANSIM): Databank Number D980238 and D980290* (Ottawa: Statistics Canada – CANSIM Division, 2000).
36 Ibid.
37 Britton, 'Is the Impact of the North American Trade Agreements Zero?' 187–8.
38 Organization for Economic Cooperation and Development, *OECD International Statistics* (Paris: OECD Publications, 1999), 45.
39 See the statistical appendix of the International Monetary Fund's website, imf.org/external/pubs/ft/weo/weo1098/pdf/1098sta.pdf
40 In 1974, the unemployment rate was 5.3 per cent. www.scotiacapital.com/english/bns_econ/canquart.pdf. datacentre.chass.utoronto.ca/cgi-bin/cansim Label D44950.
41 Schwanen, 'Trading Up,' 4.
42 www.statcan.ca/english/pgdb/people/labour/labor01a.htm
43 www.statcan.ca/english/pgdb/people/labour/labor14.htm
44 Trefler, *The Long and Short of the Canada-U.S. Free Trade Agreement*, 18.
45 Economic Council of Canada, *Good Jobs, Bad Jobs: Employment in the Service Sector Economy* (1990), 12.
46 Leah F. Vosko, 'Regulating Precariousness? The Temporary Employment

Relationship under the NAFTA and EC Treaty,' *Industrial Relations* 53, no. 1 (March 1998), 123–53.

47 Ibid., 15, 76.

48 Ibid., 15, 153.

49 Statistics Canada cited by Andrew Jackson, *Impacts of the Free Trade Agreement and the North American Free Trade Agreement on Canadian Labour Markets and Labour and Social Standards* (Ottawa: Canadian Labour Congress, 1997), 21.

50 Jackson and Robertson, *Falling Behind*, 13.

51 Britton, 'Is the Impact of the North American Trade Agreements Zero?' 187–8.

52 Ibid., 179.

53 Ibid., 180.

54 Report on presentations by Roger Gibbins and David Chaundy, *Horizons* 3, no. 6 (Dec. 1, 2000), 10.

55 This idea is developed in Roy Culpepper, 'Overview,' in Michelle Hibler and Rowena Beamish, eds., *Canadian Corporations and Social Responsibility: Canadian Development Report, 1998. North-South Institute* (Ottawa: Renouf, 1998), 10.

56 Matthew Kalman, 'Marchi Takes Canadian Trade Caravan to the Middle East,' *Globe and Mail* (Feb. 26, 1999), A16.

57 Valerie Lawton, 'Technology Aid Program Will Survive, Says Marchi,' *Toronto Star* (March 3, 1999), D3.

12. The Investing State

1 Jeanne Kirk Laux, 'How Private is Privatization?' *Canadian Public Policy* 19, no. 4 (Dec. 1993), 400–1.

2 Ibid., 403.

3 Ibid., 404–5.

4 Jorge Niosi, 'Foreign Direct Investment in Canada,' in Lorraine Eden, ed., *Multinationals in North America* (Calgary: University of Calgary Press, 1994), 369.

5 This phenomenon is affected by nationality. U.S. TNCs tend to displace trade, while German and Japanese TNCs tend to create trade. Louis W. Pauly and Simon Reich, 'National Structures and Multinational Corporate Behavior: Enduring Differences in the Age of Globalization,' *International Organization* 51, no. 1 (winter 1997), 17.

6 John Stopford and Susan Strange, *Rival States, Rival Firms: Competition for World Market Shares* (Cambridge: Cambridge University Press, 1991), 207;

Peter Morici, 'Resolving the North American Subsidies War,' *Canadian-American Public Policy* 27 (Sept. 1996), 1–34.

7 John N.H. Britton, 'Does Nationality Still Matter? The New Competition and the Foreign Ownership Question Revisited,' in Trevor J. Barnes and Meric S. Gertler, eds., *The New Industrial Geography: Regions, Regulation and Institutions* (London: Routledge, 1999), 239.

8 Morici, 'Resolving the North American Subsidies War,' 1–34.

9 Ibid.

10 Interview with Hugo Perezcano, in the Secretaria de la Economia, Mexico City, Feb. 20, 2002.

11 David Schneiderman, 'NAFTA's Takings Rule: American Constitutionalism Comes to Canada,' *University of Toronto Law Journal* 46 (1996), 535.

12 Susan Goodeve, 'Canada Commits to Trade Liberalization,' in Peter Haydan and Jeffrey Burns, eds., *Foreign Investment in Canada* (Scarborough, Ont.: Carswell, 1996), 284.

13 Lorraine Eden, 'Who Does What after NAFTA?' in Lorraine Eden, ed., *Multinationals in North America* (Calgary: University of Calgary Press, 1994), 208, 241.

14 Bruce W. Wilkinson, 'Regional Trade Blocks: Fortress Europe vs. Fortress North America,' in Daniel Drache and Meric Gertler, eds., *The New Era of Global Competition* (Montreal: McGill-Queen's University Press, 1991), 51–82.

15 Claus von Wobeser, 'El régimen legal de la inversión extranjera en el TLCAN y sus efectos en los flujos de capital hacia México,' in Beatriz Leycegui and Rafael Fernandez de Castro, eds., *Socios naturales? Cinco años del Tratado de libre comercio de América del Norte* (Mexico City: Instituto Tecnológico Autónomo de México, 2000), 268.

16 Daniel Schwanen, 'Trading Up: The Impact of Increased Continental Integration on Trade, Investment, and Jobs in Canada,' *C.D. Howe Commentary* 89 (March 1997), 18.

17 Report on paper by Bill Singleton in *Horizons* 3, no. 6 (Dec. 1, 2000), 13.

18 Shawn McCarthy, 'Business Sounds Alarm on Vulnerability,' *Globe and Mail* (May 8, 2000), B1.

19 Ibid.

20 Ibid., for 1978 and 1988 figures. Mary Janigan, 'The Fear of Losing Control,' *Maclean's Magazine* (July 1, 2000), 60–2, for percentages of GDP.

21 Janigan, 'The Fear of Losing Control,' 60–2.

22 Shawn McCarthy, 'Foreign Control of Economy on Rise,' *Globe and Mail* (May 3, 2000), B3. The increase was from 25.1 per cent in 1988 to 31.2 per cent in 1997, as measured in operating revenues.

23 Niosi, 'Foreign Direct Investment in Canada,' 370.
24 Ibid., 373.
25 Compared to 23 per cent going to the United Kingdom. Department of Foreign Affairs and International Trade (DFAIT) website, www.dfait-maeci.gc.ca
26 International Accounts Data of the Bureau of Economic Analysis, available at the U.S. Department of Commerce website, http://www.bea.doc.gov/bea/di/dia-ctry.htm
27 DFAIT's *Trade Update 2000 Report*, 34, http://www.dfait-maeci.gc.ca/eet/state_of_trade/state_of_trade0600–e.pdf.
28 Myron J. Gordon, 'Foreign Ownership: The Problem and its Solutions,' *Policy Options* (May 2000), 52–5.
29 John N.H. Britton, 'Is the Impact of the North American Trade Agreements Zero? The Canadian Case,' *Canadian Journal of Regional Science* 21, no. 2 (Summer 1998), 176.
30 Isaiah A. Litvak, 'The Marginalization of Corporate Canada,' *Behind the Headlines* 58, no. 2 (winter 2000–1), 6.
31 Britton, 'Does Nationality Still Matter?' 255.
32 M.S. Gertler and S. DiGiovanna, 'In Search of the New Social Economy: Collaborative Relations between Users and Producers of Advanced Manufacturing Technologies,' *Environment and Planning* A 29 (1997), 1585-692, cited in Britton, 'Does Nationality Still Matter?' 256.
33 M. Porter, 75, in ibid.
34 Ibid., 255.   .
35 Stephen Blank, Stephen Krajewski, and Henry S. Yu, 'U.S. Firms in North America: Redefining Structure and Strategy,' *North American Outlook* 5, no. 2 (Feb. 1995), 11.
36 Ibid., 66.
37 Ibid., 67.
38 J. Birkinshaw, 'Mandate Strategies for Canadian Subsidiaries,' Working Paper No. 9 (Ottawa: Industry Canada, 1996) cited in Britton, 'Does Nationality Still Matter?' 251.
39 Harry Arthurs,' The Hollowing out of Corporate Canada?' in J. Jenson and B. Santos, eds., *Globalizing Institutions: Case Studies in Social Regulation and Innovation* (London: Ashgate, 2000).
40 Ronald Hirshhorn, *Industry Canada's Foreign Investment Research: Messages and Policy Implications* (Ottawa: Industry Canada, 1997), 4.
41 Lorraine Eden, *Multinationals as Agents of Change: Setting a New Canadian Policy* (Ottawa: Industry Canada, 1994), 8.
42 R.A. Cameron, *Intrafirm Trade*, 33–4.

43 Juan Palacios, 'Footloose Factories in Continental Network Economies: Corporate Behaviour of Electronics Contract Manufacturers in NAFTA Settings,' paper presented to the International Political Science Association, Quebec City, Aug. 2, 2000, 6.
44 I.A. Litvak and C.J. Maule, *The Canadian Multinationals* (Toronto : Butterworths, 1981), 90.
45 Jorge Niosi, *Canadian Multinationals* (Toronto: Between the Lines, 1985), 44, translated by Robert Chodos.
46 Litvak and Maule, *The Canadian Multinationals*, 90.
47 Ibid., 92.
48 Evidence of this is conveyed in Litvak and Maule, *The Canadian Multinationals*, 92–8, and in Niosi, *Canadian Multinationals*, 51–2.
49 Elizabeth Smythe, 'Investment Rules and the WTO: Anatomy of a Campaign,' paper presented to the Canadian Political Science Association, June 1998, 6.
50 Tony Clarke and Maude Barlow, *Multilateral Agreement on Investment* (Toronto: Stoddart, 1997).
51 For an overview of the Canadian International Business Strategy, see http://strategis.ic.gc.ca/
52 Industry Canada Home page, 'Introduction: Team Canada. Working Together, We are Taking on the World,' at http://strategis.ic.gc.ca/SSG/bi17963e.htm
53 Niosi, 'Foreign Direct Investment in Canada,' 370, 380.
54 Randy Wigle, *Broad Liberalization Based on Fundamentals: A Framework for Canadian Commercial Policy. Canada in the 21st Century* (Ottawa: Industry Canada, 1998), 7.
55 DFAIT, *Trade Update 2000 Report*, 34.
56 Niosi, 'Foreign Direct Investment in Canada,' 379.
57 Ibid., 372.
58 Ibid., 383.
59 Rick Cameron, *Micro Economic Policy Analysis Branch Bulletin* (Industry Canada) 5, special issue (spring 1999), 12.
60 Mark MacKinnon, 'Capital Outflow Gains Momentum' and 'Barbados Is a Tax-haven Heaven,' *Globe and Mail* (July 5, 1999), B1, B3.
61 Someshwar Rao, Marc Legault, and Ashfaq Ahmad, *Canadian-Based Multinationals: An Analysis of Activities and Performance* (Ottawa: Industry Canada, 1994), 7.
62 Ibid., 9.
63 Niosi, *Canadian Multinationals*, 49.
64 Someshwar Rao, Marc Legault, and Ashfaq Ahmad, 'Canadian-based Mul-

tinationals,' in Steven Globerman, ed., *Canadian-Based Multinationals*, Industry Canada Research Series (Calgary: University of Calgary Press, 1994), 93.

65 Cameron, *Micro Economic Policy Analysis*, 11, and MacKinnon, 'Capital Outflow Gains Momentum,' B1.
66 Communication from Daniel Schwanen, March 1, 2002.
67 Robert Ferguson, 'Canada a "Fire Sale" for Foreign Firms,' *Toronto Star* (March 2, 1999), D1, D5.
68 Donald J.S. Brean, 'Taxation and Canadian Direct Investment Abroad,' in Globerman, ed., *Canadian-Based Multinationals*, 229.
69 The idea of 'spillover' is developed in Rao, Legault, and Ahmad, 'Canadian-based Multinationals,' 100–2.
70 David Crane, 'Mid-size Firms Deserve Funding Help,' *Toronto Star* (March 2, 1999), D2.
71 Rao, Legault, and Ahmad, *Canadian-Based Multinationals*, 33–4.
72 Litvak, 'Corporate Canada,' 8, and David Crane, 'Nortel Sets Example by Tackling Skills Gap,' *Toronto Star* (March 3, 1999), E2.
73 Litvak, 'Corporate Canada,' 7–8.
74 Ibid., 11–17.
75 Ilan Vertinsky and Rachana Raizada, 'MacMillan Bloedel: Foreign Investment Decisions and Their Welfare Consequences,' in Globerman, ed., *Canadian-Based Multinationals* 407–9.
76 I am indebted to Bruce Wilkinson for this point, which, like all counterfactual arguments, can be contested.
77 Brent Jang and Shawn McCarthy, 'Ottawa Set for Selloff of Petrocan,' *Globe and Mail* (May 19, 2000), A1.
78 Janigan, 'The Fear of Losing Control,' 60.
79 Ibid., 61.
80 Alan M. Rugman, *Multinationals and Canada–United States Free Trade* (Columbia: University of South Carolina Press, 1990), 91.
81 Stopford and Strange, *Rival States, Rival Firms*, 20.
82 Alan M. Rugman and A. Verbeke, *Global Corporate Strategy and Trade Policy* (London: Routledge, 1990), 14.
83 David Crane, 'Chrétien Beats the Drum for Investment Dollars,' *Toronto Star* (Jan. 28, 1999), D2.
84 Ibid.
85 Ann Weston, 'Ethics in the Marketplace: The Manufacturing Sector,' in Michelle Hibler and Rowena Beamish, eds., *Canadian Corporations and Social Responsibility* (Ottawa: North–South Institute, 1998), 59.
86 Data on the Loewen Case are available at http://www.citizen.org/

pctrade/nafta/Loewen.html and http://www.citizen.org/pctrade/nafta/cases/importance.html

87 Heather Scoffield and Steven Chase, 'Methanex to Sue U.S. under Free-Trade Deal,' *Globe and Mail* (June 16, 1999), B1.
88 'A New Role for a Trade Deal,' *Globe and Mail* (June 18, 1999).
89 Report on presentations by Wulong Gu, Industry Canada, and John M. Curtis, DFAIT, *Horizons* 3, no. 6 (Dec. 1, 2000), 16.
90 Stopford and Strange, *Rival States, Rival Firms*, 14.

13. The Residual State: Accommodation at the Federal Level

1 Industry Canada, *Investing in Innovation* (Ottawa, 1994). See also the Department of Finance 'purple paper' authored by Peter Nicholson in 1994.
2 Wallace Clement, 'Resources and Manufacturing in Canada's Political Economy,' in Wallace Clement and Glen Williams, eds., *Understanding Canada* (Montreal: McGill-Queen's University Press, 1997), 57.
3 R. Martin, 'Canadian Labour and North American Integration,' in Stephen J. Randall and Herman W. Konrad, eds., *North America without Borders* (Calgary: University of Calgary Press, 1992), 184.
4 D. DesRosiers, 'Automotive Marketplace: The Golden Age of Canada's Automotive Industry,' *Maclean's* (May 24, 1999), 12.
5 Ibid.
6 John Holmes, 'Industrial Reorganization, Capital Restructuring, and Locational Change: An Analysis of the Canadian Automobile Industry in the 1960s,' *Economic Geography* 59 (July 1983), 251.
7 Ibid., 262.
8 James F. Keeley, 'Cast In Concrete for All Time? The Negotiation of the Auto Pact,' *Canadian Journal of Political Science* 16, no. 2 (June 1983), 281.
9 A. Inkpen, 'Japanese Joint Ventures in the Auto Industry: Implications for North American Auto Suppliers,' in Maureen Molot, ed., *Driving Continentally: National Policies and the North American Auto Industry* (Ottawa: Carleton University Press, 1993), 35.
10 Toyota spent $600 million, more than doubling the capacity of its Corolla assembly line in Ontario to 200,000 cars a year. All the extra cars were exported to the United States. *Economist* (Jan. 14, 1995), 27.
11 Ibid. (June 26, 1998), 8.
12 W. Green, 'The Transformation of the NLRA Paradigm: The Future of Labor-Management Relations in the Post-Fordist Auto Plant,' in W. Green and E. Yanarella, eds., *North American Auto Unions in Crisis* (Albany: State University of New York Press, 1996), 161.

13 John Holmes, 'The Continental Integration of the North American Auto Industry,' *Environment and Planning* 25, no. 1 (Jan. 1993), 105–6.

14 Sam Gindin, 'Presentation,' Auto Parts Conference (Nov. 5, 1998).

15 Regional zone of preference refers to the NAFTA rule that benefits auto manufacturers that can choose to source parts in either Canada, the United States, or Mexico to meet 'North American' content levels.

16 Maureen Molot, 'Introduction,' in Maureem Molot, ed., *Driving Continentally: National Policies and the North American Auto Industry* (Ottawa: Carleton University Press, 1993), 14.

17 Simon Reich, 'NAFTA, FDI and the Auto Industry: A Comparative Perspective,' in ibid., 88.

18 Gary Hufbauer and Jeffrey Schott, *NAFTA: An Assessment* (Washington, DC: Institute for International Economics, 1993), 39.

19 Molot, 'Introduction,' 12.

20 CAW homepage, www.cawca/barg/facts/html, 5.

21 Sidney Weintraub, 'Incomes and Productivity in the Auto Industry in North America,' in Sidney Weintraub and Christopher Sands, eds., *The North American Auto Industry under NAFTA* (Washington, DC: CSIS, 1998), 231.

22 CAW homepage.

23 E. Yanarella, 'The UAW and CAW under the Shadow of Post-Fordism: A Tale of Two Unions,' in Green and Yanarella, *North American Auto Unions in Crisis*, 44.

24 Hourly CAW/GM Canada Report, Oct. 1996, 1.

25 Heather Scoffield, 'Ottawa Plots Slow, Painless Death for Auto Pact,' *Globe and Mail* (June 19, 2000), B3.

26 P. Kumar and J. Holmes, 'The Impact of NAFTA on the Auto Industry in Canada,' in Weintraub and Sands, *The North American Auto Industry*, 95.

27 Reich, 'NAFTA, FDI, and the Auto Industry,' 89.

28 Rosemarie Kanusky, 'Pharmaceutical Harmonization: Standardizing Regulations among the United States, the European Economic Community, and Japan,' *Houston Journal of International Law* 16, (spring 1994), 665.

29 Robert Weissman, 'A Long, Strange TRIPS: The Pharmaceutical Industry Drive to Harmonize Global Intellectual Property Rules, and the Remaining WTO Legal Alternatives Available to Third World Countries,' *University of Pennsylvania Journal of International Economic Law* 17, no. 4 (winter 1996), 1072.

30 Ibid.

31 P.K. Gorecki, *Regulating the Price of Prescription Drugs in Canada: Compulsory Licensing, Product Selection, and Government Reimbursement Programmes*, Economic Council of Canada, Technical Report No. 8 (Ottawa, 1981).

32 S.R. Shulman and B.W. Richard, 'The 1987 Canadian Patent Law Amendments: Revised Pharmaceutical Compulsory Licensing Provisions,' *Food, Drug, and Cosmetic Law Journal* 43 (1988), 745–57.
33 John W. Rogers, 'The Revised Canadian Patent Act, the Free Trade Agreement, and Pharmaceutical Patents: An Overview of Pharmaceutical Compulsory Licensing in Canada,'*Enforcers of Intellectual Property Rights* 10 (1990), 351–9.
34 Canada, Department of Justice, *Restrictive Trade Practices Commission Report Covering the Manufacture, Distribution,and Sale of Drugs*, Can. Cat. No. J53-62/24, RPTC 24,1963.
35 Royal Commission on Health Services, *Report of the Commission on Health Services* (Ottawa: Queen's Printer, 1964); House of Commons, *Special Committee of the House of Commons on Drug Costs and Prices* (Ottawa: Queen's Printer, 1966–67).
36 R.W. Lang, *The Politics of Drugs* (Westmead: Saxon House, 1974).
37 J. Lexchin, *Pharmaceuticals, Patents, and Politics: Canada and Bill C-22* (Ottawa: Canadian Centre for Policy Alternatives, Feb. 1992).
38 Gorecki, *Regulating the Price of Prescription Drugs in Canada.*
39 A.J. Manson, 'The Impact of Compulsory Licensing on Pharmaceutical Research,' *Canadian Intellectual Property Review* 1, no. 2 (1984), 167–8.
40 Ibid., 164–7.
41 Lexchin, *Pharmaceuticals, Patents, and Politics*, 3; also George A. Seaby, 'Drug Licensing: Should Section 41(4) Be Retained?' *Canadian Intellectual Property Review* 1, no. 1 (1984), 40.
42 Ibid., 4.
43 Margaret Smith, *Bill C-22: Compulsory Licensing of Pharmaceuticals, Mini-Review 86-36E* (Ottawa: Research Branch, Library of Parliament, Nov. 24, 1995), 2–3.
44 H. C. Eastman, *The Report of the Commission of Inquiry*, Can. Cat. No. CA CP32-46/1985E (Ottawa, 1985).
45 Linda McQuaig, *The Quick and the Dead* (Toronto: Viking, 1991), 136.
46 Smith, *Bill C-22*, 6.
47 Senate of Canada, *Proceedings of the Special Committee of the Senate on the Subject-matter of Bill C-22, Third Report of the Committee* (Ottawa: Special Committee, June 27, 1987), 12.
48 Industry Canada Health Industries Branch, *Pharmaceutical Manufacturers' Association of Canada Commitments* (Ottawa: Strategis, Government of Canada, Jan. 19, 2001).
49 Malcolm Anderson, *Evergreening in the Canadian Pharmaceutical Industry* (Toronto: Queen's Health Policy, Abramsky Hall, Jan. 21, 1997).

50 B. Champoux, *An Impact Analysis of the Regulation Pertaining to Section 55, no. 2 of the Patent Act* (Ottawa: Pharmaceutical Policy Division, Drugs Directorate, Health Canada, 1993); Queen's Health Policy, *The Economic Impact of Bill C-91 on the Cost of Pharmaceuticals in Canada* (Kingston: Queen's University, 1997).

51 Canadian Drug Manufacturers Association, *U.S. Threatens Canada at WTO for Increased Patent Protection for Brand Name Drugs* (Toronto: CDMA Press Releases, June 10, 1999).

52 Ibid.

53 Heather Scoffield and Scott Kennan, 'Trade Ruling Expected to Kill Auto Pact,' *Globe and Mail* (July 12, 1999), A1, 4.

54 Melissa K. Davis, 'Monopolistic Tendencies of Brand-name Drug Companies in the Pharmaceutical Industry,' *Journal of Law and Commerce* 15 (fall 1995), 357–73.

55 Andrew Kormylo, Sylvain de Tonnancour, and Stuart Hoover, *A Profile of Canada's Computer Services Industry* (Ottawa: Information and Communications Technologies Branch, Industry Canada, 1998).

56 *Software Products and Computer Services* (Ottawa: Industry Canada, National Sector Team – Information, March 20, 1997).

57 Kormylo, de Tonnancour, and Hoover, *Canada's Computer Services Industry.*

58 Colleen O'Brian, *Software Products and Computer Services Industry Overview* (Ottawa: Industry Canada, Information Technology Branch, March 7, 1997), http://strategis.ic.gc.ca/

59 J. Thomas McCarthy, *McCarthy's Desk Encyclopedia of Intellectual Property* (Washington, DC: Bureau of National Affairs, 1991).

60 Kormylo, de Tonnancour, and Hoover, *Canada's Computer Services Industry.*

61 Federal-Provincial Fiscal Arrangements Act, 1967.

62 Hon. Michael H. Wilson, *Securing Economic Renewal: The Agenda for Economic Renewal: Principles and Progress* (Ottawa: Department of Finance, Feb. 18, 1987).

63 Thomas Axworthy, 'Stealth Tactics Don't Belong in Higher Education,' *Globe and Mail* (Aug. 30, 2001), A14.

64 J. Robert S. Prichard, 'Federal Support for Higher Education and Research in Canada: The New Paradigm,' 2000 Kilam Annual Lecture (Halifax: Killam Trust, 2001), 27.

65 *Federal Budget 1999: Building a Strong Economy through Knowledge and Innovation* (Ottawa: Department of Finance, Feb. 1999).

66 National Research Council Canada, *IRAP: Industrial Research Assistance Program*, electronic pamphlet received from Melvin W. Chan, industry technology adviser, University of Toronto, 1999. Also *Vision to 2001: Science and*

Technology for Canada's Future (Ottawa: National Research Council, 1996); *The Communications Research Centre and Innovation in the Domestic Telecommunications Industry* (Ottawa: Corporate and Industrial Analysis Branch, Industry Canada, 1994).

67 M. Kumar and V. Kumar, *Report Prepared for the Federal Partners in Technology Transfer* (Ottawa: Information and Communications Technologies Branch, Industry Canada, 1998).

68 Gilles Paquet, 'States, Communities, and Markets: The Distributed Governance Scenario,' in Thomas Courchene, ed., *The Nation State in a Global/ Information Era: Policy Challenges* (Kingston: John Deutsch Institute for the Study of Economic Policy, 1997), 25–46.

14. The Industrial State Goes Provincial

1 This chapter benefited enormously from the research assistance of Aimée Downèy; from interviews conducted in August and September 1997 with present and former Ontario civil servants, most notably Peter Barnes, Bryan Davies, Peter Friedman, Richard Howard, Phil Howell, Gordon Jansen, Katherine McGuire, Saad Rafi, Peter Sadleir-Brown, and Anne Waddell; and from critical comments on earlier drafts by Ashley McCall, David Trick, Nelson Wiseman, David Wolfe, and an anonymous reader.

2 The National Energy Program of 1980 was a case of Tory Ontario supporting federal Liberals in a policy attacked by Tory Alberta.

3 This ministry has gone through as many changes of name as of mandate: from Industry and Trade, to Industry, Trade and Technology, to Economic Development and Trade, to Economic Development, Trade and Tourism, and again to Economic Development and Trade, and in 2002, to Enterprise, Opportuinity, and Innovation.

4 Courchene and Telmer point out that, in reality, Peterson was sending out very confused, mixed messages regarding economic policy in Ontario. On the level of rhetoric, he was advocating higher-value-added activities aimed at international trade, a better science and technology infrastructure, and the importance of human capital, but in reality he was raising taxes, fighting the trade liberalization represented by CUFTA, and co-operating with the New Democratic Party (NDP) in a social alliance. They refer to this as a split between 'a value-added and human capital philosophical agenda, on the one hand, and a socially-driven, inward-looking and high-tax legislative agenda,' on the other hand. Thomas J. Courchene and Colin R. Telmer, *From Heartland to North American Region State: The Social, Fiscal and Fed-*

eral Evolution of Ontario (Toronto: Monograph Series on Public Policy, 1998), 110–11.

5 David Cameron, 'Post-Modern Ontario and the Laurentian Thesis,' in Douglas M. Brown and Janet Hiebert, eds., *Canada: The State of the Federation 1994* (Kingston: Institute of Intergovernmental Relations, 1995), 125.

6 Office of the Attorney General, *The Impact of the Canada–U.S. Trade Agreement: A Legal Analysis* (Toronto: Queen's Park, May 1988).

7 Premier's Council, *Competing in the New Global Economy* (Toronto, 1988).

8 Cameron, 'Post-Modern Ontario and the Laurentian Thesis,' 121.

9 Ibid.

10 Jack Stilborn, 'Federal-Provincial Relations' (Ottawa: Research Branch, Library of Parliament, Nov. 1993), 86–2E; Jean-Denis Fréchette. 'Federal Transfer Payments to the Provinces for Health and Post-Secondary Education: New Trends' (Ottawa: Research Branch, Library of Parliament), 93-1E.

11 *Final Report. Cabinet Committee on the North American Free Trade Agreement* (Toronto: Queen's Printer of Ontario, June 1993).

12 Bob Rae, *From Protest to Power: Personal Reflections on a Life in Politics* (Toronto: Viking, 1996), 288.

13 Chuck Rachlis and David Wolfe, 'An Insider's View of the NDP Government of Ontario: The Politics of Permanent Opposition Meets the Economics of Permanent Recession,' in Graham White, ed., *The Government and Politics of Ontario* (Toronto: University of Toronto Press, 1997), 344–7.

14 North American Free Trade Agreement, Appendix F, Ontario's Bound Investment/Services Reservations (Annex I); NAFTA, Appendix H, Ontario's Quantitative Restrictions (Annex II); NAFTA, Appendix I, Ontario's Financial Sectors Reservations (Annex VIII).

15 David A. Wolfe, 'Networking among Regions: Ontario and the Four Motors for Europe,' *European Planning Studies* 83 (2001), 278.

16 Kenichi Ohmae, *The End of the Nation State: The Rise of Regional Economies* (New York: Free Press, 1995).

17 Speech from the Throne, Nov. 19, 1990, First Session, 35th Parliament, Hansard, 2099–2102.

18 Government of Ontario, *An Industrial Policy Framework for Ontario* (Toronto, July 1992).

19 In his memoirs, the premier describes with evident satisfaction what is probably his major achievement: his role in bringing business and labour together to hammer out rescue operations for these major enterprises. Rae, *From Protest to Power*, 144–54.

20 Confidential interview with author, Sept. 1997.

21 Neil Bradford, 'Prospects for Associative Governance: Lessons from Ontario, Canada,' *Politics and Society* 264 (Dec. 1998), 539–73.

22 *Globe and Mail*, Aug. 16, 1996, cited in Stephen McBride and John Shields, *Dismantling a Nation: The Transition to a Corporate Rule in Canada*, 2nd ed. (Toronto: Garamond, 1997), 138.

23 In his 1998 budget speech, Finance Minister Ernie Eves summed up the government's position: 'Despite the fact that the federal government reduced funding for the program that supports health care by $2.4 billion over the last three years ... Despite the fact that the federal government now spends only $125 for health care for each person in Ontario ... Despite the fact that the federal government collects twice as much in personal income tax revenue from each taxpayer in Ontario than the provincial government collects ... While the federal government has all but abandoned the health care needs of Ontarians, our Government is improving the services people have now, and expanding those that they will need in the future.' *Jobs for the Future, Today. 1998 Ontario Budget Speech*.

24 Speech from the Throne, Sept. 27, 1995, First Session of the 36th Parliament of the Province on Ontario.

25 Ibid.

26 In the 1997 budget, cuts by the Ministry of Economic Development, Trade, and Tourism ranged from $80 million (from the previous year's $164 million) for business development and tourism, through $40 million (from $154 million) for strategic analysis, sectors, and technology, to $9 million (from $34 million) for marketing and trade development.

27 Ernie Eves, *1996 Ontario Budget: Budget Speech* (Toronto: Ministry of Finance, 1996), 23–4.

28 Ernie Eves, *1997 Ontario Budget: Budget Speech* (Toronto: Ministry of Finance, 1997), 32.

29 'Innovation, Economic Growth and Job Creation,' *The 1997 Ontario Budget* (Toronto: Ministry of Finance, 1997), 161–3.

30 Ibid., 177.

31 Ibid., 174.

32 'Paper E: Strategic Skills: Investing in Jobs for the Future, Today,' *1998 Ontario Budget. Jobs for the Future, Today. Budget Papers* (Toronto: Ministry of Finance, 1998), 157.

33 *Ontario's Investment Service Design Specification*, OIS Implementation Volume 2, Request for Proposal (Jan. 5, 1994).

34 *Ontario, Canada: The Future's Right Here. Competing in the Global Market*. Government of Ontario promotional material (1996).

15. The Civil State: Social Policies under Strain

1 Figures are for 1990: Pauline V. Rosenau et al., 'Anticipating the Impact of NAFTA on Health and Health Policy,' *Canadian-American Public Policy* 21 (Jan. 1995), 3.

2 Keith G. Banting, 'Social Policy,' in G. Bruce Doern et al., eds., *Border Crossings: The Internationalization of Canadian Public Policy* (Toronto: Oxford University Press, 1996), 34.

3 Grattan Gray, 'Social Policy by Stealth,' *Policy Options* 11, no.1 (March 1990), 17, cited in Michael J. Prince, 'From Health and Welfare to Stealth and Farewell: Federal Social Policy, 1980–2000,' in Leslie A. Pal, ed., *How Ottawa Spends, 1999–2000: Shape Shifting: Canadian Governance toward the 21st Century* (Toronto: Oxford University Press, 1999), 172.

4 Prince, 'From Health and Welfare to Stealth and Farewell,' 178.

5 Sylvia Bashevkin, 'Contagion from the Right? Explaining North American Social Policy during the Clinton and Chrétien Years,' paper presented to the Canadian Political Science Association, June 1998, 15.

6 Tim Lewis, *In the Long Run We're All Dead: The Canadian Turn to Fiscal Restraint* (Vancouver: University of British Columbia Press, forthcoming).

7 Prince, 'From Health and Welfare to Stealth and Farewell,' 178.

8 Author's interview with John English, MP, Sept. 21, 1994.

9 Paul Martin said that program spending as a percentage of GDP was lower than at any time since 1951: *Budget Speech* (Canada: Department of Finance, 1995), 4. See Lewis, *In the Long Run.*

10 Lewis, *In the Long Run.*

11 Edward Greenspon and Anthony Wilson-Smith, *Double Vision: The Inside Story of the Liberals in Power* (Toronto: Doubleday, 1996), 167.

12 Ramesh Misra, *Globalization and the Welfare State* (Northampton: Edward Elgar, 1994), 39.

13 Canada: Privy Council Office, Stéphane Dion, 'Letter to Premier Lucien Bouchard,' Feb. 23, 1999, 3.

14 Allan Moscovitch, 'Social Assistance in the New Ontario,' in Diana S. Ralph et al. eds., *Open for Business, Closed to People: Mike Harris's Ontario* (Toronto: Fenwood, 1997), 82.

15 Gerard Boychuk, 'Are Canadian and U.S. Social Assistance Policies Converging?' *Canadian-American Public Policy* 30 (July 1997), 18–23.

16 Gérard Boismenu and Jane Jenson, 'A Social Union or a Federal State? Competing Visions of Intergovernmental Relations in the New Liberal Era,' in Leslie A. Pal, ed., *How Ottawa Spends 1998–99. Balancing Act: The Post-Deficit Mandate* (Toronto: Oxford, 1998), 58.

17 Larry Johnston, 'Behind the "Social Union,"' Ontario Legislative Library, Backgrounder 29, http://gateway.ontla.on.ca:80/library
18 In his speech in Verdun of October 24, 1995, and in his address to the nation the next night, Chrétien committed himself to decentralization, recognizing Quebec as a distinct society, and a veto for Quebec on constitutional amendments affecting its jurisdiction.
19 Harvey Lazar, 'The Federal Role in the New Social Union,' in Harvey Lazar, ed., *Canada: The State of the Federation 1998/99: How Canadians Connect* (Kingston: Institute of Intergovernmental Relations, 1999), 108.
20 Roger Gibbins, 'Decentralization and the Dilemma of National Standards,' in Mark Charleton and Paul Barker, eds., *Crosscurrents: Contemporary Political Issues*, 3rd ed. (Toronto: ITP Nelson, 1998), 136.
21 Ibid., 138.
22 André Dufour, 'L'Union sociale canadienne,' Ecole Nationale d'Administration Publique' (unpublished paper, October 1999), 3.
23 Claude Ryan, 'The Agreement on the Canadian Social Union,' in Alain-G. Gagnon and Hugh Segal, eds., *The Canadian Social Union without Quebec: Eight Critical Analyses* (Montreal: Institute for Research on Public Policy, 2000), 211.
24 In fact, officials in the Quebec delegation were well aware of negotiations that night between the Trudeau camp and the English-Canadian premiers but chose to let Quebec be excluded and its premier 'betrayed': Stephen Clarkson and Christina McCall, *Trudeau and Our Times, Vol. 1: The Magnificent Obsession* (Toronto: McClelland and Stewart, 1990), 384.
25 André Tremblay, 'Federal Spending Power,' in Gagnon and Segal, eds., *The Canadian Social Union without Quebec*, 181.
26 Alain Noël, 'Without Quebec: Collaborative Federalism with a Footnote?' IRPP Working Paper 1, no. 2 (March 2000), 13.
27 Roger Gibbins, 'Taking Stock: Canadian Federalism and Its Constitutional Framework,' in Leslie A. Pal, ed., *How Ottawa Spends 1999–2000* (Toronto: Oxford University Press, 2000), 216–18.
28 Tremblay, 'Federal Spending Power,' 180.
29 Noël, 'Without Quebec,' 16.
30 Government of Canada and Governments of the Provinces and Territories, *A Framework to Improve the Social Union for Canadians* (Ottawa, Feb. 4, 1999), 2. Jacques Frémont views these mobility rights, which are stronger than those in the AIT, as substituting a social logic for a free trade logic in 'Canadian Federalism: Mobility within Canada,' in Gagnon and Segal, eds., *The Canadian Social Union without Quebec*, 71–89.
31 Robert M. Campbell and Leslie Pal, 'The Rise and Fall of the Charlottetown

Accord,' in Robert M. Campbell and Leslie Pal, eds., *The Real Worlds of Canadian Politics: Cases in Process and Policy*, 3rd ed. (Peterborough: Broadview, 1994), 143.

32 Stephen Clarkson and Timothy Lewis, 'The Contested State: Canada in the Post-Cold War, Post-Keynesian, Post-Fordist, Post-National Era,' in Pal, ed., *How Ottawa Spends 1999–2000*, 346.

33 Social Union Framework Agreement, 6.

34 Wendy McKeen and Ann Porter, 'Politics and Transformation: Welfare State Restructuring in Canada,' in Wallace Clement and Leah Vosko, eds., *Changing Canada: Political Economy as Transformation* (Montreal: McGill-Queen's University Press, forthcoming).

35 In Canada, just under 70 per cent of health care costs are paid for by government and 30 per cent privately. In Sweden, the public sector pays for 84 per cent. 'Systems Side by Side,' *Globe and Mail* (June 20, 2001), A8.

36 Susan D. Phillips, 'SUFA and Citizen Engagement: Fake or Genuine Masterpiece?' *Policy Matters* 2, no. 7 (Dec. 2001), 29.

37 Federal contributions to provincial spending on health care had fallen over twenty-five years from 27 per cent in 1977–8 to between 10 and 15 per cent in 1999–2000, while health represented around 40 per cent of provincial program expenditures in 1999–2000, Alain Noël, 'Power and Purpose in Intergovernmental Relations,' *Policy Matters* (Institute for Research on Public Policy) 2, no. 6 (Nov. 2001), 14.

38 Keith G. Banting, 'Social Policy,' 52.

39 Keith Banting, 'Social Policy in a North American Free-Trade Area,' in Charles Doran and Alvin Paul Drischler, eds., *A New North America: Cooperation and Enhanced Interdependence* (Westport, Conn.: Praeger, 1996), 95ff.

40 Pauline V. Rosenau et al., 'Anticipating the Impact of NAFTA on Health and Health Policy,' *Canadian-American Public Policy* 21 (Jan. 1995), 24.

41 Canada-United States Free Trade Agreement, Appendix 1408. Louise Lussier, 'L'Accord de libre-échange et les programmes sociaux dans une perspective juridique,' *Revue Juridique Thémis* 25 (1991), 334, 340.

42 René Côté, 'L'ALENA et l'américanisatioin du droit canadien dans le secteur des services,' in Christian Deblock et al. eds., *Du libre-échange à l'union politique* (Montreal: L'Harmattan, 1996), 463.

43 Scott Sinclair, *GATS: How the World Trade Organization's New 'Services' Negotiations Threaten Democracy* (Ottawa: Canadian Centre for Policy Alternatives, 2000), 30ff.

44 Ibid., 40.

45 Ibid., 44.

46 Ibid., 33.

47 Ibid., 37.

48 Mike Moore, 'Annual Report,' *WTO Focus* 50 (December, 2000), 12.

49 'Canadian Trade Minister Pierre Pettigrew told reporters in Quebec City that his government would not open up the public education system to the FTAA, but added that Canada would be seeking commitments from other governments to get access to their education markets.' 'Forum Votes to Exclude Education from International Trade Agreements,' *CAUT Bulletin* (May 2001), A2.

50 Misra, *Globalization and the Welfare State*, 59–68.

16. The Working State: Labour Relations under Stress

1 Barrie McKenna, 'More Firms Flock to Mexico,' *Globe and Mail* (July 8, 1998), A1, A9.

2 Jock A. Finlayson, 'Whither the Trade Unions?' *Policy Perspectives* 5, no. 1 (Feb. 1998).

3 Andrew Jackson, *Impacts of the Free Trade Agreement and the North American Free Trade Agreement on Canadian Labour Markets and Labour and Social Standards* (Ottawa: Canadian Labour Congress, 1997), 11.

4 Even as late as 1987, when public service unions had surpassed private-sector unions in number and strength, when the Canadian Autoworkers had split away from the UAW, and when American unionization had fallen to less than 20 per cent of the nonagricultural labour force (compared to a Canadian rate of 38 per cent), US unions were receiving $57 million more from their Canadian members than they were spending on their benefits.

5 R.H. Babcock, *Gompers in Canada: A Study of American Continentalism before the First World War* (Toronto: University of Toronto Press, 1974).

6 Irving Abella, *Nationalism, Commuism and Canadian Labour: the CIO, the Communist Party and the Canadian Congress of Labour* (Toronto: University of Toronto Press, 1973).

7 Mackenzie King's major work, *Industry and Humanity: A Study in the Principles Underlying Industrial Reconstruction* was published in 1918 (Toronto : Thomas Allen). Harry Arthurs, 'Reinventing Labor Law for the Global Economy: The Benjamin Aaron Lecture,' *Berkeley Journal of Employment and Labor Law* 22, no. 2 (2001), 279.

8 Arthurs, 'Reinventing Labor Law for the Global Economy,' 279.

9 'International Instruments on the Right to Organize and Bargain Collectively' presentation at NAALC Workshop, Toronto, Feb. 1–2, 2001.

10 Leah F. Vosko, *Temporary Work: The Gendered Rise of a Precarious Employment Relationship* (Toronto: University of Toronto Press, 2000).

11 Roy J. Adams: 'The Impact of the Movement toward Hemispheric Free Trade on Industrial Relations,' *Work and Occupations* 24, no. 3 (Aug. 1997), 364–80.

12 Leah F. Vosko, 'Regulating Precariousness? The Temporary Employment Relationship under the NAFTA and EC Treaty,' *Industrial Relations* 53, no. 1 (March 1998), 123–53.

13 G.W. Grayson, *The North American Free Trade Agreement: Regional Community and the New World Order* (Lanham, Md.: University Press of America, 1995).

14 May Morpaw, *The North American Agreement on Labour Co-operation: Highlights, Implementation and Significance* (Quebec: Human Resource Development Canada, Office of the North American Agreement on Labour Co-operation, 1995), 113.

15 Canada, *The North American Free Trade Agreement* (Ottawa: Queen's Printer, 1992), 5.

16 Roy J. Adams and Parbudal Singh, 'Early Experience with NAFTA's Labour Side Accord,' *Comparative Labour Law Journal* 18, no. 2 (winter 1997), 161.

17 NAFTA, Annex 1, 796.

18 These were Freedom of Association and Protection of The Right to Organize, The Right to Bargain Collectively, The Right to Strike, Prohibition of Forced Labour, Elimination of Employment Discrimination, Equal Pay for Men and Women, Compensation for Occupational Injuries and Illnesses, Protection of Migrant Workers.

19 These were Labour Protection for Children and Youth, Minimum Employment Standards, and Prevention of Occupational Injuries, Illnesses.

20 Adams and Singh, 'Early Experience with NAFTA's Labour Side Accord,' 165–7.

21 Lance Compa, 'Another Look at NAFTA,' *Dissent* (winter 1997), 48, 46.

22 Adams and Singh, 'Early Experience with NAFTA's Labour Side Accord,' 168–74.

23 Jonathan Graubert, 'Emerging Soft Law Channels for Mobilization under Globalization: How Activists Exploit Labour and Environmental Side Agreements,' in John Kirton and Virginia MacLaren, eds., *Linking Trade, Environment and Social Cohesion: NAFTA Experiences, Global Challenges* (Aldershot: Ashgate, 2002), 6–7.

24 Leanne Yohemas-Hayes, 'Labour's NAFTA Complaint over Working Conditions in Mexico,' *Edmonton Journal* (March 14, 1999).

25 'Unless federal jurisdiction alone is involved, 35 per cent of the total labour force must be either covered under federal jurisdiction or by provinces and territories which have accepted the obligations before Canada can submit a complaint about the U.S. or Mexico or before they can complain about

Canadian enforcement. If a situation concerns a specific industry, 55 per cent of the work force must be subject to the terms of the NAALC.' Morpaw, *The North American Agreement on Labour Co-operation*, 121.

26 Graubert, 'Emerging Soft Law Channels for Mobilization,' 8.

27 Adams and Singh, 'NAFTA's Labour Side Accord,' 15–20.

28 Adams, 'The Impact of the Movement toward Hemispheric Free Trade,' 370.

29 Eric Gagnon, *Free Trade in North America: The Impact on Labour-Management Relations and Human Resources Management in Canada* (Kingston: Queen's University, 1998).

30 Andrew Jackson and Bob Baldwin, 'The Lessons of Free Trade: A View from Canadian Labour,' Research Paper No. 6 (Ottawa: Canadian Labour Congress, 1997), 16.

31 Steven Globerman, *Perspectives on North American Free Trade: Trade Liberalization and the Migration of Skilled Workers* (Ottawa: Industry Canada, 1999), 17, cited by Christina Gabriel and Laura Macdonald, 'Beyond the Continentalist/Nationalist Divide: Canada in North America,' in Wallace Clement and Leah Vosko, eds., *Changing Canada: Political Economy as Transformation* (Montreal: McGill-Queen's University Press, forthcoming).

32 Statistics Canada, cited by Gabriel and Macdonald, 'Beyond the Continentalist/Nationalist Divide.'

33 Ibid.

34 Morley Gunderson, 'Harmonization of Labour Policies under Trade Liberalization,' in *Free Trade 1998*, 28.

35 Daniel Drache and Harry Glasbeek, *Changing Workplace: Reshaping Canada's Industrial Relations System* (Toronto: Lorimer, 1992), 157.

36 Rodney Haddow, 'How Ottawa Shrivels: Ottawa's Declining Role in Active Labour Market Policy,' in Leslie A. Pal, ed., *How Ottawa Spends, 1998–1999. Balancing Act: The Post-Deficit Mandate* (Ottawa: Carleton University Press, 1998), 100.

37 Ibid., 103. Ottawa sold the provinces on the deal in part by emphasizing that one third of social assistance recipients would be eligible for job programs under new rules for the approximately $2 billion in EI monies transferred with the agreements. This was a seductive argument given that Martin had just eliminated the Canada Assistance Plan for social assistance, substituting a new Canadian Health and Social Transfer which slashed $7.3 billion from the provincial package for health, education, social services and social assistance spending: communication to author from Laurell Ritchie, March 28, 2002.

38 Haddow, 'How Ottawa Shrivels,' 107–10. Many experts in training argue

that the labour market agreements have had a disastrous result for lacking national standards and permitting greater privatization of training programs, including those previously offered through the public education system: communication from Ritchie.

39 The federal Liberals looked for every possible excuse not to give the labour-training money to the Harris government because they had failed to attach any effective strings when giving the money to the other provinces and feared the Tories would just use the money to make themselves look good for re-election: communication from Ritchie.

40 Andrew Jackson and David Robertson, *Falling Behind: The State of Working Canada 2000* (Ottawa: Canadian Centre for Policy Alternatives, 2000), 152; Michael J. Prince, 'From Health and Welfare to Stealth and Farewell: Federal Social Policy, 1980–2000,' in Leslie A. Pal, ed., *How Ottawa Spends, 1999–2000: Shape Shifting: Canadian Governance Toward the 21st Century* (Toronto: Oxford University Press, 1999), 181. From a maximum of $448 in 1995, Statistics Canada reported the average weekly benefit had fallen by 2001 to $280.

41 Wendy McKeen and Ann Porter, 'Politics and Transformation: Welfare State Restructuring in Canada,' in Clement and Vosko, *Changing Canada*.

42 By March 2002, Martin's poaching from EI amounted to $43 billion according to the Auditor General: communication from Ritchie.

43 Buzz Hargrove, 'Needed: A Hard Left Turn,' *Globe and Mail* (Aug. 9, 2000), A11.

44 Communication from Lynn Spink, Feb. 12, 2002, supplying figures from the Ontario Labour Relations Board and from the Ministry of Labour showing the impact of the NDP's Bill 40 – a 45 per cent increase in applications for union certification and a 59 per cent rise in workers certified from 1992 to 1993 – and the negative impact of the 'Tories' Bill 7 after one year – a 51 per cent decrease in applications for certification and a 56 per cent decline in workers certified.

45 H.W. Arthurs, 'Labour Law without a State,' *University of Toronto Law Journal* 46 (1996), 11.

46 Although Ed Broadbent remembers no explicit bargain that excluded the right to property from the Charter in exchange for not formally entrenching the right to strike (interview March 8, 2002), Harry Arthurs considers that trade-off to be implicit (interview August 15, 2001).

47 *Reference re. Public Service Employee Relations Act* (Alberta), 1987; *P.S.A.C. v. Canada* (1987); *Retail, Wholesale and Department Store Union v. Saskatchewan* (1987).

48 Ran Hirschl, 'The Political Origins of Judicial Empowerment through Con-

stitutionalization. Lessons from Four Constitutional Revolutions,' unpublished paper, University of Toronto, 1999, 31.

49 Michael Mandel, *The Charter of Rights and the Legalization of Politics in Canada* (Toronto: Thompson, 1994), 271.

50 Jim Stanford, 'Topsy-turvy Economics,' in Lynn Spink, ed., *Bad Work: A Review of Papers from a Fraser Institute Conference on Right-to-Work Laws* (York University, Centre for Research on Work and Society, 1997), 25.

51 Statistics Canada, cited in ibid., 4.

52 Statistics Canada, cited in Finlayson, 'Whither the Trade Unions?' 5.

53 Jackson and Robertson, *Falling Behind*, 96.

54 Ibid., 96.

55 Ibid., 107.

17. The (Un)sustainable State: Deregulating the Environment

1 Mark Winfield, 'The Ultimate Horizontal Issue: The Environmental Policy Experiences of Alberta and Ontario, 1971–1993,' *Canadian Journal of Political Science* 27, no. 1 (March 1994), 129–52.

2 The Canada-United States Acid Rain Treaty, signed in 1990, formalized what Congress had legislated in amendments toughening its Clean Air Act.

3 Barry Appleton, *Navigating NAFTA: A Concise User's Guide to the North American Free Trade Agreement* (Toronto: Carswell, 1994), 201–5.

4 Patricia Marchak, 'Environment and Resource Protection: Does NAFTA Make a Difference?' *Organization and Environment* 11, no. 2 (June 1998), 134, 147.

5 Michelle Swenarchuk, 'The Environmental Implications of NAFTA: A Legal Analysis,' in Ted Schrecker and Jean Dalgleish, eds., *Growth, Trade and Environmental Values* (London, Ont.: Westminster Institute for Ethics and Human Values, 1994).

6 Marchak, 'The Environmental Implications of Trade Agreements,' 148.

7 *R. v. Hydro-Québec*, [1997] 3 SCR 213.

8 Lawrence Martin, *The Antagonist: Lucien Bouchard and the Politics of Delusion* (Toronto: Viking, 1997), 12, 13.

9 George Hoberg and Kathryn Harrison, 'It's Not Easy Being Green: The Politics of Canada's Green Plan,' *Canadian Public Policy* 20 (1994), 119–37.

10 *R. v. Crown Zellerbach Canada Ltd.*, [1988] 1 SCR 401.

11 F.L. Morton, 'The Constitutional Division of Powers with Respect to the Environment in Canada,' in Kenneth M. Holland, F. L. Morton, and Brian Galligan, eds., *Federalism and the Environment: Environmental Policymaking in*

Australia, Canada, and the United States (Westport, Conn.: Greenwood Press, 1996), 37–54.

12 *Friends of the Oldman River Society v. Canada*, [1992] 2 SCR 3.

13 Karen L. Clark and Mark Winfield, *Harmonizing to Protect the Environment? An Analysis of the CCME Environmental Harmonization Process* (Canadian Institute for Environmental Law and Policy, Nov. 1996), 5.

14 Kathryn Harrison, 'Intergovernmental Relations and Environmental Policy: Concepts and Context,' in Patrick C. Fafard and Kathryn Harrison, eds., *Managing Environmental Union: Intergovernmental Relations and Environmental Policy in Canada* (Montreal: McGill-Queen's University Press, 2000), 3–19.

15 Editorial, 'Ottawa Caves in on the Environment,' *Toronto Star* (June 6, 1999).

16 Kathryn Harrison and George Hoberg, 'In Defense of Regulation: Response to Comment on "It's Not Easy Being Green: The Politics of Canada's Green Plan,"' *Canadian Public Policy* 22 (1996), 180–3.

17 Glen Toner argues that the Department of the Environment was actually spared a lot of the Liberals' budget cuts, since the reductions were based on the Green Plan's money. As a result, the department ended up with roughly the same funding in the new millennium as it had had before 1990: 'Environment Canada's Continuing Roller Coaster Ride,' in Gene Swimmer, ed., *How Ottawa Spends 1996–97: Life Under the Knife* (Ottawa: Carleton University Press, 1997), 99–132.

18 Mark S. Winfield, 'Environmental Policy and Federalism,' in Herman Bakvis and Grace Skogstad, eds., *Canadian Federalism: Performance, Effectiveness and Legitimacy* (Don Mills, Ont.: Oxford University Press, 2002), 124–37.

19 Kathryn Harrison, 'Intergovernmental Relations and Environmental Policy.' See also Kathryn Harrison, 'Prospects for Intergovernmental Harmonization in Environmental Policy' in Douglas M. Brown and Janet Hiebert, eds., *Canada: The State of the Federation 1994* (Kingston: Queen's University, Institute for Intergovernmental Relations, 1994).

20 Harrison, 'Intergovernmental Relations and Environmental Policy,' 11–12.

21 Debora L.Van Nijnatten, 'Intergovernmental Relations and Environmental Policy Making: A Cross-National Perspective,' in Fafard and Harrison, eds., *Managing Environmental Union*, 23–48.

22 Paul Muldoon and Mark S. Winfield, *Brief to the House of Commons Standing Committee on Environment and Sustainable Development Regarding the CCME Environmental 'Harmonization' Initative*, Canadian Institute for Environmental Law and Policy Brief 97/4, Oct. 21, 1997, 7.

23 Harrison, 'Intergovernmental Relations and Environmental Policy.'

24 Patrick C. Fafard, 'Groups, Governments and the Environment: Some Evi-

dence from the Harmonization Initiative,' in Fafard and Harrison, eds, *Managing Environmental Union*, 81–101.

25 Robert Hornung, 'VCR Does Not Work,' in Robert Gibson, ed., *Voluntary Initiatives: The New Politics of Corporate Greening* (Peterborough: Broadview Press, 1999).

26 Clark and Winfield, *Harmonizing to Protect the Environment?* and Muldoon and Winfield, *Brief to the House of Commons Standing Committee.*

27 Fafard, 'Groups, Governments and the Environment,' 96.

28 It changed its mind when a landfill operator in the province accepted U.S. hazardous waste, even though the dump was not licensed for the toxic material. See Martin Mittelstaedt, 'Canada Becomes Haven for Toxic Waste,' *Globe and Mail* (June 18, 2001), A1, A8.

29 Ontario Public Service Employees Union (OPSEU), *Renewing the Ministry of Environment* (Submission to Part II of the Walkerton Public Inquiry, 2001).

30 Anita Krajnc, 'Wither Ontario's Environment? Neoconservatism and the Decline of the Environment Ministry,' *Canadian Public Policy* 26, no. 1 (March 2000), 111–27.

31 Martin Mittelstaedt, 'Inspectors Told to Ignore Pollution Complaints,' *Globe and Mail* (Feb. 24, 1999), A1, A5.

32 Paul Muldoon and Mark Winfield, 'Democracy and Environmental Accountability in Ontario,' *The Environmental Agenda for Ontario Project*, available at http://www.cela.ca/dereg/democ361.htm (April 1999), 8. A similar proposed federal Regulatory Efficiency Act was defeated by environmentalists in the late 1990s. Newfoundland established a Regulatory Review Commission in 1994, and Alberta, a Regulatory Reform Task Force in 1995. Robert Paehlke, 'Environmental Policy in One Country: Canadian Environmental Policy in an Era of Globalization,' *Policy Studies Journal* 28, no. 1 (2000), 160–75. In British Columbia, Gordon Campbell's neoconservative Liberal government has outdone even Ontario and Alberta in its reduction of regulation.

33 OPSEU, *Renewing the Ministry of Environment* (Submission to Part II of the Walkerton Public Inquiry, 2001), 23.

34 Andrew Sancton and Teresa Janik, *Provincial-Local Relations and Drinking Water in Ontario*, submission to the Walkerton Inquiry, Feb. 2001, 28.

35 For a very good analysis of compliance, self-monitoring, and reporting in the aggregate and forestry sectors, see Mark Winfield and Hugh Benevides, *Drinking Water Protection in Ontario: A Comparison of Direct and Alternative Delivery Models. Issue Paper Prepared for Part II of the Walkerton Inquiry* (June 2001), Appendix 3; Tony Weis and Anita Krajnc, 'Greenwashing Ontario's Lands for Life: Why Some Environmental Groups are Complicit in the

Tories' Disastrous Plan,' *Canadian Dimension* 33, no. 6 (Dec. 1999), 34–8; and Anita Krajnc and Tony Weis, 'The New Politics of Bloodsport in Ontario,' *Canadian Dimension* 34, no. 5 (Sept./Oct. 2000), 42–5.

36 Krajnc, 'Wither Ontario's Environment?'

37 Gord Miller, *The Protection of Ontario's Goundwater and Intensive Farming*, Environmental Commissioner of Ontario's Special Report, July 2000.

38 Margaret Wente, 'Comment: It Was a Smooth but Aloof Performance by Ontario's CEO,' *Globe and Mail* (June 30, 2001), A1 and A8, and Rosie Di-Manno, 'The Long Day of No Apologies,' *Toronto Star* (June 30, 2001), A1 and A4. For the final report: The Honourable Dennis R. O'Connor, *Report of the Walkerton Inquiry: The Events of May 2000 and Related Issues, Part I* (Toronto: Queen's Printer for Ontario, 2002).

39 Richard Brennan, 'Province Angry at Receiving Blame for City Tax Increases,' *Toronto Star* (June 14, 2001), A26.

40 Laurie Monsebraaten, 'Garbage Revolution Proposed,' *Toronto Star* (June 19, 2001), A1 and A16.

41 Alan Rugman et al. 'NAFTA, Environmental Regulations, and Canadian Competitiveness,' *Journal of World Trade* 31, no. 4 (Aug. 1997), 129–45.

42 Peter M. Emerson et al., 'The Environmental Side of the North American Free Trade Agreement,' in Terry L. Anderson, ed., *NAFTA and the Environment.* (San Francisco: Pacific Research Institute for Public Policy, 1993), 53.

43 Private communication from Mark Winfield. I confirmed the Mexican government's dismay at the CEC's autonomy by two confidential interviews in Mexico City on February 19 and 23, 2002.

44 Emerson et al., 'The Environmental Side of the North American Free Trade Agreement,' 53.

45 International Institute for Sustainable Development, *Private Rights, Public Problems: A Guide to NAFTA's Controversial Chapter on Investor Rights* (Winnipeg: IISD, 2001), 91–2.

46 André Beaulieu et al., 'NAFTA/NAEEC and the Environmental Agenda of Trade,' in Pierre Marc-Johnson, ed., *The Environment and NAFTA* (Washington, DC: Island Press, 1996), 245.

47 Steven Shrybman, 'Selling Canada's Environment Short: The Environmental Case against the Trade Deal,' analysis prepared for the Canadian Environmental Law Association (Toronto: CELA, 1992), 1.

48 Elizabeth May, 'Fighting the MAI,' in Andrew Jackson and Matthew Sanger, eds., *Dismantling Democracy: The Multilateral Agreement on Investment and Its Impact* (Toronto: CCPA and Lorimer, 1998), 32–47.

49 Editorial, 'Why the Secrecy over Investor's Rights?' *Financial Post* (Aug. 29, 1998).

50 David Schneiderman, 'NAFTA's Takings Rule: American Constitutionalism Comes to Canada,' *University of Toronto Law Journal* 46 (1996), 535.

51 Editorial, 'Mad Ministers Thwarted,' *Globe and Mail* (July 21, 1998), A14.

52 Canadian Environmental Law Association, *The Environmental Implications of Trade Agreements: Final Report*. (Toronto: Queen's Printer for Ontario, 1993), 284–6.

53 John Kirton, Alan Rugman, and Julie Soloway, *Environmental Regulations and Corporate Strategy: A NAFTA Perspective* (Oxford: Oxford University Press, 1999), 211–40.

54 Konrad von Moltke, *Whither MEAs? The Role of International Environmental Management in the Trade and Environment Agenda* (Winnipeg: International Institute for Sustainable Development, 2001), 7.

55 Kirton, Rugman, and Soloway, *Environmental Regulations*, 63–4.

56 Stephen Dale, *McLuhan's Children: The Greenpeace Message and the Media* (Toronto: Between the Lines, 1996), and Paul Wapner, *Environmental Activism and World Civic Politics* (Albany: State University of New York Press, 1996).

57 Ken Conca, 'The WTO and the Undermining of Global Environmental Governance,' *Review of International Political Economy* 3, no. 2 (autumn 2000), 484–94.

58 Elly Perkins, 'NAFTA and Environmental Regulation: The Ontario Experience,' paper presented at the Canadian Association for Latin American and Caribbean Studies 27th Congress, 1996, 18.

18. The Cultured State: Broadcasting and Magazines

1 Concepts of culture 'are politically as well as culturally constructed and manipulated for a variety of ends'; Setha M. Low, 'Cultural Conversation of Place,' in Mary Hufford, ed., *Conserving Culture: A New Discourse on Heritage* (Urbana: University of Illinois Press, 1994), 19.

2 Reginald Coupland, *The Durham Report: An Abridged Version with an Introduction and Notes* (Oxford: Oxford University Press, 1945), 15.

3 Anthony Smith, *The Geopolitics of Information: How Western Culture Dominates the World* (New York: Oxford University Press, 1980), 52–4.

4 Marc Raboy et al., 'Cultural Development in an Open Economy: A Democratic Issue and a Challenge to Public Policy,' in Stuart McFadyen et al., eds., *Cultural Development in an Open Economy* (Burnaby, BC: Canadian Journal of Communication Corporation, 1994), 38.

5 Harold A. Innis, *The Bias of Communication* (Toronto: University of Toronto Press, 1964), 33.

6 Marshall McLuhan, *Understanding Media: The Extensions of Man*, 2nd ed. (Toronto: Signet, 1966), 23–35.

7 David R. Hall and Garth S. Jowett, 'The Growth of the Mass Media in Canada,' in Benjamin D. Singer, ed., *Communications in Canadian Society,* 4th ed. (Toronto: Nelson Canada, 1995), 18–21, and Mark Starowicz, 'Open Skies: The Struggle for Canada's Airwaves,' The Atkinson Lecture at Ryerson Polytechnical Institute (March 12, 1985), 3.

8 Canada, Royal Commission on Publications (O'Leary Commission), *Report* (Ottawa: Minister of Supply and Services, 1961), 5–6.

9 Marc S. Levine, *The Reconquest of Montreal: Language, Policy, and Social Change in a Bilingual City* (Philadelphia: Temple University Press, 1990).

10 Communication to the author from Paul Audley, March 5, 2002 and Claude Martin, 'Walking on a Tightrope: The Markets of Cultural Products in Quebec,' in Emile G. McAnany and Kenton T. Wilkinson, eds., *Mass Media and Free Trade: NAFTA and the Cultural Industries* (Austin: University of Texas Press, 1996), 238.

11 Marc Raboy, 'Cultural Development in an Open Economy: A Democratic Issue and a Challenge to Public Policy,' in McFadyen et al., eds., *Cultural Development in an Open Economy,* 49, 56; Michael Parker and Leigh Parker, 'Trade in Culture: Consumable Product or Cherished Articulation of a Nation's Soul?' *Denver Journal of International Law and Policy* 22, no. 155 (1993), 170, quoted in Chi Carmody, 'When 'Cultural Identity Was Not at Issue': Thinking about Canada – Certain Measures Concerning Periodicals,' *Law and Policy in International Business* 20, no. 3 (winter 1999), 8.

12 Tony Manera, *A Dream Betrayed: The Battle for the CBC* (Toronto: Stoddart, 1996), 14.

13 Frank W. Peers, 'Canada and the United States: Comparative Origins and Approaches to Broadcast Policy,' in Canadian-U.S. Conference on Communications Policy, *Cultures in Collision: The Interaction of Canadian and U.S. Television Broadcast Policies* (New York: Praeger, 1984), 15.

14 David Ellis, *Evolution of the Canadian Broadcasting System: Objectives and Realities 1926–1968* (Ottawa: Ministry of Supply and Services Canada, 1979), 1 and communication to the author from Paul Audley, March 3, 2002.

15 Canada, House of Commons, 'Speech in Support of Bill 94, Respecting Radio Broadcasting,' *Debates* (May 18, 1932).

16 Jeffery Kowall, 'Foreign Investment Restrictions in Canadian Television Broadcasting: A Call for Reform,' *Toronto Faculty of Law Review* 50, no. 1 (winter 1992), 72.

17 This amount has been reduced to 67 per cent, with speculation that it could be lowered to 54 per cent. Industry observers have suggested that much of

this drop can be attributed to years of criticism of the restriction's failing to produce more Canadian culture. Anthony de Fazekas, 'Free Trade and Culture: An Alternative Approach,' *Dalhousie Journal of Legal Studies* 2 (1993), 158.

18 Prior to the signing of CUFTA, Canadian law did not require Canadian cable companies that retransmitted U.S.-origin television signals to offer financial compensation to the original makers of American programs or their antennae broadcasters situated on the U.S. side of the border. The CRTC allowed cable companies to transmit these 'spill-over' signals because it believed that areas closer to the border were enjoying viewing advantages unavailable to more distant parts of the country. U.S. border broadcasters had initially welcomed this signal 'piracy,' because it opened up a larger market of advertising revenue – which explains their fury at Bill C-58. Berry Berlin, *The American Trojan Horse: U.S. Television Confronts Canadian Economic and Cultural Nationalism* (New York: Greenwood Press, 1990).

19 Specifically, Article 2005(2), known as the cultural 'notwithstanding clause,' states 'Notwithstanding any other provision of this Agreement, a Party may take measures of *equivalent commercial effect* in response to actions that would have been inconsistent with this agreement but for paragraph 1' (emphasis added).

20 Communication from Audley.

21 The *Wall Street Journal*'s reported retaliation targets, cited in Keith Acheson and Christopher Maule, *International Agreements and Cultural Industries* (Ottawa: Centre for Trade Policy and Law, 1996), 12.

22 Peter Morton, 'U.S. Draws up Canadian Cultural Hit List,' *Financial Post* (Feb. 4, 1995), 3.

23 John Ragosta, 'The Information Revolution: Culture and Sovereignty – An American Perspective,' *Canada-United States Law Journal* 24 (1998), 162.

24 Communication from Audley.

25 Richard Stursberg, 'New Rules Needed for Strong Canadian Voice in the Multimedia Age,' *Canadian Speeches* 12 (Sept. 1998), 43.

26 The music industry considers the activity of writing music not 'production' per se, but rather 'creation' or 'recording.' 'Production' refers to the process whereby vinyl records, tapes, CDs, and the like are manufactured. Tim Straw, 'Sound Recording,' in Michael Dorland, ed., *The Cultural Industries in Canada: Problems, Policies, and Prospects* (Toronto: Lorimer, 1996), 102.

27 'Canadian music' is defined as any piece that satisfies at least two requirements of the MAPL system
   • *music* composed entirely by a Canadian
   • *artist* principally performing the music and/or lyrics is Canadian

- *production* recorded wholly in Canada or *performed* wholly and broadcast live in Canada
- *lyrics* written entirely by a Canadian

28 Straw, 'Sound Recording,' 132.
29 See the CRTC's website, www.crtc.gc.ca/ENG/INFO_SHT/G11E.HTM
30 Communication from Paul Audley.
31 Ibid.
32 Public Notice CRTC 1998–41, www.crtc.gc.ca/eng/bcasting/notice/1998/p9841%5Fl.txt
33 Lou Dubinsky, 'Periodical Publishing,' in Dorland, ed., *The Cultural Industries in Canada*, 35.
34 Paul Audley, *Canada's Cultural Industries: Broadcasting, Publishing, Records and Film* (Toronto: Lorimer 1983), 72–3, and Ted Magder, 'Franchising the Candy Store: Split-Run Magazines and a New International Regime for Trade in Culture,' *Canadian-American Public Policy* 34 (April 1998), 10.
35 O'Leary Commission, *Report*, 6.
36 Magder, 'Franchising the Candy Store,' 12.
37 Keith Acheson and Christopher Maule, *Much Ado about Culture: North American Trade Disputes* (Ann Arbor: University of Michigan Press, 1999), 189–90.
38 Canada, Report of the Task Force on the Canadian Magazine Industry, *A Question of Balance* (Ottawa: Ministry of Supply and Services, 1994), cited in Magder, 'Franchising the Candy Store,' 13.
39 Ibid., 28.
40 Ibid., 2.
41 Ibid., 26. Magder notes that this lack of consultation itself was indicative of the shifting framework for cultural issues and Ottawa's neoconservative tendencies.
42 Edward Israel, *Final Editions? Split-Run Editions and Canada's Ailing Magazine Industry* (Toronto: Ontario Legislative Library, 1993), 8.
43 Canada, *A Question of Balance.*
44 *Canada – Certain Measures Concerning Periodicals* (Complaint by the United States) (1997), WTO Doc. WT/DS31/R (Panel Report), paras. 3.61, 3.62.
45 *Canada – Certain Measures Concerning Periodicals* (Complaint by the United States) (1997), WTO Doc. WT/DS31/AB/R (Appellate Body Report).
46 Magder, 'Franchising the Candy Store,' 49.
47 'Pitch for Bill C-55: Canadian Magazine Publishers Argue in Washington that Bill Does Not Violate Free Trade,' *Maclean's* (March 8, 1999), 42.

U.S.T.R. claims the proposed retaliation was of 'equivalent commercial effect' because, to be 'GATT-legal,' duties would have been very low. Interview with Mary Ryckman, April 9, 2002.

48 John Geddes, 'Run for the Money: With a New Deal, the Magazine Debate Shifts from Culture to How to Keep Ad Dollars in Canada,' *Maclean's* (June 7, 1999), 55–6.

49 Gerry Legaré, 'Lights, Camera, Action: The Production of Film and Television in Toronto.' Paper presented to the Association of American Geographers, New York City, February 2001.

50 Ted Magder, 'Going Global: Canada Takes the Lead in an International Effort to Rewrite the Rules on Trade and Culture,' *Canadian Forum* (Aug. 1999), 13, and Cultural Industries Sectoral Advisory Group on International Trade, *Canadian Culture in a Global World: New Strategies for Culture and Trade* (Ottawa, Feb. 1999).

51 Daniel Schwanen, 'A Matter of Choice: Toward a More Creative Canadian Policy on Culture,' *C.D. Howe Institute Commentary* 91, (April 1997), 1–37.

52 Steven Globerman, *Cultural Regulation in Canada* (Montreal: Institute for Research in Public Policy, 1983), xxiii.

53 Ted Magder, *Canada's Hollywood: The Canadian State and Feature Films* (Toronto: University of Toronto Press, 1993), 248.

19. The Diplomatic State: Lockstep under Hegemonic Dominance

1 Stephen Clarkson, ed., *An Independent Foreign Policy for Canada?* (Toronto: McClelland and Stewart, for the University League for Social Reform, 1968).

2 Quoted in John English, 'Speaking Out on Vietnam, 1965,' in John Kirton and Don Munton, eds., *Canadian Foreign Policy: Selected Cases* (Scarborough: Prentice Hall, 1992), 141.

3 Department of External Affairs, *Foreign Policy for Canadians* (Ottawa: Queen's Printer, 1970).

4 Much later, in 1983, the Pentagon got sweet revenge by forcing the reluctant Liberal to allow testing of cruise missiles over Canadian territory.

5 Department of Foreign Affairs, *Foreign Policy for Canadians*, 238.

6 Kim Richard Nossal, *The Politics of Canadian Foreign Policy,* 3rd ed. (Scarborough: Prentice Hall, 1997), 181.

7 Stephen Clarkson, '"Vive le Québec libre!" Twenty Years On,' *French Society and Politics* 5, no. 4 (Sept. 1987), 35–45.

8 Christina McCall and Stephen Clarkson, *Trudeau and Our Times, Vol. 2: The Heroic Delusion* (Toronto McClelland and Stewart, 1994), chap. 13.

9 Robert Boardman, Hans J. Michelmann, Charles C. Pentland, and Panayotis

Soldatos, The Canada-European Communities Framework Agreement, CCEA Policy Series No. 1, 1984.

10 Michael K. Hawes, 'Canada-U.S. Relations in the Mulroney Era: How Special the Relationship?' in Brian W. Tomlin and Maureen Appel Molot, eds., *Canada among Nations 1988: The Tory Record* (Toronto: Lorimer, 1989), 195–6.

11 Canada, Department of National Defence, *Challenge and Commitment: A Defence Policy for Canada – A Synopsis of the Defence White Paper* (Ottawa: Minister of Supply and Services Canada, 1987).

12 The more critical assessments of Mulroney's foreign policy are Lawrence Martin., *Pledge of Allegiance: The Americanization of Canada in the Mulroney Years* (Toronto: McClelland and Stewart, 1993), and Marci McDonald, *Yankee Doodle Dandy: Brian Mulroney and the American Agenda* (Toronto: Stoddart, 1995).

13 Nossal, *The Politics of Canadian Foreign Policy*, 183.

14 Clarence G. Redekop, 'Sanctioning South Africa, 1980s,' in Munton and Kirton, eds., *Canadian Foreign Policy*, 346.

15 Hawes, 'Canada-U.S. Relations in the Mulroney Era,' 202.

16 Royal Commission on the Economic Union and Development Prospects for Canada, *Report, Vol. 1* (Ottawa: Minister of Supply and Services, 1985), 209 (emphasis added).

17 The Gordon Foundation spent $500,000 on the Canada 21 project. Denis Stairs, 'The Public Politics of the Canadian Defence and Foreign Policy Reviews,' *Canadian Foreign Policy* 3, no. 1 (spring 1995), 94.

18 The papers were on contemporary security issues (by Denis Stairs), the challenge of global trade, investment, and finance for Canada (Sylvia Ostry and Alan Alexandroff), foreign aid and development (André Martens), and culture in foreign policy (John Ralston Saul). Special Joint Committee of the Senate and of the House of Commons Reviewing Canadian Foreign Policy, *Canada's Foreign Policy Principles and Priorities for the Future: The Position Papers* (Ottawa: Canada Communications Group, Nov. 1994).

19 Canada, *Canada in the World* (Ottawa: Queen's Printer, 1995), 14–15.

20 Louis Belanger, 'Globalization, Culture, and Foreign Policy: The Failure of "Third Pillarization,"' in *Canada in the World in the Twentieth Century* 22 (fall 2000), 185.

21 John Hay, 'Projecting Canadian Values and Culture: An Episode in the Making of Canadian Foreign Policy,' *Canadian Foreign Policy* 3, no. 2 (fall 1995), 21–31.

22 C.-P. David and S. Roussel, 'Une espèce en voie de disparition? La politique de puissance moyenne du Canada après la guerre froide,' *International Journal* 52, no. 4 (fall 1997), 53–4.

23 Department of Foreign Affairs and International Trade, *Freedom from Fear: Canada's Foreign Policy for Human Security* (Ottawa: Queen's Printer, 2000).

24 It was found that the trawler kept two log books, one for EU officials and the other with the actual amount of the vessel's catch: Donald Barry, 'The Canada-European Turbot War: Internal Politics and Transatlantic Bargaining,' *International Journal* 53, no. 2 (spring 1998), 253–84.

25 Andrew F. Cooper, *Canadian Foreign Policy: Old Habits and New Directions* (Scarborough: Prentice-Hall, 1997), 168.

26 Ibid.

27 McCall and Clarkson, *Trudeau and Our Times, Vol. 2*, 140–3.

28 Denis Stairs, 'The Policy Process and Dialogues with Demos: Liberal Pluralism with a Transnational Twist,' in *Leadership and Dialogue: Canada among Nations 1998* (Don Mills: Oxford University Press, 1998), 47.

29 Mark Neufeld, 'Democratization in/of Canadian Foreign Policy: Critical Reflections,' *Studies in Political Economy* 58 (spring 1999), 98.

30 Evan H. Potter, 'Niche Diplomacy as Canadian Foreign Policy,' *International Journal* 50, no. 2 (winter 1996–7), 29.

31 Daryl Copeland, 'The Axworthy Years: Canadian Foreign Policy in the Era of Diminished Capacity,' in *Canada Among Nations 2001: The Axworthy Legacy* (Toronto: Oxford University Press, 2001),169. Concerning DFAIT's financial woes, Copeland blames Axworthy for running the department into the ground but commends him for sparking some interest in DFAIT, which may lead to more ample resources. 'Though he drew down the reserves, ignored crucial structural issues, and was able to do little by way of new investment, he also laid a new foundation upon which it should be possible to resume construction,' 169.

32 Denis Stairs, 'The Changing Office and the Changing Environment of the Minister of Foreign Affairs in the Axworthy Era,' in *Canada among Nations 2001*, 26.

33 Lloyd Axworthy, 'Canada and Human Security: The Need For Leadership,' Department of Foreign Affairs and International Trade, 1999. http://www.dfait-maeci.gc.ca/english/foreignp/sechume.htm

34 Department of Foreign Affairs and International Trade, Notes for an Address by the Honourable Lloyd Axworthy, Minister of Foreign Affairs, 'Foreign Policy in the Information Age.'

35 Lloyd Axworthy and Sarah Taylor, 'A Ban for All Seasons,' *International Journal* 53, no. 2 (spring 1998), 197.

36 Robert Lawson, 'The Ottawa Process: Fast-Track Diplomacy and the International Movement to Ban Anti-Personnel Mines,' in Fen Osler Hampson

and Maureen Appel Molot, eds., *Canada Among Nations 1998: Leadership and Dialogue* (Toronto: Oxford University Press, 1998), 82.

37 Axworthy and Taylor, 'A Ban for All Seasons,' 189.

38 There were about 318 NGOs mobilized on land mines in the United States alone. Kenneth Rutherford, 'The Evolving Arms Control Agenda: Implications of the Role of NGOs in Banning Anti-Personnel Mines,' *World Politics* 53, no. 1 (Oct. 2000), 74–114.

39 Quoted in Allison Van Rooy, 'Civil Society and the Axworthy Touch,' in *Canada among Nations 2001*, 255. For the original citation, see Maxwell A. Cameron, 'Democratization of Foreign Policy: The Ottawa Process as a Model,' *Canadian Foreign Policy* 5, no. 6 (spring 1998), 161–2.

40 Denis Stairs, 'The Canadian Dilemma in North America,' in Joyce Hoebing, Sidney Weintraub, and M. Delol Bael, eds., *NAFTA and Sovereignty* (Washington, DC: CSIS, 1996), 8. This positive position on NGO participation notwithstanding, Stairs considers that the 'pandemic' of consultations with civil society is damaging representative democracy by 'enhancing the general level of cynicism about politicians.' Personal communication. See Denis Stairs, 'Foreign Policy Consultations in a Globalizing World: The Case of Canada, the WTO and the Shenanigans in Seattle,' *IRPP Policy Matters* 1, no. 8 (Dec. 2000), 1–44.

41 The vote took place in July 1998 in Rome.

42 Department of Foreign Affairs and International Trade, 'The International Criminal Court Agreement Bears Strong Canadian Imprint.' www.dfait-maeci.gc.ca/canada-magazine/1t1–e.htm, 2.

43 The UN General Assembly on May 25, 2000, adopted a draft of the Optional Protocol to the Convention on the Rights of the Child, which prohibits recruitment of youths under eighteen in hostilities. www.terredeshommes.org

44 Kim Richard Nossal, 'Foreign Policy for Wimps,' *Ottawa Citizen* (April 23, 1998), A19.

45 Fen Osler Hampson and Dean F. Oliver, 'Pulpit Diplomacy: A Critical Assessment of the Axworthy Doctrine,' *International Journal* 53, no. 3 (summer 1998), 405–6.

46 Stairs, 'The Changing Office and the Changing Environment,' 25.

47 Peter McKenna, 'Canada and Helms-Burton: Up Close and Personal,' *Canadian Foreign Policy* 4, no. 3 (winter 1997), 7.

48 Address by President Clinton, Feb. 26, 1999, *Foreign Policy Bulletin* 10, no. 2 (March/April, 1999), 60.

49 I developed this argument in 'Does Principle Have a Price? The Danger of U.S. Retaliation against an Autonomous Canadian Position on Nuclear Dis-

armament,' brief presented to the Canadian Centre for Foreign Policy Development, Seminar on Nuclear Weapons (Nov. 26, 1998).

50 Canada, *Canada in the World*.

51 McKenna, 'Canada and Helms-Burton,' 20.

52 Maurice J. Williams, 'Efforts and Policies of the Members of the Development Assistance Committee,' in OECD, *Review of Development Co-operation* (Paris: OECD, 1975).

53 Potter, 'Niche Diplomacy as Canadian Foreign Policy,' 29.

54 By 1994, total aid had declined to $3 billion, having peaked in 1991 at $3.5 billion. Canadian ODA was about 20 per cent lower in 1997–8 than in 1993–4. The Canadian International Development Agency's budget was cut by $309 million to $1.9 billion in 1998–9, down 29 per cent from 1995: www.acdi-cida.gc.ca/cida

55 Copeland, 'The Axworthy Years,' 167.

56 Cranford Pratt, 'Competing Rationales for Canadian Development Assistance,' *International Journal* (summer 1999), 325.

57 In January 2001, Paul Martin announced that Canada had stopped collecting interest payments from the poorest countries that were able to use debt-relief savings productively and were developing poverty reduction strategies. Department of Finance Canada website, www.fin.gc.ca

58 Van Rooy, 'Civil Society and the Axworthy Touch,' 25.

59 Norman Hillmer and Adam Chapnick, 'The Axworthy Revolution,' in *Canada among Nations 2001*, 84.

60 Jeff Sallot, 'U.S. Space Arms Plan Draws Ire of Canada,' *Globe and Mail* (July 26, 2001), A1, A10.

61 Van Rooy, 'Civil Society and the Axworthy Touch,' 255.

62 David B. Dewitt and John Kirton, *Canada as a Principal Power: A Study in Foreign Policy and International Relations* (Toronto: Wiley, 1982).

63 Peter J. Katzenstein, ed., *The Culture of National Security: Norms and Identity in World Politics* (New York: Columbia University Press, 1996) 518, n 48. I am indebted to Louis Pauly for drawing this note to my attention.

20. The Post-Globalist State: Rebalancing Corporate Autonomy and Democratic Deficit

1 Samuel E. Moffett, *The Americanization of Canada*, first pub. 1907 (Toronto: University of Toronto Press, 1972), 114.

2 Ibid., 94.

3 Roger Gibbins, 'Taking Stock: Canadian Federalism and Its Constitutional Framework,' in Leslie A. Pal, ed., *How Ottawa Spends 1999–2000: Shape Shift-*

ing: Canadian Governance Toward the 21st Century (Toronto: Oxford University Press, 1999), 218.

4 Ian D. Clark, 'On Re-engineering the Public Service of Canada: A Comment on Paul Tellier's Call for Bold Action,' *Public Sector Management – Going Global* 4, no. 4 (1994), 20–3.

5 Evert A. Linquist, 'The Bewildering Pace of Public Sector Reform,' in Jan-Erik Lase, ed., *Public Sector Reform: Rationale, Trends and Problems* (London: Sage, 1996), 47–63.

6 Frank L. Graves, 'Collaborative Government: Looking for a Canadian Way?' in Susan Delacourt and Donald G. Lenihan, eds., *Collaborative Government: Is There a Canadian Way? New Directions* 6 (Ottawa: Institute of Public Administration Canada, 1999).

7 Peter McPherson, 'A Reunion of Trade Warriors from the Canada-U.S. Trade Negotiations: Remembering How It Happened,' in Mordechai Kreinin, ed., *Building a Partnership: The Canada-United States Free Trade Agreement* (East Lansing: Michigan State University Press, 2000).

8 Graves, 'Collaborative Government,' 19. Also see Matthew Mendelsohn and Robert Wolf, 'Probing the Aftermyth of Seattle: Canadian Public Opinion on International Trade,' *International Journal* 56, no. 2 (spring 2001), 234–60.

9 Robert Wolfe, 'See You in Geneva? Democracy, the Rule of Law and the WTO,' Queen's University School of Policy Studies, Working Paper 16 (Kingston, Ont.: March 2001).

10 Donald J. Savoie, *Governing from the Centre: The Concentration of Power in Canadian Politics* (Toronto: University of Toronto Press, 1999).

11 Alasdair Roberts, 'Keeping Secrets in the Information Age' (Kingston, Ont.: School of Policy Studies, Queen's University, July 10, 2000).

12 Ian D. Clark, 'Inside the IMF: Comparisons with Policy Making Organizations in Canadian Governments,' *Canadian Public Administration* 39, no. 2 (summer), 157–91.

13 Michael J. Prince, 'From Health and Welfare to Stealth and Farewell: Federal Social Policy, 1980–2000,' in Pal, ed., *How Ottawa Spends, 1999–2000*, 160.

14 Julie M. Simmons, 'Patterns of Process: Understanding the Role of Nongovernmental Actors in the Development of the Canada Forest Accord Strategy 1998–2003,' paper presented to the Canadian Political Science Association, Quebec City, May 27–9, 2001.

15 Kathy L. Brock, 'New Ways of Governing: The Federal Government, the Voluntary Sector Initiative and Democracy,' paper presented to the Canadian Political Science Association, Quebec City, May 27–9, 2001.

16 Heather Scoffield, 'Ottawa Richer as Pinch Grows on Towns, Cities,' *Globe and Mail* (June 14, 2001), A10.
17 John Stopford and Susan Strange, *Rival States, Rival Firms* (Cambridge: Cambridge University Press, 1991), 14.
18 Martin Albrow, 'Society as Social Diversity: The Challenges for Governance in the Global Age,' *Governance in the 21st Century* (Paris: Organization for Economic Co-operation and Development, 2001).
19 Gregory Millard, Sarah Reigel, and John Wright, 'Here's Where We Get Canadian: English-Canadian Nationalism and Popular Culture,' paper presented to the Canadian Political Science Association, Quebec City, May 27, 2001.

Acronyms

AB	Appellate Body
AD	anti-dumping
AFL	American Federation of Labor
AFL-CIO	American Federation of Labor/Congress of Industrial Organizations
AIP	Anti-Inflation Program
AIT	Agreement on Internal Trade
APEC	Asia Pacific Economic Cooperation
Auto Pact	Canada-US Automotive Products Agreement
BBC	British Broadcasting Corporation
BC	British Columbia
BCE	Bell Canada Enterprises
BCG	Boston Consulting Group
BCNI	Business Council on National Issues
BILD	Board of Industry Leadership and Development
BIS	Bank for International Settlements
BIT	Bilateral Investment Treaty
BNA	British North America
CAC	Consumer's Association of Canada
Canada-Chile FTA	Canada-Chile Free Trade Agreement
CAP	Canada Assistance Plan
CAW	Canadian Auto Workers
CBC	Canadian Broadcasting Corporation
CCF	Co-operative Commonwealth Federation
CCME	Canadian Council of Ministers of the Environment
CDC	Canada Development Corporation

CDIA	Canadian direct investment abroad
CDIC	Canadian Deposit Insurance Corporation
CDMA	Chain Drug Marketing Association
CEC	Commission for Environmental Co-operation
CELA	Canadian Environmental Law Agency
CEO	chief executive officer
CEPA	Canadian Environmental Protection Agency
CHST	Canada Health and Social Transfer
CIBC	Canadian Imperial Bank of Commerce
CIBS	Canadian International Business Strategy
CIO	Congress of Industrial Organizations
CITT	Canadian International Trade Tribunal
CLC	Canada Labour Congress
CMT	Country Music Television
CNCP	Canadian National-Canadian Pacific
CNR	Canadian National Railways
CRTC	Canadian Radio-Television Commission, later Canadian Radio-television and Telecommunications Commission
CSR	Common Sense Revolution
CUFTA	Canada-United States Free Trade Agreement
CVD	countervailing duties
DFAIT	Department of Foreign Affairs and International Trade
DOC	Department of Communications
ECC	Extraordinary Challenge Committee
ECE	Evaluation Committee of Experts
ECIC	Export Credits Insurance Corporation
EDC	Export Development Corporation
EI	employment insurance
EMU	European Monetary Union
ENGO	environmental non-governmental organization
EPF	Established Program Funding
EU	European Union
FCC	Federal Communications Commission
FDI	foreign direct investment
FIRA	Foreign Investment Review Agency
FSIA	Financial Services Industry Agreement
FTA	free trade agreement
FTAA	Free Trade Agreement of the Americas

G7/G8	Group of Seven/Eight Economic Summit
GATS	General Agreement on Trade in Services
GATT	General Agreement on Tariffs and Trade
GDP	gross domestic product
GE	General Electric
GM	General Motors
GNP	gross national product
GST	Goods and Services Tax
GTA	Greater Toronto Area
HIPC	Heavily Indebted Poor Countries
IBM	International Business Machines
ICA	Investment Canada Agency
ICC	International Criminal Court
IJC	International Joint Commission
IFI	international financial institution
ILO	International Labour Organization
IMF	International Monetary Fund
IO	international organization
IP	intellectual property
IPP	intellectual property protection
IT	information technology
IT&C	Department of Industry, Trade and Commerce
ITO	International Trade Organization
ITS	Internal Trade Secretariat
MAI	Multilateral Agreement on Investment
MFN	most-favoured nation
MMT	methylcyclopentadienyl manganese tricarbonyl
MOE	Ministry of Environment
MPE	management and professional employment
MPP	member of provincial parliament
MTBE	methyl tertiary-butyl ether
MTS	Manitoba Telephone Services
MUSH	municipalities, universities, schools, and hospitals
NAAEC	North American Agreement on Environmental Co-operation
NAALC	North American Agreement on Labour Co-operation
NAFTA	North American Free Trade Agreement
NAMU	North American Monetary Union
NAO	national administrative office

NATO	North Atlantic Treaty Organization
NDP	New Democratic Party
NEP	National Energy Program
NGO	non-governmental organization
NORAD	North American Air Defense Command
NRC	National Research Council
NT	national treatment
OAS	Organization of American States
ODA	official development assistance
ODC	Ontario Development Corporation
OECD	Organization for Economic Co-operation and Development
OPEC	Organization of Petroleum Exporting Countries
PC	Progressive Conservative
PCB	polychlorinated biphenyl
PJBD	Permanent Joint Board of Defence
PMAC	Pharmaceutical Manufacturers Association of Canada
PMO	Prime Minister's Office
POGG	Peace, Order and Good Government
PQ	Parti Québécois
PRI	Partido Revolucionario Institucional
R&D	research and development
RoC	Rest of Canada
SCC	Supreme Court of Canada
SIC	*Sports Illustrated Canada*
SME	small and medium-sized enterprises – also defined as small and medium-sized firms
SPF	Sector Partnership Fund
SPS	Sanitary and Phytosanitary Measures
SUFA	Social Union Framework Agreement
SUV	sport utility vehicle
TBT	technical barriers to trade
TD	Toronto-Dominion Bank
TNC	transnational corporation
TRIMs	trade-related investment measures
TRIPs	trade-related aspects of intellectual property rights
UAW	United Auto Workers
UI	unemployment insurance

UN	United Nations
UNCITRAL	UN Commission on International Trade Law
UNESCO	United Nations Economic, Social and Cultural Organization
USSR	Union of Soviet Socialist Republics
USTR	United States Trade Representative
VCR	Voluntary Challenge and Registry
WIPO	World Intellectual Property Organization
WTO	World Trade Organization

Acknowledgments

This book is the product of work that I have been doing for several decades on the Canadian state, continentalism, and, when it emerged as a separate problematic, globalization. During this long period I have profited greatly from conversations and collaboration with many colleagues and students, while my research has been supported by various institutions in various ways. While it is impossible to identify all one's intellectual debts, since learning takes place constantly in all interactions, there are many that I can – and want to – acknowledge.

My first academic interest in the issues of war and peace raised by Canada's tortured relationship with the United States was stimulated by the members of the University League for Social Reform in the mid-1960s, when the political economist Abraham Rotstein asked me to lead the group's reflections on Canada's responses to the Vietnam War and edit the resulting volume. Shortly after its publication as *An Independent Foreign Policy for Canada?* I received my initiation into research on the hotly debated issue of foreign control of the economy with a commission from the economist Mel Watkins to do a study for the Task Force on Foreign Investment and the Structure of Canadian Industry. An opportunity to do concentrated research on the broad agenda of issues involved in the Canadian-American relationship came in 1981 when Walter Gordon asked me to prepare for the Canadian Institute for Economic Policy a study of the crisis between the Trudeau government and the Reagan administration. What I learned from writing *Canada and the Reagan Challenge* was deepened profoundly by the decade that I then spent working with my life partner, Christina McCall, on the policies and problems of the Trudeau era.

Following our long struggle to get the provocative Pierre Elliott

Trudeau between covers – as our adolescent daughters liked to put it, although it turned out to require two sets of covers to write our political biography *Trudeau and Our Times* – a Jean Monnet Fellowship at the European University Institute in Florence allowed me to spend 1995–6 examining the European Union as an alternative model of continental governance.

My present work on the Canadian state developed from a paper I wrote for Teresa Gutiérrez-Haces for a book she was editing in Mexico City, *Canada un estado posmoderno*. After revising that text with my then-doctoral student, now colleague and son-in-law, Tim Lewis, for Leslie Pal's *How Ottawa Spends: 2000*, I expanded our chapter with the help of a dozen undergraduates to produce a report for the 'Multiple Centres of Power' group. Gordon Smith at the University of Victoria ran that academic team for the federal Policy Research Secretariat's Trends Project, which was supported by the Social Sciences and Humanities Research Council of Canada (SSHRCC).

With my own SSHRCC grant received in 1997 I kept some of these students working for the summer to deepen and refine this manuscript. Undergraduate research came from Sara Boyne, Paola Cifelli, Sheila Dabu, Trevor deBoer, Franca Fargione, Daniela Follegot, Chris Giggey, Monica Misra, Karis Rae, and Brian Zeiler. Michael Hong and Ambrese Montagu made particularly outstanding contributions. SSHRCC funds helped me engage as research assistants Ambrese Montagu, Angela Van Damme, and, later, the indefatigable and exacting Graeme Norton. Matt Griem, Anita Kranjc, and Patrick Lennox provided graduate-level assistance in 2001. Research on the federal-provincial aspects of the state was supported by SSHRCC's federalism program.

It is more difficult to name colleagues who have helped bring this work to completion, because their contribution to my thinking has taken place in the course of continual exchanges in committee meetings or over lunch, in conferences, or anonymously through the daunting process of peer review. As intellectual globalization pushes scholars to interact more widely across vast spaces, I have been able to profit from a number of institutions and collaborative research endeavours, which generate stimulating interaction with academics around the country and across national borders. I have been unusually fortunate to have associations with a number of consortia and projects that have broadened my understanding and enriched my knowledge:

- The Canadian Centre for Policy Alternatives, under Duncan Cameron, its first president, and Bruce Campbell, its present director, generates a continuing flow of critical research.
- The C.D. Howe Institute, under Tom Kierans and now under Jack Mintz, provides more business-friendly research as well as periodic connections via lunchtime seminars with corporate and government leaders.
- Serving on the conseil d'administration of the Centre de Recherche en Droit Public at the Université de Montréal since 1996 has given me contact with leading legal scholars who approach the same set of issues that concern me via legal theory.
- The Centre for International Studies at the University of Toronto under a series of leaders, Len Waverman, John Kirton, and particularly Louis Pauly, its present director, has constantly encouraged me to work on emerging problems.
- Civil servants at the Department of Foreign Affairs and International Trade (DFAIT) have been generous in sharing their insights, whether in Ottawa or at their embassies in Mexico City and Washington.
- The Department of Political Science at the University of Toronto has been my permanent professional home since I started teaching in 1964. Its chair, Rob Vipond, has turned it into a community encouraging intellectual outreach and pedagogical innovation.
- The *EnviReform Project*, led by John Kirton, financed by SSHRCC, and housed at the admirable Munk Centre for International Studies at the University of Toronto, has broadened my contacts with civil society organizations coping with the environmental and labour-policy fallout from globalization.
- At the European University Institute, Francis Snyder in the Law Department involved me in his legal research on the impact of globalization on the EU's institutional order.
- 'Neo-liberal Globalism and Its Challengers: Sustainability in the Semi-periphery,' another SSHRCC-empowered major collaborative research initiative, links me through its leader, Gordon Laxer of the Parklands Institute at the University of Alberta, to a core of nineteen professors and their graduate associates in four countries of the 'semi-periphery' – Australia, Canada, Mexico, and Norway – in a five-year program to examine citizens' responses to neoconservative globalization.
- The Robarts Centre at York University under its protean director, Daniel Drache, has mounted many conferences both in Canada and

abroad bringing together scholars from different countries who are engaged in the range of issues that I tackle in this book.

- The Robarts Library at the University of Toronto generously gave me intellectual asylum with a carrel blissfully unreachable by phone, fax, or e-mail.
- The project on Trans-Atlantic Regional Market Integration, run by Reba Carruth at George Washington University, brings practitioners from the transnational corporate sector together with European and American regulators who deal with issues to which the Canadian state is connected.
- University College at the University of Toronto, with its inimitable nineteenth-century architecture and its correspondingly civil inhabitants, provides me with not just an academic home on campus but a congenial environment for leading a professorial life enhanced enormously by Eleanor Dennisson's obliging assistance.
- The University of Toronto Press itself, with its legendary editor Virgil Duff and undauntable copy editor John Parry, still provides the active engagement with both author and text that are needed for the proper birthing of a book.
- The Woodrow Wilson International Center for Scholars in Washington is a continuing source of interdisciplinary scholarly energy.

In a text covering so many areas, errors of fact and judgment abound. In order to verify information and check interpretation, I have sent individual sections of this manuscript to many colleagues who are specialists in each area. I would like to thank in particular Carolyn Andrew (University of Ottawa), Harry Arthurs (Osgoode Hall Law School), Paul Audley (cultural policy consultant), Marjorie Cohen (Simon Fraser University), Ed Comor (American University), Betsy Donaldson (Geography, Queen's University), Jacques Frémont (Faculté de Droit, Université de Montréal), Meric Gertler (Geography, University of Toronto), Peter Godsoe (ScotiaBank), Myron Gordon (Management, U of T), Marian Hebb (Writers' Union of Canada), Robert Howse (Law, University of Michigan), John Kirton (International Relations, U of T), Anita Kranjc, (postdoctoral student, U of T), Andrée Lajoie (Centre de Recherche en Droit Public, Université de Montréal), Andrew Lewis (lawyer, Paliare Roland), Tim Lewis (government of Ontario), Howard Mann (environmental law, Ottawa), Tom Oommen (DFAIT), Louis Pauly (International Relations, U of T), Douglas Peters (Toronto-Dominion Bank), Cranford Pratt (Political Science, U of T), William

Schneider (National Research Council), David Schneiderman (Law, University of Toronto), Daniel Schwanen (Institute for Research on Public Policy), Lynn Spink (co-author, *Organizing Unions*), Denis Stairs (Political Science, Dalhousie University), Richard Stren (Political Science, U of T), David Trick (University of Guelph-Humber), Leah Vosko (Political Science,York University), Marc Weiss (Woodrow Wilson Center), Bruce Wilkinson (Economics, University of Alberta), Mark Winfield (Pembina Institute for Appropriate Development), David Wolfe (Political Science, U of T), and Robert Wolfe (Political Studies, Queen's University).

I could not have completed so demanding a book in a timely way without release from teaching, so I am indebted to my unknown jurors at the Canada Council who judged me worthy of a treasured Killam Research Fellowship. Anonymous peers have also contributed to my work when reviewing my applications for various grants by SSHRCC and for a fellowship at Washington's admirable Woodrow Wilson International Center for Scholars.

Last, as well as first, I must register my incalculable debt to Christina McCall, for her insistence that learning be worn lightly and that writing be free of jargon, narratively clear, and accessible to non-specialists. She has urged me on to those elusive goals with constant encouragement and loving insight.

To readers who have managed to come so far on this journey with me, I would also like to express my gratitude. Should you wish to correct errors you have detected, make comments, or offer advice for changes that I might make to another edition of this volume, kindly write to clarkson@chass.utoronto.ca

Author Index

Abella, I., 472n6
Acheson, K., 482n21, 483n37
Adams, R.J., 473nn11, 16, 20, 22, 474nn27, 28
Ahmad, A., 460nn61, 64, 461n71
Albrow, M., 490n18
Alexandroff, A., 485n18
Anderson, M., 464n49
Anderson, T.L., 479n42
Andrew, C., 443n34
Andrews, M., 449n17
Appleton, B., 431n3, 432n6, 434n32, 437n11, 476n3
Armstrong, P., 443n34
Arthurs, H., 459n39, 472nn7, 8, 475nn45, 46
Atkinson, M.M., 454n1
Aucoin, P., 446n13
Audley, P., 483nn30, 31, 34
Axworthy, L., 486nn33–5, 487n37
Axworthy, T., 465n63

Babcock, R.H., 472n5
Babe, R.E., 451nn9, 10, 452nn17, 18, 22
Bakvis, H., 438n31, 477n18
Baldwin, R., 474n30

Banting, K.G., 439n38, 469n2, 471nn38, 39
Barber, J., 444n47
Barker, P., 470nn20, 21, 27
Barlow, M., 460n50
Barnes, T.J., 455n16
Barry, D., 486n24
Bashevkin, S., 469n5
Batt, R., 451n7
Battle, K., 446n17
Beamish, R., 457n55, 461n85
Beckton, C.F., 439n52
Behboodi, R., 438n20
Belanger, L., 485n20
Benevides, H., 478n35
Berlin, B., 482n18
Bernier, I., 440n62
Berridge, J., 444n42
Bhagwati, J., 429n3
Binhammer, H.H., 449nn7, 10
Birkinshaw, J., 459n38
Bish, R.L., 443n32
Blank, S., 431n1, 433n16, 459nn 35–7
Boardman, R., 484n9
Boismenu, G., 469n16
Bossons, J., 444n45

Boston Consulting Group (BCG), 448n1, 450n26
Boudreau, J.-A., 443n33
Bouey, G.K., 447n4
Bourne, L.S., 441n7, 442n20
Boychuk, G., 469n15
Boyer, R., 430n15
Bradford, N., 468n21
Brawley, M.R., 451n12, 452nn14, 16, 20, 21, 454n52
Brean, D.S., 461n68
Brennan, R., 479n39
Britton, N.H., 455nn9–12, 16, 18, 456n37, 457nn51–3, 458n7, 459nn29, 31
Broadbent, Ed, 475n46
Brock, K.L., 489n15
Brown, D.M., 436n6, 437n7, 467n5, 477n19
Brun, H., 439n52
Burke, R.E., 433n23
Burns, J., 433n10, 458n12

Cairns, A.C., 439nn45, 46, 49
Cameron, D., 431n2, 446n16, 467nn5, 8, 9
Cameron, M.A., 430n14, 487n39
Cameron, R., 460n59, 461n65
Cameron, R.A., 455n15, 456n28, 459n42
Camody, C., 481n11
Campbell, B., 446n23, 447n8
Campbell, R.M., 451n1, 470n31
Canada, Budget (1999), 465n65
Canada, Department of National Defence, 485n11
Canada, House of Commons, 481n15
Canada, Internal Trade Secretariat, 438n19
Canada, Privy Council Office, 469n13

Canada, Task Force on the Canadian Magazine Industry, 483nn38, 43
Canadian Drug Manufacturers Association, 465nn51, 52
Carleton, M., 470nn20, 21, 27
Castro, R.F. de, 431nn5, 6
Champoux, B., 465n50
Chapnick, A., 488n59
Chase, S., 462n87
Chaundy, D., 457n54
Clark, K.L., 478n26, 489nn4, 12
Clarke, T., 460n50
Clarkson, S., 430nn4, 10, 11, 431nn2, 7, 435n50, 444n1, 448n20, 470n24, 471n32, 484nn1, 7, 8, 486n27, 487n49
Clement, W., 445n4, 446n1, 462n2, 471n34
Clinton, W., 487n48
Coleman, W.D., 431n8, 447n13, 449nn12, 16, 18, 450n34, 454n1
Comor, E., 454n49
Conca, K., 480n57
Consumer and Corporate Affairs Canada, 451n3
Cooper, A.F., 486n25
Copeland, D., 486n31, 488n55
Corcoran, T., 454n62
Côté, R., 471n42
Coupland, R., 480n2
Courchene, T., 441n2, 442nn17, 18, 19, 444nn43, 44, 448n21, 449n20, 466nn68(ch. 13), 4(ch. 14)
Crane, D., 461nn70, 83, 84
Cribb, R., 454n61
Cross, P., 445n6
Crow, J.W., 447n7
Culpepper, R., 447n10, 457n55
Curtis, J.M., 462n89

Dale, S., 480n56
Dalgleish, J., 476n5
Davey, W.J., 433n20, 435nn36, 38, 40, 42
David, C.-P., 485n22
David, M.K., 465n54
D'Cruz, J., 451n11
Dearden, R., 434n30
Deblock, C., 471n42
de Castro, R.F., 430n8, 458n15
de Fazekas, A., 482n17
Delacourt, S., 489n6
Department of Justice, Canada, 464n34
DesRosiers, D., 462nn4, 5
de Tonnancour, S., 465nn55, 57, 60
Dewitt, D.B., 488n62
DiGiovanna, S., 459n32
DiManno, R., 479n38
Dion, S., 436n3
Doern, G.B., 430n13, 438nn22–4, 27, 29, 449n12, 451nn4, 12, 469n2
Donald, B., 441n9, 442nn13, 26, 443n31
Donner, A.W., 449n14, 450nn25, 28, 31, 32, 42
Doran, C., 433n21, 434n24
Dorland, M., 482n26, 483n33
Drache, D., 430n15, 445n3, 474n35
Drainville, A.C., 447n5, 448n22
Dubinsky, L., 483n33
Dufour, A., 470n22

Eastman, H.C., 464n44
Eden, L., 457n4, 458n13, 459n41
Ellis, D., 481n14
Emerson, P.M., 479nn42, 44
English, J., 484n2
Eves, E., 468nn23, 27, 28

Fafard, P., 477nn14, 24, 478n27

Ferguson, R., 461n67
Finlayson, J.A., 472n2
Foreign Affairs and International Trade, Department of (DFAIT), 459nn25, 27, 460n55, 486n23, 487n42
Fréchette, J.-D., 467n10
Freedman, C., 449n9
Freire, M., 441n2
Frémont, J., 470n30
Fuentes, C., 451n2

Gabriel, C., 474nn31–3
Gadd, J., 443n36
Gagnon, A.-G., 470nn23, 30
Gagnon, E., 474n29
Galligan, B., 476n11
Gamache, M., 440n62
Geddes, J., 484n48
Gera, S., 456nn25, 26
Gertler, M.S., 441n9, 442nn14, 21, 443n30, 455n16, 459n32
Gibbins, R., 457n54, 470nn20, 21, 27, 488n3
Gibson, R., 478n25
Gindin, S., 463n14
Glasbeek, H., 474n35
Glavin, T., 440n69
Globerman, S., 432n5, 456nn27, 29, 461n64, 474n31, 484n52
Gold, M., 437n14
Golden, A., 442n28
Golden Task Force, 441n4, 442nn16, 23
Goodeve, S., 433n10, 458n12
Gordon, M.J., 459n28
Gorecki, P.K., 463n21, 464n38
Grady, P., 438n32, 439n39
Graubert, J., 473n23, 474n26
Graves, F.L., 489nn6, 8

Gray, G., 469n3
Grayson, G.W., 473n13
Green, W., 462n12
Greenspon, E., 446nn18, 20, 469n11
Grennes, T., 432n5
Grieshaber-Otto, J., 432n15
Grogan, P.S., 444n41
Gu, W., 456nn25, 26, 462n89
Gunderson, M., 474n34

Haddow, R., 474nn36–8
Hall, D.R., 481n7
Hamilton, T., 454n59
Hampson, F.O., 486n36, 487n45
Hargrove, B., 475n43
Harman, J., 449n8
Harris, R.G., 448nn18, 21
Harrison, K., 476n9, 477nn14, 16, 19,
    20, 23
Hart, M., 432n14
Harvey, G., 452n24
Hawes, M.K., 485nn10, 15
Hay, J., 485n21
Haydan, P., 433n10, 458n12
Heckman, G., 453n47
Heeney, A.D.P., 430n6
Helleiner, E., 429n2(ch. 1), 446n1
Helliwell, J., 439n41
Hibler, M., 457n55, 461n85
Hiebert, J., 467n5, 477n19
Hillmer, N., 488n59
Hirschl, Ran, 475n48
Hirshhorn, R., 459n40
Hoberg, G., 476n9, 477n16
Hogg, P., 439n51
Holbein, J., 434n34
Holland, K.M., 476n11
Holmes, J., 462nn6, 7, 463nn13,
    26
Hoover, S., 465n55

Hornung, R., 478n25
Howlett, K., 450n22
Howse, R., 433n22, 434n25,
    435nn44–6, 49, 438n34, 448n15,
    450n23
Hueglin, T., 436n5
Hufbauer, G., 463n18
Hufford, M., 480n1
Huntington, D.S., 435n41

Ibargüen, C., 431nn5, 6
Industry Canada, 462n1; Health
    Industries Branch, 464n48; web
    site, 438nn26, 32, 460n52
Inkpen, A., 462n9
Innis, H.A., 480n5
Inwood, G.J., 430n12
Israel, E., 483n42

Jack, I., 439n40
Jackson, A., 429n2, 457nn49, 50,
    472n3, 474n30, 475n40, 476nn53–5,
    479n48
Jackson, J.H., 431n9
Jamieson, A.B., 449n5
Jang, B., 461n77
Janigan, M., 458nn20–1
Janik, T., 478n34
Janisch, H.N., 452n29, 453nn31–5, 39,
    42, 454nn55, 56
Jenness, R., 450nn37, 38, 40
Jenson, J., 441n10, 459n39, 469n16
Johnson, P.-M., 479n46
Johnston, L., 470n17
Jowett, G.S., 481n7

Kalman, M., 457n56
Kalwarowsky, J., 456n23
Kanusky, R., 463n28
Katz, H., 451n7

Katzenstein, P.J., 488n63
Keefe, J., 451n7
Keeley, J.F., 462n8
Kelly, J.B., 439n53, 440nn56–8
Kennan, S., 465n53
Kent, C., 433n17
Kirton, J., 473n23, 480n53, 484n2,
    488n62
Knop, K., 443n39
Knopff, R., 439n43, 440nn54, 61
Knox, P.L., 441n8
Knox, R.H., 438nn30, 33, 439nn36, 37
Konrad, H.W., 462n3
Kormylo, A., 465nn55, 57, 60
Kowall, J., 481n16
Krajewski, S., 431n1, 433n16,
    459nn35–7
Krajnc, A., 478nn30, 35, 479n36
Kresl, P.K., 442nn22, 23
Kumar, M., 466n67
Kumar, P., 463n26
Kumar, V., 466n67

Lajoie, A., 436n3, 440nn62, 67, 68
Lang, R.W., 464n36
Lapierre, A., 443n34
Lase, J.-E., 489n5
Laux, J.K., 457nn1–3
Lawson, R., 486n36
Lawton, V., 457n57
Laxer, G., 429(ch. 2)n1, 448n2
Lazar, H., 439n41, 470n19
Lee, F., 456n25
Legaré, G., 484n49
Legault, M., 460nn61, 64, 461n71
Lenihan, D.G., 489n6
Le Prestre, P., 431n10
Leslie, P.M., 436n6
Levin, R.C., 433n8, 434n31
Levine, M.S., 481n9

Levington, J., 443n29
Lewis, T., 445n5, 469nn6, 9, 10, 471n32
Lexchin, J., 464nn37, 41, 42
Leycegui, B., 431n5, 433n20, 458n15
Leyton-Brown, D., 437n14
Linquist, E., 489n5
Little, B., 446n24
Litvak, I.A., 459n30, 460nn44, 46–8,
    461nn72, 73
Lorinc, J., 444n49
Low, S.M., 480n1
Lussier, L., 471n41

Macdonald, L., 474nn31–3
MacDonald, M., 438nn22–4, 31
Macdonald Report, 438n21, 485n16
MacKay, A.W., 439n52
MacKay Report, 450n33
MacKinnon, M., 460n60, 461n65
MacLaren, V., 473n23
MacMillan, K., 438n32, 439n39
Magder, T., 483nn34, 36, 38–41, 46,
    484nn50, 53
Mahon, R., 445n4
Mailander, C.J., 449n13, 450nn36, 41
Mandel, M., 476n49
Manera, T., 481n12
Manfredi, C.P., 439n44, 440nn59, 60
Mann, H., 433n15, 434n29, 435n48
Manson, A.J., 464nn39, 40
Marchak, P., 476nn4, 6
Marin, S.E., 433n8, 434n31
Martin, C., 481n10
Martin, L., 476n8, 485n12
Martin, P., 448n16, 469n9
Martin, R., 462n3
Maule, C.J., 460nn44, 46–8, 482n21,
    483n37
May, E., 479n48
McAnany, E.G., 481n10

McBride, S., 429n4, 437n13, 445n2, 468n22
McCall, C., 430n4, 444n1, 470n24, 484n8, 486n27
McCarthy, J.T., 465n59
McCarthy, S., 450n39, 458nn18–20, 22, 461n77
McDonald, M., 485n12
McFadyen, S., 480n4, 481n11
McIntosh, T., 439n41
McKeen, W., 471n34, 475n41
McKenna, B., 431n4, 472n1
McKenna, P., 487n47, 488n51
McKinsey and Co., 449n11, 450n30
McLuhan, M., 481n6
McNally, A.G., 450n35
McPherson, P., 489n7
McQuaig, L., 464n45
Mendelsohn, M., 489n8
Merchant, L.T., 430n6
Michelmann, H.J., 484n9
Millard, G., 490n19
Miller, G., 479n37
Milroy, B.M., 443n33
Mimoto, H., 445n6
Mirandola, S., 453nn37, 38
Misra, R., 469n12, 472n50
Mitchell, B.R., 455nn4, 5
Mittlestaedt, M., 478nn28, 31
Moffett, S., 441n5, 488nn1, 2
Molot, M., 462n9, 463nn16, 19, 485n10, 486n36
Monsebraaten, L., 479n40
Moore, M., 472n48
Morici, P., 437n9, 458nn6, 8, 9
Morpaw, M., 473n14, 474n25
Morton, F.L., 439nn43, 50, 440n61, 476n11
Morton, P., 482n22
Morton, T., 440n54

Moscovitch, A., 469n14
Mulazzi, P., 440n62
Muldoon, P., 477n22, 478nn26, 32
Munton, D., 484n2
Musch, D., 434n34

National Research Council of Canada, 465n66
Neave, E., 449n20
Neufeld, E.P., 447n3
Neufeld, M., 486n29
Niosi, J., 455n17, 457n4, 459nn23, 24, 460nn45, 53, 56–8, 63
Noël, A., 470nn26, 29
North American Free Trade Agreement, 432n7, 433nn9, 14, 434nn32, 34
Nossal, K.R., 430n8, 484n6, 485n13, 487n44

O'Brian, C., 465n58
O'Connor, D.R., 479n38
Oh, J-G., 454n54
Ohmae, K., 448n17, 467n16
O'Leary Commission, 481n8, 483n35
Oliver, D.F., 487n45
Ontario, government of, 467n18, 468nn29–32, 34
Ontario, Office of the Attorney General, 467n6
Orr, D., 453n42
Ostry, S., 432n12, 443n39, 485n18

Paehlke, R., 478n32
Pal, L., 445n10, 449n12, 469n16, 470nn27, 31, 474n36, 475n40
Palacios, J., 460n43
Paquet, G., 466n68
Parker, L., 481n11
Parker, M., 481n11

Pastor, R.A., 430n8
Pauly, L.W., 457n5
Peers, F.W., 481n13
Pentland, C.C., 484n9
Perkins, E., 480n58
Peters, D.D., 449n14, 450nn25, 27, 28, 31, 32, 42
Peters, D.W., 450n27
Petter, A., 437n15
Phillips, S.D., 471n36
Poloz, S., 447n11
Porter, A., 471n34, 475n41
Porter, M., 441n3
Porter, T., 431n8, 447n13, 449nn12, 16, 18, 450n34, 459nn33, 34
Potter, E.H., 486n30, 488n53
Pratt, C., 488n56
Prince, M.J., 469nn3, 4, 7, 475n40, 489n13
Prichard, J.R.S., 465n64
Proscio, T., 444n41
Proulx, P.-P., 442nn22, 23
Putnam, R.D., 443n30

Raboy, M., 480nn4, 11
Rachlis, C., 467n13
Rae, R., 467nn12, 19
Ragosta, J., 482n23
Raizada, R., 461n75
Ralph, D.S., 469n14
Randall, S.J., 462n3
Rao, S., 460nn61, 64, 461n71
Redekop, C.G., 485n14
Redekop, J., 430n7
Reich, S., 457n5, 463nn17, 27
Reigel, S., 490n19
Richard, B.W., 464n32
Ritchie, L., 474n37, 475nn39, 42
Robert, A., 489n11
Robertson, D., 475n40, 476nn53–5

Robinson, I., 436n7
Robson, W.B.P., 433n20
Rocher, F., 437n7
Rogers, J.W., 464n33
Rosenau, P.V., 469n1, 471n40
Roussel, S., 485n22
Rowell-Sirois Report, 437n17
Royal Commision on Health Services, 464n35
Rubin, J., 447n12
Rugman, A., 451n11, 452n23, 454n58, 461nn80, 82, 479n41, 480nn53, 55
Russell, P.H., 436n2, 439nn48, 54, 440n55
Rutherford, K., 487n38
Ryan, C., 470n23
Rymes, T., 448nn3, 4

Safarian, A.E., 437n18
Sallot, J., 488n60
Sancton, A., 443n38, 478n34
Sands, C., 463n21
Sanger, M., 479n48
Santos, B., 459n39
Sassen, S., 440n1
Saul, J.R., 485n18
Savoie, D.J., 489n10
Schneiderman, D., 433nn11, 12, 434n33, 458n11, 480n50
Schott, J., 432n11, 463n18
Schrecker, T., 476n5
Schultz, R.J., 451nn4, 12, 452nn13, 14, 16, 19–21, 454nn52, 60
Schwanen, D., 438nn20, 28, 455nn8, 14, 19, 456nn24, 32, 34, 41, 458n16, 461n66, 484n51
Scoffield, H., 462n87, 463n25, 490n16
Scott, A.J., 441n2, 442n27
Seaby, G.A., 464n41

Segal, H., 470nn23, 30
Selee, J.S., 436n50
Senate of Canada, 464n47
Sennett, R., 444n52
Sewell, J., 444nn50, 51
Shields, J., 429n4, 468n22
Shrybman, S., 479n47
Shulman, S.R., 464n32
Sidak, J.G., 454n53
Simeon, R., 436n4, 443n39
Simmons, J.M., 489n14
Simpson, J., 436n1
Sinclair, S., 432nn(ch. 3)15, (ch.4)2–4,
    471nn43–6, 472n47
Singer, B.D., 481n7
Singh, P., 473nn16, 20, 474n27
Singleton, W., 458n17
Sjolander, C.T., 437n8
Skogstad, G., 438n31, 477n18
Smith, A., 480n3
Smith, G., 429n1, 431n10
Smith, Miriam, 437n7, 464n43
Smith, Margaret, 436n6
Smythe, E., 460n49
Soldatos, Panayotis, 484n9
Soloway, J., 480n53
Somerville, P., 451n8
Spink, L., 475n44, 476n50
Stairs, D., 485nn17, 18, 486nn28, 32,
    487nn40, 46
Stanbury, W.T., 452n15, 453nn40, 41,
    44–6
Stanford, J., 476nn50, 51
Starowicz, M., 481n7
Statistics Canada, 456nn35, 36,
    457n49, 474nn32, 33, 476nn51, 52
Steger, D.P., 449n19
Stein, D., 433n20
Stewart, G., 429n3
Stilborn, J., 467n10

Stopford, J., 457n6, 461n81, 462n90,
    490n17
Strange, S., 457n6, 461n81, 462n90,
    490n17
Straw, T., 482n26, 483n28
Streeck, W., 430n15
Stren, R., 441n2, 443n35
Stubbs, R., 429n2, 447n13
Stursberg, R., 482n25
Sulzenko, A., 456n23
Swenarchuk, M., 476n5
Swimmer, G., 437n8, 477n17
Swinton, K., 439n35, 443n39

Taylor, P.J., 441n8
Taylor, S., 486n35, 487n37
Telmer, C.R., 466n4
Thomson, A.J., 447n3
Todd, G., 441nn8, 11, 442n15
Tomlin, B.W., 430nn13, 14, 449n12,
    451n12, 485n10
Toner, G., 477n17
Torjman, S., 446n17
Trakman, L., 433n19, 435nn35, 43
Trebilcock, M.J., 438n20, 448n15,
    450n23
Trefler, D., 446n19, 455nn7, 13,
    456nn30, 31, 33, 44
Tremblay, A., 470nn25, 28
Tulchin, J., 436n50

Underhill, G.R.D., 429n2, 447n13
U.S. Department of Commerce web
    site, 459n26

Valpy, M., 442n24
Van Nijnatten, D.L., 477n21
Van Rooy, A., 487n39, 488nn58, 61
Verbeke, A., 461n82
Vertinsky, I., 461n75

von Furstenberg, G.M., 448n19
von Moltke, K., 480n54
von Wobeser, C., 458n15
Vosko, L.F., 446n1, 456n46, 457nn47, 48, 471n34, 472n10, 473n12

Walker, M., 432n5
Walsh, B.F., 433n23
Wapner, P., 480n56
Watal, J., 432n11
Waters, W.G., II, 452n15, 453n46
Watkins, M., 446n16
Watson, W., 429n5
Watts, G.S., 448n3
Watts, R.L., 436n6, 437n7
Weiler, J., 435n45
Weintraub, S., 463n21
Weis, T., 478n35
Weiss, M., 444n40
Weissman, R., 463nn29, 30
Wente, M., 479n38
Weston, A., 461n85
Whalley, J., 437n18

White, G., 467n13
Whittington, L., 449n15
Wigle, R., 460n54
Wilkinson, B.W., 458n14, 461n76
Wilkinson, K.T., 481n10
Williams, G., 442n25, 462n2
Williams, M.J., 488n52
Wilson, M., 446n14, 465n62
Wilson, T.A., 453n42
Wilson-Smith, A., 446nn18, 20, 469n11
Winfield, M.S., 476n1, 477nn13, 18, 22, 478nn26, 32, 35, 479n43
Winham, G.R., 432n13
Winseck, D., 451nn5, 6, 452nn25–8, 30, 453n43, 454nn48, 50
Wolfe, D.A., 445n8, 467nn13, 15
Wolfe, R., 489n9
Wolfish, D., 429n1, 431n10
Wright, J., 490n19

Yanarella, E., 462n12, 463n23
Yohemas-Hayes, L., 473n24
Yu, H.S., 431n1, 459nn35–7

Subject Index

Aboriginal nations, 15, 96, 97, 265
accounting practices and productivity rates, 195
acid rain, 334
activist state, 127; foreign policy, 388–9
adjudication, 61–70; WTO, 68–70
advocacy groups, social policy, 303–4
Agreement on Internal Trade (AIT), 76, 84, 85–9, 289, 296, 349, 411
Air Canada, 5, 208
Aird Report, 364
air pollution, 330–1
Alberta, 8, 11, 79, 84, 95, 225, 293, 317, 321, 324, 349, 385
Alberta Government Telephones, 175, 177–8
al-Qaeda, 401
American Federation of Labor (AFL), 309–10, 317
American Revolution, 407
anti-dumping actions, 55, 62–4, 223
anti–free trade coalition, 47–8
anti-globalism, 8, 10, 37, 44, 46, 47
Anti-Inflation Program (AIP), 130, 131
Anti-Personnel Mine Ban Convention, 394

Argentina, 4, 142, 146
asbestos, 352
Asia Pacific Economic Co-operation, 33
Asian financial crisis, 3, 143
AT&T, 172–3, 176–7, 181, 182
auto industry, Canadian: Auto Pact, see Auto Pact (1965); Canada's advantages, 240, 242; crisis of early 1960s, 236; CUFTA, 238, 242; effects of free trade, 236–43; Japanese 'transplants,' 237–8, 239–40, 242; Mexico, 239, 240, 242; NAFTA, 238–40, 241, 242; working conditions, 240–1
auto insurance, public, 266
autonomy: proposed for Toronto, Vancouver, 120–1; Trudeau's nationalistic efforts, 25–6, 207, 233
Auto Pact (1965), 24, 25, 32, 53, 104, 131, 237, 239, 241, 242; covers most Ontario exports, 262
Axworthy, Lloyd, 393–400

Bank Act (1967), 152, 153, 154
Bank Act, amendments (1992 and 1997), 159, 161; revisions (2000), 164

Bank for International Settlements, 43, 143–4

Bank of Canada, 23, 109, 152, 265; anti–inflationary policies under Crow, 142, 188; autonomy, 146; Canadian government and, 140–2, 148, 149; and Federal Reserve Board (U.S.), 23; functions, 138–9; interest rates, 109; monetary policy, 140, 145; money supply, 155, 167; threatened changes in late 1980s, 77

Bank of Mexico, 145

Bank of Montreal, 105, 156, 160, 164, 166–7

banks, chartered. See chartered banks

Barlow, Maude, 46, 292

Barshevsky, Charlene, 249

BC Hydro, 20

BC Tel, 170, 172, 181

Bell Canada, 105, 170, 171, 173, 175, 182, 205

Bennett, R.B., 19, 138, 364–5

Big Three auto manufacturers, 240

Bladen Report, 237

Bombardier, 10, 55, 110, 205, 226, 255, 419

books, 370

Borden, Robert, 19, 209, 254

border security, 402, 403, 404, 415

Boston Consulting Group (BCG), 164

Bouchard, Lucien, 79, 271, 285–6, 292–3, 338

Bouey, Gerald, 141

Bourassa, Robert, 84, 93, 362

brain drain, 425–6

branch-plant economy, 206, 262

branch plants, 20, 21; auto industry, 236, 237; exports and imports, 191; less R&D, 194; multiplier effects,

215; responses to continentalism, 215–16

Brazil, 142, 226; common goals with Canada possible, 419

Bretton Woods agreement (1944), 42, 139–40, 144

Britain. See Great Britain

British Columbia, 8, 84, 87–8, 97, 102, 120–1, 266, 293, 298, 322, 348, 351

British North America (BNA) Act (1867), 17–18, 90, 95, 293, 307; Judicial Committee of the Privy Council, 76

broadcasting, 104, 364–70; content, 181

brokerage houses, 155

budget balancing, 135–7

bureaucracy, downsizing, 5, 411–12; state feature, 15, 19

Burney, Derek, 30

Bush, George, 32

Bush, George W., 400

Business Council on National Issues (BCNI), 28, 174, 225, 320

cable industry, 359

Caisse de Dépôt, 214

Calgary, 46, 163, 442n23

Campbell, Gordon, 8, 120–1, 427

Campbell, Kim, 339, 413

Canada Assistance Plan (CAP), 265; transfers capped, 285

Canada-Chile Free Trade Agreement (1997), 188

Canada Council, 254, 361–2

Canada Development Corporation, 25

Canada Foundation for Innovation, 256

Canada Health and Social Transfer (CHST), 256, 286

Canada Research Chair, 256

Canada-United States Trade Commission, 38

Canada-U.S. Automotive Products Agreement. *See* Auto Pact (1965)

Canada-U.S. Free Trade Agreement (CUFTA), 4, 7, 14, 71; absence of structure, 38; auto industry rules, 238, 242; and Canadian culture, 366–7; Cancon rules strengthened, 369; constitutional aspects, 71; dispute settlement, 67–8; effects on employment, 285; on financial services, 159; issue linkage, 367; labour issues, 314; Mulroney's fight for, 14, 30–2, 413; national treatment, 51, 209; negotiations towards, 32; Ontario suffers, 262; services included, 300; tariff cuts, 108; telecommunications, 176–7; trade commission, 62; transnational governance, 4, 7

Canada-U.S. relations: annexation not likely, 11; constitution-like stability, 22–4; development in (1911–35), 20; economic links, 22; Mulroney's foreign policy, 386–9; NAFTA and continental governance, 38; rights of access, 24; Third Option, 25; trade policy faces continentalism, 26–7; and Trudeau, 25–7; U.S. hegemony in agreements, 40–1, 42–3

Canada-U.S. trade, increases under free trade, 189–92; volume, 9

Canada-wide accord on the environment, 340–1, 344

Canadian Auto Workers (CAW), 241–3, 314, 327

Canadian Broadcasting Corporation (CBC), 5, 205, 359, 365, 378

Canadian-content regulations, for radio, 368–70

Canadian-content rule, in auto industry, 237

Canadian Council for International Cooperation (CCIC), 390

Canadian Council of Ministers of the Environment (CCME), 339, 340, 341, 344

Canadian Deposit Insurance Corporation (CDIC), 152, 158

Canadian direct investment abroad (CDIA), 214–15, 217–28; Canadian control of, 222; and Canadian-dollar value, 225; and Canadian jobs, 223–5; developing world, 221; geographical distribution of, 220–1; headquarter movements to U.S., 224; sectoral distribution, 221; size, 222; taxation, 222; Trudeau government, 218

Canadian Environmental Assessment Act, 337

Canadian Environmental Law Association (CELA), 350

Canadian Environmental Protection Act (CEPA), 96, 337

Canadian Imperial Bank of Commerce, 156, 164, 166–7

Canadian Institutes for Health Research, 256

Canadian International Business Strategy (CIBS), 220

Canadian International Development Agency (CIDA), 219

Canadian International Trade Tribunal, 63

Canadian investment policy under free trade, 213–14

Canadian Labour Congress (CLC), 310, 317

Canadian National Railways, 5, 204

Canadian Payments Association, 154

Canadian Radio-television and Telecommunications Commission (CRTC), 149, 172, 173, 174, 177–8, 179, 181

Canadian Radio-Television Commission (CRTC), 365–6

Canadian state: *see also* state; direct involvement in economy, 204; effects of WTO, 33–4, 45–8; efforts to increase autonomy (1972–84), 25–6; emerging Dominion, 17–19; federal consolidation (1911–35), 19–20; and global governance, 3, 4–5, 8–9, 12; increasing continental integration (1984–), 27–33; loss of powers to TNCs, 225–6, 417; 'post-globalist': *see* post-globalist state, imagined features; role in Second World War, 20; staple-exporting colony, 16–17, 19; state Keynesianism (1935–84), 20–2; structural and functional changes, 12; weakened but not helpless, 420, 426–7

Canadian Transport Commission, 172

Cancon rules, 379

capital controls: Canada's inability to control flows, 140; deregulation, 139

capital movements, 142, 167

Carney, Pat, 31

Carson, Rachel, 332

Carter, Jimmy, 385

CCME, 344

CDC, 207

CDIA. *See* Canadian direct investment abroad (CDIA)

Cellucci, Paul, 403

Centre for Foreign Policy Development, 393

Centres of Excellence Program, 256

Chapter 11 of NAFTA, 227–8, 348–50, 353, 410, 414; Canadian defiance considered, 418, 424; cases launched by Canadian TNCs, 227–8; challenge to a Canadian province, 348–9; challenges to federal government, 228, 349, 350

Charlottetown Accord (1990), 77, 84, 92, 290–1, 296; social charter proposal, 290

chartered banks: competition, 156; continentalism to globalism, 160–2; foreign, in Canada, 153, 154–5, 161, 164; government actions, 152, 155–8, 161, 164, 165–7; importance in Canadian history, 151–2; investment in U.S. after NAFTA, 160; mergers, rejected, 110–11; mergers, successful, 153, 155, 159, 164, 165–6; offshore assets, 156, 165; owners of securities dealers, 158; owners of trusts, insurance firms, 159, 160; 'Schedule A' and 'Schedule B,' 154–5, 159; telecommunications costs, 174; Toronto's banks, 105, 162–4, 167

Charter of Rights and Freedoms, 60, 76, 325; Aboriginal rights, 97; and federal-provincial relations, 90–8; notwithstanding clause, 93; and unions, 311

Chrétien, Jean, 10, 84, 135, 226, 235, 236, 271, 293, 339, 340, 342, 404; federal-provincial relations, 77–8,

96–7; foreign policy, 389–405; neo-conservatism, 285–6; support of free trade, 46, 413; trade missions, 79; and war against terrorism, 401–4

CHST, 256, 286

CIBS, 228

cigarette packaging, 59–60, 66

cities: globalization, global competition, 100–4; and higher levels of government, 103–4; increased responsibilities, 423–4; regional government in Ontario, 115

Citizens for Local Democracy, 115–16

citizens' movements, 117–18

civil service, low morale and salaries, 422

Clinton, Bill, 33, 315, 397

Clinton, Hillary, 403

clothing manufacturers, 54

CNCP Telecommunications, 171–2, 174–5, 177–8

Codex Alimentarius, 43, 57

Cold War, 46, 384

collective bargaining, 309–10

Colombia, 70

Commission for Environmental Co-operation (CEC), 40, 41, 347–8, 352

Commission for Labour Co-operation (CLC), 39–40, 316, 320

'Common Sense Revolution' (CSR), 113, 114, 116, 289, 342, 345, 378

communications. See telecommunications; telephone systems

Communications, Department of (DOC), 149, 173–4

communications revolution, 101

communications theorists, 356–7

competition: among North American cities, 109; cities competing glo-bally, 101–3; in telecommunications, 178–83

Congress of Industrial Organizations (CIO), 309

constitution: see also supraconstitu-tion; feature of state, 15; international organizations, 44, 70; North American community, 22–4

constitution of Canada: BNA Act (1867), 17–18, 95; Constitution Act (1982), 21–2, 177

Consumers' Association of Canada (CAC), 172, 173

continental governance: and labour issues, 314–18; NAFTA, 38–42; and national distintegration, 200–2; policy making in 1950s and 1960s, 23–4

convergence in telecommunications, 182, 253, 364, 378

Copps, Sheila, 376, 379, 410

copyright, 54–5

Corel, 251

cost-sharing agreement for universities, 254–5

Council of Canadians, 46

countervailing duties, 62–4

Country Music Television (CMT), 367–8, 373

Coyne, John, 140

credit-rating agencies, 130–1

credit unions, 161

Crosbie, John, 27

Crow, John, 141–2, 147, 188

crown corporations, 21, 204; privatization, 5

CRTC, 172–3, 174, 177–8, 179, 181, 365–6

CUFTA. See Canada-U.S. Free Trade Agreement (CUFTA)

cultural assimilation, 358

cultural diffusion, 6
cultural exemption in CUFTA, 366
cultural life, 183
culture: broadcasting, 364–70; and
   CUFTA, 376; cultural content,
   357–8; cultural works considered
   'products,' 375; developing a common culture, 355; dynamic, 359–60;
   facets of every cultural industry,
   360–1; feature of state, 16; films,
   362, 379, 408; government involvement, 361–2; ideological values,
   358–9; influence of U.S., 356, 358–9;
   internal and external threats, 355–6;
   magazines, 370–7; publishing, 362;
   and state, 380; state or private control of entertainment, 359; success
   of francophone culture, 362–3;
   Toronto, 104, 105; under a post-
   globalist state, 426
currency, 138; continental, 144–8
cutbacks: by federal government, 5,
   78, 133, 135–7, 236; by Harris government in Ontario, 113–17; New
   Public Management (NPM), 411–12

Daily Food Bank, 117
Davis, Bill, 260
Davos World Economic Forum, 226,
   227
debt, 129, 135, 284; reduction of, 136,
   137, 288
Defence Production Sharing Agreements, 382
deficit, 78, 129, 130–1, 132, 133, 236,
   285; EI surpluses used for, 323; and
   interest rates, 284
deficit financing, 131, 132
deficit reduction, 135, 286
delayed licences, 247

democratic enlargement, 397–8
Department of Communications,
   173–4, 177, 179
Department of Foreign Affairs and
   International Trade (DFAIT), 177,
   390, 393, 394–5, 397, 400, 405
Department of National Defence, 104
deregulation: business in Ontario,
   272–4; environmental standards in
   Ontario, 343; telecommunications,
   149, 171–5, 178; transportation,
   food inspection, 5
Dickson, Chief Justice, 177
Diefenbaker, John, 10, 21, 140
Diefenbaker-Pearson-Trudeau era, 12,
   149, 226, 246, 281, 298, 307, 369, 378,
   399, 426
disallowance, 82
disentanglement, 291, 340; Ontario
   and municipalities, 343–4
disinvestment policy of Mulroney
   government, 204–5
disparities, 304; mitigated by Canadian tax system, 323
dispute settlement: CUFTA, 67–8;
   NAFTA, 67–8; WTO, 68–70
Doha Round (2001), 44, 47, 81, 302
dollar, Canadian, 143, 416
domestic and external forces, 5
domestic content for radio and television, 104
Dominion of Canada, 17–19, 309
downloading: federal, to provinces, 4,
   77, 111, 133, 291; province (Ontario)
   to municipalities, 113, 114, 119, 344,
   346
downsizing of civil services: federal,
   5, 411–12; municipal, 5; provincial
   (Ontario), 5, 412
drugs: generic, 244–5, 249, 250; and

intellectual property rights, 243–50; licensing system opposed by drug firms, 244–6; Mulroney delays, then eliminates, licensing, 247–9

dumping, 55, 223; split-run magazines, 371

Eastman Report, 246

economic performance under free trade, 193–200

economy: ideologies, 7–8; state feature, 15

education, 254

efficiency drives by management, 308

electoral system, 421

emotion and subjectivity in discussions, 9–10, 11

employment: affected by efforts to fight inflation, 188; affected by many variables, 189; under free trade, 196–7

employment insurance (EI), 199, 307, 322–3

energy: NAFTA, 55; National Energy Program (NEP), 25–6, 51, 131, 234, 385, 386

enforcement: GATT, 71; WTO, 71

ENGO, 333, 341, 346, 350, 351, 419; and global governance, 37, 40

entrepreneurship support organizations, 257–8

environmental issues, 328, 329–53; CEC, 347–8, 352; Chapter 11 of NAFTA, 348–50, 353; continental problem, 334–5; corporate resistance, 330; federal involvement reduced, 339–41, 352; federal legislation, 333, 337; global concerns, 331; increased awareness, 329, 330, 332, 353; MMT case, 349, 350;

negotiations, 331; post-globalism, 416–17, 418; provincial actions, 333–4, 342–4, 352–3; Supreme Court, 337, 338, 353; trade agreements, 335–7, 346–52; trade expansion, 331; Walkerton disaster, 345, 412; water for sale, 336–7, 348

environmental organizations. *See* ENGOs

Environment Canada, 333

Environment Ministry of Ontario, cuts by, 342–3

equality and social policy, 304

Established Program Funding (EPF), 255; ended, 256, 286

Estai (ship), 392

Ethyl Corporation, 227, 349–50

European Central Bank, 4

European Union (EU), 4, 7, 57, 212, 243, 314, 392, 398–9; and North American trade agreements, 30, 31, 33

European Monetary Union, 41, 145, 147

exchange rate: Canada's inability to fix, 140; continental harmonization of currencies, 145–6; flexibility, 140, 145–6, 147; labour-cost advantage, 240; and trade, 192, 416

excise tax, 374

export controls, 56–8

Export Credit Insurance Corporation (ECIC), 217

Export Development Corporation (EDC), 218

exports: growth (1987–2000), 189; manufactured end products, 190; regional variations in export success, 201; staples, 16–17, 19, 191

external and domestic forces, 5, 11;

external factors and colonial economy, 17

Extraordinary Challenge Committee, 63

exurbanization outside Metro Toronto, 111–12

FDI, 229. *See also* foreign investment in Canada

Federal Communications Commission, U.S., 172

federal government: *see also* Canadian state; poor environmental record of Chrétien government, 339–41, 352; relations with cities, 104, 110–11, 118, 119–20

federal-provincial relations: *see also* Social Union Framework Agreement; and Charter of Rights and Freedoms, 90–8; decentralizing tendencies of JCPC, 76; disentanglement, 291; and free trade, 76–80; and global governance, 80–2, 87–9; and globalization, 75–98; negotiations on economic union, 84

Federal Reserve Board (U.S.), 141, 145–6; and Bank of Canada, 23

feminist organizations, support for social programs, 303–4

film industry, 362, 379, 408

Finance Department of Canada: 28, 132, 137, 140, 177, 291; and chartered banks, 165; control over social policies, 283; generally cautious approach, 149, 234, 235–6, 261, 263; and international organizations, 144, 148; legislation, 153; not captive to Keynesianism, 129–30

financial institutions. *See* Bank of Canada; chartered banks

FIRA, 25, 219

'fish war' (1994), 392

Florence, 102–3

Fordism, 21, 103, 112, 128, 243, 260, 330

foreign direct investment (FDI). *See* foreign investment in Canada

Foreign Extraterritorial Measures Act, 387

foreign investment in Canada, 19, 20, 25, 104, 229; competitiveness of provinces and cities, 80; effects of new regime, 210–14; limited by Canadian legislation, 206; national treatment, 51; opposed by nationalists, 206; policy under free trade, 208–10, 213–14; post-globalist approach, 417–18; regulations removed, 51–2, 55, 208–9; screened by Trudeau government, 25, 207; share of North America's FDI falls, 211; significance for corporate government, 214–17; telecommunications systems, 180–2; U.S. dominance in 1990s, 212

foreign investment in North America, 210–11

Foreign Investment Review Agency (FIRA), 25, 55, 131, 207, 386

foreign policy: aid to Third World countries, 399–400; Lloyd Axworthy, 393–400; Israel-Palestine bloodshed, 405; post-globalist, 424; some independence, 398; subordinate to trade policy, 396–7, 408

Fox, Vicente, 41

free trade: ambivalent views of Ontario, 262–3, 265–6; anti-free trade coalition, 47–8: *see also* antiglobalism; Canadian investment

policy under, 213–14; considered in
early 1980s, 27; economic performance under, 193–200; effects on
auto industry, 236–43; effects on
industrial relations, 312; effects on
Toronto, 108; employment under,
196–7; environmental problems,
335–7; federal-provincial relations
and, 76–80; foreign investment policy under, 208–10, 213–14; income
stagnation under, 198–200; job
decline under, 197; limits to state
under, 53–8, 70, 231, 409, 410–11;
manufacturing and, 134, 196; manufacturing sector, 134; Mulroney's
enthusiasm for, 30, 49–50; negotiations for CUFTA, 30–2; Ontario
government views, 262–3, 265–6;
productivity under, 193–6; recommended by Macdonald, 29–30, 83;
seen as panacea, 10; theory, 54
Free Trade Agreement, Canada-U.S.
  See Canada-U.S. Free Trade Agreement (CUFTA)
Free Trade Area of the Americas
  (FTAA), 8, 72, 302, 303, 399, 419
Friedman, Milton, 141
furniture industry, 197

G7/G8 Economic Summit, 8, 45, 144,
  312
General Agreement on Tariffs and
  Trade (GATT), 7, 37, 43, 176;
  enforcement, 71; most-favoured
  nation (MFN) rule, 52, 301; negotiations on tariffs, 26; reconstituted as
  WTO, 33–4, 37, 45, 46; and tariffs,
  307; Tokyo Round, 78; Uruguay
  Round, 31, 32, 33, 45, 180, 266, 410;
  a weak forum, 30

General Agreement on Trade in
  Services (GATS), 53, 61, 81, 160,
  180, 210, 300–2, 373, 416
General Motors, 237, 309
Germany, 272, 382
Gibbins, Roger, 294
Gillespie, Alastair, 218, 219
global currency stability, 143
global governance: and Canadian
  state, 3, 4–5, 8–9, 12; concept
  explained, 7; and environmental
  organizations, 37, 40; and environmental sustainability, 346–52; and
  federal-provincial relations, 80–2,
  87–9; and labour issues, 312–14;
  and trade unions, 37, 39–40; and
  World Trade Organization, 42–5
globalism: concept explained, 7–8;
  neoconservative, 8
globalization, 67, 97, 101; and the city,
  100–4; from different viewpoints,
  6–7, 12; frustrates Keynesianism,
  133; and government cuts in
  Canada, 287; and social policy,
  303; and Supreme Court of Canada,
  96
global monetary governance, Canada's role, 142–4
global trade governance, and cultural cohesion in Canada, 363
glocalization, 117
Golden Task Force, 112–13, 115
gold standard, 138
Gompers, Samuel, 309
Goods and Services Tax (GST), 109,
  132–3, 134, 285
Gordon, Walter, 127, 154, 371
government, influence on business
  cycle (Keynesian view), 129
governmental crises, 3–4

government cutbacks, 4–5, 78;
  Ontario, 114, 115
Grafstein, Jerry, 346
Graham, Bill, 405
Graves, Frank, 414
Gray Report (1972), 206
Great Britain, 50, 212; relations with
  Canada, 17–18, 19
Great Depression, 20, 311
Greater Toronto Area (GTA), 107, 108;
  amalgamation of Toronto, 115–17;
  economy, 109, 110, 111–12; impor-
  tance of financial services, 162–4;
  infrastructure, social welfare cuts,
  114–15, 117; population growth,
  110
Greater Toronto Services Board,
  115
Greenpeace, 332–3, 351
Green Plan (1990), 338, 340

Hall, Barbara, 115
Hampson, Osler, 396
Harris, Mike, 8, 113, 114, 115, 271, 277,
  289, 342, 345, 427
Health Accord, 298
hegemon: leadership needed to main-
  tain state power, 415–16; and
  periphery, 17, 26; U.S. in trade
  agreements, 40–2, 45, 56, 71–2
Helms-Burton Act, 72, 397, 399
Holbrooke, Richard, 403
homelessness in Toronto, 113, 114, 117
Hong Kong, 252
Howe, C.D., 206, 207
Hudson's Bay Company, 17
human rights and the Charter, 90–1

IBM, 110, 251
immigration, to urban centres, 111

imports, displacing interprovincial
  flows, 200
income: see also wages; stagnation
  under free trade, 198–200
incubator initiatives, 257, 258
industrial policy: developing role for
  provinces, 258, 259–77; NDP
  Ontario, 267–8, 269–70
industrial relations, 308–11; NAFTA,
  319; neoconservative actions, 323–6
Industrial Research Assistance Program, 257
Industry Canada, 177, 179, 421
Industry, Trade and Commerce, Canada, 26, 234
inflation, 130, 141; fighting inflation
  affects employment, 188; zero inflation, 142
information, problems with government information, 421–2
infrastructure: cuts by Harris government, 114–15, 117; Harris moves to
  correct problems, 119
innovation, 222–3, 235, 268; see also
  research and development (R&D);
  Ottawa's strategy for industrial
  funding, 255–8; public and private
  sectors, 258; and software firms,
  251
insurance companies, 155, 159
insurance industry, 154
intellectual property: Super 301 legislation, 252–3; TRIPS agreement,
  243, 249, 252
intellectual property protection
  (IPP): biotechnology, 250; pharmaceutical patents, 249–50; software,
  252
intellectual property rights, 31, 33;
  and drugs, 243–50; NAFTA, 54–5

interest rates, 109, 135, 188, 265; and deficit, 284; money supply, 141; and servicing of debt, 135; and unemployment, wages, 306

Internal Trade Secretariat, 84

International Criminal Court (ICC), 395

International Labour Organization (ILO): 42, 52, 68, increased union activity in, 313–15; ineffectiveness, 312–13

International Monetary Fund (IMF), 3, 8, 42, 43, 45, 47, 139, 287

International Network on Cultural Policy, 379

international organizations, WTO contrasted with previous, 50

International Trade Organization (ITO), 43

internet, 378

interprovincial trade, falls with continental integration, 200–1

intervention by government in marketplace, 233–4

interventionist state, 231

intra-corporate trade under trade liberalization, 190–1

Investment Canada Agency (ICA), 54, 55, 208, 209, 213, 369

investment dealers, 157

issue linkage: permitted in CUFTA, 367; 'quiet diplomacy' rule against, 23

Jacobs, Jane, 99, 107, 120

Japan, 57, 272, 382; and auto transplants, 238–42

job creation, 311–12; declines under free trade, 197; neoconservatism, 321–2

JobsOntario, 268–9

Johnson, Lyndon, 383

Judicial Committee of the Privy Council (JCPC), decentralizing tendencies, 76

just society, 127, 281

Kent, Tom, 127

Keynes, John Maynard, Lord, 20, 76, 129, 152, 284, 311

Keynesianism, 8, 20–1, 27, 77–8, 111, 127–30, 136, 260, 274, 311, 330, 337, 357, 414; labour standards and employment insurance, 307; model, 103, 139; system, policy instruments, 139; welfare state, 21; versus neoconservative state, 10

King, William Lyon Mackenzie, 20, 21, 138, 206, 309, 382

Klein, Ralph, 8

Kyoto Protocol, 331, 341, 352, 401

labour, auto industry, 241

Labour Conventions case (1937), 81

labour laws, 306–7, 308; changes in Ontario, 323–5; NAALC, 315–18; and NAFTA, 39–40; neoconservative actions, 323–6

labour movement. See unions

labour standards, 308; business objections heeded by government, 319–20; neoconservatism, 320–1; temporary and part-time workers, 320

Lastman, Mel, 120

Latin America, economic crises, 3–4

Laurier, Wilfrid, 18, 309

Lévesque, René, 293, 362

Liberal (Peterson) government in Ontario (1985–90), 261–5; ambiva-

lent views on free trade, 262–3;
business-government relations,
264–5; environmental efforts, 338;
facing global interdependence,
263–4
Liberal Party of Canada, right turn
under Chrétien, 285–6
limits to state: *see also* supraconstitution; under free trade, 53–8, 70, 231,
409, 410–11; self-imposed, 188,
411–12
Loewen Group, 227, 228
Lougheed, Peter, 225

Macdonald, Donald, 29, 130, 225
Macdonald, John A., 18, 30, 200, 254
Macdonald Report (1985), 29, 83, 201,
235, 388, 396, 413
MacEachen, Allan, 283
MacLaren, Roy, 46, 396, 397
McLeod, Lynn, 288–9
McLuhan, Marshall, 356–7
MacMillan Bloedel, 224–5
Macmillan, Charles, 234
McMillan Commission, 152
McQuaig, Linda, 247
magazines, 370–7
Magder, Ted, 375
Magna International, 110
management and professional
employment (MPE), 212–13
Manitoba, 84, 227, 266, 293, 317, 321
Manitoba Telephone Service, 178
Manley, John, 400, 401, 404
Manning, Preston, 285–6, 291–2
Manpower and Immigration, Depart-
ment of, 312
manufacturing in Canada, 19–20; and
free trade, 134, 196
Marchi, Sergio, 47, 201, 397

market-share rule, in auto industry
(Auto Pact, 1965), 237
Maritime Telegraph and Telephone,
181
Martin, Paul, Jr, 78, 256, 339, 403;
authority over Bank of Canada,
142; cuts to social programs, 286–8,
322, 393, 474n37; reduction of defi-
cit, 134–7, 235–6, 340, 410; work for
global monetary governance, 144;
yielding to banks' foreign owner-
ship, 164
Martin, Paul, Sr, 127, 287
Masse, Marcel, 173, 175
Massey Report (1951), 361
Mauro, Arthur, 84
medical drugs. *See* drugs
Meech Lake Accord (1987–90), 76–7,
92, 291, 296
Merkin, Bill, 247
Metalclad Corporation, 65, 82
Methanex, 227, 228
Metropolitan Toronto. *See* Toronto
Metropolitan Toronto and Region
Conservation Authority, 106
Mexico: 17, 40–1, 58, 62, 71, 142,
attracting foreign investment, 208–
9; auto industry, 239, 240; Canadian
investment in, 220; foreign invest-
ment in, 211, 212; labour issues, 39,
305, 314–15, 317, 318; and NAALC,
317–18; supreme court, 70
Microsoft, 251–2
military integration, 382–3, 403,
404
minimal government, 10, 409
ministerial conference in WTO, 44
MMT, 349, 350
Moffett, Samuel, 407–8, 427
monetarism, 141

monetary policy, Bank of Canada, 140, 145

money supply: Bank of Canada control, 155, 167; and interest rates, 141

Montreal, 110: R&D performance, 214; surpassed by Toronto, 104, 442n23, 444n46

Moody's, 131, 284, 287

most-favoured nation (MFN) rule, 52, 300–1

Mulroney, Brian, 10, 27, 28, 49, 76, 84, 132–3, 208, 234, 247, 263, 265, 284, 314, 413; fight for CUFTA, 14, 30–2, 413; foreign policy, 386–9; goal of constitutional accord, 76–7, 92; policy advisers, 234–5

Mulroney-Chrétien era, 12, 90, 97, 107, 127, 149, 307, 413

multiculturalism, 357–8

Multilateral Agreement on Investment (MAI), 47, 220, 414; opposed by Canadian labour, 313

multilateralism, 33, 34, 385, 398–9, 405

Municipality of Metropolitan Toronto, 105. See also Toronto

musicians, 369, 379

mutual funds, 156

Myers, S.D., 350

Nader, Ralph, 173

NAFTA. See North American Free Trade Agreement (NAFTA)

National Energy Program (NEP), 25, 26, 51, 131, 234, 385, 386

National Film Board, 5

National Hockey League, 23

nationalism, noticed by Moffett (1907), 408; opposed by neoconservatism, 409; 'Third Option' of Trudeau government, 25–7, 233

National Policy: of C.D. Howe, 206, 207, 260; of John A. Macdonald, 18, 30, 200

National Research Council (NRC), 254, 256–7; and software industry, 253

national treatment, 51, 209, 255, 301, 348; CUFTA's application to services, 51; extended to investment, 209; for foreign investors, 51; investment, 235; NAFTA rule: see Chapter 11 of NAFTA; in telecommunications, 177

national unity, 291, 384, 385

NATO, 398

NDP (Rae) government in Ontario (1990–5), 111–12, 265–70; ambivalence on free trade, 265–6; environmental efforts, 338; Golden Task Force, 112–13; industrial policy, 267–8, 269–70; and international relations, 267; labour laws, 324; and NAFTA, 266–7; 'new-think' policies, 268, 269; sector partnerships, 269–70; social policies, 288; spending followed by social contract, 111

neoconservatism: characteristics of neoconservative model, 97, 117, 127–8, 133; of Chrétien Liberals, 285–6; and cultural cohesion in Canada, 363; doubt about politics, 127; globalism, 8, 89, 103; and industrial policy, 312; and labour, 320–7; minimal government, 10, 409; monetarism, 141; opposed to nationalism, 409; shift towards, 12, 27–8, 132; values of society, 412, 414

New Brunswick, 94, 102, 163, 322

New Democratic Party (NDP):
Ontario government: *see* NDP (Rae)
government in Ontario (1990–5);
relations with unions, 310, 475n44
New Direction for Canada, A, 132
New Public Management (NPM),
411–12, 421
newspapers, 370
new-think policies of Rae govern-
ment, 268, 269
New York investment bankers, 163
New Zealand, 29
Nixon, Richard, 25, 233, 384, 385
Noël, Alain, 293
Noma Industries Ltd, 305
non-governmental organizations
(NGOs), 10, 46–8, 313–14, 350, 390,
394–5, 400, 419, 425
norms, 70; in Canada-U.S. relations, 23
Nortel Networks, 10, 105, 110, 175,
223–4, 226
North American Agreement on Environmental Co-operation, 40, 347,
352
North American Air Defence Command, 23
North American Agreement on
Labour Co-operation (NAALC),
39–40, 315–18
North American community, 'constitution-like' features, 22–4
North American Free Trade Agreement (NAFTA): auto provisions,
238–40, 241, 242; Canadian banks'
gains, 160; and Canadian provinces, 80–2; Cancon rules strengthened, 369–70; Chapter 11: *see*
Chapter 11 of NAFTA; committees
and groups, 39; as continental
governance, 7, 38–42; deepening

of CUFTA, 32–3; defining cultural
industries, 367; differing effects on
members, 71–2; dispute settlement,
67–8; effects on Toronto, 108–9;
enforcement, 70–1; environmental
concerns, 347–51; foreign investment, 209–10; implementation, 40;
institutions, 38–40; intellectual
property rights, 54–5; and labour,
39–40, 314–15, 318–20; and monetary policy, 145; and NDP Ontario,
266–7; no trilateral summit, 404;
notwithstanding clause on culture,
376; review process, 53; and sovereignty, 4, 40; supraconstitutional
aspects, 37, 38–9, 42, 48, 50, 51–2,
54–6, 58–68; tariff reductions or
removals, 54, 108–9; telecommunications, 179–80; U.S. hegemon,
40–2
North American Free Trade Commission, 38–9, 62
North American Monetary Union
(NAMU), 145, 147; resisted, 41
North Atlantic Fisheries Organization, 392
Nossal, Kim, 396
notwithstanding clause in Charter, 93
Nova Chemicals, 225
Nova Scotia, 322, 325
Nunavut, 97

Oakes case, 94
OECD, 43, 45, 139, 143, 188, 209, 275,
313
offloading, 5, 133
O'Leary Commission, 359, 371
Ontario: auto industry, 242–3; industrial policy, 259–77; objections to
redistribution, 200–1; pollution-

control laws, 333–4; suffers from
CUFTA, 262
Ontario Development Corporation
(ODC), 261, 269, 273–4
Ontario government, 79, 94, 157. *See*
Liberal (Peterson) government
in Ontario (1985–90); NDP (Rae)
government in Ontario (1990–5);
PC (Davis et al.) government in
Ontario (1943–85); PC (Harris) gov-
ernment in Ontario (1995–)
Ontario Jobs and Investment Board,
119
Ontario Labour Relations Board,
324
Ontario Municipal Board, 105
Organization of American States
(OAS), 8, 47, 399
Organization for Economic Co-opera-
tion and Development (OECD), 43,
143
Ostry, Sylvia, 31, 45
Ottawa Process, 394–5
Ouellet, André, 246, 392

Palacios, Juan, 217
Palestinian trade mission (1999),
201–2
Parizeau, Jacques, 79, 157
Parliament, 56, 97
Parti Québécois, 105, 286, 298, 325,
357
Patent Act: amendment (1923),
244; amendment (1986), 247–8;
amendment (2000), 249; part of
Macdonald's National Policy, 18
patents, on medicinal drugs, 54,
243–50
PC (Davis et al.) government in
Ontario (1943–85): benign

policies, 105–6, 259–61; business-
government relations, 261
PC (Harris) government in Ontario
(1995–2002), 8, 84, 87, 113–17, 119,
270–7; downloading to cities, 113–
14; environmental mistakes, 342–4,
352–3; friendship with business,
271, 272–3; and globalization, 272,
277; government cutbacks and
deregulation, 113–17, 272–4; industrial policies, 276–7; international
relations, 272–3, 276; labour law
changes, 324–5, 475n44; opposition
to Ottawa, 271; policy adjustments,
275–6; relations with other provinces, 271–2; social welfare cuts,
113–15, 117; tax cuts and credits,
271, 274, 276
Peace of Westphalia (1648), 15
Pearson, Lester B., 10, 21, 127, 381,
383, 386, 413
Perezcano, Hugo, 458n10
periphery and hegemon, 17, 26; *see
also* hegemon; Canada as peripheral state, 16, 17; in NAFTA, 40–2;
in WTO, 45
Peters, Douglas, 132, 134
Peterson, David, 261, 263, 338
Petro-Canada, 204, 207, 225
petroleum crisis (1979), 234
Pettigrew, Pierre, 47, 397, 472n49
Pharmaceutical Manufacturers Association of Canada, 244, 246, 248
pharmaceuticals. *See* drugs
Philippines, 79
policy-making, continental. *See* continental governance
political destabilization, 6
political parties, funding, 421
pollution, 330–1, 416–17

Pollution Probe, 332

Porter, Michael, 268

postal service, 169

postal subsidies, 374–5

post-Fordism, 112

post-globalist state, imagined features: constitutional, 423–4; cultural, 426; economic, 416–20, 424; environmental issues, 416–17, 418; foreign policy, 424; governmental, 422–3; political, 420–2; societal, 425–6

post-Keynesian, 29, 130, 133–4, 141, 235

post-modernity, 406

Premier's Council (Ontario), 263–4, 265, 266

price controls, 130, 131

price stability, 142

privatization, 204–5; of Canadian foreign policy, 389–90; of crown corporations, 5; of government services, 115, 299; in telecommunications, 175; of water testing in Ontario, 344

productivity: gap with the U.S., 192; results under free trade, 193–6

Progressive Conservatives in Ontario, 106. See PC (Davis et al.) government in Ontario (1943–85); PC (Harris) government in Ontario (1995–2002)

property taxes: assessment harmonized by Harris, 119; source of cities' funds, 114

protests against globalization, 8, 10, 37, 44, 46, 47

provinces: see also Ontario; Quebec; downloading from federal, 4, 77, 111, 133, 291; downloading to

municipalities, 113, 114, 119, 344, 346; and global competition, 102; globalization and domestic pressures, 8; international promotion of companies, 227; protectionism, 82–3; talk on social policy, 292–3; and trade agreements, 78; training, 321–2, 323

public domain, 16

public-sector unions, 326

publishers, 362

Quebec: 79, 84, 94, 317, 322; federal strategy to placate (1995), 291; industrial relations, 325; law, 93; referendum (1995), 78; securities legislation, 157–8; separatism, 384, 385; success of francophone culture, 362–3; and Social Union Framework Agreement, 293–4; sovereignists, 11; and Supreme-Court, 96–7

'quiet diplomacy,' 23

Quiet Revolution, 131

radio: Canadian-content rules, 368–70; state presence in, 364–5, 408; strengthened by CUFTA and NAFTA, 369–70

Radio Canada, 104, 363, 365

Rae, Bob, 265–72, 288

Rand check-off formula, 309–10

Reagan, Ronald, 27–8, 71, 129, 247, 385, 386, 387

recession of early 1980s, 130, 234

recession of early 1990s, 108, 132–3, 134, 142, 268

reciprocity and telecommunications, 175

record industry in Canada, 368–9

regional governments around Toronto, 108, 115
regional variations in export success, 201
Reisman, Simon, 30, 129, 176, 262
representative democracy, 15
research and development (R&D): basic research, 257; Canadian software firms, 253; federal support for, 255–8; foreign and domestic firms compared, 194–5; medical drugs, 243, 245; R&D Challenge Fund (Ontario), 276; tax credits, 205
Revenue Canada, 63
right of establishment, 52
rights, 15, 70; property rights, 60; rights of access, 24, 175; social rights, 290
rights of access: Canada-U.S. relations, 24; telecom companies, 175
Robarts, John, 260
Roosevelt, Franklin Delano, 382
Royal Bank, 105, 156, 164, 166–7, 174
Ryckman, Mary, 484n47

St Laurent, Louis, 21, 254
St Lawrence Seaway, 104
Sanitary and phytosanitary measures (SPS), 57, 58
Saskatchewan, 84, 266, 293, 298, 322, 325, 349
Sasktel, 178, 181
satellites, 171; transmission of magazine copy, 373
schools in Toronto, 114
Schwanen, Daniel, 379
Science Council of Canada, 233–4
Scotiabank, 156, 160, 166–7
Seattle protest (1999), 10, 37, 44, 46, 47

Sector Partnership Fund (SPF), 269–70
secure access, 62
securities industry, 157
semi-peripheral country, Canada as, 303
separatism: and the Charter, 91, 92; in Quebec, 384, 385
service sector, growth in Canada, 192
Shamrock Summit (Mulroney-Reagan, 1985), 247
shared-cost programs, 290, 292
Sharp, Mitchell, 46
Sharpe, Andrew, 194
simulcasting, 366
Singapore, 252
small and medium-sized enterprises (SMEs): innovation, 222–3; support from government, 261, 275
Smith, Anthony, 356
social commons, 304
social contract (NDP Ontario), 111, 288
social dumping, 313, 319
social policies, 281–304; advocacy groups, 303–4; CHST reduces funding, 256, 286; compared with U.S., 282; enlightened federal and provincial policies, 104, 106, 281–2; federal cutbacks, 282–8; Finance controls social policy, 283; and globalization, 303; intergovernmental rules: see Social Union Framework Agreement; job losses from CUFTA, 285; Liberals' right turn, 285–6; neoconservative attitudes, 414; Ontario cuts, 113, 114, 115, 117, 288–9; value changes in society, 412
Social Sciences and Huymanities Research Council of Canada, 254
Social Union Framework Agreement

(SUFA), 289–98, 411; and Quebec, 293–4

software: Canadian firms, 251, 252, 253; new global trade norms, 250–4; standard, 251–2

softwood lumber, 62–3

South Korea, 29, 79, 252

sovereignty: of Canadian state, 16, 43–4; emergence of concept, 15; and global financial stability, 144; internal and external, 34, 35; loss of, by small countries, 43; and multinational organizations, 3, 43–4, 50; and NAFTA, 40, 43; provincial, 18, 80–2, 94–8

split-run editions of U.S. magazines, 371–2, 373, 376

Sports Illustrated Canada (SIC), 372–3

Spry, Graham, 365

stagflation, 130, 139

Stairs, Denis, 396

staple-exporting economy, 16–17, 19, 191

state: see also Canadian state; activism, 20–1; anxiety about, 3; change in structures, 15; coercion by, 16; common culture, 355, 380; features of the modern state, 15–16; labour legislation, 306–7, 308; regaining powers in crisis, 415–16, 417

Statistics Canada, 421, 422

Stentor, 171, 175, 181

stock exchanges: Canadian and U.S., 23; losing autonomy, 216; Toronto stock exchange, 163

strikes, 310, 325

subjectivity of discussions, 11

subsidy programs, 255, 419

Summit of the Americas, 47

Sun Belt Water Inc., 348

Super 301 legislation, 252–3

SuperBuild Corporation in Ontario, 119

supraconstitution: adjudication, 61–70; constraints on state, 4, 53–8, 70, 231, 409, 410–11; enforcement, 70–1; NAFTA, 37, 38–9, 42, 48, 51–2, 54, 68, 70–1; norms, 50–3; rights, 58–61; WTO, 52–3, 56–8, 61, 410–11

Supreme Court of Canada, 70, 81, 90, 93, 404; Aboriginal rights, 96, 97; autonomy for cities, 121; bargaining rights not protected, 325–6; environmental rulings, 337, 338, 353; and federal government, 95–6, 97–8; federal jurisdiction over telecommunications, 177–8; globalization, 96; national security, 404; power strengthened by Charter, 92, 93–4; provincial sovereignty, 94–8; Quebec secession rights, 96–7; sexual orientation, 94–5; test of NAFTA's Chapter 11, 424

Taiwan, 28, 252

tariffs: effects of cuts under free trade, 190; and GATT, 26, 307; NAFTA, 54; National Policy (1879), 18; on telecommunications goods, 176; U.S. use of, 22

Task Force on the Future of the Canadian Financial Services Sector, 165

taxes: cuts, 129–30, 137, 283, 288; excise tax, 374; Goods and Services Tax (GST), 132–3, 134; redistributive tax policies, 323

tax evasion, corporate, 415–16

Team Canada trade missions, 79, 201–2, 221, 227, 228, 272

technical barriers to trade (TBTs), 57, 58, 81

technological developments, 7, 19–20; and cities, 112; and cultural cohesion in Canada, 363–4; and environmental concerns, 331–2; satellite transmission evades tariffs, 373; telecommunications, 171–3, 182, 183, 253

Technology Fund (Ontario), 264

telecommunications: competition, 178–83; continental consolidation, 182; convergence, 182, 253, 364; CUFTA, 176–7; deregulation, 149, 171–5, 178; federal jurisdiction over, 177–8; foreign ownership, 180–2; globalization, 182–3; government control, 179; international context, 175–7, 178, 179–80; NAFTA, 179–80; national treatment, 177; privatization, 175; tariffs on, 176; technological developments, 171–3, 182, 183; WTO, 180

Telecommunications Act (1993), 179, 182

Teleglobe, 171, 175, 205

telegraph, 169

telephone, 169

telephone systems: cell phones, 173; deregulation, 149, 174, 175; from monopoly to competition, 171–8; regulation of, 170, 171, 172, 173–4, 177–8; success, 170; terminal equipment, 172

Telesat, 171, 175

television, 359, 365; state presence in, 365–8, 408

Telus, 175, 181

territorial state, 15

terrorism: attacks against the U.S., 6, 16, 401; effect on border controls, 41, 402, 403, 404, 415; and NAFTA, 42; war against terrorism, 401, 415–16, 417

Thailand, 79, 142

Thatcher, Margaret, 27–8, 115, 363, 385, 387

Thiessen, Gordon, 142

Third Option, 25, 30, 131, 233, 385; rejected by Mulroney, 386

three-pillared model for Canadian diplomacy, 390–1

Time-Warner, 372

TNCs. See transnational corporations (TNCs)

Tobin, Brian, 392

Tokyo Round of GATT negotiations (1973–9), 262–3

Toronto: amalgamation, 115–17; continental competitiveness, 109–10; decline in schools, 114; effects of free trade, 108; evolution in late twentieth century, 103; Fordist state (1945–80), 104; future, 118–21; homelessness, 113, 114, 117; population growth, 107–8; problems with downloading, 113–14, 346; quality of urban life, 114–15; R&D performance, 214; ranking among North American cities, 109; regional municipalities surrounding, 115; social services cut, 114–15, 117, 288–9; subway, 105; two-tier government (1950–80s), 106; urban sprawl, 346

Toronto-Dominion Bank, 156, 164, 166–7

Toronto Stock Exchange, 163, 224

trade agreements: *see also* Canada-
U.S. Free Trade Agreement
(CUFTA); North American Free
Trade Agreement (NAFTA); World
Trade Organization (WTO); and
Canadian political system, 4, 33–4;
primary mechanism of neoconservative state, 187; problems anticipating consequences, 187; protecting TNCs from government pressure, 215; seen as strengthening
investment rules for CDIA, 219–20;
supraconstitutional aspects: *see*
supraconstitution; U.S. hegemony
in, 40–2, 45, 56, 71–2
trade disputes, 62–4
trade liberalization. *See* free trade
trade ministers, meetings, 38, 39
trade missions. *See* Team Canada
trade missions
trade performance, increase in trade
(1987–99), 189–92
trade policy, 78, 187; dual action, 188
Trades and Labour Congress, 309
trade unions. *See* unions
training: 'offloaded' by federal government, 321, 323; Ottawa's role,
235, 236; programs of NDP Ontario
government, 268–9; provinces,
321–2, 323
transfer pricing, 195
transnational corporations (TNCs):
see also Chapter 11 of NAFTA;
cross-border trade within, 191–2;
development in Canada, 19–20, 24;
foreign-controlled TNCs and Canada's trade, 191; labour standards,
318; and loss of Canadian government powers, 225–6; loss of state
powers to, 3, 6, 7, 206, 225–6, 417;

new powers under NAFTA, 33, 52,
55, 209–10; in Toronto, 104, 110;
U.S.-led action needed for control,
416
treaties. *See* trade agreements
Trefler, Daniel, 195–6
TRIMs, 210, 220
TRIPs agreement, 61, 210, 243, 249,
252
Trudeau, Pierre Elliott, 10, 21, 27, 79,
93, 99, 127, 131, 207, 233, 255, 263,
281, 333, 357, 413; bureaucratic
shifts, 396; and Canada-U.S. relations, 25–6; and Charter of Rights
and Freedoms, 90, 91–2; foreign
policy, 383–6; revenues and spending, 283
trust companies, now owned by
banks, 159, 160
Turbot War, 392
Turner, John, 27, 29, 129, 132, 284

unemployment, 134, 136, 197, 285,
413; changes in calculation of,
421–2; effect on collective bargaining, 306; in Toronto, 108
unemployment insurance (UI), 307,
322
UNESCO, 42, 45, 50
unions: continental influences, 308–9,
310, 408; failures and successes,
326–7; and global governance, 37,
39–40; lost cases on bargaining
rights, 325; NAALC, 315–18; and
NDP, 324; part-time workers, 327;
public-service unions, 310; relations with NDP, 310; women, 327
United Auto Workers, 241, 309, 472n4
United Kingdom. *See* Great Britain
United Nations, 398; ancillary organi-

zations, 42; ineffective in labour standards, 313

United States: annexation of Canada not likely, 11; Congress, 11, 24, 43, 49, 63, 314; federal support for cities, 119; government, 32, 50, 55, 57, 118; health system compared with Canada's, 282; hegemon in trade agreements, 40–2, 45, 56, 71–2, 415–16; influence on Canadian culture, 356, 358–9; leadership needed for global action, 416; wage rates higher than Canada, 199–200

United States Trade Representative (USTR), 67, 247

universities: Access to Opportunities Program (Ontario), 276; federal support, 295; government retreat, new programs, 256; relations with industry, 257–8; shared costs, 254–5

Uruguay Round of GATT talks, 31, 33, 180, 266, 410

value-added jobs, 192

values: and neoconservative attitudes, 412; and views of globalization, 9

Vancouver, 110, 442n23

Vaughan region, 112

Voluntary Sector Initiative (VSI), 423

Volcker, Paul, 141

wages: controls, 130, 131, 142, 310; gap between men and women, 199; and interest rates, 306

Walkerton disaster (May 2000), 345, 412

War of 1812, 407

water: pollution, 333–4; safety problems, 345–6, 412; sales under

NAFTA, 348; and trade agreements, 336–7

Watkins Report (1968), 206

Weber, Max, features of the Weberian state, 15–16

welfare state, 104, 106, 134, 281–2; see also social policies

White, Bob, 314

Wilson, Michael, 28, 29, 132, 284–5, 413

withdrawal by Ottawa from programs, 4, 236, 411

women: unions, 327; wage gap with men, 199; in the workforce, 198–9

working conditions, 306–8; auto industry, 240–1; NAFTA, 319–20; neoconservative actions, 322–3

World Bank, 8, 42, 43, 47

World Health Organization, 42

World Intellectual Property Organization, 43

World Petroleum Association, 8

World Trade Organization (WTO): 8, 33, adjudication, 68–70; adverse rulings on magazines, 373–5, 410; agreement on agriculture, 57; agreement on intellectual property: see TRIPS; agreements on foods, 57; Appellate Body, 69–70, 373–5; on Auto Pact (1965), 241, 242; constitution, 44; constraints on Canadian policies, 34, 35, 52–3, 56–8, 61, 410–11; created from GATT, 33–4, 37, 45, 46; dispute settlement, 68–70; Doha: see Doha Round; effects on Toronto, 108–9; enforcement, 71; export controls, 56–8; Financial Services Industry Agreement, 160; on foreign investment, 210; GATS: see General Agreement on Trade in Services; and global governance, 4, 7, 42–5, 72; invalidation of cultural regulations, 363; ministerial conference, 10, 44, 46; most-favoured-nation (MFN) rule, 52; and national monetary policy, 145; opposed by environmentalists, 351–2; and provincial governments, 81; review process, 53; scope and authority, 50; structure and operation, 44–5; subsidies, 57–8; supra-constitutional, 48, 51–3, 56–8, 61; telecommunications services, 180; Uruguay: *see* Uruguay Round

Yukon, 88

zero inflation, 142

Other Books by Stephen Clarkson

Trudeau: L'illusion héroïque
(with Christina McCall). Montreal: Boréal, 1995.

Trudeau and Our Times. Volume 2: The Heroic Delusion
(with Christina McCall). Toronto: McClelland and Stewart, 1994.

Trudeau: L'homme, l'utopie, l'histoire
(with Christina McCall). Montreal: Boréal, 1990.

Trudeau and Our Times. Volume 1: The Magnificent Obsession
(with Christina McCall). Toronto: McClelland and Stewart, 1990.

Canada and the Reagan Challenge: Crisis and Adjustment, 1981–85. 2nd ed.
Toronto: James Lorimer, 1985.

The Soviet Theory of Development: India and the Third World in Marxist-Leninist Scholarship.
Toronto: University of Toronto Press, 1978; London: Macmillan, 1979.

City Lib: Parties and Reform.
Toronto: Hakkert, 1972.

L'analyse soviétique des problèmes indiens du sous-développement (1955–64).
Paris and The Hague: Mouton, 1971.

Edited Volumes

Visions 2020: Fifty Canadians in Search of a Future.
Edmonton: Hurtig, 1970.

An Independent Foreign Policy for Canada?
University League for Social Reform
Toronto: McClelland and Stewart, 1968.